# Century of the Marathon
## *1896-1996*

Riël Hauman

# Century of the Marathon
## *1896-1996*

HUMAN & ROUSSEAU
Cape Town   Pretoria   Johannesburg

This book is dedicated to
the memory of my great friends
Harry Beinart and Arrie Joubert
whose love of athletics was an inspiration
to me and many others

Cover photographs: Elana Meyer and Uta Pippig in Boston, 1994
(Touchline Media/Ace Lyons), Dorando Pietri
in London, 1908, and Zithulele Sinqe and Willie Mtolo at Stellenbosch, 1987

Copyright © 1996 by Riël Hauman
First edition in 1996 by Human & Rousseau (Pty) Ltd
State House, 3-9 Rose Street, Cape Town
Text electronically prepared and typeset in 10 on 12 pt Plantin by
Human & Rousseau, Cape Town
Typography and cover design by Annelize van Rooyen
Printed and bound by Colorcraft, Hongkong

ISBN 0 7981 3554 9

The marathon is a romantic accident.
  – George Gretton: *Out in Front*

. . . the screen [depicting Bruce Fordyce in the 1983 Comrades marathon] bore witness to something that was intangible, something that was beyond words. The great runner oblivious of the moment, entranced by his own most private thoughts, showing that man is indeed most marvellously made.
  – Tim Noakes: *Lore of Running*

I make the marathon beautiful for myself and for others. That's why I am here.
  – Uta Pippig, marathoner, in an interview in *Runner's World*

# CONTENTS

# FOREWORD

The enigmas of the marathon race are threefold. First, why did this race ever come into existence? Second, why is the race distance such an odd one of 26 miles and 385 yards (42.195 km)? And why, beginning in the 1970s, did the popularity of this race suddenly increase at a time when humans, according to all the available evidence, were generally becoming more sedentary, slothful and glutinous?

It is appropriate that in the centenary year of the inaugural running of the first modern marathon race at the 1896 Olympic Games in Athens, author and marathon runner Riël Hauman should turn his considerable literary and statistical talents to the compilation of a definitive history of the first century of marathon running. And so provide if not answers, then at least solid clues to the solution of these enigmas.

Here we learn that the race is, in reality, a historical or – as Hauman records – a romantic accident. In retrospect, the inclusion of the first marathon in the 1896 Olympic Games owes much to mythology and little to reliable historical fact. Pheidippides, the messenger whose name is most often linked to the origins of the race, may well have lived. But, as again confirmed here, it is probable that he never ran the 40-odd kilometres from Marathon to Athens in 490 BC. So the bigger question becomes: Why *really* was the marathon race introduced into the first modern Olympic Games and as the result of *whose* vision?

Could it have been an ingenious coup of the world's original sports marketing executive who wished to add the heroic to those first Games; an inspired bonus that would distinguish the modern from the ancient Olympic Games? Indeed our romantic perceptions of the race and its origins are somewhat dimmed when we learn that the winner of the first race, the Greek shepherd Spiridon Louis, ran solely in the quest of a victory that would earn him sufficient to purchase a horse and cart. So that he would never again have

to run for recreation, or to walk as part of his daily work!

Perhaps the message from this definitive history is that the romance we perceive in the race is no more nor less than that which we each bring to it. And the result of what happens when the dreams of many find physical expression in a uniquely demanding event.

For the race distance of 26 miles, 385 yards we are indebted to the British Royal family who wished to have the 1908 Olympic Games marathon start on their property at Windsor Castle and finish in front of their Royal Box at the White City Stadium in London. To achieve this, an extra 365 yards had to be added to the then unofficial distance of 26 miles. Subsequently this new distance was accepted as the official marathon distance. Without the addition of the extra distance at least two famous races – the 1908 Olympic marathon and the 1954 Empire Games marathon – would have ended with different results and two of the great moments of high drama produced by the race would have been lost. Indeed the extra distance – the bane of all marathon runners – still continues to add moments of the highest drama to this already most dramatic race. For it was the extra distance in the marathon leg of the triathlon in a race run as recently as October 1995 that robbed Paula Newby-Fraser of an unprecedented eighth Hawaiian Ironman Triathlon victory. Such is the legacy of history and the reason why it must be preserved in books like this.

But why does the race continue to grow in popularity? Here the answer may also be found in these pages. Perhaps the reasons are not much different from those given by the author for his own fascination with the race – the inspiration provided by fellow South African Ferdie le Grange as he finished one of the great marathon performances run on the African continent. The vision of such exceptional brilliance was enough to thrill the author and ignited a 21-year-long passion for the race. This book will be the most enduring legacy of that moment and will itself become a source of motivation for future runners of this most inspiring race. Such indeed is the power of the marathon and the inspiration that its great runners provide to sustain interest in their own passion.

That perhaps is the explanation for the lasting attachment that so many have with the marathon. It is a race that provides the theatre for greatness and so fulfils our human need for noble heroes. Not for common heroes fashioned in less demanding exploits, but for those whose courage has been proven in the one athletic event that is the supreme measure of physical endurance, willpower and courage. And it is these heroes who excite us to find the heroism buried deep inside each of us.

So the great value of this book is that is records the wonderful races and the majestic heroes that the event has produced; those gifted few with the courage to devote their athletic careers in search of the most ephemeral achievement in sport – the perfect marathon race. And through the actions of those individuals we follow the first hundred years of the most unusual sport as it has grown from what may have been a publicist's gimmick in the 1896 Olympic Games to one of the most popular modern sports that allows the common person to discover and express his or her heroism.

The author has written his book with the passion of the true believer and the accuracy of the statistician, a most rare combination. The result is a book of real scholarship, remarkable in its completeness and full of the unusual information and insights which distinguish that which is classic and enduring.

For all those who have ever agonised in the glorious excess of the marathon, this is a book to savour. It is a book of infinite delight that records and so sustains all that is great about this inspiring example of human athletic endeavour.

TIM NOAKES
Professor in the Liberty Life Chair of Exercise and
Sports Science and
Director of the MRC/UCT Bioenergetics of Exercise
Research Unit, University of Cape Town,
and Sports Science Institute of South Africa

# ACKNOWLEDGEMENTS

I first became aware of the magic of the marathon on 23 April 1974 in Port Elizabeth. I remember it as if it were yesterday: In the gathering darkness of the evening the winner of the South African Open marathon came onto the brick-red track on the far side of the stadium and ran around the bend and into the home straight with light, seemingly effortless strides. He was a slim, long-limbed runner clad in the maroon and gold colours of Stellenbosch University and he wore lightweight blue racing shoes. The main lighting of the stadium was not yet switched on, but at the finish he was illuminated briefly by a pool of strong light as he raised his arms to head height in triumph.

A thrill went down my spine then and I shivered, not only from the cool night air. I was one of a lucky few (the explosion in the popularity of marathon running would only happen a few years later) who had witnessed one of the truly great achievements in South African athletics history.

The runner was Ferdie le Grange; his time was 2:12:47, the seventh fastest in the world that year. It was his sixth national record, and it stood for five years.

Seventeen months later I ran my first marathon, more than an hour slower than Le Grange. This book is the result of a 21-year-long fascination with and study of the marathon. It has been made possible by the assistance of many people, of whom I would like to mention seven by name.

First of all my friend Gert le Roux, an indefatigable researcher and collector of information on all branches of athletics. There is no one in South Africa who knows more about the sport, but he does not always receive the credit he deserves for his immense work on the documentation of athletics – even in his so-called "retirement".

Then my friends-in-writing, Dr David E. Martin and Roger Gynn, whom I have never met but have exchanged countless letters with over the years. They are the authors of the classic *The Marathon Footrace: Performers and Performances* and have always been extremely willing to provide information and answer queries on international events.

My knowledge of athletics was formed, nurtured and developed by two magnificent mentors – two of the world's greatest authorities on athletics – Harry Beinart and Arrie Joubert. Although both died long before I even started writing this book, their influence on its outcome was indispensable.

I am also grateful to many other friends, fellow statisticians and acquaintances in road running who, directly or indirectly, helped to shape the book. One of them is that erudite writer on and student of running, Tim Noakes, who has generously consented to write the Foreword.

Lastly I am deeply indebted to my wife, Suzette, who unselfishly kept the household running (no pun intended) while I was sitting in front of my mistress, as she calls my computer.

RIËL HAUMAN
Cape Town
November 1995

# INTRODUCTION

One of the earliest descriptions of a footrace is in the *Iliad*, attributed to the Greek epic poet Homer around 800 BC, where he gives an account of the race between Ajax and Odysseus. Evidence of athletic competitions have been found in Egyptian art dating from ca. 3500 BC, and in Crete sports competitions were held before 2000 BC, while the earliest documented reports of athletic events in the Ancient World originated in Greece and Ireland. Races were held in Greece a thousand or more years before the Christian era, usually coinciding with religious festivals. In Ireland the Lugnas games, later called the Tailteann games, developed from local festivals and were held well before Homer's time.

Ancient Greece had many cultural festivals, such as the Pithian, Nemeian and Isthmic games, but the Olympic Games, so called because they were held at Olympia in the northwest Peloponnesus, became the most famous. Some historians trace the origins of these games to 1222 BC, but the earliest victor we know by name is Coroebus, who won the sprint, or *stade*, race in 776 BC. This event was the only one on the programme of the ancient Games – it was the length of the stadium, about 192 metres. In 724 BC a race of double this distance, the *diaulos*, was added, and in 720 BC a race of 24 stade (about 4.5 km), the *dolichos*, appeared on the programme.

The four-yearly Games gradually grew in size as more events were added, and vast crowds from all over the Greek world attended. However, no women were allowed to participate – or even watch. The Olympic Games were stopped in 393 AD by the Roman Emperor Theodosius.

During the Middle Ages organised sport did not play the important role it had in antiquity, although athletic competitions did survive on the European continent, especially in the British Isles. Activities that grew into the sport of today started to develop among the common people in Britain around the twelfth century. Footraces, jumping and hurling weights became well established, with men and women competing for prizes ranging from shirts and hats to cheese and meat – even, it is said, a marriage partner!

The upper class, of course, saw athletics in a different light: for them running, jumping and throwing were "sundrye forms of exercise necessarye for a gentilman" and "bothe a good exercise and a laudable solace", as Sir Thomas Elyot put it in his *The Boke Named the Governour* (1531).

Between the seventeenth and the nineteenth century pedestrianism flourished in Britain. This consisted of running events for wagers and was promoted by the aristocracy – but the running was usually done by the servants. The footmen of the time were professional runners who carried messages between towns, and on the rough roads of the period did so more quickly than horses, horse-drawn carts or coaches.

By the beginning of the nineteenth century the aristocracy no longer controlled pedestrianism. One of the most famous "peds" of the period was a Scottish landowner, Robert Barclay Allardice, known as Captain Barclay. In 1809 he walked 1 000 miles in 1 000 hours, winning the huge amount (for those days) of £16 000.

In the course of time pedestrianism brought with it many dubious practices, but it led to the establishment of athletics meetings as we know them today. By 1850 at least a dozen purpose-built tracks existed in the main cities of Britain. The athletes sometimes competed in front of crowds of 25 000 who came to watch running events like 110, 440 and 880 yards, the mile, 4 miles, 6 and 10 miles, as well as jumping and throwing events.

Pedestrianism, which experienced its heyday around 1810, caused a revolution, but it was mainly a sport for the working classes. In the middle of the nineteenth century athletics took hold in the universities, and in 1861 the famous

American Indian Deerfoot (or Hagasadoni, also known as Louis Bennett) came to Cambridge to run, and win, a race over 6 miles at Fenner's Ground. Among the spectators was the Prince of Wales, and the future king dined with the flamboyant runner in Trinity College afterwards.

This event sparked an immense interest in the sport. It became a solidly middle-class activity, and soon civil servants, army officers, solicitors and the like were taking part. The first match between Oxford and Cambridge, held at the Christ Church Ground, Oxford, on 5 March 1864 (with eight events), is regarded by many as the foundation meeting of modern athletics.

Athletics at Cambridge University were managed by John Graham Chambers (1843-83), who can be described as the architect of modern athletics. He brought order to the sport and was a leading member of the committee of the Amateur Athletic Club, which held its first championships in 1866. The announcement of this meeting stated that the competition would be "open to any gentleman amateur, and the club lays down the following rule, which will be strictly enforced: 'That no gentleman who has ever run in any open race or handicap can enter for the club races.'".

What was an amateur? The club defined it in typically Victorian terms: "An amateur is any person who has never competed in an open competition, or for public money, or for admission money, and who has never at any period of his life taught or assisted in the pursuit of athletic exercises as a means of livelihood." In 1867 the following was added: ". . . or is a mechanic, artisan or labourer", and the following year the first words were changed to: "An amateur is any gentleman . . ."

In 1866 the first national championships, those of England, were held; the Americans followed ten years later. The first national body for athletics, the Amateur Athletic Association, was founded in Oxford in 1880. By then it had been decided that competition would be open to all classes. Eight years later the Amateur Athletic Union of the United States was established.

Distance running at these early athletics meetings was very popular, due in large measure to the exploits of the famous peds and the awe in which the performances of men like Walter George, William Cummings and Alfred Shrubb were held. The longest championship distance at the time was 10 miles, and the earliest long-distance world record officially recognised by the International Amateur Athletic Federation was Shrubb's 50:40.6 for this distance, run on 5 November 1904 in Glasgow. Shrubb actually set seven world records in the race, ranging from 29:59.4 for 6 miles to 18 742 m for the hour.

Both amateurs and professionals also competed over distances such as 15 miles, 25 km and 30 km, with the British professional Richard Manks covering the latter distance in 1:52:51 in 1851 on his way to the finish of a 20-mile race, but marathon running (meaning, initially, races over a distance of about 40 km) in the contemporary sense was born with the decision to include a race of this length in the programme of the first modern Olympic Games in 1896.

This book traces the history of the marathon from that race a century ago to the present day.

# 1

## *It started with*
# PHEIDIPPIDES

IT ALL BEGAN with the Athenian messenger Pheidippides (or so they say). According to legend this professional runner ran from the plain of Marathon to Athens to bring tidings of the famous victory of General Miltiades over the invading Persians. There, after gasping out his message, "Joy to you, we've won", he expired. And thus the classic marathon footrace was born.

But legend, alas, is not always truth. Or the whole truth.

Our basic knowledge of the events of 490 BC comes from the Greek historian Herodotus, who lived from approximately 484 to 425 BC. Herodotus wrote his history towards the end of his life, and probably obtained his information from men who were alive at the time the battle at Marathon took place.

In August 490 BC the Athenians were informed that a huge Persian army had landed at Marathon on the east coast of modern Greece, about 38 km from Athens. Although they were heavily outnumbered, the Athenians decided to march out and meet the enemy but also sent a messenger to Sparta to ask for assistance.

The man selected for this task was "a herald, one Philippides, who was by birth an Athenian, and by profession and practice a trained runner" (according to Herodotus). In his biography of General Miltiades the Roman historian Cornelius Nepos called the runner Phidippus and described him as belonging to the "class known as hemerodromoi", meaning men who ran for a day, or longer. These runners were especially valued by the army as a means of communication, for they could cover prodigious distances. (There is evidence of one runner covering about 177 km in fifteen hours.)

Pheidippides was told to ask the Spartans to come directly to the plain of Marathon and meet the Athenians there. Herodotus wrote that the runner "reached Sparta on the very next day after quitting . . . Athens".

This means that he ran the distance in about 24 hours. According to Solinus the distance was 1 240 *stades*, or 1 240 times the length of the track in a stadium. This measurement varied in different places but was usually about 210 yards. Pheidippides therefore ran about 238 kilometres over extremely mountainous terrain – a stupendous achievement, even if one takes into account that he was a "professional runner". (The current world 24-hour track record is 283.6 km.)

What is more, according to the legend, Pheidippides then ran back to Athens to tell the city fathers that the Spartans had declined to march out immediately in aid of the Athenian cause because they never did so before the moon was full. Having delivered his message, Pheidippides then followed the Athenian army over the Pentele heights and informed General Miltiades of the Spartans' reply.

Despite the enormous odds, the Athenian generals decided to attack the yet unconquered Persians the next day. The invaders were taken by surprise and although violent, the battle was over before noon. Pheidippides then immediately returned to Athens to carry the news of the miraculous victory.

That is the story of the legendary herald. But there does not even seem to be certainty about his name. One historian even ascribed the feat to Eucles. Most likely his name was as it is given by Herodotus, because this means "the son of a lover of horses" and the corruption to Pheidippides may have been decided upon by someone who thought the former form to be unfitting for one of the great heroes of Athens.

So what are the facts?

The eminent marathon historians David E. Martin and Roger Gynn have pointed out that four points in Herodotus's account should be considered carefully. Three have already been mentioned: the name of the runner (Herodotus called him Philippides), his profession and the distance he covered. The fourth factor is that Herodotus tells us about his run from

Athens to Sparta but nothing about the rest of his feat. All of this, wrote Martin and Gynn in their authoritative book *The Marathon Footrace: Performers and Performances*, "would have made precisely the kind of tale that Herodotus enjoyed so much; one cannot imagine him omitting such uplifting material had he known it and had it happened. Clearly our hero did return to Athens to report that his mission [to Sparta] was unsuccessful, but that is all of which we can be sure."

The fact that Herodotus does not even mention someone who ran from Marathon to Athens is usually forgotten – or not mentioned – when the story of Marathon is told; thus most people think that it was also Herodotus who told the story of Pheidippides completing this run.

There may be a very simple reason why Herodotus is silent on this score. In his standard work *A World History of Track and Field Athletics 1864-1964* Roberto Quercetani mentioned that Professor Lauri Pihkala of Finland was of the opinion that the historian may have left it out because the runner was a deserter!

Pausanias, who wrote in the second century AD, reported the run from Sparta back to Athens, while two other Greek writers of the same period – one of them Lucian, in his rather ironically named *A Slip of the Tongue in Greeting* – are the only sources for the journey from Marathon to Athens. Lucian called the runner Philippides, while Plutarch (who lived about four centuries after the battle) ascribed the run to Eucles, but said that other writers called him Thersippus.

In his excellent study in *Olympic Review*, "The true course run by the Marathon messenger", Dr Ion P. Ioannides wrote that, although there is no clear historical proof about the messenger who brought the news of the victory, it would have been a very natural thing to do. There is ample evidence for such runs, even in earlier periods. One such run took place more than five centuries earlier, when a Hebrew messenger ran a distance of 35 km to bring news of the battle at Even-Heazer between the Philistines and Israelites.

Although one tends to agree with Ioannides that the battle and events of Marathon marked an era in its "manifestations of an unusual human power and will [firing] the imagination of men in later times very vividly" and that this led to the climate which gave birth to the marathon as a race, it seems a pity that the run from Marathon to Athens has come to overshadow the truly heroic, far longer and far more difficult – and seemingly authentic – run from Athens to Sparta.[1]

This feeling is heightened by the fact that the route which is today regarded as that taken by Pheidippides – and along which the so-called Classic marathon is run – is probably the wrong one!

Ioannides has studied the battlefield, the camping grounds of both armies, the topography of the area and the various pathways to Athens. He is of the opinion that the most probable route was from the Tymbos, the burial place of the Athenian soldiers, through the ruined Vrana settlement, past the monastery of Agios Georgios, ascending through a dense pine forest to the famous Dionysos Sanctuary (350 m above sea level). It then descends gently through the suburbs of Athens – among them Amaroussion, the home village of the first Olympic marathon champion, Spiridon Louis.

The total distance of this route across the Pentele heights to the Panathenaic Stadium is about 34 km (8 km less than the modern standard distance) and among the reasons put forward by Ioannides for the probability of this route is its shortness and the safety it secured for the messenger in comparison with the easier but more dangerous route along the coast. The fact that it passes by the sanctuary would have made it the one most used at the time and therefore the shortest in the area.

One does not know why the organisers of the first Olympic marathon in 1896 chose the route which they did, but this route has become the one accepted as being Pheidippides's.

And this brings us back to the legend. Whether it was Pheidippides who ran from Marathon to Athens, or someone else, whether the run took place at all, and whatever other runs preceded it, does not really make any difference. The mythical messenger gave the world a race which has maintained its fascination over the past century and presented thousands with its magical challenge.

1. This run is commemmorated today with what is called the world's most challenging endurance race – a distance of 246 km from the Acropolis in Athens over five mountain ranges to Sparta. At the time of writing the course record is held by the Greek Yannis Kouros with 20:25:00.

# 2

# *1896*

# THE FIRST OLYMPIC MARATHON

THE IDEA OF INCLUDING a distance race in the programme of the first Olympic Games in Athens in 1896 came from the French historian and linguist Michel Bréal. In 1892 Baron Pierre de Coubertin had announced at the Sorbonne Amphitheatre in Paris that the ancient Olympic Games would be revived. The International Olympic Congress was convened on 16 June 1894 and the International Olympic Committee was founded a week later with de Coubertin as its first President. Bréal, a friend of de Coubertin, strongly advocated a race to commemorate the legendary run of the Athenian messenger and offered a prize for the winner. When de Coubertin and Bréal went to Athens to discuss the programme of the Games, the Greeks immediately accepted the idea.

Not only that, but they started planning to ensure a victory by a Greek. They scheduled two "marathons" to prepare their runners, but even before these took place, two men ran from Athens to Marathon. This was in February 1896, and Georgios Grigoriou finished in 3:45:00 – ten minutes after J. Vanoulis. The latter, however, had taken a lift in a cart for 5 km. Thus cheating in distance running got an early start!

The first authenticated "marathon" race was run from Marathon Bridge to the Panathenaic Stadium in the Greek capital on 10 March 1896. It was part of the Pan-Hellenic Sport Celebration. Twelve runners took part and the winner was Harilaos Vasilakos in 3:18:00. (He was also known as Haralambos Vasilakos and some sources give his name as Charilaos.) Behind him came Spiridon Belokas 3:21:00, Dimitrios Deliyannis 3:33:00, Dimitrios Christopoulos 3:33:50, Georgios Grigoriou 3:36:00 and Evangelos Gerakakis 3:37:07.

Two weeks later there was another race over the same route and this time there were 38 contestants. Ioannis Lavrentis improved on Vasilakos's time by winning in 3:11:27; he was followed by Ioannis Vrettos 3:12:30, Eleftherios Papasimeon 3:13:37, Elias Kafetzis 3:15:50, Spiridon (also known as Spyros) Louis 3:18:27 and S. Moussouris 3:19:15. A fortnight later Louis would be famous.

The first Olympic Games of the modern era were opened on 6 April. The Games were funded primarily by a gift of one million drachmas from the wealthy Greek Georgios Averoff. Averoff also added an antique vase to the silver cup offered by Bréal as the prize for the marathon winner. A total of thirteen nations were represented by 311 competitors – all male, of course.

The marathon, over a distance of 40 km, was run on 10 April. Twelve of the sixteen starters were Greeks.[1] Until then the athletics events at the Games had not been very successful for the host nation – it had even lost that most classical of events, the discus throw. But the Greeks felt assured of a victory in the marathon and various gifts were offered to a Greek winner, among them a barrel of sweet wine, lifelong free haircuts, and free clothing for life, while the owner of a chocolate factory offered more than 2 000 pounds of chocolate. Averoff offered the hand of his daughter in marriage and a dowry of a million drachmas. (One wonders if the daughter was consulted!)

The competitors were transported to the village of Marathon on 9 April, and the next day gathered at Marathon Bridge for the start at 14:00. The starter, Major M. Papadiamantopoulos, made a speech and then they were off.

The four foreigners in the field were Gyula Kellner of Hungary, who had run a 40 km trial in Budapest, Edwin Flack of Australia, winner of both the 800 and 1500 metres (the only two running events on the track not taken by the American team), Arthur Blake of the USA, winner of the sil-

---

1. This is according to Martin and Gynn, *The Marathon Footrace*. Other sources, such as *Athletics: A Modern History of Track and Field Athletics (1860-1990)* (Quercetani), give the number of entrants as eighteen. All sources give the number of foreigners as four. A total of nine runners finished.

ver medal in the 1500 m, and Albin Lermusiaux of France, who had been third in the 1500 m. Flack's victory in the 800 m had come on the day before the marathon!

There is some evidence that a Greek woman, Melopene, ran despite a ban on women participants (see Chapter 9), but this has not been established beyond doubt.

Only a few hundred people were at the start, but there was much excitement and expectation from the Greek spectators, for this was the final event of the Games and the host nation's last chance to win a gold medal. However, things did not look too bright for the Greek runners in the early stages of the race. Lermusiaux took the lead and set the pace for the first half of the distance. By 15 km, it is said, he had a lead of 3 km, although this sounds unlikely. At this stage Flack was in second place and Louis in sixth. Between Louis and Flack were Blake, Kellner and the first Greek, Lavrentis.

When Lermusiaux reached the village of Palini he passed through a triumphal arch erected by the villagers and received a floral victor's wreath. But by this time the steady incline had taken its toll and the runners started to drop out, among them Blake. Vasilakos, the winner of the race exactly a month before, was now running third.

Then the uphill became even more severe and Lermusiaux stopped for an alcohol rubdown. Flack passed him. The Frenchman started to run again, but about 8 km later he retired and was carried to a carriage. Meanwhile the Greek hopes had shifted to Louis, who was running steadily and passed Flack at 32 km. For the next 4 km Flack hung on grimly a few metres behind Louis. Kellner was now third, Vasilakos fourth and the young Greek Belokas fifth.

The road was choked with dust from the runners' feet, an entourage of soldiers on horseback to clear the way, handlers on bicycles and carts carrying doctors and nurses.

Louis, whose job as a water carrier involved walking kilometres alongside his mule every day, had dreamt that he would win the Olympic marathon. It is said that he did nothing but pray on the day before the race and ate nothing. On race day he ate a whole chicken.

Now, nearing the end of the marathon, he proved to be the better runner and tactician and when he increased his pace outside Ambelokipi (37 km), with the crowds lining the road cheering him on, he left the gallant Flack behind. The Australian's helper asked a Greek spectator to keep the runner from falling over while he went in search of a wrap, but the utterly exhausted Flack thought that he was being attacked and hit the Greek with his fist! Flack then dropped out and was taken to the stadium where he received a drink of egg and brandy.

Soon afterwards the starter of the race, a dust-covered Major Papadiamantopoulos, entered the stadium on horseback and hurried to the King in the royal box to tell him that the marathon would probably have a Greek winner. The crowd was overcome with elation when the small, dusty figure of Louis appeared in the marble entrance to the stadium. The winner was given a tumultuous reception and Crown Prince

## LOUIS, THE ORIGINAL HERO

The Greeks were thrilled with their first modern athletic hero. At the time of his victory over the dusty roads between Marathon and Athens Spiridon Louis was 24 years old. Many legends surround him: he has variously been described as a shepherd, a water carrier, and the postman of his village. He had also been in the army.

Louis, a tough man, had apparently prepared well for the Olympic marathon, and ran a tactically shrewd race. He did not follow the suicidal pace of the early leaders but bided his time until the second half. At one stage he confidently told spectators: "Everything is going to plan. My turn will come yet." His tactic of even pace and outlasting the "hares" is still as sound today as it was then – although one cannot say the same about the one or two glasses of wine which he drank along the route!

Pandemonium took over the Panathenaic Stadium, where 70 000 spectators were amassed, when Louis ran through the marble entrance. According to some reports, women tore off their jewellery and threw it at his feet. The jubilant Greeks showered him with a variety of gifts. As he was already married (with two children), he could not accept the offer of Miss Averoff's hand in marriage. When the King offered him a gift, however, he chose a horse and cart to make it easier for him to transport fresh water from his village to Athens.

Louis died on 27 March 1940.

Constantine and Prince George went onto the track and accompanied the exhausted runner to the finish, where he bowed to the King. The King waved back with his naval cap.

Louis had run the first official sub-3 hour marathon: 2:58:50. It took more than seven minutes for the next runner to enter the stadium . . . and he was also a Greek! It was Vasilakos in a time of 3:06:03. Less than half a minute later the third runner finished: Belokas. Greek joy knew no bounds, but there was a shock waiting. Belokas had overtaken Kellner near the end but the Hungarian accused the Greek of having taken a ride in a carriage. The Crown Prince investigated the allegation, found that Kellner was speaking the truth (Belokas admitted as much), and stripped Belokas of his medal. Kellner was the only foreign runner to finish.

To this day Louis's victory margin of 7:13 is the biggest in Olympic history. After the race Louis went back to his home village of Amaroussion and never ran again. Forty years later he was guest of honour in the Olympic Stadium in Berlin.

RESULT:[2]

1 Spiridon Louis GRE 2:58:50
2 Harilaos Vasilakos GRE 3:06:03
3 Gyula Kellner HUN 3:06:35 [3]
4 Ioannis Vrettos GRE
5 Dimitrios Deliyannis GRE
6 Eleftherios Papasimeon GRE

2. Modern abbreviations for countries are used, such as RSA for South Africa. See also the Results and Statistics section.
3. Kellner's time is given as 3:09:35 by some sources (such as Ekkehard zur Megede, *Die Geschichte der Olympischen Leichtathletik*), but is generally accepted (*inter alia* by Martin and Gynn) as 3:06:35.

# 3

# *1896-1918*
# TWO DRAMATIC OLYMPIC RACES

THE 1896 OLYMPIC MARATHON provided the impetus for worldwide marathoning. Although the participation of the United States in the first Olympic Games was largely due to the efforts of athletes and officials of the Boston Athletic Association (the club of Arthur Blake, who ran the marathon in Athens but did not finish), it was New York that took the lead. The Boston officials decided to organise a marathon but were upstaged by the New York City Knickerbocker Athletic Club. This club held the first marathon in America on 20 September 1896 as part of one of its regular meetings.

The thirty runners were taken by train to Stamford, Connecticut, from where they started out at 12:26 on the 25-mile (40.2 km) journey to Columbia Oval in the city. For the first 8 miles they "plowed along through mud and slush", as *The New York Times* put it, with John McDermott in the lead. The last part of the route was perhaps the most difficult because, although there was no more mud, it consisted of a steady climb up Mount Vernon Avenue. The road was full of small cobbles, making the progress of the already very tired runners even more difficult. This hill was only one of the "many heart racking hills" the contestants had to negotiate.

McDermott had kept the lead the whole way, beating off the challenge of cross-country runner Hamilton Gray, and entered the track accompanied by a cyclist. The women spectators "fairly screamed with excitement", while the men left their seats and ran down to the track. "There was a pandemonium of joy."

McDermott's time was 3:25:55.6. He was followed by Gray (3:28:27) and Louis Liebgold (3:36:58). A total of ten runners finished the race and the attention the event received ensured the growth of the marathon in the United States.

The first Boston marathon took place on 19 April the next year – Patriots' Day, which commemorates Paul Revere's famous ride in 1775 during the American War of Indepen-

dence to warn inhabitants of the area of the approach of British troops. The race did not follow Revere's ride at all and was run from Metcalfe's Mill in Ashland to the Irvington Street Oval in Boston. The distance was 24 miles, 1 232 yards (39.7 km). Fifteen runners started from a line scraped in the road. The topography of the route was much the same as that of the Olympic race, although it was about 250 m shorter. It went through towns and villages that would become famous through their association with the race: South Framingham, Natick, Wellesley. It ended with one lap around the Oval, which was next to Exeter Street.

The race started at 12:19. Richard Grant, a track athlete from Harvard running his first marathon, took the lead with Gray. McDermott was about 400 m behind at Natick, but was closing the gap steadily. At the hill between Wellesley and Newton Lower Falls he caught the leaders and soon passed them. He received tremendous support from the crowds as he ran resolutely to the finish. Although he walked twice, he ran up the last hill "like a half miler, down the other side . . . breaking a funeral procession and stalling two electric cars", as the reporter of *The Boston Daily Globe* wrote, and reached the finish in the packed Oval in 2:55:10. The crowd swamped him, but he succeeded in escaping to the BAA clubhouse.

| RESULT: | 1 | J.J. McDermott 2:55:10 |
|---|---|---|
| | 2 | J.J. Kiernan 3:02:02 |
| | 3 | E.P. Rhell 3:06:02 |
| | 4 | H. Gray 3:11:37 |
| | 5 | H.D. Eggleston 3:17:50 |
| | 6 | J. Mason 3:31:00 |
| | 7 | W. Ryan 3:41:25 |
| | 8 | L. Brignolia 4:06:12 |
| | 9 | H. Franklin 4:08:00 |
| | 10 | A.T. Howe 4:10:00 |

## AMERICAN DOUBLE WINNER

John J. McDermott was 24 years old when he won the first marathon on US soil. In the inaugural Boston event he was one of six New Yorkers attempting to show the Bostonians how to run the marathon. The runners had to contend not only with the tough course, but also with dust kicked up by the accompanying horse-wagons and bicycles. But once McDermott had passed the two leaders, Gray and Grant, there was nothing stopping him. A newspaper report of the time waxed lyrical about his easy, fluid style and single-minded determination.

"He was running like clockwork. His legs seemed to rise and fall like a phantom Greek and . . . his arms were at full length at his side, and his face was set with determination. He breasted the long hill meaningfully, still maintaining his beautiful form, and he laughed at the wheelmen who were pounding their pedals in their endeavor to keep their machines in motion. [At the] Evergreen cemetery . . . he stopped running for the first time since he started just 20 miles back."

McDermott then walked for about 200 m, ran for another 200 m and suffered a cramp in his left leg. His leg was massaged and he started running again, but had to stop once more. His leg was rubbed and then he set off, walking once more for a short distance. He was almost hit by cars in a funeral procession, but "churned on, exasperated but unstopped, but several of the delicate horseless carriages, in appropriate funeral fashion, stalled".

He finished with severe blisters and promptly announced that he had run his last long race. But like other runners after him he could not keep his promise, for in the next year's Boston he finished fourth in 2:54:17.4.

Boston was the only US race which was to continue uninterrupted into the twentieth century. In 1901 there was a Pan-American Exposition marathon in Buffalo and in 1905 races were staged in Chicago and St Louis, with the Yonkers marathon in New York starting in 1907 (see p. 23).

In the meantime the marathon was also becoming popular in Europe and Canada. The first European race after the Olympics was held on 4 October 1896 in Hungary. Gyula Kellner dropped out; the winner over the 40 km distance was Bela Janko in 3:29:00. Kellner did win the following year over the same distance, in 3:52:00. No further races were held there until 1922.

Regular races were held in Sweden, although they were restricted to members of the organising clubs. The first open competition, over 40.2 km, was held on 13 August 1899 between Stockholm and Södertälje. Johan Nyström, a groom, won in 2:54:14.2. Norway's first marathon, on 4 October 1896 over the same distance, was won in 3:34:36 by Hallstein Bjerke. According to Martin and Gynn the 28 runners started at three-minute intervals.

Bjerke won the first Norwegian championship in 1897 and was third in the first Danish race in 1898. In Germany a race over 40 km was staged in 1898 (the winner was Arthur Techtow in 3:19:05), but no further events took place until 1905. France held a race over approximately 40 km for professional athletes in 1896. The route was from Paris to Conflans and 191 runners started. The British go-as-you-please expert Len Hurst (who had become a professional at the age of fifteen) won in 2:31:29.8. Four years later the race was run in the reverse direction and Hurst won in a marvellous 2:26:47.4. Amateurs were allowed to take part (the winner was Touquet in 2:38:00).

The 1898 Boston marathon was won by debuting Ronald McDonald, who was born in Canada and ran in bicycle shoes. McDonald started prudently at the back of the 21-man field and made his move on the Newton hills. He did not take any fluid and lost eight pounds during the race, but won in 2:42:00. The 1899 race started about 400 m from the previous point and finished at the BAA clubhouse on Exeter Street. (This start was to be used until 1907 and the finish until 1965.) The winner was the only man to have finished the first three races, and also – at 173 pounds (78.5 kg) – the heaviest victor ever: Lawrence Brignolia, an oarsman from Massachusetts. Despite falling and losing five minutes, Brignolia beat Grant easily in 2:54:38.

The Canadians had had long-distance races for years[1] and in 1900 came to Boston with the intention of winning. They did not only win, but claimed the top three places. The race was also memorable for another reason: it had a false start! This was caused by the Canadians who started sprinting after starter John Graham had made his speech and before he could set them off officially.

James Caffrey reached the finish first in 2:39:44.4 after a battle with his countryman William Sherring. Sherring ran 2:41:31.6 and F. Hughson finished third in 2:49:08.[2]

Controversy surrounded the 1900 Olympic Games in Paris, held together with the Paris Exposition and described at best as "a failure" and at worst as "the worst-organized and most vitriolic" Olympics. The Games were stretched out over a five-month period and matters were not helped much by the cool attitude of the French organisers of the Exposition towards athletics. The venue for the Games was the Racing Club de France in the scenic Bois de Boulogne and the track was a hastily laid out 500-metre oval on the club's lawn! In their book *Fast Tracks: The History of Distance Running* Raymond Krise and Bill Squires wrote that "'makeshift' was the order of the day".

It has been said that the marathon course was tailor-made for the French runners (it was changed at the last minute). The fact that France took the first two places and that the winner, Michel Théato, was a baker's roundsman who knew the intricate, poorly marked course through the streets and lanes of the capital very well, did not improve feelings after the race. With marvellous understatement Martin and Gynn wrote in *The Marathon Footrace* that ". . . many believe that [Théato's knowledge of Paris] contributed to his victory". Others were more forthright and accused Théato of cheating.

---

1. The *Hamilton Herald* organised a go-as-you-please event over 30.6 km on the east coast of Lake Ontario in 1894. This race has been held ever since, except in 1917-1919 and 1925-1935.
2. Sherring's day of glory would come six years later when he won the marathon at the Athens Intermediary Games in 2:51:23.6.

It was an extremely hot day, with temperatures reaching 39 °C and heavy traffic as well as sheep and pedestrians hindering the competitors. Ernst Fast of Sweden held the lead until 5 km before the end, but then took a wrong turn. He finished third (more than 37 minutes behind the winner) to become, at 19 years, 179 days, the youngest ever marathon medal winner. The American Arthur Newton claimed after the race that he had led from halfway and that no one had passed him. Newton was only one of many who criticised the way in which the race was conducted and the tactics of the French.

RESULT:
1 Michel Théato FRA 2:59:45
2 Emile Champion FRA 3:04:17
3 Ernst Fast SWE 3:37:14
4 Eugene Besse FRA 4:00:43
5 Arthur Newton USA 4:04:12
6 John Cregan USA
7 Richard Grant USA
8 Ronald McDonald USA

Théato was said to have been born in 1877, but the French athletics historian Alain Bouillé has claimed that he was actually born in Luxembourg in 1878. He turned professional in 1902 after having finished third in the 1901 Paris marathon in 2:42:43.4.

In the years of the third Olympiad between Paris and St Louis inaugural marathons were held in Austria (40 km at Vienna on 14 July 1901), Switzerland (40.2 km at Geneva on 27 October 1901), Belgium (36 km at Brussels in 1903), and Finland (40.2 km at Tikkurila on 16 September 1906). Italy's first marathon race had taken place over 40 km on 30 October 1898 in Milan.

The 1901 Boston event again went to Caffrey (in 2:29:23.6, the fastest yet), but the next year the Americans were back at the top. New Yorker Samuel Mellor, winner of the Buffalo race the previous year, finished first in 2:43:15.4 and he was followed by nine other Americans! There were 38 starters and an estimated 100 000 spectators along the route.

Boston had its first local winner in 1903, which was also the first year that the race was run on 20 April (Patriots' Day was on the Sunday). The Cambridge runner John Lorden beat Mellor by almost 6 minutes in 2:41:29.8. It was an exciting race between Mellor and Caffrey, with the lead changing nine times in the first 17 miles and the two runners trading insults. On the Newton hills Mellor ran away from Caffrey, only to be caught near the end by a storming Lorden. In fourth place in the results appeared a name which was to become famous: Fred Lorz.

The 1904 Olympic Games were once again attached to an international exposition, despite the lessons learned in Paris four years earlier. The Games had been awarded to Chicago, but because of the plans of St Louis to stage the Louisiana Purchase Exposition Chicago decided to relinquish its right.

Unfortunately the marathon runners were once again given scant consideration in the planning of their event.

Twelve nations sent 687 athletes (six women) to the Missouri city. Americans were the stars of the athletics events, with the brilliant James Lightbody taking the 800, 1500 (in a world record) and 3000 metres steeplechase. Archie Hahn won three sprints – 60 m (discontinued after these Games), 100 and 200 m, while Harry Hillman was first in the 400, 400 hurdles and 200 m low hurdles (also discontinued) and Ray Ewry first in the standing high, long and triple jumps (as he had been in 1900). The regular long and triple jump events were won by Myer Prinstein. No wonder the Games were called an American club championship!

Among the favourites for the marathon were the Americans Thomas Hicks, second in Boston that year in 2:39:34.2 behind Michael Spring, and Lorz, fifth in Boston. Two Zulus and a certain B.W. Harris became the first athletes from South Africa to take part in the Olympic Games (see Chapter 8). Another interesting entry was the tiny Cuban Felix Carvajal, who as a mail carrier had run from one end of his country to the other. He came to the United States by boat (he had raised money for the trip by running in circles around a public square in Havana) but lost all his money in a gambling game in New Orleans. He then hitchhiked to St Louis and appeared on the starting line of the marathon in heavy street shoes, long trousers and a long-sleeved shirt. Martin Sheridan, who was to win the discus throw three days later, cut off his pants at the knees.

The marathon was run on 30 August over 40 km[3] and in 32 °C heat. There were 32 starters. The only water along the route, which included seven hills and sections paved with cracked stone, was at a well 12 miles into the race. A cloud of dust was kicked up by the accompanying vehicles. Martin and Gynn (The Marathon Footrace) called it "the most devastating marathon environment ever seen" and referred to the "brutality of conditions". It has also been called one of the most bizarre events in Olympic history.

Lorz led initially, but was soon caught by Spring, Mellor, Newton and Hicks. After 9 miles Lorz developed cramps, stopped and got into a car. Newton and Mellor were leading, but soon afterwards Mellor started walking while Hicks was moving up. By 14 miles Mellor had recovered, increased speed and caught Newton, moving into the lead. Hicks was third, followed by the Frenchman Albert Corey, a professional strikebreaker, and William Garcia running together, and then Carvajal.

Over the next few miles Corey started to tire. Garcia and Mellor pulled out (Garcia was found unconscious at the roadside and nearly lost his life because of a stomach haemorrhage caused by the dust), while in the lead Hicks ap-

---

3. According to Roger Gynn, The Guinness Book of the Marathon, modern reconstruction has shown that the course was closer to 26 miles (41.8 km) in length.

peared close to collapse. With 10 miles to go Hicks was sponged down and his mouth rinsed out with distilled water. Seven miles from the end his attendant, Charles Lucas, gave him $\frac{1}{60}$ grain of strychnine sulphate with raw egg white. Hicks wanted to lie down and rest, but his helpers spurred him on. At 19 miles he was in the lead by 1½ miles and was then given a concoction of strychnine, egg and a sip of brandy. His whole body was also bathed in hot water, kept warm alongside the boiler of a steam-engined automobile. He was having hallucinations and was moving mechanically. His helpers did have beef tea with them but did not give it to the runner because they feared it might upset his stomach!

Then something dramatic happened.

Hicks was suddenly passed by Lorz, who was running fluidly. He sped over the last two hills and entered the stadium alone, about 15 minutes ahead of Hicks. Even though Hicks had to walk the rest of the way (he was given more brandy and eggs) and slowly jogged into the stadium, no other runner could catch him.

Lorz thoroughly enjoyed his hero's welcome (he was photographed with the daughter of the US President, Alice Roosevelt), but his fame was short-lived. The officials who had accompanied the runners lodged a protest and Hicks was declared the winner. Lorz admitted that he had played a practical joke (he jogged to the finish because the car he was travelling in had broken down!) and was banned by the Amateur Athletic Union. However, he was later reinstated and in 1905 won the Boston marathon.

The irrepressible Carvajal, who ran with no assistance at all, finished a remarkable fourth – after having taken some peaches from an official and green apples from a farmer's orchard and stopping a couple of times to talk to spectators.

The modern marathon runner can only shudder at the effects of the "refreshments" given to Hicks. He lost more than 20 kg during the race and afterwards told reporters that he would rather have won the race than be president of the United States. He never ran a marathon again.

| RESULT: | | | |
|---|---|---|---|
| | 1 | Thomas Hicks USA | 3:28:53 |
| | 2 | Albert Corey USA | 3:34:52 |
| | 3 | Arthur Newton USA | 3:47:33 |
| | 4 | Felix Carvajal CUB | |
| | 5 | Demeter Velouis GRE | |
| | 6 | David Kneeland USA | |
| | 7 | M.A. Brawley USA | |
| | 8 | Sydney Hatch USA | |
| | 9 | Lentauw RSA | |
| | 10 | C.D. Zahuritis GRE | |
| | 11 | F.P. Devlin USA | |
| | 12 | Yamasani RSA | |

It is still the only time in Olympic history that the first three runners have come from the same country, although there is some doubt whether Corey had in fact obtained American citizenship, as the British-born Hicks had.

Lorz won the 1905 Boston race by nearly 90 seconds. About three weeks later the first Missouri Athletic Club marathon, which actually started in the Illinois town of Freeburg, was won by Joseph Forshaw in 3:15:57.8. Carvajal was third. The same year the Illinois A.C. also staged a marathon, won by Rhud Metzner in 3:15:00.

The Greeks wanted the Olympic Games to be held in Athens every four years. De Coubertin reached a compromise with them: an Intermediate Games would be staged in the middle of an Olympiad. These Games were never given the official title of "Olympic" and were held only once, in 1906.

The 1906 Games were not part of any other event and were planned well. The marathon was held on a course more or less parallel to the earlier one and was 41.86 km long. The date was 1 May and 53 runners took part. A Greek victor would receive a statue of Hermes, a loaf of bread every day for a year, three cups of coffee a day for a year, free shaves for life, and a free lunch for six every Sunday for a year! But it was not to be.

The winner was the Canadian Sherring, a railwayman from Hamilton. His savings were supplemented by a donation of $75 from his club, but it wasn't enough to get him to Europe. So he gave the $75 to a friend, who bet the money on a horse named Cicely. The horse duly won and paid 6-1 odds. Now Sherring had enough money. Once in Greece he supported himself through a part-time job as a railway porter. When the Greeks staged a trial over the marathon course on 17 March, Sherring must have chuckled, for he had covered the same course in a training run 20 minutes faster than the winning time of 3:04:29.6.

In the Games race Sherring took the lead for good after 29 km. Although not a Greek, he was greeted at the stadium gates by Prince George, who ran the length of the track with him to the finish in front of the royal box, and by the thunderous roar of the 80 000 spectators.

| RESULT: | | | |
|---|---|---|---|
| | 1 | William Sherring CAN | 2:51:23.6 |
| | 2 | John Svanberg SWE | 2:58:20.8 |
| | 3 | William Frank USA | 3:00:46.8 |
| | 4 | Gustav Tornros SWE | 3:01:00 |
| | 5 | Ioannis Alepous GRE | 3:09:25.4 |
| | 6 | George Blake AUS | 3:09:35 |
| | 7 | Constantinos Karvelas GRE | 3:15:54 |
| | 8 | Andre Roffi FRA | 3:17:49.8 |
| | 9 | Hermann Muller GER | 3:21:00 |
| | 10 | C.H. Natabaris GRE | |

Back in Hamilton Sherring's financial troubles were over, for he received $5 000 from the city, as well as $400 from Toronto.

One of the athletes who did not complete the Athens race was Dorando Pietri, who retired after 24 km because of stomach problems. Only two years later his name would become part of the Olympic marathon lore.

In Finland the first marathon on 16 September 1906 was won by Kaarlo Nieminen in 3:01:06. Nine months later he won a marathon in Viipuri in 2:49:15. In this race over 40 km two of the three Kolehmainen brothers who were to achieve fame in later years made their debut. Tatu was second in 3:04:15 and Hannes, only seventeen, third in 3:06:19. (The next year he improved to 2:52:36, and in 1909 he clocked 2:42:59 for a 40.2 km track race in Göteborg.) In the trial race for the 1908 Olympics, on 24 May 1908, Nieminen won over the same distance in 2:47:19.4, beating Tatu by 12½ minutes. The Finnish selectors decided that Tatu was not good enough to go to London, so a month later he showed them by clocking 2:39:04 over 40 km!

In the United States interest centred on the Boston marathon in the years between Athens and London. The 1907 race was won by an Onondaga Indian teenager, Thomas Longboat from Toronto. It was Longboat's first marathon and he ran through rain and sleet to victory in 2:24:20.8 – a course record. Longboat was one of a group of nine who managed to cross a railway line in front of a train in South Framingham, while Robert Fowler and John Hayes had to wait for the train to pass and then chased the leaders the rest of the way. Fowler and Hayes finished second and third in 2:27:54.8 and 2:30:38.6 respectively.

Later in the year (28 November) Hayes won the first Yonkers marathon in New York in 2:43:00 and the next year was second at Boston in 2:26:04, beaten by 20.8 seconds by Thomas Morrissey. Fowler was third.

While the marathon was gaining in popularity in the US, England was also preparing for an assault on the Olympic title. In April a trial race was held from Windsor to Wembley Park. It was organised by Polytechnic Harriers and included a part of the Olympic route. The distance was 22½ miles (36.2 km). The winner in terrible conditions of heavy rain, hail and snow accompanied by a cold wind was Alex Duncan in 2:15:45. The first six were selected for the Olympics.

The first national championship in Italy was held in Rome on 3 June 1908; it was also the Olympic trial. There were only three competitors, with Pietri the favourite. But he failed again, dropping out at 33 km despite excellent performances in 1907. However, he was selected for the Olympic marathon after he had proved himself with a time of 2:38:00 in a 40 km run only seventeen days before the Olympic marathon.

Other countries were also busy preparing their runners for the Olympic race. Among them was South Africa, who sent Charles Hefferon to London even though he could not complete the official trial (see Chapter 8).

The Olympic race of 1908 was one of the most dramatic marathons of all time. The Polytechnic Harriers' organisation of the April trial was so impressive that the club was given the responsibility of staging the Olympic event. As things turned out, the odd distance used for the race was

## YONKERS

The first Yonkers marathon, on 28 November 1907, was won by John Hayes in 2:43:00. After a break from 1918 to 1934 the race was again held regularly and won mostly by North Americans. The late 1950s and early 1960s was the era of John J. Kelley, who had an uninterrupted winning streak from 1956 to 1963. His fastest time was 2:20:13.6 in 1960. His near-namesake John A. Kelley won the race in 1935 and again in 1950. From 1949 to 1966 the race incorporated the American national championship.

Gary Muhrcke, winner of the first New York City marathon in 1970, also won Yonkers in 1968 and 1969.

to become the official marathon distance. The start was on the East Terrace of Windsor Castle and the route stretched 26 miles to the White City Stadium in Shepherd's Bush. In order to have the finish line directly in front of the royal box, another 385 yards were added (the track was 536.45 m long) to make the distance of 26 miles, 385 yards (42.195 km).

According to the Official Report of the Games the Oxo Company was the official caterer and would provide the following refreshments along the marathon route: hot and cold Oxo, Oxo and soda, rice pudding, raisins, bananas, soda and milk. The Oxo representatives stationed at intervals would also provide eau de Cologne and sponges. (No wonder the *Official Centenary History of the Amateur Athletic Association* states that the competitors were "the best fed and most fragrant marathon runners in history"!) The runners had to be properly attired, wearing "complete clothing from the shoulder to the knees (i.e. jersey sleeved to the elbows and loose drawers with slips)".

"Dressing accommodation" was available at Great Western Railway, Windsor Station, where all the waiting rooms and cloakrooms were at the runners' disposal.

For the first time more than 2 000 competitors took part in the Games, and the 23 nations represented was also a record. Two days before the marathon the South African Reggie Walker won his country's first-ever gold medal when he took the 100 m in an Olympic record time of 10.8 seconds. The American Mel Shepperd repeated the feat of Edwin Flack and James Lightbody at earlier Games by winning both the 800 and 1500 m. On the day before the marathon there was big drama in the 400 m final, contested between three Americans and one Briton, Wyndham Halswelle. John Carpenter impeded Halswelle and the race was declared no contest. When it was rerun two days later, the Americans refused to participate and Halswelle, who had fought in the Boer War, ran alone, winning in 50.0 seconds.[4]

So there was no love lost between the Americans and the British when the marathon started at 14:30 on 24 July, with 56 runners lining up. It was a hot, humid afternoon and the

---

4. The events of the 1908 Games were run entirely by the British, and the controversy in the 400 m was just one of many disputes between the organisers and participating countries, especially the United States.

initial pace set by the British runners was far too fast. Tom Jack ran the first mile in 5:02.4 and continued this pace for the first 3 miles. At 5 miles his time was 27:01. He was 6 seconds ahead of Jack Price, who was followed by Fred Lord, Duncan, Hefferon and Pietri. By 10 miles Price was leading, just ahead of Lord. Hefferon was 19 seconds behind them in third place, with Pietri on his heels. Soon afterwards the strong South African, who had placed fourth in the 5 miles earlier in the Games, overtook Lord and at the halfway mark was 41 seconds behind the leader.

Hefferon was running extremely well and his determination to emulate Walker carried him into the lead soon after 14 miles. Price gave up and by 15 miles (88:22) the South African's lead over Lord was exactly 2 minutes. Pietri was 6 seconds further back. Then Lord stopped for a rest and both Pietri and Longboat passed him. Before the Games the United States had protested that Longboat was a professional (although there were no details), but this was denied by Canada and the athlete was allowed to run.

Longboat could not sustain the pace and started to walk. Hefferon was now almost 4 minutes ahead of the Italian and looked like the winner. He passed 20 miles in 2:02:26. But, surprisingly, despite the heat Pietri started to speed up and behind him the Americans, who had been running conservatively, were also moving up. By 22 miles Pietri was only 2:47 behind and by 24 miles he had cut another 47 seconds from Hefferon's lead. Behind him came the Americans Hayes, Joseph Foreshaw and Alton Welton.

## THE MAN FROM CARPI

Dorando Pietri's loss in the 1908 Olympic Marathon brought him more fame than victory brought John Hayes. Pietri's valiant struggle on the White City track resulted in an outpouring of sympathy and on the initiative of Sir Arthur Conan Doyle he was presented with an exact replica of the gold cup won by Hayes. The inscription read: "To Pietri Dorando In Remembrance of the Marathon Race From Windsor to the Stadium July. 24. 1908 from Queen Alexandra." Songs were written about him, including one by Irving Berlin.

In Italy Pietri was celebrated with poems and festivals. His home town of Carpi collected 1 496.65 lire for him.

Pietri was born in Mandrio on 16 October 1885. His first sport was cycling, but he soon abandoned this for running. He won his first national title over 25 km in 1905 and in his international debut won the Paris 30 km race. Early in 1906 he won a 42 km race in Rome in 2:42:00.6.

After the Olympic Games he turned professional and ran with mixed success in the USA, beating Hayes four times, but losing some races and failing to finish others. His best time over 42.195 km was the 2:44:20.4 with which he beat Hayes in Madison Square Garden on 25 November 1908. The runners had to negotiate more than 260 laps of the track!

In Buenos Aires on 24 May 1909 he clocked 2:38:48.2 over 42.4 km. This was his last marathon. When he retired in 1911 he had won 38 of 59 amateur races and 50 of 69 as a professional. His marathon record was eight victories in seventeen starts (not counting the 1908 London race).

Unfortunately Pietri's brother relieved him of most of his winnings, and he had to spend the rest of his days as a taxi driver. He died in San Remo on 7 February 1942.

Pietri's pursuit of the South African from 20 miles was relentless; this was one race he was going to finish – and win. The progress of the pursuit can be seen in their mile times: 16th mile – Pietri 7:06, Hefferon 6:38, 17th mile – Pietri 7:11, Hefferon 6:47, 18th mile – Pietri 7:24, Hefferon 7:04, 19th mile – Pietri 6:51, Hefferon 6:38, 20th mile – Pietri 7:18, Hefferon 6:57, 21st mile – Pietri 5:58, Hefferon 6:32, 22nd mile: Pietri 7:51, Hefferon 8:22.

Dorando's time for 23 miles is not available, but he ran the two miles from 22 to 24 miles in 25:21 against Hefferon's 26:08. Two miles from the stadium Hefferon made the mistake of accepting a drink of champagne. He started getting cramps and became dizzy. Pietri saw the leader for the first time in Old Oak Common Lane and less than a mile from the stadium he swept into the lead. In the meantime Hayes, who had enjoyed a light lunch of two ounces of beef, two slices of toast and a cup of tea but had taken nothing on the route, was actually running much better than either Pietri or Hefferon.

When Pietri came down a ramp into the stadium, the race that had been rather uneventful up to that stage suddenly changed to high drama. The small moustached Italian with his white cap, white shirt and long, red shorts turned right onto the cinder track instead of left. Offficials pointed him in the right direction, but before he could go much further, he stumbled and fell. The crowd of nearly 100 000 started screaming. Officials and doctors ran to help him. He got to his feet and set out again to run the remaining distance he still had to cover – about 385 yards, the distance added to the race to have the finish in front of Queen Alexandra.

Pietri fell four more times as he struggled desperately to achieve the coveted victory. Each time he was helped by his handlers, who sponged him down in an effort to revive his strength. According to a newspaper report of the time he was practically delirious, his movement being "simply a flounder, with arms shaking and legs tottering". When he fell for the fifth time, just short of the finish, he was held by Jack Andrew, the chief organiser of the race, who assisted him across the line. By this time Hayes had also appeared on the track, having passed Hefferon mere metres from the stadium gates.

Pietri collapsed as soon as he was across the finish and was taken away on a stretcher, close to death. Just over half a minute later Hayes crossed the line, with Hefferon finishing another 48 seconds later. The race was a triumph for North American runners, with the home athletes suffering from their rash start. Only 27 of the 56 starters finished.

The Italian flag was immediately run up the victory pole but, quite naturally, the Americans lodged a protest and Pietri was disqualified. Andrew stated that he was only carrying out the instructions of the race doctor, Doctor Bulger. Martin and Gynn quote him from *The Polytechnic Magazine*: "As regard the actual finish, most of the reports of same are absolutely erroneous regards my assisting the winner – the doctor's instructions were emphatic, carrying them out caused disqualification; as the animated photographs show,

I only caught Dorando as he was falling at the tape. What I did then I would do again under similar circumstances."

RESULT:
1. John Hayes USA 2:55:18.4
2. Charles Hefferon RSA 2:56:06
3. Joseph Foreshaw USA 2:57:10.4
4. Alton Welton USA 2:59:44.4
5. William Wood CAN 3:01:44
6. Frederick Simpson CAN 3:04:28.2
7. Harry Lawson CAN 3:06:47.2
8. John Svanberg SWE 3:07:50.8
9. Louis Tewanima USA 3:09:15
10. Kaarlo Nieminen FIN 3:09:50.8.
Disq.: Dorando Pietri ITA 2:54:46.4

By the next day Pietri had recovered remarkably from his gruelling effort. He appeared in the stadium to receive a special gold cup from the Queen and charged that the British officials should have left him alone because he could have finished without their aid. However, photographs of the events in the stadium show that this was most unlikely.

The 22-year-old Hayes, whose winning time became the first world record for the marathon, returned to the US a hero. He had prepared for the Olympics mostly by running on the cinder path on the roof of Bloomingdale's Department Store in New York, where he worked. On his return he was promoted to manager of the sporting goods department.[5]

Hayes and Pietri soon became professional runners. Pietri won the first race between them, on the indoor track of Madison Square Garden, New York. The two contestants tossed a coin for the starting position; Hayes won and took the inside position. Pietri pulled away after 25 miles. After the 26th mile spectators, thinking the race was over, streamed onto the track and blows had to be resorted to in order to clear a path for the runners. After the race Pietri indicated that he had shown that he was indeed the better runner.

Less than a month later he tackled Longboat at the same venue. In almost a repeat of the London race Pietri collapsed in the 26th mile and was carried unconscious to the dressing room. He and Longboat each received $3 750.

An unusual event took place on Christmas day 1908 when eleven sailors ran a marathon on the warship *Wyoming* in the harbour of San Francisco. They had to cover 355 laps of the 130-yard track laid out on the deck!

A plethora of races, amateur and professional, sprung up as the marathon increased in popularity. One of the most

remarkable was the duel between Longboat and the famous English runner Alfred Shrubb on 5 February 1909 in Madison Square Garden. At one stage Shrubb, in his first marathon, was nearly a mile ahead, but he started to tire and collapsed at 24½ miles.

On 15 March 1909 Pietri and Hayes met for the second time, again in the Garden, and again the Italian won. But on 3 April, this time outdoors, both Pietri and Hayes, as well as Longboat, were beaten in 2:40:50.6 by the French waiter Henri St Yves. Pietri finished almost 5 minutes behind the Frenchman, but beat Hayes by almost 4 minutes.

Meanwhile Fowler had set a new world amateur record of 2:52:45.4 on 1 January in a chaotic marathon in Yonkers. The race started – in -18 °C! – with a 5 km run from Getty Square to the Empire City race track, followed by laps around the track. Crowd control was poor and the race was stopped after seven runners had finished. Fowler's time was beaten on 12 February by James Clark USA, who recorded 2:46:52.6 on a course from Brooklyn to Coney Island and back. On 8 May Albert Raines USA improved the mark further when he ran 2:46:04.6 in the Bronx marathon (start and finish in the Bronx Oval). On the same day the professionals contested a derby with prize money of $10 000 at the New York Polo Grounds. St Yves won the first prize of $5 000 in 2:41:05, with Pietri finishing only sixth.

In November 1909 the Amateur Athletic Union decided at its convention in New York that no runners of fifteen years and younger would be allowed to enter ultradistance races. Entrants in all races longer than 5 miles were required to be examined by a licensed physician before they could participate.

In Britain there was big disappointment about the performances of its runners in the Olympic marathon, and the newspaper *Sporting Life* donated a trophy for the winner of an annual race of not less than 25 miles in an effort to promote distance running. The first race, on 26 May 1909 from Windsor Park to Stamford Bridge, was organised by Polytechnic Harriers and won by one of the club's runners, Harry Barrett, in a new world record of 2:42:31. He beat Lord by exactly 2 minutes.

A little more than three months later, on 31 August in Stockholm, the Swede Thure Johansson clocked 2:40:34.2 on a 368 m track inside the Idrottsparken velodrome. According to the International Athletic Foundation's *Progression of World Best Performances and Official IAAF World Records* the distance was 1 m short of 42.195 km. Johansson turned professional soon thereafter and the next year ran 2:36:55.2 indoors in New York.

In other parts of the British Commonwealth, Australia and South Africa, the marathon was also taking root. Down under the first marathon was run on 12 April 1909 in Sydney. The winner was Andrew Sime in 3:05:30.2, but four months later the first Australian championship was won in Brisbane by Andrew Wood in 2:59:15.4. Hefferon's performance in Lon-

5. A different view on Hayes is given by Krise and Squires, *Fast Tracks: The History of Distance Running*. According to them Hayes was paid by Bloomingdale's to train as a full-time runner (the result of a deal between the firm and Hayes's club, the Irish-American A.C.). He actually trained on a track outside Manhattan, not on the store roof. But in *The Complete Book of The Olympics* David Wallechinsky merely says that when Hayes was chosen for the Olympic marathon, his employer gave him a full vacation with pay to train.

## THE "POLY"

The Polytechnic Harriers club was formed in 1883 as the running section of the Hannover Athletics Club (founded in 1873). The Harriers held their first cross-country event in October 1883.

The club's first marathon, staged in conjunction with *Sporting Life*, had 68 competitors. The unfavourable conditions did not stop the club's own Henry Frederick "Harry" Barrett from establishing the first world record by an Englishman.

The race was interrupted during World War I (it did not take place in 1910 either because of the King's health), but resumed in 1919 and was then held without a break until 1974.

In 1924 both Duncan McLeod Wright and Sam Ferris debuted in the Poly, with the former winning in 2:53:17.4 and Ferris finishing second. Six years later they were to finish in the same order in the first Commonwealth Games marathon. In 1925 Ferris scored his first victory and he repeated this in 1926, 1927, 1928, 1929, 1931, 1932 and 1933. In 1930 he missed the race through injury; in 1933, when the race finished in the White City for the first time, he won for the eighth time in his last marathon.

Jim Peters won on his debut in 1951 and then took the next three races, each in world record time (see pp. 48, 51-52). Peters's 1954 course record 2:17:39.4 stood until 1963 when the American Buddy Edelen broke it – with a world record 2:14:28! In the next two years further world records were set: 2:13:55 by Basil Heatley in 1964 and 2:12:00 by Morio Shigematsu in 1965. (From 1946 to 1972 the Poly finished in Chiswick.)

Other runners who won three times were Bobby Mills (1920-22), Bert Norris (1935-37), Leslie Griffiths (1940, 1942-43), Jack Holden (1948-50). Women first took part in 1978, with Gillian Adams winning in 2:54:11.

don gave marathon running a significant impetus in South Africa, too. In November 1910 Kenneth McArthur ran 2:42:58.2 in Cape Town – the fastest time yet recorded anywhere in the world on an out-and-back course (see Chapter 8).

In the US the Boston marathon of 1910 heralded the start of the phenomenal career of one of the all-time greats, Clarence DeMar. He finished second, but the next year won in 2:21:39.6 after the race leader, Festus Madden, had been hit by a car 2 miles from the end. Although DeMar was not to win the race again until 1922, he became one of the most famous runners of Boston.

The professionals continued battling it out over the marathon distance and running fast times, culminating in the 2:32:21.8 run by Hans Holmer CAN on 3 January 1911 in Edinburgh.

The Japanese were starting to gear up for the 1912 Olympic marathon in Stockholm, with the first race over an approximate marathon distance (25 miles) held in November 1911. It was won in 2:32:52 by Shizo Kanaguri, who was to win the first three Japanese championship races, although he could not finish the Stockholm marathon. In Britain the 1912 Polytechnic Harriers marathon, or "Poly" as it became known, was won by Holmer's countryman James Corkery, who beat the South African Christian Gitsham. This race had an unfortunate ending, as the runners were directed the wrong way on entering the stadium and thus completed only 480 yards on the track instead of 840. Corkery's time of 2:36:55.4 could therefore not be recognised as a new world record. Gitsham finished a fine second in 2:37:14.6.

The Finns were also ready. Between July 1909 and the Olympic trial at Oulukyla on 19 May 1912 Tatu Kolehmainen did not run a single marathon (after he had completed eight between June 1907 and 1909), but he won the trial on a muddy course in a brilliant 2:29:07.6.

The Games of the fifth Olympiad started in Stockholm on 5 May 1912, with 28 nations taking part. It was the first Games where electric timing devices and a public address system were used. The hero, and tragic figure, of these Games was the American Indian Jim Thorpe. He won the decathlon by a huge margin (with a world record), and was also placed first in the pentathlon, but the next year was disqualified for having played semiprofessional baseball in 1910. (The Stockholm decathlon was the only three-day contest in Olympic history.) Both short sprint titles were won by American Ralph Craig, while Tatu Kolehmainen's brother Hannes won the first 5000 and 10000 m races contested at the Olympics. (He also won the individual cross-country title.)

On 14 July at 13:45, four days after his brother's victory in the 5000 m, Tatu stood on the starting line of the marathon. He himself had dropped out of the 10000 m six days earlier. It was very hot when the 68 runners gathered for the race. The course was out and back to Sollentuna, but was only 40.2 km. All wheeled traffic was prohibited for the duration of the race.

Kolehmainen, Alex Ahlgren SWE and Carlo Speroni ITA (who was only seventeen) went into the lead. The two South Africans, the slender Gitsham and the sturdily built McArthur, were in the second group. By the second control point at Tureberg Kolehmainen was 13 seconds ahead of the South Africans. Then followed Lord, Ahlgren and his countryman Sigge Jacobsson.

Between Tureberg and the turn at Sollentuna Gitsham moved to the front, putting 15 seconds between him and the struggling Kolehmainen. Gitsham reached the halfway mark in 72:40. McArthur was third, 35 seconds behind Gitsham. But the Finn rallied and when they reached Tureberg again (94:40) he pulled even with Gitsham. McArthur was running strongly and confidently one second behind. Speroni was fourth, ahead of Jacobsson and Lord. The Americans, among them the winner of the silver medal in the 10000 m, Louis Tewanima, Gaston Strobino, Andrew Sockalexis and DeMar, were well back.

The effort proved too much for Kolehmainen and he started to fade again, eventually dropping out. When McArthur and Gitsham passed the control point at Stocksund in 2:14:20 they were 30 seconds ahead of Strobino and Jacobsson. The Canadian James Duffy was moving through the field after having paced himself very well in the tough conditions and moved into fourth. Speroni was still there, followed by the American Indians Tewanima and Sockalexis. But the battle was still to come, and this Olympic marathon was to be no less dramatic than those that had gone before.

McArthur and Gitsham stuck together, neither prepared to

give his countryman an edge. But when they reached a long hill near the stadium, Gitsham stopped for a drink. McArthur had apparently said that he would wait for his team-mate (he took no refreshment during the entire race), but now he seized the opportunity and opened a small gap. This proved to be decisive and he steadily increased it to the finish. Gitsham, his rhythm gone, tried everything he could, but there was no stopping the policeman from Potchefstroom.

Behind them Strobino and Sockalexis passed Jacobsson, who had made the mistake of wearing new shoes, but Speroni collapsed and Tewanima was jogging along slowly.

A tired McArthur ran into the stadium to the roar of the crowd and circled the track. A laurel wreath tied with the colours of South Africa was placed over his shoulders, throwing him off-stride. However, he kept going, although he staggered after reaching the tape and was carried away to receive attention. His time of 2:36:54.8 beat Gitsham by 57.2 seconds. DeMar finished twelfth.

Since 1912 no other country has been able to equal the South African feat of winning both the gold and silver medal in the marathon. McArthur's triumph "over ruwe wegen en heuvels" (over rough roads and hills) was reported in the Potchefstroom newspaper *Het Westen* under the heading "Champion of the world". The reputed agreement between the two South Africans to stay together until the end caused a fair amount of controversy later. According to one version given by H.B. Keartland, manager of the South African team, McArthur did not wait when Gitsham drank water near the end. But, according to another source, Keartland seemed to indicate that McArthur had indeed waited, but drew away when Gitsham started developing cramps in his legs soon after he had taken water.

Keartland said that after the race harsh words were exchanged between McArthur and Gitsham, whose relationship had not been good even beforehand. However, it seems unlikely that two runners would arrange to finish together in an Olympic championship – even if they were team-mates. And Keartland's story that they did not have much to say to each other and were jealous of the other's performances made it even more unlikely.

RESULT:
1 Kenneth McArthur RSA 2:36:54.8
2 Christian Gitsham RSA 2:37:52
3 Gaston Strobino USA 2:38:42.4
4 Andrew Sockalexis USA 2:42:07.9
5 James Duffy CAN 2:42:18.8
6 Sigge Jacobsson SWE 2:43:24.9
7 John Gallagher USA 2:44:19.4
8 Joseph Erxleben USA 2:45:47.4
9 Richard Piggott USA 2:46:40.7
10 Joseph Forshaw USA 2:49:49.4

Tragedy struck the marathon for the first time when, in the latter stages of the race, the Portuguese record holder, Francisco Lazaro (21), collapsed in the stifling heat. He was given first aid and then taken to hospital, where everything possible was done to revive him. It was all in vain, however, and Lazaro died the next day. According to Martin and Gynn, hospital records were not available and it is not certain whether an autopsy was carried out. Lazaro may have had a heart problem, but the heat of the afternoon surely contributed to his death.

McArthur, who was 30 years old and born in Derbock, Northern Ireland, received offers to become a professional runner and participate in the US, but he refused. He retired from running, but Gitsham continued to run on the track.

The 1912 Olympics were the last Games until 1920. World War I intervened and, whereas in ancient times wars were interrupted when it was time for the Olympics, it was now the other way around. The 1916 Olympics, scheduled for Berlin, were cancelled.

The 1912 Games were also significant because they saw the founding of the International Amateur Athletics Federation (IAAF) on 17 July. Representatives from seventeen countries were at the meeting.

Willie Kolehmainen had a somewhat more successful 1912 than his brother Tatu. Willie, a professional, first clocked 2:32:56.5 and then went to America, where he brought the world best down to 2:29:39.2 in a track race in Vailsburg, New Jersey.

One of the best races of the period between Stockholm and the War occurred in the "Poly" on 31 May 1913. Only 35 runners toed the line, but there were some big names among them: Tatu Kolehmainen, Ahlgren, Johannes Christensen DEN, Louis Pautiex FRA, John Westberg SWE, and Lord. Nineteen days before, the Frenchman had run a brilliant 2:36:19.8 for 42 km, which would have been a world record if the course was the full distance. On the same day, on a track at Shepherd's Bush, Harry Green GBR set a new world record of 2:38:16.2. But the Polytechnic race was to be a battle among the foreigners. Kolehmainen, Ahlgren, Christensen and Pautiex exchanged the lead for the first half until Pautiex started to tire after 27 km. Not long afterwards Christensen could not keep up either and, as if this were a signal, Ahlgren surged away from Kolehmainen. Accompanied all the way by the Swedish ambassador, Ahlgren increased his lead to the finish, reached in 2:36:06.6. It was a new world record and he had beaten the Finn by more than 5½ minutes.

RESULT:
1 Alexis Ahlgren SWE 2:36:06.6
2 Tatu Kolehmainen FIN 2:41:48
3 Johannes Christensen DEN 2:44:30.4
4 John Westberg SWE 2:44:54
5 Fred Lord GBR 2:49:07.8

At the next year's "Poly" Ahlgren's chances of defending his title evaporated because of an upset stomach. The winner in

2:46:50.8 was the French Algerian Ahmed Djebelia, who had run in the first, albeit unofficial, French championship only six days previously.

The first marathon in Russia was held on 20 August 1913 as part of the All-Russian Olympic festival at Kiev. The distance was 40.5 km and although the winning time was slow (Aleksandr Maksimov 3:03:00), the marathon had gained a foothold in the country.

Across the Atlantic the 1914 Boston was won by Duffy with another good performance – 2:25:01. For the next four years, with war raging in Europe, the marathon focus was in North America. The 1915 Boston was also won by a Canadian, Edouard Fabre, in 2:31:41.2. But in 1916 the famous race saw its first home-town winner when Arthur Roth (who hailed from the Boston neighbourhood of Roxbury) beat Ville Kyronen by less than 11 seconds after a desparate sprint by the latter. In 1917 DeMar returned, but had to settle for third (2:31:05) behind William Kennedy 2:28:37.2 (at 35 the oldest winner ever) and Sydney Hatch 2:30:19.2 (his third consecutive top-three finish). Hannes Kolehmainen was fourth.

In 1918, with the US part of the global conflict and priorities shifting to the war effort in Europe, Boston still went ahead, but this time fourteen teams of ten soldiers each ran it as a relay – in full military uniform. Thus the tradition of a race on Patriots' Day was maintained.

# 4

# 1919-1945
# A STANDARD DISTANCE

THE WAR WAS over, but the countries of Europe were devastated and the people had priorities other than marathon running. Both the 1919 "Poly" and Boston produced slow winning times. Gradually, however, as the process of rebuilding gained momentum, sport grew in importance again. The 1920 Olympic Games were to have been held in Budapest, but as Hungary was one of the defeated nations it was decided to award the Games to Antwerp. Because of the ravages of war there was a lack of facilities – the Games started less than two years after the end of the War. A new stadium was built in the Belgian capital, but was never more than about a third full for the duration of the Games. These are also the only Games never to have produced an official report.

The new Olympic flag, designed by Pierre de Coubertin and depicting the five rings on the altar at Delphi to represent the five continents, was displayed for the first time.

The Americans held four marathon trial races, with Hannes Kolehmainen and two of his Finnish countrymen running in the last one. Kolehmainen was then living in the US. He won in 2:47:49.4 on a difficult course said to be about 26.5 miles (42.6 km). It was the Finn's first marathon since the 1917 Boston, when he finished fourth. Second was Joseph Organ, who was to be the top American finisher in Antwerp.

Kolehmainen's team-mates in the Olympic marathon would be his brother Tatu, who won the Finnish trial over 40.2 km in 2:39:03.5, Urho Tallgren and Juha Tuomikoski. The top British contender would be Arthur ("Bobby") Mills, who on 17 July 1920 won the Polytechnic marathon in a British record of 2:37:40.4. It was his debut marathon!

The first Olympic Games in eight years started on 20 April. Despite the War, a record number of competitors and nations (29) took part. Austria, Hungary, Germany, Bulgaria and Turkey were not allowed to participate. The American team was involved in a controversy that nearly caused the end of US participation. The team travelled to Europe on the *Princess Matoika*, a ship which had been used to transport American dead from World War I. Conditions were unbearable, but the team's protests were largely ignored. The team was promised better accommodation in Antwerp, but when this did not materialise the world record holder in the triple jump, Dan Ahearn, refused to stay in the team quarters. He was suspended and the entire team threatened to withdraw from the Games. (Ahearn could only finish sixth in his event.)

The undisputed superiority of the American athletes in all previous Olympics was challenged by tiny Finland. The Finns' tally of nine gold medals equalled that of the USA and their total of sixteen medals was only thirteen fewer than the Americans won. The USA won only three track events. The long-distance races marked the emergence of one of the greatest athletes of all time, the phenomenal Finn Paavo Nurmi. Nurmi was second in the 5000 metres and took gold in the 10000 m. He also won the individual cross-country and was a member of the winning Finnish team.

So when Hannes Kolehmainen started the marathon with 41 other runners just after 16:10 on 22 August, he carried the hopes of his nation on his shoulders: he was expected to win to add to the glory of Finland. For the first time in the history of the Games the marathon was run in cool conditions, but at 42.75 km the course – out and back to Runspi – was the longest ever.

One of Kolehmainen's strongest rivals was Christian Gitsham, the South African who had won the silver medal eight years before. He had trained over the course for several weeks and was confident. This showed in his tactics, for he went into the lead immediately with the Belgian August Broos. Gitsham shook off his rival before the 10 km mark, where he led from Ettore Blasi ITA, Broos, Kolehmainen, Jüri Lossmann EST and Tuomikoski. Kolehmainen gradually started to move up, and by 15 km he had caught Gitsham. He started applying pressure and although they were still together at 20 km, the South African was having problems. It was said that he had a leg injury, but it was generally felt that he had overtrained. Other reports said that one of his shoes tore open.

Gitsham kept pace with the easily running Finn, but it was to cost him dearly. They reached halfway in 73:10 – very fast running indeed – which gave them a lead of 48 seconds on Broos and Blasi. The determined Kolehmainen then went to the front and by 27 km he had broken clear of the South African. Lossmann, who used to train with lead weights in his shoes, was now in third and Broos fourth. The next 8 km proved decisive for Gitsham – he could not maintain the pace and was passed by three runners. He retired after 35 km.

Kolehmainen and Lossmann were now well clear, with the Estonian putting everything into his effort of catching the leader. Tuomikoski was third, followed by Broos. The Italian champion Valerio Arri, who had been second in the "Poly", was charging through the field and running in sixth. Broos passed Tuomikoski at 40 km, but both were passed by the flying Arri. At the finish Lossmann was only 12.8 seconds behind Kolehmainen, who broke the tape in 2:32:35.8 – a world record made even more remarkable by the fact that the course was more than 500 m too long! Had the distance been the standard 42.195 km, Kolehmainen would have run about 2:30:37 – a time that was to be achieved only five years later. It is still the closest finish ever in Olympic history.

Arri celebrated his bronze medal by performing three somersaults once he had crossed the finish line!

RESULT:
1  Hannes Kolehmainen FIN 2:32:35.8
2  Juri Lossmann EST 2:32:48.6
3  Valerio Arri ITA 2:36:32.8
4  August Broos BEL 2:39:25.8
5  Juha Tuomikoski FIN 2:40:10.8
6  Sofus Rose DEN 2:41:18
7  Joseph Organ USA 2:41:30
8  Rudolf Hansen DEN 2:41:39.4
9  Urho Tallgren FIN 2:42:40
10 Tatu Kolehmainen FIN 2:44:03.2

Lossmann later said that had the Estonian team supported him instead of going on an excursion for the day, he would have won. He misunderstood a signal given to him within sight of the stadium and thought that he still had 2 km to run.

Kolehmainen, who had been living in the USA since after the Stockholm Games and had also married there, returned to his native country after his Antwerp success and continued to race, setting two world records for 25 km and one for 30 km (beating Lossmann again). He competed in the Olympic marathon in 1924, but failed to finish.

Kolehmainen, who had an effortless, smooth running style, is regarded as the father of Finnish distance running. His feats inspired those who followed him and whose names in turn became synonymous with running excellence: Paavo Nurmi, Albin Stenroos, Lauri Lehtinen, Taisto Mäki, Ville Ritola, Viljo Heino and, ultimately, Lasse Viren.

Mills, who finished 14th in Antwerp, won the Polytechnic marathon again in 1921 and 1922, both times by at least 7 minutes. In 1923 he met his match when he was defeated by Aksel Jensen DEN in a fine 2:40:46.8. The time remained a Danish record for more than 23 years.

Across the Atlantic the 1921 Boston race saw a new record when Frank Zuna's increase in pace after the Newton hills brought him to the finish on Exeter Street in 2:18:57.6. He was the first man to complete the course in under 2:20, easily beating Chuck Mellor. The distance was 24 miles, 1 232 yards (39.7 km),[1] which would have given Zuna, a plumber and one of the heaviest men ever to win Boston, a converted time of about 2:27:48 for the standard distance.

But what nobody knew at the time was that the era of Clarence DeMar's dominance was about to start. DeMar had taken a few years off between the Stockholm Olympics and 1917, when he ran Boston again. World War I interrupted his career, but in November 1921 he was forced by a sleet storm to run from his home in Melrose to his work in Medford, about 4½ miles. He then started to think seriously about returning to the famous race.

He did so on 19 April 1922. DeMar started conservatively and only made his presence felt after 20 miles. He picked up the pace from his position near the front (James Henigan was leading) and went into the lead. DeMar had the record in his sights and finished with a sprint to the cheers of the thousands of spectators along the last stretch of the route. His time of 2:18:10 smashed Zuna's year-old record.

RESULT:
1  Clarence DeMar 2:18:10
2  Ville Ritola 2:21:44.8
3  Albert Smoke 2:22:49.6

A year later DeMar was there once more and followed the same race plan. Although Albert Michelsen, who was to become one of DeMar's greatest rivals, had a lead of 150 m at one stage, DeMar kept his steady pace and waited until after 20 miles before he picked it up. He won in 2:23:47.4 despite being hindered by photographers. Zuna was second, almost 2 minutes behind. After the marathon DeMar went out to play two hours of baseball!

1. This distance was used from the inception of the race until 1923. In 1924-26 it was 26 miles, 209 yards (42.02 km), in 1927-52 and from 1957 the standard distance of 42.195 km, and in 1953-56 25 miles, 938 yards (41.08 km).

In 1924 DeMar had a medical examination after having suffered knee and back pains for a number of years. It was found that one leg was shorter than the other and the problem was solved by some adjustments and attention to his spine. In the Boston race he took the lead at Wellesley (just after halfway) and won his fourth title in 2:29:40.2, beating Mellor by almost 5½ minutes in what was called his greatest Boston victory.

The course had been lengthened – to the standard distance, it was said, but a remeasurement in February 1927 showed it to be 26 miles, 209 yards. DeMar was therefore credited with a new world record – only to lose it three years later when the mistake was discovered.

Like the Americans the Japanese were also getting ready for the 1924 Olympics. They recorded a series of fast times, culminating in the 2:36:10 by Shizo Kanaguri six days before DeMar's Boston victory. Kanaguri had taken part in both the 1912 and 1920 Olympic marathons, finishing 16th in the latter in 2:48:45.4.

Apart from Boston the Americans held another trial, over the standard distance in Baltimore. This was won in 2:41:39.4 by Zuna. He and the first six Americans at Boston were selected, but then a final trial over 16 miles was run in Paris in June to eliminate one runner!

The inexperienced Ralph Williams did not complete the trial (dropping out after only 3 miles), but in a controversial decision he was included in the final team ahead of Carl Linder, who had beaten him at Boston. In his autobiography, *Marathon*, an obviously irritated DeMar commented: "This trick destroyed any hope and morale that any of the men had left."

The Finns had no such problems. The great Kolehmainen was selected, although he had run only two marathons since Antwerp. With him in the team was 35-year-old Albin Stenroos, whose marathon experience was far more meagre: his last race over the distance (on the track) was in 1909! His Olympic credentials consisted of a bronze medal in the 10000 m in 1912 – the race won by Kolehmainen.

Stenroos, a woodcutter, had set Finnish track records for 5000 and 10000 m when only eighteen and a world 30 km record in 1915, but between 1918 and 1920 he did not race at all – or even train. Then he came back and set another world record, over 20 km, in 1923. His preparations for the Olympic marathon were thorough: he walked up to 120 km a week.

The Polytechnic race was won by the Scot Duncan McLeod Wright in 2:53:17.4 – the slowest winning time ever. Wright was chased by Samuel Ferris in the debut of what was to be a sterling career. His time was 2:54:03.

The Games of the eighth Olympiad started in Paris on 4 May and the French capital thus became the first city to host the Games twice. (Only two cities, London and Los Angeles, have since shared this honour.) For the first time the Games had more than 3 000 competitors, while the 44 participating nations was also a record.

The indomitable Nurmi was now at the peak of his powers. He achieved one of the greatest feats in the history of athletics by winning the 1500 m in Olympic record time and then coming back less than an hour later to repeat the performance in the 5000 m. He won more gold medals in the individual 10000 m cross-country and 3000 m team events, and in both races he was also a member of the winning

## DEMAR – A BORN COMPETITOR

Clarence DeMar was born in Ohio on 7 June 1888 and moved to Massachusetts at the age of ten. He ran more than a hundred marathons in a career spanning from 1909 to 1954. His first race was Boston in 1910, where he finished third and then started serious training.

Shortly before his record-breaking win in the 1911 Boston he was diagnosed as having a heart murmour. Nevertheless, he continued running until after the Stockholm Olympics. Then he stopped, partly because of fears of damage to his heart, but also because he had developed an intense interest in religion. "As a member of the Baptist church I had a suspicion that the whole game of running was a selfish vain-glorious search for praise and honor," he wrote in his book, *Marathon*. He added that he also did not have the time to train properly due to his work and study commitments (he was taking classes at Harvard and Boston University). Furthermore, he was teaching a Sunday school class.

But DeMar never stopped running completely, although it was often only the mile from North Station to his work at a printing house in Franklin Street, which he ran both ways – in his working clothes. He could cover this distance in "under six minutes through traffic".

He did run short races, but only went to watch the Boston race once, in 1915. That was also the year he received his Associate in Arts degree. He took off from work for the occasion, and when he returned one of his colleagues asked him why he had taken time off, since they were very busy.

"Although it was none of his business", DeMar showed him the rolled degree certificate. The man then said: "Don't you suppose the boss will give you another dollar a week on that?"

Two years later DeMar decided that his period of "rest" was over, and he started preparing for Boston – running three times a week. He finished third. During the war years and immediately thereafter he took another break, but in 1922 he was back to start his marvellous series of victories. He won that year, as well as in 1923, 1924, 1927, 1928 and 1930 for a total of seven victories, and was in the top ten on another eight occasions. His last Boston marathon was in 1954.

He lost to John Miles's course record in 1926, but then had an immensely successful streak of five victories, beating Albert Michelsen four times, as well as Miles (in the 1927 Boston) and Olympic champion Albin Stenroos. He won the AAU title in 1926, 1927 and 1928. In 1929 and 1930 he won five out of six marathons.

In an ironic twist DeMar was extensively tested at the Harvard Fatigue Laboratory in 1926 and 1928 and found to have no heart problem at all, and phenomenal cardiovascular stamina.

The last sentence of his book, published in 1937, summed up how this great competitor, to whom a sense of balance and proportion in his life was everything, felt about his running: "I still enjoy the long grind of the marathon." He died in 1958 of cancer.

Finnish team. His six gold medals stood as a record for one Games until 1972. Another historic achievement was the American Harold Osborne's golds in the high jump and decathlon. Only one other athlete – Jackie Joyner-Kersee in 1988 – has since won an individual and multi-event at the same Games. The organisation of the Games was much better than in 1900, but aggressive nationalism among the spectators led to several incidents.

The marathon was run on 13 July. The starting time was set back from 15:00 to 17:00 because of the intense heat of the previous day, when the cross-country race was held. Fortunately it was not nearly as hot. The 58 starters – among them the South African champion Henry Phillips – were to run 42.195 km, now the standard distance after a decision by the International Olympic Committee. The runners completed 710 m on the track in the stadium and then ran out to the village of Pontoise le Chou, where they turned.

Right from the start it was evident that Hannes Kolehmainen would not be a factor. A Greek runner, Kranis, was in the lead during the early stages, but was soon joined and passed by the Frenchman Verger. After about 12 km DeMar was running in second, 15 seconds behind the leader, with Kranis, Mellor and Jean Manhes FRA following. Stenroos was 54 seconds behind Verger, but Kolehmainen was more than 3½ minutes behind.

Over the next 8 km Stenroos started to move up until he passed DeMar and caught Verger before the 20 km mark. Changes in the order were also taking place behind him, with Blasi and his countryman Romeo Bertini catching Manhes, and Boughera El Ouafi, the French Algerian winner of the French title earlier in the year, running with Mellor, Lossmann and Marcel Alavoine BEL. Stenroos accelerated away from the Frenchman and at the turn he was already half a minute ahead in 80:00.

At this stage DeMar was 58 seconds behind in third and running well. Behind him came Bertini, just ahead of Blasi, Manhes and Lauri Halonen FIN. Then followed El Ouafi, Mellor and Lossmann. DeMar passed Verger, who was soon to drop out (as was Blasi), but his fellow American Mellor was beginning to suffer. A strong Wright moved up into ninth.

When the Finn reached the control point at 27.75 km he had increased his lead dramatically to 2:50 and DeMar had come under pressure from Bertini. Halonen was fourth. The top order remained virtually unchanged except that Lossmann was in fifth after Wright had dropped out because of sore ankles (he had bound them on the advice of the British coach as a means of support on the cobbled section of the course). But Ferris, in his second marathon, was improving the British standings, having moved up from 30th to 13th. He continued this progress and with 7 km to go he was ninth.

It became clear that Stenroos would not be challenged – he was in excellent condition – but it was just as clear that Ferris had left his challenge too late. Between 35 and 38 km he was the cause of much excitement, for he passed Lossmann, the Swedish champion Gustav Kinn and the Chilean Manuel Plaza. Only Stenroos, Bertini, DeMar and Halonen remained ahead of the gallant Briton, but he could do no more. Stenroos won by almost 6 minutes and broke Hayes's Olympic record by nearly 14 minutes. The average age of the medal winners was 34.

RESULT:

| | | |
|---|---|---|
| 1 | Albin Stenroos FIN | 2:41:22.6 |
| 2 | Romeo Bertini ITA | 2:47:19.6 |
| 3 | Clarence DeMar USA | 2:48:14 |
| 4 | Lauri Halonen FIN | 2:49:47.4 |
| 5 | Samuel Ferris GBR | 2:52:26 |
| 6 | Manuel Plaza CHI | 2:52:54 |
| 7 | Boughera El Ouafi FRA | 2:54:19.6 |
| 8 | Gustav Kinn SWE | 2:54:33.4 |
| 9 | Dionisio Carreras ESP | 2:57:18.4 |
| 10 | Juri Lossmann EST | 2:57:54.6 |

Phillips finished 19th in 3:07:13, while Mellor faded to 25th in 3:24:07. The great Kolehmainen failed to finish, and also did not finish the last of his thirteen career marathons – in 1928 in Kauhava. He had returned to live in Finland in 1920 and died in 1966, one of the giants of athletics.

After the Olympics Stenroos regained the world record for 30 km from Kolehmainen, running 1:46:11.6. He lived in the US in 1925 and 1926, finishing second in Boston in 1926 behind John Miles CAN but beating DeMar again. He retired when he could not make the 1928 Finnish Olympic team.

A number of Czechoslovakian officials had attended the Paris Games and soon afterwards it was decided that an annual race should be established in their country. The first Czech marathon had been held in 1920. On 28 October the new race was run from Turna to Kosice. The recent nation-

## KOSICE

The first Kosice marathon in 1924 was run from Turna to Kosice, but thereafter the course has been from Kosice to Sena and back (except for 1925 and 1952, when different routes were followed). The eight athletes in the first race were all from Czechoslovakia, but the race has had an international flavour since then and it was 1934 before a Czech (Josef Sulc) could win again.

In 1931 the Argentinian Juan Carlos Zabala made his marathon debut at Kosice and won by more than 14 minutes in 2:33:19. The next year he became Olympic champion in Los Angeles.

The first sub-2:20 came in 1959 when the Soviet runner Sergey Popov won in 2:17:45.2. Popov had set a world record of 2:15:17 the year before. In 1961 the Olympic champion and world record holder, Abebe Bikila ETH, won in 2:20:12. Two years later the winner was again the world record holder, Buddy Edelen USA, in 2:15:09.6 (beating Popov).

The only man to win Kosice four times was Jozsef Galambos HUN, in 1927, 1928, 1932 and 1933.

Women first took part in 1980, with Sarka Balcarova TCH taking the honours.

*Left*: Spiridon Louis, the first Olympic marathon champion, after his victory in 1896.

*Below*: The two Zulus Yamasani (left) and Lentauw who took part in the 1904 Olympic marathon in St Louis, dressed in their race outfits. (The Missouri Historical Society)

*Above*: Dorando Pietri is helped to his feet by the medical attendant Dr M.J. Bulger (with cap), after having fallen for the first time near the end of the 1908 Olympic marathon. The official with the megaphone is Jack Andrew, the chief clerk. The two men eventually assisted Pietri across the finish line.

*Left*: The South African Charles Hefferon won the silver medal after Pietri had been disqualified. Hefferon was in the lead until less than a mile from the stadium.

*Above*: An already fatigued Kenneth McArthur, South Africa's only Olympic marathon victor, was burdened with the winner's laurel wreath well before he reached the end of the 1912 race in Stockholm.

*Left*: Chris Gitsham finished second behind his countryman. No other country has since filled the first two places in the Olympic marathon.

The two Springboks Sydney Luyt (left) and Johannes Coleman lead the world record holder, Yun Bok Suh, through the streets of Stanmore, London, in the 1948 Olympic marathon. Coleman finished fourth and Luyt sixth, both far ahead of the Korean.

## THE UNITED STATES CHAMPIONSHIP

The Amateur Athletic Union (AAU) of the United States was founded in 1888. Because it was an established annual race, the Boston marathon was considered the national championship, but the first official AAU championship was only contested in 1925 – appropriately in Boston. Boston had the honour again in 1928 and 1929, while from 1938 to 1966 (except 1948) the championship was incorporated in the Yonkers marathon.

After Charles Mellor's victory in 1925 the race was won three times in a row by Clarence DeMar, and also three times by Pat Dengis and Gérard Côté, although not consecutively. Then, in 1956, the era of John J. Kelley started. He won an unprecedented eight times in a row, his fastest victory being 2:20:13.6 in 1960. (He finished 19th in the Rome Olympics that year.)

The oldest winner was the unrelated John A. Kelley, who was 43 when he scored his second win in 1950.

In 1964, two years after he had become the first American to run under 2:20, Buddy Edelen won.

In recent years the only runners who have won more than once are Gary Tuttle (1975, 1976), Ken Martin (1984, 1985), Bill Reifsnyder (1989, 1991) and Steve Spence (1990, 1992). The first women's championship was held in 1974; Judy Ikenberry won in 2:55:18.

al record setter with 3:09:05.6, Frantisek Fiala, was not among the eight starters. Karol Halla took Fiala's record away with his winning time of 3:01:35.

Marathoning was growing ever more popular and in 1925 four countries held official national championships. First was the USA, and the Amateur Athletic Union decided to stage the first championship race in conjunction with Boston. It was a bitterly cold day with a strong wind and most runners wore long underwear as protection. Not so DeMar and Mellor (they did wear gloves). One report said that Mellor had that day's edition of the Boston *Globe* stuffed into the front of his running shirt as insulation. DeMar was going for his fourth consecutive victory, but it was not to be. Mellor, chewing a piece of tobacco, was superb and won in 2:33:00.6. DeMar was second in 2:33:37 and Zuna third in 2:35:35.

Zuna was also on the starting line when the first British Amateur Athletic Assocation championship was decided as part of the "Poly" on 30 May. The initial battle was between Mills, Wright and Zuna, with Ferris as usual biding his time. Mills had started too fast (56:22 at 10 miles) and was overtaken first by Wright and then by Zuna and Ferris. The determined Ferris took the lead at 22½ miles, reaching 25 miles in 2:28:25 and the finish in 2:35:58.2 – a new British record. Zuna's 2:38:27.4 in second was the fastest American time ever on a standard course. Wright was third in 2:42:28.4.

A German marathon had been held annually since 1905, but the first official championship was decided on 6 September in Leipzig. Paul Hempel had run a national record 2:47:05.2 the previous year in Berlin, and he also won in Leipzig in a slightly slower time, 2:48:25.5.

On 27 September the Czechs held their first official championship in Prague. The winner was Josef Maly in 2:51:08. Exactly a week later Maly ran in the second Kosice marathon. This time the race started in Kosice itself and the runners went through Cana and Haniska before returning to Kosice. The Hungarian record holder and champion Pal Kiraly (he had won his first of three consecutive titles three weeks earlier) won easily in a national record 2:41:55. His compatriot Jozsef Galambos was second and Maly third.

In 1925 the world record fell to unheralded Albert "Whitey" Michelsen. Michelsen had many tussles with DeMar, beating him often before 1926 and losing to him most of the time after that, but on 12 October 1925 Michelsen was supreme. He beat DeMar easily after an exciting battle in the Port Chester marathon (from Columbus Circle, New York, to Liberty Square, Port Chester) and became the first man officially to run sub-2:30. It was to remain a world record for almost ten years.

RESULT:
1 Albert Michelsen 2:29:01.8
2 Clarence DeMar 2:31:07.8
3 Frank Zuna 2:37:21.6

Their rivalry at Port Chester continued: in 1926 DeMar won and the next year it was Michelsen's turn. In the words of Martin and Gynn, Michelsen "seemed almost to be haunting DeMar: he was always there, race after race, finishing consistently second or third. But he so seldom won the big races." (*The Marathon Footrace*)

The 1926 Austrian championship went to Frank Tuschek in a national record 2:43:53. He would win the title eight more times.

The year 1926 was also notable for the performance of

## THE AAA MARATHON

The Amateur Athletic Association (AAA) was formed in 1880 as the governing body of men's athletics in England and Wales and held its first championships that year.

As was the case in the US, the first marathon championship race in Britain was held in conjunction with an existing marathon, in this case the 1925 Polytechnic marathon. Sam Ferris won this and the following two title races, while in the thirties the race was dominated by two Scotsmen, both members of Maryhill Harriers: Duncan McLeod Wright (winner in 1930 and 1931) and Donald McNab Robertson (1932-34, 1936, 1937, 1939). Other multiple winners were Jack Holden (1947-50), Jim Peters (1951-54) and Brian Kilby (1960-64).

Holden, who was world cross-country champion four times, also won the Empire and European marathons in 1950. In fact, Holden lost only three of his seventeen career marathons: the 1948 Olympic race (he did not finish), Kosice in 1947, and the 1951 Poly.

Peters (see p. 51) set world records in his 1952 and 1954 victories.

In recent years the race has been won twice in faster than 2:09:00: Steve Jones 2:08:16 in 1985 and Dionicio Cerón MEX 2:08:53 in 1994.

The first women's champion was Margaret Lockley, who clocked 2:55:08 in 1978. In 1983 the incomparable Grete Waitz NOR set a world record: 2:25:28.7.

Violet Piercy, who set the first unofficial world record for women (see Chapter 9).

The eighteen-year-old Miles, from Nova Scotia, became the first Canadian in eleven years to win Boston (up until then only Americans and Canadians had won the race; the first "outsider" to win was Paul de Bruyn GER in 1932), beating both the Olympic champion and DeMar (as well as the latter's course record), but in 1927 DeMar was back in front. The course was now the standard distance after the measuring error had been discovered. DeMar won for the fifth time in a slowish 2:40:22.2.

The 1928 Boston, the first of three trials for the Olympic team, was an amazing race. Pitted against DeMar was James Henigan in his eighth Boston. Henigan had been running marathons since 1911, but had finished only one marathon as he always fell prey to his rash tactic of starting too fast. There was also Joie Ray, a top middle-distance runner who was eighth in the 1920 Olympic 1500 m. It was Ray's first marathon and he finished an admirable third (2:41:56.8). DeMar won in 2:37:07.8, but the surprise was between them: Henigan completed the race in 2:41:01!

The next month Ray did even better: he won the second trial, the New York to Long Beach marathon, in 2:34:13.4. The last trial, in Baltimore, was won by William Agee in 2:57:04.4.

The Finnish trial at Kauhava went to Martti Marttelin in 2:38:56, but neither Kolehmainen nor Stenroos could finish. However, the latter was given another chance to qualify for the Amsterdam Olympics. He finished second in this race over 41.6 km behind Yrjo Korholin-Koski but was not selected.[2]

In Britain Ferris continued to run well, but a new challenger appeared on the scene. Harry Payne, a vegetarian who had suffered gas poisoning in World War I, made his debut in the Poly. He was 36 and had only begun running nine years earlier. Ferris won without any trouble for his fourth victory and Payne finished fourth, but less than two months later Payne took the AAA title in Ferris's absence (he had a slight injury). The race was run over the Poly course and Payne improved Ferris's 1927 British record of 2:35:27 to 2:34:34.

RESULT:    1   Harry Payne 2:34:34
           2   Ernest Harper 2:37:10
           3   Duncan Wright 2:38:09

The Amsterdam Games were the first to allow women to take part in the athletic events. Germany was present for the first time since 1912. Other "firsts" were the fact that de Coubertin did not attend, and that an Olympic flame burnt for the duration of the Games. The 46 participating nations were a record. Despite the fact that General Douglas Mac-

2. Two years later Korholin-Koski, then living in the USA under the name Karl Koski, won the AAU championship.

Arthur, President of the US Olympic Committee, had said before the Games that his country was sending "the greatest team in our athletic history", the US team could win only one of ten individual running events, the 400 m. The Americans fared better on the field, though. The women's team won one of the five events on the programme.

The Finns performed even better than in any previous Games: their fourteen medals were only seven fewer than the Americans'. Douglas Lowe GBR became the first man to retain the 800 m title, but the Finns won every race longer than two laps. Ville Ritola and Nurmi played musical chairs with first and second place in the 5000 and 10000 m and Nurmi was also second in the steeplechase.

The marathon was held on 5 August and the 68 runners got under way just after 15:00. Among the favourites were the well-known runners El Ouafi, Ferris, DeMar, Michelsen, Plaza and Payne – but there was also the lesser-known Japanese champion, Kanematsu Yamada, who had run 2:43:22. El Ouafi had not done much running between the previous Olympic marathon and 1927, but on 1 April 1928 he had won a 35 km race and then had been victorious three months later in the French marathon championship (over 38.5 km), clocking 2:20:03.

The lead was taken immediately by Ray, with the one-armed South African Marthinus Steytler on his heels.

A large group of runners soon took over and the lead kept changing, with Eino Rastas FIN, Franz Wanderer GER, Jean Linsen BEL and Ray all taking a turn at the front. At 20 km Ray was leading the Finns Marttelin and Vaino Laaksonen, followed by the Japanese Yamada and Seiichiro Tsuda.

After the turn Yamada and Tsuda made a move, but could not quite shake the American. At this stage Ferris was running conservatively, far back, because he had felt muscle twinges in his legs early on and had decided not to risk anything. At 30 km Yamada was leading alone, with Ray second and Marttelin third. Fifty metres further back came Tsuda and El Ouafi, with Plaza just behind them. However, the strongly running French Algerian soon picked up the pace and after 39 km ran into second, with Plaza still in his wake. Yamada was struggling and it was no surprise when El Ouafi passed and ran away from him close to the stadium. The Japanese could not hold off either Plaza or Marttelin and thus, despite leading with 3 km to go, did not even get a medal. He did set a new Asian record.

Ferris's initial leg trouble did not develop into anything more serious and he no doubt could have finished much higher than his eighth position. His countryman Payne disappointed with 2:42:29 in 13th; DeMar was only 27th (in what was probably his most decisive loss against Michelsen), Henigan 39th. Steytler ended up 40th in 2:57:21. The first five places were taken by runners born on five different continents.

Ray was in severe pain afterwards from leg cramps and blisters. He was philosophical about the outcome: "I lost because I ran too slow."

RESULT:
1  Boughera El Ouafi FRA 2:32:57
2  Manuel Plaza CHI 2:33:23
3  Martti Marttelin FIN 2:35:02
4  Kanematsu Yamada JPN 2:35:29
5  Joie Ray USA 2:36:04
6  Seiichiro Tsuda JPN 2:36:20
7  Yrjo Korholin-Koski FIN 2:36:40
8  Samuel Ferris GBR 2:37:41
9  Albert Michelsen USA 2:38:56
10 Clifford Bricker CAN 2:39:24

El Ouafi, a car mechanic, took revenge on three of the athletes who had beaten him in Paris: DeMar, Ferris and Plaza. He soon became a professional. In 1959 he was shot dead in a café in Paris.

On 26 September a confident Ferris, his leg problems now behind him, ran the Liverpool marathon. He took command after 10 miles and simply ran away from his rivals. At the finish the watches read 2:33:00 for a new British record. However, about two weeks later he was beaten by Marttelin in Turin, as had been DeMar two days earlier by Arthur Gavrin in a very hot Port Chester race.

At Leningrad Aleksandr Lavrov established the first official Soviet marathon record when he won in 3:03:04. Jozsef Galambos won his second Kosice to make amends for his 49th place in Amsterdam.

The 1929 Boston was once again won by Miles, who ran a course record 2:33:08.8 with DeMar only fourth. Later in the year at Port Chester Michelsen scored one of his rare victories over DeMar, beating him by 43 seconds in 2:38:31.

In May Ferris was first (for the fifth time) in the Poly, with Payne fourth. The two big rivals met again on 5 July to decide the British title over the Poly course. The race was held in the evening and Ferris made an uncharacteristic fast start. He went through 5 miles in 28:55, then slackened off and allowed C.E. Leatherland to take the lead. By 15 miles (86:32) Ferris was in front again. Payne was fourth, a minute behind. But suddenly he accelerated and covered the 5 miles between 15 and 20 miles in a searing 27:33. This gave him a lead of almost 2 minutes on Ferris – and he stretched this to more than 8 minutes at the finish, coming within a minute of the world record. His new British and European record was 2:30:57.6. He had covered the final 6 miles, 385 yards in a brilliant 35:51!

The 1930s marked the emergence of Japan as a marathon power (in 1935 the seven fastest marathoners were all Japanese). In South Africa the first runners since the days of Hefferon, McArthur and Gitsham reached world class (see Chapter 8).

When DeMar started Boston on 19 April 1930 he was already 41 years old. He had married late in 1929 and changed his work. In his book he commented as follows on the former event: "... I heard continually from all sides that I should give up running. However, even a married man needs some recreation and I can see no reason why I shouldn't take my fun in any way that pleases me most." He duly won the race, beating the Finnish Americans Ville (Willie) Kyronen and Koski. He wrote that this was the start of a very good year. He won several races, capping it with an emphatic start-to-finish victory at Port Chester, albeit in the slow time of 2:46:15.

Less than a month before Boston Koski had won the AAU race over a ridiculously difficult course on Staten Island. He took the lead from Harvey Frick just past the 13-mile mark on the aptly named Dead Man's Hill and finished in an almost incredible 2:25:21.2. It was nearly 4 minutes faster than Michelsen's world record. *The New York Times* reported that "careful survey of the distance by officials ... indicated that the course was the full 26 miles 385 yards ..." However, Martin and Gynn argued that the course must have been short, one of their reasons being that Koski's performance trend at the time was about ten minutes slower. "The question probably never will be answered with unequivocal accuracy," they wrote.

In the meantime there were strong feelings in the British Empire that a sports festival for member countries should be held. An intra-Empire championship had been held in the British capital in 1911, but only the host country, Canada, South Africa and Australia attended and the programme did not include a marathon. After the Amsterdam Olympics it was decided that the first Empire Games would be staged in Hamilton, Ontario, from 16-23 August 1930.

British marathon runners were sure to make their presence felt in the first Empire Games marathon. The AAA title went to Wright in a personal best (PB) of 2:38:29.4, with a not fully fit Ferris third behind Marttelin.

The race in Hamilton was on 21 August and fourteen runners started. Payne had been knocked down by a car when training before the race and would not be a factor. At 6 miles Herbert Bignall, who had been second in the Poly, was leading, but he was soon passed by Wright, who was never headed again. He had finished two of the three laps in the stadium when Ferris entered and gallantly shook Wright's hand in congratulation as he passed him.

RESULT (only the winner's time was given):
1  Duncan McLeod Wright Sco 2:43:43
2  Samuel Ferris Eng
3  John Miles CAN
4  Percival Wyer CAN
5  Herbert Bignall Eng
6  Norman Dack CAN
7  Silas MacLennan CAN
8  Ross O'Toole NFL
9  James O'Reilly Ire
10 Ezra Lee CAN

In the Far East the Japanese were improving their standards every year. In 1929 the Asian record was lowered to 2:35:24 by Kozo Kusunoki, but this time was bettered twice toward the end of 1931. Then, on 30 April 1932 Tanji Yahagi established a new world best for out-and-back courses with his 2:31:31 in Tokyo. A week later Norio Suzuki ran 2:29:20, but the course was probably short. None of these runners made the Japanese team, however. One of those who did was Tsuda, sixth in Amsterdam. He was to be accompanied by Taika Gon, who had won the official trial in 2:36:49.6, and Onbai Kin (who had run 2:34:58 in 1931).

In South America another runner was getting ready for the 1932 Olympics. Juan Carlos Zabala of Argentina was an orphan who was turned into a great runner by Alexander Stirling, a physical training instructor who had adopted him. On 10 October 1931, the day before his twentieth birthday, Zabala set a new world record for 30 km. He then went to Kosice for his marathon debut, where he hit his rivals like a bolt from the blue. In driving rain he charged through 30 km less than 7 seconds slower than his recent track record and finished in an amazing 2:33:19 – leaving Galambos almost 15 minutes behind! His course record would stand for nineteen years.

But Ferris, who in Amsterdam had not run to his potential, was not going to hand the Olympic title to Zabala on a plate. He won both the 1931 and 1932 Poly, in the latter beating the South African Thomas Lalande, 2:36:32.4 against 2:43:30.4. Lalande was there again when the AAA title was contested just over a month later. He improved to 2:42:28.4, but was far behind the first two, Robertson (2:34:32.6) and Wright (2:34:34).

The Americans held no fewer than three trial races: Boston, a race in Salisbury, Maryland, and one in Los Angeles, site of the Olympic Games. The 1931 Boston had been won on a very hot day by Henigan, at last scoring the victory which had so long eluded him. Koski, who had made the mistake of staying with the man who knew the Boston course so well – DeMar – until it was too late, finished third and DeMar fifth. Later in the year, in the Port Chester marathon, Henigan almost got his second victory. He was leading when a car hit him. He slowed and was passed by Dave Komonen, the Canadian champion. Henigan caught him again, but Komonen's finishing spurt was too good. Michelsen was third and DeMar fourth.

In the 1932 Boston race Henigan was up against a German living in New York, Paul de Bruyn, who had his sights set on Los Angeles and had finished eighth the previous year. He was a boiler room fireman at the Wellington Hotel and regularly ran up and down the 26 flights of stairs to do repairs.

RESULT:
1 Paul de Bruyn 2:33:36.4
2 James Henigan 2:34:32
3 Willie Kyronen 2:34:55
4 Albert Michelsen 2:36:23.4

In the second trial Hans Oldag beat Michelsen by more than 5 minutes, so the latter had to run the third trial to secure a place in the team. It was a hot day in Los Angeles on 25 June when Michelsen faced Zabala, but that did not deter the Argentinian. Only two weeks before he had failed in his attempt to break the 30-year-old world record for 15 miles when he beat Michelsen by more than 6 minutes in Chicago. His time for the same distance in Los Angeles was about 4½ minutes slower, but he was more than 8 minutes in the lead. It did not last, however, and he pulled out with foot problems. Michelsen went on to win in a slow 2:44:11.

The next day a remarkable race took place thousands of kilometres away. Finland held its trial in Viipuri. Among the starters in light rain was Paavo Nurmi, running his first marathon – in spikes! (The first and last 10 km sections were on the track, but the middle part was on the road.) Nurmi performed . . . well, like Nurmi. At 20 km he asked Armas Toivonen if the pace was too fast. The reply was that they were running at the usual pace. Seven kilometres later Nurmi asked if the pace was too slow. The answer was the same, and Nurmi then pulled away. He reached 40.2 km unchallenged in 2:22:03.8 – and stopped! This time means that he could have completed the full distance in about 2:29:07. Of course he was selected for the Olympics, together with the trial winner, Toivonen (2:35:50.2), and Kyronen.

But it was not to be. Two days before the start of the Games, on 28 July 1932, the executive council of the International Amateur Athletic Federation decided to suspend Nurmi on the grounds that he had received money in excess of his expenses when he ran five exhibition races in Germany the previous year. The statement by the council read simply that, "having carefully reviewed the evidence before it and having heard the representatives of Finland", the council had "unanimously rejected the entry of Paavo Nurmi, under authority given it in the seventh paragraph of Rule 2 of its general rules for Olympic events". No appeal was allowed. The Finns, however, did allow Nurmi to continue competing in his home country as a "national amateur".

The competitors in Los Angeles numbered less than half of those in Amsterdam and only 37 nations entered teams – a result, no doubt, of the worldwide depression. For the first time the participants were housed in an Olympic village. American sprinter Eddie Tolan won both the 100 and 200 m and the Finnish dominance in the distance events was broken. Lauri Lehtinen did win the controversial 5000 m race which almost caused the spectators to riot because of what they felt were the Finn's unfair tactics against his US rival Ralph Hill. American schoolgirl Mildred "Babe" Didrikson won the 80 m hurdles with a world record as well as the javelin throw (the first time these events were contested) and finished second in the high jump. The excellent track, called "the fastest in the world" by the *New York Daily News*, helped the athletes to set many world and Olympic records.

Only 29 runners contested the marathon, run on a warm 7 August. Zabala forged to the front immediately, accompanied by Margarito Pomposo Banos MEX and Bricker. They were followed closely by Michelsen, Jose Ribas ARG and Tsuda. When Zabala reached the second control point at

15.2 km in 57 minutes he was leading by half a minute.

The three Japanese were running together just behind Bricker. However, they were making no impression on the leader. Zabala reached 23 km in 80:00, a minute ahead of the Finns Toivonen and Lauri Virtanen. The latter, Nurmi's replacement, had won the bronze medal in the 5000 m only two days before, and the bronze in the 10000 m five days before that. After another minute Tsuda and Kin reached the control point, followed a minute later by Oldag and Michelsen. Bricker was not in the picture any longer.

But Zabala was not going to have it all his own way. Virtanen used his track speed (30:35 for 10 km) to overhaul the Argentinian at 31 km and boldly set out for victory. He built a lead of 300 m, while behind him Wright had moved into fourth. Ferris, following his usual tactics, had come from far back into sixth.

Now it was Wright's turn. He accelerated, went past both Zabala and Toivonen and caught Virtanen. By 35.5 km he had a gap of one minute on Zabala – a spent Virtanen could not hold his position and was soon to drop out. Toivonen held third, but Ferris was now fourth, running hard. Toivonen had no answer to the Englishman's charge, and Ferris also passed Wright who had in the meantime been repassed by Zabala. He put everything into his effort of catching Zabala, who was having difficulties. Ferris was gaining, but the South American was not going to let victory slip from his grasp and he entered the Coliseum still a minute ahead. Never before had the first four finishers circled the track at the same time.

Zabala was completely spent and Ferris was cutting the gap with every stride. But Zabala managed to hold on and collapsed beyond the finish line. He had beaten Ferris by only 19 seconds and set a new Olympic record of 2:31:36. Only twenty runners finished – the smallest number since 1904. Japan was the only country with three runners in the top ten.

RESULT:
1  Juan Carlos Zabala ARG 2:31:36
2  Samuel Ferris GBR 2:31:55
3  Armas Toivonen FIN 2:32:12
4  Duncan McLeod Wright GBR 2:32:41
5  Seiichiro Tsuda JPN 2:35:42
6  Onbai Kin JPN 2:37:28
7  Albert Michelsen USA 2:39:38
8  Oskar Heks TCH 2:41:35
9  Taika Gon JPN 2:42:52
10 Anders Hartington-Anderson DEN 2:44:38

To this day Zabala at 20 years, 301 days is the youngest winner of the Olympic marathon.

Ferris said later that during a training run before the race he had seen a large milk advertisement about a mile from the finish and had decided that he would use it as a marker for his final effort, if needed. On the day of the race, however, the sign was covered by a viewing stand and he did not see

it. Ferris, who was born in Northern Ireland and served in the Royal Air Force from 1918 to 1950, was now nearing the end of his career and this was his last Olympics. He had a remarkable record, having finished fifth in Paris and eighth in Amsterdam. He had also won the Polytechnic marathon an unprecedented eight times, as well as the first three AAA marathons. His marathon successes came on a training regimen which seldom exceeded 40 miles a week. Between 30 May 1925 and 18 May 1929 he lost only two of his twelve marathons and of his last four marathons he only lost in Los Angeles. He ended his career with a win in the 1933 Poly, his closest ever in this classic.

The 1933 Boston race produced a new star in Leslie Pawson, who broke Miles's course record with a magnificent 2:31:01.6. Second was Komonen, who went on to win both the AAU and the Canadian titles in slow times later in the year.

The best European race in 1933 was the tenth Kosice, where Galambos defended his title. He had tough competition in Arturs Motmillers of Latvia and Josef Sulc, the Czech record holder (2:37:31). The Hungarian was too strong in the later stages and won in a national record of 2:37:53.2. Motmillers clocked 2:41:38.2 and Sulc 2:42:43.[3] Thirteen days before, in the last Turin marathon (the race started in 1919), Aurelio Genghini ITA had run 2:38:39.2 for the 42.75 km course.

In 1934 Turin was the venue for the first European athletics championships, held in the Stadio Comunale. But first came the second Empire Games marathon. This took place on 7 August in London. Robertson, who had won the AAA championship for the third consecutive year, was the favourite. But the Canadian Harold Webster, who was born in England and had beaten Komonen in the national trial, took the lead after 12 miles and ran away from the others. He won easily in 2:40:36 – a good time for the very humid conditions.

RESULT:
1  Harold Webster CAN 2:40:36
2  Duncan McNab Robertson Sco 2:45:08
3  Duncan McLeod Wright Sco 2:56:20
4  Harold Wood Eng 2:58:41
5  Percival Wyer CAN 3:00:40
6  Wilfred Short Wal 3:02:56

On 9 September only fifteen runners started the European race on the long Turin course. There were no British runners. The Swedish champion, Thore Enochsson, took the lead at 11 km. Behind him came Rudolf Morf SWI, followed by Heinrich Brauch, the German champion, Michele Fanelli ITA and Toivonen, in his first outing since the Olympic race. Seven kilometres later Enochsson was still in front, but the

---

3. Although Sulc was to fail in the first European championships, finishing only ninth, he beat both Galambos and Motmillers in the 1934 Kosice race in 2:41:26.3. He again failed in the 1936 Olympic marathon, but won the Czech title in 1940, 1941 and 1942.

Italian was now third. Then the Finn speeded up, moved into second by 21 km, and passed the leader after 30 km. Genghini also passed Enochsson.

The year before, on the same course, Genghini had beaten Enochsson by just under 2 minutes . . . and Enochsson was determined not to let that happen again. He stayed in contact with the Italian, never allowing him a gap of more than 10 m, and finally repassed him. He finished 27.8 seconds ahead, albeit more than 2 minutes behind the leader.

RESULT:
1  Armas Toivonen FIN 2:52:29
2  Thore Enochsson SWE 2:54:35.6
3  Aurelio Genghini ITA 2:55:03.4
4  Jozsef Galambos HUN 2:55:14
5  Heinrich Brauch GER 2:58:40.2
6  Hans Wehrli SWI 2:58:45

But 1934 and 1935 belonged to runners who had not run in either London or Turin. Already in 1933 Kozu Kusunoki had won the Japanese title in Tokyo in a brilliant 2:31:10, a world best on an out-and-back course. He beat Shoryu Nan (2:32:33) and Tamao Shiaku (2:32:44). These were the fastest times of the year behind Pawson's Boston performance. Near the end of 1934 Shiaku ran 14 seconds slower than he did in 1933, but it was still the fastest Japanese time of the year and third on the world list.

The two men ahead of him were the North Americans Pat Dengis USA and Komonen. Dengis, an aeroplane mechanic who was born in Wales, had been fourth (2:52:10) in the 1933 Port Chester race won by De Bruyn, but in 1934 he was a totally different runner. He again went to Port Chester and simply ran away from the opposition, recording the world's fastest time for the year: 2:31:30.

Komonen won Boston in 1934 in shoes of his own design (he was a cobbler), running 2:32:53.8 to earn second spot on the world list. He beat John A. Kelley, whose second place was the first of seven such runner-up slots.

Then in 1935 the Japanese took over. On 21 March an unknown Japanese, Kitei Son, ran 2:26:14 in Tokyo, beating his countryman Fusashige Suzuki. This was ruled a short course, as was that on which in 1933 he had completed his first marathon in 2:29:34.4. In April 1934 he was timed in 2:24:51.2, also not over the full distance. His fourth marathon was again on a short course, in October 1934, and he scored his fourth victory, this time in 2:32:19.8.

On 31 March Son was not in the field when Suzuki ran on an out-and-back course from Jingu Stadium in Tokyo. The course was checked thoroughly beforehand to make sure that it was the correct distance. Just as well, because the tiny Suzuki stormed to a new world record of 2:27:49.

Son, who also competed on the track over distances from 800 to 5000 m, ran his first full-distance marathon on 4 April 1935 . . . and lost. The course was the same as for Suzuki's record, and both Suzuki (who was running his third marathon in two weeks) and Son succumbed to Yasuo Ikenaka – and yet another world record! Ikenaka had been third in the race on 21 March.

RESULT:
1  Yasuo Ikenaka 2:26:44
2  Fusashige Suzuki 2:33:05
3  Kitei Son 2:39:24

Across the Pacific Johnny Kelley won Boston on a perfect day. In the hope that he could beat Pawson's course record he took fifteen glucose tablets before the race. This caused havoc in his stomach and he had to stop twice in the last 3 miles. He still won, in 2:32:07.4, with Dengis second in 2:34:11.2. Komonen dropped out.

Thirteenth in this race (in his second attempt at the distance) was a remarkable runner. The twenty-year-old Narragansett Indian Ellison "Tarzan" Brown ran barefoot and in a shirt made from the dress of his mother, who had died two days earlier. He grew up in a poor family who lived in a dilapidated shack near Westerly, Rhode Island. He liked swinging in trees and this earned him his nickname.

Dengis ran to victory in the AAU marathon (his first of three titles) and then also won a marathon from Valley Forge to Philadelphia in adverse conditions in 2:38:24. He beat, among others, DeMar and De Bruyn. Their best days were over, but the runner in fourth place was just starting his career: "Tarzan" Brown clocked an unremarkable 2:53:11, but he was soon to run much faster.

Kelley, who had missed Pawson's record by just more than a minute in Boston, lost to the man himself in the Port Chester marathon – but by less than 3 seconds: 2:37:49.2 against 2:37:52.

Seven weeks later Kelley met Dengis in the Yonkers marathon. The race had not taken place for eighteen years and was revived by the Chippewa Athletic Club. The hilly course was now the full standard distance and Kelley ran one of the best races of his career, setting a course record of 2:38:43 that was to withstand the efforts of Dengis until 1939.[4] Pawson was second and Kelley thus avenged the Port Chester defeat; Dengis finished fourth.

In England the 1935 Poly was won by a member of the host club, Albert Norris. He had been second to Ferris in 1931 and gave him his toughest battle in the Poly in 1933, losing by only 70.2 seconds in 2:43:34.4. A month later he was also second in the AAA championship behind Robertson. Only nine days after that he had recovered sufficiently to go to Amsterdam, where he improved to 2:42:54.6. Now 36, Norris was ready for a big win. After an exciting duel with the South African Lalande, who once again collapsed toward the end of the race (see Chapter 8), Norris took his first Poly in 2:48:37.8 despite having to walk twice in the

4. Dengis won Yonkers in 1937, 1938 and 1939, running 2:33:45.2 in the latter year.

final mile. Norris once more showed his remarkable powers of recovery when he started the AAA championship only seven weeks later. He had been second the previous two years, but this time he came out on top. It was an extremely hot day and this was reflected in his time: 3:02:57.8, the slowest in the history of the event.

Still Norris wasn't satisfied. Ten weeks later he was in Paris for an international race. He ran well, clocking 2:44:47.2, but finished only fourth. The winner in an excellent 2:37:04 was François Begeot FRA, who had represented his country in Los Angeles. Second was the Swedish champion of 1934 and 1935, Henry Palme.

The first official Soviet championship was held on 12 September and won by Nikolay Babaryshkin in the record time of 2:48:23.

With the pre-Olympic year drawing to a close, attention shifted to the east. Son ran 2:42:02 and 2:33:39 nine days apart (the latter second to Choshun Ryu's 2:31:24), but he was merely warming up. On 3 November, in perfect conditions, he blitzed the Jingu course in Tokyo in a new world record of 2:26:42. The depth of talent behind him was an eye-opener, with the next two runners finishing in the same time.

RESULT:  1  Kitei Son 2:26:42
2  Tamao Shiaku 2:31:21
3  Shinichi Nakamura 2:31:21
4  Shoryu Nan 2:36:52

The next salvo was fired less than three weeks later when Nakamura improved by a further 86 seconds, beating Kusunoki in Osaka in 2:29:55. Kusunoki, a previous holder of the Asian record and world best for an out-and-back course, had run 2:26:51 in July on a short course.

Early in the Olympic year another unauthorised, and probably short, course gave Shiaku a time of 2:26:53. Son put his cards on the table with a 2:28:32, but when the Japanese trial was held on 21 May – in less than ideal conditions – Nan was the winner in 2:36:03, followed by Son (2:38:02) and Suzuki (2:39:41). The fourth man, Shiaku, was also added to the team, with the team coach to decide the final threesome for the Olympic marathon.

Eight days before Boston, in faraway Port Elizabeth, Johannes Coleman won the national title by narrowly defeating Henry "Jack" Gibson, 2:31:57.4 against 2:32:09. Coleman's time was a new South African record and gave him the fourth place on the world list for the year, one spot ahead of Gibson. (See Chapter 8.)

The Boston marathon produced one of those classic battles that make the marathon special. The protagonists were Kelley and Brown. The latter set a mad pace, reaching 11 miles in 55 minutes. He was caught by Kelley and they waged a ding-dong battle through the Newton hills. Amazingly, Kelley cracked first (he would finish only fifth) and Brown, a stone-mason, went on to take his first victory in 2:33:40.8. He was

sponsored by the Rhode Island Tercentenary Committee and showed that their trust in him was not misplaced by making the Olympic team.

The rest of the team was selected after the AAU race held in Washington. William McMahon, second in Boston, won this one from Kelley, 2:38:14.2 against 2:40:07. They would join Brown in Berlin.

Norris was already in the British team,[5] and his teammates were decided in the AAA race. After a battle reminiscent of Boston, Robertson and Ernest Harper ran onto the White City Stadium track shoulder to shoulder. They were both in the team, but neither would relent and they sprinted to the tape, Robertson gaining the edge in 2:35:02.4 against 2:35:03.6.

The Games of the eleventh Olympiad started in the German capital on 1 August. A record of more than 4 000 competitors turned up; the number of participating nations (49) was also the highest ever. When the Games had been awarded to Berlin, no one could have foreseen the rise of Nazism, characterised – among other things – by its virulent anti-Semitism. The German leader, Adolf Hitler, saw in the Olympics the perfect vehicle to expound the achievements of his nation and the superiority of the Aryan race. According to Krise and Squires in *Fast Tracks* Hitler "perceived the Games as a means of placing the entire world under the same sort of spell that he wove in his highly ritualized and symbolic mass rallies". The United States' participation in the Games was controversial, and the *New York Times* published an editorial against it. The Germans put on a magnificent display throughout the Games, and Avery Brundage, president of the US Olympic Committee, declared: "No nation since ancient Greece has captured the true Olympic spirit as has Germany." An insensitive statement, perhaps; certainly a debatable one.

An excellent tradition which the Germans did introduce was the Olympic torch relay in which a lighted torch is carried from Olympia in Greece to the Olympic stadium. Hitler opened the Games in front of 110 000 spectators in the magnificent new stadium bedecked with swastikas after 3 000 runners had carried the torch across Europe. The Games were also the first to be televised.

The Americans easily won the most medals in athletics, followed by Finland and Germany. Although Germans won three of the throwing events, Hitler's ideal of Aryan dominance was dealt a blow by the superb performances of Jesse Owens, who won four gold medals – his gold in the long jump coming after a fierce battle with the German Luz Long.

The marathon was run on 9 August, a warm, sunny day, and started at 15:00. There were 56 competitors. Zabala, the defending champion, had come to Europe a few months ear-

5. He had won the Polytechnic race in a PB of 2:35:20. Lalande was second, giving him the third place on the South African team with Coleman and Gibson. (See Chapter 8.)

lier and set a new world record of 1:04:00.2 for 20 km in Munich. He took the lead immediately, with Manuel Dias POR, Lalande and Brown on his heels. After 6 km Harper and Son moved into third and fourth. Zabala responded and surged away, creating a gap of 43 seconds on Dias by 8 km.

Then it was Brown's turn to react and 2 km later he was in third, but 1:25 behind the leader. Harper and the world record holder were running steadily and when Zabala reached 15 km in 49:45, 1:40 ahead of the Portuguese, they were only 30 seconds behind Dias. Behind them followed Enochsson, Palme, Brown, Coleman and Gibson. When Zabala reached the turn (71:29) his initial fast pace had started to count against him, and Harper and Son had cut his advantage to 50 seconds. They were now in the silver and bronze medal positions, having passed a fading Dias, the Portuguese champion. Enochsson was running strongly behind Dias, but he was just ahead of the South Africans.

Zabala recovered somewhat and over the next 4 km stretched his lead to 90 seconds, reaching 25 km in 83:17. Brown was back in fourth, but in the end the effort proved too much for him. Coleman had broken away from Gibson and Enochsson and Dias were now between them.

Three kilometres later the inevitable happened. Son accelerated and left the Englishman behind. He was gaining on the leader when, just past the 28 km mark, the exhausted Zabala fell and was passed by both Son and Harper. Son reached 31 km in 1:46:20, 16 seconds in front of the surprising Harper. Zabala had not given up yet, but in reality his race was run and he quit a kilometre later. Coleman was now fourth in front of Gibson and the three Finns, Erkki Tamila, Vaino Muinonen and Mauno Tarkiainen. This trio was not going to let the high Finnish standards in Olympic distance events slip. (Finnish runners had won the steeplechase, 5000 and 10000 m earlier in the Games.)

Son and Harper were still moving away from the rest, though. The Japanese went past 33 km with a lead of 25 seconds. Harper was three minutes ahead of Muinonen, Tamila and the tenacious Coleman. But now the second Japanese, Nan, started his final move. He had the confidence of having beaten Son in the Japanese trial, and although he had left his challenge too late, he was still determined to get a medal.

By 35 km Nan had surged past Gibson, the debuting Tarkiainen, Coleman, Tamila and Muinonen. But Son was almost four minutes ahead. In fact, even Harper – suffering from a bad blister on one foot – was safe from the Japanese attack. He was only 45 seconds behind the flying Son, but over the last 7 km Son increased his lead to more than 2 minutes.

Son reached 40 km in 2:19:40 and went on to a new Olympic record – the first sub-2:30 winner. Behind the first three Tamila was safe in fourth, a medal out of reach, while Gibson shook off Tarkiainen and a slow-starting Robertson passed them both.

Harper, the 1926 international cross-country champion,

## HE WAS ACTUALLY KEE-CHUNG SOHN

Kee-Chung Sohn was born on 29 August 1914 in Sinuiju, a port in northwestern Korea. He won his first four marathons, all on short courses, but he also competed with success in track events. In 1935 he ran 10000 m in 32:54, not good enough for the top 50 on the world list, but it provided him with the necessary speed to run a new world marathon record of 2:26:42 in November.

Because Korea was occupied by Japan at the time of the 1936 Olympics, Sohn was selected for the Japanese team. He had to change his name to Kitei Son, but always signed his Korean name during the Berlin Games. And he always took pains to explain that Korea was a separate nation. On the rostrum after the marathon both Sohn and his compatriot Sun-Yong Nam (Shoryu Nan) bowed their heads when the Japanese flag was raised and the Japanese anthem played.

In Korea the newspaper *Dong-a-Ilbo* printed a picture of Sohn on the rostrum but with the Japanese flag on his tracksuit obliterated. As a result, the Japanese government jailed eight employees of the paper and suspended it for nine months.

At the opening ceremonies of the 1948 Games, the first to be attended by an independent Korea, Sohn proudly carried the Korean flag. In 1988, when the Games came to Seoul, they opened with a wonderfully poignant moment when the 76-year-old marathon champion of 52 years earlier carried the torch into the stadium.

Sohn lost only three of his twelve marathons and never placed worse than third.

never won a marathon, but here he ran a PB when it counted most. Kelley could only manage 18th in 2:49:32.4. In sixth Coleman achieved the best result by a South African since Kenneth McArthur in 1912.

| RESULT: | | | |
|---|---|---|---|
| | 1 | Kitei Son JPN | 2:29:19.2 |
| | 2 | Ernest Harper GBR | 2:31:23.2 |
| | 3 | Shoryu Nan JPN | 2:31:42 |
| | 4 | Erkki Tamila FIN | 2:32:45 |
| | 5 | Vaino Muinonen FIN | 2:33:46 |
| | 6 | Johannes Coleman RSA | 2:36:17 |
| | 7 | Duncan McNab Robertson GBR | 2:37:06.2 |
| | 8 | Henry Gibson RSA | 2:38:04 |
| | 9 | Mauno Tarkiainen FIN | 2:39:33 |
| | 10 | Thore Enochsson SWE | 2:43:12 |

This was Son's last marathon. In an interview he said: "The human body can do so much. Then the heart and spirit must take over." After World War II he settled in the land of his birth, Korea, where he trained the country's marathoners. (Nan was also born in Korea.)

The remaining three major marathons of the year were won by Georg Balaban AUT (Kosice), Brown (Port Chester) and Melvin Porter USA (Yonkers). In the latter race the Canadian Gérard Côté, a former boxer who was to come into his own four years later, was second and Dengis third.

The top ten on the world list for 1936 consisted of four Japanese, two South Africans (both in the top five), two Britons, a Finn and an American.

In 1937 Dias, who was only 17th in Berlin, improved his national record by almost 7 minutes when the won the Portuguese title by nearly 13½ minutes in 2:30:38. In the Polytechnic marathon he was soundly beaten by Norris. In the tremendous heat only seven of the 92 starters finished. Norris in turn lost to Robertson in the AAA race.

In the US Kelley tried to run away with the Boston title by surging hard on the Newton hills, but he was caught and passed by former snowshoe-racing champion Walter Young CAN in the 24th mile. Young won in 2:33:20, with Pawson third. Pawson came back to win the next year and repeated this in 1941, improving on his 1933 time (then a course record) with 2:30:38. Six weeks later Young also won the first Lawrence-to-Salisbury Beach marathon, beating no less a personage that the great DeMar, now 49. Their times were 2:50:52.4 and 2:55:35.

DeMar, who had been seventh in Boston, was also there for the Port Chester event. He ran faster (2:48:48), but could only finish seventh once more as Dengis won. This was the start of a magnificent series of wins by Dengis which saw him triumph at Yonkers in 1937, 1938 and 1939 (the latter two also giving him the AAU title), at Port Chester in 1938 and 1939 and at Salisbury in 1938 (with the world's fastest time for the year, 2:30:27.6) and 1939. He could never win Boston, though, finishing second in 1935 and 1938.

The 1938 Central American and Caribbean Games, staged in Panama City, featured a marathon for the first time. The winner was Jose Thompson PAN in 3:01:03.4. The Games would not include a marathon again until 1970.

Three days before this race, on 7 February, marathon runners from the Britsh Empire met in Sydney to decide their regional title. South Africans and Australians took part for the first time. Gibson was the favourite after he had bagged the national title in Bloemfontein the previous year in a brilliant 2:30:45, the second fastest time in the world (see Chapter 8). Of course Norris was also there, as was the man who had placed sixth in Berlin – Coleman. He had lost to Gibson in Bloemfontein, but was the man for the big moment.

Gibson threw down the gauntlet immediately after the start and led Coleman by 9 seconds after 5 miles, reached in 26:31 – a sub-2:20 pace. This was too fast, and Gibson slowed, giving Coleman the chance to close the gap. They arrived at the 10-mile mark in 54:32, still world record pace. Norris was fourth behind Lloyd Longman CAN. Coleman ran with his countryman for another 3 miles and then moved away soon after the halfway mark. He ran strongly (15 miles in 83:58, 30 seconds ahead of Gibson) and although Norris passed both Gibson and the Canadian, Coleman went even faster than the Englishman. He raced through 20 miles in 1:53:46, 27 seconds ahead of Norris. Then the Englishman started to struggle and had to walk. At the finish Coleman just missed Gibson's South African record time, but crushed Norris by more than 7 minutes.

RESULT:
1 Johannes Coleman RSA 2:30:49.8
2 Albert Norris Eng 2:37:57
3 Henry Gibson RSA 2:38:20
4 Duncan McNab Robertson Sco 2:42:40
5 James Bartlett CAN 2:50:51
6 Lloyd Longman CAN 2:50:54

This would remain Coleman's fastest time, but a full decade later he would score another international triumph.

Seven months later only sixteen runners toed the line in Paris for the second European championship. Palme had won the Poly in 2:42:00, beating British debutant Squire Yarrow and Lalande. Yarrow took the lead at 31 km. He was followed by the fifth-placer in Berlin, the Finnish champion Muinonen. The experienced Finn bided his time until near the end, where he passed the Englishman. Palme came through too late to win the bronze medal on his 31st birthday.

RESULT:
1 Vaino Muinonen FIN 2:37:28.8
2 Squire Yarrow GBR 2:39:03
3 Henry Palme SWE 2:42:13.6
4 Maurice Waltispurger FRA 2:44:28
5 Erich Puch GER 2:45:08.8
6 Eugen Bertsch GER 2:45:21

This was the start of a long career in top competition for Yarrow, because eight years later, at the age of almost 41, he would win the AAA marathon in the colours of Polytechnic Harriers. But he could never win his club's marathon.

Muinonen, however, exceeded even Yarrow's longevity. In 1949 he ran 2:36:23 at the age of fifty! (See p. 46.)

Boston provided the first big news of 1939, the year which was to see the second global war severely curtail sporting activities. The day was cold and rainy when several top contenders started the trek to Exeter Street: among them Brown, Côté, Dengis, Young, Kelley and Pawson.

Brown, who had won the race in 1936 and represented the United Sates in the Olympics, was initially denied entry because he did not have the dollar entry fee! The talented runner was unemployed and hoped that a good performance would result in a job offer. But even in his wildest dreams he probably could not have foreseen how the race would end.

On the day no one could match him. A superbly fit Brown went through the tape in a new course record, American record and the fastest time ever by a non-Japanese. It was the first time that the standard distance had been covered in less than 2½ hours in Boston and it would remain, by more than 2½ minutes, the fastest time in the world for 1939.

RESULT:
1 Ellison Brown 2:28:51.8
2 Donald Heinicke 2:31:24.6
3 Walter Young 2:32:41.2
4 Patrick Dengis 2:33:22.6
5 Leslie Pawson 2:33:57.6

Martin and Gynn described Brown's performance as follows: "The quality of performance by this austere and humble but incredibly talented athlete warmed the spirits of the soaked and shivering spectators as few other sporting achievements ever could."

Dengis's victories at Salisbury Beach (2:32:44.4) and in the AAU race at Yonkers (2:33:38.2) mentioned above came against Kelley and Côté (who was eighth in Boston). Kelley and Côté finished in that order in the former race and traded places in the latter.

The Poly was won for the second consecutive year by Palme after a tough duel with Lalande, who was passed by Norris near the end. Palme's time was a PB of 2:36:56. He was by far the best Swede of his generation, winning ten national marathon titles between 1934 and 1944 (nine consecutively).[6]

Faster European times were turned in later in the year when Savino Resta ITA set a national record of 2:33:25 and his countryman Francesco Roccati ran 2:35:23.6.

The year ended with the tragic death of Dengis when the small plane in which he was flying over Baltimore crashed on 17 December. An outstanding career was cut short.

Sport obviously had to take a back seat during World War II and the fighting in Europe made it impossile to use most of the existing courses. In the USA, however, races still took place even though military service hampered the availability of participants. The dominant figure in North America in the 1940s was the French-Canadian Côté.

After Tarzan Brown's scintillating run at Boston in 1939 probably nobody expected his record to fall soon. But it lasted for only one year, because on 19 April 1940 Côté utilised the perfect conditions to run 2:28:28.6. Kelley (2:32:00.6) was second once more, followed by Heinicke and Pawson.

Cramp forced Brown to retire, but only six weeks later he had his revenge on the road between Lawrence and Salisbury Beach. His main opponents were the top four runners in Boston . . . and he showed them all his heels in a new US record, surpassing even Côté's time on the downhill Boston course. Only Kelley could stay reasonably close.

RESULT:

| | | |
|---|---|---|
| 1 | Ellison Brown | 2:27:29.6 |
| 2 | John Kelley | 2:28:18 |
| 3 | Don Heinicke | 2:31:29 |

Côté finished nearly 8 minutes behind Pawson and he again lost to Heinicke at Port Chester, but then made amends by winning the AAU title at Yonkers in 2:34:06.2. This meant that he became the first man to win the two oldest US races plus the AAU marathon in the same year – a feat that he was to repeat in 1943![7]

The 1940 Poly took place in Windsor Great Park and was won by Leslie Griffiths GBR in a slow time of 2:53:41.6. Over the next five years the race was run on a four-lap course in Chiswick, with Griffiths and the Welshman Thomas Richards each winning twice. Richards's second victory, in 1945, came against Côté, who was a member of the Canadian forces in Europe.

The Kosice marathon did not take place again until 1945.

The 1940 Olympics were scheduled for Tokyo, but were cancelled and rewarded to Helsinki. When Soviet troops invaded Finland, these also fell by the wayside. The 1944 Games, awarded to London, were likewise cancelled.

It was ironic that the first Soviet sub-2:40 time was run in 1940, when Yakov Punko and Nikolay Kopilov dead-heated in 2:39:35 in Moscow. In Japan a significant race took place in Fukuoka in March. Toshio Kawaguchi ran 2:33:44 at a venue which would become famous in the future. The fastest Japanese time during the war years was 2:31:38 by Zaiten Kimoto in 1942. In Germany Wilhelm Borgsen clocked 2:33:30.8 in Berlin in 1941.

In the US races continued, albeit with depleted fields. As already mentioned, Pawson won Boston in 1941 after training very hard for two months, beating Kelley, Heinicke and Côté. The same four contested the Salisbury Beach event; this time Pawson was ahead of Côté, Kelley and Heinicke. In 1942 Boston was won by Bernard "Joe" Smith in the unexpectedly fast time of 2:26:51.2, a new US record and the third fastest time ever. Lou Gregory was second in 2:28:03.4. (Smith had won the AAU title the previous November in very difficult conditions of rain and hail.) The following year it was Côté's turn again – he repeated his 1940 victory, once again defeating Kelley on the Newton hills. The Yonkers race was an intense struggle, with a mere 2 minutes covering the first five. Côté won in 2:38:35.3, with Kelley fourth and Pawson fifth. In 1944 Côté went for his second victory in a row at Boston, something which only James Caffrey and DeMar (twice) had managed. He and Kelley once more battled each other, with Côté taking the honours in 2:31:50.2.

Kelley also took second at Yonkers on Armistice Day (11 November 1945) after he had easily won Boston for the second time, in 2:30:40.2.

In Europe the first postwar Kosice marathon, now called the International Marathon of Peace, was won on 28 October by Antonin Spiroch TCH in 2:47:21.8. On the same day Palme's Swedish record fell in Göteborg when Sven Hakansson finished in 2:36:37.6.

These early events stimulated competition in Europe and resulted in many nations quickly returning to full marathon activities soon after the cessation of hostilities on the continent. Plans were made for the third European Championships in Oslo in 1946.

---

6. With this feat he equalled that of Gustav Kinn, who also won ten titles between 1917 and 1929 and competed in the Olympics in 1920, 1924 and 1928 (finishing 25th in his best time, 2:47:35).

7. In 1940 Côté also held the world 10-mile snowshoe record.

# 5

# *1946-1969*

# GROWTH AROUND THE GLOBE

THE NORTHERN SUMMER of 1946 saw the British and Finnish marathon runners getting ready for the first post-war regional showdown. The Finns had won both marathon titles at the first two editions of the European Championships – and the defending champion, Vaino Muinonen, now 47, was still active and running well! He clocked 2:33:03 in a race in Vuoksenniska on 21 July. He didn't win, however. Ahead of him Mikko Hietanen ran a new national record of 2:31:37, thus establishing himself as one of the early favourites for the European title.

The previous month Horace "Harry" Oliver had won the Poly, once again run from Windsor to Chiswick, and started by the King himself. Oliver's winning time was 2:38:12, with defending champion Tom Richards fourth and Squire Yarrow fifth. In the AAA championship, run on 20 July, there was a replay of the stirring duel between Robertson and Ernest Harper on the White City track ten years earlier. This time Robertson and Yarrow entered the same stadium together (it was to be the last time the race would finish there) and ran shoulder to shoulder to the finish. Robertson, the Scottish champion, just could not hold his slightly older rival and lost by a yard. Yarrow's 2:43:14.4 gave him a team spot to Oslo. The 51-year-old Duncan McLeod Wright was fifth.

However, the times run in Europe were not the fastest by European athletes. On a different continent, in Boston, a Greek shocked the running world with a new European record. Stylianos Kyriakidis (36), who had finished eleventh in Berlin and won the Balkan title in 1934, 1936, 1937 and 1939, beat both Johnny Kelley and Gerard Côté in 2:29:27! Kyriakidis ran the race to focus attention on the deprivation suffered by his country in the War. He became the first runner from outside North America to win since 1932.

Seventeen athletes competed in the Norwegian capital for the European title on 22 August – the Soviets for the first time. The race was run over the usual Scandinavian distance of 40.2 km. The halfway leader was Pierre Cousin FRA, but he was followed closely by Yakov Punko, the Soviet record holder, Muinonen and Hietanen, Klaus Schiesser, the Swiss champion, and Oliver. At 30 km the unfortunate Kyriakidis dropped out. Five kilometres further Hietanen, who had been a skier until 1937, had assumed command, leading Cousin by 20 seconds. Muinonen was holding on in third; Punko was fourth.

Over the last 5 km Hietanen drew away from Muinonen, who passed the Frenchman but won the silver medal by only 13 seconds. Still, it was an amazing performance at his age.

RESULT:
1. Mikko Hietanen FIN 2:24:55
2. Vaino Muinonen FIN 2:26:08
3. Yakov Punko URS 2:26:21
4. Pierre Cousin FRA 2:27:05
5. Karl Gosta Leandersson SWE 2:28:30
6. Erik Jonsson SWE 2:30:08

Punko returned to his home country to win the ninth Soviet championship the next month in a slow 2:49:53.8 and then went to Kosice to face the other five finishers in Oslo again. Leandersson led from Hietanen at 30 km (1:49:25), but then the European champion showed his class and took the lead. He won in 2:35:02.4 against the Swede's 2:37:00.2. In third place Henning Larsen DEN set a new national record of 2:38:36.8. Larsen, who had been eighth in Oslo, had already won the Danish title five times (the last four consecutively) and would eventually take his tally to nine.

In the US Côté won Yonkers for the third time, beating Kelley, but at Boston in 1947 he faced tremendous competition. He dearly wanted his fourth victory, but Boston had now turned into a truly international event. Cars were banned from the course for the first time.

Among the starters were the all-conquering Hietanen, Muinonen, Kyriakidis and the first Oriental to enter Boston – the Korean Yun Bok Suh. Suh came to the race with the aid of funds donated by American servicemen. The unknown Korean was not intimidated by his more experienced opponents and ran with Hietanen from the start. On Heartbreak Hill Suh, who was only 1.55 m tall, was attacked by a dog and knocked to his knees. He got up immediately and started chasing the Finn despite the bleeding gash in his leg and a broken shoelace. He not only caught Hietanen, but passed him and reached the finish in a wonderful new world record of 2:25:39. To this day Suh is the shortest man ever to win Boston. Côté was only fourth, but he would get his desired victory the next year.

RESULT:  1  Yun Bok Suh 2:25:39
         2  Mikko Hietanen 2:29:39
         3  Theodore Vogel USA 2:30:10

In England the brilliant marathon career of Jack Holden was beginning. Holden, an accomplished cross-country runner in the true British tradition (he had won the international championship in 1933, 1934, 1935 and 1939) and as track runner good enough to secure four AAA distance titles, won the AAA marathon in 2:33:20.2 from Richards and Robertson. In September Holden finished second in Kosice.

Across the English Channel a new race was born in the Netherlands. The first Enschede marathon took place on 12 July as part of an athletics meeting between the host country and Czechoslovakia. The winner was a Finn, Eero Riikonen, in 2:44:13.

Later in the year the top Finn, Hietanen, retained his national title and in September easily won a Nordic race in Stockholm in a fast 2:30:58. He beat Olle Larsson, who set a Swedish record of 2:36:08.

The AAU title went to Ted Vogel at Yonkers in 2:40:11. Côté, torn between becoming a professional and running in the 1948 Olympics, was fourth.

The last month of the year produced another new race, this time in Japan, where the *Asahi Shimbun* newspaper sponsored a marathon at Kumamoto. This event would become one of the premier annual marathons of the world, better known under the name of its venue since 1964, Fukuoka. The winner on 7 December was Toshiichi Wada in 2:45:45. Behind him came a much better known athlete, Shinzo Koga, in 2:48:06. Koga had won yet another new race sponsored by a newspaper, *Mainichi Shimbun*, at Osaka in 1946 (he would also win there in 1947 and 1948 and the Asahi race in 1949). About a month before the first Asahi race Koga had run 2:36:33 in Kanazawa.

At the end of the year the first three in Boston were first, second and fourth on the world list. In third was the Italian Salvatore Costantino, who had run 2:29:51 in Rome on 27 October – just missing the continental record. His time was to stand as an Italian record for more than a decade.

Côté got his fourth victory at Boston in 1948, but it was not easy. He could only shake off Vogel in the last 3 miles and won by 44 seconds in 2:31:02. He repeated his victory a month later in a marathon race held with the Coliseum Relays in Los Angeles. This was almost as hard as Boston: when he arrived at the stadium gate, it was still locked – and when he finally got inside, he had to share the track with a hurdles race then in progress! As usual after a win, the extrovert Côté lit a cigar. His winning time was 2:42:07. Less than a month later the indefatigable Canadian also won his country's Olympic trial.

Inexplicably the Finns held their trial race for the London Olympics less than a month before the Games, incorporated in the national championship in Vuoksenniska on 11 July. Hietanen won once more, in 2:31:02. Second was Jussi Kurikkala. The third place in the team was given to a man who had not run in the trial: Viljo Heino, world record holder in the 6 miles, 10000 metres, 10 miles and the hour.[1] It is perhaps no coincidence that Heino (coached by Paavo Nurmi) placed highest of the Finns in London.

The British team for the Olympic marathon comprised Holden (winner of the Polytechnic marathon which doubled as the AAA championship), Richards and Stan Jones. The Soviets were not going to be in London, but shortly before the Games Feodosiy Vanin set a new Soviet record of 2:31:55, beating Vasiliy Gordienko by only 29 seconds. Soviet runners were clearly ready to join the world's elite.

The Games of the fourteenth Olympiad were opened by King George VI in the British capital on 29 July. There were marginally more competitors than in Berlin, but the number of nations increased from 49 to 59. Not everyone in Britain was in favour of the Games so soon after the devastating war which had crippled Britain's economy. Existing facilities were generally used, but on the whole the Games were organised well. Germany and Japan were not invited. This time the Finns did not win a single distance event. The Swedes surprised by finishing second to the USA in the medals table. The star of the Games was the Dutchwoman Fanny Blankers-Koen, who took home gold medals from the 100, 200, 80 m hurdles and relay. No other woman before or since has been able to win three individual golds. At 17 years, 263 days Bob Mathias USA became the youngest male winner in the history of the Olympics when he won the decathlon. The Games also heralded the emergence of one of the greatest athletes in history: Emil Zatopek TCH, who won the 10000 m in Olympic record time (Heino dropped out after 6 km) and finished second over half that distance.

---

1. When Heino set the hour record of 19.339 km in 1945, Hietanen was second with 18.083 km. Hietanen himself established five world records for 15 miles, 25 km and 30 km in 1947 and 1948 – the record in the longest distance (1:40:46.4) coming only three weeks before the trial race.

The marathon started in Wembley Stadium on a humid 7 August. Among the 41 runners to attempt the rather difficult course was Suh, but he was destined never to feature. There were also the two South Africans, Johannes Coleman and the much younger Sydney Luyt, as well as the Argentinian track runner Delfo Cabrera, a fireman running his first marathon.

The early lead was taken by another first-timer, the Belgian paratrooper Etienne Gailly, who reached 10 km in 34:34. He had a gap of 12 seconds on Lou Wen Ngau CHN, and then came Rene Josset FRA and Eusebio Guinez ARG, 19 seconds further back. Gailly kept the lead for the next 10 km, passing 20 km in 69:29. The prerace favourites were still far behind: Holden was ninth with, among others, Cabrera and Luyt ahead of him. Hietanen had injured his foot and was falling back (eventually to retire), while Costantino and Cousin had already dropped out. Holden, suffering from blisters, stopped at 24 km.

At 25 km Gailly, running a superb race, was 41 seconds ahead of Guinez in 87:27, with Gustav Ostling SWE third and Cabrera fourth. Luyt was fifth, 1:25 behind the leader. Over the next 5 km the Korean Yoon Chil Choi moved through the field into third, only 52 seconds behind the leader. Between them, 30 seconds behind Gailly (1:47:01), Guinez was still in second. His inexperienced countryman Cabrera wasn't far away, though, trailing Choi by one second. Then followed Ostling, Luyt and Richards, with Empire champion Coleman in eleventh but ready to begin his charge.

Then, suddenly, it all changed. Choi sped past Gailly, reaching 35 km 28 seconds ahead of Cabrera. Gailly was now third, with Guinez just behind him, but Richards was moving fastest of all. Luyt had overtaken Ostling and Coleman was just behind him. But, just as suddenly, the race changed again. A kilometre later Choi was spent and soon dropped out. Cabrera was in the lead, while Gailly and Richards battled it out behind him. The strong Coleman moved into fourth and it looked as if he could get the bronze medal. But the race was far from over – indeed, the most dramatic phase was just beginning.

The Belgian found some hidden reserves and surged past Cabrera at 40 km. Less than a kilometre from the stadium Gailly was 50 m ahead of Cabrera and 100 m ahead of Richards. He reached the stadium first for the final lap, but he was exhausted and going very slowly. Cabrera was now just behind him and easily passed him to win by 16 seconds. Richards was also looking strong when he appeared and he relegated Gailly to third, to the delight of the home crowd. Gailly almost collapsed 60 m from the end, but recovered.

The 38-year-old Coleman was fourth and Luyt an excellent sixth for South Africa's best showing since 1912. Argentina was the only country with three runners in the top ten. Heino finished 11th, Côté 17th, and Kyriakidis 18th, while Suh barely broke 3 hours.

RESULT:
| | | |
|---|---|---|
| 1 | Delfo Cabrera ARG | 2:34:51.6 |
| 2 | Thomas Richards GBR | 2:35:07.6 |
| 3 | Etienne Gailly BEL | 2:35:33.6 |
| 4 | Johannes Coleman RSA | 2:36:06 |
| 5 | Eusebio Guinez ARG | 2:36:36 |
| 6 | Sydney Luyt RSA | 2:38:11 |
| 7 | Gustav Ostling SWE | 2:38:40.6 |
| 8 | John Systad NOR | 2:38:41 |
| 9 | Alberto Sensini ARG | 2:39:30 |
| 10 | Henning Larsen DEN | 2:41:22 |

Kelley finished only 21st, but five months later he won his first AAU title. The Yonkers marathon did not take place in 1948 and the national championship was held on a new course in New York City. Crowds estimated at a million lined the streets and Flushing Meadow Park in great heat to watch Kelley win by more than 10½ minutes in 2:48:32.3. Côté could not break three hours in fourth.

In Sweden the national championship was contested for the first time over the standard distance, on 5 September. Leandersson, who had won the title in 1945 but did not run in London, beat his three countrymen who did in a new record of 2:31:12. Ostling was second, followed by the defending champion and previous record holder, Larsson (who was also left out of the Olympics). Leandersson's next race was Kosice, and again he was unstoppable, winning in 2:34:46.4. In fourth was the Czech record holder, Vaclav Weisshautel, who claimed his third consecutive national title.

Leandersson was at a peak and crossed the Atlantic for a tilt at Boston and the Americans. He won easily in 2:31:50.8, leaving the top American, Victor Dyrgall (in his first marathon), in his wake. But the Swede nearly met disaster when a motorist pulled out of a side street in Auburndale and the runner had to take hasty evasive action.

Dyrgall, who had done well over shorter distances in the past, attempted his second marathon a month later in the AAU race – and promptly won. (He was to regain his title three years later.) The two races had remarkably similar results:

| | BOSTON | AAU |
|---|---|---|
| 1 | Gosta Leandersson 2:31:50.8 | Dyrgall 2:38:48.9 |
| 2 | Victor Dyrgall 2:34:42 | Kelley 2:39:30 |
| 3 | Louis White 2:36:48 | White 2:40:47 |
| 4 | John Kelley 2:38:07 | Côté 2:42:38 |
| 5 | Bernard Smith 2:38:30 | Smith 2:43:30 |
| 6 | Gérard Côté 2:42:55 | |

Two weeks later Kelley won the Salisbury Beach marathon in 2:36:32 against White, but by only 2 seconds.

Holden did not spend much time contemplating his London disappointment. He won a marathon in Sheffield, two months later the Poly and six weeks after that the AAA marathon (2:34:10.6). Then he went to Enschede and scored his fourth consecutive victory, running 2:20:52 for the 40 km course (the only time this race has not been over the full distance). An amazing success story had started.

Leandersson was less fortunate. In the first all-Nordic championship, held on 11 September in Stockholm, he was beaten by Martti Urpalainen FIN, 2:32:18 against 2:33:55.

Then, in Turku on 2 October, another Finn shocked the world. Salomon Kononen sped to a new European record of 2:28:39.4 and behind him the quality was deep: Paavo Laine ran 2:30:46.2 and Vilho Partanen 2:31:04 . . . and in eighth place the half-century-old Muinonen finished in 2:36:23!

The Finns were not through yet: Urpalainen entered Kosice and won in 2:33:45.6 against a record number of foreign entrants. But a local runner, Jaroslav Fiala, finished second in 2:35:42 to clinch the national title.

While the Finns and the Britons were sharpening up for the two main events of 1950, the Empire Games and European Championships, the Japanese were not idle. The 1949 Mainichi and Asahi marathons were won by Saburo Yamada and Shinzo Koga respectively, but the fastest time came from Fumio Babasaki, who ran 2:35:31 in Tokyo in November.

The annual performance list for 1949 was topped by three Finns (Kononen, Laine and Partanen), while two more Finns followed in fifth and seventh places. Luyt was ninth with the 2:34:16.5 which won him the national title.

As the decade closed, the all-time list (all the athletes who had run sub-2:30) was:

| 2:25:39 | Yun Bok Suh KOR | 1947 | |
|---|---|---|---|
| 2:26:42 | Kitei Son JPN | 1935 | |
| 2:26:44 | Yasuo Ikenaka JPN | 1935 | |
| 2:26:51.2 | Joseph Smith USA | 1942 | |
| 2:27:29.6 | Ellison Brown USA | 1940 | |
| 2:27:49 | Fusashige Suzuki JPN | 1935 | |
| 2:28:03.4 | Lou Gregory USA | 1942 | |
| 2:28:18 | John Kelley USA | 1940 | |
| 2:28:25.8 | Gerard Côté CAN | 1943 | |
| 2:28:39.4 | Salomon Kononen FIN | 1949 | (10) |
| 2:29:01.8 | Albert Michelsen USA | 1925 | |
| 2:29:27 | Stylianos Kyriakidis GRE | 1946 | |
| 2:29:39 | Mikko Hietanen FIN | 1947 | |
| 2:29:51 | Salvatore Costantino ITA | 1947 | |
| 2:29:55 | Shinichi Nakamura JPN | 1935 | |

The marathon was to undergo a dramatic transformation in the fifties. The race assumed a much more global character than in the past and times plummeted. The major event of the decade was the crashing of the 2:20:00 barrier. Two runners, one a Briton and the other an Asian Russian, respectively dominated the first and the second half of the fifties.

The 1950 British Empire Games were held in Auckland as early as February, with the marathon on 11 February. Holden soon took command in the rain, but he was followed closely by Luyt who even at 17 miles was less than 2 minutes in arrears. Luyt was pressed by two runners from the host nation, which was taking part in the Games for the first time, Jack Clarke and George Bromily, but although he fell further behind Holden as the race progressed, he remained in a safe second.

As in London, Holden's feet were giving him trouble. This time he took care of the problem by removing his shoes about 8 miles from the finish and continuing barefoot – on cut and blistered feet. Two miles from the stadium Holden also had to contend with that eternal runners' bane, a dog. But he shrugged off all hindrances and ran resolutely to the gold medal and a PB, helped somewhat by the sun appearing toward the end of the race – and, of course, the grass track at Eden Park.

RESULT:
1   Jack Holden Eng 2:32:57
2   Sydney Luyt RSA 2:37:02.2
3   Jack Clarke NZL 2:39:26.4
4   Gordon Stanley AUS 2:40:49
5   Thomas Richards Wal 2:42:10.6
6   Paul Collins CAN 2:45:01.4

In 12th, just one place behind Côté, was a runner who was to become famous as a successful coach some years later. His name was Arthur Lydiard and he finished in 2:54:51.6.

Six months later, half a world away in Brussels on 23 August, Holden was carrying the hopes of Britain to end the domination of the Finns in the European Championships. He won, but it was a close thing . . . and a new Finnish star appeared on stage.

The race started just after the Heysel Stadium had been hit by a thunderstorm. Gailly and his countryman Jean Leblond went to the front and reached 5 km in 18:35. By 10 km Holden and the Frenchmen Charles Cérou and Josset were with them, and in the next 10 km the two Soviets Gordienko and Vanin also joined in the fray. Five weeks before Vanin had set a new Soviet record of 2:29:09.4 – but he had only just beaten Gordienko, who ran 2:29:20.8!

Now Holden decided that he had to do something, and he pulled away from his rivals. He ran the second half of the race alone, gradually enlarging the gap. But farther behind him Veikko Karvonen, an inexperienced Finnish postal worker in only his third marathon, was slicing through the field. He eventually caught both Russians and failed to overhaul Holden by a scant 200 metres.

RESULT:
1   Jack Holden GBR 2:32:13.2
2   Veikko Karvonen FIN 2:32:45
3   Feodosiy Vanin URS 2:33:47
4   Karl Gosta Leandersson SWE 2:34:26
5   Vasiliy Gordienko URS 2:34:37
6   Charles Cérou FRA 2:36:09

At 39 Holden crowned a superb career.[2] The succinct remark by Martin and Gynn in *The Marathon Footrace* contains a message for all aspiring marathon runners: "[Holden] was another example of an athlete who developed a profound base of endurance training at the shorter distances, which then served well to allow him to move up relatively injury-free to a successful marathon career."

The 1950 Boston made history: for the first time three foreign runners from the same country took the top positions. The winner, the youngest since John Miles in 1926 in the slowest time since 1938, was the Korean Kee Yong Ham (19). At the finish to meet him was his coach: Kee-Chung Sohn, or Kitei Son as he had been known when he won the last prewar Olympic marathon.

RESULT:
1 Kee Yong Ham 2:32:39
2 Kil Yoon Song 2:35:58
3 Yoon Chil Choi 2:38:47

Kelley was only fifth, but a month later he again won Yonkers (and the AAU title), in a slow 2:45:55.3 on a very hot day. At 43 he was the oldest-ever champion, and it was his last victory. Before the end of the decade there would be another John Kelley on the scene.

Brilliant running through the Newton hills gave the Boston victory in 1951 to the Japanese star Shigeki Tanaka. His acceleration on the most difficult part of the famous course brought him home in 2:27:45. However, his three countrymen could not hold off the Americans and John Lafferty finished second (first American, as in 1950). Kelley was still there, in sixth. Tenth was Jesse Van Zant, who the next month beat Lafferty in a rainstorm for the AAU title, 2:37:12.5 against 2:37:36.

Two significant developments in 1951 were the staging of the first Pan-American Games and Pan-Asian Games marathons. The former was won by the 1948 Olympic champion, Delfo Cabrera, in 2:35:00.2 and the latter by Chhota Singh IND in 2:42:58.6. Cabrera beat his countryman Reinaldo Gorno by eight-tenths of a second less than ten minutes, but Gorno's moment of glory would come a year later in Helsinki. Singh had won his seventh national title in nine years earlier in the year (and would add another one two years hence) and easily beat the top Japanese in the race, Katsuo Nishida (2:49:03).

The best Japanese times, however, were achieved in their home country. On 9 December the Asahi marathon was held at Fukuoka for the first time. The winner was Hiromi Haigo in 2:30:13, 30 seconds ahead of Tadashi Asai. The next year the *Mainichi* newspaper sponsored a second race, this one at Beppu and over only 35 km (although in subsequent years it

was over the full distance). It was won by Hideo Hamamura (2:01:50). The newspaper's established race at Osaka went to Yoshitaka Uchikawa in a fast 2:29:55.4. Here Nishida fared better, running 2:30:15 – but he was only two seconds faster than Hamamura.

These times were not the best in the Orient early in the Olympic year, however. On 16 March, at Pusan in Korea, Choi had established the fastest time ever on an out-and-back course with his 2:26:07. The previous year (when he won the Asian Games 1500 m title) he had run even faster at the same venue (2:25:15.6), but the course was regarded as short.

The 1951 Poly was a case of "The King is dead, long live the King". Holden went through 5 miles (28:00) in the lead but, surprisingly, with him was Jim Peters (32), running his first marathon. They stayed together for another 8 miles, but by 18 miles Holden had a lead of about 200 yards. Then Peters's tenacity brought him first even and then ahead within a very short distance. Holden, suffering from a bad stitch, retired and the new star went on to a remarkable British record of 2:29:28.

Although it was his first marathon, Peters had already won the AAA 6-mile title in 1946 and the 10-mile crown the following year. He could finish only ninth in the Olympic 10000 m in 1948, and this led him to the marathon and fame. Five weeks after the Poly Peters, running for the Essex Beagles club, lined up for his second marathon and won that too. It was the AAA championship, held over a hilly course, and he romped home in 2:31:42. He was to win four titles in a row, a feat which equalled that of his predecessor.

But Karvonen was not sitting still either. On the first day of July he won his first Finnish title, clocking an amazing 2:28:46. He missed the Finnish record by less than 7 seconds. On 3 August the top Scandinavians met in the second Nordic marathon in Tampere. Conditions were ideal and Karvonen strengthened his reputation with a new Finnish standard of 2:28:07.4. He had to run hard to beat the new Swedish star Gustaf Jansson (2:29:19). Karvonen then went to Enschede for his third top marathon in two months. Totally in command, he won yet again, this time in 2:29:02. He was far ahead of the French champion Cerou (2:35:31.4).

A few weeks later, on 29 September, Zátopek sent a signal to the world's marathoners which at the time they probably did not realise was meant for them. On the track at Stara Boleslav the Czech set a new world record for 10 miles and then proceeded to become the first man under an hour for 20 km (59:51.8) and the first to exceed 20 km in the hour run (20.052 km). These records would stand for a month short of twelve years. He ran the *second* 10000 m of the 20 km in 29:58.3 – faster than his winning time for the distance in the 1948 Olympics! Zátopek was getting ready to shock the world in Helsinki.

Boston marathon day in 1952 was hot and this played into the hands of Doroteo Flores from Guatemala, who won in 2:31:53. Dyrgall was the first American, finishing

2. A mere month before the European title race, on 22 July, the Tipton Harrier had won his fourth AAA title in a PB of 2:31:03.4 – the fastest ever by a British athlete on an out-and-back course.

second in 2:36:40. He then won Yonkers in 2:38:28.4, earning a spot in the Olympic team.

In Britain the AAA championship and Olympic trial were incorporated into the Polytechnic marathon, run from Windsor to Chiswick. The date was 11 June, and it was to be a significant day in the history of marathoning.

Peters, returning to the scene of his triumph the previous year, charged into the lead. By 10 miles he was 49 seconds in front of his closest pursuer, Stan Cox – and this despite being hit by a car at 8 miles. His time was 51:35, a 2:15:00 pace! Peters had been wise to stay away from Enschede, and now he was full of running. He continued at the same pace and ran the next 5 miles in 25:48; his lead was now 1:49. Over the last 11 miles even the brilliant Peters could not maintain this tempo (20 miles in 1:44:00) and Cox cut his lead to a minute, but Peters's time was astounding: he had broken the world record by almost 5 minutes! His 2:20:42.2 was the biggest improvement on the world best since James Clark's time in 1909. Behind him there were more fast times, with Cox also smashing the world record.

RESULT :  
1 James Peters 2:20:42.2  
2 Stanley Cox 2:21:42  
3 Geoffrey Iden 2:26:53.8  
4 Charles Robertson 2:30:48  
5 Robert McMinnis 2:31:42  

A remeasurement of the course found it to be slightly longer than the required distance.

The race was only six weeks before the Olympics, and no doubt this, as well as Peters's tactics, contributed to his undoing in Helsinki.

On the same day in Ghent, Belgium, the local runners underscored the higher standard of the continent's marathoners when Charles de Wachtere won the Belgian championship on a point-to-point course in 2:23:07.8. Leblond was just behind: 2:23:35.

In the Finnish championship (run on the Olympic course) there was a huge upset when an injured Karvonen could only finish sixth. He was nevertheless selected for the Olympic Games, together with the first two in the trial, Erkki Puolakka and Hietanen.

The Olympic Games in Helsinki were attended by almost 5 000 sportsmen from a record 69 nations. One of these, for the first time, was the Soviet Union. But the Soviets did not make themselves very popular by refusing permission for the Olympic torch to be carried across Estonia. The final carrier of the torch received a tremendous ovation when he entered the stadium for the highlight of the opening ceremony – and rightly so: it was Paavo Nurmi, the greatest of the Finnish greats.[3] The assembled sportsmen and women on the infield left their places and ran to the side of the track to watch him

pass. Nurmi circled the track and lit the flame that would burn for the duration of the Games. Then he handed the torch to an even older runner: Hannes Kolehmainen. He ran to the top of the Olympic tower and lit another flame.

It was more than a little ironic that, at the Games where the American millionaire Avery Brundage, passionate campaigner for the maintaining of amateurism, was elected president of the IOC, the Games honoured the man who had been banned for professionalism twenty years before.

Nurmi was the hero of the 1924 Games; now, with the Games in his homeland, they belonged to Zátopek. Stars like the Americans Bob Mathias, who at only 21 retained his decathlon title with a world record, Mal Whitfield, who again won the 800 m – in exactly the same time as in 1948, Horace Ashenfelter, who all of a sudden improved his PB in the steeplechase by a massive 22 seconds and won in world record time against the cream of the event, and, of course, Esther Brand, who in the high jump won South Africa's last Olympic gold medal, all had their moments. But centre stage was taken by the great Czech. (One should not forget his wife, Dana, who won the javelin throw.) Zátopek first won the 10000 m in the Olympic record of 29:17.0 and four days later – the same day as his wife's victory – took a wonderfully exciting 5000 m in another Olympic record of 14:06.6.

Kolehmainen had won the two longest track races in 1912, but nobody had yet attempted to win the treble of 5000 m, 10000 m and marathon. But that is exactly what Zátopek, who had joined the Czech army in 1944, planned to do. Only three days after the final of the 5000 m, on 27 July, he started his fourth race in seven days. He had already logged 20 km of exhausting racing against the top distance runners in the world, and many people thought that he was now undertaking the impossible. But, as he himself said: "If I didn't think I could win, I wouldn't have entered."

The start of the marathon, Zátopek's first, was at 15:30, with the Czech being joined by 65 other runners on the stadium track for 3½ laps. It was warm, but Peters threw caution to the wind and went through 5 km in 15:43. He was aleady 19 seconds ahead of Cox, Jansson and Zátopek. Zátopek was followed by the world record holder for 30 km, the 1951 Soviet champion Yakov Moskachenkov (whose record the Czech would smash three months later), with a gap of 18 seconds to Flores and Gorno. Peters was only slightly slower over the second 5 km, but his time of 31:55 was still a 2:15:00 pace. He was 16 seconds ahead of Jansson, who was followed within a second by Zátopek, with a further 7 seconds to Cox. Gorno was fifth and behind him were Cabrera, the defending champion, and Iden.

Although the next 5 km was the most difficult section of the route with a number of hills, it went slightly faster (15 km in 47:58). Despite the quickening pace, Jansson was now with the Briton, and Zátopek was immediately behind. These three were 64 seconds ahead of Gorno, who was followed closely by Cox and Cabrera.

---

3. Nurmi was also honoured with a bronze statue outside the stadium.

The Czech wonder athlete Emil Zátopek triumphed in the marathon – his first – at the 1952 Olympics after gold medals in the 5000 and 10000 metres. He set an Olympic record in each of his three victories.

Wally Hayward on his way to a new world 24-hour record at Motspur Park in 1953. Timing him is another running great, previous record holder Arthur Newton. Hayward, who won the SA marathon title in 1946 and 1952, set six world records in this race.

On 13 June 1953 Jim Peters ran the first sub-2:20 marathon when he clocked 2:18:40.4 in the Polytechnic Harriers race. He won the race four times in a row, the last three in world record times.

On 21 October 1964 Abebe Bikila became the first man to defend the Olympic marathon title successfully. Four years before, on Rome's historic Via Appia, he had won the gold medal in world record time. Running barefoot (*right*), he only pulled away from Rhadi ben Abdesselem in the last mile. In Tokyo he ran with shoes (*below*) and broke the world record again, trouncing his rivals by more than 4 minutes.

It was at this stage of the race that a famous conversation is alleged to have taken place. There are various versions of it, but according to the eminent historian Roberto Quercetani in his magnificent *Athletics: A History of Modern Track and Field Athletics (1860-1990)* Zátopek told him years after Helsinki: "In a way, [the marathon] was probably my easiest victory. It was not the 'new' distance that frightened me, but rather the possibility of certain paces – which nobody chose to impose." So, according to Quercetani, sometime between 15 and 20 km Zátopek asked Peters (in English): "I know virtually nothing about marathon running, but don't you think we ought to go a little faster?" He received no reply, and then answered his own question by increasing the pace! (In a different version of the story, told by Krise and Squires in *Fast Tracks*, Peters replied: "It's too slow, Emil." Zátopek then made sure by repeating the question: "You say 'too slow'. Are you sure the pace is too slow?" To which the Englishman replied: "Yes.")[4]

When Zátopek took the initiative the tall Jansson went with him and they quickly opened a gap of 10 seconds on Peters. They reached 20 km in 64:27 after the slowest 5 km of the race. Gorno was still fourth (65:50) and running steadily, followed about a minute later by Cabrera. The runners turned at Ruotsikylä and headed into the wind back to the stadium.

Shortly afterwards Cox collapsed and was taken away by ambulance. (Before the race his pulse rate had been 120 and he was advised by a Finnish doctor not to run.) The fifth 5 km was even slower (17:03), but Zátopek had succeeded in opening a five-second gap on the Swedish champion. "He stopped at one feeding station," Zátopek later said, "and picked up a slice of lemon to suck. I was not so sure. I had never taken anything before in racing or training. But I thought, 'If he runs well, at the next feeding station I will take two lemons.'" (David Wallechinsky, *The Complete Book of the Olympics*). Zátopek's dilemma was solved for him by Jansson slipping further behind, and the Czech did not take any refreshments during the race.

Peters was suffering from his rash start, but was still in third, 28 seconds behind the leader. The Argentinians were

running very well: Gorno was fourth, 1:25 behind Zátopek, Cabrera fifth and Corsino Fernandez sixth.

The next 5 km proved decisive. Zátopek covered it in 17:12 and reached 30 km in 1:38:42 – 12 seconds faster than Moskachenkov's world record for the distance on the track! He was now 26 seconds in front of Jansson, who was leading Peters by 45 seconds. Then a cramp in his left leg forced Peters to stop near the 20-mile mark – incidentally, close to where Sam Ferris was standing. Ferris shouted encouragement and Peters hobbled on, but he lasted for only about 200 m and then had to admit defeat, his race finished.[5]

At the head of the field even the Czech wonder athlete was slowing down (30-35 km took him 18:08), but he was increasing his lead all the time. He was 65 seconds ahead of Jonsson, who was losing ground to Gorno (49 seconds behind). Cabrera was still in the hunt for a medal, only 31 seconds behind his countryman. Choi was now fifth and Karvonen sixth after a slow start; they were running fastest of all.

The last full 5 km of the race took Zátopek 18:08, but the others were slowing down even more. Gorno moved into second, but he was more than 2 minutes behind Zátopek, who was assured of victory. Cabrera was still hanging onto fourth, but over the last 2 km he tired rapidly and both Choi and Karvonen passed him.

The top South African and world's foremost ultrarunner, Wally Hayward, was doing well in tenth.

The spectators in the stadium had been waiting patiently for the winner to appear. They could hear the cheering in the streets leading to the stadium, and it gradually swelled in volume as the marathon leader approached. Then the Olympic fanfare resounded through the stadium, and the next moment he was there, running out of the tunnel. The crowd was on their feet and welcomed him with a roar of ZÁ-TO-PEK! ZÁ-TO-PEK! "The miracle had been worked," Peter Lovesey wrote in *The Kings of Distance*. The balding Czech in the red vest, which he had earlier rolled up to his armpits to aid in cooling him down, broke the tape with a smile to complete the most exceptional feat in the history of athletics – one that will probably never be equalled. Zátopek's time was a new Olympic record and world best on an out-and-back course. He had set an Olympic record in each of his three victories.

Cabrera (who ran more than 8 minutes faster than in 1948) missed fifth place by six-tenths of a second, but his placing was nevertheless the best by any defending marathon champion up till that time. It would be equalled in 1956 by Zátopek.

4. There is also the story that Zátopek had decided beforehand to stick to Peters during the race because he was the favourite. "I didn't want to follow a nobody," he is supposed to have said. So he checked that Peters was wearing number 187 and at the start went up to the runner with this number on his chest and stuck out his hand. "Hello, I am Zátopek." The other runner replied: "I'm Jim Peters." (*Fast Tracks*) This story is also quoted by George Gretton in *Out in Front*. According to him, Zátopek said: "When we took our places in front of the grandstand, I caught sight of a runner with his number, and I immediately went and asked if he really was Peters. After all, there is nothing like making sure." In 1992, on a visit to the US, Zátopek told more or less the same story, and added that he did not quite know what to do after having heard that the pace was too slow. "I could not decide to let him alone. If he's not able to run more, who can help me? Then he fell more and more behind. It was new for me." Even the great have doubts!

5. According to Martin and Gynn, Peters and Cox travelled to Helsinki in an old World War II transport plane which took nine hours to reach the Finnish capital because of bad weather. They had only a few sandwiches to eat and there was a cold, uncomfortable draught through the plane. This may have had something to do with Peters's poor performance, although he undoubtedly started too fast.

RESULT:
1   Emil Zátopek TCH 2:23:03.2
2   Reinaldo Gorno ARG 2:25:35
3   Gustaf Jansson SWE 2:26:07
4   Yoon Chil Choi KOR 2:26:36
5   Veikko Karvonen FIN 2:26:41.8
6   Delfo Cabrera ARG 2:26:42.4
7   Jozsef Dobronyi HUN 2:28:04.8
8   Erkki Puolakka FIN 2:29:35
9   Geoffrey Iden GBR 2:30:42
10  Wallace Hayward RSA 2:31:50.2

The champion was lifted onto the shoulders of the victorious (and world record setting) Jamaican 4x400 relay team, ran to the stands to greet his wife, and then went to the finish line to greet Gorno with an orange slice. Afterwards he declared that the marathon was "a very boring race". But on another occasion he said: "If you want to run, then run a mile. If you want to experience another life, then run a marathon."

The Japanese failed dismally: Nishida could only finish 25th in 2:36:19. But on 7 December he won the Asahi race, this time held at Ube, in 2:27:59. This was the year's fastest time by a Japanese.

When the Russian title was decided on 25 August it went to a runner who did not compete in Helsinki, Vasiliy Davidov, and he set a national record of 2:23:59. In October Karvonen clocked 2:25:19.2 in Turku to show that he was over his injury.

The year 1953 was to prove one of the most dramatic in the history of the marathon. The first important race was, as usual, Boston. There was a top-class foreign field: Yamada, Nishida, Kurao Hiroshima and Hamamura from Japan, Leandersson from Sweden and Karvonen from Finland. Because of construction along the route, it was only 25 miles, 938 yards long. (This course was used until 1957.) The runners had a strong wind at their backs and Leandersson used this to create a gap of 400 yards by 20 miles. He was overhauled on the hills by Yamada and Karvonen, and the Japanese went on to win in 2:18:51, against Karvonen 2:19:19, Leandersson 2:19:36 and Nishida 2:21:35.

There were only two Americans in the top eight, and they had almost identical names: John A. Kelley was seventh and John J. Kelley (no relation) eighth.

Leandersson then won the AAU race at Yonkers over a very difficult course in a slow 2:48:12.5.

But 1953 was to belong to an athlete training and racing far away from the east coast of the USA.

Jim Peters trained according to the methods of Alfred Shrubb and Nurmi and did not set much store by the interval training of Zátopek. He usually ran at even pace in his training, covering long distances, although he did run short races for speed. In the words of George Gretton (*Out in Front*), Peters, a pharmacist, did not train intelligently enough. "He was also, perhaps, a victim of the excessive 'amateurism' of the British attitude to athletics. In 1954 he continued to do a full-time job

## THE GREATEST RUNNER

Emil Zátopek is regarded by many as the greatest runner who ever lived, and his triple performance in Helsinki the greatest feat in the history of the sport. The incomparable Czech did more than just win Olympic gold medals; he revolutionised running. As Peter Lovesey put it in *The Kings of Distance*: "We were totally unprepared for Zátopek. In 1948 we were still spellbound by that fantastic figure, Nurmi." But Zátopek's victory over 10000 m in the London Olympics soon changed that.

Zátopek was born in Koprivnice, Northern Moravia, on 19 September 1922 (the same day as his future wife Dana Ingrova). His first race was over 1 400 m in 1941; he clocked 4:24.6. He soon discovered that he had an extraordinary ability to run – and to take on prodigious training loads.

He once said in an interview that he based his training on what he could find out about the way Nurmi went about it. ". . . I never spoke with Paavo Nurmi, but running is easily understandable. You must be fast enough – you must have endurance. So you run fast for speed and repeat it many times for endurance." His philosophy about running and racing was really simple: one had to combine a trained physique with an intense mental and psychological effort – and that would bring success.

He did not believe in steady runs and gradually refined an interval training regimen which he intensified as the years went by. By 1948 he was doing sessions of 5x200, 20x400, 5x200, with 200 m recoveries. (Unlike Nurmi he never timed his runs.) He often trained in heavy army boots. He ran his first 10000 m on the track in May 1948; the Olympic final was his third race over the distance.

In 1949 he alternated three sessions: 5x200, 40x400, 5x200 and 5x200, 20x400, 5x400 and 5x200, 10x400, 5x400, again with 200 m recoveries. Because he did not improve his times between 1950 and 1953, he increased the training load to sessions of 70x400, with only 100 m jog intervals. This went up to 100x400 (100 m recoveries) in the early part of 1954 – and on 30 May he broke Gunder Hägg's world record for 5000 m with a time of 13:57.2, while two days later he became the first man under 29 minutes for 10000 m when he ran 28:54.2 in Brussels.

Zátopek, gregarious and friendly, was never secretive about his training methods and shared them freely. He always emphasised, however, that he had intensified his training over a number of years and that it should not be attempted by novices. His methods have certainly had a significant influence on training, even to the present day.

From May 1948 to July 1954 Zátopek ran 38 races over 10000 m and won them all. Between October 1948 and June 1952 he was never beaten over 5000 m. His awkward running style, lolling head and contorted face belied the wonderful efficiency of his running . . . and his tremendous fitness. When asked about his style, he replied: "I was not talented enough to run and smile at the same time."

Zátopek set eighteen world records, from his first in 1949 to his last, over 25 km in October 1955. The latter also lasted the longest – until 1965.

as a pharmacist and took his two weeks annual leave just before the Vancouver Games for his final burst of training, into which he probably put too much effort in too short a time."

However, when Peters toed the line on 13 June at Windsor for the 1953 Poly, Vancouver was still more than a year away. He had not lost a marathon which he completed and he was at the start of the most remarkable series of races seen up to that time.

He had recorded a number of very fast times for shorter races, among them a PB of 29:01.8 for 6 miles, while he had also placed eleventh in the international cross-country championships. He started rather conservatively (5 miles in 27:05), but then speeded up and by 10 miles (52:40) was 2 minutes ahead of Cox. The next 5 miles took 25:40 and at the 15-mile mark he was almost a minute slower than the previous year. He reached 20 miles in 1:45:07, 5 minutes in the lead. He continued strongly until the finish, and encountered no problems at all. History was made: the world's first legitimate sub-2:20.

RESULT :
1 James Peters 2:18:40.4
2 Stanley Cox 2:26:19
3 Geoffrey Iden 2:26:39

When the course was remeasured later, it was found to be 42.337 km.

A few weeks later Peters ran 29:07.4 in the AAA 6 miles, and on 25 July he was ready for another marathon. This was the British championship in Cardiff, and the race started in pouring rain. The rain lessened later, and eventually stopped, but when Peters turned for the journey back, he had to contend with a headwind. He also encountered two herds of cows on the road! He finished in 2:22:29, a world best for an out-and-back course (bettering Zátopek's Helsinki time).

In September, having prepared assiduously, Peters went to Enschede. Once more there was rain and wind, but the weather did not deter the flying Englishman. He reached halfway in 69:07 and at the finish was only slightly slower than in Chiswick: 2:19:22. This course record (on an out-and-back course) was broken only in 1971, by fellow Briton Bernard Allen. Cox was second in 2:24:38.

Peters did not let up on his punishing schedule, for three weeks later, on 4 October, he was in Turku to prove himself. Many of the world's best, who had been casting doubt on his fast times, were there. Among them was the newly crowned Nordic champion, Karvonen, who had run 2:30:16 a month earlier; Puolakka, the national champion, was also there. The course was unusual: the competitors left Turku stadium, ran a loop in the countryside which took them back to the stadium for a lap around the track, followed by another loop in the country and then twelve more laps on the track!

This time Peters started fast, flashing through the first 10 km in 32:02, a 2:15:00 pace. The second 10 km took only 31:14, giving him a gap of 200 m on Karvonen. He could not maintain this pace, however, and went through 30 km in 97:01. He slowed all the time, and his world record seemed relatively safe. In the end he just managed to beat it after having run the last 40 km all on his own. He beat Karvonen by more than 7 minutes and vindicated himself in no uncertain style.

RESULT :
1 James Peters 2:18:34.8
2 Veikko Karvonen 2:25:47
3 Onni Koskinen 2:32:53.6

Peters had been setting new standards, but a 2½-hour marathon was still the yardstick of quality for the rest of the world. In the Asahi race on 6 December four Japanese ran under that barrier: Hamamura 2:27:26, Hiroshima 2:28:07, Nobuyoshi Sadanaga 2:28:44 and Nishida 2:29:40. But they made no impression on the world list for 1953:

| 2:18:34.8 | James Peters GBR | Turku |
|---|---|---|
| 2:24:38 | Stanley Cox GBR | Enschede |
| 2:24:46 | Roland Guy AUS | Sydney |
| 2:25:47 | Veikko Karvonen FIN | Turku |
| 2:26:00 | Keith Ollerenshaw AUS | Sydney |
| 2:26:39 | Geoffrey Iden GBR | Chiswick |
| 2:26:43 | Alan Lawrence AUS | Sydney |
| 2:27:01 | Alan Lawton GBR | Chiswick |
| 2:27:04 | Gustaf Jansson SWE | Falkoping |
| 2:27:13 | Robert McMinnis GBR | Liverpool |

Thus Peters's slowest time of the year was more than two minutes faster than the time of the next athlete on the list. The next year he went to the US for his first Boston marathon as the firm favourite, but there was strong opposition. Apart from the Japanese and Karvonen, Cabrera was also in attendance, and he took the early lead. He could not withstand the Englishman's onslaught, however. Karvonen, fully aware of the effects of the Newton hills, kept Peters in his sights. He went by at the foot of the hills and was 100 yards ahead when he crested the final hill. Peters could not close the gap and the Finn had his revenge. Peters collapsed after finishing in 2:22:40, 2:01 behind Karvonen. Puolakka was third in 2:24:25, Cabrera sixth and John J. Kelly seventh.

Peters returned home, because he had an appointment on the world's fastest course for the British championship on 26 June. He was the only man who had broken 2:21, and he knew that his main challenge would come from the only other man who had broken 2:22 – his countryman Cox. The question was: could he improve on his world record of the previous year?

He fully intended to try. It was a warm day with a following wind when the 181 runners started the trek to Chiswick. Peters began faster than the previous year and reached 5 miles in 26:40. Only Cox and Jack Broughton were with him, but after another 3 miles Broughton had to let go. The second 5 miles went only slightly slower; Peters and Cox recorded 52:53 there. Cox then slowed down. Peters went past 15 miles in 78:35 and 20 miles in 1:44:25 – his lead then was 4½ minutes and he was 42 seconds ahead of his pace in 1953. When Peters reached the finish, he had clocked his – and the world's – fourth sub-2:20 time and broken his world record by 55.4 seconds.

RESULT :
1 James Peters 2:17:39.4
2 Stanley Cox 2:23:08
3 Eric Smith 2:27:04

A few weeks later Peters improved his PB for 6 miles to 28:57.8 in the AAA race.

Then he went to Vancouver and the British Empire and Commonwealth Games for the climactic race of his career. Peters, in superb condition, ran the 6 miles and won a bronze medal. That gave him confidence, but it may also have contributed to his downfall in the marathon. The long race was on 7 August – a very hot day. The noontime start and the difficult course did nothing to make it easier for the twelve entrants. Peters started fairly slowly and found himself in the lead at 3 miles with Cox and Joseph McGhee, the Scottish champion. But then the impatient Peters made the error of picking up the pace. After 9 miles he surged away from the other two and quickly opened a gap of 300 yards.

Very soon the intense heat started to have its effect on the runners. When Peters ran up the last hill to the stadium, he began to sway from side to side. He fell as soon as he hit the track, got up, stumbled forward and fell again. The crowd watched in stunned anguish as the pale runner, with less than a lap to go, fell repeatedly, staggered to his feet each time and

## THE TRAILBLAZER

James Henry Peters was born in London on 24 October 1918. After his disappointment in the 1948 Olympic 10000 m he turned to the marathon and set a British record on his debut. In his fifth marathon he broke the 2:20:00 barrier – and he was to do it another three times and end his career before anyone else could follow him. Peters was a hard trainer, and after his defeat by Karvonen in the 1954 Boston he followed a programme of more than 100 miles per week. This resulted in his fastest time, a new world record in the Polytechnic marathon.

But it was to be his last completed marathon. The Vancouver race ended his career on a tragic note – and very nearly ended his life. The English steeplechaser Chris Brasher, who earlier in the afternoon had seen his friend Roger Bannister win the "Mile of the Century" against the Australian John Landy, described the finish of the marathon in *Fast Tracks*: "It was a hell of a scene, one of the most horrific in athletic history. They took his temperature right there and his brain temperature was about 107 or 108 degrees. It is something that is still absolutely unbelievable in medical circles."

The well-known South African researcher Professor Tim Noakes wrote that the flow of blood to the skin, which assists with heat dissipation, is severely limited in athletes running at world class speeds. These athletes run in a "'micro-environment' in which their ability to maintain heat equilibrium depends entirely on the prevailing environmental conditions". If the conditions are against the runner, he "will . . . accumulate heat until his body temperature reaches the critical level at which heat-stroke occurs. This physiological 'quirk' is the prime reason why among marathon runners the problems of heat-stroke have largely been confined to the highly-trained competitive athletes such as Pietri and Peters who are able to maintain high running speeds for prolonged periods despite adverse environmental conditions." (*Topsport*, April 1977)

Peters completed nine marathons between June 1951 and June 1954. He lost only one of them and set five world bests for out-and-back and point-to-point courses. Unfortunately he did not finish the two most important races of his career, in Helsinki and Vancouver – primarily because he did not follow the advice he gave in his book *Modern Middle and Long-distance Running*, to always run at even pace "within yourself".

slowly, excruciatingly slowly, moved forward. The harrowing spectacle, reminiscent of the 1908 marathon, continued as the minutes ticked by agonisingly and Peters crept around the track. No one helped him until at last, when he had almost reached the finish line for the track events (but not the marathon), sanity prevailed and he was taken from the track. John Savidge, who had won the shot put for England, carried the unconscious runner to an ambulance. Peters only regained consciousness about 24 hours later and remained in hospital for a week. He never raced again.

Cox also suffered badly, running into a telegraph pole at 24 miles and collapsing. McGhee prudently took a rest along the side of the road. He reached the stadium twenty minutes after Peters had entered it and won the gold medal in front of two South Africans, Jack Mekler and Jan Barnard. The extreme conditions caused Barnard to run more than 26 minutes slower than the national record time which had won him the South African trial race earlier in the year. (See Chapter 8.)

| RESULT: | 1 | Joseph McGhee Sco 2:39:36 |
|---|---|---|
| | 2 | Jack Mekler RSA 2:40:57 |
| | 3 | Johannes Barnard RSA 2:51:49.8 |
| | 4 | Barry Lush CAN 2:52:47.4 |
| | 5 | George Hillier CAN 2:58:43.4 |
| | 6 | Robert Crossen NI 3:00:12.2 |

Only eighteen days later the European Championships marathon was held in Berne. There were 22 starters in the cool afternoon, among them the Finns Karvonen and Puolakka, who had finished first and second respectively in their national title race (Karvonen's time was 2:28:36.6), and the Soviet champion, Boris Grishayev, who took his country's title in 2:27:05.6. The first clear leader was the Swede Jansson, but he was closely followed by Grishayev and his countryman Ivan Filin. The Soviets were leading by 4 seconds at 10 km (33:32), but over the next 10 km were joined by Puolakka, Jansson, Adrianus van der Zande NED and Jose Araujo POR. The group's time was 67:02 at 20 km, with Karvonen 15 seconds in arrears.

Over the second half of the race Karvonen increased his pace, caught the leaders, and then he and the two Soviets got rid of the rest. They reached 40 km in 2:17:02. Puolakka was 63 seconds behind, safely in fourth but without a medal.

Approaching the stadium, Filin surged and opened a gap of 20 m. But he was to be the victim of one of those unfortunate incidents that sometimes happen in marathons all over the world. When he entered the stadium, the officials seemed not quite ready and he turned left instead of right. By the time he was told of the mistake and turned around, he had lost about a hundred metres and had been passed by his rivals. Karvonen's kick carried him past Grishayev and he won by 5 seconds in a new national record. He received both cheers and boos from the crowd.

The Soviets' appeal on behalf of Filin was rejected, but he was awarded a special gold medal. The Soviets continued their good showing in the European Championships, and they would fare even better four years later.

RESULT:
1 Veikko Karvonen FIN 2:24:51.6
2 Boris Grishayev URS 2:24:55.6
3 Ivan Filin URS 2:25:26.6
4 Erkki Puolakka FIN 2:26:45.6
5 Gustaf Jansson SWE 2:27:27.8
6 Geoffrey Iden GBR 2:28:02.8

Puolakka and Jansson clashed again in the Kosice marathon, the Finn winning in a race record of 2:27:21 after a stirring battle.

The Asahi race, which took place on 5 December at Kamakura, had its first international winner. Both Puolakka and Karvonen travelled to Japan, where they came up against Gorno and Choi. The Korean led in the rain at the halfway mark (72:57), with Karvonen, Tanaka, Gorno, Puolakka and Yamada behind him. Over the second half Gorno and Karvonen applied pressure and by 30 km they had a considerable lead. They had to run into a cold wind which sapped their strength. The Argentinian was the eventual winner in the South American record of 2:24:55, with Karvonen second in 2:26:10 and Puolakka third (2:29:17).

Beaten on their own course, the Japanese then aimed for the 1955 Boston. It was a windless day, although it rained. Gorno and Jansson were there again, but the race belonged to Hamamura. He finished strongly and won in 2:18:22 (the course was still short, and would also be short in 1956). Behind him came Eino Pulkkinen FIN (2:19:23) and Nicholas Costes USA (2:19:57). Gorno was fifth and Jansson sixth. But Gorno was to taste victory at last in Enschede, where he won in 2:26:33 – one second ahead of his compatriot Osvaldo Suarez. Cox was third.

The Pan-American Games marathon had taken place in Mexico City a month before Boston. The altitude was too much for the younger Kelley and the title went to Flores in a very slow 2:59:09.2.

There was no Jim Peters at the Poly in 1955, and that meant a definite lack of sparkle. McMinnis won in 2:26:22, beating the more experienced Iden. He repeated the win in the AAA race, defeating Iden by 10 minutes.

In the Finnish championship Karvonen had been beaten soundly by Paavo Kotila (fourth in Boston). When they met in the Nordic championship in Copenhagen on 4 September the European champion was out for revenge. He controlled the race throughout and clocked the year's fastest time: 2:21:21.6. Kotila was almost 3 minutes behind in a PB of 2:24:18.6, with Pulkkinen third (2:26:29.8). None of the other Scandinavian runners could come close.

Almost a month later Karvonen scored another signifi-

## THE CLASSICAL MARATHON

The first Classical marathon on the course from the village of Marathon to the Panathenaic Stadium was held on 2 October 1955. The first half of the race is fairly flat, but from 20 to 32 km the course climbs about 65 m. The rest of the route is downhill.

Runners from Europe have dominated the race over the years, although there have been winners from all over the world. In 1961 a barefoot Abebe Bikila, the Olympic champion, won. The first sub-2:20 was run in 1969 when Bill Adcocks clocked 2:11:07.2 – a magnificent performance on this challenging course.

The first Greek winner was Theopanis Tsimigatos in 1977. In 1965 Jozsef Suto HUN (2:30:40.4) won by almost 18½ minutes – the largest margin of victory ever in a major marathon.

cant victory. The first International Classical Marathon was staged over the legendary course from Marathon to Athens. The idea was to hold the race every second year. The Finn won easily in 2:27:30.

The Scandinavians also contested the 25th Kosice marathon in October. This time the Finns were beaten, as the Swedish champion, Evert Nyberg, running in only his second marathon, beat Kotila narrowly in 2:25:40 for a new national record. Kotila was only 3 seconds behind, followed another 4 seconds later by his countryman Eino Oksanen. The Czech Jaroslav Sourek won his fourth consecutive national title behind the visitors.

Then it was time for the Asahi race again, held at Fukuoka for the second time. Nyberg went, but so did Karvonen – intent on re-establishing Finnish superiority. There was also a top-class runner from the southern hemisphere: the Aussie Ollerenshaw, who had run 2:22:17 a few months earlier.

Unfortunately the Aussie dropped out at about 18 miles because of stomach problems. He had been leading for nearly 10 miles, but was then passed by Hiroshima, Karvonen and Pulkkinen. Hiroshima turned in 71:14, but despite having the crowds along the route behind him, he could not stave off Karvonen's challenge in the last part of the race. The Finn won in 2:23:16, but Hiroshima established a new Asian record of 2:23:51. Pulkkinen and Nishida were both under 2:28:00.

In the Beppu race in February 1956 Hiroshima was again better than Nishida, 2:26:24 against 2:27:26.

The 1956 Poly was a vastly different race than the 1955 edition – in fact, it evoked memories of the great Peters, for Ron Clark raced to a remarkable 2:20:15.6 in unfavourable conditions of cold and rain. More excellent times followed: Fred Norris clocked 2:21:48.6, and both Arthur Keily and Harry Hicks ran 2:22:37.2! Hicks was given fourth, but secured the third place in the team for the Melbourne Olympics with a victory in the AAA championship (2:26:15) against Cox.

Other top Europeans selected by their nations to go south were Filin, who won his second consecutive Soviet title in a national record of 2:20:05.2, Thomas Nilsson, who won both the Swedish championship and Kosice, the latter in a national record of 2:22:05.4 and, of course, the defending champion.

But none of them could boast the times of the Finns. The Finnish trial race took place at Pieksamaki on 12 August, less than four months before the Olympic marathon. It turned out to be the best marathon in history as no fewer than four runners sped through the 2:20:00 barrier!

After the race the all-time list of sub-2:20 times looked like this:

| | | |
|---|---|---|
| 2:17:39.4 | James Peters GBR | 1954 |
| 2:18:04.8 | Paavo Kotila FIN | 1956 |
| 2:18:34.8 | Peters | 1953 |
| 2:18:40.2 | Peters | 1953 |
| 2:18:51 | Eino Oksanen FIN | 1956 |
| 2:18:56.4 | Veikko Karvonen FIN | 1956 |
| 2:19:22 | Peters | 1953 |
| 2:19:27 | Eino Pulkkinen FIN | 1956 |

One of the most amazing aspects of the race was Kotila's pace judgement. His splits for each 10 km were 33:10, 33:41, 33:05 and 32:32. The Finnish times were brilliant, but behind them a national record was also set by the East German Lothar Beckert, who clocked 2:21:44.8.

In America John J. Kelley set a new Yonkers course record of 2:24:52.2 in winning the AAU title. Earlier in the year at Boston he had waged a tremendous battle with the Finn Antti Viskari, which the Finn decided in his favour on the Newton hills to win in 2:14:14 – 19 seconds in front of the American. Kelley was accompanied to Melbourne by Nick Costes and Dean Thackwray, but it was clear that the Americans would be no match for the quick Europeans.

The first (and so far only) Olympic Games in the southern hemisphere began in Melbourne on 22 November. The city's remoteness resulted in the smallest number of participants since 1932. Because of Australia's quarantine laws the equestrian events were held in Stockholm, while Egypt, Iraq, Lebanon, the Netherlands, Spain and Switzerland boycotted the Games for various political reasons. Earlier in the year Russian forces had invaded Hungary and many Hungarian team members made their way to the Games independently. After the Olympics many remained in the West. In another political development the I.O.C. forced East and West Germany to field a combined team.

The major figures were three athletes who won two or more gold medals. The American Bobby Morrow won both short sprints and helped his relay team to a gold medal and world record, the Soviet distance runner Vladimir Kuts took over from Zátopek in winning the two longest track races, and the golden girl of the host country, Betty Cuthbert, exactly duplicated Morrow's feat. The US discus thrower Al Oerter started his phenomenal string of Olympic successes with a gold medal and Olympic record, while Chris

Brasher GBR won a highly dramatic steeplechase.

The marathon was held on 1 December and, as could be expected in the Australian summer, it was hot. Before the race much attention centred on the man who had won in Helsinki, the wonder athlete Zátopek. In 1954 he had won the European title in the 10000 m, but was also defeated over this distance for the first time in his career. In 1955 he bounced back (after training which was severe even by his standards) by setting world records for 15 miles and 25 km, but his records for the shorter distances were taken away by Kuts and Sándor Iharos HUN. Six weeks before the Games the Czech suffered a hernia and underwent surgery. His doctor told him to rest for two months, to which the tough Zátopek replied that he did not have enough time before the Games. "So I went directly from the hospital to the track."

Sadly, Zátopek was to play little part in the events in Melbourne. The race started on a curious note when one of the runners false-started – the only time this has happened in the Olympic marathon. The 46 competitors completed 2½ laps of the track and then headed out on the out-and-back course. Kotila took the lead, but he had the Kenyan Arap Sum Kanuti with him. The Finn reached 10 km in 33:30, two seconds ahead of Filin and Albert Ivanov, who had run 2:21:52 in the Soviet championship behind Filin. Just behind them came the man who had won silver medals behind Zátopek in the 1948 10000 m as well as the Helsinki 5000 and 10000 m races, the French Algerian Alain Mimoun.[6] His real name was Ali Mimoun O'Kacha and he had actually retired in 1954, but decided to run the Olympic marathon in 1956.

Mimoun was followed by Norris, Karvonen, Kanuti, the Balkan Games champion, Franjo Mihalic YUG, Oksanen and the Australian Les Perry – surprisingly in front of Ollerenshaw.

Mimoun, running his first marathon one month short of his 36th birthday, moved to the front and went past 15 km in 50:37, just ahead of Filin and Kelley. They were followed closely by Kotila, Norris, Mihalic, Ivanov and Nyberg.

The runners now started climbing to the turning point, but it did not do much to break up the leading group. The next 5 km took a rather slow 17:26, with Mimoun, Mihalic, Karvonen, Kelley and the Soviets running together. Zátopek was tenth, not quite out of contention yet.

Now Mimoun, wearing his lucky number 13, decided that it was time to do something. On reaching a sharp hill just before halfway, he surged away. He continued pulling away to a lead of 50 seconds at 25 km (84:35), increasing the pace

6. Mimoun, who was wounded in the leg during World War II, was also beaten twice by the Czech in the European Championships of 1950 – in the 10000 m by 69 seconds! In Melbourne he finished twelfth over this distance, but Zátopek said that he believed Mimoun could win the marathon. Mimoun also thought so, saying that a French runner had won in 1900, again in 1928 – and Melbourne was another 28 years later.

by almost a minute over that 5 km section. Mihalic and Karvonen were running alone in second, 20 seconds in front of a group which now included the Japanese Yoshiaka Kawashima. He had run the last 5 km only 6 seconds slower than Mimoun, but unbeknown to him – and quite a distance behind – his Asian compatriot from South Korea, Chang Hoon Lee, was also beginning a charge.

Nyberg and Zátopek had passed the Soviets, while Kotila and Kelley were running together. Mimoun slowed down over the next 5 km, but so did the others. Kawashima had caught Mihalic and Karvonen, while Zátopek had passed Nyberg and was looking as if he could still join in the fray at the head of the field. Lee was moving fastest of all and had jumped from 18th to eighth.

The heat was affecting even Mimoun and the 5 km to 35 km took him almost 18 minutes. Mihalic had left the flagging Karvonen behind and was 1:16 behind the leader. There was a gap of 8 seconds to Karvonen, 38 seconds to Kawashima and 20 seconds to Zátopek. The Czech was less than 2 minutes behind his old track adversary. Lee was sixth and still chasing with grim determination. But the crowds along the route were willing Zátopek on; they wanted the great man to succeed where no one else had before.

But it was not to be. While Mimoun reached 40 km (2:17:30) with his lead intact and the medals seemed more or less settled, the Korean had passed the defending champion and was gaining on Kawashima, only 21 seconds ahead. Over the last 2 km Mimoun was unassailable, enlarging his lead to 92 seconds, but the Japanese could not stay ahead of the Korean, who finished 58 seconds out of the medals. Karvonen finished two places higher than in Helsinki and not much slower; the top thirteen included six Scandinavians. Ollerenshaw ended up 25th in 2:48:12.

RESULT:
1 Alain Mimoun FRA 2:25:00
2 Franjo Mihalic YUG 2:26:32
3 Veikko Karvonen FIN 2:27:47
4 Chang Hoon Lee KOR 2:28:45
5 Yoshiaki Kawashima JPN 2:29:19
6 Emil Zátopek TCH 2:29:34
7 Ivan Filin URS 2:30:37
8 Evert Nyberg SWE 2:31:12
9 Thomas Nilsson SWE 2:33:33
10 Eino Oksanen FIN 2:36:10

The Olympic victory was not Mimoun's only big international win of the year: earlier he had also won the world cross-country title for the fourth time.

Zátopek equalled the achievement of Cabrera four years previously in finishing sixth and also had the consolation that his Olympic record remained intact. When he arrived at the finish he was greeted by loud cheering – and by Mimoun, who was waiting for him. The two old rivals embraced, smiling. Later Zátopek said: "I realized I was licked at the halfway point [and] about all that was left was to go out like a champion. That was when I decided it was no use breaking my neck with any more speed and risk collapse . . . This was my last race." (Cordner Nelson, *Track and Field: The Great Ones*) Like others before and after him, Zátopek could not keep to the last statement, and went on running in 1957. (In 1968 Zátopek and his wife supported the Prague Spring uprising and were discredited and vilified, and even suffered material deprivation, until the fall of the Communist government in 1990.)

Mimoun also kept on running and won the French marathon title in 1958, 1959, 1960, 1964, 1965 and 1966, and placed 34th in the Rome Olympic marathon. Sixteen years after his Melbourne triumph he still managed to run sub-2:35.

The fastest Japanese time of the year was run in the Asahi race in Nagoya only eight days after the Olympic event. Keizo Yamada won in 2:25:15.

The next year the Boston distance was correct again – and what a race it was! For the first time since 1945 there was an American winner – and his name was almost identical to that of the previous US victor: John J. Kelley, who beat Karvonen and a number of top Asians in a course record 2:20:05. Then followed seven foreigners, led by Karvonen (2:23:54). A month later Kelley easily retained his AAU title at Yonkers in 2:24:55.2, becoming the third man after his elder namesake and Côté to win Boston, Yonkers and the AAU title in the same year.

In Britain the AAA title was won in 2:22:27.8 (a PB) by Edward Kirkup, repeating his victory over Keily in the Poly – but by only 6.2 seconds. Across the Channel the Enschede race, run over an out-and-back course to Haaksbergen, was won in 2:32:39 by Piet Bleeker NED, who thus retained his Dutch title.

The Olympic silver medallist Mihalic, like Zátopek and Mimoun a converted track runner, won the first international marathon in the Soviet Union on 4 August when he beat Ivanov in 2:21:23.4. In third place was a runner who was soon to set new standards: the Soviet Sergey Popov (26). He clocked 2:24:04.2, but a month later he was much faster. The same Moscow course was used for the Soviet championship, and Popov ran away from his better known countryman to become the sixth runner under 2:20:00. His time was 2:19:50 and he beat Filin 2:21:39, Ivanov 2:22:00 and Grishayev 2:23:02. (Popov was born on 21 September 1930 in Irkutsk, close to Lake Baikal in the central Soviet Union.)

After his Moscow win Mihalic went to Greece for the second Classical marathon and won again, in 2:26:27.8. He easily beat Kotila, who had won the Nordic title in Göteborg in 2:24:04. As a matter of fact, the Finns took the first three places, trouncing the Swedes in their own back yard.

For the first time the Soviets entered Kosice. His quick Moscow time had evidently taken much out of Popov, for he was beaten by Filin (2:23:57.8) and Kirkup (2:25:54.8), running 2:26:09.2. But the Soviets took fourth, fifth and seventh. The last big international event of the year, the Asahi contest, was won in an Asian record of 2:21:40 by Hiroshima. He battled Kotila all the way, the Finn finishing in 2:22:29 ahead of Kawashima and the Czech Kantorek, the best runner from that country since Zátopek.

Mihalic's success continued into 1958, when he won a hot Boston in 2:25:54. Kelley was second, but then won the AAU title for the third year in a row. His time was fast because of cool conditions: a course record of 2:21:00.4.

On 27 May the Korean Lee, who had run such a great second half in Melbourne, beat the Japanese in the second Asian Games marathon in 2:32:55. Second place was interesting: it was taken by the Burmese Myitung Naw in a national record of 2:42:46.

Then it was time for the British Empire and Commonwealth Games marathon. The Games were held in Cardiff and the marathon started from the famous Cardiff Arms Park at 14:40 on 24 July. Among the favourites were the South African champion, Barnard (who had run the world's eighth fastest time of 2:21:37.2 in 1956, but had failed to finish the Melbourne marathon), the Welsh champion, Rhys Davies, and Dave Power AUS, who had won the 6 miles only five days earlier and was running his first marathon. Davies led at 10 miles (53:48), followed by Power and Colin Kemball, winner of the Poly. Shortly after the turn Power assumed the lead and moved away from Davies. He reached 15 miles in 80:03, but now he was only 10 seconds ahead of Barnard, Kirkup and Gordon Dickson, the Canadian record holder with 2:21:50.5. A cramp had forced Davies to fall back.

Over the next 5 miles Power increased his lead slightly, to 16 seconds, but the South African had shaken off the other two. The Englishman Peter Wilkinson was third, and this order remained unchanged to the end. Barnard cut the Australian's lead by 4 seconds, though, and he finished one position higher than four years previously.

RESULT:
1 David Power AUS 2:22:45.6,
2 Johannes Barnard RSA 2:22:57.4
3 Peter Wilkinson Eng 2:24:42
4 Edward Kirkup Eng 2:27:31.2
5 Gordon Dickson CAN 2:28:42.2
6 Colin Kemball Eng 2:29:17.2

Exactly a month later, on 24 August, Wilkinson, accompanied by Norris, had to represent Great Britain in the European Championships marathon in a rainy Stockholm and on a difficult course. At 5 km the two leading "M's" from Melbourne, Mimoun and Mihalic, were at the front of a strong contingent: Popov, the Soviet title holder, Filin, Nilsson, Arnold Vaide SWE, Aurele Vandendriessche BEL and Miguel Navarro ESP. Popov moved ahead, and by 15 km the tiny runner was leading Mimoun, with the rest strung out behind. The wily Mimoun kept up with the Soviet and by 20 km (62:30) they

were 27 seconds ahead of Mihalic. At this stage they were running about 10 seconds per kilometre faster than Peters had done when he set the world record.

The two passed 25 km in 78:23 and then Popov surged again. He had covered the previous 5 km in 15:53 and the 5 km to 30 km took him 16:12. He was slowing (whereas Peters had picked up the pace), but he was still running 5.5 seconds per kilometre faster than the Briton in his world record.

Norris was in second, and Mimoun dropped out before 35 km was reached. Popov went through that mark in 1:51:03. Behind him Filin was running very well, going from fifth to third and then overtaking Norris outside the stadium for the silver medal. Filin set a new PB, but his countryman set a world record by more than 2 minutes – and on a much tougher course than Peters had done four years earlier.

The two British runners performed extremely well, beating the might of Finland and Sweden.

RESULT:
1 Sergey Popov URS 2:15:17
2 Ivan Filin URS 2:20:50.6
3 Fredrick Norris GBR 2:21:15
4 Peter Wilkinson GBR 2:21:40
5 Lothar Beckert GDR 2:22:11.2
6 Veikko Karvonen FIN 2:22:45.8.

Popov's time would not be bettered by a Soviet runner until 1970. His winning margin remains the biggest ever in a European championship marathon.

For the first time a Japanese athlete was invited to Kosice, but Hiroshima was no match for the Czech star Kantorek, who won in 2:29:37.2 – 5 seconds ahead of Beckert. The Asahi race was a thriller, with Karvonen and the Japanese Nobuyoshi Sadanaga entering the track shoulder to shoulder. The spectators were behind the local runner and he did not disappoint them, outsprinting the Finn by three seconds in 2:24:01. Mihalic and Kantorek followed.

Ten days before the end of the year the first Chinese runner of note, Li Tun-Yung, delivered a bolt from the blue when he ran 2:19:55.6 in Tsinan to become the eighth athlete under 2:20:00.

In the first major marathon of 1959, on 8 February in Beppu, the Japanese debutant Yoshitaka Tsuiji clocked an outstanding 2:23:40 to beat Hiroshima – the only Japanese to have bettered the winning time. Hiroshima was only third behind Kenji Fujiki's 2:24:04.

On a very cold April day Oksanen won in Boston, 2:22:42 against Kelley's 2:23:43. Karvonen could not quite match them, finishing fourth in 2:24:37. No one was ahead of Kelley in the AAU marathon, however, and he clinched his fourth consecutive title, this one in 2:21:54.4. Kelley prepared well for the Pan-American Games in Chicago in September, establishing a US record for 10 miles on the track and winning the AAU 20 km race. Conditions in

Chicago were difficult, but Kelley scored the first US victory in an international race since Johnny Hayes in the 1908 Olympic marathon. His time was 2:27:54.2, an excellent performance in the circumstances.

In Europe Kantorek closed the decade on a high note. First he won in Enschede (2:26:48), then he clocked a marvellous 2:19:06 to win the Czech championship in Ostrava on 13 September, and then was defeated badly in Kosice (11 October). Popov showed his class in no uncertain terms by winning in a wonderful 2:17:45.2, the second best on an out-and-back course (behind his own world record).

RESULT:  1  Sergey Popov URS 2:17:45.2
         2  Dennis O'Gorman GBR 2:23:08
         3  Ivan Filin URS 2:23:55.4

Kantorek was only seventh, but in the Asahi race in December (held at Fukuoka, the venue used to the present day with the exception of 1963) he finished second to Hiroshima, 2:29:34 against 2:30:48.

In the Marathon-to-Athens race the Finns, who had not gone to Kosice, were up against a new force, the Kiwis. Bill Baillie had set an Australasian record of 2:20:13 in Auckland on 22 August, beating Jeff Julian by a mere 24 seconds. Both were trained by Lydiard. In the Greek event Julian proved the stronger, but he still had to admit defeat against Oksanen (2:26:30). Baillie was seventh.

At the end of the decade the all-time list looked like this:

| 2:15:17 | Sergey Popov URS | 1958 | |
|---------|------------------|------|------|
| 2:17:39.4 | James Peters GBR | 1954 | |
| 2:18:04.8 | Paavo Kotila FIN | 1956 | |
| 2:18:51 | Eino Oksanen FIN | 1956 | |
| 2:18:56.4 | Veikko Karvonen FIN | 1956 | |
| 2:19:06 | Pavel Kantorek TCH | 1959 | |
| 2:19:27 | Eino Pulkkinen FIN | 1956 | |
| 2:19:55.6 | Li Tun-Yung CHN | 1958 | |
| 2:20:05 | John J. Kelley USA | 1957 | |
| 2:20:05.2 | Ivan Filin URS | 1956 | (10) |
| 2:20:06.6 | Nikolay Rumyantsev URS | 1958 | |
| 2:20:13 | William Baillie NZL | 1959 | |
| 2:20:15.8 | Ronald Clark GBR | 1956 | |
| 2:20:37 | Jeffrey Julian NZL | 1959 | |
| 2:21:15 | Fredrick Norris GBR | 1958 | |
| 2:21:17.8 | Olavi Manninen FIN | 1956 | |
| 2:21:23.4 | Franjo Mihalic YUG | 1957 | |
| 2:21:23.8 | Symen Kuznetsov URS | 1955 | |
| 2:21:29 | Cheng Chao-Hsin CHN | 1958 | |
| 2:21:37.2 | Johannes Barnard RSA | 1956 | (20) |

The first major shots of the Olympic year of 1960 were fired not in the venerable Boston marathon, but in a race of much less importance, the Doncaster-to-Sheffield affair on 18 April. In the years since Peters's retirement a number of British runners had shown that they were on the verge of following him through the 2:20:00 barrier. It happened on this day . . . and two Britons achieved the feat. Keily won the race

for the third time, in 2:19:23, and he was only 31 seconds ahead of Wilkinson (2:19:54). Less than two months later, in the Polytechnic marathon on 11 June, Keily improved again – to 2:19:06. Behind him was an upcoming star, making his debut: Brian Kilby finished in 2:22:53. A month later, on 9 July, Kilby went one better when he ran away with the AAA title, winning in 2:22:44.8 on a warm day. Within two years he would be the best marathon runner in Europe and the British Empire.

The day after Keily's win in Sheffield the Boston race went to Kotila in 2:20:54. Kelley had to retire because of a blistered foot and that placed his trip to the Rome Games in jeopardy, because of the AAU's ridiculous policy that a runner had to complete both Boston and the national championship. This ruling was later changed after pressure was brought to bear on the AAU, and Kelley won the AAU title at Yonkers in a scintillating 2:20:13.6 – a course record broken only in 1974!

The 1960s heralded a tremendous increase in the popularity of the marathon in the United States. Whereas the US had only five marathon races in 1959, there were 44 in 1969. More and more people started running long distances – even women, who were still barred from entering marathons. The 1961 report by the President's Council on Physical Fitness in Sport, which announced the decline in the nation's fitness, and President John F. Kennedy's subsequent campaign to rectify matters, had much to do with the increase in interest. The organisation of road races shorter than a marathon was still a very informal affair. Krise and Squires describe it as follows in *Fast Tracks*: "[These] races emphasized socializing nearly as much as competition. Road race prizes ran the gamut of variety from meat or poultry to motorcycles or pianos. Neither t-shirts nor beer appeared on the lists of prizes and accoutrements of 1950s' road races. A special race would offer juice, soda, coffee, and cookies to athletes and their families after the competition, usually back at the gym where everyone had left his sweat clothes."

Worldwide the sixties brought a huge increase in quality, as can be seen in the rest of this chapter and in the summary at its end.

The fast times run by Keily and Wilkinson motivated Britain's other top runners, who still had to fight for the third spot on the Olympic team. They got their chance near Liverpool on 30 July, where Norris, O'Gorman, Brian Cooke and Kemball took the initiative. It was a circular two-lap course and the leaders passed 15 miles in 1:18:43. Rain over the next 5 miles helped to cool them down. Norris and O'Gorman ran this section in 25:51, shaking off the others. Over the last 2 miles Norris could not stay with his rival and had to concede first place, but both were quicker than 2:20:00.

RESULT:  1  Dennis O'Gorman 2:18:15.6
         2  Fredrick Norris 2:19:08
         3  Colin Kemball 2:21:22

O'Gorman was now fourth on the world all-time list and secured his place for Rome, where he would be the top British finisher.

The Games of the seventeenth Olympiad were opened in Rome on 25 August. For the first time more than 5 000 sportsmen and women competed and the 83 participating nations were also a record. The Games went off without any major incidents, but it was the last in which South Africa would take part until 1992. The country's last medal was won by Malcolm Spence, who earned a bronze in the 400 m. The star of the Games was the graceful American sprinter Wilma Rudolph, nicknamed "La Gazelle" by the French. Born in 1940 as the twentieth child in a poor family of 22 children, she could not walk normally until she was ten because of paralysis in one leg. She was a determined girl, however, and followed an exercise programme which enabled her to win a bronze medal in the relay at the 1956 Olympics! Two years later in Rome she won both sprints easily and was a member of the USA's winning relay team.

In the 200 m for men the Italian Livio Berruti ran into the hearts of his partisan countrymen by upsetting the Americans and equalling the world record. The incomparable Australian Herb Elliott pulverised the 1500 m field in a wondrous new world record and Oerter took his second discus gold. The Soviets won only one less gold medal than the Americans. And, of course, for the first time an African nation won a gold medal.

The marathon was run on 10 September and started at 17:30 to escape the intense summer heat. For the first time in Olympic history neither the start nor the finish was in a stadium. The 69 runners lined up beneath Capitol Hill and after a few kilometres four men were in the lead. They were Keily and Vandendriessche, who had won the Belgian title for the fifth consecutive time, and two Africans: Rhadi ben Abdesselem, a soldier from Morocco, and Abebe Bikila, a member of the bodyguard of Emperor Haile Selassie of Ethiopia. Bikila was running barefoot.

They passed 5 km in 15:35 and 10 km in 31:07. By now Kilby had joined them, as well as Rhadi's team-mate Allal Saoudi. They were 3 seconds ahead of Albert Messitt IRL. Over the next 5 km the leading group remained the same, except that Saoudi was losing ground. The split at 15 km was 48:02. Then Bikila and Rhadi really started moving, covering the 5 km to 20 km in an astounding 14:37! They were 9 seconds behind Popov's pace in his world record.

The world record holder and favourite was also in the race, running in a group 62 seconds behind the leaders. Vandendriessche was 26 seconds behind Bikila and Rhadi, with Keily following him by 15 seconds. Then came Popov, Barry Magee NZL, Benaissa Bakir MAR and Franz Kunen NED.

However, even the amazing Africans had to slow down. They reached 25 km in 78:47, now 24 seconds behind Popov's schedule, but they had a massive lead of 3:24 on Magee and Popov. Keily was in fifth, just ahead of Bakir and Mihalic. Vandendriessche was in trouble and would drop out. With 12 km to run the athletes turned into the ancient Appian Way; the leaders had passed 30 km in 94:29. Magee and Popov were somewhat closer now, passing in 96:52, but Keily had dropped back. Bakir and Mihalic were a minute behind Magee and the world record holder. For the first time in the race Bikila and his rival were ahead of Popov's record pace, if only by 6 seconds.

Magee was running well, proving the efficacy of the training methods of New Zealand coach Lydiard, whose other protégés Peter Snell and Murray Halberg had won the 800 m and 5000 m respectively at these Games. At 35 km he was 2:02 behind the leaders' 1:50:27. Bikila and Rhadi were now 36 seconds faster than Popov and heading for a new world record. The question was: who would win?

Bikila, who was 27 or 28 (see box on p. 63), was the novice – he had not started running until he was 24 – but he had run two trials over the marathon distance before the Games, clocking 2:39:50 and then a brilliant 2:21:23 in high-altitude Addis Ababa (2 440 m above sea level). Rhadi (31) had won the international cross-country title earlier that year. Four weeks before the Olympics he had run a personal best time of 29:20.8 for 10000 m, but in the Olympic race over this distance he finished only fourteenth.

Popov, although still in fourth (68 seconds behind the black-clad Kiwi) was struggling and was challenged by his countryman and Soviet titlist, Konstantin Vorobyev. But between 35 and 40 km the race took a significant turn. The Africans were slowing down further and the world record was slipping from their grasp. They needed 18:06 for that section (reaching 40 km in 2:08:33), whereas Popov had covered it in 16:40 and Magee now did it in 17:30. Lydiard's stamina training was paying off.

Vorobyev passed Popov, but he was too far behind. At the head of the field Bikila and Rhadi stormed down the ancient torch-lit Via Appia toward the Arch of Constantine in a dramatic scene witnessed by thousands. They were cutting their deficit on the world record with every stride.

Less than a mile from the finish Bikila had noticed, when he checked out the course with his coach a few days before the race, the obelisk of Axum, which Italian soldiers had taken from Ethiopia and brought to Rome. There was a slight uphill after the runners passed the obelisk, and Bikila had decided that that was the right place to make his final move in the race. He had no doubt that he would be in contention at that point, and so it now proved. It had been a titanic struggle, but he got the upper hand in that last mile and was rewarded with a new world record. There was a moment of drama 60 metres from the end when a local unexpectedly drove his scooter onto the course, but fortunately Bikila managed to avoid him. Over the last 2 km Bikila had finished 50.8 seconds faster than Popov two years before and he broke the record by only 0.8 seconds. Rhadi was a fraction more than 25 seconds behind and the first fifteen runners broke Zátopek's Olympic record.

RESULT:
1   Abebe Bikila ETH 2:15:16.2
2   Rhadi ben Abdesselem MAR 2:15:41.6
3   Barrington Magee NZL 2:17:18.2
4   Konstantin Vorobyev URS 2:19:09.6
5   Sergey Popov URS 2:19:18.8
6   Thyge Togersen DEN 2:21:03.4
7   Abebe Wakgira ETH 2:21:09.4
8   Benaissa Bakir MAR 2:21:21.4
9   Osvaldo Suarez ARG 2:21:26.6
10  Franjo Skrinjar YUG 2:21:40.2

After the race Bikila said: "We train in shoes, but it's much more comfortable to run without them." The first three runners took positions one, three and four on the all-time list. Back in the pack in this great race were such luminaries as Mihalic (12), Kantorek (14), Kelley (19), Oksanen (24), Keily (25), Hiroshima (31), Mimoun (34) and Beckert (56). Kilby finished in 2:28:55.

One fact was clear: with four men from that continent in the first ten, the African running revolution had begun.

Less than three months later Magee was in Fukuoka. He had recovered sufficiently to record the first sub-2:20 in the race, finishing in 2:19:04. The second runner, Kotila, also ducked under the barrier with 2:19:21. Exactly three months after the Japanese race, on 4 March 1961, Magee was under 2:20:00 again when he won the New Zealand title in 2:18:54.

Somewhat surprisingly no Japanese had yet run faster than 2:20:00, but this was rectified by Takayuki Nakao when he clocked 2:18:54 at Nagoya on 21 March.

Then came Boston. John J. Kelley had tuned up with an easy victory in 2:25:27 in the Cherry Tree marathon. He was up against his nemesis of 1959, Oksanen, as well as Norris. And there was also a dog . . .

It was a very cold day, with snow falling during the race. Oksanen and Kelley ran together for most of the way, and they also had the company of a dog for part of the distance. Kelley fell over the dog at 17 miles and was helped up by Norris. A determined Kelly caught Oksanen again, but the Finn edged away from him near the end and won by 25 seconds in 2:23:29. Norris was third.

This was Oksanen's second Boston victory and the third one in a row by Finland. In 1962 Oksanen would score his third, and easiest, win when he beat his countryman Paavo Pystynen in 2:23:48. After these four victories Finland would have to wait until 1972 for another one.

Kelley ran almost exactly 3 minutes slower when he won his sixth consecutive AAU title at Yonkers in 2:26:53.4 a month after Boston.

In Britain Wilkinson won both the Doncaster-to-Sheffield race and the Poly, in the latter beating Kilby. Wilkinson ran 2:20:25, with Sam Hardicker second in a PB of 2:20:58. But

Kilby defended his AAA title successfully, winning in 2:24:37 in difficult conditions. Wilkinson then took the Enschede race against a good field, beating both the previous year's winner, Kantorek, and the Austrian champion, Adolf Gruber, in 2:24:11.

Kantorek had his revenge in Fukuoka, where Wilkinson ran a gutsy race, coming back towards the end after a difficult patch between 25 and 30 km. The Czech won in 2:22:05 from Oksanen 2:22:18, Sadanaga 2:22:19 and Wilkinson 2:23:24.

The Olympic champion scored three major victories in 1961 (see box on p. 63).

Kelley won the Cherry Tree race again in February 1962, but the first American in Boston was the marine Alex Breckenridge. Kelley, however, took his seventh AAU title. His time of 2:27:39.8 was the slowest of his eight victories, but he beat Breckenridge by more than 3 minutes. The "other Kelley", John A., was fourth in 2:37:42.

On the same day the Mainichi marathon in Osaka incorporated the Japanese trial for the Asian Games. Masayuki Nagata won in 2:27:37, beating Nakao, and then went on to clinch the Asian title in Djakarta. Only four of the eight starters finished on a hot and humid day; the winning time was 2:34:54.2.

As British runners were gearing themselves up for the European Championships marathon the Poly was won by a fresh face on the scene: Ron Hill (23). Hill had debuted in Liverpool the previous year, winning in 2:24:22, and now he ran faster: 2:21:59. He was to have a miserable European race, failing to finish, but his day would come. Kilby, the defending champion, won the AAA race in atrocious conditions of strong wind and rain, clocking an admirable 2:26:15. He beat the Scottish champion, Alastair Wood (2:26:35).

The European race was held in Belgrade on 16 September. It was a warm day and the 28 athletes were not keen to run too fast. The serious contenders were quite happy to watch proceedings at the front of the field from a distance. The early leader was Stanislaw Ozog POL, who was running his first marathon. By 15 km Kilby was more than 2 minutes behind, but he moved up over the second 15 km. At 30 km Rumyantsev, one of three Soviets (the others were Popov and Viktor Baikov, who had won the national title in 2:19:17.8), led from Kilby and Vandendriessche in 1:42:37. Kilby took over as the Soviet fell back, but then faced a challenge from Baikov. The two had a tremendous battle, but it tired Baikov to such an extent that Vandendriessche managed to overhaul him near the end for the silver medal.

RESULT:
1   Brian Kilby GBR 2:23:18.8
2   Aurele Vandendriessche BEL 2:24:02
3   Viktor Baikov URS 2:24:19.8
4   Alastair Wood GBR 2:25:57.8
5   Pavel Kantorek TCH 2:26:54.4
6   Sergey Popov URS 2:27:46.8

This win gave Kilby the first leg of his phenomenal double for 1962. Oksanen finished twelfth.

The Kosice race on 7 October was a thriller. The experienced Kantorek came up against a newcomer, Leonard Edelen from South Dakota. "Buddy", as he was called, had set US records for one hour and 10 miles earlier in the year and had won the Welsh marathon title in 2:22:32. He and Kantorek ran shoulder to shoulder before the American succeeded in opening a small gap before 40 km. But Kantorek, before his "home" crowd, came back at him when they reached the stadium. His finishing sprint was too good for Edelen and he barely won: 2:28:29.8 against 2:28:31.4.

In October Nakao improved on his Japanese (and Asian) record by 2 seconds with 2:18:52 in Auckland. He had worked on his speed by running a new Japanese 10000 m track record two weeks before. Toru Terasawa was second in 2:19:15, with Baillie only fourth (2:22:35). But four days later Nakao's time was shattered by the Korean Yu Mang Hyang in Pyongyang. His 2:16:09.6 was the fourth fastest ever run.

The British Empire and Commonwealth Games marathon was held on 29 November in Perth. This time there were no South Africans among the twenty competitors.

Kilby and the defending champion, Power, ran in a pack behind the early leaders, and Kilby went to the front just before 10 miles (54:36). He was accompanied by Mohamed Yousouf of Pakistan and Mel Batty of England. Over the next 5 miles they were passed by a new group, with Power, Wood and Bruce Kidd CAN, who had won the 6 miles five days earlier, prominent. Kilby was close by, but then accelerated, and by 20 miles he had a lead of 30 seconds over Batty. A further 30 seconds back was a group which included the Australians Rodney Bonella, Power and Ollerenshaw (who had won the national title over the same course).

By 25 miles (2:14:49) Kilby had stretched his lead to one minute over Power. The gap remained constant over the remainder of the race and Kilby finished in a PB (as did Power). Like Holden in 1950, he had won the AAA, European and Empire titles in the same year.

RESULT:
1 Brian Kilby Eng 2:21:17
2 David Power AUS 2:22:15.4
3 Rodney Bonella AUS 2:24:07
4 Keith Ollerenshaw AUS 2:24:59
5 Melvin Batty Eng 2:25:51
6 John Stephen TAN 2:28:39

Edelen and Kantorek again met in Fukuoka, but the race went to Terasawa . . . in a new Japanese record of 2:16:18.4! He only shook off the challenge of Nakao in the last 5 km and the latter was also rewarded with a sub-2:17 – 2:16:53.4. Nakao was followed by a third Japanese: Kenji Kimihara, who clocked 2:18:01.8 in his debut. Although well beaten, Edelen and Kantorek staged a replay of their

fight at Kosice. They appeared in Heiwadai Stadium together and sprinted for the tape. Edelen prevailed in 2:18:56.8, but only by a whisker. At last an American had run sub-2:20.

RESULT:
1 Toru Terasawa 2:16:18.4
2 Takayuki Nakao 2:16:53.4
3 Leonard Edelen 2:18:56.8
4 Pavel Kantorek 2:18:57.4
5 Makoto Nakajima 2:19:09.2
6 Masayuki Nagata 2:19:51.8

Thus 1962 ended with three runners under 2:17:00 and a further three under 2:19:00 for the year – both the best ever.

In 1963 a number of new marathons started in Japan (and six in the USA), but early in the year attention focused on Beppu, where Japan's best duelled on 17 February. The result was astonishing.

Ideal conditions led to a quick pace from the beginning. The first 10 km were covered in 32:43 and the second in 32:52. This was well behind Bikila's pace in Rome, and the turn at Oita was reached in 69:09. The 5 km between 20 and 25 took only 15:55 . . . and then things started happening! Terasawa and Kimihara raced through the next 5 km in 15:19; their time at 30 km was 96:49 – still 2:20 behind Bikila, who had run the same section in 15:42.

The two leaders flashed through 35 km in 1:52:24 (1:57 behind Bikila), having run 15:35 for the previous 5 km. Then Kimihara could not maintain the furious pace any longer and slipped back. He was soon overhauled by Kazumi Watanabe and Haruo Otani, while Terasawa ran on unperturbed. His split at 40 km was 2:08:10 – he had caught up to and passed Bikila, who had reached this point in 2:08:33. A new world record was in the offing, but of course the Ethiopian had covered the last 2.195 km in a quick 6:43.2. Watanabe was 47 seconds behind Terasawa, also on course for a world-class time.

With the timekeepers' watches ticking on relentlessly, Terasawa inevitably started to tire (he had run the previous 5 km almost 2½ minutes faster than Bikila). The record started slipping from his grasp. But he held on, albeit barely, and behind him nine athletes ducked under 2:20:00 (six were under 2:18:00).

RESULT:
1 Toru Terasawa 2:15:15.8
2 Kazumi Watanabe 2:15:39.4
3 Haruo Otani 2:15:57
4 Kenji Kimihara 2:16:19
5 Jyuichi Sato 2:16:33.8

In a single race the world's number of 2:15:00 marathons had been doubled. But it was only the beginning of 1963's wonders.

Boston had a formidable field. Bikila was there, and so were Vandendriessche, Kilby, Oksanen and Kelley. The unbeaten Olympic champion brought along compatriot Mamo Wolde. Kelley must have looked forward to the race, because the Massachusetts SPCA put a number of vehicles on the course to collect stray dogs! Kelley did not win, and he was beaten not by Bikila but by Vandendriessche. The Belgian set a new course record of 2:18:58, with Kelly second in 2:21:09. Then followed Kilby 2:21:43, Oksanen 2:22:43 and Bikila 2:24:43.

Bikila and Wolde had set a fast pace from the beginning, but Bikila suffered from leg cramps and was passed by Vandendriessche at Coolidge Corner (24 miles). The Boston marathon thus maintained its jinx over Olympic champions – none had ever won there.

Five weeks later Kelley took his unprecedented eighth consecutive AAU title, this one in 2:25:17.6 with a cushion of almost eight minutes.

The rest of the year, however, would belong to another American, one living in England since 1960, and to a Briton. Buddy Edelen won the Classical marathon in 2:23:06.8, breaking Bikila's course record, and then entered the 50th Poly, where he had finished ninth in 1962. The race was on 15 June and Edelen had the company of 139 runners – although not for long. Edelen, Hill and Juan Taylor passed 5 miles in 26:15, a faster pace than the Japanese had run at Beppu but much slower than Bikila had in Rome. They picked up the tempo, but were joined by Wood and Don Shelley. The split for 10 miles was 52:20. By 15 miles (77:40) Edelen, Taylor and Hill were leading. They were still about 4 seconds per kilometre slower than Bikila, but Edelen, full of confidence, was running faster all the time. The next 5 miles took only 25:12 and at 20 miles he was alone in 1:42:52. He completed the last 6.2 miles in 31:36 (3:09/km pace) and finished in a new world record of 2:14:28. His record brought back memories of the fabulous running of the great Jim Peters, and he was given a rousing welcome.

RESULT:  1  Leonard Edelen 2:14:28
         2  Ronald Hill 2:18:06
         3  Juan Taylor 2:22:08

Rumours soon circulated that the course was short. According to Martin and Gynn two measurements showed that this was indeed the case, by 103 and 36 yards respectively, but it was also said that the athletes had run an extra 70 yards because they had been diverted around a traffic circle instead of running straight across it. "These errors were all within generally accepted ranges of deviation from the exact figure . . ., and thus the unfavourable arguments were put to rest."

On 6 July in Port Talbot Kilby made an assault on Edelen's record – and almost succeeded. It rained, but this did not deter the Briton. He sped through 5 miles in a fantastic 24:20, then slowed down to 26:12 and reached 20 miles in 1:41:15 – still more than a minute ahead of the American's schedule. He could not quite maintain this blistering pace and finished in

2:14:43, missing the record by 15 seconds. But he was now the British as well as the European record holder.

Just more than five weeks later Kilby attempted to win his fourth consecutive AAA title. Another fast time seemed unlikely so soon, but Kilby did not hold much back and won in 2:16:45 after a very even pace. One of his club mates from Coventry Godiva Harriers, Basil Heatley, was second in 2:19:56.

The Enschede race went to Czech champion Vaclav Chudomel in 2:25:10.4, with compatriot Kantorek third.

Two big races remained in 1963. Edelen had been training hard for Kosice. His world record was the result of very high mileage: He ran to work each day over either a route of 4½ miles or one of 7 miles, and added to this a session of two hours. On Sundays he ran 23 miles in the morning and did a jogging or striding session of between 3 and 5 miles in the afternoon. It was warm on race day. Edelen took the lead and passed the 5 km markers in 16:27, 32:43, 49:15 and 65:34 into a headwind. When they turned at Sena, he increased the tempo and soon got rid of the Ethiopians Demissie Wolde and Wami Biratu, as well as Heatley. He covered the next 5 km in a scintillating 15:41 and had only Popov with him. The 5 km to 30 km were only slightly slower (15:57), but this was the end of the Soviet. Then the American accelerated once more, needing only 15:13 between 30 and 35 km! He reached 40 km in 2:08:15 (15:50 for the previous section) and set a new course record of 2:15:09.6. In second Popov repeated the time which gave him victory in 1959.

RESULT:  1  Leonard Edelen 2:15:09.6
         2  Sergey Popov 2:17:45.2
         3  Vaclav Chudomel 2:18:02.6

The Asahi race had a surprise winner. The marathon was held only two days after Kosice, and in Tokyo as part of a special Olympic rehearsal for the real thing the next year. The New Zealander Jeff Julian surged away from a top field after 30 km and went on to win in 2:18:00.6 from Kimihara (2:20:25.2) and Vandendriessche (2:20:31.4). In December, round about the usual Asahi date, Julian won the Owairaka race in Auckland in 2:21:10 and in February 1964 repeated the win in the Auckland championship, running 2:19:58.

At the beginning of the Olympic year the top ten runners on the all-time list were:

| 2:14:28 | Leonard Edelen USA | 1963 |
| 2:14:43 | Brian Kilby GBR | 1963 |
| 2:15:15.8 | Toru Terasawa JPN | 1963 |
| 2:15:16.2 | Abebe Bikila ETH | 1960 |
| 2:15:17 | Sergey Popov URS | 1958 |
| 2:15:39.4 | Kazumi Watanabe JPN | 1963 |
| 2:15:41.6 | Rhadi ben Abdesselem MAR | 1960 |
| 2:15:57 | Haruo Otani JPN | 1963 |
| 2:16:09.6 | Yu Mang Hyang KOR | 1962 |
| 2:16:19 | Kenji Kimihara JPN | 1963 |

The Japanese chose their team on 12 April, with the Mainichi marathon the trial (over the Olympic course). The inconsistent Terasawa was not only beaten by Kimihara, but also by the newcomer Kokichi Tsuburaya. Their times were 2:17:11.4, 2:18:20.2 and 2:19:43 respectively. In February Terasawa had won the Beppu race, scene of his world record in 1963, in 2:17:48.6. In August the Japanese threesome for Tokyo ran another marathon, Kimihara winning in 2:17:12 against Tsuburaya's 2:19:50.[7]

In the US Vandendriessche again won in Boston, running 2:19:59 in extremely cold conditions. For the first time the venerable race attracted more than 300 participants. The Yonkers race (the first of two US trials) attracted only 128 starters, but among them was one who was to end Kelley's string of victories: world record holder Buddy Edelen. He was running his first marathon in the US and promptly won in conditions exactly the opposite of those at Boston. Edelen's time was 2:24:25.6 and the quality of this performance can be seen in the time of the second runner, Adolph Gruber AUT, who clocked 2:44:11.4. Kelley was third in 2:44:46.4.

For the second successive year the Poly provided a world record. The date was 13 June and the weather was ideal. Hill, Barry Collins and Chudomel led early (5 miles in 25:10), 10 seconds in front of a group which included Heatley and James Alder. Hill went through 10 miles in 50:20, 2 minutes ahead of Edelen's pace and 45 seconds ahead of the next group. He still had Chudomel and Batty with him, and they reached 15 miles in 76:35 – but now only 17 seconds in front of Heatley and Alder. Hill tried surging, but to no avail. Heatley caught him just before 20 miles. Edelen had arrived at 20 miles in 1:42:52; Heatley's split was 1:42:08. He was 5 seconds in front of Hill; Chudomel came through in 1:42:35.

The gritty Hill did not succumb and reached Chiswick in the second fastest time ever, but the accolades went to Heatley. He had beaten Edelen's record by 33 seconds and established himself as the favourite for Olympic gold. Chudomel set a new national record with the fastest third-place time ever (but two months later lost the Czech title to Kantorek at Kosice).

RESULT:
1 Basil Heatley 2:13:55
2 Ronald Hill 2:14:12
3 Vaclav Chudomel 2:15:26

Two weeks later Taylor won the Welsh title in 2:15:37, with another Coventry Godiva runner, Bill Adcocks, second in his first official marathon (2:19:29). The third place in the British team went to Kilby, who won the AAA title in 2:23:01.

Bikila's only venture outside his home country between October 1961 and the spring of 1964 had been his unsuccessful trip to Boston. On 3 August he won Ethiopia's trial at high-altitude Addis Ababa in an excellent 2:16:18.8, with Mamo Wolde second in 2:16:19.2! However, his appendectomy only six weeks before the Tokyo race put a big question mark over his chances.

The number of competitors in Tokyo for the Games of the eighteenth Olympiad was down on the figure for Rome, but a record 93 nations entered teams. The Japanese had waited 24 years after the Games had originally been scheduled for Tokyo in 1940, and they did a superb job of organising the festival. The powerful New Zealand middle-distance runner Peter Snell became the first man since Albert Hill in 1920 to win both the 800 and 1500, while US distance runners won the 5000 and 10000 m for the first time ever. Billy Mills's victory in the 10000 m, which he achieved by beating a host of more fancied runners (among them Mamo Wolde), was one of the most sensational of the Games. Betty Cuthbert came back after eight years to win the first 400 m gold medal. Oerter won his third discus gold (only the second athlete to win three successive titles) and the infamous Press sisters took the shot put, discus throw and pentathlon.[8] The USA won fourteen gold medals; no other country had more than five.

The marathon was held on 21 October, a cloudy and humid day. There were 68 competitors and they were to run an out-and-back course. Ron Clarke AUS, who had been beaten in the two longest track races, took the lead. Clarke, who was already the holder of the world record for 10000 m and would start his amazing assault on the world record book the next year, went through 5 km in 15:06. Ireland's Jim Hogan was 2 seconds behind. Hill was fifth behind two unknown Tunisians. Bikila was only 11 seconds behind Clarke. Clarke was spread-eagling the field and reached 10 km in a very fast 30:14 – in fact, much faster than any world record race had been run up to that point. But Hogan was with him, probably realising that Clarke was running his fourth race in a week. Bikila was just behind, and the scene was set for a memorable race.

Clarke, Hogan and Bikila went through 15 km in 45:35, a massive 2:27 ahead of Bikila's pace in Rome. They were followed more than a minute later by a large group which included Jozsef Suto HUN, Naftali Temu KEN, Antonio Ambu ITA and Robert Vagg AUS. But even this amazing pace was not fast enough for the man who had had his appendix taken out a few weeks earlier. Bikila, wearing shoes this time, surged away from his rivals and ran the next 5 km in 15:23. He got to 20 km (60:58) with a lead of 5 seconds on Hogan and an advantage of 1:41 on his Rome pace. He was running almost 6 seconds per kilometre faster than Heatly had done!

7. Three days later Tsuburaya beat Kimihara over 10000 m on the track, setting a national record of 28:52.6 to earn 13th spot on the world list for the year.

8. It was the last Olympics before sex tests were instituted for women competitors.

Clarke was 41 seconds behind and fading. Demissie Wolde and Tsuburaya, carrying the hopes of the whole of the host nation, passed 20 km in 62:46.

Bikila turned in 64:28, making it look very easy. He steadily increased his lead, although Hogan was hanging on grimly. The Ethiopian reached 25 km in 76:40 (15:42 for the fifth section of 5 km), 2:07 ahead of his Rome performance. Hogan was 15 seconds in arrears and Clarke still third (78:02), but he was under pressure from Tsuburaya, Suto and Wolde. Then came Kimihara, Mills, Kilby and Heatley, but they were nearly 3 minutes behind Bikila.

## A TRUE MARATHONER

Others before him had tried, but on 21 October 1964 Abebe Bikila secured his place in history when he became the first runner to defend the Olympic marathon title successfully. Unlike other Olympic champions before him, Bikila was not a track runner turned marathoner. And although he completed thirteen marathons (losing only once), he will always be remembered mainly for the two he ran in Rome and Tokyo.

For many years it was believed that he was born in Mout on 7 August 1932, which was according to his entry for the 1960 Olympic Games. (Statisticians before and after Bikila's time have been exasperated by the confusion over birth dates of African athletes.) But on his tomb in Addis Ababa the inscription reads: "Here lies the hero Capt. Abebe Bikila. Born at Jatto, Debre Birhan, in 1933. Died at Addis Ababa in 1973." The inscription is in Amharic, English, Italian and Japanese (Bikila's name means "budding flower" in Amharic).

Bikila joined the Ethiopian Army when he was nineteen. He became a member of the Imperial Bodyguard and was already 24 when he started running under the influence of the Swedish sports adviser Onni Niskanen, who had a government training camp at altitude. Niskanen's runners trained over the country and mountains, on the road (runs of more than 30 km with and without shoes), and on the track (intervals, mainly 1500 m).

Bikila regarded physical exercise as an essential part of his training and did gymnastics before every training session. Directly after his Tokyo victory he astounded the crowd by doing callisthenics on the grass.

Bikila, who in 1967 was described as a self-composed man who greatly depended on his own methods and judgement, was almost completely unknown when he arrived in Rome for what was to be his third marathon. Between the Rome and Tokyo Games he ran six marathons, losing only in Boston in 1963. (This was his only marathon between October 1961 and May 1964.) His major wins came in Athens, Osaka and Kosice (2:20:12).

On 3 August 1964, about ten weeks before the Tokyo marathon, Bikila ran an astounding 2:16:18.8 in high-altitude Addis Ababa. This proved that he was ready, but soon after that he had an appendectomy which left him with only six weeks to recover. In Tokyo he showed no ill-effects, however, and raced to a magnificent new world record. His victory margin was the biggest since Albin Stenroos had won forty years before.

In 1969 Bikila, who loved riding horses, broke his neck in a car accident which left him almost completely paralysed. He received intensive treatment, but without much success. In an interview in 1973 he said: "It was the will of God that I won the Olympics, and it was the will of God that I met with my accident. I accepted those victories as I accept this tragedy. I have to accept both circumstances as facts of life and live happily."

That same year he suffered a severe brain haemorrhage and died on 25 October.

Bikila only very rarely ran on the track. His best 10000 m time, 29:00.8, was achieved in 1962; it was good enough for fourth on the world list. He did not finish his last two marathons, in Zarauz in 1967 and in Mexico City.

By 30 km Clarke was only fifth. Bikila was still drawing away from Hogan as he continued his unrelenting chase after the record. No runner had ever won the Olympic marathon twice, but it was certain that, barring something unforseen, Bikila was going to achieve this feat. His time at 30 km was 92:50; his lead was 40 seconds. Tsuburaya was 89 seconds behind the Irishman.

By now even the great Bikila was slowing. The next 5 km took him 16:11, the slowest of the race. Hogan, Tsuburaya and Suto came next and Heatley had shaken off Kilby. Clarke was struggling in seventh, followed by Wolde, Vandendriessche and Edelen, who had waited much too long to start his challenge.

The killing pace of the first half proved too much for Hogan and he withdrew from the race. Suddenly Bikila's lead was almost 3 minutes, the Japanese now being in second. Bikila's time at 40 km was almost 3½ minutes faster than in Rome, and although he did not finish nearly as fast as in 1960 he regained the world record and secured his place in history.

Bikila's reception was overwhelming, but the crowd was delighted 4 minutes later when the second runner entered the stadium: Tsuburaya. However, the silver medal had not yet been won. In a dramatic finish he was followed closely by the previous world record holder, Heatley. The wily Briton waited until the final bend and then charged around his exhausted rival. In the meantime, on the grass infield, the winner and new record holder was amusing the crowd with a vigorous set of callisthenics to loosen up.

Over the last 7 km Edelen, of whom much more was expected, had moved into sixth. Clarke was ninth, turning the tables on his 10000 m conqueror Mills, who finished 14th.[9]

RESULT:

| | | |
|---|---|---|
| 1 | Abebe Bikila ETH | 2:12:11.2 |
| 2 | Basil Heatley GBR | 2:16:19.2 |
| 3 | Kokichi Tsuburaya JPN | 2:16:22.8 |
| 4 | Brian Kilby GBR | 2:17:02.4 |
| 5 | Jozsef Suto HUN | 2:17:55.8 |
| 6 | Leonard Edelen USA | 2:18:12.4 |
| 7 | Aurele Vandendriessche BEL | 2:18:42.6 |
| 8 | Kenji Kimihara JPN | 2:19:49 |
| 9 | Ronald Clarke AUS | 2:20:26.8 |
| 10 | Demissie Wolde ETH | 2:21:25.2 |

Oksanen was 13th, Terasawa 15th, Hill 19th and Kantorek 25th.

At the medal ceremony the stadium band did not know the Ethiopian anthem, so they played the Japanese one!

A comparison between Bikila's splits for each 5 km and the last 2.195 km in Rome and Tokyo makes interesting reading:

9. After the 10000 m, when Clarke was asked whether he had worried about Mills before the race, he replied: "Worry about him? I never heard of him!"

| | 1960 | | 1964 | |
|---|---|---|---|---|
| 5 km | 15:35 | | 15:17 | |
| 10 km | 31:07 | (15:32) | 30:14 | (14:57) |
| 15 km | 48:02 | (16:55) | 45:35 | (15:21) |
| 20 km | 62:39 | (14:37) | 60:58 | (15:23) |
| 25 km | 78:47 | (16:08) | 76:40 | (15:42) |
| 30 km | 94:29 | (15:42) | 92:50 | (16:10) |
| 35 km | 1:50:27 | (15:58) | 1:49:01 | (16:11) |
| 40 km | 2:08:33 | (18:06) | 2:05:10 | (16:09) |
| 42.195 km | 2:15:16.2 | (6:43.2) | 2:12:11.2 | (7:01.2) |

The 24-year-old Tsuburaya's medal was Japan's first in athletics since 1936 and the only one of the 1964 Games. Tragically, the expectations of his countrymen after Tokyo proved too heavy to carry. Following the Olympics Tsuburaya, who was very despondent after his "humiliation" in front of an estimated half a million people, was forced to abandon his fiancée and start training for the 1968 Games. In 1967 he injured his right Achilles tendon and spent three months in hospital. When he started running again, he soon realised that his body was not the same any more and would not be able to take the strain of trying to win the next Olympic marathon. On 9 January 1968 he ended his life; with his body was found this note: "I cannot run anymore." In the words of Quercetani, possibly the only explanation for Tsuburaya's suicide is the fact that "in the Empire of the Rising Sun [the marathon] is looked upon almost as a religion".

Six weeks after the Olympic marathon Terasawa made amends for his performace in Tokyo by winning the Asahi race in 2:14:48.2, with Nakao second in 2:15:42.

The remarkable Olympic year ended with the world list looking like this:

| | | |
|---|---|---|
| 2:12:11.2 | Abebe Bikila ETH | Tokyo |
| 2:13:55 | Basil Heatley GBR | Chiswick |
| 2:14:12 | Ronald Hill GBR | Chiswick |
| 2:14:48.2 | Toru Terasawa JPN | Fukuoka |
| 2:15:26 | Vaclav Chudomel TCH | Chiswick |
| 2:15:37 | Juan Taylor GBR | Port Talbot |
| 2:15:42 | Takayuki Nakao JPN | Fukuoka |
| 2:16:19.2 | Mamo Wolde ETH | Addis Ababa |
| 2:16:22.8 | Kokichi Tsuburaya JPN | Tokyo |
| 2:17:02.4 | Brian Kilby GBR | Tokyo |

Eight weeks after his victory at Fukuoka Terasawa had a much tougher task at Beppu. He could only break away from his pursuers after 32 km and went on to set another Japanese record – this time 2:14:38. Behind him was unprecedented depth: Nakao 2:15:37, Hideaki Shishido 2:16:07.8, Morio Shigematsu 2:16:15, Yoshikazu Funasako 2:16:26 and Kazuo Matsubara 2:16:57. The man in seventh, Hirokazu Okabe, had run 2:16:59 three weeks earlier. This meant that, five weeks into 1965, Japan had seven runners faster than 2:17:00!

The Japanese stars journeyed to Boston for a major assault on North America's premier marathon. The finish was moved from Exeter Street to the Prudential Center on Boylston Street. In perfect weather the Japanese took five of the top seven positions, Shigematsu winning in 2:16:33. Vandendriessche ran a PB 2:17:44, but three Japanese finished ahead of him: Shigematsu, Shishido 2:17:13 and Nakao 2:17:31.

The Japanese were also to dominate in 1966, Kimihara winning in 2:17:11 from Seiichiro Sasaki (2:17:24) and Terasawa (2:17:46). In fifth Norm Higgins ran 2:18:26, the fastest ever by an American in the race.

Bikila defended his Mainichi title in the heat, his 2:22:55.8 being an extraordinary feat in the conditions. The race was run in Otsu for the first time. Mamo Wolde once again could not finish a race.

Then came the Poly and, of course, a fast time. Edelen was there, as was a strong Japanese contingent. Race day, 12 June, was overcast and there was a slight following breeze. The American went through 10 miles in 50:34 with Shigematsu, Terasawa and Okabe (the latter was second behind Bikila in Otsu). The foursome covered the next 5 miles in 25:06 and their split at 15 miles was 55 seconds faster than Heatley's the previous year. Excitement was mounting along the route, because the Poly's sixth world record seemed a distinct possibility.

Three miles later Edelen started to slow, while Alder dropped out. The Japanese were left to battle it out among themselves and Shigematsu proved the stronger. He reached 20 miles alone in 99:04 – more than 3 minutes faster than Heatley's pace. Terasawa went by in 1:40:00, 2 minutes ahead of the American. The spectators at the finish saw Bikila's record wiped from the book: Chiswick's third consecutive global best. But, sadly, it was also the last (and the last in Britain).

RESULT:
1 Morio Shigematsu 2:12:00
2 Toru Terasawa 2:13:41
3 Leonard Edelen 2:14:34

The first three places in the AAA race were taken by Coventry Godiva runners: Adcocks 2:16:50, Kilby 2:17:34, Taylor 2:18:57. His club mate therefore prevented Kilby from taking his sixth consecutive national title. In Belgium Vandendriessche had an even better record, having won his country's title nine times in a row. But he, also, was defeated in 1965 after suffering an injury. Adcocks and Kilby tackled the Belgian at Kosice, where it was so hot that little puddles of tar formed on the road. Vandendriessche (who had also won a race in Switzerland and the Enschede marathon earlier), handled the conditions the best and came home in 2:23:47, with Adcocks second and Kilby third.

The Asahi race was moved to October and the weather was much warmer than it usually was in December. Clarke was not bothered by this and streaked away from the finish. Three months earlier he had become the first man to run 10000 m under 28:00 with 27:39.4 at the famous Bislett Games in Oslo. He had also set two world records for 3 miles, three for 5000 m, one for 6 miles, one for 10 miles, one for 10 km and one for the hour run. He seemed intent to add the marathon to the list. He flashed through halfway in 66:35 and went past 25 km in 79:09, but then slowed down. The next 5 km took 17:15, but he was still 1:47 ahead of Hidekuni Hiroshima. Then Clarke "blew" and never reached the 35 km mark; Hiroshima went on to win in 2:18:35.8.

The Beppu race of 1966 was much faster because conditions were much better. Terasawa won in 2:14:35, but Okabe was only 17 seconds behind. It was another typically deep Japanese event: Shigematsu clocked 2:16:16, but placed only ninth! A total of 24 men ran sub-2:20.

RESULT:
1 Toru Terasawa 2:14:35
2 Hirokazu Okabe 2:14:52
3 Kenji Kimihara 2:15:28
4 Seiichiro Sasaki 2:15:32
5 Isamu Sugihara 2:15:35
6 Kazuo Matsubara 2:15:44

In the US the AAU started taking steps towards course certification and established a set of guidelines to measure courses with the calibrated bicycle method. The maximum error allowed was 0.37 per cent.

In the British Commonwealth runners were preparing for their regional championship, to be held in Kingston. Early in the year New Zealander Dave McKenzie won his provincial title in 2:17:22 in very hot conditions and then also won the national title in 2:16:15.

The Polytechnic marathon was won by debuting Graham Taylor on an extremely hot day in 2:19:04. Hogan ran 2:19:27 and Hill was third in 2:20:55. It was only his second marathon since Tokyo. Scotsman Wood ran only 2:28:29, but a month later he astounded the world with an exceptional 2:13:45 in Inverness in Scotland – a new British and European record, and the second fastest time ever run. However, there was no place for him in the Scottish team for Kingston, nor in the British team for the European Championships later in the year.

Seventeen runners started the Kingston race at 05:30 on 11 August. The humidity was tremendous. Clarke was running, and after two more defeats in his track specialities (when everyone had expected him to win) he dearly wanted a gold. Again he threw down the gauntlet, surging away from the pack shortly after 5 miles. He reached 10 miles in 53:33, 12 seconds up on James Wahome KEN, Michael Ryan NZL, Adcocks and Kilby, the defending champion. (McKenzie could not run because of an injury.)

By 15 miles Clarke (80:32) was just a few yards ahead of

Adcocks and Alder, who led Kilby, Ryan and Wahome. Once again the Australian did not last and Alder and Adcocks took the lead, with Ryan in third. Clarke retired after 20 miles, as did Kilby, who was nowhere near his form of four years previously. The temperature was climbing steadily while the runners were ascending the hill towards the stadium. Alder was 50 yards in front of Adcocks, but then he was pointed in the wrong direction near the entrance. When he came onto the track, he saw Adcocks 30 yards ahead of him. The tired Alder dug down into his reserves and overhauled his rival on the back straight to take a well-deserved gold medal.

RESULT:
1 James Alder Sco 2:22:07.8
2 William Adcocks Eng 2:22:13
3 Michael Ryan NZL 2:27:59
4 David Ellis CAN 2:31:46.8
5 Jeffrey Julian NZL 2:32:45.4
6 Ronald Wallingford CAN 2:35:13

The European Championships race was only three weeks later in Budapest. The afternoon of 4 September was warm when 34 athletes started. Among the contenders were the East German champion of 1962, 1964 and 1965, Gerhard Honicke, who had won the 1964 title in 2:19:52, and the 1966 champion, Gerhard Lange (2:17:32.2). Zdzislaw Bogusz POL led at 5 km (a cautious 16:19), but by 10 km (33:11) he had been swallowed by the pack. Carlos Perez ESP was ahead by 3 seconds at 15 km (50:07), and by 20 km (66:48) there were still thirteen in the lead group. Gyula Toth HUN tested the others with a couple of surges and led past 25 km in 83:30. At 30 km Hogan, Toth and Kalevi Ihaksi FIN (1:40:27) were leading Perez and Anatoliy Sukharkov URS by one second, followed a second later by Vandendriessche and Gioacchino de Palma ITA.

Then matters changed suddenly. Hogan accelerated and ran the next 5 km in 16:05. He reached 35 km 30 seconds ahead of the Hungarian, with the Belgian, one of the big favourites, passing Toth over the next 5 km. Hogan, often an unpredictable runner, sailed on to win in 2:20:04.6. Kantorek still managed to finish in the top ten (eighth in 2:23:49.4), while Hill was a disappointing 12th.

RESULT:
1 James Hogan GBR 2:20:04.6
2 Aurele Vandendriessche BEL 2:21:43.6
3 Gyula Toth HUN 2:22:02
4 Carlos Perez ESP 2:22:23.8
5 Anatoliy Skripnik URS 2:23:14.6
6 Anatoliy Sukharkov URS 2:23:33.8

Many of the top runners went to Kosice, where a headwind in the first half slowed things down somewhat. With the wind behind the runners after the turn Toth broke away and no one could catch him, although Alder tried hard. Toth beat the Briton by 56 seconds in 2:19:11.

Because of its reputation as a fast course which attracted many international stars the Fukuoka race had acquired unofficial world championship status. In 1966 the Japanese governing body designated the race as an International Open Marathon Championship. The marathon saw one of its most exciting finishes as Ryan and Hiroshima entered the stadium practically together. Ryan was slightly in front, but the Japanese, spurred on by the spectators, closed the gap. They raced around the track in an all-out sprint. Ryan's kick in the final straight was decisive and he won by 0.6 second in 2:14:04.6, a new national record. Toth (2:16:36.2) and Perez (2:17:20) both set national records as well, while Rodney McKinney became Australia's first runner under 2:20:00 with his 2:19:06. Chudomel finished last; Hogan was tripped and dropped out.

RESULT: 1 Michael Ryan 2:14:04.6
2 Hidekuni Hiroshima 2:14:05.2
3 Hirokazu Okabe 2:15:09.2
4 Masatsugu Futsuhara 2:15:36.2
5 Toru Terasawa 2:15:51.2

Two other runners, Kimihara and Shigematsu, represented Japan in the Asian Games marathon on 15 December in Bangkok. As expected, they finished the heat-affected race first and second respectively, in 2:33:22.8 and 2:35:04.2.

Serious racing in 1967 started, as usual, at Beppu on 5 February. It was a cool and cloudy day as the top Japanese clashed. Terasawa tried to get rid of his companions after 25 km, but to no avail. It tired him out and it was left to Kimihara, Sasaki, Takahashi Inoue and Akio Usami to continue the battle. After 30 km the former twosome drew away and each applied surges to gain the upper hand. When Sasaki took a drink at 41 km Kimihara pulled away to a victory in 2:13:33.4. Sasaki was only 5.2 seconds behind and Usami clocked 2:14:50.2 in third. Inoue finished in 2:15:17.2.

In New Zealand McKenzie again won the Canterbury as well as the national marathon and then went to Boston to face the Japanese. The cold was aggravated by wind and a light rain fell. Nevertheless, there were 600 starters. The Japanese probably did not like the conditions, because instead of dominating affairs they could do no better than third. McKenzie won in a course record 2:15:45, with American Tom Laris second in 2:16:48. Then came Yutaka Aoki in 2:17:17. Fourth was another American, Louis Castagnola, in 2:17:48.

This edition of the Boston marathon was memorable for the famous incident when a female runner, Katherine Switzer, was discovered on the course and an effort was made to remove her from the race (see Chapter 9).

For the first time in eighteen years the AAU title was not decided at Yonkers, but in Holyoke. The Yonkers race was won by the virtually unknown James McDonagh and the AAU title by Ron Daws, who beat McDonagh in a slow time. Both were selected for the Pan-American Games marathon in Winnipeg on 4 August, where McDonagh finished fifth and Daws failed to complete the race. Only thirteen runners contested the marathon, with Canadian Andrew Boychuk winning in 2:23:02.4.

Earlier, on 7 May, the first Karl Marx Stadt marathon had taken place in East Germany (the German Democratic Republic). It was a unique race, for it was run entirely on a 5.22 km loop in a park free of traffic. The surface was of packed earth. The race was meant to give the East German runners good international competition. In fact, the foreign entrants were no match for the locals, who took the first six places.

RESULT: 1 Jurgen Busch 2:16:09.2
2 Paul Krebs 2:16:44.4
3 Gerhard Honicke 2:17:37.8

Even before this race, in April, Busch had triumphed in the Classical marathon, winning in 2:20:40 and beating Toth, Kantorek, the Turk Ismael Akcay and Honicke. After Karl Marx Stadt he continued in the same vein, scoring wins in the national championship and in the first Vltava marathon in Prague.

In Britain the national championship developed into a struggle between Alder and Wood, who seven weeks before had run 2:16:16 on the same course where he had recorded his fast time the previous year. He now ran only 5 seconds slower, but Alder beat him by 13 seconds in 2:16:08.

The other major European races of the year all produced relatively slow winning times: Enschede 2:20:54, the Mediterranean Games 2:21:33, and Kosice 2:20:53.8.

But Fukuoka was quite a different story.

A top field converged on the Japanese city. Mike Ryan, the defending champion, was there, as well as Sasaki, Boychuk, Alder, McKenzie and his fellow national champion from Australasia, the Aussie Derek Clayton. The big-boned Clayton had won the Australian title in 2:21:58, but less than a month before that he had taken the Victoria state title in 2:18:28. However, these times gave no indication of what he was really capable of. Later in his career his superhuman and uncompromising training methods would lead to numerous injuries and he was to undergo nine major operations, but on this day, 3 December 1967, and again eighteen months later in Belgium, he was to reign supreme and break new ground in the marathon.

Ryan and Clayton started at a stupendous pace. They covered the first 5 km in 15:06 and the second in 14:51 for a 10 km time of 29:57. By 15 km (44:57) they were 38 seconds ahead of Bikila's pace in Tokyo. Ryan could not maintain this tempo, but the powerful Clayton slackened off only marginally and reached 20 km in 59:59. He was on course for a 2:06 marathon. The valiant Ryan was only

23 seconds behind, with Sasaki a further 13 seconds back.

Clayton went through halfway in 63:22. By now Sasaki had actually gained two seconds on the leader, and he cut Clayton's lead even further over the next 5 km! At 25 km, where the Australian arrived in 75:11, Sasaki was only 20 seconds behind. With a dramatic acceleration Sasaki caught Clayton and they went through 30 km together in 90:32. Sasaki had run the previous 5 km in 15:01. Ryan was third in 91:36, and even McKenzie in fourth (92:10) was faster than Bikila.

But Sasaki's surge was too much and he slowed again, letting Clayton get away. Clayton's seventh 5 km was only 15:39, but he had a gap of 12 seconds at 35 km (1:46:11). Ryan was exactly two minutes behind, with McKenzie now just 12 seconds adrift. Alder (1:49:52) was next.

Clayton slowed even further and the next 5 km took him 16:05, but his lead grew to 54 seconds. He reached 40 km in 2:02:16, almost 3 minutes ahead of Bikila's pace, and it was clear that he would run the world's first sub-2:10 marathon. McKenzie was now in third.

Clayton needed 19 seconds more than Bikila did for the last 2.2 km, but that mattered little as he finished in 2:09:36.4. He was the first man to run a marathon at a pace of faster than 5 minutes per mile. The first three runners were now first, second and fifth on the all-time list.

RESULT:
1 Derek Clayton 2:09:36.4
2 Seiichiro Sasaki 2:11:17
3 Dave McKenzie 2:12:25.8
4 Masatsugu Futsuhara 2:14:40
5 James Alder 2:14:44.8
6 Yoshiaki Unetani 2:14:49.6

The year 1968 was an Olympic one, but this time there was the added pressure of altitude. Mexico City is 2 225 metres above sea level, and the 1955 Pan-American Games held in the city proved that severe strain is put on athletes from sea-level environments. On the other hand, athletes from high-altitude countries such as Ethiopia and Kenya benefit. The air at such levels of altitude is approximately 23 per cent thinner than at sea level and thus the shortage of oxygen is to the detriment of runners in the endurance events.

This fact was in the back of the minds of all marathon runners as they prepared for the Olympic race. Two months after Fukuoka Sasaki won the Beppu race in another quick time: 2:13:23.8. Unetani was second in 2:15:22. The Japanese trial was won in Sasaki's absence by Usami in 2:13:49 from Unetani and Kimihara.

One of the runners who was preparing himself for the demands that Mexico City would make was the Irishman Patrick MacMahon, who won a race in Artesia, New Mexico, in 2:19:49.8. The US trial was held at Alamosa, Colorado, which is at approximately the same altitude as Mexico City. George Young won in 2:30:48; the two other mem-

bers of the team were Kenneth Moore and Ron Daws.

The winners at Boston and Yonkers were Ambrose Burfoot in 2:22:17 and Gary Muhrcke in 2:32:41 respectively. Two years later Muhrcke would become famous as the first winner of the New York City marathon. Burfoot was coached by John J. Kelley, the last American to win Boston. Muhrcke, a fireman from New York City, was to win again the next year.

An American who did not make the Olympic team was Eamon O'Reilly, who had become the country's second fastest ever by clocking a debut 2:16:39.8 – and this at altitude in Santa Rosa, New Mexico!

In Europe Adcocks won the Karl Marx Stadt marathon in a brilliant new European record time of 2:12:16.8. Behind him Rumanian Nicolae Mustata, Busch and Toth set national records. Fourteen athletes achieved personal bests.

RESULT:
1 Bill Adcocks 2:12:16.8
2 Nicolae Mustata 2:13:26.2
3 Jurgen Busch 2:13:45.2
4 James Alder 2:14:14.8
5 Gyula Toth 2:14:59

The Poly had Kimihara as winner (2:15:15), while Tim Johnston took the AAA title in 2:15:26. With him to Mexico would go Adcocks and Alder.

The Olympic Games were opened on 12 October, with a record number of 112 nations competing. For the second time in a row South Africa was not one of the invited nations. The SA National Olympic Committee (SANOC) had been instructed by the International Olympic Committee in 1963 that it had to dissociate itself from its government's apartheid policies. In 1964 this was deemed not to have happened, and South Africa was not invited to Tokyo. By 1966 SANOC included black representatives and declared that its teams would be selected on merit. The IOC sent a commission of enquiry to South Africa in 1967 and thereafter voted to invite South Africa to Mexico City. But the Supreme Council for Sport in Africa opposed this decision and threatened to boycott the Games if South Africa participated. Pressure on the IOC mounted, and at a meeting of its Executive on 21 April in Lausanne it was decided unanimously that the invitation be withdrawn. IOC members voted 47-16 (8 abstentions) in favour of the Executive's decision. At the IOC's 69th Congress in Amsterdam in May 1970 South Africa's membership was terminated with a vote of 35-28 (three abstentions).

The Mexico Games will forever be linked to the name of one man. With his stupendous leap of 8.90 m the American long jumper Bob Beamon achieved what has been called the greatest performance ever seen in athletics. Oerter became the first athlete to win an event four times when he claimed the gold medal in the discus throw, while Wyomia Tyus was the first sprinter ever to retain the 100 m title. African runners absolutely dominated the distance events, winning everything from the 1500 m to the marathon, the only exception being the 800 m. Their five *gold* medals were equal to *all* medals previously won by them. American sprinters Tommie Smith and John Carlos caused a furore with their Black Power salute on the rostrum after the 200 m.

The marathon was run on 20 October on a point-to-point course. Before the race a supremely confident Clayton said: "I'm the fastest marathon runner in the world, so why should I worry about anybody else?" But in reality he should not have run (see box), and was not a factor. Apart from Clayton, most attention was centred on the defending champion, who was going for an unprecedented triple. But Bikila had an injury and pulled out at 17 km with a fracture of the fibula in his left leg.

The leader at 5 km was Busch (16:44). In the leading group were also Moore, Gaston Roelants BEL and Johnston, who had trained at altitude for an extended period. The 10 km marker passed in 33:55 with Moore leading Roelants, Pablo Garrido MEX, Johnston and John Farrington AUS. Then came Ryan, Adcocks, Alfredo Penaloza MEX and Nedo Farcic YUG.

Over the next 5 km Sasaki joined in the fray, and by 15 km (50:26) Johnston and Farcic were just ahead of Roelants and the Japanese. They were followed by Moore and Ryan and a group which included Naftali Temu, the Kenyan who had won the 10000 m only a week before (he also won bronze in the 5000 m). With Temu were Busch, Akcay and Mamo Wolde, who had finished less than a second behind Temu in the 10000 m after having led until 50 m from the end. Roelants moved up to Johnston and he too pulled away from the others slightly. They reached 20 km in 66:02, a mere second ahead of the Kenyan. The next pair, Akcay and the Ethiopian Merawi Gebru, followed 17 seconds later. Ryan, Sasaki, Wolde, Kimihara and Clayton all moved through the checkpoint less than 30 seconds behind Roelants and Johnston. Moore was just behind Clayton.

Temu now took the initiative, passing 25 km in 82:29, while Wolde (8 seconds behind) had also passed a struggling Johnston. Gebru, who had beaten Perez, Wolde and Akcay in July in 2:18:58.8, was in fourth in the company of Kimihara. They were 68 seconds behind the leader and 6 seconds in front of Ryan. The world record holder was ninth; his countryman Farrington was out of contention. Over the next 5 km Wolde turned his eight-second deficit into a lead of six seconds. He reached 30 km in 99:20; Kimihara was now third. Sasaki and Alder had both left the race. Ryan had passed Gebru, who had caught a struggling Johnston (he was suffering from stomach cramps). They had Akcay with them.

Temu slowed drastically and was passed by one runner after another. By 35 km the medal winners looked secure: Wolde 1:55:54, Kimihara 1:57:45 and Ryan 1:57:50. Johnston was now fourth, Akcay fifth and Roelants, previous

holder of the world steeplechase record, sixth. By 40 km Wolde's lead was unassailable; he led Kimihara by 2½ minutes in 2:12:59. Ryan was only 6 seconds behind the Japanese. Adcocks had been running conservatively and now started moving up, passing Roelants, Gebru and Johnston.

Wolde (36), who had first competed in the Olympics in 1956 (he ran in the 4x400 m relay, the 800 and 1500 m!), won Ethiopia's third successive gold medal by more than 3 minutes, looking as fresh at the finish as Bikila had done in Tokyo. Temu faded to 19th; McKenzie was 37th. There were only three Africans in the top twenty – fewer than expected.

| RESULT: | 1 | Mamo Wolde ETH 2:20:26.4 |
|---|---|---|
| | 2 | Kenji Kimihara JPN 2:23:31 |
| | 3 | Michael Ryan NZL 2:23:45 |
| | 4 | Ismael Akcay TUR 2:25:18.8 |
| | 5 | William Adcocks GBR 2:25:33 |
| | 6 | Merawi Gebru ETH 2:27:16.8 |
| | 7 | Derek Clayton AUS 2:27:23.8 |
| | 8 | Timothy Johnston GBR 2:28:04.4 |
| | 9 | Akio Usami JPN 2:28:06.2 |
| | 10 | Andrew Boychuk CAN 2:28:40.2 |

With this victory Wolde at last emerged from the shadow cast by his great countryman. Unlike Bikila, Wolde loved running on the track. He competed in 10000 m races with great success between 1962 and 1964, but after finishing fourth in Tokyo seemed to lose interest. He only regained good form again in 1967, and then progressed on an upward curve to the highlight of his career in Mexico.

A memorable event of 1968 which took place not on the track nor on the road was the publication of Dr Kenneth Cooper's best-selling book *Aerobics*. This, coupled with the formation of the American Medical Joggers Association the same year, would have a significant impact on the growth of the sport in the seventies. Two years later, in 1970, the tremendously popular magazine *Runner's World* appeared for the first time to start a boom in running media in the US.

Fukuoka once more did not disappoint. The weather was optimal and Adcocks took full advantage of the conditions. He allowed Unetani to set the pace, clocking 15:46, 31:11 and 46:37, and then pulled the bunch up to the Japanese. They reached 20 km in 61:57 after having run the previous 5 km in 15:20. Adcocks led from Unetani, Tadaaki Ueoka, Burfoot, Futsuhara, Kazuo Yamashita and Akcay. Over the next 5 km all but Adcocks, Unetani and Ueoka faded; the threesome clocked 77:19 at 25 km. Ueoka and Adcocks passed 30 km in 92:38, with Unetani 3 seconds behind. The next 5 km took only 15:21 as Adcocks and the Japanese tried to get rid of each other. Adcocks was the one who succeeded and reached 35 km with a gap of 14 seconds over Unetani, who had passed his countryman. Adcocks finished considerably faster than Clayton had done (his time at 40

## AN IRON WILL

Derek Clayton was too slow for the mile, so he became a marathon runner instead. At this event he became the best in the world – the first to run a sub-2:10 marathon and the first to run an average of sub-five minute miles all the way. His immense training loads and exhaustive racing caused numerous injuries, but Clayton was philosophical about it: "I've got a damn good surgeon," he said after his knee operation following the Mexico City Olympics, "and that's the only reason I'm still running."

In Mexico Clayton, the world record holder, was the overwhelming favourite. He finished only seventh, and later it was revealed that he had run with a cyst on the cartilage of his right knee. Before the race doctors had told him that he needed an operation. "Sure I needed an operation," Clayton said when he arrived back in Australia, "but that would have meant giving the Games away. I told them I'd run even if it meant losing the leg."

Clayton was born in Lancashire on 17 November 1942, lived in Belfast for a time and settled in Australia in 1963. He ran his first marathon in 1965 and won. He didn't finish the second one, claimed the national title in the fourth, and crashed through the 2:10:00 barrier in the fifth.

Part of Clayton's success obviously stemmed from the high percentage of his $VO_2$ max (maximum oxygen uptake capacity) that he could utilise for long periods. According to Martin and Gynn his $VO_2$ max was 69.7 ml/kg/min, and Clayton used up to 86 per cent of this (compared to an average of 75 per cent for good runners). Clayton's maximum cardiac output was about 34.5 litres per minute, compared to an average of 23 l/min for normally active men.

His best 5000 m time was 13:45.6 and for 10000 m 28:32.2.

The powerfully built Clayton (1.88 m/73 kg) was bigger than most marathoners and this, combined with his punishing training schedules and iron will to succeed, led to breakdowns in his body which required nine major operations. He occasionally reached 200 miles per week. He usually ran a marathon every week in training – and "I never ran slowly; really bombed it every time". At his peak, before his brilliant race in Antwerp in 1969, Clayton followed a ten-week training cycle in which he ran five weeks of 160 miles, "resting with three 100-mile weeks".

When he stood on the starting line in Antwerp, he knew that "everything had peaked at the perfect time. I knew I was . . . facing a once-in-a-lifetime chance".

And so it proved. Clayton was never quite the same again (he admitted as much), although he ran 2:11:08.8 in winning the Australian title in 1971. He twice dropped out of the Commonwealth Games marathon and in the Munich Olympics finished 13th. He won his last completed race, the Australian championship in 1973, in 2:12:07.6. He was only 31 when he retired, his body exhausted.

km was 2:03:47) and secured the second spot on the all-time list with his 2:10:47.8. His first 5 km (15:49) was his slowest and he ran the second 20 km faster than the first (61:44 against 62:03).

RESULT:

| | | |
|---|---|---|
| 1 | William Adcocks | 2:10:47.8 |
| 2 | Yoshiaki Unetani | 2:12:40.6 |
| 3 | Tadaaki Ueoka | 2:13:37.6 |
| 4 | Ismael Akcay | 2:13:43.6 |
| 5 | Akio Usami | 2:13:51.8 |
| 6 | Ambrose Burfoot | 2:14:28.8 |

In Beppu Ueoka crushingly turned the tables on Unetani, 2:14:03.2 against 2:17:38.6. Five weeks after Beppu Seiji Fukada won the first Kyoto marathon in 2:17:43.8.

The phenomenal growth in road running in the USA was evident when 1 152 runners congregated on the Hopkinton town green for the 1969 Boston marathon. For the first time in history the race was run on 21 April. Unetani was unchallenged from the Newton hills and raced across the finish line in a magnificent new record of 2:13:49. Garrido was far behind in 2:17:30.

On the tough Marathon-to-Athens course on 6 April Adcocks delivered one of the most spectacular performances of all time. After a tremendous battle with Ryan, Akcay, Demissie Wolde and Kimihara over the uphill section of the route, Adcocks pulled away when the runners started descending towards the finish. He completed the race in the third fastest time ever: 2:11:07.2. Kimihara finished second in a PB 2:13:25.8.

In Karl Marx Stadt another British runner, the champion, Tim Johnston, also scored a hard-fought victory. His time was much slower (2:15:31.2), but he beat Farcic, Busch and Lajos Mecser HUN.

In the meantime Clayton was getting ready for another all-out effort. On 19 May he ran a warm-up 2:17:26 in the heat of high-altitude Ankara and only eleven days later he started – at the unusual time of 19:35 – a marathon in Antwerp. It was a two-lap course beginning at the Beerschot stadium. Clayton was in the lead by 9 km and reached 10 km in 30:06, nine seconds slower than in Fukuoka. Usami was still with him, but did not last long.

Clayton wrote in his book *Running to the Top* that he had prepared himself for a 2:07 marathon. "I ran nothing but quality miles, never letting up on myself once during training. I knew that to set the record I wanted, I would have to train on the very brink of injury. After ten weeks of this incredibly arduous training, I knew I was ready for the record attempt." (His mileage for the week of the race was 100!)[10]

The Australian, who "was feeling like a well-oiled machine", sped through 15 km in 45:17 and 20 km in 60:30 – now 31 seconds behind his previous record tempo. When he went through halfway in the stadium before starting the loop for the second time, he had a lead of 70 seconds. By 25 km (75:41) and 30 km (90:56) he had not yet caught up with his record pace, but by 35 km (1:46:14) he was only 3 seconds behind.

Clayton, running with a string of motorcars and cyclists

10. In an interview in *New Zealand Runner* Clayton said: "I never considered myself getting beaten in that race, because I was running so well – I thought I could beat anyone in the world . . . it was just a supreme feeling of power I had within myself . . . I just didn't think there was a man alive at that time [who] could get near me anywhere from 10 miles onwards up to 26 miles."

in attendance, could not hear the splits being called. Doubts set in as the exhaustion crept into his legs. "I began to speed up, to push through this wall of exhaustion. Those last six miles blended together in a nightmare of horns, shouts, bicycles, exhaustion, pain, and fear." In an interview he said that he started losing his rhythm at 20 miles. "Then I panicked even more. And the more I panicked, the more effort I put into it. It became one excruciating effort . . ."

The tremendously tough Clayton, who never took any liquid during his marathons, pushed his body to the limit over the next 5 km and passed 40 km in 2:01:55 – 21 seconds faster than in Japan. The world record was within his grasp . . . if he could last. He did more than last, finishing faster than any other world record setter had done before, with the exception of Bikila in Rome. His new world standard was 2:08:33.6 and behind him Usami set a national record.

RESULT:   1   Derek Clayton 2:08:33.6
2   Akio Usami 2:11:27.8
3   James Alder 2:16:34.4

There were rumours that the course was short, and these have persisted to the present day. Unfortunately the course was never remeasured, but various observers have pointed out that Belgian courses were notoriously short. In a 1980 report in *Track & Field News* it was stated that the head of the Belgian Athletic Federation had admitted that marathon courses in Belgium were measured with four cars, and the average measurement taken. When an investigation was conducted into the accuracy of the course, the Belgian federation indicated that no documentation was available and that the race was organised by a club and not the federation!

Clayton told *Track & Field News* that he had warned the Belgians before the race that he was going for the record, and that they had indicated that the course had been measured by a calibrated wheel attached to a car, both before and after the race. Both times "there was 6 metres difference in the damn thing – we're not going to worry about 6 metres – so they assured me it was checked out," Clayton said in the *New Zealand Runner* interview.

It is a tragedy that such a performance will always be clouded by doubt, but it should be remembered that the race was run at a time when course certification was not as stringent as it is today – and it is unfair to single out this performance as being on a short course. According to Martin and Gynn "the evidence brought forward by the rumor-mongers has not been sufficient to cause the measured distance to be seriously questioned. Race conditions were such that performances recorded by most of the top athletes were comparable to what they had achieved or would achieve during the coming months."

A comparison between the splits in Clayton's two world records is revealing and shows his even pace up to 35 km in the second race:

| | FUKUOKA | | ANTWERP | |
|---|---|---|---|---|
| 5 km | 15:06 | | 15:00 | |
| 10 km | 29:57 | (14:51) | 30:06 | (15:06) |
| 15 km | 44:57 | (15:00) | 45:17 | (15:11) |
| 20 km | 59:59 | (15:02) | 60:30 | (15:13) |
| 25 km | 65:11 | (15:12) | 75:41 | (15:11) |
| 30 km | 90:32 | (15:21) | 90:56 | (15:15) |
| 35 km | 1:46:11 | (15:39) | 1:46:14 | (15:18) |
| 40 km | 2:02:16 | (16:05) | 2:01:55 | (15:41) |
| 42.195 km | 2:09:36.4 | (7:20.4) | 2:08:33.6 | (6:38.6) |

The AAA title was decided at a new race in Manchester on 20 July, a hot and humid day. Clayton was there, but it was clearly a mistake to race again so soon after his effort at Antwerp, where he had blood in his urine and vomited black mucus. In his book he wrote that the race left him "so totally spent that it took me six months to recover". The world record holder was up against Hill, Adcocks, Hogan, Unetani, Kimihara and Busch. As usual Clayton tried hard, leading at 10 miles, but by 15 miles Hill had taken over. By 20 miles Clayton was losing contact and later experienced stomach cramps. Hill went on to victory in 2:13:42, with the Aussie second in 2:15:40. Alder was third, Kimihara fourth and Adcocks fifth.

The European marathon was run in Athens on 21 September (only three years after the previous edition of the event). Although it was overcast, the temperature was quite high when the race started at 16:00. Farcic took the runners through 10 km in 32:10, but soon afterward Roelants joined him. They ran together for a while, but then the former track star surged on the uphill part of the course and by 25 km he was more than a minute clear of Farcic and Hill. Alder was fourth and Busch fifth.

Roelants stayed ahead on the climb, but Alder passed the struggling Hill and Farcic. Once the runners reached the top Hill felt better and he moved back into second. He made little impression on the leader, though, and at 35 km Roelants was still 80 seconds ahead. But now Hill was running hard and he cut the gap to 21 seconds by 40 km. Both were giving everything for victory, but Roelants could not stave off the challenge. Hill passed him with 800 m remaining and increased his pace further, winning by 34.4 seconds. Adcocks, who had run such a brilliant time on the same course in April, had to retire with a foot injury.

RESULT:   1   Ronald Hill GBR 2:16:47.8
2   Gaston Roelants BEL 2:17:22.2
3   James Alder GBR 2:19:05.8
4   Jurgen Busch GDR 2:19:34.8
5   Ismael Akcay TUR 2:22:16.8
6   Denes Simon HUN 2:22:58.8

About a month later, on 19 October, a remarkable race took place on the North American continent, in Detroit. The weather was ideal and the course flat. The runner who took the lead from the start had an interesting background: He was born in Germany from Ukranian parents and had been a resident of Canada since 1958. He ran in the Olympic marathon in Mexico City, but did not complete it (the same fate befell him in the 1969 Boston). In March 1969 he changed his name from Peter Buniak to Jerome Drayton and in August ran a 2:16:11 marathon in Ontario. Drayton's splits in Detroit (where he had won the previous year in 2:23:57) were 50:30 for 10 miles, 76:05 for 15 miles and 1:40:38 for 20 miles. He was running at 2:12:00 pace! And that was precisely what he finished in for a new North American record.

Drayton then went to Fukuoka, where one of the best fields in the history of the prestigious race was assembled. It rained at the start and it was cool throughout. Drayton was full of confidence and showed it by going into the lead immediately. He ran 15:11, 30:42 and 46:12 for a lead of 21 seconds – and then stretched it to more than 30 seconds at 20 km (61:45). He reached halfway in 65:08 and continued to pull away – to 39 seconds at 25 km (77:00) and 45 seconds at 30 km (92:29). Hayami Tanimura was second, with Hill only 4 seconds adrift. The pouring rain did not deter the flying Canadian, who passed 35 km in 1:49:08. Tanimura had shaken off Hill, but the Englishman came back at him and caught him at 40 km. Drayton (2:04:02) was 59 seconds ahead of Hill, who now put everything into his final charge. But he had left it too late and was beaten by 41.6 seconds as the first thirteen runners clocked personal bests! Drayton's PB, of course, was another North American record.

RESULT:
1  Jerome Drayton 2:11:12.8
2  Ronald Hill 2:11:54.4
3  Hayami Tanimura 2:12:03.4
4  Pablo Garrido 2:12:52.8
5  Toshiharu Sasaki 2:13:06.4

In seventh Kenny Moore, who had been the first US runner in Mexico City (14th), set a new US record of 2:13:27.8.

This wonderful event ended a decade in which marathon standards worldwide had been totally transformed. Interest in racing the marathon had increased and as more and more athletes with a track and cross-country background tackled the event, it became less daunting and less of a race for slow runners who could not compete at shorter distances. This not only led to higher quality, but also broadened the base as thousands of formerly sedentary people tried their hand at the traditional event.

Japan was definitely the top marathon nation, with five runners in the top ten on the world all-time list at the end of 1969. According to Martin and Gynn Japanese marathoners clocked 46 per cent of the total number of sub-2:20 times during the decade, followed by Great Britain with 14 per cent. While Japan, Britain, the Soviet Union, New Zealand and East Germany dominated the all-time list with 76 per cent of the total number of sub-2:20s, the rest of the times on the list were recorded by runners from no fewer than 25 countries.

The top twenty on the all-time list were:

| | | | |
|---|---|---|---|
| 2:08:33.6 | Derek Clayton AUS | 1969 | |
| 2:10:47.8 | William Adcocks GBR | 1968 | |
| 2:11:12.8 | Jerome Drayton CAN | 1969 | |
| 2:11:17 | Seiichiro Sasaki JPN | 1967 | |
| 2:11:27.8 | Akio Usami JPN | 1969 | |
| 2:11:54.4 | Ronald Hill GBR | 1969 | |
| 2:12:00 | Morio Shigematsu JPN | 1965 | |
| 2:12:03.4 | Hayami Tanimura JPN | 1969 | |
| 2:12:11.2 | Abebe Bikila ETH | 1964 | |
| 2:12:25.8 | David McKenzie NZL | 1967 | (10) |
| 2:12:40.6 | Yoshiaki Unetani JPN | 1968 | |
| 2:12:52.8 | Pablo Garrido MEX | 1969 | |
| 2:13:06.4 | Toshiharu Sasaki JPN | 1969 | |
| 2:13:21 | Akio Yoshida JPN | 1969 | |
| 2:13:25.8 | Kenji Kimihara JPN | 1969 | |
| 2:13:26.2 | Nicolae Mustata HUN | 1968 | |
| 2:13:27.8 | Kenneth Moore USA | 1969 | |
| 2:13:37.6 | Tadaaki Ueoka JPN | 1968 | |
| 2:13:41 | Toru Terasawa JPN | 1965 | |
| 2:13:43.6 | Ismael Akcay TUR | 1968 | (20) |

# 6

# *1970-1989*
# THE INSPIRATION OF SHORTER

WHILE AFRICAN DISTANCE runners won the last three Olympic marathons of the sixties and also dominated the long track events at the 1968 Games – albeit with a huge amount of help from the altitude – there was no real consolidation of the Africans' position at the top of the marathon ladder. The boycott by the Organisation of African Unity of the Olympic Games of 1976 (because of the tour by an All Black rugby team in South Africa) set back the development of African athletics – and this took quite a while to overcome. Ethiopia (the country of Abebe Bikila and Mamo Wolde) and Kenya remained the top nations and annihilated their rivals at the annual World Cross-country Championships, and runners from Ethiopia and Tanzania won several big marathons worldwide, but Africa had to wait until 1985 for its next victory in a major championship marathon. And then the victor did not come from one of the major powers, but from a tiny country without a single track!

In America road running entered a new phase, one which would see the sport explode in the seventies. Running drew thousands upon thousands of new runners or joggers, and although factors such as more leisure time, greater affluence and a growing awareness of the importance of healthy living played a part, even more important perhaps were the writings of running gurus such as Dr Kenneth Cooper, James Fixx, George Sheehan, Joe Henderson and others. And, of course, the phenomenal success of the first United States winner of the Olympic marathon since 1908.

In 1970 a Gallup Poll found that approximately two million Americans were running regularly. And money poured into the hitherto relatively poor sport. As Martin and Gynn put it so well in *The Marathon Footrace*: "Running paraphernalia literally exploded in quantity and innovativeness as entrepreneurs sought to capture, and as runners were delighted to provide, the dollars that were being poured out in enjoyment of a newfound sport. To run a marathon became a profound ambition of many people."

The marathon did not grow only as far as participation was concerned; the standard also rose dramatically. In 1969 the 100th best all-time performance was 2:16:07.8; in 1975 it had already jumped to 2:13:40. Fast times followed one another in such rapid succession that it becomes almost impossible to discuss them all in detail.

The first two big races of the new decade took place in Japan – both on the same day! In Kyoto Kokichi Uchino won in 2:16:55.8 and in Beppu Kenji Kimihara was first in 2:17:12. But these times were soon surpassed by the consistent British runner Bill Adcocks, who clocked 2:13:46 in Otsu in April.

An amazing race took place in Seaside, Oregon, on 28 February. Kenny Moore won the Trail's End marathon in 2:20:58, but the limelight fell on a woman – more precisely, a sixteen-year-old girl. Caroline Walker destroyed the women's world record with her 3:02:53. Her performance ushered in a remarkable period of women's marathoning, one which would result in a world record of faster than 2½ hours at the end of the decade. (See Chapter 9.)

The dominant male figure in the early part of the decade was Adcocks's countryman Ron Hill. He came to Boston to renew his rivalry with Jerome Drayton, who had beaten him in the marvellous Fukuoka marathon the previous year. It was a cold, windy day with rain and this might have contributed to Drayton's problems. He suffered a muscle pain in his leg and withdrew in Wellesley. The American Eamon O'Reilly chased Hill all the way and was rewarded with a US record of 2:11:12, but ahead of him Hill sped to a Boston course record of 2:10:30, the first Briton to win the race. Nobody else would run faster in 1970.

RESULT:  1 Ron Hill 2:10:30
2 Eamon O'Reilly 2:11:12
3 Pat McMahon 2:14:53

In the United Kingdom, where Hill and Adcocks had been selected for the English team for the Commonwealth Games in Edinburgh, Alastair Wood failed to make the Scottish team. Jim Alder won the trial over the championship course in 2:17:11. Hill and Adcocks would be joined by Don Faircloth, who won the Polytechnic marathon in his debut in 2:18:15.

When the 30 runners gathered in Meadowbank Stadium on 23 July one figure stood out: Derek Clayton, the world record holder, had qualified for the Australian team with an excellent 2:13:39 in Melbourne, but here his injuries caught up with him again and he (as well as Drayton) failed to finish.

Drayton started fast and reached 5 miles in 23:21 in the company of Clayton, Hill and Kenyan Philip Ndoo. Hill opened a small gap and went through 10 miles in 47:45. He was followed 5 seconds later by Drayton, then came Ndoo another 5 seconds back, and then Alder and Adcocks (they were 55 seconds behind the leader).

Hill was running superbly and passed halfway in a scintillating 62:35. Drayton was now 30 seconds in arrears, leading Alder and John Stephen TAN by 25 seconds. Five seconds later came Adcocks and Faircloth. The flying Hill ran through 15 miles in 72:18, 59 seconds ahead of the Canadian. In the next 5 miles both Drayton and Clayton stopped (the latter because of chest pains), leaving Alder in second barely ahead of the Tanzanian.

In his book *The Long Hard Road* Hill describes how he started suffering from 16 miles. "I got a white plastic cup of water and poured it over my head. I kissed my lucky ring on my left little finger and immediately got cramp in my left elbow through bending it. Christ, I was getting into a hell of a state."

He passed 20 miles in 97:32, more than a minute ahead of Alder. Faircloth was ahead of Adcocks, and the New Zealander Jack Foster, an ex-cyclist, had charged into sixth and would improve further.

Hill was well clear at 25 miles, which he reached in 2:03:10. He kept his rhythm right up till the end and won in a new British, Commonwealth and European record.

RESULT:  1  Ronald Hill Eng 2:09:28
2  James Alder Sco 2:12:04
3  Donald Faircloth Eng 2:12:19
4  John Foster NZL 2:14:14
5  John Stephen TAN 2:15:05
6  William Adcocks Eng 2:15:10

Hill's time was the fastest ever in a major competition and Adcocks was the only one of the top eight who did not run a personal best. This was to be Hill's best race, although he continued to run fast times for a number of years.

Hill was born in Lancashire and trained as a textile chemist before moving into the sports goods trade. He played a role in the introduction of carbohydrate loading as a dietary preparation to competition and also designed a whole new range of running equipment, in particular the string vest. In the sixties he set world records for 10 and 15 miles as well as 25 km. With the doubts cast over Clayton's time in Antwerp, Hill's performance in Edinburgh was regarded by many as the world's best. He won the AAA title for the second time in 1971 (2:12:39) and twice more finished second. By 1975 he had won sixteen of his 38 marathons; by the end of 1979 he had run 29 sub-2:20 marathons, then a world record. His last major victory was in Enschede in 1975 (2:15:59.2). In major championships after 1970 he finished third in the 1971 European race, sixth in the Munich Olympics and 18th in the 1974 Commonwealth Games.

Exactly a month after the Edinburgh race the second Maxol marathon was staged in Manchester. There was a strong Japanese contingent, and they dictated the fast pace from the start. Akio Usami proved the stronger, beating Yoshiaki Unetani in 2:13:45.

In other top European races during the rest of the year John Newsome GBR won the Vltava race in Prague in a course record of 2:16:07.8 and Mikhail Gorelov URS took Kosice in 2:16:26.2. Kimihara was second and Clayton fifth.

In the USA 13 September was one of the most significant dates in the history of the marathon. The first New York City marathon, the brainchild of Fred Lebow, was held in Central Park. The glorious future of this race, about which nine-time winner Grete Waitz would say, "If I had to pick the one event that most completely changed my life, it would certainly be the New York City marathon", was still a few years away, but the seeds of its tremendous growth and stature were sown that day. Lebow, a tennis player who had started running a few years before, was impressed after running through Central Park for the first time. "I've never lost a tennis match since," he said. The first race was held entirely inside Central Park, with four big loops plus a small one. There were 127 starters – 126 men and Nina Kuscsik, who failed to finish. Gary Muhrcke won in 2:31:38.

Over the next five years the race would grow steadily. In 1973 (on 30 September) the finish line was at the same Columbus Circle spot where the very first marathon in the USA, on 20 September 1896, had finished. In 1975, the last time the marathon was held in Central Park, Tom Fleming ran the first sub-2:20 on the course when he won in 2:19:27. A total of 534 runners started; the next year the field would grow to 2 090!

Another three years later there would be almost 12 000 competitors and Chris Brasher, the 1956 Olympic steeplechase champion, would say: "Last Sunday, in one of the most violent, trouble-stricken cities in the world, 12,000 men, women, and children from 40 countries of the world, assisted by 2.5 million black, white, and yellow people, Protestants, Jews, Muslims, Buddhists, and Confucians, laughed, cheered, and suffered during the greatest folk festival the world has ever seen." Brasher then established the London marathon and this resulted in city marathons appearing all over the world.

John Farrington, who had recovered from injury, won the 1970 Australian title in 2:15:27 and then went to Fukuoka for the annual unofficial world championship on 6 December. As usual it was a strong field, with Moore being there as well as two strong Soviets and of course the Japanese. Unetani took the early lead on a somewhat windy day and passed 5 km in 15:20, 4 seconds ahead of the pack. Shortly thereafter the pack swallowed him, and fifteen runners reached the halfway point together in 65:39. The 5 km between 20 and 25 km took only 15:12 and this reduced the bunch to seven.

Two kilometres later Usami broke away. Moore went with him and was 5 seconds behind at 30 km, reached by the leader in 92:26 after a 14:59 split! Unetani was third, Yuriy Volkov URS fourth, Tadaaki Ueoka JPN fifth and Foster sixth. Usami slowed down somewhat (15:06 for the next 5 km), but nevertheless stretched his lead over the American to 43 seconds. Unetani had pulled himself up to just 3 seconds behind Moore, and Foster was now fourth.

Usami drew away even further to win easily in the third fastest time ever – also a new Asian record. Moore became the quickest American on an out-and-back course.

RESULT:    1  Akio Usami 2:10:37.8
           2  Kenneth Moore 2:11:35.8
           3  Yoshiaki Unetani 2:12:12

Foster ran a New Zealand record of 2:12:17.8 in fourth and Volkov a Soviet record of 2:14:28 in eighth.

Nine days later Kimihara won the Asian Games marathon in a hot and humid Bangkok in 2:21:03.

The authoritative magazine *Track & Field News* ranked Hill first in the world for 1970.

In February 1971 the races in Kyoto and Beppu were once again on the same day, a most unfortunate state of affairs. In the former race, run in snowy conditions, Hayami Tanimura beat Faircloth, 2:13:45.2 against 2:14:58.6. The Beppu race was slower, with Kimihara scoring another victory (2:16:52). The third major Japanese race, the Mainichi marathon in Otsu, resulted in about the same winning time – 2:16:45.4 for Unetani.

In the USA the number of marathons had grown from 44 in 1969 to 73 in 1970 to 102 in 1971. The times were generally much slower than in the rest of the world, and the fastest pre-Boston time in 1971 was run by a Colombian, Alvaro Mejia, who won the West Valley Track Club marathon

(his debut) in the South American record time of 2:17:22.2.

In Boston Mejia was up against Irishman McMahon, and on a hot day the two of them broke away from the pack after the Newton hills. Mejia went ahead only in the last 200 metres and won by the smallest margin in Boston history: 2:18:45 against 2:18:50. Third in 2:22:23 was the South African Johnny Halberstadt, who was studying in the US.

On 6 June Eugene hosted the AAU race, which was also the trial for the Pan-American Games marathon. Running in this race was the man who was destined to be the next North American star and who was to play an immense role in the growth in popularity of the marathon in the years to come. The pinnacle of his career was still a year in the future, but on this day Frank Shorter showed a glimpse of his talent. He was already AAU 3-mile and 6-mile champion and although he could not stay with the more experienced Moore, who broke away at 22 miles, he finished second in 2:17:44.6 – excellent considering the warm and windy conditions. Moore was 56 seconds ahead.[1]

In *The Frank Shorter Story* Henderson wrote about the aftermath of this race: "Afterwards, Frank sat across from me at a banquet. He looked distinctly green in the face. I asked him how he felt. 'I'm just happy to be done,' he moaned. He looked down at his untouched plate and quickly left, holding his hand over his mouth." In the race itself, Shorter had begun struggling at 20 miles, and had asked Moore: "Why couldn't Pheidippides have died here?"

Two months later, after Shorter had retained his AAU 6-mile title, he and Moore, great friends, went to high-altitude Cali for the Pan-American Games. Shorter won the 10000 m and despite having to pull off the road for a few minutes in the marathon, he won that too.[2] His time was 2:22:40 – almost 4 minutes faster than the second man. The heat proved too much for Moore and he dropped out.

A week after this race the European Championships marathon took place in Helsinki. The British team had been chosen after the Maxol marathon in Manchester on 13 June (also the AAA marathon). It was an intriguing race in which the best British runners (with the exception of the injured Adcocks) ran away from the winner of the Karl Marx Stadt race, the German Jurgen Busch. Hill won in 2:12:39, but he could secure the victory only in the last couple of kilometres having had the company of newcomer Trevor Wright since the start. Wright finished in 2:13:27, the fastest debut

1. Shorter started the 1968 US Olympic trial marathon in Alamosa, but did not finish.
2. Shorter described this race in humorous vein in *The Frank Shorter Story*: "When it got really bad I jumped off in a ditch . . . I guess while I was down there only one guy passed me [and] I caught him pretty fast. Then all of a sudden I came upon the whole group of them. I ran up behind them as softly as I could. I got right behind Kenny and said, 'Yoo hoo, I'm back!' Mejia just dropped his load right there. I could tell he was through."

ever. Busch was third in 2:14:03 and New Zealander Jeff Julian fourth in 2:15:19. The third member of the strong British team was Colin Kirkham (2:15:21).

A week later the Belgian trial was won by a runner whose international career would begin in Helsinki: Karel Lismont, who clocked 2:15:48.2.

It was cool and cloudy when the 52 runners lined up on 12 August in Helsinki's venerable stadium. Pat McMahon went through 5 km in 15:33 with a bunch of twelve competitors 8 seconds behind him. McMahon did not last long and by 10 km Huseyin Aktas TUR (31:12) led from two groups of five separated by a second.

By 15 km the race had become even more interesting, for now 21 runners were sharing the lead in 47:05. The pace was very constant, and yet when 20 km was reached in 62:45 the lead group was down to eleven. Roelants, winner of the silver medal in the previous edition of the race, and Wright went through halfway in 65:30, followed by Hill, Kirkham and Lismont. Over the next 5 km (25 km passed in 78:34) Lismont joined his countryman and Wright and by his easy running showed he was a big danger. Hill, Pentti Rummakko FIN and Kirkham were 18 seconds behind. The next 5 km was quick (only 15:36) and the leading trio had stretched the advantage to 44 seconds.

Then Lismont showed his talent with a decisive surge. He

## MR CONSISTENT

Karel Lismont, the son of a cafe proprietor in the small village of Burgoon, was born on 8 March 1949. He started running in 1966 and took part in his first marathon in 1970, winning the national title in 2:25:46 and beating Aurele Vandendriessche. Helsinki was his first taste of international success and over the next decade he established himself as a competitor par excellence in big races. No other runner has equalled his string of top placings in championship races.

The Flemish-speaking Lismont, who worked as a tax collector, had his greatest day in Munich in 1972, when he finished second in the Olympic marathon behind Frank Shorter. He ran much faster in Montreal four years later, but again was beaten by the American – and by Waldemar Cierpinski.

In Moscow in 1980 he ran one of his worst races and blamed the course. "...the course was pretty uninteresting, indeed bleak, and it was also dead-flat, diminishing my appetite for running," he said in an interview.

His critics wrote him off, but two years later the consistent Lismont won his second consecutive bronze medal in the European Championships in Athens behind Gerard Nijboer NED and his countryman Armand Parmentier.

Lismont's international championship career:

| | | |
|---|---|---|
| 1971 European Championships | 2:13:09 | 1 |
| 1972 Olympic Games | 2:14:31.8 | 2 |
| 1974 European Championships | did not finish | |
| 1976 Olympic Games | 2:11:12.6 | 3 |
| 1978 European Championships | 2:12:07.7 | 3 |
| 1980 Olympic Games | 2:13:27 | 9 |
| 1982 European Championships | 2:16:04 | 3 |
| 1983 World Championships | 2:11:24 | 9 |
| 1984 Olympic Games | 2:17:09 | 24 |

sped through 35 km in 1:50:18 and had a lead of 12 seconds on Wright. The two inexperienced runners had drawn away from the veteran Roelants, who was 30 seconds behind the Englishman. Next came the most experienced marathoner of all, Hill, 14 seconds behind Roelants.

Lismont easily accelerated and covered the 5 km between 35 and 40 km in a speedy 15:47. He was now 44 seconds ahead and the gold medal seemed secure. Hill passed Roelants, who barely stayed ahead of the Finn.

| RESULT: | 1 | Karel Lismont BEL 2:13:09 |
|---|---|---|
| | 2 | Trevor Wright GBR 2:13:59.6 |
| | 3 | Ronald Hill GBR 2:14:34.8 |
| | 4 | Colin Kirkham GBR 2:16:22 |
| | 5 | Gaston Roelants BEL 2:17:48.8 |
| | 6 | Pentti Rummakko FIN 2:17:58.8 |

The first five runners were all from Great Britain and Belgium. Lismont had become the best in Europe in only his third marathon. A marvellous career awaited him.

In Enschede Jim Peters's eighteen-year-old record fell to his countryman Bernie Allen, who ran 2:16:54.2. On 12 September the course for the Munich Olympic marathon was tested with a race won by Akio Usami in 2:15:52. The course received much criticism because of its sharp turns and different road surfaces.

In the US Norm Higgins (34) became the oldest winner (to this day) of the New York City marathon when he clocked 2:22:54.

Three runners who had filled lesser positions in Helsinki met in a stirring competition in Kosice on 3 October. Gyula Toth HUN won in 2:21:43.6 (he was tenth in the European race), beating the Finns Kalle Hakkarainen and Rummakko. Toth then went on to win the international race between Szeged and Ferencsallas in his home country for the sixth time.

Far to the south, in Hobart, Tasmania, Clayton and John Farrington met on 25 September in a race that proved that the big Australian could still run superbly. They raced through halfway in 63:55 and Farrington kept pace with Clayton until the 20-mile mark. Then the world record holder pulled away to win in 2:11:08.8, with Farrington second in 2:12:14. These two times would remain the best in the world that year. Clayton would approach this time only once more.

A month later Farrington ran another fast time, 2:15:46, in Hamilton. This was perhaps a bit too much, for he could not keep his form until Fukuoka.

Shorter was in Fukuoka for the first time to run in the event he would dominate for four years. The date was 5 December, and there was a strong wind. Usami, the defending champion, set the initial pace. It was fast – faster than Clayton in Antwerp; he reached 5 km in 14:42 and 10 km in 29:47. Not intimidated at all, Shorter, Farrington, Seppo Nikkari FIN and Foster joined Usami before 15 km (45:20). This group gradually drew away from their rivals and split 61:41 at 20 km and 65:17 at halfway.

Then Shorter increased the pace, covering the next 5 km in 15:11. Even the more experienced (and faster) Usami could not stay with him and by 25 km he had a lead of 9 seconds. Amazingly, the American maintained the pace for another 5 km (15:18) and gained another 25 seconds. Usami, eleven years younger than the 39-year-old Foster, shook off the New Zealander and clawed back 4 seconds on Shorter, but when Shorter reached 35 km in 1:48:26 he seemed assured of victory. The gritty Foster, however, caught the Japanese again and they went through 40 km in 2:06:48. By then Shorter was out of reach. His 2:12:50.4 was the slowest winning time since 1966, but it was an emphatic victory and gained him favourite status for Munich, his birthplace.

RESULT:    1   Frank Shorter 2:12:50.4
           2   Akio Usami 2:13:22.8
           3   John Foster 2:13:42.4

This victory secured first place on the 1971 world ranking for Shorter. Usami repeated his second spot of 1970 and Lismont was third.

The early 1972 races in Japan were affected by bad weather, with the winning times in Beppu (Yoshiro Mifune 2:19:10.4), Kyoto (Susumu Sato 2:17:37) and Otsu (Usami 2:20:24) being much slower than usual. Usami would be joined in Munich by Kimihara and Unetani.

In Boston on 17 April women could participate officially for the first time. (The women's numbers were preceded by a big "F" – "presumably to help nearsighted finishing chute workers", as Krise and Squires put it in *Fast Tracks*.) The winner in 2:15:30 was the Finn Olavi Suomalainen in his first marathon. The women's race was won by Kuscsik (who had run 2:59:43 a month earlier) in 3:10:26.4. (See also Chapter 9.)

The AAU title was won in a slow 2:24:42.8 by Edmund Norris, son of the British star of the fifties Fred Norris. But all attention was focused on the US Olympic trial, held on 9 July in Eugene. It was a remarkable race, with the first four runners tieing in pairs! Shorter and Moore tied in 2:15:57.8 for first, and then Shorter's club mates from the Florida Track Club, Jeff Galloway and Jack Bacheler, tied in 2:20:29.2 for third. Since Galloway had already qualified for the team in the 10000 m, Bacheler got the third marathon spot.

Shorter had prepared very hard in high-altitude Colorado, putting in some 170-mile weeks. He won the 10000 m trial easily and went to Munich to run well in both events. "I think I wanted the American record for the 10,000 meters, but I was counting on the marathon for real results."

Shortly after the Boston marathon fast times were turned in in Europe. Igor Shcherbak set a Soviet record of 2:13:16.2

in Uzhgorod on 28 April (Vladimir Moiseyev was a close second in 2:13:59) and the next day in Karl Marx Stadt Eckhard Lesse clocked an East German record of 2:13:19.4. With Shcherbak in the Soviet team would be Anatoliy Baranov, who won the Soviet championship in 2:14:19.6, and Yuriy Velikorodnikh (both of them beat Shcherbak for the title). The Maxol marathon (and British trial) went to Lutz Philipp FRG in 2:12:50; he beat Hill by a second. The next two British runners were Don Macgregor in third and Colin Kirkham in fourth.

The Games of the twentieth Olympiad in Munich were the most tragic in the history of these festivals. Everything that happened in the competition arenas was overshadowed and the Olympic ideal itself shattered when, on the morning of 5 October, ten days after the biggest Olympics ever had been opened, eight Palestinian terrorists killed two Israeli team members inside the Olympic village and took nine others hostage. The group wanted 200 prisoners released from Israeli jails. They took their hostages to a military air base, where three of the terrorists were killed by German sharpshooters. A gun battle broke out in which all the hostages were killed, as well as another two terrorists and a policeman. With their obscene act the terrorists focused world attention on their aims – and what better place to do it? – but their methods horrified the world and they achieved nothing. The Games were suspended for a day and a memorial service was held in the main stadium – and then the world's sportsmen honoured the twelve people who had died innocently by continuing, albeit under a pall, to test themselves in the world's greatest exhibition of youthful talent. The continuation of the Games was a highly controversial decision but, ultimately, the right one.

The star of the Games was the Finnish long-distance ace Lasse Viren, who won both the 5000 m and 10000 m – the latter in a world record time of 27:38.4 despite a fall in the 12th lap – thus becoming the first man since Vladimir Kuts in 1956 to achieve the double. Two sprinters won both the 100 m and 200 m: Valeriy Borzov URS and Renate Stecher GDR. The 1500 m for women was contested for the first time, and won in a world record by Lyudmila Bragina URS. Kip Keino, winner of this event for men four years previously in Olympic record time, turned to the steeplechase and won that with an Olympic record. His country, Kenya, which claimed second place on the medal table in 1968, could only finish fifth this time.

Five days after the massacre, on the last day of the Games, the marathon was run in hot, humid – although cloudy – conditions. Shorter had already achieved the first part of his goal: he finished fifth in the 10000 m in the US record time of 27:51.4. Now he was up against 72 other runners, among them the defending champion, Mamo Wolde, his friend Moore, Hill, Clayton, the world record holder, Lesse, and a host of other stars. It was probably the best field ever assembled for an Olympic marathon.

The night before the marathon Shorter had had "a liter and a half or two of beer" before he went to bed ("That German beer is great . . ."). The next morning he did not run but "went to fill up on carbohydrates: pancakes, cereal and breads, honey and syrup".[3]

The runners did two laps of the track. Outside the stadium Shorter got into a tangle with the camera truck ("I pounded on the truck, swore a few times, and then stopped and went around the truck. I lost 20 or 30 yards . . . but I caught up pretty soon.") A huge bunch passed 5 km in 15:51.

At the first refreshment table Shorter's drink was taken by one of the Ethiopians. Shorter took the next bottle on the table, which was Moore's, but could not give it to him; that would have been "aiding". He then ran after the offender, grabbed the bottle out of his hand and said, "That's mine!"

Hill, wearing shoes and clothing of his own design, led at 10 km in 31:15. Just behind him came Clayton, intent on winning the gold medal which had eluded him in Mexico City, and then followed Foster, Nikkari, Roelants, Usami, and the two Woldes, Mamo and Demissie. Then Shorter, who was already suffering from blisters, made his move. He covered the next 5 km in under 15 minutes and led by 5 seconds at 15 km in 46:21. He later admitted that the break was very early – "I don't think I ever want to go that early again". But at the same time he was confident: "I hardly ever die when I run from the front."

In the group following him were Lismont, Mamo Wolde, Foster, Nikkari, Usami, Reino Paukkonen FIN, and Roelants. Then came the other two Americans, Moore and Bacheler – and only then Clayton and Hill.

The next 5 km took Shorter 15:09 and it resulted in a gap of more than 30 seconds. Second was Lismont, just ahead of Usami, Wolde and Nikkari. Bacheler had overtaken the more favoured Moore, who was running with Clayton.

Shorter, who had had a pair of racing shoes made to his specifications (and described Hill's outfit as his "space costume"), slowed down slightly (15:35 for the next 5 km), but his lead increased to 57 seconds at 25 km. He was running fluidly and already looked like the victor. Clayton, Moore and Wolde were running together in second; Lismont and Bacheler were 6 seconds in arrears. The next two sections of 5 km were covered in 15:44 and 15:51 respectively and no one was gaining on the American. Running on the gravel

section in the English Garden between 30 and 35 km Shorter concentrated on running as straight a line as possible on the weaving path. Shorter later wrote that this section made the course slower by about two minutes. In his book *Best Efforts* Kenny Moore wrote about this part of the course: "We [he and Wolde] dipped and rolled and sometimes stumbled on the dusty, rutted path. In a clearing the trail widened. Trotting straight at us was a long-haired dachshund. I went left. So did he. I cut back. So did he. To the amusement of the crowd, I had to hurdle him."

By now the world record holder had fallen behind. A cramp attacked Moore's right hamstring and Wolde moved away. While still in the park, Moore was passed by Lismont. "The last medal was disappearing ahead of me," Moore wrote. Bacheler was fifth, followed by Kimihara.

Over the last full 5 km Shorter slowed drastically, needing 16:51 to 40 km. At 41 km he said to himself: "'My God, I've really done it.' You almost can't believe after all that work, training, worry and direction that finally there it is. From there on in, it was just a victory lap."

Lismont had passed the Ethiopian, while Moore (who had fallen soon after the runners left the stadium) was just outside the medals. Bacheler was losing ground and was passed by Kimihara, a resurgent Hill, Macgregor and Foster.

Shorter's moment of glory in the beautiful stadium was clouded by an imposter – a German student who ran onto the track ahead of him – but the American went through the finish unperturbed in what was to be the crowning moment of his momentous career. He was the first American winner of the Olympic marathon in 64 years. His winning time of 2:12:19.8 was a PB and he won by more than 2 minutes. Although he knew, once he had entered the stadium, that he could get the Olympic record by sprinting, he didn't do so. He wrote in *The Frank Shorter Story*: ". . . I didn't want to do that. I figure that's bush league. The last half-mile is not the race. It isn't demonstrative of anything to sprint there. The real race is out there between 15 and 40 kilometres."

RESULT:

| | | |
|---|---|---|
| 1 | Frank Shorter USA | 2:12:19.2 |
| 2 | Karel Lismont BEL | 2:14:31.8 |
| 3 | Mamo Wolde ETH | 2:15:08.4 |
| 4 | Kenneth Moore USA | 2:15:39.8 |
| 5 | Kenji Kimihara JPN | 2:16:27 |
| 6 | Ronald Hill GBR | 2:16:30.6 |
| 7 | Donald Macgregor GBR | 2:16:34.4 |
| 8 | John Foster NZL | 2:16:56.2 |
| 9 | Jack Bacheler USA | 2:17:38.2 |
| 10 | Lengisse Bedane ETH | 2:18:36.8 |

It was the best Olympic race ever, with the 20th runner finishing in under 2:22:00 and 32 athletes under 2:25:00. Wolde ran superbly for a PB at age forty (the same age as Foster). Clayton was 13th in 2:19:49.6.

---

3. The night after the marathon Shorter, his wife Louise, author Erich Segal (*Love Story*), Shorter's classics professor at Yale University, and some friends went out to celebrate. This time they drank champagne because Segal had told them that it never gave one a hangover. Shorter, whose drinking of a large quantity of beer the night before the race had received much publicity, wrote that he preferred beer: "I don't worry about it; it's good carbohydrates, a few calories and a lot of water. You can rationalize it real well. I like it and it's the way I like to relax." Immediately after the race Shorter drank three gins while taking a bath!

## MARATHONER FROM MUNICH

Frank Shorter was beaten in the Montreal marathon by an athlete from the Eastern bloc. A few years later he played a major role in the establishment of a trust fund system in the United States in an effort to help top runners make something of their talent. "I became concerned with the trust fund issue," he said in an interview published in *Marathon and Distance Runner*, "because I wanted US athletes to be able to compete on an equal footing with athletes from the Eastern Bloc. All I want is to be able to stand on a start line, look right and left and not feel that I've been at any disadvantage to the Russians or the East Germans. After all, I got beaten by an Eastern Bloc runner and I didn't like it."

Even before Montreal Shorter, a qualified attorney, had negotiated a deal with the AAU which allowed him to appear in advertisements without losing his amateur status – a major breakthrough in those days.

Shorter was born on 31 October 1947 in Munich, where his father was an army doctor. He went to Yale University in 1965, where the coach, Bob Giegengack, told him in 1968 that he could be the best marathoner ever. At that time Shorter "was less than completely dedicated to track and field".

Giegengack wrote that the coach's prime responsibility is to help each athlete find his best possible event. "Speed may be inborn, and maybe you can't do much about improving it. I suspect you can't. What you have to do is develop the ability to hold your native speed over a longer distance. This is what Frank did." (*The Frank Shorter Story*)

Shorter himself said that in high school he was "one of your 4:30 mile types. They turn them out in a factory in heaven and drop them onto college campuses every fall."

In his senior year he won the NCAA cross-country and 6-mile titles. In 1971 he moved to Gainesville and entered law school at the University of Florida. By that time he had already won the AAU 3 and 6 miles (the latter a tie with his friend Jack Bacheler) and the AAU cross-country. He would retain his 6-mile title that year and would win the national cross-country another three times in succession.

In Florida Shorter trained with the runners of the Florida Track Club (Bacheler, Jeff Galloway, Marty Liquori and others). But he liked doing his morning work-outs alone, 8-10 miles at about 6:30-7:00 minute per mile. On the track he would do twenty quarters, with 110-yard runs (not jogs) between. As Roy Benson, assistant track coach at the university, put it: "Frank

doesn't put much variety into his workouts. His work is quite straightforward. He just burns through it."

Shorter had definite ideas about training and competition strategies. He admired Lasse Viren and the way the Finn could peak. Of the rumours that Viren used "blood.doping" he said: "The mere fact that everyone is so concerned about that shows what kind of control he has over his competitors. I mean, the best thing you can have is everybody thinking about you. What you might be doing, what you might be eating, what you might be taking. It's great, let them think about that. You go train.

"[Sebastian] Coe's the same way. I love Coe. You read all the running magazines; if everyone was to believe everything that Coe says, they'd all be trying to run 3:49 by jumping up and down on boxes. He's a sly guy."

He feels that road racers "have to have started on the track, period. It's basic training theory," he said in *Track & Field News*. "You have to make your legs go faster in training than they will go in a race. The wider you can have that variance, the more comfortable you'll be in the race. Simple."

Between his defeat in the AAU marathon in 1971 (the second marathon he started) and his second place in Montreal Shorter ran twelve marathons and lost only once (while not finishing one). In both of his non-winning races he suffered from injury.

In 1977 he injured his left foot and this later required surgery. He did not finish his only marathon of the year (New York). If one discounts the marathon he did not finish in 1973, his marathon record during his golden years of 1971-1976 reads: fourteen races, ten victories, three seconds, one fourth. His four consecutive wins in Fukuoka have never been equalled. The average of his five fastest races is 2:11:16.8.

He continued to run competitively into the nineties, participating in veterans' athletics after he had turned forty. In the 1980 Olympic trial he finished a very disappointed 85th in 2:23:24 and said, "My time is past. I should just stick to the track and have fun." Yet the following year he was third in Chicago in 2:17:27.7. At the end of 1987 he could still clock 2:36:54 – and 4:21.95 for an indoor mile, beating Jim Ryun and Peter Snell!

By that time he was both a successful businessman with his own chain of running stores and line of sports clothes and a respected TV commentator. Shorter can indeed say that, while running has made him, he in turn has made a major contribution to the sport as we know it today.

---

"The really great thing about having won," Shorter wrote soon after his victory, "is the influence it has on my running philosophy. The pressure is off. I can now do it because I like it. I'm going to run however I feel. I won't ever feel the need to press it as hard as I did before."

But press it he did when he went to Japan for the Fukuoka race on 3 December. From the beginning the pace was much faster than in Munich, with Clayton leading through 5 km in 14:51. Shorter, Nikkari, Farrington and Yasunori Hamada JPN reached 20 km in 60:16 and by the halfway point Shorter was slightly ahead in 63:38. Clayton retired shortly afterwards, and by 30 km Shorter (91:03) was 5 seconds ahead of Farrington. The American was invincible on the day and by 35 km (1:46:56) he had widened the gap to more than 30 seconds. Shorter was now clearly going for the US record, and although he was slowing, he reached 40 km in 2:03:21 (more than 2 minutes faster than in Munich).

He won in 2:10:30, equalling the fourth fastest time ever and setting his second national record of the year.

RESULT:
1 Frank Shorter 2:10:30
2 John Farrington 2:12:00.4
3 Kimio Otsuki 2:14:00.6

The world-famous physiologist Dr David L. Costill ascribed Shorter's success to the large fraction of his aerobic capacity ($VO_2$ max) that he used in a marathon. Shorter's $VO_2$ max was only 71.4 ml/kg/min, fully 13 ml/kg/min less than that of ace distance runner Steve Prefontaine, but Shorter utilised 86-90% of that for long periods (as did Clayton, whose $VO_2$ max was even less than Shorter's).

Shorter's Munich triumph, televised throughout the world, had a magical effect on the growth of running in his homeland. It became the inspiration for one of the most popular races in the USA, the Falmouth event, started by a bartender who watched the Munich marathon in faraway Massachusetts. Americans watched Shorter and were inspired by the grace of his running, his personality and his articulateness. Krise and Squires wrote that Shorter served as a focal point for American running – "people began to think of competition in terms of *fun* instead of pain".

Road racing in the US entered a new phase. In 1971 a total of 1 120 Americans had run faster than 3 hours for the marathon; by 1975 this figure would be 3 005. The 100th best US performance in 1970 had been 2:34:39; in 1975 it would be 2:24:22. The image of the sport also changed: big money flowed into road running as more and more sponsors became involved. The running boom swept across the US and, soon, across the world. Prize money increased and so did the fees being paid to top runners for appearing in high-profile races.

Shorter was again ranked first for the year, followed by Farrington and Lismont.

Shorter was back in Japan on 18 March 1973 to contest the Mainichi race in Otsu, which was also the national championship. In February Foster had defeated the Japanese in Kyoto (2:14:53.6), and this time the local runners had to surrender to the Olympic champion. Shorter showed his class by setting a course record of 2:12:03, easily beating Yoshiaki Kitayama (2:13:24).

Boston went to American Jon Anderson in a heat-slowed 2:16:03, while a rainy Maxol marathon was won by Lesse in a national (German Democratic Republic) record of 2:12:24. In fourth place Ferdie le Grange set a South African record of 2:13:58. (See Chapter 8.) He and Lesse were separated by Kitayama (2:13:29) and Brian Armstrong CAN (2:13:30).

The traditional course for the Polytechnic marathon was changed to a loop starting and finishing at Windsor Castle. It proved to be somewhat short. The race was won in 2:19:48 by Robert Sercombe.

In the Enschede race Hill scored a fine victory in 2:18:06.2, but on 27 October he had to bow to an exciting newcomer in the AAA championship (also the trial for the Commonwealth Games). Ian Thompson, eleven days past his 24th birthday, was running his first marathon – in fact, he had never run beyond 10 miles before! He finished in 2:12:40, the best debut ever, and beat Hill (2:13:22) and Kirkham (2:15:25).

Fukuoka, on 2 December, saw another bold move by the world's number one marathon racer. This time Shorter pulled away even before 5 km was reached. His split at that mark was faster than the previous year: 14:36. But his early and easy getaway must have taken the motivation away, for he slowed and the expected new record did not materialise. While the others were fighting for the lesser places, Shorter sailed on unpressed: 29:46, 61:03, 64:27 at halfway, 92:04 at 30 km, and 2:11:45 at the finish. He won by almost 2 minutes from Armstrong (2:13:43.4), with Lesse third in 2:13:53.8. Drayton, who had beaten Anderson in 2:13:26.8 for the Canadian title, dropped out.

The Commonwealth's best gathered in Christchurch on 31 January 1974. The 33 starters relished the cool conditions at 17:00. Thompson was ready, but he was up against

Farrington, who had won the New South Wales title the previous year in 2:11:12.6, and Clayton, who had beaten Farrington in the Australian trial race in a fine 2:12:07.6 and had shown that he was still a force to be reckoned with.

A large group passed 5 km in 15:12, and at 10 km (30:15) there still sixteen contenders. At the halfway mark near the airport Thompson – running with a confidence belying his inexperience – and Foster were leading from Welshman Bernie Plain, Farrington and the Swazi Richard Mabuza. Then Thompson accelerated and moved ahead. He had reached 20 km in 60:30 and now ran the next 10 km in 30:25. His lead was 1:15 over Foster, with Mabuza running third ahead of Farrington. Once again Clayton had dropped out. By 40 km Thompson (2:02:12) was almost 2 minutes ahead of the New Zealander in his all-black outfit. Foster's countryman Terry Manners had passed Farrington.

Thompson further increased his lead over the last 2 km and was clocked in 2:09:12 – the fastest ever in a major championship. Foster, who had started running at the age of 33, ran another brilliant race to set a world record for a veteran. Hill, failing to break 2:30:00, finished 18th, one place behind Drayton.

RESULT:
1. Ian Thompson Eng 2:09:12
2. John Foster NZL 2:11:18.6
3. Richard Mabuza SWA 2:12:54.4
4. Terry Manners NZL 2:12:58.6
5. John Farrington AUS 2:14:04
6. Donald Macgregor Sco 2:14:15.4

Thompson scored another victory when he won the Classical marathon in Athens in 2:13:50.2.

Shorter's two victories in Japan gave him his third consecutive first place in the *Track & Field News* ranking.

The early Japanese races of 1974 were also fast: Hamada won Beppu in 2:13:04.2, Matti Vuorenmaa FIN Kyoto in 2:15:10.6 and Usami Otsu in 2:13:24. In Boston a record fifteen men were faster than 2:20:00, with Irishman Neil Cusack winning in 2:13:39. Fleming was second (2:14:25) and Drayton third (2:15:40). Cusack was beaten by Foster in the Los Angeles Times marathon, but then won the Rice Festival marathon in 2:14:27.

In Europe the AAA championship was incorporated into the Poly marathon (same course, but now measured correctly); it was also the trial race for the European Championships. Thompson had been preselected. Usami was there, and he was unbeatable. Despite the warm weather and high humidity he won easily in 2:15:16, beating Plain by more than 3 minutes.

On the continent Lismont won his nation's title race in 2:11:13.2; he was expected to present a challenge to the favoured Thompson.

Thirty athletes started the Rome European championship race at 17:15 on a very hot 8 September. Thompson led early, but by 10 km (32:44) he had been joined by Lismont, Lesse, Roelants, Cusack, Jose Reveyn BEL, Plain and Ferenc Szekeres HUN. The next 10 km was much faster, and Thompson, Roelants and Lesse reached 20 km in 62:12. Two kilometres further Thompson broke away and opened a gap of 16 seconds by 25 km (78:59). Lesse was alone in second, with Roelants a minute behind. The British runner passed 30 km in 97:38 and increased his lead to the end. Roelants again finished in the medals, but Lismont dropped out.

| RESULT: | 1 | Ian Thompson GBR 2:13:18.8 |
|---|---|---|
| | 2 | Eckhard Lesse GDR 2:14:57.4 |
| | 3 | Gaston Roelants BEL 2:16:29.6 |
| | 4 | Bernard Plain GBR 2:18:02.2 |
| | 5 | Jose Reveyn BEL 2:19:36.4 |
| | 6 | Ferenc Szekeres HUN 2:20:12.8 |

Thompson's three brilliant victories would give him the top ranking position ahead of Shorter, with Lesse third.

A month later Keith Angus GBR scored an upset victory in Kosice, beating men like Hill, Farrington, Foster and the East German Hans-Joachim Truppel in atrocious conditions in 2:20:09. Truppel was second, with another East German third in 2:20:28.4. His name was Waldemar Cierpinski, and he was running his first marathon. Earlier that year he had clocked 8:32.4 for the steeplechase, but now he had turned to the marathon. Six years later his name would be mentioned alongside that of the great Abebe Bikila.

In Fukuoka Shorter attempted an unprecedented fourth victory. No one had won the race more than twice, and Shorter had already claimed three consecutive wins. The Olympic champion had not run a marathon since the 1973 Fukuoka. He was more cautious this time and remained in the leading group until after the turnaround point. The leaders had passed 5 km in 15:00, 10 km in 30:20, 15 km in 46:00 and 20 km in 61:47. Shorter's time at halfway was 65:15, 48 seconds slower than the previous year. He had the company of Manners and the Finn Pekka Paivarinta, who had set a national record of 2:12:10.6 late in September.

When Shorter surged, Lesse went with him, and by 25 km (76:54) they had a lead of 13 seconds on the Finn. Shorter was running hard and reached 30 km (92:31) with a two-second lead, but still 27 seconds behind his 1973 time. Over the next 5 km Shorter could not increase his lead over the tenacious Lesse, passing 35 km in 1:48:21. Then the pace started to affect the East German and at 40 km (2:04:33) he was 17 seconds behind Shorter. Behind them Manners, Paivarinta and Chris Stewart GBR were fighting for third. Shorter finished in 2:11:31.2 after having covered the second half in 66:16 (as against 66:52 in 1972, when he had started much faster).

| RESULT: | 1 | Frank Shorter 2:11:31.2 |
|---|---|---|
| | 2 | Eckhard Lesse 2:12:02.4 |
| | 3 | Pekka Paivarinta 2:13:09 |
| | 4 | Terry Manners 2:13:11.2 |
| | 5 | Chris Stewart 2:13:11.8 |

On his way home Shorter ran the Honolulu marathon where a foot injury slowed him to fourth in 2:33:22 – only his third loss over the distance in eleven starts. (He had failed to finish a race in Korso in May 1973, also because of injury.)

On 2 February 1975 Kenichi Ozawa won in Beppu in a sterling debut time of 2:13:10.4 and in April the Otsu race went to Usami in 2:12:40. He recorded his 21st sub-2:20 time, the most by any runner. A third Japanese, Sueki Tanaka, won the Asian title in Seoul in tremendous heat; his time was 2:32:05.8.

On 21 April Boston had more than 2 000 athletes for the first time. One of them was a Boston schoolteacher who had started running seriously late in 1972. He did not finish the 1973 Boston race and came 14th in 1974 (2:19:34). His name was Bill Rodgers and he took the lead near 10 miles, after having discarded the gloves he was wearing against the cold. He was running his sixth marathon (he had won two of the previous five) and no one was prepared for what he was to deliver that day.

Earlier in the race he had run with Hill. "He was an awe-inspiring figure," Rodgers wrote in his book *Marathoning*. "Just to match strides with Hill was an experience. I then found out I could move in front and Hill wasn't responding. I was moving out and I could sense it was going to be my day. You have days like that."

It certainly was his day. At 9 miles he was in the lead with Drayton and heard a woman encourage the Canadian. This made him furious. ". . . I had Boston and GBTC written across my shirt [but] nobody knew me. I'd finished third in the International Cross-Country run and nobody knew it. So I just really poured it on."[4]

Rodgers stopped twice to take a drink and once to tie a shoelace, yet still flashed through the finish in an American record 2:09:55. He described the last few hundred metres of the race as "dreamlike", but there was nothing dreamlike about the quality of his performance: he had improved by almost 10 minutes and became the fourth fastest runner in history.

| RESULT: | 1 | William Rodgers 2:09:55 |
|---|---|---|
| | 2 | Steve Hoag 2:11:54. |
| | 3 | Tom Fleming 2:12:05 |

The Pan-American Games marathon was held in Mexico

---

4. Rodgers was running for the Greater Boston Track Club, which was formed in 1973 by seven Boston runners with Billy Squires as coach. Nine weeks after it was formed, the club won the AAU 20 km championship, with Rodgers taking the individual title in 63:58.

## FROM FAIR-WEATHER RUNNER TO SUPERSTAR

Bill Rodgers, once called a "gentle radical", was born two days before Christmas in 1947. He started running in 1963, but he was "a fair-weather runner", as he calls himself in his book *Marathoning*. He ran in college (2 miles in 8:58.8), but quit running in 1969. He moved to Boston after graduating in 1970, watched two Boston marathons and started running again in 1972 with the intention of tackling the marathon.

He entered the 1973 Boston race, but failed to finish. Six months later (after having won the national 20 km title) he finished – and won – his first marathon, the Bay State race, in 2:28:12. A year later he was back at Boston, finishing 14th in 2:19:34 – and another year later he won the race in an American record of 2:09:55.

In his account of this amazing performance in *Track & Field News* Rodgers (whose goal was to improve to 2:16) wrote that he had planned to run the Newton hills smoothly, rather than attacking them. "I stopped twice, once on the pretext of tying my shoe and once for water. The thought of winning entered my mind as I went up the hills."

He could not believe his time. "This course must be short," was his first reaction. But it was not, and the time was merely the start of one of the biggest success stories in the history of the marathon, which included four consecutive victories in New York (1976-79), four wins in Boston (1975 and 1978-80), as well as a victory in Fukuoka in 1977. His 1979 Boston victory came with another American record, 2:09:27.

Rodgers ascribed his phenomenal improvement in the 1975 Boston to more speed work. ". . . 4:55, sometimes 4:45, maybe even a little better, repeat miles and stuff. Bill Squires had us doing repeats; we might run something like 6 or 7 or 8 repeat miles . . . at around 4:45 pace."

Rodgers set American records on the track for 15000 m (43:39.8), 20000 m (58:15), the hour run (12 miles, 1351 yards), 25000 m (1:14:11.8) and 30000 m (1:31:50). His time for 25 km was also a world record. He was third in the World Cross-country Championships in 1975 and in 1976 won

a marathon in Sado, Japan, in 2:08:23 on a course 200 m short.

He won the American title for 30 km on the road in 1976 in 1:29:04 at a time when the world track record for the distance was 1:31:30.4.

The Montreal Olympic marathon was an agonising experience. He was not in good condition (he denied later that he was running with a foot injury), but went with the leaders and hit the wall at 25 km. He finished 40th in 2:25:15. Later the same year he won the first New York City marathon, easily defeating Frank Shorter.

Although he did not finish the 1977 Boston (after two knee injuries), he set his US track records in the same city later that year and rounded off the year with victories in New York and Fukuoka. In 1978 he won Boston in his seventh clocking under 2:12:00 when he had to sprint to beat Jeff Wells by 2 seconds in 2:10:13.

"I never had to gut it out so hard at the end of a race. The last six miles I was just maintaining – well, I was falling apart. I was wishing they could cut off those last 385 yards!"

Rodgers, a humble and engaging personality who once worked with retarded people in a state institution and later owned a chain of running stores and marketed his own running gear, was a junk food addict when at his peak and ate four meals a day. "Sometimes I wonder," he said to his friend Kenny Moore, "whether I run high mileage so I can eat like this, or do I eat like this so I can do high mileage?"

He never ran well in the heat. His gloves in cold weather became something of a trademark. "No gloves, no good race," he said.

Rodgers was also in the forefront of the struggle for open payments to athletes. He once described the US governing body, The Athletics Congress, as "a bunch of bloodsuckers and parasites". He admitted in 1981 that he made more than $250 000 a year from running and running-related business.

In 1984 Rodgers tried to make the Olympic team again, but finished eighth in the trial in humid conditions. In 1994 he could still clock 1:40:02 for 30 km.

City. The winner in 2:25:02.9 was Rigoberto Mendoza CUB. In Europe the Karl Marx Stadt marathon went to Lesse in 2:14:49.6, the Uzhgorod race in the Soviet Union to Aleksandr Gozki URS in 2:14:23.4 and the Soviet title race to Grigoriy Vinjar in 2:15:27.8. Hill did not run the AAA marathon, but won the Debno marathon in Poland in a scintillating 2:12:34.2, his fastest since the Edinburgh victory in 1970. Behind him Edward Legowski set a Polish record of 2:13:26.

On 30 August Hill was in Enschede, up against Cusack and Rodgers. Four weeks earlier Hill had finished third in a race on the Montreal Olympic course. The heat had bothered the runners and slowed the times (Noriyasu Mizukami JPN won in 2:25:45.9). In Holland it was somewhat cooler, but not cool enough for Rodgers. He could not match Hill and dropped out (as did Cusack); the Briton went on to score a significant win in the course record time of 2:15:59.2.

A remarkably strong field was assembled for the Fukuoka race. Rodgers was the favourite, but lining up with him were Lesse, Truppel, Drayton, Legowski, David Chettle AUS, Giuseppe Cindolo ITA, Jerzy Gross POL and Takeshi Soh JPN. The latter was one of a set of twins; he and his brother Shigeru had first caught the world's attention in 1973 when

they ran first and second in Nobeoka, Shigeru winning by 20 seconds in 2:17:28.6.

The unpredictable Drayton controlled the race from the beginning. He reached halfway in 64:22 ahead of a group which included Mario Cuevas MEX, Chettle, Rodgers, Lucian Rosa SRI and Soh. The lead changed a few times after this, but by 30 km Drayton and Soh were 6 seconds ahead in 91:54 (51 seconds slower than Shorter in 1972). The Australian, who had run 2:16:39 for 12th the year before, took the initiative, his surge and 5 km in 15:06 taking him away from Drayton. Chettle went through 35 km in 1:47:11 (now only 15 seconds behind Shorter's split), leading the Canadian by 5 seconds. Soh came past 20 seconds later, with Rodgers 2 seconds behind him.

Chettle kept the gap constant, reaching 40 km in 2:03:00. Rodgers was now third and Cindolo fourth. Drayton was not beaten, however. He went after Chettle, quickly overhauled him and ran the last 2.195 km in just over 7:03 to win in 2:10:08.4, a national record.

| RESULT: | 1 | Jerome Drayton | 2:10:08.4 |
|---------|---|----------------|-----------|
| | 2 | David Chettle | 2:10:20 |
| | 3 | William Rodgers | 2:11:26.4 |
| | 4 | Giuseppe Cindolo | 2:11:45 |

The Polish record fell again, this time to Gross in 2:13:05. A record 29 runners finished in under 2:20:00.

Rodgers was ranked above Drayton for the year, with Chettle third. The year ended with five runners under 2:12:00, the best since Clayton's world record year of 1969. Five of the top ten times of 1975 were run in Fukuoka, proving again the high standard of this unofficial world championship event.

But 1976 was to prove even better than 1975.

The serious part of the Olympic year began with the Japanese selection race on 18 April. Usami won easily in 2:15:22; joining him in the team were Mizukami and Shigeru Soh. The next day in an unseasonably hot Boston the winner was Jack Fultz in 2:20:19 – good enough to beat Cuevas and Foster.

In Europe Cierpinski ran two magnificent races. He first won in Karl Marx Stadt, clocking 2:13:57.2 in his third marathon, and then won the trial six weeks later in 2:12:21.2. He would be the only East German in Montreal; Lesse and Truppel were not regarded as good enough by the GDR selectors.

The Soviet trial, held as part of the Debno race in Poland, resulted in a superb performance by Leonid Moseyev. He ran an even pace to win in 2:12:19.8 from Gozki (2:12:40) and Yuriy Velikorodnikh (2:12:58.2). Suddenly the Soviets were back in the forefront of world marathoning. The top Pole was Kazimierz Orzel (2:13:18.6).

The largest field ever for a British race started the country's trial in Rotherham. It was an amazing race, with unheralded Barry Watson running away from Thompson (who admittedly was suffering from tight thigh muscles) to win in 2:15:08. Thompson was seventh and both he and Hill (fourth) had to stay at home – the British selectors in their wisdom decided to ignore completely the previous records of two of the world's best marathoners.

The American trial in Eugene featured the defending Olympic champion, Rodgers, Fleming, Don Kardong and Anthony Sandoval – the best among the top US runners. Shorter won in 2:11:51, 7 seconds ahead of the national record holder. Kardong completed the team with his 2:13:54 PB. Shorter's five fastest marathons now averaged 2:11:32 – a time beaten in a single race by only thirteen other runners.

The Games of the 21st Olympiad opened in Montreal on 17 July – the earliest in the year since 1928. The number of participants was down on the 1972 figures, and for the first time since Tokyo the number of countries was less than a hundred. The Organisation of African Unity organised an African boycott because of a New Zealand rugby tour in South Africa. The International Olympic Committee claimed – quite correctly – that it had no influence over rugby tours since rugby was not an Olympic sport, but this made no impression on the hard-line African states. They were joined by Iraq and Guyana. The boycott deprived won-derful runners such as Filbert Bayi, Mike Boit and Ben Jipcho of the chance to display their talents for the world to see.

*Track & Field News* hit the nail on the head (under the heading "See the 4-ring circus"): "The political value of the African withdrawal remains to be seen. The inertia of the Games is too large to be swayed by such a small action. And less than a month later, does one remember Filbert Bayi because he didn't run the 1500, or does one remember John Walker because he ran and won?"

South Africa was illegally expelled from the International Amateur Athletics Federation at this body's Congress in Montreal. Although the Council of the IAAF had proposed that the *status quo* of South Africa's limited membership be retained, the Russian proposal (after a campaign funded with United Nations money) to drive the country out was adopted with a simple majority, thus ending South Africa's membership after 63 years.

The Games, the most expensive ever, resulted in heavy financial losses for the host city.

The hero of the Games was the phenomenal Finn Lasse Viren. He won the 5000/10000 m double again – the first man to do so – with a superb display of driving acceleration in the closing stages. (Not even his great countryman Nurmi had won the 5000 m twice in succession.) Two other athletes scored doubles: Alberto Juantorena became the first man to win both the 400 and 800 m, the latter in a world record, and Tatyana Kazankina the first woman to win the 800 and 1500 m, the former in a world record. Seven other world records were established – one by Irena Szewinska in the 400 m when she won her seventh medal in five events.

The most interesting of the 67 entrants in the marathon, run on 31 July, was Viren – in his first marathon. He was clearly the best distance runner on the track of the past two Games, but the question was: Could he do what the great Zátopek had done 24 years earlier? The Czech had had two advantages: there were no heats in the 10000 m in 1952, and Zátopek enjoyed two days of rest between the final of the 5000 m and the marathon. Viren had to start the marathon the day after his 5000 m triumph. Although publicly saying that he just wanted to finish, it was certain that the flying Finn was in the long race to win.

Rodgers, nursing an injured foot, led a group of nine through 5 km in 15:19. The group included Shorter and Drayton. A light rain fell as the runners reached 10 km in 30:48. Soon thereafter Cindolo, also injured, retired. (With his 2:11:50.6 in April he was the fastest marathoner of 1976.) By 15 km Shorter led in 46:00, but he had eleven rivals with him. Shorter managed to thin the pack out to eight by 20 km (61:24) with a few surges. He was 6 seconds faster than in Munich, but this time he had some of the best athletes in the world around him: Rodgers, Lismont, Drayton, Viren . . . and Cierpinski, who had arrived in Montreal a month before the Games to acclimatise. The champion clearly had a battle on his hands.

Just before 25 km Shorter accelerated and pulled clear. Viren followed him for about 200 m, but then eased off the pace. Shorter covered the 5 km between 20 and 25 km in 15:11, the fastest of the race. He had a gap of 30 m, but soon Cierpinski came back at him and they passed 30 km in 92:08 (5 km in 15:33). It was raining heavily.

"It was a wonderful feeling when I came alongside," Cierpinski later said. "I glanced at Shorter as I did so, and looked right into the eyes of the man who was my idol as a marathon runner. I knew all about him. And yet I could tell by the return glance that he didn't know much, if anything, about me. The psychological advantage was mine."

Shorter later admitted that he did not know who Cierpinski was (the East German did not wear the usual dark blue national outfit). The American thought he was Carlos Lopes of Portugal.

Shorter repeatedly tried to shake off his rival, but to no avail. Then the East German, clad all in white, attacked and decided the outcome. At 35 km (1:47:24) he was 13 seconds in front and 1:16 up on Shorter's split four years before. Cierpinski was running well and a very fast time seemed certain.

Drayton, Viren and Lismont followed 50 seconds behind Shorter, but Rodgers was only a shadow of his best. For him the second half of the race was "agony". Kardong was moving up, running the race of his life.

Shorter was going as well as he had in Fukuoka in 1972, but he could make no impression on Cierpinski, running his fifth marathon. At 40 km he was 32 seconds behind the leader (2:03:12) and over the last section he was to lose another 18 seconds as Cierpinski stormed towards the finish. Kardong passed Lismont and was in the medals, while the amazing Viren was fifth and Drayton, running with a heavy cold, sixth. Right near the end the American had to give way to the dogged Belgian when cramp assailed him, but he finished less than 4 seconds behind.

As in Munich a confusing situation developed in the stadium. Cierpinski ran the requisite lap of the track and when he reached the finish he saw the lap counter indicating that he had another lap to go. In fact this was for Shorter (who was on the back stretch), but the German made sure by running another lap! When he crossed the line a second time, Shorter was waiting there to shake his hand.

Thus the ultimate prize eluded Shorter, but he had the satisfaction of knowing that he had run close to his best and that his victor had to run an Olympic record and PB to beat him. It was a magnificent race, with the first four beating Bikila's Olympic record and the first eight faster than 2:15:00. Only three men had ever run faster than Cierpinski.

RESULT:
1  Waldemar Cierpinski GDR 2:09:55
2  Frank Shorter USA 2:10:45.8
3  Karel Lismont BEL 2:11:12.6
4  Donald Kardong USA 2:11:15.8
5  Lasse Viren FIN 2:13:10.8
6  Jerome Drayton CAN 2:13:30
7  Leonid Moseyev URS 2:13:33.4
8  Franco Fava ITA 2:14:24.6
9  Aleksandr Gozki URS 2:15:34
10  Henri Schoofs BEL 2:15:52.4

Foster was 17th, Soh 20th, Usami 32nd and Rodgers 40th.

"I knew Cierpinski was a good steeplechaser," Shorter said later, "and I knew he had run a 2:12, but to tell you the truth I just never thought of him before as a marathon contender. I could do no more than I did . . . I will just have to accept the fact that I was second best."[5]

Shorter also said that he did not run well in the rain. "I get tight [and] didn't feel as well as I normally do." Foster, watching a film of the race the next day, commented on Shorter's "elegant" style. "I still think he's the greatest marathon runner in the world. If he and Cierpinski were to race against each other over and over, I think Frank would beat him nine times out of ten." On the day, however, it was not to be.

Cierpinski said that he had decided some time previously that he didn't enjoy the steeplechase. "The hurdles were not a pleasant part of running. But I have always loved running. I just drifted into the marathon one day in 1974 and tried it out . . . I decided that from then on this would be my race."

On 24 October a major episode in the development of the marathon as a worldwide popular event took place in New York City, the Big Apple. It was America's bicentennial year and on that day the race, held in Central Park for the previous five years, became an extravaganza as 2 090 runners made their way around the five boroughs of the city, from Staten Island through Brooklyn, Queens, Manhattan and the Bronx to finish in Central Park.

Rodgers, at his best again, had Shorter to contend with.[6] Paivarinta led for the first half, but then Rodgers, Shorter and Stewart passed him. Rodgers moved away from the rest and Stewart briefly led Shorter, but at 23 miles Shorter surged in pursuit of his countryman and left the Englishman behind. Rodgers (who was paid $2 000 by Lebow out of his own pocket to run the race) was unbeatable, though, and Shorter could not get close.

In the course of the race Rodgers's illegally parked car was towed away. The New York Road Runners Club, organisers of

5. In an interview Shorter said that when he and Cierpinski shook hands, the German said: "*Sprechen Sie Deutsch?*" "I thought to myself, 'That's a funny thing for a Portuguese guy to say.' When I was told who he was I couldn't believe I'd been beaten by a steeplechaser!"

6. Shorter agreed to run because "I just wanted to show up and see how the police would clear the streets. That alone would be an accomplishment." Clear the streets they did, but Lebow narrowly averted being arrested when he rearranged police barricades that had been put up incorrectly near the Pulaski Bridge.

the marathon, paid the ninety-dollar fine. Meanwhile the owner of the car clocked the world's second fastest time of 1976.

RESULT:
1  William Rodgers 2:10:09.6
2  Frank Shorter 2:13:12
3  Chris Stewart 2:13:21

The Fukuoka event on 5 December pitted the new Olympic champion against the fastest man of 1974, Commonwealth and European champion Thompson. The latter had finished only 22nd in New York, but in Japan he ran a different race. Drayton and Cierpinski were together at the turn (65:12), but then the Canadian surged away and opened a gap of 13 seconds by 30 km (93:18). Thompson was sixth, 41 seconds behind, but then he ran the next 5 km in 15:28 and moved up to within 28 seconds of the leader. He continued to run hard, but could gain only another 9 seconds as Drayton finished in 2:12:35. Thompson clocked 2:12:54.2, while Cierpinski only just held off Shigeru Soh, 2:14:56 against 2:14:59.

Despite Cierpinski's loss he was ranked first for 1976, followed by Shorter and Lismont.

The day after Fukuoka Rodgers won the Maryland marathon in 2:14:22. Early in 1977 he won the Kyoto race in an almost identical time: 2:14:26.2.

Drayton's winning streak continued until Boston where on a hot day Rodgers retired near the top of Heartbreak Hill. The Canadian won in 2:14:46 from the Turk Veli Balli (2:15:44). Balli had run a rather suspect 2:11:30 in Lahore in November 1976.

Rodgers performed much better in the first Amsterdam marathon on 21 May, beating both Hill and Thompson in 2:12:46.6. The course was almost the same as the old Olympic course. Thompson ran 2:17:47.4 in fourth. Hill was no better than 14th, but three weeks later he met Thompson again in the Polytechnic marathon and finished second, 2:14:32 against 2:16:37. Then the action moved back across the Channel, where Brian Maxwell CAN, who had been third in Boston, took the hot-weather Enschede race in 2:15:14, a course record.

The number of starters in the second New York marathon was more than double that of the previous year (4 823), and they were greeted on 23 October by ideal weather. There was some wind, but it did not seem to bother the international field of star performers too much (four of the top six finishers in Montreal were running). Rodgers stayed with the large pack which included Shorter, Thompson, Viren, Stewart, Drayton and Kardong for the first part of the race, pulling away after 25 km to win in 2:11:28.2. Shorter, hampered by a foot injury, did not finish, while Viren ran 2:19:33.1.

RESULT:
1  William Rodgers 2:11:28.2
2  Jerome Drayton 2:13:52.2
3  Chris Stewart 2:13:56.8

In fifth place in his second marathon was Garry Bjorklund USA. Early in December he improved to 2:13:46 in winning the Baltimore marathon. On the same day, in faraway Japan, Rodgers ran an amazing race. He seemed fully recovered from New York and won Fukuoka in the year's fastest time. He led slightly at halfway (64:22) and then shook off all company to finish in 2:10:55.3. Moseyev was second in 2:11:57, Massimo Magnani ITA third in 2:13:04, while Thompson added to his spotty record with 44th place in over 2½ hours. (Three weeks earlier he had run 2:03:31 in the Choysa marathon in Auckland, but the course turned out to be only 39.7 km. Chettle won in 2:02:24.) Viren clocked 2:20:40.

The year ended (almost literally) with a marathon run in Israel – entirely below sea level. It was run on 31 December at the Sea of Galilee and was won by Werner Dorrenbacher FRG in 2:19:33.

The early part of 1978 belonged to the Soh twins. On 5 February Shigeru showed that Clayton's Antwerp time was beatable. He went out to break the record and at 25 km he was timed at 74:19 – an almost unbelievable 1:22 ahead of the Australian at the same point in his world record. He slowed, but still had a margin of 40 seconds at 40 km (2:01:15). Then, unfortunately, he ran into a headwind which put paid to a new record. Nevertheless, he finished in 2:09:05.6 – the fastest time on a course about which there was no doubt as to its length. His 10 km splits were 29:47, 29:42, 30:01 and 31:45. Takeshi was second in 2:12:48.6, completing a remarkable brotherly double.

In Otsu on 23 April Takeshi turned the tables on his brother, 2:15:15.4 against 2:17:13.4.

Six days before this race Shorter had started in his first Boston. No Olympic champion had ever won the prestigious event, and much of the media attention before the race was focused on this fact, and on the duel between Shorter (who had not fully recovered from his injury) and Rodgers. Shorter stayed with the leading pack (the others were Rodgers, Kevin Ryan NZL and Esa Tikkanen FIN) beyond the tenth mile, but then dropped behind. Rodgers went to the front just before the Newton hills and won for the second time, but he was almost caught by an exciting newcomer, Jeff Wells. Wells charged over the last few miles, running much faster than the American record holder, and failed to win the race by a mere two seconds! It was the closest finish ever at Boston, and in depth it was the best marathon ever, with six under 2:12:00. Tikkanen ran a new Finnish record.

RESULT:
1  William Rodgers 2:10:13
2  Jeff Wells 2:10:15
3  Esa Tikkanen 2:11:15
4  Jack Fultz 2:11:17
5  John Thomas 2:11:25
6  Kevin Ryan 2:11:43

Rodgers had won the three premier marathons in a row: New York, Fukuoka and Boston, but at the 1978 Fukuoka, run on 3 December, his image of invincibility was shattered by Toshihiko Seko, two other Japanese, a Briton (Trevor Wright) and a Soviet (Leonid Moseyev)! Seko, running in his fourth marathon, passed Shigeru Soh after 37 km and went on to win in 2:10:21. Rodgers did beat Cierpinski, though – the Olympic champion had a disastrous race (he suffered from cramps) and could only finish 32nd. The American's time was 2:12:51 and he suffered only his second road loss of the year (the other was at the hands of Henry Rono in the San Blas half marathon).

The race marked the return to the top of the Japanese for the first time since their heydays in the sixties.

RESULT:
1  Toshikio Seko 2:10:21
2  Hideki Kita 2:11:05
3  Shigeru Soh 2:11:42

Fukuoka was not Moseyev's only excellent performance of the year. On 3 September he had won the European title in Prague in an even faster time. In this race he came up against the 1971 winner, Lismont, who once again showed his toughness. The Belgian led a group of five at 40 km. In the group was Cierpinski, but he could not hold the pace over the last 2 km. Moseyev and his relatively unknown countryman Nikolay Penzin entered the stadium together, with the former's sprint prevailing by a whisker. It was the closest finish ever in a major championship race.

RESULT:
1  Leonid Moseyev URS 2:11:57.5
2  Nikolay Penzin URS 2:11:59
3  Karel Lismont BEL 2:12:07.4
4  Waldemar Cierpinski GDR 2:12:20
5  Catalin Andreica ROM 2:12:29.4
6  Massimo Magnani ITA 2:12:45.3

Three weeks earlier, on 11 August, the Commonwealth Games marathon had been run in Edmonton. Drayton, who had dropped out in Boston and was to drop out in Fukuoka, took the lead at 40 km and seemed certain to win, but just outside the stadium he was passed by hard-running Tanzanian Gidamis Shahanga (20), who had made up 50 seconds from 35 km. The time was slow, but it was the first Commonwealth marathon win by a runner from Africa since Johannes Coleman RSA won in 1938.

RESULT:
1  Gidamis Shahanga TAN 2:15:39.8
2  Jerome Drayton CAN 2:16:13.5
3  Paul Bannon CAN 2:16:51.6
4  Kevin Ryan NZL 2:17:16
5  Greg Hannon NI 2:17:25
6  Paul Ballinger NZL 2:17:46

On 22 October Rodgers went to New York to try to win Lebow's race for the third time in succession. The number of starters doubled again – to a massive 9 875. While the spotlight was mainly on the new world record run by Grete Waitz in the women's race, Rodgers easily defeated Thompson by exactly 2 minutes in 2:12:12, the slowest of his four victories. Wright was third in 2:14:35 and the 46-year-old Foster sixth in 2:17:28.

Three weeks later Thompson ran slightly faster when he won in Auckland in 2:13:49. This time the course was the correct distance.

*Track & Field News* ranked Moseyev as the best marathoner of the year, with Rodgers second. The second to tenth times on the world list were run at Boston and Fukuoka.

The early Japanese races in 1979 did not reproduce the fast times of 1978, with Kita winning in Beppu in 2:13:29.1. Seko, however, was saving himself for his confrontation with Rodgers in Boston. It was a cool, drizzly day when Rodgers, Seko and Bjorklund set off at the head of the field. After about 15 miles Bjorklund could not stay with the two star racers and fell back. He shouted to his countryman: "2:08! Go for it!"

Two months before, in Saratoga, Rodgers had set a world record of 1:14:11.8 for 25 km, but this of course paled in comparison with Seko's track 10000 m of 27:51.61 in 1978. They were clearly the two best marathoners of the year; the question was: who would win?

Rodgers, wearing white gloves and a woollen cap, made his move going into the Newton hills. He applied relentless pressure, and at the top of Heartbreak Hill he broke away. Seko could not respond and Rodgers arrived at the Prudential Center with a lead of almost a minute. He broke his course and American record and became the fourth fastest marathoner ever. Seko's runner-up time was the third fastest ever on the course.

RESULT:
1  William Rodgers 2:09:27
2  Toshihiko Seko 2:10:12
3  Robert Hodge 2:12:30

Frank Shorter was 79th in 2:21:56.

In May Hannon took the AAA title in 2:13:06 and in July the pre-Olympic marathon in Moscow was won in 2:13:19.6 by Moseyev. But the main marathon wars started again in September. On the ninth day of the month, in Eugene, Wells proved that his Boston performance was no fluke. He and Tony Sandoval took the lead at 38 km in the Nike/Oregon Track Club marathon and finished together in 2:10:20. In fourth was New Zealand track star Dick Quax, running a national record and world best debut of 2:11:13, and in eleventh (2:15:04) one Bernard Randall of the West Valley Track Club. In reality he was South African Bernard Rose, running under a pseudonym because of the IAAF's ban on South African athletes.

Five days later the Belgian national championship was held in Berchem. In a big surprise Marc Smet, a 28-year-old runner whose previous best was 2:13:23 run in 1978, clocked a magnificent 2:10:00 to win. It would be the second fastest time of the year.

Rodgers had now won Boston three times and New York three times in a row. On 21 October he lined up at New York's Verrazano Narrows Bridge again. The number of starters had increased once more, but not as impressively as in previous years: Rodgers had the company of Shorter plus 11 531 other runners. One of them, a reporter from the *New York Post*, broke away when only 5 seconds of the ten-second countdown had elapsed and was followed by a large part of the men's field. Kirk Pfeffer USA, who had won the Enschede race in 2:11:50 two months before, went through halfway in an astounding (considering the heat) 63:50. He kept going until the 22-mile mark, but then his body started paying for his rashness. Rodgers caught the exhausted leader after 23 miles and stormed to a 2:11:42 win. No one has yet equalled his feat of four successive victories. Pfeffer managed to stay in second, clocking 2:13:09. Thompson was fourth (2:13:43) and Shorter seventh (2:16:15).

The 1979 New York marathon made history when large amounts of money were offered ("under the table") to the top athletes on the basis of finishing positions. An amount of $10 000 was offered to the first man, and the prizes went down to $800 for eighth. A similar scale (with smaller amounts) was used for the women's competition.

A distinguished athlete who attended the New York marathon but did not run was Emil Zátopek, on his first visit to the US. "It was like a miracle for me," he said of the event. "All those people jogging!" He also offered his opinion of the running boom, as quoted in *Fast Tracks*: "The modern world is much troubled and in stress. Also, the world is increasingly more technical; and many do not want to lose contact with natural movement and nature. Running is the simplest and most natural movement, like swimming for fish and flying for birds. It is possible to jog till the last day of life."

Then the scene shifted east for Fukuoka on 2 December. The Soh brothers had been quiet for the major part of 1979, but they were ready for the year's premier race. However, so was Seko, who had already run an all-out effort earlier in the year. The race was the Japanese championship and Olympic trial, and a tremendously strong field that included Cierpinski had been assembled. It developed into a thrilling battle, but the leader in the latter stages was not one of the Japanese: the British runner Bernie Ford, a sub-27:50 10000 m athlete in his second marathon, led the Sohs and Seko at 35 km. At 40 km (2:03:55) Takeshi Soh accelerated, and he entered Heiwadai Stadium first. Ford had fallen back slightly. Seko waited until 200 m from the finish and then used his track speed to overhaul his countryman and score his second win, in 2:10:35. Ford clocked a PB 2:10:51 in fourth.

RESULT:
1. Toshihiko Seko 2:10:35
2. Shigeru Soh 2:10:37
3. Takeshi Soh 2:10:40

Seko ended the year as the only runner with two sub-2:11 times. There were four Americans in the top ten on the world list (Rodgers, Wells and Sandoval being joined by John Lodwick, who had run 2:10:54 in Eugene), but their run of successes at Fukuoka had come to an end (there was no US runner in the top ten). Rodgers returned to the top of the ranking list in front of Seko; Moseyev was third on the strength of his Moscow win, where he outkicked Shigeru Soh by 0.2 seconds.

In 33rd place on the world list was the next great Australian star: Robert de Castella had won the national title in 2:13:23 in his second marathon.

At the end of the sixties no runner from the previous decade had survived on the all-time list. At the end of the seventies two from the sixties remained on the list:

| 2:08:33.6 | Derek Clayton AUS | 1969 | |
| 2:09:05.6 | Shigeru Soh JPN | 1978 | |
| 2:09:12 | Ian Thompson GBR | 1974 | |
| 2:09:27 | William Rodgers USA | 1979 | |
| 2:09:28 | Ronald Hill GBR | 1970 | |
| 2:09:55 | Waldemar Cierpinski GDR | 1976 | |
| 2:10:00 | Marc Smet BEL | 1979 | |
| 2:10:08.4 | Jerome Drayton CAN | 1975 | |
| 2:10:12 | Toshihiko Seko JPN | 1979 | |
| 2:10:15 | Jeff Wells USA | 1978 | (10) |
| 2:10:20 | David Chettle AUS | 1975 | |
| 2:10:20 | Tony Sandoval USA | 1979 | |
| 2:10:30 | Frank Shorter USA | 1972 | |
| 2:10:37.8 | Akio Usami JPN | 1970 | |
| 2:10:40 | Takeshi Soh JPN | 1979 | |
| 2:10:47.8 | William Adcocks GBR | 1968 | |
| 2:10:51 | Bernard Ford GBR | 1979 | |
| 2:10:54 | John Lodwick USA | 1979 | |
| 2:11:05 | Hideki Kita JPN | 1978 | |
| 2:11:12 | Eamon O'Reilly USA | 1970 | (20) |

The Olympic year of 1980 started rather slowly. Nothing much happened until 21 April, when Rodgers took a very hot Boston ("a psychological ordeal", as he described it) in 2:12:11, his third win in a row. He was the first runner since Clarence DeMar in 1924 to achieve this feat. Only one other runner had won Boston four times – Canadian Gérard Côté, who was at the finish to congratulate Rodgers.

Five days later 24-year-old Dutchman Gerard Nijboer started his third marathon in Amsterdam. The previous year he had won the Dutch title in Enschede (the race won by Pfeffer), running 2:16:48 in his debut. In New York he had finished eleventh, clocking 7.6 seconds slower. The Amsterdam course was out and back, flat and certified, and it was a cool day. Nijboer, a public relations agent, took the lead at 27 km and simply ran away from his opposition. He finished in a phenomenal 2:09:01, the second fastest time ever, and

proved that Clayton's record was not so inhuman after all. Szekeres was second in 2:12:35. The course was remeasured three times after the race.

A month later, on 24 May, both the US "Olympic trial" and Soviet championship race took place. By that time, of course, the US Olympic Committee (USOC) had already decided to comply with the call of US President Jimmy Carter to boycott the Olympic Games because of the Soviet invasion of Afghanistan. Despite protests by the athletics community (*Track & Field News* accused the President of coercion), Congress voted 474-16 for a boycott and after "nothing less than blackmail and bribery and fanciful flights of hyperbole" from the White House, the USOC followed suit.

At Niagara Falls Sandoval won a fast and exciting race in 2:10:18.6; his "team-mates" would be Benji Durden (2:10:40.3) and Kyle Heffner (2:10:54.1).

The Soviet race in Moscow went to Vladimir Kotov in 2:10:58, a national record. He beat Satymkul Dzhumanazarov by 18 seconds, but the latter would run the best race of his career just over two months later and take revenge.

Earlier in May Cierpinski had won his second successive Karl Marx Stadt marathon, showing that Fukuoka – his only real failure in thirteen marathons – had been just a minor hiccup and that he was ready to defend his Olympic title. He won in 2:11:17, his fastest since Montreal. It was a tight race: Norway's Oyvind Dahl was second (2:11:40) and Cierpinski's countryman Truppel third (2:11:56).

The first Olympic Games behind the Iron Curtain were opened in Moscow on 19 July, with 81 nations participating – the lowest number since 1956. Athletes from Great Britain and Australia attended, although their governments supported the Carter-led boycott. Among other strong countries not present were West Germany, Kenya and Japan. Security was particularly tight, with winners on the athletics track physically prevented from taking victory laps. The Soviet spectators did not endear themselves to their visitors by constant booing and whistling – especially when competitors from certain countries were in action. They were even called "the rudest . . . at a major track meet anywhere in the world" and accused of "boorishness".

The competition, however, was excellent. Six world records were set, while the women set twelve Olympic records in their fourteen events. Not surprisingly, all the world records came from athletes from Eastern Bloc countries. The only double winner of the Games was Ethiopian Miruts Yifter (nicknamed "Yifter the Shifter" because of his fearsome kick), who had been prevented from running in Montreal by another boycott. He won "Viren's events", the 10000 m after a last lap of 54.4 seconds. Viren himself finished fifth.

But to many fans the highlights of the Games were the 800 and 1500 m in which the superb British duo Steve Ovett and Sebastian Coe traded wins, each taking the "wrong" event – Ovett the 800 and Coe the 1500.

The marathon was on 1 August, a hot day. There were 74

## MARATHONER FROM HALLE

Between 1976 and 1980 Waldemar Cierpinski did little to indicate that he would be the first man since Abebe Bikila to retain the Olympic marathon title. Yet he did so with consummate ease.

Cierpinski was part of the GDR sports system from an early age. He started training at the sports school in Halle in 1962 (he was born in Neugattersleben on 3 August 1950), where it was decided to make him a steeplechaser – although that was not what he wanted. He had been doing endurance runs from the age of seven. He came under the tutelage of Peter Conrad at the Karl Marx Stadt High School in Nienburg and used to run the 6 km from Jesar, where he lived with his parents, to Nienburg. Thus he saved on bus fare, and he became very fit. Bikila was his idol; the Ethiopian's Rome victory had shown him the way he wanted to take.

He won the national steeplechase title in 1972, but was not selected for the Olympic Games. This convinced him that his future lay elsewhere, and in 1973 he ran the 52.5 km between Halle and Jesar as a trial. By then he belonged to the club SC Chemie Halle and on 6 October 1974 he entered his first marathon, the Kosice race. It was one of only three annual marathons in the whole of the Eastern bloc. On a cold, rainy day he finished third in 2:20:28.4 and his career was launched.

He returned the next year for his second marathon. This time he ran 2:17:30.4, but finished only seventh. He improved dramatically in 1976, first to 2:13:57.2 and then to 2:12:21.2. His defeat of Frank Shorter in Montreal came as a surprise to everyone except his countrymen. He beat his idol's Olympic record.

Between 1976 and 1980 he had mixed success, failing badly (as favourite) in the Prague European marathon. He scored a few wins, but retired from the 1979 Fukuoka race. The previous year he had been 32nd in the Japanese classic, explaining that he had pulled a calf muscle.

But he was ready for the defence of his Olympic title. He had won the national 10000 m title in 1979 and 1980 and was confident. He won the GDR marathon trial in 2:11:17, but despite the boycott which resulted in the Americans and Japanese not being in Moscow, there were quite a few runners who were ready to challenge him. However, his surge at the 35 km mark destroyed all opposition.

Voices were heard in the world's media criticising the GDR sports system after Cierpinski's victory. Writing in *Athletics Weekly*, Ivan Berenyi pointed out that Cierpinski had twice won the GDR 10000 m title in mediocre times in the absence of the country's top track runners. He asked whether these races were not perhaps arranged "to keep Cierpinski's name in the eyes of the international public, so that when he emerges in his supercharged Olympic shape people will not be too surprised? The impression that a lot of people are being manipulated somehow, possibly including Cierpinski himself, is hard to escape."

In a 1984 article in *Marathon and Distance Runner* Berenyi wrote that after his 1976 victory Cierpinski's status in the GDR sports establishment ensured that he could select his opponents – keeping dangerous GDR rivals out of races. Berenyi mentioned that "[it] also helped" that Cierpinski and national distance coach Manfred Matuschewski, as well as both the president and the vice president of the GDR track and field association, were of Polish origin.

In 1980 Cierpinski again failed at Fukuoka (sixth) and only went back there in 1983, when he finished 15th. In between he could only manage sixth in the European marathon, but earned a bronze medal in the first World Championships race. His country's 1984 boycott robbed him of a chance of a third Olympic win. He planned to finish his career in the 1985 World Cup marathon, but by then he had been surpassed in the GDR by Michael Heilmann.

He kept on running, though, and in August 1995 clocked 2:45:22 in a marathon in Sydney.

starters but, sadly, with no Japanese or Americans among them. All eyes were on Cierpinski (who would turn thirty two days later): Could he do what Bikila had done and what he had prevented Shorter from doing? With him on the starting line were some of the best marathon racers in history: Nijboer, Moseyev, Lismont, Thompson, Ford and Kotov, as well as a few exciting newcomers: De Castella, Dzhumanazarov and Dereje Nedi ETH. Viren was also there.

The early leader was the Dane Jorn Lauenborg (15:48 at 5 km). Cierpinski, Nijboer, Dzhumanazarov and Kotov were part of a large pack that passed this mark in 16:10. Kotov then went to the front and he had a gap of more than 20 seconds at 10 km (a slow 31:16). The Soviet champion still led at 15 km (46:45), but by 20 km (63:42) he had been caught by his pursuers. Viren was still in the main bunch, but would drop out at 27 km with stomach problems.

The route now went along the Moscow River. Rodolfo Gomez MEX, who had run 2:16:18 in 1979, surged forward and reached 25 km in 77:55. He had covered the 5 km in a very quick 14:13 and was 6 seconds ahead of Nijboer. Dzhumanazarov, Kotov and European champion Moseyev followed 3 seconds later, but Cierpinski had let them all go and was 48 seconds behind the Mexican. The heat suited Gomez and although he slowed down appreciably (30 km in 93:27 and 35 km in 1:49:47), he still increased his lead to 30 km. Nijboer and the Soviets were 23 seconds behind, but they had been joined by Cierpinski, Nedi and Magnani.

The champion now started to stamp his authority on the proceedings. He took Nijboer with him as he set off after the slowing Gomez. By 35 km they were only 3 seconds behind him and had a gap of 2 seconds on the others. Then Nijboer made a move of his own, going past Gomez. But the East German was not to be denied. He waited a short while, then accelerated easily away at 36 km. By 40 km (2:04:35) his lead had grown to 19 seconds. The last 2 km were "particularly painful" for Cierpinski and Nijboer cut 2 seconds from his lead (running away from Dzhumanazarov in the process). Despite his discomfort Cierpinski sprinted the last 200 m on the track in 33.4 seconds and claimed his place in history alongside the great Ethiopian of the sixties. Dzhumanazarov proved stronger than his more favoured countrymen and won the Soviet Union's first marathon medal with his solid third. The Soviets also took the unofficial team competition.

| RESULT: | 1 | Waldemar Cierpinski GDR 2:11:03 |
|---|---|---|
| | 2 | Gerard Nijboer NED 2:11:20 |
| | 3 | Satymkul Dzhumanazarov URS 2:11:35 |
| | 4 | Vladimir Kotov URS 2:12:05 |
| | 5 | Leonid Moseyev URS 2:12:14 |
| | 6 | Rodolfo Gomez MEX 2:12:39 |
| | 7 | Dereje Nedi ETH 2:12:44 |
| | 8 | Massimo Magnani ITA 2:13:12 |
| | 9 | Karel Lismont BEL 2:13:26 |
| | 10 | Rob de Castella AUS 2:14:31 |

The British runners had a disastrous day: Thompson, Ford and David Black all failed to finish. Smet was 13th.

Two major races remained in 1980. Both would produce very fast times, in the first by the most gifted rookie to appear on the scene in many a year, and in the second – a race such as there had never been before – by a host of seasoned campaigners.

The New York City marathon took place on 26 October, and the field increased to more than 14 000. One of the most interesting entrants was the Tanzanian Filbert Bayi, former world record holder for the mile. And there was Alberto Salazar, running his first race longer than 8 miles. He said he would break 2:10: "Some people tell me you have to run a lot of times to be able to run a good marathon. I'm not at all sure that's true. It's just a race." (Peter Gambaccini, *The New York City Marathon: Twenty-five Years.*)

And, of course, there was Bill Rodgers. But the four-time champion fell at 14 miles (another competitor clipped his heel) and could not get back into the race. Rodgers said that he remembered Viren's fall in the 1972 Olympics and how the Finn got up and set a world record. "I tried to emulate Viren, but I guess I'm not gold-medal material."

Nijboer fared even worse; he developed leg cramps and dropped out.

At the front of the race Salazar, in the green and yellow uniform of the University of Oregon, pushed the 21st mile into the wind in 4:57 and got rid of Gomez and John Graham GBR. His winning time of 2:09:41 showed that he was not just talking before the event. It was a course record, the fastest debut in history and the second fastest by an American. It was clear that Salazar would be a force to be reckoned with. He would improve further, but on the international front the honours would go to others.

| RESULT: | 1 | Alberto Salazar 2:09:41 |
|---|---|---|
| | 2 | Rodolfo Gomez 2:10:13.9 |
| | 3 | John Graham 2:11:46.5 |

Rodgers, his knees bloodied, finished fifth in 2:13:20.

Three of the first ten in the Olympic race went to Fukuoka for the 7 December event. The top Japanese were all there, hungry for victory after having been denied the opportunity in Moscow. The race started at noon; the runners had a slight tailwind. But the initial pace was rather slow – the halfway point was reached in 66 minutes. At 30 km De Castella led (93:02), but then the Japanese started to take the initiative and increase the pace.

At 35 km Seko, the two-time defending champion, Takeshi Soh and Kunimitsu Itoh led by 6 seconds. Over the next 5 km Seko and Soh pulled away from their countryman, leading him by 6 seconds at 40 km (2:03:08). They had run the previous 10 km in 30:05. In almost an exact replay of the previous year, Seko and Soh entered the stadium together. Seko, who had set a national 10000 m record in

Derek Clayton shattered the world record and became the first man to run a sub-2:10 marathon when he won the 1967 Fukuoka race. Eighteen months later, after training "on the very brink of injury", he ran more than a minute faster in Antwerp.

A flying Frank Shorter runs on the blue line indicating the route near the end of the 1972 Olympic marathon in Munich, where he was born. His victory, the first by a United States athlete since 1908, started a running revolution in his homeland.

Four years after Shorter's win he failed to emulate Bikila with a repeat victory when Waldemar Cierpinski unexpectedly beat him in Montreal. But in 1980 Cierpinski succeeded when he retained the title in Moscow.

*Next page:* The strain shows as Ferdie le Grange races to his magnificent 2:12:47 in Port Elizabeth in 1974. It gave him seventh spot on the world list for the year. Behind him is Gabashane Rakabaele.

Thompson Magawana's audacious run in the SA marathon of 1980 took everyone by surprise. In 1987 he achieved an incredible double by finishing third in the SA marathon two weeks after winning the Two Oceans ultramarathon in record time.

*Previous page:* Grete Waitz won the New York marathon a record nine times between 1978 and 1988 and set three of her four world records in the Big Apple. In 1983 she became the first world champion. (Touchline Media/Bob Martin)

The powerful Rob de Castella in full flight. He set a world record in the 1981 Fukuoka race, won the Commonwealth title in an epic tussle in 1982 and became the first world marathon champion in 1983. (Touchline Media/David Cannon)

*Next page:* Joan Benoit holds the Stars and Stripes aloft in the Los Angeles Coliseum moments after her victory in the first Olympic marathon for women in 1984. Her time was a world best for a women-only marathon. (Touchline Media/Tony Duffy)

A triumphant Carlos Lopes wins the 1984 Olympic marathon, the second leg of a remarkable double – earlier the same year he had won the world cross-country title. He became the oldest ever Olympic winner in a running event. (Touchline Media/Tony Duffy)

Europe earlier in the year, sprinted away from his rival for a narrow win by 4 seconds.

The times were magnificent: Only two of the first nine (Shigeru Soh and Cierpinski) failed to set personal bests and the times for places 2-22 were the best ever for these positions! For the first time two runners had dipped below 2:10:00 in the same race. Pfeffer ran the fastest ever by an American on foreign soil.

RESULT:
1 Toshihiko Seko 2:09:45
2 Takeshi Soh 2:09:49
3 Kunimitsu Itoh 2:10:05
4 Garry Henry AUS 2:10:09
5 Shigeru Soh 2:10:23
6 Waldemar Cierpinski 2:10:24
7 Kirk Pfeffer 2:10:29
8 Robert de Castella 2:10:44
9 Yutaka Taketomi JPN 2:11:27
10 Dave Cannon GBR 2:11:35

The first five times were among the top ten performances in the world for 1980. *Track & Field News* ranked Cierpinski first for the year, followed by Nijboer, Seko and Salazar.

At the end of the year a new organisation, the Association of Road Running Athletes, was formed in the USA to promote "open" road racing, i.e. with payments "over" rather than "under" the table. At the time, the best road racers received about $3 000 in appearance fees for a 10 km race. The first ARRA race was the Cascade Run Off on 29 June 1981, where Greg Meyer and Anne Audain each received $10 000 for winning. Many athletes were suspended, but others placed their winnings in special accounts from which they were allowed to withdraw money for expenses.

Seko did not run in Beppu in 1981 and the race went to the Soh brothers, Shigeru beating Takeshi by 2 seconds in 2:11:30. A month later Gomez took another Japanese race, in Tokyo, in 2:11:00. Later in March Dick Beardsley USA and Inge Simonsen NOR tied in the first London marathon in 2:11:48. The race started on the famous Meridian Line at Greenwich Park; there were 6 700 competitors.

Seko went to Boston, where he ran with Rodgers and his countryman Craig Virgin (in his second marathon) until the bottom of Heartbreak Hill. Surprisingly, it was Rodgers who faltered first. At the top of the hill Virgin was ahead, but he could not shake off Seko. The Japanese, on the other hand, knew that the American was faster over 10000 m[7] and that he had to get away. So Seko surged at 22 miles and was so strong that he won by exactly a minute in 2:09:26 for another PB. He had covered the second half

7. Virgin's 27:29.16 made him the third fastest ever over this distance, compared to Seko's 27:43.44. Two weeks before Boston Virgin had run the fastest road 10 km ever, 28:06.

in 64:01 and was now the fifth fastest runner in history.

Rodgers finished third in 2:10:34, his sixth time under 2:11:00 – the most by any runner.

"Old" Johnny Kelly, who had won the race twice, ran his fiftieth Boston and received a tumultuous welcome when he finished in 4:01:25. He was 73 years old.

Seko, who had been Japanese schools champion over 800 and 1500 m, had been coached by Kiyoshi Nakamura since he was nineteen. Nakamura said: "God gave Seko to me and I want to thank God by making Seko the best." Nakamura's approach was spiritual as much as it was physical. "The idea is to clear your mind of everything and to let your body function naturally, undisturbed by thoughts. We must study the Bible, Scriptures and all famous works. We must study nature: mountains, rivers, the stars, sun and moon. All of them are our teachers; and more specifically, we must study the other top runners. That way he's still Seko, but he has a part of all his competitors in him, which will enable him to beat them." (*Fast Tracks*)

In May a new marathon was established in Frankfurt, West Germany. It was won in 2:13:20 by Kjell-Erik Ståhl SWE. Six days later, on 23 May, the first running of a race which would become famous for its fast course took place in Rotterdam. Graham won in a PB 2:09:28, becoming the eleventh runner under 2:10:00.

The first half of the year was also significant for the announcement that women would run the marathon in the 1984 Olympic Games in Los Angeles.

Less than a month after Graham's performance Beardsley also improved tremendously and followed the Briton under 2:10:00 when he won the Grandma's marathon on a point-to-point course in Duluth in 2:09:36.2. It was his fourth marathon of the year and his fourth PB.

Before the New York marathon on 25 October Salazar predicted he would run 2:08. In fact, he had the world record in his sights. Early in September he had finished third in the World Cup 10000 m in a PB 27:40.69 and shortly before the marathon he had completed a training session in which he ran three mile intervals in 4:12 with less than 3 minutes rest between them.

The race was televised nationally for the first time and millions of Americans watched Salazar, Graham and José Gomez MEX reach halfway in 64:10. Salazar's coach Bill Squires had said: "There are three things that you don't bet against. They are taxes, death – and Alberto." His charge started surging in Manhattan and ran the 17th mile in 4:33. That was enough to break his rivals, but could he keep going?

Salazar ran the next 3 miles in 4:42, 4:51 and 4:46 and went through 20 miles in 97:29, a few seconds faster than Clayton's approximate time at the same point. He kept pushing, the determination etched on his face. His form held and he stormed through the finish in 2:08:12.7 (rounded off to 2:08:13). Jukka Toivola FIN was second in 2:10:52.2 and Hugh Jones GBR third in 2:10:59.8.

Clayton's record, set on a course which was believed by many to have been short, had fallen at last. "It's like Roger Bannister's first 4-minute mile," exulted Allan Steinfeld, the marathon's technical director. The women's race also produced a new world record when New Zealand's Allison Roe clocked 2:25:28.7.

But, sadly, it was not to be. When the course was validated much later, it was found to be 148 metres short. At the time[8] certified courses were allowed to be short within a tolerance of 0.2% (84.3 m in a marathon). Before the 1982 New York race 89 m were added to the course, which brought it within the allowable tolerance.

Fortunately, Fukuoka set matters straight – and this time there was no doubt at all. After three consecutive Japanese victories the local runners tasted defeat when the powerful Aussie De Castella ran away from everyone. Seko was not there, but Cierpinski and the Soh brothers were.

The leader for most of the race on 6 December was Bjorklund, who went through 5 km in 15:31 and 10 km in 30:31. There were nine runners in the front pack (including the Sohs, Itoh, Kotov and Gianni Poli ITA) and they were 25 seconds behind Clayton's world record schedule. But then the American picked up the pace even further and they reached 15 km in 45:29, cutting 13 seconds from Clayton's "lead".

The next 5 km took 15:02, but it had taken Clayton 15:13 and they were only one second behind record pace. Bjorklund was still leading at halfway (63:48) and at 25 km (75:33), and he had brought the pack of seven under Clayton's pace by 8 seconds.

Two kilometres later De Castella and Itoh moved ahead. The battle was now between these two, and Itoh had the knowledge that he had beaten the Australian the previous year, when De Castella has set his 2:10:44 PB. But Deek, as De Castella is nicknamed, was a different runner this time. Their next 5 km were slower then Clayton's (30 km in 91:09). Bjorklund was now 6 seconds behind, just ahead of the Sohs. At 34 km De Castella accelerated and drew away from his rival. He was clocked in 1:45:08 at 35 km, having run the previous 5 km in an amazing 13:59! He was 15 seconds ahead of Itoh and more than a minute ahead of Clayton's split at the same point.

De Castella slowed down dramatically and reached 40 km in 2:01:32, now 50 seconds ahead. The record was secure, although his last 2.2 km was almost 8 seconds slower than Clayton's. He finished in 2:08:18 which meant, with the course being out-and-back and certified, that for the first time in twelve years there was not the least uncertainty about the world record. He had broken his countryman's record by 15.6 seconds.

Despite De Castella's fabulous time the standard of per-

8. This was also the case in 1982 and 1983.

formances was not as deep as the previous year – although the runner-up did go through the 2:10:00 barrier for the first time.

RESULT: 
| 1 | Robert de Castella | 2:08:18 |
| 2 | Kunimitsu Itoh | 2:09:37 |
| 3 | Shigeru Soh | 2:10:10 |

The shortness of the New York course produced another unfortunate result when *Track & Field News* ranked Salazar ahead of De Castella on the strength of his "world record". The fact that the Australian ran on an out-and-back course (the New York course is point-to-point) and beat a far stronger field was ignored in this seemingly partisan decision.

With the European Championships and Commonwealth Games being late in 1982, fireworks were not expected early in the year. On the last day of January Vadim Sidorov URS beat Jones by 8 seconds in 2:10:33 in Tokyo.

The next major race was Boston on 19 April. Salazar had been outkicked by Mohamed Kedir in the World Cross-country Championships (De Castella was tenth), but in Boston there was no stopping him . . . almost. There was a following breeze on the journey from Hopkinton, but it was hot and many runners had to be treated afterwards for heat-related exhaustion. It was Salazar's first Boston (although he had grown up near the course), and he led at halfway in 64:04 – just ahead of Beardsley and Rodgers.

Rodgers lost contact on the hills, and thereafter Salazar and Beardsley fought each other. The heat affected Salazar more than Beardsley, but he held on and finally took the lead with about 800 m to go. Beardsley came back at him, but with 150 m to go Salazar surged ahead for good. Salazar's celebrated toughness gave him the win, but by only 2 seconds in 2:08:51. "You go all that distance, so it would be crazy to let someone break you in the last few yards," he said. He had won his third marathon out of three.

It was the first time that two men had broken 2:09:00 in the same race. They were more than 3 minutes ahead of the third runner.

Salazar was one of the competitors who had to receive medical treatment. Four years previously his temperature had soared to 42° C after the Falmouth race; he was packed in ice and given the last rites of the Roman Catholic Church. This time his temperature plummeted to 31°, but once again he recovered.

Three weeks after Boston Jones won the London marathon by almost 3 minutes in 2:09:24. Later in May Gomez took Rotterdam in 2:11:57 (he had won the Classical marathon in Athens in 2:11:49) and New Zealand track star Rod Dixon (fourth in the Montreal 5000 m) won in Auckland in 2:11:21.

Then the big races followed. First was the European Championships, run on 12 September in Athens. Women competed for the first time.

The race over the difficult course started at 17:00 when

## RUNNING ON THE EDGE

Alberto Salazar was born in Havana on 7 August 1958, but was taken to the USA by his parents in 1960. He started running at the age of thirteen and in 1977 won the national junior titles over 5000 and 10000 m. On the last day of 1978 he set a world best of 22:13 for 5 miles. In 1980 he broke 28 minutes for 10000 m for the first time and ran his first marathon, in New York. In 1981 he broke the world record in New York, but unfortunately the course was found to be short. He set a phenomenal course record of 31:56 for the 7.1-mile Falmouth race; in 1982 he broke this with 31:54. Also in 1982 he finished second in the World Cross-country Championships and won New York for the third consecutive time.

Coached by Bill Dellinger in Eugene, Oregon, Salazar became known as a fearless competitor who drove himself to – and sometimes over – the limit, as happened at Falmouth in 1978. Dellinger said of him: "We've never had anyone at [the University of] Oregon handle the load Alberto has shown he can handle, not even Steve Prefonteine."

His battles with Rodolfo Gomez in New York and Dick Beardsley in Boston in 1982 have become legendary. "I believed that I could take as much as anyone else. I was willing to pay more than anyone else. Someone would have to break, and I thought it would be the other guy."

The year 1982 was probably his best. Apart from winning New York (by 4 seconds) and Boston (by 2 seconds) and the magnificent cross-country performance, he set US records of 13:11.93 and 27:25.61 (the third fastest time in the world) on the track. Pressure to excel mounted – and the peak could not last. The first setback came in the 1983 Rotterdam race, where he was beaten by De Castella and Lopes (he finished fifth).

Knee and hamstring problems hit him – and then an even worse malady:

his body started suffering from an endocrine imbalance and New York in 1982 was to be his last major win for twelve years. He would later say in *Runner's World*: "My immune system was totally shot. I caught everything. I was always sick, always run-down." In the 1984 Olympic marathon he could only finish 15th. His career then went rapidly downhill.

In 1994 Salazar said in *Runner's World*: "In hindsight, I started running poorly after the Boston Marathon in 1982. . . It was the beginning of my long, gradual decline. Training for the Olympics in 83 and 84, I was sick constantly. I had 12 colds in 12 months."

He went from doctor to doctor. Nothing helped. He tried a number of comebacks, also changing his rather peculiar style, but his body would not respond (although he did win some races). Then, in 1993, on the advice of a friend, he started taking the antidepressant drug Prozac, which boosts levels of the neurotransmitter serotonin. Two days later he ran six repeat miles in 4:42.

"I thought my watch was broken." But it wasn't – it was merely the Salazar of old coming back.

In 1994 the intensely religious Salazar, who works for Nike and lives in Portland, Oregon, entered South Africa's Comrades ultramarathon – the first time he would run longer than the marathon distance – and delivered an amazing performance. He broke away from the field after about 25 km and at one stage was 10 minutes ahead. But he suffered on the monstrous hills: "At one point, I even walked a little. I've never done that in a race. I just asked the Lord to help me through. I prayed more during this race than I've prayed in a year." He won by more than 4 minutes in 5:38:39, one of the most dramatic performances ever in ultradistance running.

---

the heat had by no means dissipated. Nijboer had been struggling with a knee injury and set off conservatively, running with the main pack for the first half of the race. From 25 km he moved to the front, gradually stretching his lead until he was 35 seconds ahead at 35 km. The heat and tough course took their toll and Nijboer tired towards the end ("I've never felt so weak before"), but he held onto his lead, winning the Netherlands' first gold medal in a major championship, albeit in a slow time.

Runners from northern European countries took the first five places, with Belgium capturing its seventh and eighth medals in the last seven European marathons. Lismont won the bronze eleven years after his victory in Helsinki.

| RESULT: | 1 | Gerard Nijboer NED 2:15:16 |
|---------|---|---------------------------|
| | 2 | Armand Parmentier BEL 2:15:51 |
| | 3 | Karel Lismont BEL 2:16:04 |
| | 4 | Pertti Tiainen FIN 2:16:27 |
| | 5 | Jukka Toivola FIN 2:17:31 |
| | 6 | Waldemar Cierpinski GDR 2:17:50 |

On 8 October the best runners in the Commonwealth gathered in Brisbane. It was to be one of the best duels in the history of marathoning. Shahanga (who had already won the 10000 m) defended his title against the world record holder, but there was also his countryman, the newcomer Juma Ikangaa (who actually is a few months older than Shahanga). The race began at 06:00 and was televised in its en-

tirety without any commercials. The two Tanzanians flew away from the start and covered the first 10 km in 30:11, 20 seconds faster than De Castella had done in Fukuoka!

The next 10 km took only slightly longer; they passed 20 km in 60:33. They reached halfway in 63:50 and were timed in 91:10 at 30 km, with De Castella almost a minute behind. Ikangaa, a lieutenant in the Tanzanian army, then dropped his team-mate, but Shahanga fought back again. All the while De Castella, following his race plan to the letter, was cutting their lead with every stride. The leaders were now on the hilly part of the course, and the initial reckless pace began to tell. Shahanga fell behind again, and at almost the same time the hard-charging Aussie caught sight of them for the first time in a long while.

De Castella sped the 10 km between 30 and 40 km in 30:31 – only slightly slower than in Fukuoka – and caught the champion with 4 km to go. Over the next kilometre he cut Ikangaa's lead of 70 m to nothing . . . and went straight past. Thousands of Australians glued to their television sets then saw Ikangaa pass De Castella again. De Castella regained the advantage . . . but Ikangaa came back and went into the lead once more. In an amazing show of guts the two men were slugging it out, with the finish looming ahead.

Finally, agonisingly, Deek's power carried him into the lead for the last time. He stretched the gap to 10 m, then 20, and then pulled away from the struggling Tanzanian to win by 12 seconds.

It was a superb race and a tremendous victory. De Castella's 2:09:18, just a minute slower than his world record and the eighth fastest time ever run, would have been much faster on a flat course. Ron Clarke, the great Australian track runner, called it the best marathon ever run. "The Brisbane course is the toughest I have ever seen . . . it must be the greatest run in history. Rob paced himself to absolute perfection."

RESULT:
1 Robert de Castella AUS 2:09:18
2 Juma Ikangaa TAN 2:09:30
3 Mike Gratton Eng 2:12:06
4 John Graham Sco 2:13:04
5 Kevin Ryan NZL 2:13:42
6 Gidamis Shahanga TAN 2:14:25

Ikangaa's time was a new Africa record, and he was philosophical about his loss. "He's a runner, I'm a runner. We both did our best," he remarked.

Sixteen days after this thriller Salazar and Rodolfo Gomez staged their own in New York. Rodgers, who had won the Melbourne marathon the previous week in 2:11:08 (his first victory in seven starts), was absent, but Salazar was to have his hands full with Gomez. The Mexican was brimming with confidence, having won three marathons earlier in the year (he was also first in Eugene in September, clocking 2:11:35). Early in the second half Salazar threw in a couple of 4:44 miles and got rid of all his pursuers except Gomez, Carlos Lopes POR (running his first marathon), Jon Sinclair USA and David Murphy GBR. By the time he reached the Bronx he had only Gomez for company (Lopes would fail to finish, but his time would come).

In 1980 Salazar had beaten the Mexican by 32 seconds, but now he was a much tougher nut to crack. The finish was getting closer, and still Gomez clung to the American. In Central Park Salazar, who earlier had suffered from a side stitch, dug deep and put in a few 150-metre surges. After each one he tried not to return to the previous pace, thus constantly picking up the tempo. With a mile to go they were still level, but on re-entering Central Park for the final stretch, Salazar tried once more. This time he broke Gomez, and he was helped by a small piece of lawn over which they ran as well as a dust cloud kicked up by their motorcycle escort. He won by 4 seconds in 2:09:29.

Third in 2:11:54 was American Dan Schlesinger, a Yale graduate, Marshall scholar at Oxford and Harvard law student who spoke Japanese, Korean and French.

Salazar was now undefeated in four marathons. He and Gomez had run the final 10 km in 30:13 and the 26th mile in an almost unbelievale 4:35.

"I did whatever I had to do to be the best," Salazar later said of his running career. "It really was an obsession." Unknown to him and the world, this was to be his last marathon victory.

In Fukuoka the standard was considerably lower than in the last two years, with Paul Ballinger NZL winning in 2:10:15 from Hideki Kita JPN (2:11:09) and Bruno Lafranchi SUI (2:11:12). Itoh was fourth.

Salazar and De Castella were again ranked first and second in the world by *Track & Field News*, with Gomez third.

The year 1983 was an important one in the history of athletics. For the first time a world championships meeting would be staged; the venue was Helsinki. Everything else that happened did so in the shadow of the main event of the year.

On 13 February Seko delivered a warning that he should not be forgotten (although in the end he did not go to Helsinki, preferring somewhat inexplicably to save himself for Fukuoka) when he won the Tokyo marathon in 2:08:38. Behind him came Takeshi Soh in 2:08:55 and Gomez in 2:09:12. All three ran personal bests.

De Castella prepared for Helsinki by choosing Rotterdam (9 April) over Boston and London, and he gave a glimpse of the fast times that could be achieved on this course when he won in 2:08:37 – and he had to run this fast to beat Lopes, who was only 2 seconds behind him! It was the first marathon meeting between De Castella and Salazar.

Graham, the course record holder, set the pace to halfway (64:27) in ideal conditions, with Salazar, who had been suffering from a groin strain since February, leading at 25 km (76:25), 30 km (91:48) and 35 km (1:47:43). De Castella, Lopes and Gomez (running his sixth marathon in thirteen months) pulled away at 37 km, but then even the strong Mexican found the pace too fast. No wonder, because the 5 km between 35 and 40 km were run in 14:39!

De Castella knew that Lopes's 10000 m time was about a minute faster than his (the Portuguese was second in the 1976 Olympic 10000 metres), so he kept the pressure on.[9] It worked: "With 500 m to go, I just put my head down and ran as hard as I could. Almost a sprint."

RESULT:
1 Robert de Castella 2:08:37
2 Carlos Lopes 2:08:39
3 Rodolfo Gomez 2:09:25
4 Armand Parmentier 2:09:57
5 Alberto Salazar 2:10:08

De Castella and Seko were now the only two runners with two sub-2:09 times.[10] Salazar, beaten for the first time, had said before the race that whoever won should be considered the world's premier marathoner.

Eight days later Gratton scored his first big win, clocking 2:09:43 in London. The next day, across the Atlantic, Meyer won Boston in a PB 2:09:01. Two more runners were under

9. Three weeks earlier Lopes had outsprinted Salazar (fourth, only one second behind) and De Castella (sixth) to win the world cross-country silver medal.
10. It should be noted that Salazar's New York time of 1981 would have been about 2:08:41 on a full-length course.

## THE FIRST WORLD CHAMPION

In 1986 Robert de Castella won Boston in 2:07:51, the third fastest marathon at the time. He called it his best performance, but added: "I'm still not at my peak. Once you reach one peak it gives you a better sight or an improved perspective of another, higher peak."

De Castella, or Deek as he is called, would never run faster and would never win the Olympic marathon, but he was the dominating figure during the first half of the eighties. His place in history is secure for having won the first world title and setting a world record in Fukuoka in 1981.

"I don't have any limitations on what I can do," he said in an interview in *Athletics Weekly*. "Boston has some of the hardest sections of any marathon course. I was pleased to be able to run the same splits up the hills as I ran down them. The . . . knowledgeable Boston people said it was unheard of."

De Castella was trained by Pat Clohessy from the age of fourteen (he was born on 27 February 1957) and set seven Australian junior records on the track, among them 2 miles in 8:49. He improved steadily, but really started training hard in 1979, doing a variety of work-outs. He won his marathon debut in 1979 in 2:14:44, ran 13 seconds faster to place tenth in the 1980 Olympic race, finished eighth that year in Fukuoka in a PB 2:10:44 and a year later returned to Japan to finally erase Derek Clayton's Antwerp time with a new world record of 2:08:18.

In an interview in *Marathon and Distance Runner* he commented: "Everything . . . just really came together in a climax. I felt strong and powerful during the whole race. In all my other marathons over the last five miles I've been pretty wiped out [but] in Japan I was still running strongly. I also got back to 100 miles training a week more quickly than after any other marathon. [My recovery] probably infers that I can run faster."

De Castella was criticised for taking a drink at 40 km (his usual drink was plain water with 2% of glucose syrup dissolved in it) and then also missed the turn into the stadium. He thought that this had cost him about 6 seconds.

De Castella, who worked as a biophysicist at the Australian Institute of Sport in Canberra, had definite ideas about marathon running. "Once you are running around 2:08 you've got everything mental under control. I think the improvements you can make in your mental approach are fairly limited [and] the main breakthrough is going to come in training and mental preparation. Training for the marathon is getting close to the ultimate in dedication." He added that 130 to 140 miles per week was probably enough training, but he'd like to try to run the miles faster.

He also felt strongly about eating correctly. He restricted his intake of salt, sugar, dairy products and gluten and preferred rice, boiled potatoes and a little pasta as his main sources of carbohydrates.

Deek's first marathon after Fukuoka came ten months later in the Commonwealth Games in Brisbane. In near 100% humidity the Aussie ran a brilliant tactical race to win in 2:09:18. Six months later he again dipped under 2:09:00, beating Carlos Lopes and Alberto Salazar in 2:08:37. Four months after that came the crowning moment of his career when he won the world title in convincing fashion. He had scored four superb victories in a row and *Track & Field News* ranked him sixth among the world's elite in all events for the year.

He placed third in both Steve Jones's brilliant Chicago races: when Jones broke his world record in 1984 (he was also beaten by Lopes), and when Jones failed to equal Lopes's world record by one second in 1985 (Djama Robleh was second).

De Castella's best Olympic performance came in 1984, when he finished fifth; in 1988 he was eighth. (He is the only man to have completed four Olympic marathons.) The only blemishes on his career were his failures to finish the 1987 World Championships race and the Tokyo marathon in 1992, and a disappointing 2:18:50 in the 1990 Commonwealth event (after having won the previous two editions). He ran faster than 2:10:00 eight times. He twice finished sixth in the World Cross-country race, in 1981 and 1983.

His last major marathon win was Rotterdam in 1991 (2:09:42).

2:10:00, Americans Ron Tabb (2:09:32) and Benji Durden (2:09:58). Rodgers finished tenth in 2:11:59.

Then the scene shifted to the Finnish capital for the first World Championships, where the marathon was scheduled for 14 August.

Once again the strength of De Castella was decisive. The Japanese stayed away and Lopes decided not to run after a disappointing performance in the 10000 m. But Cierpinski was running well again, and the field also included Parmentier, Lismont, Nijboer and Ikangaa. And there was the Ethiopian Kebede Balcha, who had run a sub-2:12 in 1981.

A huge pack of about thirty runners were together for the first half, but after 25 km (77:35) Agapius Masong TAN, Balcha and Djamah Robleh DJI accelerated away. They quickly opened a gap of 70 m, but the others pulled them back and by 30 km there were twenty runners together again. The time was 93:08.

Then, suddenly, the world record holder and Commonwealth champion was away. At 34 km the course turned into the wind and also went uphill. De Castella surged and only the far less experienced Balcha could go with him. But, exactly as in Brisbane and Rotterdam, De Castella's prolonged increasing of the tempo proved too much. With 3 km to go the Ethiopian let go and De Castella went through 40 km (2:03:28) with a lead of 12 seconds. He had run the last 5 km in 14:54, much faster than he had in his world record and just 15 seconds slower than in Rotterdam.

He cruised to the finish, waving to the crowd. "My plan was to get rid of my competitors on the way up the hills, and that's how I lost Balcha," the first world champion said later.

Balcha's performance was the best by an Ethiopian in a major marathon since Wolde's third in the 1972 Olympics. Cierpinski won the bronze medal by one second, while Lismont added to his reputation with a solid ninth.

| RESULT: | 1 | Robert de Castella AUS 2:10:03 |
|---|---|---|
| | 2 | Kebede Balcha ETH 2:10:27 |
| | 3 | Waldemar Cierpinski GDR 2:10:37 |
| | 4 | Kjell-Erik Ståhl SWE 2:10:38 |
| | 5 | Agapius Masong TAN 2:10:42 |
| | 6 | Armand Parmentier BEL 2:10:57 |
| | 7 | Pier Giovanni Poli ITA 2:11:05 |
| | 8 | Hugh Jones GBR 2:11:15 |
| | 9 | Karel Lismont BEL 2:11:24 |
| | 10 | Stig Roar Husby NOR 2:11:29 |

None of the main placers in Helsinki was in New York for the 23 October event. Dixon had been third in the 1500 metres in Munich, but after New Zealand's boycott of the 1980 Olympics he established himself as a road runner in the US, with notable success. In 1982 he set a course record in the San Francisco Bay to Breakers race. In New York, chasing Shahanga and Geoff Smith GBR, he slipped coming off the Queensboro Bridge (it was raining) and aggravated a hamstring injury. He was 35 seconds behind Smith with 20 miles covered, but by then his hamstring problem was over and Smith, in his debut, was having problems of his own (cramps in his legs). The New Zealander steadily cut the deficit and went into the lead with less than a quarter of a mile to go. He finished in 2:08:59. Behind him Smith fell across the line – the fastest nonwinner ever in New York.[11] His time was 2:09:08 – a world best for a debut; Tabb was third in 2:10:46.

Dixon knelt down and kissed the pavement. Ten years later he would say: "That win . . . was the topping off of my whole career. New York is the one you have to win."

A week earlier the first edition of the revamped Chicago marathon, now called the America's marathon, was held. Joseph Nzau TAN beat Hugh Jones in a thrilling finish, 2:09:44.3 against 2:09:44.8. Rodgers was 30th.

Seko had stayed out of the marathon battles all year after his win in Tokyo, but was ready for Fukuoka on 4 December. He had a stellar field to contend with: Salazar was there, and so were the Soh brothers, Cierpinski, a host of top Japanese runners (the race was the Japanese Olympic trial) and Ikangaa. The Tanzanian led from the start and reached 20 km in 61:30 and 30 km in 91:53. By 34 km his pursuers – Salazar, the Sohs, Itoh, Kita and Seko – had caught up with him.

Seko, who had sustained a leg injury three weeks before, showed no sign of it as he and Ikangaa broke away after 40 km. They reached the track together and stayed together for another 300 metres. Then the Japanese star accelerated into a furious sprint to which Ikangaa had no answer. Seko clocked his second sub-2:09 of the year, with Ikangaa just 3 seconds behind him.

RESULT:
1 Toshihiko Seko 2:08:52
2 Juma Ikangaa 2:08:55
3 Shigeru Soh 2:09:11

Six runners were faster than 2:10:00 – the highest number ever in a single race. For the third time ever two were under 2:09:00 (equalling the 1982 Boston and the 1983 Rotterdam). Takeshi Soh (fourth) would join his brother and Seko in Los Angeles. Salazar finished fifth again, but set an American loop course record of 2:09:21.

The year ended with 21 performances faster than 2:10:00, more than three times the previous record, and seven under 2:09:00 – five more than in any previous year. De Castella was finally ranked first by *Track & Field News*, ahead of Seko and Lopes.

The Olympic year 1984 started slowly, as one might have

11. Both men were excellent milers. Dixon had a 3:53.62 to his credit and Smith 3:55.8.

## LEBOW VS BRIGHT

The Chicago marathon – along the city's famed lakefront – was first held in 1977 as the Mayor Daley marathon. It made its mark, however, in 1983 when it attracted a top-class international field. In 1984 the field was even better because a big sponsor provided Bob Bright, the race director, with the opportunity of offering prize money of $250 000 as well as appearance fees.

This, together with Fred Lebow's squabbles with New York mayor Ed Koch, resulted in Chicago being by far the higher quality race of America's two major marathons. Steve Jones ran a new world record in Chicago, and that was enough to establish the event's reputation. And it started the battle of the marathons – not quite as deadly as the Battle of Marathon two and a half centuries before, but, in the road-running world, just as serious.

Bright said: "Our goal is not to be better than someone else [but] to be just as good as we can be here." And Lebow countered: "What makes the New York City Marathon is not the name runners."

In 1985 Chicago offered $270 000 in prize money, including $35 000 for first, as well as incentives for breaking certain times and bonuses for records ($50 000 for a world record). Jones was back, commanding $25 000 in appearance money.

In New York Lebow was offering $273 800 in prize money (likewise with additonal amounts for fast times and records) and it was reported that Olympic champion Carlos Lopes, who had broken Jones's world record in Rotterdam in April, would be getting $75 000 in appearance fees. (In the end he did not run.) The previous year both Lopes and female Olympic champion Joan Benoit had been offered $50 000 to enter Chicago. She did run in 1985 and could have received more than $100 000 if she had won and broken Ingrid Kristiansen's world record. She missed by 15 seconds.

The "war for the stars" continued throughout the eighties, with Lebow and Bright flying all over the world to procure top runners. The Chicago race was not held in 1987, and by the end of the decade was in decline. From 1991 its prize money was drastically reduced – and with that, of course, its winning times became slower.

expected. The first sub-2:10 from a runner eligible to go to Los Angeles came in the London marathon on 13 May when Charlie Spedding GBR won in 2:09:57 in his second marathon. (In January he had won the Houston marathon.) A month earlier Shahanga had triumphed in Rotterdam (2:11:12) and Smith in Boston (2:10:34). A week before London Lismont had won in Munich in 2:12:50.

On 31 March the South African title had gone to Ernest Seleke in a national record 2:09:41 – the first time a South African had run under 2:11:00. The point-to-point course in Port Elizabeth dropped 129 metres – 13 m more than Boston. (See Chapter 8.)

On 21 July two men ran faster than 2:10:00 in a close race in Grünau: Jörg Peter GDR 2:09:14 and his countryman Michael Heilmann 2:09:30.

With runners aiming for the Olympic test, no other fast times were recorded until the Games.

The Games of the 23rd Olympiad were opened in Los Angeles on 28 July. When the festival was last held in the USA, in the same city in 1932, 37 nations had sent 1 408 competitors. This time 7 078 contestants from 141 nations – the latter a record – turned up. One of the absent nations was the Soviet Union, who staged a tit-for-tat boycott. The

Soviets were not very successful in getting other countries to join them (thirteen did) but nevertheless some of the sports (noticeably women's athletics) were severely affected. Strong athletics nations who boycotted were the Soviet Union, East Germany, Poland, Czechoslovakia, Ethiopia and Cuba.

The main stadium was the Los Angeles Memorial Coliseum, and it was the first time in the history of the Olympics that a stadium had twice been used to house the Games.

The man of the Games was the incomparable American Carl Lewis, who emulated the feat of his countryman Jesse Owens in 1936 by winning four gold medals: in the 100 and 200 metres, long jump and relay. In the 800 m Joaquim Cruz won Brazil's first track gold medal and Sebastian Coe, recovered from a debilitating illness, scored a brilliant repeat victory in the 1500 m with a last lap in 53.3 seconds and a last 300 m in 39.3 seconds. Edwin Moses won his second gold medal in the one-lap hurdles eight years after the first and Ulrike Meyfarth hers in the high jump twelve years after the first (when as a sixteen-year-old she had become the youngest Olympic winner ever). Daley Thompson was the second man to retain the decathlon title and Valerie Briscoe-Hooks the first (man or woman) to win the 200 and 400 metres – and then added the 4x400 m relay.

The first Olympic marathon for women went to Joan Benoit (see Chapter 9). Seven days later, on 12 August, 107 runners started the men's race. The favourites were De Castella and Seko, but a number of other runners were ready to challenge them. Among them was Lopes, who had finished only one of his previous three marathons but had the track credentials to be a serious contender.[12] Spedding was also there, as well as Smith, Nijboer, Salazar, Ikangaa, the Sohs and Dixon.

Earlier in the year Lopes had reclaimed the world cross-country title which he had won eight years before. He dropped out in Rotterdam at 28 km with cramp, but in July ran 10000 m in 27:17.48 in the Stockholm race in which his mercurial countryman Fernando Mamede set a new world record of 27:13.81. He certainly was in top form, but many observers felt that his age would count against him in the marathon, especially as it was very hot. But the tough Portuguese, who had been struck by a car while training in Lisbon three weeks before the marathon and suffered cuts and bruises on his elbow and leg, was in the lead group from the start. Cor Lambregts NED and Ikangaa reached 5 km in 15:35 with all the main contenders just behind them. They went through 10 km in 31:12 and Salazar was already in trouble.

12. In 1976, five months after having bagged the world cross-country title, he won the silver medal behind Lasse Viren in the 10000 m in Montreal. The next year he developed severe Achilles tendon problems which were eventually cured by acupuncture. In 1982 he set a European 10000 m record of 27:24.39, beating Salazar and world record holder Henry Rono with a last lap of 58.6 seconds.

Then the pace picked up and the next 5 km were covered in a fast 14:48. Ahmed Mohamed Ismail SOM, Shahanga and Ikangaa led at 15 km in 46:00, one second ahead of Nzau and 2 seconds ahead of Lopes, De Castella and Robleh.

The Irishman John Treacy now also showed at the front. First to reach 20 km were Lopes and Nzau, in 61:26, with Treacy, Spedding, De Castella and Robleh just behind. Takeshi Soh followed 3 seconds behind the two frontrunners. The heat started to take its toll and the pace slowed. Twelve runners were still together at 25 km (77:12) and the situation remained unchanged to 30 km, which was reached in 93:02. Ikangaa was mostly responsible for setting the pace.

Everyone was waiting for De Castella to make his move. It did not come, and at a refreshment station Deek lost some ground at the same time as Lopes accelerated. But the others (there were now seven) went with him and at 35 km Spedding led Lopes, Treacy, Soh, Ikangaa, Nzau and Seko in 1:48:23. De Castella was 5 seconds further back and appeared to be struggling; Robleh was 19 seconds behind him. Seko, Salazar and Jones had dropped out of contention.

Now Lopes really started moving. "Everything was hitting just perfectly . . . all the cylinders were on go," he would later say in an interview with *Track & Field News*. Treacy (in his debut) and Spedding tried to keep contact, but could not maintain his relentless pace. The Portuguese quickly got rid of them and when he reached 40 km in 2:02:56 they were 22 seconds behind. As exhaustion set in, the runners began to string out: Soh was 36 seconds behind Treacy and Spedding, and De Castella and Ikangaa followed after a further 32 seconds.

"After 37 km," Lopes said later, "I was convinced I would win." He ran the 5000 m between 35 and 40 km in a magnificent 14:33 and won by 35 seconds. Despite the adverse conditions his time was a new Olympic record. At 37 years, 176 days he was the oldest ever Olympic winner in a running event, but he was unconcerned about his age: "I have followed the same program for 15 years. The keys are endurance and happiness. I bet on my youthfulness."

Treacy, ninth in the 10000 m six days earlier, pulled away from Spedding (who had decided not to drink any alcohol for the week before the race) 600 m from the end.

RESULT:
1 Carlos Lopes POR 2:09:21
2 John Treacy IRE 2:09:56
3 Charles Spedding GBR 2:09:58
4 Takeshi Soh JPN 2:10:55
5 Robert de Castella AUS 2:11:09
6 Juma Ikangaa TAN 2:11:10
7 Joseph Nzau KEN 2:11:28
8 Djama Robleh DJI 2:11:39
9 Jerry Kiernan IRE 2:12:20
10 Rod Dixon NZL 2:12:57

For the first time all three medal winners ran faster than 2:10:00. A very disappointed Seko finished 14th in 2:14:13, 6 seconds ahead of Salazar. Rodolfo Gomez, Nijboer and Smith all failed to finish. The last runner, Dieudonne Lamothe of Haiti, finished almost exactly 43 minutes behind Lopes!

Lopes had run the race in a new pair of shoes. He had been given a pair, but one of the shoes was too tight. So he was fitted for a new pair five days before the race, the shoes were then made in Japan and hand-delivered two days before the marathon! There were actually two pairs, and his wife Theresa said that he should wear the pair with the gold trim as that was the colour of the medal he would win.

"I always run hard when I am in a race that is important to me. But the most important thing to me is also the most simple – I like to win," the new champion said.

Steve Jones GBR, who had not run in the Olympic marathon (he was eighth in the 10000 m), was in superb form when it was time for the America's marathon in Chicago on 21 October – his second attempt at the distance. The previous year he had dropped out of the Chicago marathon with a sore foot (later identified as a stress fracture) and tried to return his expense money ($1 500) because he felt he did not deserve it. Race director Bob Bright refused to accept it.

The self-coached Jones said in an interview in *Track & Field News* that those 16 miles in Chicago (before he dropped out) "were the easiest 16 miles I had ever run. I really couldn't see what all the fuss was about over the marathon. I respected the distance, yes, but I wanted to try it again."

For the 1984 race he trained in high-altitude Utah and ran a half marathon and 15 km to sharpen up. (He had only once run beyond 20 miles – a 22-mile training run.) Lopes and De Castella were also lured by the wonderful prize money available (it was said that they each received a $50 000 appearance fee), but it was probably too soon after their strenuous efforts in the Olympic marathon and on the day they were no match for the 29-year-old Welsh novice.

The weather was far from ideal, with strong winds and rain. De Castella wanted a fast race and led early. With him in the large pack were Lopes, Jones, Smith, Nzau and South African 2:12:08 performer Ewald Bonzet, running under an alias but in his Bellville club vest. Lopes stopped momentarily to fix his shoe after his heel had been clipped, but quickly caught the pack again.

They reached 15 km in 45:14 – 15 seconds faster than De Castella had done in his world record. Jones, whose best for 10000 m (27:39.14) was the fastest in the field with the exception of the Olympic champion, thought it felt much slower. He was confident and wanted to start racing with 6 miles to go. The pack of ten turned into the wind after 10 miles and slowed. The time at 20 km was 60:57. Smith led at halfway in 64:20 and Deek at 25 km in 75:00. They were now 33 seconds faster than world record pace and the bunch had been thinned out to six: De Castella, Lopes, Jones, Smith, Gabriel Kamau KEN and Martin Pitayo MEX.

At about 28 km a remarkable event occurred which showed how poised and in control Jones was. Kamau fell and Smith tumbled over him. Without breaking his stride Jones grabbed his countryman's arm and brought him back on his feet.

At 30 km Jones, looking very comfortable, led in 91:51. The pace had dropped so much against the wind that they were 42 seconds behind De Castella's time in Fukuoka. But all of a sudden the serious racing started. Along a stretch of road shielded partially from the wind, Jones surged and caught everyone but Kamau by surprise. He blitzed the 21st mile in 4:43 and the next one in 4:46.

De Castella recovered quickly and started chasing as Kamau dropped behind. But it was to no avail. "I held with Jones for a while, but he was running too fast. He just made a sensational run."

Soon the flying RAF corporal had a lead of 100 m. He had to run the last three full miles each in under 4:50 to get the world record. He was grimacing from the effort, his face strained in pain, but had no trouble doing it, speeding the 26th mile in 4:45 to make sure. His new world record (by 13 seconds) came twenty years to the day after Abebe Bikila had set a world record in winning the Tokyo Olympic marathon.

It was an almost unbelievable run by Jones, who beat the world record holder and Olympic champion and got the record to boot. Lopes caught De Castella in the last 200 m; the Australian clocked the fastest time ever for third place.

RESULT:

| | | |
|---|---|---|
| 1 | Steve Jones | 2:08:05 |
| 2 | Carlos Lopes | 2:09:06 |
| 3 | Robert de Castella | 2:09:09 |
| 4 | Gabriel Kamau | 2:10:05 |
| 5 | Geoff Smith | 2:10:08 |

Jones's mile splits were: 4:55, 5:03, 4:49, 4:48, 4:50, 4:50, 4:48, 4:44, 4:52, 5:07, 5:07, 5:01, 4:55, 4:52, 5:10, 4:55, 4:54, 4:54, 5:03, 4:46, 4:43, 4:46, 4:41, 4:47, 4:47, 4:45.

Jones said afterwards that he did not consider himself a marathoner just because he had broken the world record. But he was to run faster still.

Jones had missed making the British Olympic team as a steeplechaser in 1980. He had been running internationally since 1977 and earlier in 1984 had finished third in the World Cross-country Championships (won by Lopes). His main aim for Chicago was to run faster than 2:12 and break the Welsh record. He did not know exactly what the world record was, only that it was "in the low 2:08s", and watched the clock ticking away over the last 200 m.

When asked later about how he fitted in his training with his work, Jones commented that "the frustrating aspect is that at present I still have to get permission to go to a race at which I might win $10,000 or $15,000, far more than I earn in a whole year with the RAF".

After this race Fukuoka was somewhat of an anticlimax.

It was won in 2:10:00 by Takeyuki Nakayama JPN.

Lopes was ranked first for the year, with Jones second and Treacy third.

At the end of the year the magazine *The Runner* asked a panel of experts to select the greatest marathon runners of all time. The result was: 1 Abebe Bikila, 2 Frank Shorter, 3 Waldemar Cierpinski, 4 Bill Rodgers, 5 Clarence DeMar, 6 Rob de Castella, 7 Alberto Salazar, 8 Carlos Lopes, 9 Ron Hill, 10 Derek Clayton. Pheidippides was placed twelfth!

The post-Olympic year was supposed to be quiet, but no one told the top runners: it was to be a magnificent year, the start of an upsurge in the development of the marathon. The first major race was the inaugural World Cup marathon, held in Hiroshima on 14 April. The tiny nation of Djibouti made everyone grab for their atlases when Ahmed Salah won in 2:08:09, the second fastest time ever. His countryman Robleh, who had finished eighth in Los Angeles and described himself as a desert nomad who had herded cattle, goats and sheep before joining the army, was third in 2:08:26 and they (with Abdillahi Charmarke, 11th) took home the team prize. The race set a new record for sub-2:09 times; the favourite, Nakayama, was second in a national record 2:08:15 after the African runner had passed him just before the stadium. The runners in positions four, five and six all set national records too: Heilmann 2:09:03, Abebe Mekonnen ETH 2:09:05 and Orlando Pizzolato ITA 2:10:23.

The day after the World Cup Smith won Boston in 2:14:05 and five days later, at 15:00, Lopes stood on the starting line in Rotterdam. De Castella had shown the way in 1983; now the Portuguese wanted to go one better. Less than a month earlier he had won the world cross-country title for the third time. (In 1966 he had represented Portugal for the first time when he competed in the junior race at this event.)

The weather was not really ideal, for there was a breeze – but the effect of this was minimised by Belgium's Vincent Rousseau and Luc Waegemans who ran in front of Lopes. They went through 5 km in 14:57 and 10 km in 30:04, faster than Jones had done in Chicago. The chasing pack included Nijboer. Unfortunately the pace then slackened and the time at 15 km was 45:24. Rousseau increased the tempo again and they reached 20 km in 60:10 after a 5 km split of 14:46, the fastest of the race. They were 47 seconds ahead of Jones's time.

Waegemans had fallen behind and Rousseau and Lopes were alone at the front. Halfway was reached in 63:24 and Rousseau stopped, his job done. Now it all depended on the Olympic champion – could he run the second half all on his own and maintain the tempo?

Lopes quickly dispelled any fears when he covered the next 5 km in a blistering 14:47, reaching 25 km in 74:57. He was 3 seconds ahead of record pace. Graham was in second place, but far behind.

Even the superbly fit Lopes could not keep going at the same rate and his next 5 km took 15:02 – but Jones had taken 16:51, and in the end this section of the race made the difference. With the support of 600 000 spectators lining the course Lopes pushed himself to the limit. Could he run under 2:08:00? The wind was constantly changing direction, sometimes helping him, sometimes hindering his progress. He ran the next 10 km in 30:04 and stormed across the finish in 2:07:12. It was a magnificent performance – one of the great marathon performances of all time by a man 38 years old.

"Naturally, it would have been better to have competition for the second half of the race," Lopes said. "But when I found myself alone . . . I didn't panic. Yes, it was very hard, but habitually I run races in my head and don't become preoccupied with my opponents."

RESULT:
1 Carlos Lopes 2:07:12
2 John Graham 2:09:58
3 Cor Lambregts NED 2:11:02

Not surprisingly, the length of the course was questioned after Lopes's run. Unfortunately it was not checked immediately, but six months later three course measurers of the Association of International Marathons (AIMS) certified the course to be the correct length.

The London marathon was held the day after Rotterdam. Jones said that he was not out to regain his world record; the important thing was to win. He battled defending champion Spedding for most of the way, and stomach cramps from 4 miles before the finish. At one stage Jones asked Spedding if he had any advice for the cramps during a race. "Sure, stop running," the helpful Spedding said. Jones did not follow this advice; instead, he surged ahead and won in a course record. Although the course was not nearly as fast as Rotterdam, the next four runners all set personal or national bests.

RESULT:
1 Steve Jones 2:08:16
2 Charles Spedding 2:08:33
3 Allister Hutton 2:09:16
4 Cristoph Herle FRG 2:09:23
5 Henrik Jorgensen DEN 2:09:43

The race set a world record of sorts, with about 17 000 starters and 15 841 finishers.

Jones was not yet through for the year. In August he set a new world best of 61:14 for the half marathon and on 20 October, exactly six months after Lopes had broken his world record, he returned to Chicago. He had only one purpose: to get his record back. He started aggressively, racing through the first three miles in 4:46, 4:42 and 4:48. By then he had already left the appointed rabbit behind – at the prize-giving the announcer would say: "Jones killed the rabbit at three miles." He proceeded with miles in 4:39 and 4:34, and

reached 10 km in 29:30 – 34 seconds faster than Lopes had done in Rotterdam. His second 5 km took an amazing 13:43! He had Simeon Kigen KEN with him, but Kigen fell behind soon after 7 miles and Jones was on his own. De Castella led the pursuing pack which also included Robleh. Jones did not have the help Lopes had in setting the pace; nevertheless, he went through 15 km in 43:52 (previous 5 km in 14:22!) and halfway in 61:43 – the fastest split ever.

It was too fast, however. He lost ground to Lopes all through the second half. By 30 km he was only 79 seconds ahead. The 5 km between 25 and 30 km took 15:10 and the next 5 km 15:19. His time at 40 km was 1:59:53 (5 km in 15:54) and although he did not run slower than 5 minutes per mile before mile 21, all his remaining miles were slower than that.

Jones found it increasingly hard to maintain his rhythm, yet succeeded in picking up the pace when he came into the finishing straight and saw how close he was to the record. "I realized that I still had a chance at the record. So I sprinted." It was not to be, however, and he missed Lopes's time by a scant one second. Robleh set a new Africa record in third. Chicago became only the fifth race ever with three runners under 2:09:00.

RESULT:  1  Steve Jones 2:07:13
2  Djama Robleh 2:08:08
3  Robert de Castella 2:08:48

Jones's mile splits showed quite a different pacing pattern from the previous year's event: 4:46, 4:42, 4:48, 4:43, 4:59, 4:34, 4:39, 4:37, 4:39, 4:38, 4:44, 4:42, 4:44, 4:50, 4:51, 4:54, 4:51, 4:54, 4:54, 4:57, 5:02, 5:07, 5:06, 5:05, 5:13.

The Welshman was not too disappointed with his near miss. "I didn't get the bonus for the record, but I picked up a bit of money for winning the race. The money and the fame are irrelevant, really. I'm just a hamstring injury away from oblivion; you've got to look at it like that."

Reliable sources indicated that Jones's earnings in the race, including appearance money, prize money and time incentives, were $88 000. On top of this, he probably also received a large bonus from his shoe company, Reebok. De Castella took home about $51 000. In contrast, American Joan Benoit-Samuelson, who won the women's race in 2:21:21 and received a larger appearance fee than Jones, earned $108 000.

Seven days later Pizzolato won a hot New York for the second consecutive time, in 2:11:34, after having passed the front-running Salah in the 25th mile. Nijboer was fifth and Rodgers seventh (2:15:33).

Fukuoka did not have the resources to compete with the big-money US races, and Japanese runners dominated again. The time was slightly faster than in 1984, Masanari Shintaku winning in 2:09:51.

The year ended with a record ten times faster than

2:09:00 and, of course, a record two performances faster than 2:08:00. The other sub-2:09 not mentioned above was the 2:08:58 national record which gave South African Mark Plaatjes his country's title in Port Elizabeth. (See Chapter 8.)

Jones deservedly ranked first in the world, followed by Lopes and Salah.

The first major marathon of 1986 was Tokyo, and Ikangaa improved on his PB when he won in 2:08:10 and led three other runners under 2:09:00 – the first time this had happened. He was followed by another new face from Africa, Ethiopian Belayneh Dinsamo, who ran 2:08:29 in his first outing over the distance. His countryman Mekonnen was third in 2:08:39 and Nakayama fourth in 2:08:43. Ikangaa pulled away from Nakayama at 39 km, and then the two Ethiopians also passed the Japanese. Lopes had dropped out at 18 km. It was a brilliant start to the year, but more was to follow, and both Ikangaa and Mekonnen would run two more very fast races.

Scarcely two months later Mekonnen won Rotterdam in 2:09:08, beating Dinsamo by one second. They were the only two runners under 2:11:00. The very next day Seko showed that he had put the Los Angeles disappointment behind him when he scored an easy 2:10:02 victory in London. A day later, across the Atlantic, it was time for Boston.

For the first time the venerable race offered prize money. Both male and female winners would receive $30 000 plus a new Mercedes Benz. (The irony was that both winners ran the televised race in Mazda Track Club vests!) There was a $50 000 bonus for a world record and $25 000 for a course record, as well as cumulative time bonuses.

De Castella, who after losing to Jones in Chicago had said, "I've been very consistent, but I hope next time I'm not consistent and that I run a PR", set a tough pace from the gun and was alone at the head of the field after 20 km (even Itoh could not stay with him). Deek reached halfway in 63:38. At 15 miles he was still behind Smith's course record pace (by 30 seconds), but he ran the hills like a man possessed and went through 30 km in 90:28. The next two sections of 5 km took only 15:23 and 15:14 (40 km in 2:01:05) and at the finish he had achieved his goal: a new PB of 2:07:51 and a victory by more than 3 minutes. "I'm pleased . . . it might just be my best run ever," he declared.

The time was of course also a yearly world leader and it earned the Australian $60 000. Rodgers finished fourth in 2:13:36, his best in two years, one place ahead of debutant Arturo Barrios MEX, who earlier in the year had set a world record of 27:41 for 10 km.

In May the South African title race on the Port Elizabeth course produced the number two and number four times on the world list for the year when Zithulele Sinqe won in 2:08:04 with Willie Mtolo second in 2:08:15. (See Chapter 8.)

Two regional championships were held in August, but neither was very exciting. On the first day of the month Edinburgh hosted the Commonwealth Games marathon. A total of 32 African and Caribbean nations (out of the 58 Commonwealth countries) boycotted the festival because the British government did not impose strong economic sanctions against South Africa (which was not a member of the Commonwealth). Among the boycotters were Kenya, Tanzania, Nigeria and Jamaica. De Castella had no trouble in retaining his title with a victory in 2:10:15 over a lacklustre field. The only significant aspect of the race was the appearance of the next great Australian star, Steve Moneghetti.

RESULT:
1 Robert de Castella AUS 2:10:15
2 David Edge CAN 2:11:08
3 Stephen Moneghetti AUS 2:11:18
4 John Graham Sco 2:12:10
5 Art Boileau CAN 2:12:58
6 Philip O'Brien Eng 2:14:54

On the penultimate day of the month the European Championships marathon was run in Stuttgart. Jones "did a Chicago" by going out hard in his first championship marathon. He ran the second 5 km in 14:27 – much too fast in the humid conditions. His time at 10 km was 30:11 and when he went through 15 km in 45:02 he was 90 seconds in front. His 27 pursuers were led by Italian Gelindo Bordin, who had never won a marathon in eight starts. With Bordin was his countryman Pizzolato, winner of the previous two New York marathons. The Italians started cutting Jones's lead over the second half, and they were helped by the Welshman falling victim to his own impetuous pace and the heat. By 30 km (91:49) Jones was struggling desperately and the Italians were only 64 seconds behind.

Over the next 5 km the race took a dramatic turn. The Italian duo passed Jones and when he reached 35 km (1:49:08) he was eighth! The bearded Bordin sprinted away from his countryman, who had done all the hard work to catch the leader, over the last 150 m. He had covered the distance from 40 km in 6:55.

RESULT:
1 Gelindo Bordin ITA 2:10:54
2 Orlando Pizzolato ITA 2:10:57
3 Herbert Steffny FRG 2:11:30
4 Ralf Salzmann FRG 2:11:41
5 Hugh Jones GBR 2:11:49
6 Gerard Nijboer NED 2:12:46

Steve Jones finished a painful 20th in 2:22:12.

On 28 September Mekonnen ran his third fast marathon of the year when he won in Montreal in 2:10:31.

October was the second "marathon month" of the year and it produced two magnificent races in Asia. On the fifth day the year's third regional championship marathon was held at the Asian Games in Seoul. Nakayama wanted to improve on both his time and position in the Tokyo event and he did so admirably. He won easily in a scintillating 2:08:21, beating Hiromi Taniguchi JPN (2:10:08). It was the fastest time ever in a major Games marathon and the third fastest of 1985, but fourteen days later Nakayama was relegated to fifth!

Many observers were immediately sceptical when the results of the Beijing marathon were circulated around the world. Taisuke Kodama JPN had gone into the race with a PB of 2:10:34 set earlier in the year in Beppu, yet he won in a time that was almost unbelievable: 2:07:35, the third fastest ever! He was followed by Itoh, who cut his PB from 2:09:35 all the way to 2:07:57, the fifth fastest time ever.

RESULT:
1 Taisuke Kodama 2:07:35
2 Kunimitsu Itoh 2:07:57
3 Juma Ikangaa 2:08:39

It was the first time that the 2:08:00 barrier had been broken twice in the same race. The times were greeted with incredulity, but in *Athletics: The International Track and Field Annual 1987* the well-known marathon authority Roger Gynn wrote: "The route . . . had been accurately measured but when the results were published it appeared that the markers at 20 km and 40 km were, in all likelihood, wrongly placed. The very fast times . . . were attributed to exceptional weather conditions and the ultra fast course, little concern being apparent over the fact that Kodama had improved by a startling 2:59 and Itoh, a veteran of some 20 marathons in nine years, by 1:38 from his best which dated back to 1981!" (The latter date should have been 1983.)

In the 1991 *Annual* it was stated that "intensive investigation by Tatsumi Senda has led him to the conclusion that the Beijing course has been c. 400 m short", but the times were retained in the all-time list. In a letter to the author dated 29 June 1993 Peter Matthews, editor of the *Annual*, wrote: "With regard to the Beijing marathon – we just do not know. The Chinese authorities still recognise times made in the race, and we just do not know whether the course has been measured according to AIMS methods – probably not? The problem is that while Mr Senda's work showed clearly that the split times did not make sense and that there had to be a shortfall of some 400 m if the previous placings of kilometre points were correct, that did not mean that the overall race distance was necessarily short – it might simply have been that the intermediate points were out."

Seko was probably sorry that he did not take part in this fast race. Seven days later he ran his first sub-2:09 time since 1983 when he won in Chicago, his second major win of the year. He beat Salah, 2:08:27 against 2:09:57, with Spedding third in 2:10:13. Rodgers finished 11th in 2:15:31.

A week later the New York marathon was held in November for the first time, and Poli beat De Castella, who was running his third marathon in seven months, 2:11:06

against 2:11:43. Pizzolato was third. For the first time more than 20 000 runners started.

The race was called "Car Wars". There had been a major controversy after both Ingrid Kristiansen and De Castella were photographed in Mazda track suits with their Mercedes cars following their wins in Boston. The Mercedes people, who were putting huge amounts of money into the sport, naturally felt slighted and Fred Lebow, organiser of the New York City marathon, did not want to alienate the German manufacturer. De Castella was allegedly paid $40 000 to wear the Mazda logo in New York, but after negotiations between the parties it was agreed to reduce the logo to an almost insignificant size.

In Fukuoka Ikangaa scored his own second big victory, clocking 2:10:06.

In terms of depth it was not the best year ever (only sixteen sub-2:10 times compared to 21 in 1983), but at the top the two "B's" – Beijing and Boston – made it an unforgettable year. There were twelve times faster than 2:09:00, the most ever.

The year 1986 was also significant for the congress of AIMS held in Berlin in September. It was decided that a marathon course should not be one centimetre short, but that it could be slightly long – a maximum of 42 metres. The congress decided that it was possible to establish official world records for the marathon provided certain criteria were met. One of the criteria was that the drop in altitude between start and finish should not exceed 42 metres.

Money played an ever bigger role in the sport. The top runners tended to avoid one another – "the prime cause could only have been money," wrote Gynn, "and the wheeling and dealing of the entrepreneurs in their greedy attempts to buy the biggest names for their particular races, to which Boston succumbed . . . Now only Fukuoka remains out in the cold, and one wonders for how much longer that classic can afford to stay aloof from the rabble." Gynn's conclusion was that money was "rightly beneficial" to the runners, but that it was "possibly detrimental" to the sport.

Ikangaa's two victories and fast time in Beijing gave him first place on the ranking list. He was followed by De Castella and three Japanese, Kodama, Seko and Itoh.

The Tokyo marathon of 1987 did not provide the same fireworks as the previous edition, with Taniguchi winning in 2:10:06. Nakayama was second in 2:10:33. The winning time, almost 2 minutes slower than Ikangaa's in 1986, was in fact an indication of what the overall standard for the rest of the year was to be. The world had to wait until 10 May for the first sub-2:10 of the year when the same runner won the London marathon in a PB. The race in the British capital was a remarkable and closely fought one: Spedding ran 2:10:32 and finished only eighth.

| RESULT: | 1 | Hiromi Taniguchi 2:09:50 |
|---|---|---|
| | 2 | Mustapha Nechchadi MAR 2:10:09 |
| | 3 | Hugh Jones 2:10:11 |
| | 4 | Gianni Poli 2:10:15 |
| | 5 | Geir Kvernmo NOR 2:10:17 |
| | 6 | Mehmet Terzi TUR 2:10:25 |
| | 7 | Boguslaw Psujek POL 2:10:26 |
| | 8 | Charles Spedding 2:10:32 |

The only other times that would make the top ten for the year were Taniguchi's in Tokyo and the Fukuoka winning time (see below).

A month earlier Salah had won the World Cup marathon again (in 2:10:55), but this time he had had no support and Italy had taken the team title. Kodama, a shadow of the man who had run sub-2:08 the year before, could only manage 2:11:23 in second.

Rotterdam and Boston were held in the traditional mid-April weekend. The former went to Dinsamo in 2:12:58 and the latter to Seko in 2:11:50. Six days later Lismont showed that he could still run well when he won in Hamburg in 2:13:46.

Eight days before the London marathon the South African championship had been decided on a standard, point-to-point course for the first time since 1983. The race was at Stellenbosch, and Sinqe and Mtolo again finished one-two, but in 2:10:51 and 2:11:01. (See Chapter 8.)

The second World Championship race was held in Rome on 6 September. It was hot and humid when the 65 starters were led out of the stadium by the irrepressible Ikangaa, but he was soon overtaken by Canadian Peter Maher. The race was run almost entirely within the Aurelian Walls, which marked the perimeter of imperial Rome at its largest. The pace was not very fast, yet Maher was 300 m ahead of the field when he went through halfway in 65:37.

By this time top runners like defending champion De Castella, Robleh, Smith and Mekonnen were suffering in the conditions and would all fail to finish. The six-man chasing group started cutting Maher's lead and by 25 km (after 5 km in 15:56 by Maher) they were only 50 m behind. Less than 3 km further the pack – Ikangaa, Tefera Guta ETH, Hugh Jones, Jorgensen, Moneghetti and an unknown Kenyan – caught and passed Maher.

The Kenyan was 23-year-old Douglas Wakiihuri, running his third marathon. He had travelled to New Zealand to find a coach and then went to Japan, where he came under the tutelage of Seko's coach, Nakamura. At the time of the World Championships he was living in Tokyo; he spoke English, Swahili and Japanese. His best was 2:13:34, run in Beppu in February (and before that 2:16:26).

At 30 km Ikangaa led in 94:08. By 35 km (Moneghetti in front in 1:49:45) the lead pack had grown to seven as Bordin, who had been coming from quite a distance back, joined them. This acted as a warning for the others and

Wakiihuri, Salah and Moneghetti quickly broke away. Bordin could not respond; he had expended too much energy in working his way up to the front. Soon Moneghetti also had to let go.

Just before 38 km Wakiihuri accelerated away from the more experienced World Cup winner. He passed 40 km in 2:04:58 and at the finish he had created a gap of 42 seconds. The winning time was unexceptional, but it was a PB by more than 1½ minutes. Behind him Bordin delighted the home crowd by passing Moneghetti for the bronze – just 10 seconds short of silver.

RESULT:
1  Douglas Wakiihuri KEN 2:11:48
2  Ahmed Salah DJI 2:12:30
3  Gelindo Bordin ITA 2:12:40
4  Stephen Moneghetti AUS 2:12:49
5  Hugh Jones GBR 2:12:54
6  Juma Ikangaa TAN 2:13:43
7  Orlando Pizzolato ITA 2:14:03
8  Ravil Kashapov URS 2:14:41
9  Henrik Jorgensen DEN 2:14:58
10 Dirk van der Herten BEL 2:16:42

European champion Bordin had run well despite faulty pace judgement, but his biggest moment was still in the future.

The Beijing marathon this time produced a very ordinary winning time: Ikangaa's 2:12:19. In second place Negash Dube ETH ran a world junior best of 2:12:49.[13]

On 1 November another Kenyan, Ibrahim Hussein, won New York in 2:11:01. After the relative stagnation of the early eighties, the field was growing again: this time the finishers (21 244) were more than 20 000 for the first time.

The fastest race of the year took place in Fukuoka on 6 December. Race day was rainy and windy, but it did not bother Nakayama. He had waited since February to avenge his defeat by Taniguchi. He was on his own after 15 km and passed halfway in 61:55 – an amazing 1:29 faster than Lopes had run in his world record. But the weather and the lack of competition was against him (he was more than 700 m ahead at 35 km) and he slowed to 2:08:18 – 3 seconds slower than his PB but the world's fastest time for 1987. It equalled De Castella's 1981 course record – a world record at the time.

Shintaku was second in 2:10:34, Dinsamo fifth and Taniguchi a disappointing sixth. Kodama again failed, running 2:16:49 for 24th. The world record holder for 10000 m on the track, Mamede, did not finish his first marathon. Seko was absent because of an ankle fracture. Nakayama and Shintaku were selected for the Japanese team

for the Olympic Games in Seoul, with one place left open.

Japan was clearly the top marathoning nation with 118 performances faster than 2:20:00 for the year, followed by the USA with 95.

Questionable status was accorded the times run in Venice (Salvatore Bettiol ITA first in 2:10:01) and Belaja Cerkov (Igor Braslavskiy URS first in 2:10:05 and six others under 2:12:00).

Not surprisingly, Nakayama was ranked first for the year, followed by Taniguchi and Wakiihuri.

The year 1988 was to be another significant one in the annals of the marathon. As was the case in 1986 the first fast time of the year was clocked in Tokyo, on 14 February, when Mekonnen just beat Ikangaa after a tough battle. Two more runners were under 2:09:00 – equalling the achievement of the 1986 edition of the race and setting the tone for the year.

RESULT:
1  Abebe Mekonnen 2:08:33
2  Juma Ikangaa 2:08:42
3  Jörg Peter 2:08:47
4  Robert de Castella 2:08:49

Mekonnen was to have as busy a year as in 1986, and an even better one. De Castella, however, would not run faster than here. Peter's time was a national record. Wakiihuri was seventh, but he was also to run better later in the year.

Early in March Martin Mondragon MEX won the Los Angeles marathon in 2:10:19, but more interesting were the two men in 21st and 59th places: Bill Rodgers (2:20:29) and Lasse Viren (2:27:31).

The third weekend in April was again Marathon Weekend, with the Rotterdam and London events both on 17 April. In London, the selection race for the British team to the Olympic Games in Seoul, a foreigner took the honours. Jorgensen won in 2:10:20, with Kevin Forster GBR second in 2:10:52.

The race was rather unspectacular (except that it had more than 20 000 finishers), but then everything else in 1988 would be in the shadow of what was happening that same day across the English Channel. The 1985 Rotterdam race had shown what the course in the Dutch city was capable of. This time a group of extremely talented African runners lined up with Lopes's world record firmly in their sights. Ethiopia had decided to boycott the Olympics and its marathoners came to Rotterdam to show the world that they were the best. In windless conditions five Ethiopians, Itoh, Salah and two pacesetters went through 5 km in 15:05 and 10 km in 30:05. They were one second slower than Lopes in his record race.

The Ethiopians included Dinsamo, the 23-year-old policeman who had won the year before and whose best was the 2:08:29 he ran for second in the 1986 Tokyo marathon (his debut), Mekonnen and Wodajo Bulti, who

13. This time was equalled by his compatriot Tesfayi Dadi in the 1988 Berlin marathon. At the time of writing these performances still stand as the world record.

had run 27:29.41 for 10000 m the year before. He was contesting his first marathon.

At 15 km, reached in 45:06, they were 21 seconds faster than Lopes, but they lost this over the next 5 km, which Lopes had covered in 14:43 (his fastest split of the entire race). The leaders went through this point in 60:12 (Lopes 60:10). They covered the next 5 km in 15:00 – but Lopes had done so in 14:47! They lost another 2 seconds to 30 km, but then cut back 9 seconds with a 15:09 split to 35 km. At this point Salah threw in a surge, but Dinsamo went with him. Mekonnen and Bulti could not maintain the pace, leaving the other two to fight it out. Dinsamo proved the stronger and by 40 km, where he clocked 2:00:20 (14 seconds faster than Lopes), he had a lead of 25 m. He covered the last 2.195 km in a scintillating 6:30 and was rewarded with a new world record of 2:06:50. His two halves were almost even – the most efficient way to run a marathon – at 63:22 and 63:28.

In second place Salah also broke Lopes's record, again confirming the merits of the course. Bulti set a new world best for a debut marathon. The depth of performances, however, was rather disappointing, with only these three running sub-2:09.

RESULT:

| | |
|---|---|
| 1 | Belayneh Dinsamo 2:06:50 |
| 2 | Ahmed Salah 2:07:07 |
| 3 | Wodajo Bulti 2:08:44 |
| 4 | Abebe Mekonnen 2:09:33 |

The next day African runners also reigned supreme in Boston, albeit in slower times. The race was the Olympic trial for Kenyan and Tanzanian athletes. Hussein added the crown to the one he had won at New York in 1987 when he broke away from Ikangaa in the final 100 m to win by one second in a national record 2:08:43. Hussein was Boston's first African winner. Behind them came a host of famous names, among them Treacy 2:09:15 (national record), Bordin 2:09:27 (national record) and Steve Jones 2:14:07, as well as Shahanga and Rodgers (2:18:17).

There were no further fast times before the Olympic marathon, which took place in Seoul, South Korea, on 2 October (there would still be a number of fast times in October after the Games, though).

For the first time more than 9 000 contestants from 159 nations[14] vied for Olympic honour. The Games were opened on 17 September. North Korea boycotted the proceedings and was joined by Ethiopia and Cuba, among others. Despite marvellous performances the Games of the 24th Olympiad will forever be remembered by the Ben Johnson steroid scandal. The Canadian won the 100 m in an almost unbelievable 9.79 seconds, but a few days later he was dis-

14. There were actually 160, but the Brunei delegation, which marched in the opening ceremonies, did not include any competitors.

qualified after he had tested positive for stanozolol, an anabolic steroid. The gold medal went to Carl Lewis, who also won the long jump, thus becoming the first man to score repeat wins in these events. The 800, 1500, steeplechase and 5000 m were all won by Kenyans (a Moroccan took the 10000). After having won seven Olympic, World Championship and World Cup titles in the 400 m hurdles Edwin Moses could only manage third this time. Among the women the star was the stunning Florence (Flojo) Griffith Joyner, who had set a phenomenal world record of 10.49 for 100 m in the US Olympic trials. In Seoul she won this event with ease and four days later set a world record of 21.34 in also winning the 200 m (after an American record in the quarterfinals and a world record 21.56 in the semifinals!). All but one of the other women's track events went to runners from Eastern bloc countries. Jackie Joyner-Kersee, Flojo's sister-in-law, won both the long jump and the heptathlon, the latter in a world record.

The marathon started in the stadium, in hot and humid weather. It was clear that fast times would not be possible. The favourites were world champion Wakiihuri, European champion Bordin, Salah and Hussein, but there were also De Castella, Seko, Nakayama and Ikangaa.

Ikangaa led the 118 runners out of the stadium and controlled the pace for much of the first half. Halfway was reached by a group of twenty in 64:49, with Mondragon leading. Over the next 4 km the pack thinned out to thirteen and Ikangaa led again at 25 km (76:57). Hussein had dropped out.

De Castella and his countryman Moneghetti were not comfortable and when Bordin increased the tempo they dropped behind. The Italian went past 30 km in 92:49 and a kilometre later Seko also had to let go. The pack now numbered only six: Bordin, Nakayama, Salah, Ikangaa, Wakiihuri and the surprising Spedding.

At 35 km, reached in 1:48:25, Nakayama and Salah were in front. Soon after, Spedding could not keep up and then Ikangaa faded. When Nakayama also fell off the pace only the three medallists from the last World Championships remained. The conditions were much the same as in that race, which Ikangaa had also led for a considerable distance (he finished sixth). Would the Rome order of Wakiihuri, Salah, Bordin change this time? Who would handle the conditions and the last 7 km best?

In the 37th kilometre, which was slightly downhill, the two Africans surged and opened a gap on Bordin, who was suffering from leg cramps. Salah kept the heat on and Wakiihuri let him go. At 39 km Salah was 20 m in front of the Kenyan and 40 m ahead of Bordin. Was the race over?

Then the tough Italian came back. With Wakiihuri "a little bit tired", Bordin took over second spot before 40 km and started chasing Salah, who was struggling. The Djiboutian could sense Bordin coming and called on his reserves to stay in front. At 40.5 km he glanced over his left shoulder and then his right and saw his rival just 3 metres behind. This completely demoralised Salah and within 50 m he was beaten. As Bordin raced toward the stadium Wakiihuri also went past the luckless Salah – and even Nakayama was gaining on him.

Bordin smiled as he ran around the track and waved to the crowd. Immediately past the finish he knelt down and kissed the track. Fifteen seconds later Wakiihuri arrived in a PB. It was the closest Olympic marathon since Hannes Kolehmainen had won by 12.8 seconds in 1920. Salah barely managed to stay among the medallists.

RESULT:
1  Gelindo Bordin ITA 2:10:32
2  Douglas Wakiihuri KEN 2:10:47
3  Ahmed Salah DJI 2:10:59
4  Takeyuki Nakayama JPN 2:11:05
5  Stephen Moneghetti AUS 2:11:49
6  Charles Spedding GBR 2:12:19
7  Juma Ikangaa TAN 2:13:06
8  Robert de Castella AUS 2:13:07
9  Toshihiko Seko JPN 2:13:41
10 Ravil Kashapov URS 2:13:49

Jogging a victory lap, Bordin said: "I'm too tired even to be happy." Salah, who had won the World Cup race on the same course, said that his shoelaces were too tight, otherwise he would have won. Among the runners who did not finish were Peter and Treacy. The last finisher was Polin Belisle from Belize in 3:14:02 (see also p. 109).

Having finished in the first three in the last two major

## THREE UNIQUE ACHIEVEMENTS

Gelindo Bordin has three unique distinctions: He is the only Olympic marathon champion ever to have won the Boston marathon, he is the only man to have won both the European and Olympic marathons, and he is the only male runner to have retained the European title. He became European champion in 1986, Olympic victor in 1988 and won both Boston and the European race two years later.

Bordin, born in Longare on 2 April 1959, first appeared on the international scene when he finished fifth in the 10000 metres in the 1979 World Student Games. He ran his first marathon on 7 October 1984 in Milan, winning in 2:13:20. He lost his next three marathons (the 1985 World Cup, the 1985 European Cup and the 1986 Italian championship), but then took the European title in a PB 2:10:53.4.

In his first attempt at the Boston marathon, in 1988, he finished fourth but ran a national record of 2:09:27. Two years later he returned and this time he succeeded and ran into history, setting another Italian record (2:08:19) in the process.

His win in Seoul came eighty years after the ill-fated "victory" by countryman Dorando Pietri in London.

Bordin always raced sparingly, contesting only two marathons each in the years 1985-1988 and only one (third in New York) in 1989. In 1990 his Boston win came in the first of his three marathons that year. The average of his five fastest marathons is 2:09:46.4.

international championship events, with each having won once, Bordin and Wakiihuri could justly claim to being the world's most successful competitors of the second half of the decade. It is true, of course, that Dinsamo was not in Seoul – neither was Mekonnen, or the men who were to win New York and Chicago later in the year.

At the end of the year Dinsamo would be ranked first by *Track & Field News*, followed by Bordin, Salah, Mekonnen, Ikangaa, Wakiihuri and Jones.

Two more major marathons were held in October. Two weeks after the Olympic race Mekonnen and Taniguchi duelled in Beijing. It was almost a replica of the 1986 race – the winning time was exactly the same – with the winning margin considerably less. The 24-year-old Mekonnen, running in his 19th marathon, sped past Taniguchi after 41 km and finished in 2:07:35 – five seconds ahead and a PB by 58 seconds. Compared to men like Lopes, Salazar, Nakayama and Jones the first two were slow 10000 m runners: Mekonnen had just barely broken 29:00 and Taniguchi had not broken 28:30. Yet they were less than a minute slower than the world record. Takeshi Soh was third in 2:10:30.

A further two weeks later Alejando Cruz MEX, unknown and only twenty years old, won Chicago in 2:08:57. It was more than 4 minutes faster than his PB. He surged away from the opposition with a 4:42 20th mile. "When it was time to go, I went," he said afterwards. The first seven runners set personal bests and the first two national records.

RESULT:
1  Alejandro Cruz 2:08:57
2  Yakov Tolstikov URS 2:09:20
3  Richard Kaitany KEN 2:09:39

A week later it was time for New York. The field had grown to more than 23 000. One of them was Jones, who wanted to regain some lost prestige. He had retired from the RAF and recovered from injury. His disappointing Boston run had resulted in his being left out of the British Olympic team. Later he was asked to run, but declined because he felt that the request had come too late. Now he was ready for a fast time again. He threw down the gauntlet to Treacy, Shahanga and the others by speeding the 14th mile in 4:47 and the 17th in 4:28. "I just put my head down . . . and I never looked back," he said later.

He reached the finish in 2:08:20 – a course record. He regarded it as his best race ever and his friend Treacy commented that it was probably worth around 2:06:00 on the much faster Rotterdam course. Jones was now the only man to have won Chicago, London and New York.

Salvatore Bettiol ITA was second in 2:11:41. Rodgers failed to finish.

In Fukuoka Toshihiro Shibutani produced the slowest winning time since 1976 when he clocked 2:11:04. It was quite a change from the marvellous 1983 event – in fact, the race would not see a sub-2:09 again until 1993.

It was a remarkable year: a record thirteen times under 2:09:00 were achieved and two races each produced two sub-2:08s, also a record for a single year. The twenty sub-2:10s were one less than the 1983 total.

With no major championship titles to be won in 1989 (except the World Cup), it was to be an "off" year. Taniguchi won Tokyo by almost 3 minutes in 2:09:34 and Dinsamo repeated his Rotterdam victory in a time almost 2 minutes slower than in 1988: 2:08:40. Cruz, who had led until 32 km (when stomach cramps slowed him down), was an excellent second in 2:09:25 with Dutchman Martin ten Kate third in a PB 2:10:04. The times were affected by a troublesome wind.

On the same day an almost unknown Ethiopian showed his country's immense depth by winning the World Cup event in Milan. Metaferia Zeleke, winner of the 20 km at the World Junior Championships the previous year, ran 2:10:28. He beat compatriot Dereje Nedi (35) by 8 seconds and Ethiopia took the team title.

The next day Mekonnen won Boston in 2:09:06, beating the equally peripatetic Ikangaa (2:09:56). The leading pack (Ikangaa, Mekonnen, Hussein and Simon Robert Naali TAN) set a new course record of 62:23 at halfway and the winner only went ahead in the final 2 km.

Six days later London was a battle royal. Conditions were excellent and Salah, Moneghetti and Wakiihuri made full use of them as they led the field after the first half (covered in 64:42). The trio stayed together until the 26th mile marker as the suspense mounted. Who would kick first?

It was Wakiihuri. But the other two went with him. The finish line was looming ahead when the Kenyan found that little bit extra, accelerated again and drew away to win in a PB. Moneghetti's time was also his best.

RESULT:
1 Douglas Wakiihuri 2:09:03
2 Stephen Moneghetti 2:09:06
3 Ahmed Salah 2:09:09
4 Manuel Matias POR 2:09:43
5 Suleiman Nyambui TAN 2:09:52
6 Tony Milovsorov GBR 2:09:54

It was only the second time that a race had produced six runners under 2:10:00. In seventh Pat Petersen, who had been fourth in New York in 1987, clocked 2:10:04 – the fastest time by an American since Salazar ran 2:09:21 in the 1983 Fukuoka race.

The London marathon was selected to host the 1991 World Cup race – the first time the international event would be held in conjunction with an existing race.

The only other race of the year to produce a sub-2:10 winning time – sub-2:09 and the fastest of the year, in fact – was New York. It was run on 5 November. Ikangaa, who had last won in Beijing in 1987 and had set an Africa record of 2:08:55 in 1983, was intent on dipping under 2:08:00. But he faced the world record holder, the Olympic champion, the defending champion, previous winner Poli, and new American hopeful Ken Martin, a converted steeplechaser. Also in the field was South African Mark Plaatjes, who had immigrated to the USA in the hopes of competing internationally (something which his country's sports isolation prevented him from doing).

When someone commented to Jones that his knowledge of the course might help him, he answered: "I can't remember a single bit of it."

Ikangaa, who had finished second in Boston three times in a row, this time did not lead early but was part of a pack which covered the first half in 63:44. With the Tanzanian were all the big names: Jones, Dinsamo, Bettiol, Poli and Plaatjes. Then Jones, in a repeat of the previous year's race, surged. On this occasion, however, it was not going to be so easy. Ikangaa went with him – and went ahead. He knew that he was vulnerable in a sprint finish. He ran the 14th mile in 4:34.

"He ran incredibly," Jones later said. "He looked so good, it was demoralising."

There was no stopping the flying Tanzanian army major. He won in 2:08:01, a course record, PB and national record. He was elated, winning a Mercedes Benz for his efforts and finally satisfying an important member of his family: "My mother had complained that I never win the car."

Ikangaa had prepared at high-altitude Alamosa and ascribed his success to this, as well as to running a more even pace than usual. He had been "learning from my mistakes", he said afterwards.

The untested 31-year-old Martin, who had reportedly been offered a very small appearance fee, was second in the first sub-2:10 by an American since 1983 – and received an adjustment in his fee. Bordin finished strongly, but ran out of ground and required medical attention afterwards. Jones was eighth in 2:12:58 and Dinsamo one place behind in 2:13:42.

RESULT:
1 Juma Ikangaa 2:08:01
2 Ken Martin 2:09:38
3 Gelindo Bordin 2:09:40

Briton Paul Davies-Hale won Chicago in 2:11:25 and Matias a wind-plagued Fukuoka in an even slower 2:12:54. Kashapov was second in the same time – a rare occurrence in a premier marathon. Earlier, in August, Ten Kate had broken the ten-year-old Enschede course record when he clocked 2:10:57.

Ikangaa was deservedly ranked first for the year, followed by Mekonnen (who had slumped to seventh in Fukuoka), Wakiihuri, Dinsamo and Moneghetti.

The decade closed with no runner from the seventies on the all-time performers list but, amazingly, Clayton's 1969 time still made the top twenty!

| | | | |
|---|---|---|---|
| 2:06:50 | Belayneh Dinsamo ETH | 1988 | |
| 2:07:07 | Ahmed Salah DJI | 1988 | |
| 2:07:12 | Carlos Lopes POR | 1985 | |
| 2:07:13 | Steve Jones GBR | 1985 | |
| 2:07:35 | Taisuke Kodama JPN | 1986 | |
| 2:07:35 | Abebe Mekonnen ETH | 1988 | |
| 2:07:40 | Hiromi Taniguchi JPN | 1988 | |
| 2:07:51 | Robert de Castella AUS | 1986 | |
| 2:07:57 | Kunimitsu Itoh JPN | 1986 | |
| 2:08:01 | Juma Ikangaa TAN | 1989 | (10) |
| 2:08:04 | Zithulele Sinqe RSA | 1986 | |
| 2:08:08 | Djama Robleh DJI | 1985 | |
| 2:08:15 | Takeyuki Nakayama JPN | 1985 | |
| 2:08:15 | Willie Mtolo RSA | 1986 | |
| 2:08:27 | Toshihiko Seko JPN | 1986 | |
| 2:08:33 | Charles Spedding GBR | 1985 | |
| 2:08:34 | Derek Clayton AUS | 1969 | |
| 2:08:43 | Ibrahim Hussein KEN | 1988 | |
| 2:08:44 | Wodajo Bulti ETH | 1988 | |
| 2:08:47 | Jörg Peter GDR | 1988 | (20) |

Apart from Clayton's performance all the other times on the list were set in 1985 or later. Another interesting aspect of the all-time performances list was that the top thirty times had been run by only seventeen athletes, with Jones appearing four times, De Castella and Nakayama three times each, and Ikangaa, Seko, Mekonnen, Salah, Robleh and Dinsamo twice each. Of those seventeen seven were Africans and five Japanese – those with one performance each were Lopes, Kodama, Taniguchi, Itoh, Sinqe, Mtolo, Spedding and Clayton.

When *Track & Field News* asked road-racing writer Jack Welch to choose the marathoners of the decade, he named Alberto Salazar and Joan Benoit. Motivating the choice which he admitted was "personal stuff", he described Salazar's two titanic duels with Dick Beardsley in Boston and Rodolfo Gomez in New York. "The Finns call it *sisu*. In Japanese, it's *konjo*. Guts. A defiance of defeat as much as a determination to win. Surely there have been faster runners, athletes with golden prizes. But there is only one Salazar."

# 7

# *1990-1995*
# STRIKING CHANGES

MARATHONING IN THE nineties has been characterised by a wider global growth of interest in the sport. A number of major city races played an important role in this, but it was also influenced by larger amounts of money put into developing the sport, especially as far as coaching is concerned. The changing political scene also had an effect, because runners from Eastern European countries became free to venture beyond their borders and seek out fast races with large amounts of prize money. In 1991 all but four of the 59 sub-2:20 times by Polish runners were recorded outside Poland; seventy of the 135 Soviet sub-2:20s were run outside the Soviet Union.

The first major race of the new decade took place in Auckland on 30 January 1990 when the Commonwealth Games marathon was held in high humidity and warm weather. It was a closely fought contest on a flat point-to-point course, with the first three runners finishing within 11 seconds. Douglas Wakiihuri was the victor, but he had to run hard to hold off Steve Moneghetti and Simon Robert Naali. Wakiihuri only took the lead with 600 metres remaining. They were the only runners under 2:12:00.

RESULT:
1  Douglas Wakiihuri KEN 2:10:27
2  Stephen Moneghetti AUS 2:10:34
3  Simon Robert Naali TAN 2:10:38
4  Steve Jones GBR 2:12:44
5  Ibrahim Hussein KEN 2:13:20
6  Daniel Nzioka KEN 2:13:27

It was the fourth time that the Kenyan had beaten Moneghetti in a major marathon (the previous victories came in the World Championships, the Olympic Games and the London marathon, where the margin was only 3 seconds). Wakiihuri was an unknown when he won the world title in

Rome, and he remained an enigmatic figure all through his very successful career. He was born in Mombasa, but grew up at 2 000 m altitude. His home was about a mile from the school he attended, but he ran it four times a day: because the family was very poor he could not afford the school meals, so he ran home to eat lunch and then ran back to school for the afternoon session.

In 1982, at the age of nineteen, he came under the influence of Koyoshi Nakamura, the legendary coach of Toshihiko Seko, and moved to Japan. "You absorb the culture," he later said. "I was very happy with how I was brought up. Not by books, but by learning with my eyes and ears and head. Reading a book, you don't feel it."

He added: "I am Kenyan, but think and feel Japanese."

At his best he possessed an air of invincibility and had strong feelings about the marathon, once telling a reporter: "There is the truth about the marathon and very few of you have written the truth. Even if I explain it to you, you'll never understand it, you're outside of it."

A friend of both Wakiihuri and Ikangaa explained the difference between the two: "Ikangaa is a diplomat. When he's not running, he's watching CNN for hours. He understands *you* much better. Douglas understands *himself*."

Early in 1990 the US governing body, The Athletic Congress, decided that road courses would fall into three categories: a loop course, where the start and finish cannot be more than 30 per cent of the race distance apart, a point-to-point course that is not downhill (such as New York), and a point-to-point course that is downhill (such as Boston, with a drop of 139 m). The drop in elevation between start and finish cannot exceed more than 1 m/km.

The other important regional contests of the year were the European Championships in Split and the Asian Games in Beijing. The former race took place on 1 September, and

106

once again Gelindo Bordin took the gold medal. The conditions favoured him: the race was run in the tremendous heat of the afternoon, in what *Track & Field News* called "a travesty of scheduling for the unfortunate athletes".

The test of attrition over the difficult four-lap course was dominated by the defending champion and his countrymen Gianni Poli and Salvatore Bettiol – until Bettiol faded towards the end.

RESULT:
1 Gelindo Bordin ITA 2:14:02
2 Gianni Poli ITA 2:14:55
3 Dominique Chauvelier FRA 2:15:20
4 Salvatore Bettiol ITA 2:17:45
5 José Montiel SPA 2:17:51
6 Geoff Wightman GBR 2:18:01

The Asian Games marathon on 30 September was won by Korean Kim Won-tak in 2:12:56. In March he had also been first in the Seoul marathon (2:11:38).

On the same day the Berlin marathon produced the fastest race of the year. This time there was no one in front of Moneghetti, but his victory over Gidamis Shahanga was as close as some of his losses had been. The race was run over a new course which went through both sections of the once-divided city, starting under the Brandenburg Gate (there were 34 000 starters).

Moneghetti's 2:08:16 was a PB. Shahanga finished 16 seconds later, with the East German runners Jörg Peter and Stephan Freigang third and fourth in 2:09:23 and 2:09:45 respectively.

Earlier in the year, on 16 March – two weeks after Bordin's 31st birthday – he had become the first Olympic champion ever to win the Boston marathon. A foursome of Africans, including – of course – Juma Ikangaa, went through halfway in an insane 62:01. Bordin took the lead from Ikangaa in the 21st mile ("They run crazy. I just run by myself, control my pace," the Olympic winner said) and sped to the second fastest time ever on the course and second best time for the year: 2:08:19. Ikangaa was second in 2:09:52.

In fourth place the amazing 41-year-old New Zealander John Campbell set a world veterans' record of 2:11:04. He beat the previous record, set by his countryman Jack Foster in 1974, by 15 seconds. One place and 24 seconds behind him came Robert de Castella.

There were very few fireworks in London and Rotterdam (both run on 22 April). Allister Hutton GBR took the former in 2:10:10 (Belayneh Dinsamo did not finish) and Hiromi Taniguchi the latter in 2:10:56 (Abebe Mekonnen was second in 2:11:52).

There was yet a third city marathon on the same day: Shahanga won in Vienna in 2:09:28. His second place in Berlin later in the year made him the only runner with two sub-2:10 times in 1990. Only three other sub-2:10s were run during the course of the year. Martin Pitayo MEX and Antoni Niemczak POL[1] both clocked 2:09:41 in Chicago, but the Mexican was given the win. In February David Tsebe had won the South African title in Port Elizabeth in 2:09:50. (See Chapter 8.)

Bordin claimed his third big race of the year when he took the Venice marathon in October in 2:13:41 and Wakiihuri his second when he won New York in 2:12:39 (Ikangaa was fourth). Fifth-placer Campbell took the veterans' division in 2:14:34, a course record, and received a $75 000 bonus as the winner in Los Angeles, Boston and New York.

"Today is probably going to change my life," said the New Zealander, who used to work seven days a week in a convenience shop and trained "when it's convenient".

Dinsamo redeemed himself with a 2:11:35 win in Fukuoka, 2 seconds ahead of Tsutomu Hiroyama JPN.

Bordin's undefeated campaign gave him the top ranking for the year; Wakiihuri was second and Moneghetti third.

The standard of performances in 1991 was much the same as in the previous year, but there were two crucial international championships to contest: the World Championships and the World Cup.

The latter, run in conjunction with the London marathon on 21 April, produced by far the best race. Yakov Tolstikov URS won in a national record 2:09:17, beating Manuel Matias POR by 64 seconds. The first British runner, Dave Long, was fourth, but Great Britain won the team title.

The World Championships race was run in Tokyo on 1 September in very difficult conditions of heat and humidity, although the start was at 06:00 (24 of the sixty starters were to drop out). Wakiihuri was absent because of injury, as was Ikangaa.

Taniguchi was in the lead pack from early on. They reached 15 km in a slow 15:38, an indication of how the race would develop. Takeyuki Nakayama and Moneghetti were also in the group, which was joined by Mekonnen before 15 km (46:55). They went through halfway in 66:25. Shortly thereafter Taniguchi started testing his rivals with surges which gradually reduced the pack. When he accelerated at 30 km (1:35:34) only Futoshi Shinohara JPN and Jan Huruk POL went with him. Moneghetti and Nakayama dropped back, but Bettiol and Bordin made a valiant attempt to come back into the race. They rejoined the bunch, but at 37 km Taniguchi surged again. Ahmed Salah, who had been battling with an injury since the 1989 London race, Shinohara and Huruk all responded, but at 38 km Taniguchi accelerated for the final time and pulled away to win the gold medal in Tokyo's Olympic stadium. At 31 years, 150 days he became the oldest man to win the marathon title.

American Steve Spence, who called the conditions "like a

1. Niemczak had tested positive for steroids at the 1986 New York City marathon and received a two-year suspension. In 1995 he tested positive for the drug ephedrine after a second place finish in the Tokyo marathon.

sauna", ran an excellently judged race to win the bronze medal.

| RESULT: | 1 | Hiromi Taniguchi JPN 2:14:57 |
|---|---|---|
| | 2 | Ahmed Salah DJI 2:15:26 |
| | 3 | Steve Spence USA 2:15:36 |
| | 4 | Jan Huruk POL 2:15:47 |
| | 5 | Futoshi Shinohara JPN 2:15:52 |
| | 6 | Salvatore Bettiol ITA 2:15:58 |
| | 7 | Maurilio Castillo MEX 2:16:15 |
| | 8 | Gelindo Bordin ITA 2:17:03 |
| | 9 | Tekeye Gisilase ETH 2:18:37 |
| | 10 | Konrad Dobler GER 2:19:01 |

Among those who failed to finish were Mekonnen, Nakayama, Niemczak, Peter and Tolstikov.

The first sub-2:10 of 1991 was run on the thirteenth day of the year when Osmiro Souza Silva BRA won the Marrakech marathon in 2:09:55. The fastest race of the year followed on 3 February when Koichi Morishita JPN ran 2:08:53 in the Beppu-Oita marathon, beating Nakayama by 19 seconds. Toru Mimura JPN was third (2:09:23).

Six days before the World Cup Ibrahim Hussein won his second Boston marathon (his previous win was in 1988; in 1990 he did not finish). The pace was slow from the start ("I just wanted to avoid running crazy like we did last year," Hussein said afterwards), but Hussein, who had had a year's lay-off because of an Achilles injury, ran the 5 miles between 14 and 19 miles in 24:33 and won in 2:11:06. Mekonnen's late charge gave him second in 2:11:22; Wakiihuri was sixth. Ikangaa and John Treacy failed to finish. Johnny Kelley (83) ran his 60th and last Boston marathon in 5:42:54.

On the same day as the World Cup Robert de Castella scored his first major win since Boston in 1986 when he beat the new Mexican star, Dionicio Cerón, in Rotterdam. It was very cold – it actually snowed during the race – and De Castella had to run by himself after 20 km (60:27). It was the eighth time he had dipped under 2:10:00 and the sixth fastest time of the year. Dinsamo finished fifth in 2:11:34.

| RESULT: | 1 | Robert de Castella 2:09:42 |
|---|---|---|
| | 2 | Dionicio Cerón 2:10:02 |
| | 3 | Tesfaye Dadi ETH 2:10:08 |

The only other sub-2:10 time of the year came in New York, where Cerón's countryman Salvador García, second the previous year, won in 2:09:28. Another Mexican, Andrés Espinosa, was second (2:10:00) and Hussein third (2:11:07). For the first time more than 25 000 (25 797) finished. Josef Galia became, at the age of 93, the oldest finisher in the history of the race. He clocked 7:59:34.

On the first day of December Shuichi Morita JPN won the Fukuoka race, which had lost much of the prestige it had enjoyed in earlier years, in 2:10:58.

Taniguchi, who had been ninth in the February Tokyo marathon (won by Mekonnen), was ranked first for the year, followed by Mekonnen, despite his failure to finish the World Championships race (he was fourth in Fukuoka, though) and Huruk. Mekonnen had the best three-race average for the year: 2:11:09.

Another record by Foster fell during 1991 when South African Titus Mamabolo (born 7 January 1941) ran 2:19:29 in July – the first sub-2:20 ever by a 50-year-old.

The year 1992 was important for two reasons: it was an Olympic year, and South African athletes returned to the international arena. Because the nature of the Olympic marathon course in Barcelona made fast times impossible, the latter event had a much more visible impact on the world performance list. Two South Africans, Tsebe and Willie Mtolo, scored major international victories – Tsebe with the world's fastest time for 1992.

The Beppu race on 2 February resulted in an even faster winning time than in 1991. Cerón had to do all he could to hold off Hwang Young-cho KOR, winning in a national record 2:08:36 against 2:08:47. The 21-year-old Hwang, the 1991 University Games champion, had a previous best of 2:12:35 (in his debut in 1991). Later in the year he would run almost 5 minutes slower, yet win the Olympic gold.

A week later Morishita won the Tokyo race in 2:10:19 in a sprint finish against Nakayama (2:10:25) and debutant Toshiyuki Hayata (2:10:37). Both De Castella and Dinsamo failed to finish.

García resumed where he had left off the previous year by winning in Rotterdam (2:09:16), beating yet another Mexican, Isidro Rico, by 12 seconds. (The Mexican team selectors had told the athletes that they had to run sub-2:10 to be selected. Three of them did so, but Rico was the only one to finish the Olympic race, in 29th place.) The first 15 km were run in 45:06, the same time recorded by Dinsamo in his world record race, but thereafter the pace slowed. García, who had trained above 3 600 m in the Bolivian Andes for the race, took the lead from Rico at 40 km and scored a PB.

Six days later Spence won the US trial in 2:12:43. The next day António Pinto POR ran 2:10:02 in London to beat Huruk by 5 seconds. It was a very exciting finish: on their heels followed Naali (2:10:08) and Tena Negere ETH (2:10:10).

On 20 April Hussein won his second consecutive (and third overall) Boston in 2:08:14, moving ahead of Bordin into second place on the performance list of the venerable race. There were no top Americans present because of their trial, but it was the Kenyan Olympic trial. Simon Karori, in his debut, was timed in 62:41 at halfway; he would finish in 2:53:56! Hussein was far in front by 21 miles, but he continued running in the same tempo and was rewarded with a PB – a tactic which probably cost him a better performance, maybe even a medal, in Barcelona.

Joaquim Pinheiro POR was second (2:10:39), Espinosa

third (2:10:44) and Ikangaa, a bit luckier this time, fourth (2:11:44).

South Africa's first international victory was scored by Mtolo on 21 June when he won the Enschede marathon in 2:13:39.

The Games of the 25th Olympiad were opened in Barcelona on 25 July. The main stadium was situated on top of Montjuïc hill (102 m) – a fact not relished by the marathon runners, who had to run up it to finish their already gruelling event.

South Africa took part for the first time in 32 years, fielding a team which was – understandably – outclassed in the high-pressure Olympic cauldron. A number of firsts were scored: Spain, China, South Korea and Algeria won their first gold medals, Paraskevi Patoulidou became the first woman from Greece to win gold when she scored a stunning victory in the 100 m hurdles, and Ethiopian Derartu Tulu was the first female Olympic winner from an African country other than South Africa when she beat Elana Meyer in the 10000 m.

Linford Christie (32) became the oldest man to win the 100 m; Fermin Cacho thrilled the host country by winning the 1500 m in a dramatic upset; Kenyans won all three medals in the steeplechase; Kevin Young set a brilliant world record of 46.78 in the 400 m hurdles and Carl Lewis became the first man to win three gold medals in the long jump. In the women's 1500 m Hassiba Boulmerka won Algeria's first gold medal. Jackie Joyner-Kersee again won the heptathlon, but her attempt to repeat in the long jump was foiled by her archrival Heike Drechsler, as well as by Inessa Kravets. A women's walk (10 km) was included for the first time; the title went to China's Chen Yueling.

The marathon was run on 9 August. Among the 110 starters were Taniguchi, De Castella, Wakiihuri, Ikangaa, Moneghetti, Hussein, defending champion Bordin, Cerón, Nakayama and Hwang. The latter had two formidable teammates: Kim Jae-ryong had beaten Kim Wan-ki in March, 2:09:30 against 2:09:31.

It was hot and nobody seemed to be in a hurry – it was almost as if they were trying to put off the climb up Montjuïc for as long as possible. The halfway point was passed in 67:22 and still there was no sign of any runner wanting to increase the pace to thin out the pack. Shortly afterwards Taniguchi lost a shoe at a refreshment station. He pulled it back on, but had lost contact with the group.

Bettiol tried to get away at 24 km, but was unsuccessful. Then Morishita surged and drew Hwang and Kim Jae-ryong with him. Ninety minutes into the race Kim surged away from the others, but he was not strong enough to stay ahead and the other two caught him again. Nakayama was now in fourth and Freigang in fifth.

The battle up front became a fight in which neither runner thought of giving up. Morishita and Hwang surged and countersurged, their faces lined in grim determination.

As they started the climb up Montjuïc, Freigang had moved into third and he was running strongly only 11 seconds behind the two Asians. Morishita and Hwang climbed the tortuous hill together and it was only with less than 2 km left that Hwang could pull away, slowly widening the gap until Morishita's spirit was broken.

Hwang's winning time of 2:13:23 was the slowest since 1968, but it did not matter. It was a tremendously satisfying victory for him, especially because it came at the expense of a Japanese. Fifty-six years before, a Korean runner had won the Olympic marathon – but in the colours of the invader, Japan. Kee-Chung Sohn had to accept a Japanese name, Kitei Son, and the Japanese anthem was played to celebrate his victory. This time Hwang won for Korea and he could stand to attention for his own anthem.

One of the most telling aspects of Hwang's victory was that he ran the second half faster than the first, despite the heat and the climb at the end. Behind him Nakayama caught Freigang again, but on the track the German kicked away from his opponent.

RESULT:
1 Hwang Young-cho KOR 2:13:23
2 Koichi Morishita JPN 2:13:45
3 Stephan Freigang GER 2:14:00
4 Takeyuki Nakayama JPN 2:14:02
5 Salvatore Bettiol ITA 2:14:15
6 Salah Kokaich MAR 2:14:25
7 Jan Huruk POL 2:14:32
8 Hiromi Taniguchi JPN 2:14:42
9 Diego García SPA 2:14:56
10 Kim Jae-ryong KOR 2:15:01

Of the three medal winners in 1988 Bordin did not finish, Wakiihuri was 36th and Salah 30th. De Castella was 26th (2:17:44), Hussein 37th and Moneghetti 48th. Among the other nonfinishers were Cerón and Mekonnen.

"I was certain of having a medal, but only the gold interested me," Hwang said later. "It was important for me to win this for Kee-Chung Sohn . . . It was also for my mother who during the entire race was at the temple praying that I would win the gold for Korea."

The 22-year-old Korean had prepared for the marathon in the Korean training camp sponsored by the giant Korean company Kolon. The athletes had access to a coach, physical therapist, psychologist/dietician, two cooks and a one-kilometre asphalt training track. The runners' daily schedule was worked out meticulously by the coach – down to the time for their showers!

One of the most bizarre stories of modern marathoning was told by David Martin in *Athletics 1993* about the man who finished last in Seoul (see p. 103). Polin Belisle was born in Honduras, brought up in Belize and later became a naturalised US citizen. He got into the Belizean team for Seoul with a qualifying time of 2:36:18 in the Long Beach marathon. In 1992 he finished 11th in the Los Angeles marathon in 2:18:38, but was disqualified because he was not picked up on check-point videos. (The same thing had happened to him when he finished fifth in 2:17:39 in the 1991 Long Beach marathon!) He requested permission from Honduras to compete on its team in Barcelona. He signed a loyalty oath to Honduras, but when Belizean officials told their Honduran counterparts about his membership of the Belizean team in 1988 he was banished from the Honduran team. He was permitted to keep his identity card and race numbers, and by some strange quirk of fate his name remained on the entry list . . . and he started the marathon! He was the first to drop out.

On 27 September Tsebe lined up in Berlin against Freigang, Turbo Tumo ETH, Matias and Karori. They went through halfway in 63:04 and the South African, whose best was 2:09:50, took the lead at about 32 km. He stormed away and won in what was to be the world's fastest time for the year: 2:08:07. Matias was second in 2:08:38, also a PB.

On 1 November Tsebe's compatriot Mtolo ran more than a minute slower, but received far more publicity when he won the Big Apple ahead of 28 655 other runners. More than anything else, this victory showed the world that South Africa's marathoners could compete with – and beat – the best in the world. The 28-year-old Mtolo, two years older than Tsebe, had caused consternation in his hotel the previous night when his preparation of his favourite prerace meal, maize porridge, set off a smoke alarm.

The field started running moments before the gun went off. The wind was blowing strongly as the rabbit, Paul Pilkington, led them through halfway in 64:10. Lameck Aguta KEN and Espinosa then took over and ran hard along First Avenue, with Mtolo and Kim Wan-ki following 80 m behind. After the 19-mile mark Espinosa got rid of the Kenyan, but by then Mtolo had started to close. The earlier effort had cost the Mexican dearly, and just after 21 miles Mtolo caught him. After another mile and a half the South African accelerated and drew away. A gap opened quickly and Mtolo ran through Central Park unchallenged to score what was perhaps the most significant South African marathon victory since Johannes Coleman's win in Sydney in 1938.

Kim almost caught Espinosa at the finish, and might have done so if a television motorcycle had not impeded him.

RESULT:  1  Willie Mtolo 2:09:29
         2  Andrés Espinosa 2:10:53
         3  Kim Wan-ki 2:10:54

Mtolo won the first prize of $20 000 plus a time bonus of $30 000 and a $36 000 Mercedes Benz car.

The originator of the New York City five-borough marathon, Fred Lebow, who was suffering from brain cancer, ran "his" race for the first time. He was accompanied by Grete Waitz, nine-time winner (see Chapter 9), and finished in 5:32:34.[2]

One more sub-2:10 time was clocked during the remainder of the year: Negere won Fukuoka in 2:09:04. South African Lawrence Peu was a magnificent second in 2:10:29, one second ahead of Diego García. Cerón was fourth (2:10:42).

The last big race of 1992, Honolulu (13 December), was won for the second year in a row by Benson Masya KEN, who in September had claimed the first world half-marathon title in 60:24, a world best (on a slightly downhill course). His time in Honolulu was 2:14:19.

The first four in the Olympic race were ranked in that order: Hwang, Morishita, Freigang and Nakayama. Then followed Huruk, Negere, Cerón and Mtolo. As in 1986, South Africa had two runners in the top ten on the performance list – but this time their performances came in international competition and on internationally accepted courses.

World marathoning continued at its constant level in 1993. The seven performances under 2:10:00 for the year was the lowest number since the two in 1987, but the 50th performer on the world list was at 2:11:44, compared to 2:11:50 in 1992.

The World Cup in San Sebastián on 31 October was one of the fastest races of the year, and in depth definitely the best. It was run in ideal conditions on a flat, fast three-lap course. Richard Nerurkar GBR won in 2:10:03 and behind him came another nine runners under 2:11:00, a record. Ethiopia won the team competition.

RESULT:  1  Richard Nerurkar 2:10:03
         2  Severino Bernardini ITA 2:10:12
         3  Kebede Gemechu ETH 2:10:16

In May Nerurkar had won his debut marathon in Hamburg in 2:10:57, easily beating Naali.

The big race of 1993 was the World Championships in Stuttgart on 14 August, where the prize for the winner was a Mercedes. Conditions were just the opposite of those in Barcelona.

Among the competitors was ex-South African Mark Plaatjes. He had set a South African record of 2:08:58 when winning the national title in 1985, but had then relocated to the USA. He became an American citizen in July 1992 and Stuttgart was his first international competition.

The race started in the early evening. The first clear leader was German Kurt Stenzel, who covered the first 10 km in 31:26. He was followed as leader by Naali, who went through 20 km at the head of a large pack. By halfway only seven runners remained, with Namibian Lucketz Swartbooi

2. Lebow, who was born as Fischel Lebowitz in Romania in 1932 and arrived in the USA in 1951, died in 1994, four weeks before the 25th New York City marathon.

## WORLD CHAMPION FROM CORONATIONVILLE

Mark Plaatjes ran only slightly more than 42 kilometres to win the world marathon title in Stuttgart, but he had in fact come a very long way to claim the victory. He had endured death threats, insults, poverty, political ostracism and relocation to a foreign country and culture before he could achieve his goal: to be the best marathon runner in the world.

Plaatjes was born on 1 June 1961 in Coronationville, near Johannesburg, into a family of ten children. He is coloured, and at the time when he grew up South Africa was experiencing the full force of the apartheid system and the sports boycott. Plaatjes ran his first race in his final high-school year when he entered a 3000 metre event at an interschools meeting on a dare – and won in 9:03!

His next race was the ultramarathon over 50 km between Johannesburg and Pretoria. Only seventeen, he finished 15th overall and first junior.

In his community, where the South African Council on Sport (Sacos) dictated on all sports matters, Plaatjes was vilified because he ran in races organised by the "white" SA Amateur Athletics Union. But he is full of disdain for Sacos: ". . . they never did anything. They were just a body in name."

In 1980 Plaatjes appeared on the SA marathon performance list for the first time with 2:19:55. The next year he shot right to the top when he won the national title in dusty, windy, high-altitude (1351 m) Potchefstroom in 2:16:17. He clinched the race with a scorching surge between 20 and 25 km (covering this section in 15:13). It was a remarkable run in the conditions. Five weeks before he had set a PB by winning the Stellenbosch marathon in 2:17:06.

In 1983 he won the SA cross-country title – a feat he would repeat in 1985.

By 1984 he had improved his marathon time to 2:14:03 in finishing fourth in the SA marathon.

In 1985 he went to Port Elizabeth for the national marathon intent on winning. He did so – and smashed Ernest Seleke's national record with a scintillating 2:08:58 on the downhill course (the drop between start and finish

was 129 m). He beat Willie Mtolo by more than 1½ minutes and his time was the tenth fastest in the world that year.

The next year he ran 2:16:55 in Johannesburg (1748 m).

On a Christmas trip to the USA in 1987 he and his wife, Shirley, decided to stay and applied for political asylum. They had had a comfortable life in South Africa, but "I didn't want my daughter to grow up feeling inferior".

At first he had difficulty adjusting to his new life and his political status did not exactly open doors for him as far as racing opportunities were concerned. But a breakthrough came in 1988 when he clocked 2:10:41 for third in the Los Angeles marathon. Two years later he finished fourth (2:13:44). He scored a magnificent victory in 1991, running 2:10:29, and also finished second in Berlin.

In 1992 Plaatjes, who by then had qualified as a physical therapist and set up a practice in Boulder, Colorado, was assured that he would be able to run for his adopted country in the Barcelona Olympics, even though his citizenship had not yet been approved, but two weeks before the US trial it all came to naught when the decision on South Africa's readmission to the international fold was delayed.

He went to London to use his fitness and run a fast time, but he was "just emotionally so drained" that he only finished 20th.

For five years he had been officially stateless, but he became a US citizen in mid-1992. It was rather ironic that by that time South Africa, the country he had left to seek a better life, was already back in the Olympics.

A year after his severe disappointment about Barcelona he finally got his chance to prove himself against the best in the world and the rest, as they say, is history. Mark Plaatjes, the youngster from Coronationville who once had to run away from an angry black mob who wanted to kill him because he was running on Labour Day when a strike had been called, was champion of the world.

and Kim Jae-ryong leading. These two had finished second and third in Boston after a tough duel and now they threw down the gauntlet to each other again.

Plaatjes, the first American in both the Houston and Boston marathons, was content to follow and wait. Swartbooi, running in his third marathon (the first had been the Olympic race the previous year, where he did not finish), broke away at 25 km (78:23). Along the Neckar River he ran, speeding away from the others. By 30 km he was 57 seconds ahead of Naali, Boniface Merande KEN and Kim. Plaatjes was another 11 seconds further back.

Gradually Plaatjes closed the gap, and at 35 km he caught Kim. He only saw the leader when he reached 40 km – "I saw the van in front of me – and he must have had about a minute. At 41 km I had closed the gap to 30 seconds, and only then did it enter my mind that I could actually win."

Plaatjes drew alongside the leader with a kilometre to run. His initial reaction was one of sympathy for his fellow African. He "felt terrible", because Swartbooi had been doing all the work. "Then I thought, 'He's only 26 years old, he's a youngster, and I'm 32 years old. This might be my last chance, he's got lots of opportunities,' so I just went hard past him."

Plaatjes put 14 seconds between himself and Swartbooi and won the gold in 2:13:57. "I can't express it any other

way except to say that I've waited for 12 years to be able to do this, to be able to compete against the best in the world, and I finally got a chance," the new champion said.

| Result: | | | |
|---|---|---|---|
| | 1 | Mark Plaatjes USA | 2:13:57 |
| | 2 | Lucketz Swartbooi NAM | 2:14:11 |
| | 3 | Bert van Vlaanderen NED | 2:15:12 |
| | 4 | Kim Jae-ryong KOR | 2:17:14 |
| | 5 | Tadao Uchikoshi JPN | 2:17:54 |
| | 6 | Konrad Dobler GER | 2:18:28 |
| | 7 | Boniface Merande KEN | 2:18:52 |
| | 8 | Aleksey Zhelonkin RUS | 2:18:52 |
| | 9 | Tahar Mansouri TUN | 2:18:54 |
| | 10 | Peter Maher CAN | 2:19:26 |

The times were the slowest in an international championship marathon since the Olympic Games in 1968. Steve Jones finished 13th and Ikangaa 21st, while Freigang, Mekonnen and Mtolo retired.

Plaatjes was the fourth American to win an Olympic or World Championships marathon. Only one, however, was born in the USA: the 1908 Olympic titlist John Hayes.

Earlier in the year action had been fairly slow: 2:13:04 was enough to win the Beppu race, while Mekonnen won in Tokyo in 2:12:00. The first quick times came in the now-famous Marathon Weekend in mid-April, when the London, Rotterdam, Vienna and Boston marathons were run.

In London on 18 April Eamonn Martin GBR contested the first marathon in a career that had started twenty years before. He kicked away from Rico just before Westminster Bridge and won in 2:10:50 – a fine time in very windy conditions. Martin had prepared for the race by reading all the books he could find by marathon greats "to see how they coped with the pain and how they got through it". Rico finished 3 seconds behind him. De Castella was 33rd in 2:19:44.

That same day in Rotterdam Rico's countryman Cerón ran 16 seconds slower than Martin to win from Naali (2:11:06 against 2:11:44). The weather was even worse than in London – the wind blew strongly (against the runners in the second half) and it rained. Mtolo was a disappointing fourth in 2:12:33. Further to the east, also on 18 April, Carlos Patricio POR won the Vienna race in 2:11:00.

The next day the action shifted to the Boston marathon, the Kenyan trial for Stuttgart. Kenyan Cosmas Ndeti was running his second marathon (his first was a 2:14:28 the previous year in Honolulu), so he was content to stay in the company of Masya, the man who had beaten him in Honolulu. Up ahead Swartbooi went through halfway in 65:12; he had the company of fifteen others.

On the Newton hills both Samuel Lelei KEN and Kim Jae-ryong tried to break away, but Swartbooi was having none of it. He went to the front again at 22 miles. A considerable distance behind him Masya told his friend to start moving. Ndeti did so . . . at such a rate that he was only 50 m behind the leader at 23 miles. The Namibian's lead lasted just another mile; he had no reply when Ndeti stormed past.

Ndeti's strong surge resulted in a second half of 64:21 – the second fastest in the history of the race behind De Castella's 64:13 in 1986. Swartbooi had to relinquish second to Kim.

RESULT:
1. Cosmas Ndeti 2:09:33
2. Kim Jae-ryong 2:09:43
3. Lucketz Swartbooi 2:09:57
4. Hiromi Taniguchi 2:11:02
5. Samuel Lelei 2:12:12
6. Mark Plaatjes 2:12:29

Masya, who sixteen days before had equalled his half-marathon best of 1992 when he ran 60:24 in The Hague,[3] finished 33rd in 2:23:25. Ikangaa was 22nd; Freigang, Hussein and Spence did not complete the race.

On 29 August Cerón won a marathon at high-altitude (2300 m) Mexico City in 2:14:47. On 26 September, three days before his 31st birthday, South African Xolile Yawa

---

3. On the same day, 3 April, Masya's countryman Moses Tanui became the first man to run the half marathon in under an hour. He clocked 59:47 in Milan. Earlier in the year Moneghetti had clocked 60:06 in Tokyo ahead of Cerón's 60:17.

---

scored an easy win in the Berlin event, running a PB 2:10:57. The defending champion, Tsebe, was third in 2:12:07. Yawa had debuted in Boston with 2:15:28.

Two more sub-2:11 races followed in October (one of them, the Venice affair, went to Artur Castro BRA in 2:10:06), but there was only one more sub-2:10 before the end of the year. This came on 17 October in Reims when 31-year-old Belgian soldier Vincent Rousseau, who only fourteen days before had won the World Half-marathon Championship in 61:06, set a national record of 2:09:13. Leszek Beblo POL was second in 2:10:24. Rousseau's time was the second fastest of the year. Earlier in the year he had also set national records for 5000 and 10000 m (27:23.18). His only previous completed marathon had been a 2:13:07 in the 1992 Rotterdam.

The Chicago marathon was plagued by strong wind and snow falling during the race – making the winning time, 2:13:14 by Luiz dos Santos BRA, an excellent performance.

On 14 November Espinosa returned to New York to try to improve on his two consecutive second places. Lined up against him were new American hope Bob Kempainen, Mexican Arturo Barrios, the holder of the world records for 20 km and one hour (21 101 m), Lelei and Moses Tanui KEN in his debut.

It was the warmest 14 November ever recorded in New York (22 °C at noon). Espinosa had trained near Mexico City for the event and took the lead at 20 miles. But 2 miles further on Kempainen, who had won the US cross-country title in New York's Van Cortlandt Park in 1990, pulled even. It was almost a replay of the 1992 race, when Mtolo caught Espinosa, but this time the Mexican was the stronger. He surged – "Espinosa had another gear left," Kempainen said later, "I clearly didn't."

The victor's comment was: "When someone takes something very seriously and works very hard, this is the result. I didn't know who [Kempainen] was. But I had thought about the last two years a lot, and I decided I was not going to finish 2nd again."

Barrios moved from seventh to third in the last 3 miles.

RESULT:
1. Andrés Espinosa 2:10:04
2. Bob Kempainen 2:11:03
3. Arturo Barrios 2:12:21

Tanui finished tenth in 2:15:36, showing again that a blistering half-marathon time does not necessarily point to a top marathon performance.

Marathon fans had to wait until 5 December and Fukuoka for the year's fastest race. For the first time since 1987 the winning performance was under 2:09:00. Cerón, with two victories for the year to his credit, wanted to make it three. After 32 km he was running together with Toshiyuki Hayata JPN, Negere and Gert Thys RSA in the lead, but 3 km further he accelerated and covered the next 5 km in a fast 14:58. He dropped Hayata and Negere, but the inexperienced Thys (he was running only his third marathon) stayed with him. The South African, whose best was the 2:11:40 he ran in Otsu earlier in 1993, lasted until 39 km and then he had to let go. Cerón increased his advantage to 40 seconds at the finish, becoming the first Mexican to win the famous race. Thys clocked the fastest time by a South African for the year.

RESULT:  1  Dionicio Cerón 2:08:51
         2  Gert Thys 2:09:31
         3  Valdenor dos Santos BRA 2:10:20

Negere faded to 11th; Ikangaa was 18th, Tolstikov 31st, Mtolo 34th in another unimpressive run, and Taniguchi 38th.

A week later stormy weather prevailed in Honolulu, where 23 000 runners braved the conditions. Lee Bong-ju KOR beat Ndeti by 24 seconds in 2:13:16; Masya was eighth.

Cerón's three wins and quickest time gave him the number one ranking for the year. He was followed by Plaatjes and Swartbooi (who had failed to finish in New York).

After ten years the membership of the Association of International Marathons (AIMS) reached 100. This influential body, to which almost all the major marathons belong, works together with the International Amateur Athletic Federation to improve race conditions and management.

The year 1994 was the best since 1988. While development had remained stagnant since Dinsamo's 1988 world record with no sub-2:08 times in the interim (Ikangaa missed a sub-2:08 by two seconds in 1989), there was a turnaround in 1994. When the year began, the world had seen nine sub-2:08s (two in 1985, three in 1986 and four in 1988). Another three were added in 1994, although two of them were aided by the downhill course and strong following wind in Boston.

The Tokyo race was the early performance leader. The night before the race the Japanese capital had been hit by its first snowstorm in 25 years and 2 000 volunteers were called in to clear the course. Moneghetti showed that he was still a force to be reckoned with when he won in 2:08:55, only 39 seconds slower than his PB and his first victory since he set that best in the 1990 Berlin race. Rousseau, starting what was to become a marvellous year, was second in 2:09:08, another PB. Hayata followed in 2:10:19. Moneghetti only took the lead at 40 km.

In the Beppu marathon the previous week defending champion Maurilio Castillo MEX had finished first in 2:11:15, but was told that he had followed a press truck that cut 280 m off the course. Hajime Nakatomi JPN also made the wrong turn, but quickly turned back and was the official winner in 2:11:28.

An unusual race took place in Los Angeles on 6 March. Pilkington, who had a best of 2:11:13, was paid to set a 65:00 halfway pace. He reached his goal in 65:02, nearly a minute ahead. Pilkington felt good and instead of dropping out as he was expected to do, he continued . . . to win in 2:12:13! In addition to his rabbiting fee, Pilkington won a

Mercedes and $27 000, as well as the US title. Responding to criticism from Italian Luca Barzaghi (second in 2:12:52), who had expected him to retire on completion of his assigned job, the American said: "He made a tactical mistake. It's still a race."

A fortnight later a high-quality race took place in Kyongju, South Korea. The Dong-A marathon had been held since 1931,[4] but it was the first time that the Koreans had allowed foreigners to compete. Kim Wan-ki ran the first half in 64:22 – and then sped the second half even faster. But he did not win, for he could not get away from Matias. The Portuguese tried a break at 40 km, but it did not work and he waited until he could outsprint his rival on the track. The first three runners all broke Kim's course record.

RESULT:  1  Manuel Matias 2:08:33
         2  Kim Wan-ki 2:08:34
         3  Isidro Rico 2:09:14

Plaatjes had to jump over a group of runners who had fallen early in the race. He strained a hamstring and stopped at 12 km.

Marathon Weekend in April surpassed anything produced during this festival of marathon running in previous years.

The Rotterdam marathon took place on 17 April, with the course being run in reverse. This time Rousseau was not the rabbit, but one of the elite runners. It was cold and windy, but the Belgian record holder was in superb form; the Tokyo marathon had only been a warm-up. He passed 25 km in 76:45 behind the pacemakers, but decided that this was too slow. He ran the next 10 km in 29:30 (30 km in 91:20) and by 35 km (1:46:15) he was 78 seconds ahead of Jose Marquez MEX (whose best was 2:18:23). The 5 km between 35 and 40 km took 15:05 (40 km in 2:01:20) and Rousseau ran the last kilometre in 2:48. He finished in 2:07:51, the fastest time in the world since 1988. His halves were 64:55 and 62:56 – phenomenal running in the conditions. He was the second runner to run three successive sub-2:09 marathons (Rodolfo Gomez was the first).

RESULT:  1  Vincent Rousseau 2:07:51
         2  Willie Mtolo 2:10:17
         3  Benjamin Paredes MEX 2:10:40

"I always wanted to go out faster," Rousseau said later, "but it shows that taking off slower you can still run a fast time."

Earlier the same day the wind was blowing even harder in London. Cerón had wanted to run a world record, but the

4. The first marathon in Korea was held in September 1927; it was won in 3:29:37 by Bong Ock Ma. The Dong-A marathon was sponsored by the newspaper with the same name – the same one which published the picture of Kee-Chung Sohn in 1936 with the Japanese flag on his vest obliterated.

weather made this impossible. He settled into the large pack that followed the rabbits to halfway in 64:41. In the group was also the defending champion, Martin. Mekonnen stretched the pack out with a 19th mile in 4:45, at the conclusion of which he had only Cerón, German Silva MEX (in his debut), Grzegorz Gajdus POL and Bettiol as company. The 5 km splits up to that point had been 15:23, 14:58 (30:21), 15:13 (45:34), 15:38 (61:12), 15:50 (77:02) and 15:22 (92:24). The next 5 km went by in 15:25 and by 23 miles only Cerón and Mekonnen remained at the front. The Mexican charged through the next 5 km in a brilliant 14:41 (40 km 2:02:30) and this ensured his victory. He clocked 6:23 for the last 2.195 km and won in 2:08:53 – his fourth consecutive win. In third place Silva, better known as a track runner (he was sixth in the 1992 Olympic 10000 m), completed his first marathon in 2:09:18.

Cerón's second half was 64:12. Mekonnen's performance was his best since winning Boston five years previously.

RESULT:
| | | |
|---|---|---|
| 1 | Dionicio Cerón | 2:08:53 |
| 2 | Abebe Mekonnen | 2:09:17 |
| 3 | German Silva | 2:09:18 |
| 4 | Salvatore Bettiol | 2:09:40 |
| 5 | Grzegorz Gajdus | 2:09:49 |

The depth of performances was almost as good as the 1989 London marathon, when six men were under 2:10:00. Wakiihuri ran 2:19:25 for 38th, while Ikangaa finished 59th.

The best was yet to come. The next day Ndeti defended his Boston title against one of the best fields ever assembled for the race. Espinosa was there, so were Olympic champion Hwang, Barrios, Kempainen, exciting newcomer Jackson Kipngok KEN, whose only previous marathon was a 2:16:33, and Swartbooi.

Ndeti had prepared in the Japanese training camp in Chiba (in the company of Rousseau), but suffered a heel injury which made him a doubtful starter a week before the race. Then he received treatment in Boston (he had brought his infant son, Gideon Boston Ndeti, with him), and this worked wonders. He was ready.

The main contenders started relatively slowly and were content to follow Keith Brantly USA, who took them through 15 km in 46:03 and halfway in a modest 64:52, 8 seconds ahead. Then García accelerated, taking Swartbooi, Boay Akonai TAN, Barrios, Hwang, Espinosa, Kempainen, Ndeti, Kipngok and Sammy Nyangincha KEN with him. They caught Brantly at 15 miles. On the Newton hills Swartbooi and Kipngok were 5 m ahead of Espinosa and Hwang. Ndeti was still biding his time.

"This year I was not concerned with quick splits, only on winning the race. I wasn't looking at the clocks. I was watching the competition," he was to say later.

At the top of Heartbreak Hill Akonay stormed into the lead. But behind him Ndeti had also started to move. He flu-

idly increased the tempo and soon he was in second. Just a hundred seconds later, at 36 km, he drew alongside the leader. He looked at Akonay a couple of times and then, inevitably, he was away.

What Ndeti did not know at that stage was that Espinosa, the New York champion, had begun a move of his own and was actually running faster than the Kenyan. With 2 miles to go he was 50 m behind, but down the crowd-lined Boylston Street near the finish he was gaining with every stride. Ndeti took quick looks over his shoulder a few times and ran just fast enough to secure the victory. At the finish Espinosa was just 4 seconds behind. Ndeti had run the second half in 62:15 and just missed Jones's Commonwealth record.

Both smashed De Castella's eight-year-old course record of 2:07:51, but this was not the only record-setting aspect of this amazing race.

- The average of the first ten (2:08:28.4) was the fastest ever recorded in any marathon.
- Seven finished under 2:09:00 – three more than in the 1986 and 1988 Tokyo marathons.
- Eleven athletes ran faster than 2:10 – five more than in the 1983 Fukuoka and the 1989 London.
- The two under 2:08:00 equalled the number in Beijing in 1986 and 1988 and Rotterdam in 1988.
- Seven men set national records: Ndeti, Espinosa, Hwang, Kempainen, Swartbooi, Martin Fiz ESP (2:10:21) and Carlos Tarazona VEN (2:12:49).

RESULT:
| | | |
|---|---|---|
| 1 | Cosmas Ndeti | 2:07:15 |
| 2 | Andres Espinosa | 2:07:19 |
| 3 | Jackson Kipngok | 2:08:08 |
| 4 | Hwang Young-cho | 2:08:09 |
| 5 | Arturo Barrios | 2:08:28 |
| 6 | Boay Akonay | 2:08:35 |
| 7 | Bob Kempainen | 2:08:47 |
| 8 | Lucketz Swartbooi | 2:09:08 |
| 9 | Sammy Nyangincha | 2:09:15 |
| 10 | Moses Tanui | 2:09:40 |

Ndeti's total prize money was $95 000.

Kempainen became the fastest American since Salazar had run 2:08:52 in 1982.

One has to bear in mind, though, that conditions were extremely favourable. The runners were aided by a tailwind estimated by some sources as between 6 and 16 km/h and by others as about 30 km/h.[5] Furthermore, the Boston course drops by 3.2 m/km, three times more than the maximum allowable for a road record.

Fiz was to have his day of days four months later (on 14 August) when he won the European title in Helsinki.

5. According to *On the Roads*, the official publication of the Road Running Information Center of USA Track and Field.

Almost exactly a year before, on 7 August and in the same city, he had run his debut in 2:12:47. Conditions were warm and humid (84%) – "ideal marathon weather for those that had trained in hot and humid Spain", as one report put it. The race started at 09:30 and the roads were still wet from earlier rain. A pack of twenty runners completed the first half in a pedestrian 66:06. Then Chauvelier surged and reduced the group to twelve.

Soon afterwards Fiz, brimming with confidence after his Boston performance, broke from the pack. His countrymen Diego García and Albert Juzdado followed in the company of the two Portuguese Antonio Rodriguez and Pinto. They lasted until about 30 km and then the Spaniards were alone to fight out the medals. Nerurkar was making a valiant attempt to catch them and came to within 7 seconds, but then fell back.

The first of the Spaniards to drop off the pace was Juzdado, and 2 km from the finish Fiz surged just enough to drop García. He clocked 10 seconds slower than in Boston, but considering the conditions and the nature of the four-lap course this performance was in fact far superior.

Runners from warm-weather countries took seven of the first ten places. It was the first time in the history of the race that runners from the same country scored a clean sweep of the medals.

RESULT:
1  Martin Fiz ESP 2:10:31
2  Diego García ESP 2:10:46
3  Alberto Juzdado ESP 2:11:18
4  Richard Nerurkar GBR 2:11:56
5  Luigi di Lello ITA 2:12:41
6  Antonio Rodriguez POR 2:12:43

The Commonwealth Games marathon took place in Victoria, British Columbia, on 28 August. The thirty starters faced unpleasant conditions – heavy rain (including a thunderstorm) and wind. Moneghetti had previously won bronze (1986) and silver (1990) and very much wanted to complete his medal collection. The weak opposition made it easy for the Aussie. He led through 15 km (48:25) and 20 km (64:09) and was in the pack of fifteen that passed halfway in 67:36. After 25 km Moneghetti began to stamp his authority on the race, with only Englishman Mark Hudspith and Kenyan Nicholas Kioko being able to go with him. Neither could maintain the tempo and by 30 km Moneghetti was 13 seconds clear. He continued to increase the gap, running the second half in 64:14 for an emphatic win – his first in a major championship and his second victory of the year.

RESULT:
1  Stephen Moneghetti AUS 2:11:49
2  Sean Quilty AUS 2:14:57
3  Mark Hudspith Eng 2:15:11
4  Dale Rixon Wal 2:16:15
5  Patrick Carroll AUS 2:16:27
6  Nicolas Kioko KEN 2:16:37

Moneghetti's victory margin was the biggest since Jack Holden had won the title by more than 4 minutes in 1950. His 5 km splits showed how he achieved the win: 16:27, 16:14, 15:44, 15:44, 15:33, 15:17, 15:16, 14:58 (6:36 for the final 2.195 km).

Rousseau scored an easy victory in the Brussels marathon in September, his 2:12:59 being nothing more than a gentle jog for him. A week later, on 25 September, Pinto won in Berlin in 2:08:31, beating Nyangincha by 19 seconds. Hu took the Beijing race in 2:10:56, while the African Championships marathon in Abidjan went to South African Andries Pilusa in a somewhat ridiculous 2:25:13. Hwang won the only regional championship open to him, the Asian Games in Hiroshima on 9 October, in 2:11:13.

The Chicago marathon on 30 October was won for the second time in a row by Luiz dos Santos, in 2:11:16. Ndeti, suffering from a blister, dropped out after 20 miles.

On 6 November Pilkington was again the pacemaker in New York. But the adverse conditions (intermittent rain and high humidity) resulted in the large pack following at an almost respectful distance as he covered the first 8 miles in a 2:08:30 pace. In Brooklyn Luis da Silva BRA took off alone after Pilkington, reaching halfway in 65:03, but the pack soon caught him again. In the bunch were training partners German Silva and Rico, Barrios (trying once more to win a major marathon after he had become a US citizen in September), Domingos Castro POR, Rousseau, William Koech KEN, Lelei and Paredes.

The pace increased, with the 6 miles from 16 to 22 run in 28:50. One of the first to let go was race favourite Rousseau, who earlier in the week had said that he could not run well in temperatures above 18 °C. The Belgian would eventually drop out.

By 22 miles Barrios could not stay in contact, and now the race was down to Silva and his countryman Paredes, who had won the Central American and Caribbean Games marathon (2:14:23) and had run sub-2:11 in Rotterdam. They ran shoulder to shoulder until 25 miles, with Silva relying on his speed to beat Paredes at the finish (six weeks earlier he had finished second in the World Half-marathon Championships in 60:28).

But suddenly a dramatic event almost cost him the race. In Central Park South he went off-course by following a camera motorcycle, while Paredes, after hesitating slightly, continued on the correct course. Silva soon realised his mistake ("I could see people's faces and I knew, 'Oh, mistake'. I didn't have to ask anybody."), but by the time he returned to the route, he was 50 m behind with only a kilometre to run. He was not going to be beaten though, and simply put everything he had into that last kilometre. ("I had done too much work. I was thinking, 'Even if I break myself, I will catch him'.") He ran his countryman down, passing him 150 m from the finish, and beat him by 2 seconds in 2:11:21. His tenacity brought him $35 000 plus a Mercedes. It was the closest finish in the history of the race – halving Salazar's margin over Rodolfo Gomez (coach of Silva and Paredes) in 1982.

RESULT:
1. German Silva 2:11:21
2. Benjamin Paredes 2:11:23
3. Arturo Barrios 2:11:43

The race remained the largest marathon in the world with a record number of 29 735 finishers.

Akonay ran his second sub-2:10 of the year when he won Fukuoka in 2:09:45, beating a tough field that included Cerón, the defending champion, Espinosa, Nakayama, Matias and Ikangaa. In ideal weather Akonay and Matias broke away from their rivals after 35 km (Cerón had dropped behind after 33 km), opening a gap of 7 seconds on Valdenor dos Santos by 40 km (2:03:04). The Tanzanian's kick from 41 km brought him the victory.

RESULT:
1. Boay Akonay 2:09:45
2. Manuel Matias 2:09:50
3. Valdenor dos Santos 2:10:15

Espinosa was fourth, Ikangaa tenth and Cerón 16th. Plaatjes failed to finish.

The year's last important marathon, in Honolulu, was won for the third consecutive time by Masya, in a wind-slowed 2:15:04.

*Track & Field News* changed the period for its marathon rankings to cover what the magazine called the marathon "season", September to August, and thus ranked marathon runners for the period 1 September 1993 to 31 August 1994 (which, of course, included the 1993 New York and Fukuoka races – for which runners had already been ranked at the end of 1993). Cerón was adjudged the top marathoner, followed by Rousseau, Ndeti, Espinosa and Moneghetti.

The year ended with fourteen times faster than 2:09:00 – one more than the previous record year of 1988. The 28 times under 2:10:00 were seven more than in 1983 (1988 had twenty), while the three sub-2:08s were one behind the four of 1988.

The all-time list included twelve sub-2:08 times (no runner had more than one):

| | | |
|---|---|---|
| 2:06:50 | Belayneh Dinsamo ETH | 1988 |
| 2:07:07 | Ahmed Salah DJI | 1988 |
| 2:07:12 | Carlos Lopes POR | 1985 |
| 2:07:13 | Steve Jones GBR | 1985 |
| 2:07:15 | Cosmas Ndeti KEN | 1994 |
| 2:07:19 | Andrés Espinosa MEX | 1994 |
| 2:07:35 | Taisuke Kodama JPN | 1986 |
| 2:07:35 | Abebe Mekonnen ETH | 1988 |
| 2:07:40 | Hiromi Taniguchi JPN | 1988 |
| 2:07:51 | Robert de Castella AUS | 1986 |
| 2:07:51 | Vincent Rousseau BEL | 1994 |
| 2:07:57 | Kunimitsu Itoh JPN | 1986 |

The main race in 1995 was the fifth World Championships marathon. As usual, serious marathoning started early in the year in Japan. On 5 February Aussie Pat Carroll, who had finished almost 5 minutes behind Moneghetti in Victoria, scored a huge PB (previously 2:10:44 in 1988) when he won the Beppu marathon in 2:09:39 from Freigang (2:10:12). Two months before Carroll had failed to finish in Honolulu, but this time he ran confidently (speeding the 5 km between 35 and 40 km in 14:56). The world record holder dropped out.

A week later Eric Wainaina, another runner in the long line of fine Kenyan marathoners, clocked 2:10:31 to win in Tokyo, beating Tolstikov, Salah, Mekonnen and Taniguchi. It was after this race, in which he had finished second in 2:10:44, that Niemczak tested positive for ephedrine.

A strong field contested the Los Angeles marathon on 5 March, but wind and rain – not to mention a difficult course – kept times down. Pilkington was – surprise! – the pacesetter, but the defending champion stepped in a pothole and retired after 4 miles. Rolando Vera ECU won by 20 seconds from Kempainen, 2:11:39 against 2:11:59, and they were followed by Pitayo, Barrios and Plaatjes.

On 12 March much faster times were run in Rome, where the city's marathon was resurrected after a gap of four years: Belayneh Tadesse ETH won in 2:10:13, with Ikaji Salum TAN second in 2:10:25. A week later Lee Bong-Ju won the Dong-A race in Kyongju in 2:10:58, with Nerurkar following 5 seconds later and Espinosa after another 5 seconds in third. Matias was fourth. On 25 March Paredes took the Pan-American Games marathon in Mar del Plata in 2:14:44.

The London marathon was moved to 2 April for its 15th edition, following just a day after the 141-year-old Oxford vs Cambridge boat race. Before the race Cerón talked about breaking Dinsamo's world record if conditions were favourable. There was a bonus of £100 000 for such a feat. When Pinto heard that the Mexican and Moneghetti were going to chase the record, he said: "I will follow after them with a sack. When they collapse, I will load them in and continue on."

The designated rabbits were Gary Staines GBR and Huruk, and they passed 5 miles in 24:07, 10 miles in 48:21 and halfway in 63:31 – more or less on record pace. But with their job done, the pace slackened. Until Pinto came to the rescue.

He blitzed the 15th mile in 4:37 and continued to attack, with the result that he quickly had a 200-metre advantage. Cerón and Moneghetti were not worried, however. "The pace was too fast for the wind," the Mexican later said.

Up ahead Pinto pressed on; at 22 miles near the Tower of London his lead was a minute. Then he turned into the wind and slowed. His miles dropped to over 5 minutes, while his pursuers were running faster than that. But it remained a nail-biting affair, for Cerón and Moneghetti only caught the gallant Portuguese in the 26th mile. He tried to hang on, but was too tired.

In the final stretch Moneghetti was outkicked by Cerón,

## HOW MANY ARE TOO MANY?

Frank Shorter believes a runner can run only five or six top-level marathons. "A similar question is, how many times can you *really* give 100%? And even if you know how to regulate that, why squander them by racing too much?" He added that he "went 100%" in four races, of which two were the Olympic marathons in which he won gold and silver.

"Those four times I know I was mentally and physically peaked, I was ready, I had trained right for the particular race and I got everything out of myself that I could have gotten," he said in an interview in *Track & Field News*.

The question of how many marathons a top runner can run hard is a vexing one, especially in view of the many temptations in the form of huge money prizes available in today's major marathons. Overracing is a real danger – not only in terms of possible injuries, but also with a view to a long-term career.

One way to arrive at a possible rule of thumb in this regard is to look at the number of marathons Olympic winners had run before victory at the Games. The results of such a study were published by Roger Gynn in the 1985 *International Athletics Annual*. The first three post-World War I champions, for instance (Delfo Cabrera 1948, Emil Zátopek 1952 and Alain Mimoun 1956), all won the Olympic gold in their first attempt at the distance.

After the War the average number of marathons run by the Olympic champions before their victory (in the case of Abebe Bikila and Waldemar Cierpinski before their first win) was just 3.1! When Bikila and Cierpinski won for the second time, they had nine and fourteen marathons respectively behind them. The only other champions who deviated considerably from the average were Mamo Wolde and Gelindo Bordin – both won in their ninth marathon.

Derek Clayton ran his first world record in his fifth marathon and Jim Peters set his world records in his third, fifth, eighth and tenth marathons. Clayton had completed eight marathons when he set his second world record – and never approached this time again. Rob de Castella's record 2:08:18 came in his sixth, Alberto Salazar's nonrecord 2:08:13 in his second, while Steve Jones ran his record 2:08:05 also in his second marathon. Carlos Lopes's 2:07:12 came in his fourth marathon (he became the oldest Olympic winner ever in his second).

When Lopes won in Los Angeles, the three medallists had only previously completed three marathons between them! Hwang Young-cho won the 1992 Olympic title in his fourth marathon.

As usual, there are exceptions: Ron Hill clocked his 2:09:28 in his 18th marathon, Bill Rodgers his 2:09:27 in his 23rd and De Castella his 2:07:51 in his 13th.

De Castella may have given the best summary of the effect of too many marathons when, after finishing 33rd (2:19:44) in his last serious marathon, the 1993 London, he said: "My body is starting to get a little beat up and a little bit weary."

as he had been by Wakiihuri in 1989 – and, as had been the case then, he lost by 3 seconds. "When you get beaten by the number 1, you want to come back, even if Antonio thinks I'm an old-timer," the Australian said.

It was Cerón's fifth victory in six marathons. He became the first man to win London two years in a row, and his time was a PB by 6 seconds. He was also the first man ever to run sub-2:09 four years in succession.

RESULT:  1  Dionicio Cerón 2:08:30
2  Stephen Moneghetti 2:08:33
3  Antonio Pinto 2:08:48

The first six ran under 2:11:00; Yawa improved his PB to 2:10:22 in fourth. Neither Mekonnon nor Ikangaa could break 2:20:00.

The same day, across the Channel, Domingos Castro – one of a set of twins – won the Paris marathon in a PB 2:10:06 from Negere in 2:10:59 and Lelei in 2:11:11.

A week later the World Cup marathon took the same route as the 1896 Olympic race, finishing in the Panathenaic Stadium. Among the honoured guests were Olympic champions Kee-Chung Sohn, Emil Zátopek, Gelindo Bordin and Hwang Young-cho. The man Bordin had beaten for the Olympic title in 1988, Wakiihuri, was the victor. He ran 2:12:01 in light rain, winning by more than a minute over a weak field. "After the World Championships [of 1987] and the Olympics, I can ask for no more," he said. Wakiihuri's time was still almost a minute slower than the magnificent course record (2:11:08) set by Bill Adcocks over the testing course as long ago as 1969. It was the Kenyan's first win since the 1990 New York race.

On 17 April it was cool and sunny when 9 416 runners gathered in Hopkinton at noon for the 99th Boston marathon. The weather was different from the previous year – there was much less wind. Two-time winner Ndeti also ran differently – he mostly stayed at the front of the lead group. The man setting the pace most of the time was Kenyan Barnabas Rotich, who reached halfway in 64:52. He was caught by the large bunch, which included Ndeti, Aguta, Kim Jae-ryong, Nyangincha and Tanui, between 14 and 15 miles. The Kenyans then joined forces to get rid of the Korean. By the 19th mile, after the Newton hills, Kim was still with them, but soon after cresting Heartbreak Hill, in the 22nd mile, Ndeti surged hard.

Kim and Aguta had to let go, but Tanui stayed in contact. Not for long, though. Ndeti's relentless pressure started to tell and a small gap developed which became bigger and bigger as they raced on Beacon Street. "At 35 km I could see that Moses, Lameck and that Korean guy . . . that I felt strong and that I would win," said Ndeti later. "The race last year and in '93 were very tough, but this year was not tough."

He reached the finish in Copley Plaza in 2:09:22, joining Clarence DeMar and Bill Rodgers as three-in-a-row winner. Unlike the others, his three wins came in his first three attempts. Once again he ran the second half (64:30) faster than the first.

RESULT:  1  Cosmas Ndeti 2:09:22
2  Moses Tanui 2:10:22
3  Luiz dos Santos 2:11:02

When asked about his preparation for the race, Ndeti, who had been observed having scrambled eggs and rice for breakfast, replied: "I have my own training in Kenya and it is a secret. I don't want to tell my secret."

Kenyans took six of the first ten places. Dos Santos came

from 12th with 10 km to go to beat Aguta by one second.

On 23 April the quick Rotterdam course again produced a fine race, and Fiz ran a remarkable time – establishing himself as one of the favourites for the world title. He improved his PB set in Boston the previous year by almost 1½ minutes and won easily in 2:08:57 for the fourth sub-2:09 time of the year.

The European champion's task was made somewhat easier by the temperature – Rousseau decided not to defend his title because he felt it was too hot. The first half was covered in almost exactly the same time as in Boston (64:53), with Pitayo setting the pace. Fiz still had some company at 30 km (91:54), but at 32 km he accelerated and pulled steadily away. He set a new Spanish record, breaking Antonio Serrano's 2:09:13 from the 1994 Berlin marathon.

RESULT:
1  Martin Fiz 2:08:57
2  Bert van Vlaanderen 2:10:36
3  Isaac Garcia MEX 2:10:54

Serrano did not finish – nor did Silva and Paredes.

Fiz said that he had dreamt of "winning one of the best marathons in the world. In August I hope to win a medal again at the World Championships in Göteborg."

The last major marathon before the World Championships was run on the final day of the month in Hamburg, where the Argentine track star Antonio Silio set a national record of 2:09:57. He was the only runner under 2:11:00.

Fiz and his Spanish team-mates were in top form for the world title race on 12 August. There were 78 starters, and they were to find the hot conditions (the race started at 14:00 in a temperature of 29 °C) exceptionally trying. It was clear that runners used to hot weather would be at an advantage: it was a replay of the European Championships which had taken place, incidentally, two days short of a year before. There were many strong contenders, among them Cerón, Moneghetti, Espinosa, Lee, Salah and Akonay – the question was, who would cope best with the conditions?

Englishman Peter Whitehead took the lead soon after the first half of the three-lap course was completed in a slow 66:53. Making liberal use of sponges to cool himself, Whitehead set about thinning out the lead pack. He succeeded, but just before 27 km Dos Santos broke away and opened a lead of 30 m over Cerón. Then the real racing began when Fiz accelerated to go after the two leaders. The effect was immediate: only Nerurkar, Whitehead and Juzdado could respond as they joined Cerón and Dos Santos. Whitehead was not done yet and again started to force the pace, running the section between 25 and 30 km in a splendid 15:18 (94:44). Then Fiz went to the front and covered the next 5 km in 15:43.

It was too much for Juzdado, and soon also for Whitehead. But Cerón was lurking menacingly behind the Spaniard, and Fiz must have had visions of Cerón storming past

as he had done against Pinto in London. Dos Santos first lost contact, then came back with a supreme effort, only to fall behind for good. Fiz and Cerón continued matching strides in one of those classic confrontations seen in truly great marathons.

Then Cerón took the initiative. He did not surge away from the Spaniard, but gradually a gap developed which he increased to 20 m. Fiz looked at his watch a couple of times, then pulled up his shorts – and set out after Cerón. "When Cerón raced by me, I was confident I could hold my pace to the end," he said later. "I thought it might be a quick move and if I could just hold on to Cerón I had a chance."

He easily drew level and went past just after 39 km. Surprisingly Cerón, who had thought 2:15:00 would be fast enough to win, could not respond. Fiz ran the 5 km between 35 and 40 km in 14:48 and showed his strength by running the second half more than 2 minutes faster than the first (66:54 and 64:47).

Fiz, who has a sub-8:30 steeplechase to his credit (he was born on 3 March 1963 in Vitoria), excitedly ran around the Ullevi Stadium track, waving to the crowd as he completed a remarkable three-race streak of wins (and his fourth victory in five races). Spain continued its excellent showing in major championships, with the same three runners who had won the medals in the European Championships again finishing in the top six.

RESULT:
1  Martin Fiz ESP 2:11:41
2  Dionicio Cerón MEX 2:12:13
3  Luiz dos Santos BRA 2:12:49
4  Peter Whitehead GBR 2:14:08
5  Alberto Juzdado ESP 2:15:29
6  Diego García ESP 2:15:34
7  Richard Nerurkar GBR 2:15:47
8  Stephen Moneghetti AUS 2:16:13
9  Andrés Espinosa MEX 2:16:44
10 Steve Plasencia USA 2:16:56

The arduous conditions were reflected in the slow times; only eighteen runners broke 2:20:00. Lee finished 22nd, Salah 25th, Ikangaa 43rd, while Akonay could not complete the race.

Six weeks later, on 24 September, 16 677 runners converged on Berlin for the city's marathon. At the start the temperature was 14 °C (it was to increase to 18 °C later) and a world record attempt was on the cards. The two main protagonists were Lelei and Rousseau. Rousseau, with a best of 2:07:51 – against Lelei's 2:11:11 in Paris – was the favourite. Among their challengers were defending champion Pinto and Nyangincha.

Two Kenyans and two Germans were the pacemakers and they sped through 2 km in 5:59. The main group behind them comprised Rousseau, Lelei, Pinto, Nyangincha, Gilbert Rutto KEN and Davide Milesi ITA. Six seconds behind came a second group led by Yawa, the 1993 winner, and Freigang.

The leaders reached 5 km in 14:55, 10 seconds faster than Dinsamo had done in his world record. Soon afterwards Milesi could not keep contact. The time at 10 km was 29:58, 7 seconds ahead of world record pace. By 15 km (45:09) the chase pack was already a full minute behind. Dinsamo had run the same 5 km in 15:01 – 10 seconds faster; the leading group was now 3 seconds behind his pace.

Realising this, the rabbits picked up the tempo, running the next 5 km in 14:54 to reach 20 km in 60:03 (Dinsamo 60:12) and then went through halfway in 63:21. They maintained the pace to 25 km (75:08) and then dropped out, leaving the stars to their own devices. They were now 4 seconds "ahead" of Dinsamo and the record was still clearly in their sights.

The pace remained constant, but nevertheless Rutto and Nyangincha found it too much and lost contact. Now only Rousseau, Pinto and Lelei remained and they reached 30 km in 90:15 (Dinsamo 90:13). Soon after 32 km Rousseau implemented his race plan: he started surging and gained a gap of 20 m. Despite the surges he lost ground on world record pace, for Dinsamo had run the 5 km between 30 and 35 km in 15:09. In contrast Rousseau took 15:19, placing him 12 seconds behind the Ethiopian's tempo.

Behind him the diminutive 33-year-old Lelei started chasing in earnest. The much taller Belgian (also 33) ran both the 39th and 40th kilometre in 3:00, but Lelei was even faster and caught his rival at 40 km, reached in 2:00:30. Rousseau had covered the last 5 km in 14:56, which gained him 2 seconds on the world record. But he had no answer to the superior speed of the Kenyan, who in 1993 had run a "world best" of 59:24 on the Lisbon half-marathon course which was later found to be 97 m short.[6]

Lelei completed the last 2.195 km of the race in a storming 6:29 – one second faster than Dinsamo in Rotterdam, but it was not enough. His 2:07:02 was still the second fastest on record, though, and a Commonwealth record. He beat his previous best by a massive 4:09! Rousseau ran a national record in second and became the first – and so far only – man with two sub-2:08s to his credit. It was only the fifth time that two runners had finished under 2:08:00 in the same race.

RESULT:  
1 Samuel Lelei 2:07:02  
2 Vincent Rousseau 2:07:20  
3 Antonio Pinto 2:08:57  
4 Samuel Nyangincha 2:09:36  

Lelei's coach Dieter Hogen, whose other pupil Uta Pippig won the women's event in 2:25:36, said afterwards: "We were looking for a 2:07 time and I am happy that Sammy stayed relaxed . . . You can't ask for more if you have both winners at such a marathon." Lelei's first notable performances on the world scene was in 1992, when he won the Cascade Run Off (15 km) and Peachtree (10 km) races in the USA. His brilliant Berlin race stamped him as an early favourite for Atlanta.

In the Chicago marathon Martin, holder of the British record for 10000 m (27:23.06) showed that the knowledge he had gained from books and from his 1993 London win certainly gave him the right kind of experience. He waited (in the company of Carlos Bautista MEX and Leonid Shvetsov RUS) until the last few hundred metres and then used his tremendous leg speed to win by 3 seconds in 2:11:18.

On 22 October two sub-2:10 times were recorded in the Reims marathon when Beblo and John Kipkoskei KEN both set personal bests, the Pole winning in 2:09:41 against 2:09:54. Six days later a number of famous names took part in the Chunchon marathon in Korea, but none of them won. Vera was first in 2:11:30, with Hwang second (2:11:32), Salah fifth, Dinsamo seventh (2:14:39), and Mekonnen 11th, while Kipngok did not finish.

The next day, in Venice, there was a chaotic start to the men's race. After the women's start, the men pushed forward into the top runners' zone and the race got under way five minutes before the official start. Two Italians, Danilo Goffi and Giacomo Leone, finished first and second in 2:09:26 and 2:09:34 respectively.

On 12 November Silva was back in a very cold, windy New York to defend his title. During the year he had suffered a personal loss when his father died, but he had prepared meticulously in the Desert of the Lions near Mexico City and was ready. There would be no going off course this time. His decisive surge in the 23rd mile got rid of two-time winner Salvador García. Two miles later the defending champion kicked again and dropped William Koech KEN. Only the tenacious Paul Evans GBR, holder of his country's half-marathon record, hung on – but less than a kilometre from the end even he had to let go. Silva won in 2:11:00, 5 seconds ahead of Evans.

A stellar field assembled in Fukuoka for the 49th running of the race. Luiz dos Santos was there, as well as Serrano, Taniguchi, Diego García, Ndeti and – of course – Ikangaa. It was an immensely exciting race, with García, Dos Santos, Serrano and Masaki Oya JPN reaching 40 km together. A confident Dos Santos (31), by far the most experienced after his two Chicago wins, thirds in Boston and the World Championships and victory in the São Paulo marathon, waited until the final bend on the track in stadium to outsprint Serrano and Oya – despite the fact that Serrano's best for 10000 m is more than a minute faster than his! His time was a new national and South American record, while Oya improved his PB by more than 3 minutes.

---

6. That same year Lelei ran 60:42 – incidentally, also in Berlin. Rousseau's best half-marathon time is 60:23 on the aided Tokyo course.

RESULT:   1   Luiz dos Santos 2:09:30
2   Antonio Serrano 2:09:32
3   Masaki Oya 2:09:33
4   Diego García 2:09:51

Despite the two magnificent sub-2:08s at the top of the performances list, 1995 could not match 1994 for depth. Six runners were under 2:09:00 (Lelei, Rousseau, Cerón, Moneghetti, Pinto and Fiz) compared to fourteen in 1994 (but this figure included seven in Boston). Pinto was the only one with two sub-2:09s. There were only seventeen times faster than 2:10:00 (1994 had 28).[7]

As the first century of the modern marathon drew to a close, one of the most striking aspects of the development of the event was the demise of the once dominant Japanese and the power of the African, European and Mexican runners. At the end of 1987, 735 different runners from 56 countries had recorded 1 009 performances faster than 2:20:00. Japan's 118 performances led the USA by a huge margin. Since then, however, the Japanese have been in decline: there were no Japanese in the top twenty on the world list in 1993 and 1994, only one in 1992 and two in 1995.

Africa emerged as a strong marathon entity in the early eighties and has continued to make its presence felt, often placing five or more runners in the top twenty on the yearly list over the last fifteen years (nine in 1988; eight in 1989). Kenya has supplanted Ethiopia as the continent's major force. Europe, of course, has always been at the forefront of the event (ten Europeans made the top twenty in 1985; nine in 1990; eight in 1995). Three new powers doing well were Mexico (since 1991), Korea (since 1992) and Spain (since 1994). Seventeen countries had national records faster than 2:09:00.

The sport continued to grow in popularity. In 1994 the largest marathon in the world was the New York City marathon with 29 735 finishers. Two other marathons, Honolulu (25 799) and London (25 206), had more than 25 000 finishers. In 1995 more than 34 000 runners (thousands would become walkers in the heat) started in Honolulu. Thanks to the exhaustive statistics of the USATF Road Running Information Center, the growth in marathon participation in the USA can be clearly seen. In a study of the hundred largest races (of which eleven were marathons) it was found that 79 906 runners finished the marathons in 1986. The figure was 92 646 in 1989, 112 824 in 1992, 110 763 in 1993 and 126 429 in 1994. (The 10 km was by far the most popular distance.)

What about the standard of performances? If one looks at the times of the 10th and 100th performers on the annual world lists, the dramatic progress of the sixties and seventies certainly levelled off during the eighties and early nineties – with a very promising upturn in 1994, especially at the top . . . but once again bearing in mind the optimal conditions of that year's race in Boston. The distorting effect Boston had on the 1994 list can be seen in the 1995 times, which fit the trend of the last few years.

Here is a comparison:

|      | 10th    | 100th   | under 2:12:00 |
|------|---------|---------|---------------|
| 1960 | 2:19:54 | –       | 0             |
| 1970 | 2:13:32 | 2:20:58 | 4             |
| 1980 | 2:10:23 | 2:14:25 | 33            |
| 1985 | 2:09:05 | 2:13:39 | 52            |
| 1986 | 2:09:57 | 2:13:38 | 42            |
| 1987 | 2:10:34 | 2:13:34 | 38            |
| 1988 | 2:08:49 | 2:13:08 | 55            |
| 1989 | 2:09:40 | 2:13:37 | 40            |
| 1990 | 2:10:10 | 2:13:30 | 40            |
| 1991 | 2:10:08 | 2:13:13 | 55            |
| 1992 | 2:09:30 | 2:13:22 | 55            |
| 1993 | 2:10:06 | 2:12:50 | 62            |
| 1994 | 2:08:35 | 2:12:24 | 82            |
| 1995 | 2:09:33 | 2:12:32 | 82            |

At the end of 1995 Derek Clayton did not make the top thirty on the all-time list any more (compare the list on p. 105). Thirteen runners had clocked fourteen times under 2:08:00 (all run in Rotterdam, Boston, Chicago, Beijing and Berlin) and the 30th performer on the list was at 2:08:33. An all-time list as at the end of 1995 appears in the Results and Statistics section on p. 190.

7. This total does not include the Venice times mentioned above.

# 8

# *Ninety years in*
# SOUTH AFRICA

THE INAUGURAL MEETING of the SA Amateur Athletic Association took place on 26 March 1894 at the grounds of the Wanderers Club in Johannesburg. The notice convening the meeting announced its two objectives:

"*First.*–To establish the S.A.A.A.A. on a firm basis.

"*Second.*–To hold a General Meeting of Representatives from all centres of Sport, to finally pass and confirm the Rules, which have been provisionally adopted, and under which this Meeting is being held."

Five clubs joined the Association that day: Wanderers, Zoutpansberg, Kimberley, Bloemfontein and Pietermaritzburg. Henry Nourse was elected President. The founding meeting coincided with the first South African Championships, held on 24 and 26 March at the Wanderers' Club Grounds in Kruger's Park (site of the city's present-day main railway station).

Nine events were contested at the meeting, the longest of which was the 3 miles walk. The mile title went to Geo Melville in 4:48.

The next year South African athletes undertook their first overseas trip when four competed in the English Championships in London. They were reported as being the first South Africans to receive Springbok colours. In his book *South African Sports*, published in 1897, G.A. Parker called the foursome "the men who donned the green and orange".

South Africa was not represented at the first Olympic Games, held in Athens in 1896, although *The Star* did state in an editorial that "despite present political turmoil, South Africa should contemplate the proceedings".[1] In 1900 the country was in the throes of the Anglo-Boer War and in 1904 it was still reeling under its effect, so no teams were sent to these Games either.

1. The turmoil referred to was the aftermath of the Jameson Raid.

But South Africa was represented at the 1904 Games, albeit unofficially (see p. 21). Lentauw and Yamasani, two black South Africans working at the Louisiana Purchase Exposition in St Louis, which was held concurrently with the Games, and one B.W. Harris decided to run the marathon. How the two black men made their way to the USA is not known, but South Africa thus became the first African country to have runners in the Olympic marathon. Lentauw and Yamasani ran with ordinary working shirts, the sleeves rolled up, and knee-length trousers. Lentauw was barefoot, but his compatriot wore shoes and socks.

In his book *The Olympic Games 1904* Charles J.P. Lucas described the marathon course as "the most difficult a human being was ever asked to run over".

While running near the front, the two South African runners were attacked by a large dog which, according to one report, chased Lentauw almost a mile off course. Nevertheless, the gallant runner returned to the route and managed to finish ninth, with Yamasani 12th. Their times were not recorded. It may well have been that, but for the canine intervention, South Africa would have won its first Olympic medal in this race! In the results Lentauw and Yamasani were indicated with the designation "Kaffir, South Africa".

That same year the governing bodies for athletics and cycling amalgamated to form the SA Amateur Athletics and Cycling Association. In November the Orange River Colony AA and CA enquired about participation by blacks in competitions. The national board of the SAAA and CA discussed "Native Competition" and informed the Orange River body that there were no rules regarding the matter. The provincial body was discouraged from including such events in meetings, though.

The General Olympic Committee was established on 3 January 1908 and it was decided to send a team to the

Olympic Games in London. The previous year the Cape Town club Spartan Harriers had announced that it would organise a marathon race in preparation for the Games. Doug Coghlan, who researched the history of athletics in South Africa, called this race, held on 15 August 1907, "almost certainly the first official marathon in South Africa". It was run over 26 miles and sixteen runners competed in dusty, windy conditions. The main cause of the dust was the cyclists accompanying the runners – even the officials travelled by cycle because the four cars promised by the Automobile Club did not arrive.

C.T. Childs won in 3:12:55 despite encountering problems with the crowds in Salt River. "From Mowbray Childs and the officials had to force their way through to the finish."

On 30 September Celtic Harriers organised a marathon in Cape Town, and this was won in 3:10:32.8 by James Lambrechts.

A marathon race was scheduled for 13 March in Bloemfontein, but it was cancelled because there were only three competitors. Instead Charles Hefferon ran a 25-mile training run on the Maselspoort road, recording 2:56:00 despite the dust and leg cramps. On the same day the SAAA and CA executive decided to stage a marathon as part of the SA Championships in Cape Town.

Early in April the Transvaal AAA held a race over 20 miles from the Krugersdorp Sports Ground to Johannesburg. Ken McArthur won over rutted roads in 2:20:30 from J.M. Baker and J.N. Cormack.

The first SA marathon was held on 22 April in Cape Town. The distance was announced as being 26¼ miles, but after protests by two of the runners it was changed to 25 miles. The race was run on the Durban road and started at 15:00. The conditions were "terrible", according to the SAAA and CA minutes – it was extremely hot, and dust, petrol fumes and the loose road surface hampered the runners. A horse-drawn cart stayed ten yards in front of McArthur from Goodwood to the finish and would not give way to the runner.

Hefferon and McArthur fought for the lead, with Hefferon setting the pace for the first 10 miles. Then McArthur, the Transvaal cross-country champion, took over and reached the turn in 78:44. He had drunk some champagne at the Early Morning Market and slowed drastically over the second half, eventually finishing in 3:18:27.4. Lambrechts was second and J.W. Connor third. Hefferon dropped out.

The report in *The Cape Argus* stated that McArthur "ran a game race and proved his stamina, although it is evident he lacks the pace to win a race such as the Olympic Marathon". Inexplicably he was not selected for the team, but Hefferon, who had won the mile and 4 miles (both for the fifth successive time) at the Championships, was. J. Mitchell-Baker would join him in the London race.

Hefferon's tactics in the dramatic Olympic marathon (see p. 23) have been questioned, and he himself said on his return to South Africa that he made a mistake in forcing the pace when he was not "severely pressed". Both he and the country's gold medal sprinter, Reggie Walker, returned as heroes and Hefferon was given a rousing reception in Bloemfontein. He claimed that he lost the race because of the drink of champagne he took, that he lost six pounds in weight during the race, and that some of the 135 letters and 350 telegrams he received included proposals of marriage.

The Bloemfontein runners formed a club which they called Hefferon Harriers. Hefferon's performance in the Olympic race resulted in an increase in the popularity of both road and cross-country running in South Africa.

Some South Africans participated in a professional marathon held over the Olympic route on 10 October. They were Charlie Meekoms, Walter Ewins, Richard Ford and a prominent amateur who used the pseudonym James Walsh. A professional race was held in South Africa on 18 March 1909 and won by Arthur Preston, a miner, in 3:10:24. The *Transvaal Leader* called it the "Race of the Century". Preston used the alias Wilson. A month later he won a race over 25 miles in 2:59:01.

Because of the furore created by McArthur's omission from the Olympic team, Hefferon challenged him to a race over any distance between 1 mile and 26 miles. McArthur agreed to meet the Olympic silver medallist in a 5-mile cross-country race at the Wanderers on Boxing Day 1908. He was given 35 seconds start, but Hefferon still passed him and McArthur then dropped out.

Several "marathons" were held over various distances in towns all over South Africa, but these were mostly shorter than the Olympic distance.

Hefferon became a professional in July 1909, but ran only one marathon, on 12 March 1910, when he beat Preston over the standard distance in 3:07:40. The race was held on a 7-laps-to-the-mile track at "The Stadium" in Johannesburg.

On 4 September 1909 McArthur, who worked in the mounted branch of the SA Police, won the Wanderers marathon in 3:03:54. The race started at Zuurfontein and finished with 9 miles on the track. McArthur's time was the fastest on record by a South African amateur. On 23 October he ran an incredible 2:44:36 in Durban, but when the course was rechecked (by motorcycle) it was found to be 1 mile, 16 yards short. However, in 1911 Dr R.D. Howden measured the course three times, using a speedometer ordered from the manufacturers of the new De Dion automobile – guaranteed to be accurate – and found it to be the correct length. At the time the world record was 2:42:31. The second runner, Ramos, clocked 3:10:51 – "a time that seems reasonable when compared with his other performances", according to Coghlan.

The race started at 14:00 from the Old Town Hall and finished with 2 miles on the Lords Ground track. McArthur and eighteen other runners attempted the hilly course and he "finished fresh and walked off the ground smoking".

On 5 February 1910 Ramos won a marathon held with the Camps Bay Gala in 3:22:19, putting his Durban time in perspective. Three days later a marathon for Coloured runners was held over the same course. The winner in 3:38:17 was W.R. Henry.

Nine months later, on 5 November, *The Cape Argus* sponsored a marathon in Cape Town and McArthur got his chance to prove that the Durban time might have been legitimate after all. It was a perfect day when the 175 starters went on their way. McArthur took the lead from the start, joined by Chris Gitsham and A.J.C. Reynolds. By the halfway mark McArthur's lead was already 6 minutes; Gitsham had already withdrawn. The Potchefstroom policeman (who had to run twenty laps of the Green Point track at the end of the race) finished 36 minutes ahead of Reynolds in an amazing 2:42:58.2 – the fastest time yet on an out-and-back course achieved anywhere in the world and less than 30 seconds slower than the world record.

McArthur's prize was £10; he also received "Messrs. Stuttaford and Co.'s Thermos flask for first at the turning point".

In 1912 both McArthur and Gitsham were selected for the Olympic marathon in Stockholm, where they conquered the rest of the world's marathoners by winning the gold and silver medals (see p. 26). Two months before the Games Gitsham had been robbed of a national record when he clocked 2:37:14.6 in the Polytechnic Harriers marathon – but the runners ran only 480 yards on the track at the finish instead of 840.

In 1914 South Africa affiliated to the International Amateur Athletic Federation (IAAF) and paid its affiliation fee of £5. During the war years activities in South Africa, as in the rest of the world, were limited.

In 1920 Gitsham was again selected for the Olympic marathon, and although he spent several weeks training on the Antwerp course and took the lead from the start, he did not finish (see p. 29).

The year 1921 was significant for the establishment of the Comrades ultramarathon between Pietermaritzburg and Durban. The winner was W. "Bill" Rowan. It is interesting to note that walking and running competitions had been held on the road between the two Natal towns as early as the nineteenth Century. In 1876 a Lieutenant Bradshaw of the 13th Regiment walked from Fort Napier, Pietermaritzburg, to Durban in 13 hours, 37 minutes. In 1914 the *Natal Witness* wanted to organise a race from Pietermaritzburg to Drummond and back (52 miles), but the SAAA and CA decided that it was too long.

Harry Phillips, the SA marathon champion in 1923 and 1924, was the country's sole representative in the 1924 Olympic marathon in Paris. He finished 19th in 3:07:13.

In 1928 South Africa again sent only one runner to the Games in Amsterdam. He was the one-armed marathoner

## A UNIQUE MARATHONER

Very little is known about Ken McArthur, who has the unique distinction of being South Africa's only Olympic marathon champion and was one of its earliest athletic heroes. He was born in Derbock, Northern Ireland, on 10 February 1882. While Erich Kamper in his book *Lexikon der 12 000 Olympioniken* gives his names as Kenneth Kane, his gravestone reads Kennedy K. McArthur.

McArthur was an excellent track and cross-country runner. At the SA Championships of 1912, held in Cape Town a week before the team's departure to Stockholm for the Olympic Games, he won the 10 miles (55:11.2), beating Chris Gitsham, and came second in the 4 miles, again beating Gitsham. The selectors did not want to include Gitsham in the team, but H.B. Keartland, the team coach, insisted that Gitsham was not a natural track runner and should be entered for the marathon (although he had never run one).

In England the team stayed at Preston Park near Brighton, but McArthur struggled to acclimatise and was sent to Uxbridge with a specified training schedule to follow. There he found a friend and adviser in A.B. George, a journalist and ex-running champion, who accompanied him on long training runs. McArthur immediately improved.

Meanwhile Gitsham's excellent performance in the Polytechnic marathon justified Keartland's confidence in him. The story of the dramatic race between them in Stockholm is related on p. 26.

After his victory in the Olympic marathon McArthur received a bronze statue of Pheidippides from the Crown Prince of Sweden. This had to be returned to the IOC but, unbeknown to McArthur, found its way to Johannesburg. It was located in the Johannesburg Museum twelve years later and returned to Lausanne.

In 1956 McArthur was named as South Africa's best-ever marathoner by the eminent statistician Harry Beinart. Gitsham was placed third.

McArthur died on 13 June 1960.

McArthur's marathons (not all were over the standard distance):

| 2:20:30 | Johannesburg | 1 | 11.04.08 |
| 3:18:27.4 | Cape Town | 1 | 22.04.08 |
| 3:03:54.2 | Johannesburg | 1 | 04.09.09 |
| 2:44:36 | Durban | 1 | 25.10.09 |
| 2:42:58.2 | Cape Town | 1 | 05.11.10 |
| 2:36:54.8 | Stockholm | 1 | 14.07.12 |

from Vryheid, Marthinus Steytler. Earlier in the year he had run a phenomenal 2:26:37 at Paarl, breaking the world record by almost 2½ minutes, but the course was found to be 2 miles short. On 13 May he did succeed in breaking McArthur's national record when he ran 2:41:35 in Durban. In Amsterdam Steytler was 40th in 2:57:21.

The decade of the thirties was characterised by the immense rivalry between two of the greatest marathon runners ever produced in South Africa, Johannes Lodewyk Meyer ("Johnny") Coleman and Henry Alfred ("Jackie") Gibson. The first SA marathon of the new decade was won by Steytler in 2:57:35.2, but the foremost runner of the early part of the decade was Thomas Lalande, who finished second behind Samuel Ferris in the 1932 Polytechnic marathon in 2:43:30.4. Just over a month later, on 1 July, Lalande clocked 2:42:28.4 in the AAA race.

In 1933 Lalande again ran in the "Poly", but failed to finish (he was unemployed at the time and could not eat adequately). In the AAA marathon he led by almost 3 minutes at 15 miles, but just past 20 miles he collapsed again. In the 1934 AAA race he started more prudently and came home third in 2:58:37. However, the next year he once again could not complete the Polytechnic race.

No South African went to the Olympic Games in 1932, and in the years 1931-34 the winning time in the national championship was never below 3 hours. But then, in 1935, a new era started.

In October 1934 Coleman had run his first marathon, winning in 2:54:45. In September 1935 he won the Natal Championship in 2:41:50. Earlier in the year Gibson had won the SA title in Pretoria with ease in 2:52:40.4. (He also won the 10 miles.) Hardy Ballington was second in 3:04:25.2.

About two months after his Natal win, on 16 November, Coleman tackled another marathon in Durban. He shattered Steytler's SA record by more than 3 minutes, winning in 2:38:32. But even this was nothing compared to what he had in store for 1936, the Olympic year.

At the SA Championship on 11 April in Port Elizabeth Coleman met Gibson for the first time. Thirteen runners started at 08:00, but it was essentially a three-man race to halfway. Wallace ("Wally") Hayward was the only competitor who could keep up with the flying Coleman and Gibson, but after 16 miles even he found the pace too fast. With a slight breeze behind them on the return trip, Coleman and Gibson really piled on the pressure. They were still together when they entered the Westbourne Oval. Then Coleman sprinted and gained the upper hand. His 2:31:57.4 was a new Africa record and at the time the fastest in the world for the year (he would end up fourth on the world list for 1936). Gibson clocked 2:32:09. The third runner was more than 11 minutes behind Gibson.

There is an interesting story about this race. Coleman always ran without his dentures, but also did not want to finish a race without them. So he had his sister standing with them at the small gate through which the runners had to enter the stadium. When he and Gibson reached the gate, spectators were surprised to see Coleman stand back so that Gibson could run through first! He assured his frantic sister that Gibson was tired and that he would catch him. He then took his teeth from her, put them in his mouth and set off after his rival.

The next day, Sunday, Coleman completed a 10-mile training run and on the Monday he won the title over this distance in a championship record 53:53.8!

The exciting Port Elizabeth marathon was the start of a remarkable series of six battles between the two men. They were both selected, with Lalande, for the 1936 Olympics. Lalande ran an excellent 2:36:18 in the Poly on 13 June.

In Berlin Coleman was in fourth position until the last 7 km (see p. 40). When he entered the stadium, he waved to his team-mates – with an amazing result. To the thousands of German spectators the wave looked like a Hitler salute . . . and they jumped to their feet with a thunderous "Heil Hitler!"

Coleman finished sixth in 2:36:17, Gibson eighth in 2:38:04 and Lalande (who was struck by a cramp in his calf soon after the start) 27th in 2:57:20.

On 27 March 1937 Coleman and Gibson met for the third time. After two losses Gibson was eager to take revenge. Coleman was undefeated in four marathons on home soil and had not been beaten by a South African yet. The course for the SA marathon in Bloemfontein consisted of five laps, and the two men again ran shoulder to shoulder until the closing stages. Then Coleman faded – a victim, probably, of the high altitude (1 392 m). Gibson reached the finish in the Ramblers Stadium in a wonderful new continental record of 2:30:45 – the second fastest time in the world that year (a mere 7 seconds behind list leader Manuel Dias POR). This phenomenal record would stand for seventeen years.

Coleman was a well-beaten second in 2:36:29, with A.J. Reeve third in 2:54:07.5.

Gibson was born in Johannesburg on 31 March 1914 and started running track races in 1930. He joined Johannesburg Harriers in 1932 and ran his first marathon the same year. A slight, wiry athlete, he won the SA 10-mile title in 1935 and the 6 miles in 1940.

After serving as a gunner with the SA Air Force in the Middle East during World War II he returned in 1943 and was commissioned as an observer navigator. On a reconnaisance flight near Durban on 15 January 1944 his plane crashed and he and three other officers were killed.

Coleman and Gibson were selected for the 1938 British Empire Games in Sydney. The team arrived in Sydney on 2 January and Coleman, a prodigious trainer, immediately launched into a strenuous programme. In the first week he ran 77 miles and by the fourth week he was up to 126 miles, including runs of 26 and 27 miles. His total for the last week before the race on 7 February was 100 miles, despite resting for two days – a rare occurrence for him! His five sessions for the week were 27, 13, 22, 22 and 16 miles (the latter "cross-country").

Two days before the race Coleman had a sore throat. The next day he read in a newspaper that the English runner Al Norris had brought his wife with him to Australia to see him win the marathon. This was the best motivation the South African could have received.

With the marathon at sea level there was no stopping Coleman. He won a brilliant race, his seventh in nine marathons, by more than 7 minutes and failed to better Gibson's record by 4.8 seconds (see p. 41). It was the second-fastest time of the year and placed Coleman eighth on the all-time list. Gibson won the bronze medal in 2:38:20.

The only refreshment Coleman took in the course of the race was a small bottle of glycerine. At 20 miles he saw Norris's wife waiting for him with a glass of orange juice; he

## RACING OSTRICHES AND TRAINS

A strong case could be made that Johannes Coleman was the greatest marathoner South Africa has produced. He never won an Olympic gold like Ken McArthur did, but he performed at a consistently high level from 1935 to 1949 – a long time in the life of a marathon runner.

The rivalry between Coleman and Jackie Gibson in the years 1936-40 pushed South Africa's marathon standard to new heights, and Coleman, Gibson and Sid Luyt laid the foundation for the country's proud tradition in the event.

Two years after Gibson's tragic death the Jackie Gibson Memorial marathon was established to honour him. The first race was won by Wally Hayward in 2:43:52 and the second, in 1947, by Coleman in 2:47:04.

Coleman believed in training . . . and more training. A conductor on the railways, he travelled by ship from Durban to Cape Town en route to Berlin for the 1936 Olympics. The ship docked in East London, and Coleman went ashore to run 9 miles. In Port Elizabeth he ran 18 miles . . . and then again in Cape Town. On the *Athlone Castle* to Southampton he ran one to two hours on the deck every day.

Coleman was born in Oudtshoorn on 5 June 1910. He discovered his talent for running on his father's farm when he stole ostrich eggs from the nests and had to escape the wrath of the male ostriches. He said that he had been caught only once, and has borne the scar on his back ever since! He also competed in the local *Boeresport*, but the adults were not very keen on his participation and he had to stand right at the back at the start of races. He always won, however, and his prize was a tickey (three pennies).

Coleman used to race the horse-drawn cart back home when he and a labourer were sent to either Calitzdorp (22 miles from their farm) or Oudtshoorn (12 miles) to buy provisions. He always won, running the former distance in 2 hours, 40 minutes and the latter in 1 hour, 25 minutes. He also raced the train (the farm was next to the Kerkrand line) to Calitzdorp.

Criticism that the jovial, happy-go-lucky Coleman (who strongly believed in his own training methods and never accepted advice) followed the wrong tactics in the 1948 Olympic marathon is probably justified. Near the finish he was accompanied by two police motorcycles. Every time Coleman accelerated, the riders did the same, and to Coleman the noise of the powerful engines was so impressive that he made a game of it, continuously varying his pace. Once inside the stadium, he moved to the outside of the track to be nearer the spectators, waving and smiling. Ahead of him the third runner was staggering, completely exhausted, but Coleman didn't notice. He finished only 32.4 seconds behind the bronze medallist and 74.4 seconds behind the winner. That night he danced until two o'clock the next morning.

Coleman also won the Comrades marathon in 1937 and 1939, both in record times, but his greatest accomplishment must be the fact that he earned fourth spot on the world list in 1936, then second with his wonderful victory in Sydney in 1938 . . . and ten years later was still good enough to place seventh on the list. It was only in 1992 that a South African runner surpassed his 1938 list position!

merely smiled as he ran past, for he was sure of victory.

Nine months later Coleman won the Natal marathon for the fourth time. In an interview with Arrie Joubert many years later Coleman told the story of this race in Pietermaritzburg: "When I arrived at the finish, there were no timekeepers. I found them in the nearby tearoom at Alexander Park and the chief timekeeper, Harold Sulin, told me they had not expected the winner home so quickly. I laughed but I felt like crying, because it must have been my fastest ever marathon. The conditions were ideal. It was a cool, misty day. According to my wrist watch my time was 2 hours 23 minutes and my nearest rival arrived more than 10 minutes later."

Earlier in the year Lalande had been third in the Poly in 2:45:35. He finished in the same position in the AAA marathon the next year.

In 1939 the SA marathon was held at altitude again, in Krugersdorp. As was the case in Bloemfontein two years previously, Gibson was too strong for his rival, beating Coleman 2:35:07 against 2:45:53.

The next year, in the last championship race before the War intervened, Coleman turned the tables in sea-level Durban. He won in 2:37:30, with Gibson second in 2:43:05. This was the last race between the two and the score was 4-2 in Coleman's favour.

Athletics resumed again in 1946 and the first postwar SA marathon was won in 2:39:02 by Hayward. The 1948 marathon, also the Olympic trial, was held in Port Elizabeth on 27 March, eleven years to the day since Gibson's defeat of Coleman in Bloemfontein. Coleman had only been beaten three times, but the question was whether, at almost 38, he could again make the Olympic team.

He was up against newcomer Sydney Luyt (22), a carpenter from Springs who had run his first marathon in 2:39:27 the previous November. The wily Coleman not only won, but ran 2:32:30 against Luyt's 2:38:43.6. Coleman's time was seventh on the world list for the year.

In London bad pace judgment probably cost Coleman a medal (see p. 45). He started much too slowly: at 25 km he was 79 seconds behind Luyt and 2:44 behind the leader, Etienne Gailly BEL, and at 35 km he was eighth, 2:16 behind the first runner. He completed the last 8 miles 77 seconds faster than winner Delfo Cabrera ARG, 40 seconds faster than silver medal winner Tom Richards GBR and nearly 3 minutes faster than Gailly. His last 7.195 km took only 27:48 – 34 seconds faster than Cabrera. Afterwards criticism was levelled at Coleman that he had not taken the race seriously enough.

Coleman finished fourth, looking fresh, in 2:36:06, with Luyt, who had been troubled by a leg injury, a magnificent sixth in 2:38:11. Coleman was only the sixth runner to place in the first six in two Olympic marathons – and he did it twelve years apart!

Two years later Luyt was South Africa's best when it was time for the Empire Games in Auckland. The previous year he had decisively defeated Coleman for the national title in Queenstown, a PB 2:34:16.5 against 2:39:08. He repeated this victory in the trial race at Paarl in November, running 2:39:27 – exactly the same time as in his debut. In Auckland he ran a plucky race against Jack Holden GBR, gaining the silver medal in 2:37:02.2 (see p. 46).

In 1951 Luyt again won the SA title, running an excellent 2:35:42.2 in high-altitude Pretoria, but in 1952 he was beaten by Hayward (2:37:00.5) and William ("Bill") Keith. At the same meeting in Cape Town, held in conjunction with the Van Riebeeck Festival, Luyt retained his 6-mile title.

In the Olympic marathon in Helsinki Hayward also finished as top South African: an astonishing tenth in 2:31:50.2 – and this despite a leg injury for which he had to receive a pain-killing injection the day before the race. The night after the marathon he was treated in hospital. Luyt was one place behind in a PB 2:32:41, with Keith 19th in 2:34:38 (see p. 48).

Hayward's time was the third best by a South African and just over a minute slower than Gibson's national record. After 1952 he turned to the ultradistances and in 1953 at Motspur Park set world records for 50 miles, 100 km, 150 km, 100 miles, 200 km and 24 hours in one race – two months after his course record for the London to Brighton race. In the latter event he broke the record by almost 23 minutes and in the 24-hour race he ran 45 km further than the previous record. That same year he had become the first runner to complete the "down" Comrades ultramarathon in under 6 hours when he won in 5:52:30. In 1954 he won the Comrades for the fifth time – 24 years after his first victory – and became, at 45 years, 10 months, 21 days, the oldest winner in the history of the race.

Hayward (born on 10 July 1908) was a tremendously versatile runner, for he could also boast three SA 10-mile titles (1930, 1932 and 1937) and one at 4 miles (1937). In his four SA marathons he finished first, second, first and second.

In 1954 the SAAA and CA took away his amateur status after he had received 100 guineas from the SA Olympic and Empire Games Association and an equal amount from a liquor company, as well as other amounts from private individuals and the SA Boxing Association, to finance an overseas tour. The money was paid to him directly instead of via the Association, as the rules stipulated. His total expenses were £395 19s 4d, while he only received £285 5s.

There was an outcry, but to no avail. Hayward was bitter: "It was a tremendous shock. I had gone overseas to do my best, to represent my country. And then they did this to me. I never forgave them."

In 1978 he returned to competitive running and at the age of 70 clocked 3:06:24 for the marathon. He followed this up three weeks later with 3:08:35 in the Jackie Gibson Memorial marathon (a race he had won in 1946). In 1988, at the age of 79 years and 10 months, Hayward beat 4 869 runners in the Comrades to finish in a stunning 9:44:15 and win the Founders Trophy for the oldest finisher.

In a long interview the author had with him in 1979 Hayward said that he enjoyed long training sessions – "I'm actually a loner, understand?" He usually got up at 03:00 on a Sunday to do a training run of 80 km or so. His favourite road was the Old Main Road between Johannesburg and Pretoria, and he would stop at a café at Halfway House to drink "a few cups of tea" and eat a piece of sponge cake.

The 1954 SA marathon was won by Jackie Mekler, the Southern Transvaal champion, in 2:35:25.1. Hayward was second and newcomer Jan Barnard third. Mekler (born 4 March 1932) would win the Southern Transvaal title three more times in succession and the Comrades five times (1958, 1960, 1963, 1964 and 1968). In the trial race for the Empire Games in Vancouver he was no match for Barnard, though. Barnard, like McArthur and Gibson a member of Johannesburg Harriers, started his career as a track and cross-country runner. Although he only ran 2:48:18 in the SA marathon, he shattered Gibson's national record in the trial, run on 31 May in Port Elizabeth. He won in 2:25:31.8, the seventh fastest time in the world in 1954. Mekler also bettered the previous record in second, clocking 2:28:58. Gerald Walsh was third in 2:31:50, with Hayward just 8 seconds behind him in another marvellous performance. Twelve days later he would win his final Comrades, setting a record for the "up" run; Walsh would again be third.

Barnard (born 21 October 1929) thus went to Vancouver for the marathon on 7 August as one of the strongest medal contenders. In the dramatic race in which Jim Peters GBR collapsed on the track (see p. 52) Mekler and Barnard ran conservatively in the heat and took the silver and bronze medal respectively in 2:40:57 and 2:51:49.8.

This defeat by his countryman only made Barnard more determined to show that he was the best, and in 1955 he started a four-year period of huge success. He won the national title in Pretoria in 2:36:39.6 and was also first in the 6 miles. At the end of the year he led the all-time lists in the 2 miles, 6 miles, 10 miles and marathon. McArthur's 52:46.2 of 1911 was still second on the 10-mile list.

In July Walsh was timed in 2:22:38 and Mercer Davies in 2:24:28 in a 38-mile race between King William's Town and East London. Walsh's time, however, was not accepted as a national record. In the 1956 SA marathon Barnard beat Davies, 2:37:36 against 2:38:05.

Mekler spent most of 1955 in Britain, but suffered a knee injury which prevented him from doing his best. He placed 12th in the Poly (2:40:21), third in the AAA marathon, second in the Scottish championship (2:39:28) and second in the Turku marathon.

On 6 October 1956 Barnard brought South Africa a little closer to the 2:20:00 barrier when he sped to a tremendous 2:21:37.2 in Port Elizabeth. This was the eighth fastest time in the world for the Olympic year. Davies was second in 2:25:06.

Barnard, who was injured, had a disastrous race in the Melbourne Olympic marathon. While he started well and was in the first fifteen after 5 km, he steadily fell off the pace and at 25 km was more than 4 minutes behind the leader, Alain Mimoun FRA. He dropped out after 35 km. Davies ran a well-judged race, moving from 22nd at 25 km to finish 14th in 2:39:48.

In 1957, the year that the SA Amateur Athletic Union (SAAAU) was formed, Mekler won his second national title, running 2:33:06.8 for the fastest SA time of the year. He and Davies received Springbok colours to represent South Africa in the Classical marathon in Athens, where Mekler was fourth (2:36:04.6) and Davies sixth (2:39:49.6). They ended the year with the five fastest times in South Africa between them. In 1958 Barnard regained the SA title (and also won the 6 miles). His time was 2:28:04, the best ever in the Championship, and he was followed by Marthinus Wiid (2:30:45) and Mekler (2:32:32). The trial for the Empire Games was held in Durban on 17 May and again Barnard won, in 2:36:30.2. It was a narrow victory, though: Wiid was only 8.8 seconds behind. Keith James finished third and Mekler fourth.

In the Empire Games marathon in Cardiff Barnard had a great run and although he put everything into his charge in the last part of the race, it was not enough to catch David Power (see p. 56). Barnard won the silver medal in 2:22:57.4, 11.8 seconds behind the Australian. Wiid was 13th in 2:36:07.2.

James won both the 1959 and 1960 SA titles, the latter in Bloemfontein in an excellent 2:29:14.6. Mekler was second (2:32:03.4) and Barnard third (2:34:27.2). James placed second in the first Seoul marathon on 28 September 1959, clocking a PB 2:27:52. He ended the year with the three fastest times by a South African.

In 1960 South Africa took part in the Olympic Games for the last time for many years. James performed exceptionally well in Rome, running another PB of 2:22:58.6 for 13th – the second fastest time ever by a South African.

At the end of the year the South African all-time list was:

| 2:21:37.2 | Jan Barnard | Port Elizabeth | 1956 |
| 2:22:58.6 | Keith James | Rome | 1960 |
| 2:25:06 | Mercer Davies | Port Elizabeth | 1956 |
| 2:26:47.4 | Marthinus Wiid | Durban | 1960 |
| 2:28:58 | Jackie Mekler | Port Elizabeth | 1954 |
| 2:30:45 | Jackie Gibson | Bloemfontein | 1937 |
| 2:30:49.8 | Johannes Coleman | Sydney | 1938 |
| 2:31:50 | Gerald Walsh | Port Elizabeth | 1954 |
| 2:31:50.2 | Wally Hayward | Helsinki | 1952 |
| 2:32:05.5 | Oelof Vorster | Durban | 1960 |

The growing isolation of South Africa since 1960 (see also pp. 67 and 82) struck its athletes a cruel blow. In the years 1961-65 the top performance on the SA performance list was never faster than 2:24:00, and Barnard's national record was ten years old by the time it was broken in 1966 by South Africa's first dream miler, De Villiers Lamprecht, who ran 2:20:42.5 on the difficult Stellenbosch course. In the period 1961-70 the SA title (for whites) was won five times in over 2½ hours. In the same period the fastest time by a black runner was 2:23:32 by Bennett Makgamathe in 1967 – the second fastest time of the year by a South African.

In 1962 Barnard became the first athlete to receive Springbok colours in all three branches of athletics: track, road and cross-country.

In 1965 two separate trials were held for white and black runners to select a team for the Classical marathon in Athens. The two races were held on the same day and over the same course in Potchefstroom! Cornelius van Antwerp won the race for whites in 2:30:43.8 and Clifford Malope the race for blacks in 2:30:34.8, 3.6 seconds ahead of Johannes Metsing. The two blacks were selected, and in the tremendous heat of Athens Malope came fourth in 3:04:52. Metsing failed to finish.

In 1966 the first noteworthy performance by a woman came from Sarie van der Westhuizen, who clocked 3:39:27. That same year Malope became the first black runner under 2½ hours when he clocked 2:28:53 at Libanon.

In 1968 track and cross-country star Willie Olivier, who had been second in Lamprecht's record run, broke the record by running 2:20:21 on the last day of May. Still, the record had only progressed by a little more than a minute since Barnard's day, while the world record was already under 2:10:00. The time was ripe for the next marathon star to appear on the scene.

He did so on 6 March 1971 in the Western Province (WP) Championship. Ferdinand ("Ferdie") le Grange, a medical student at Stellenbosch University, chose an undulating course at Durbanville, near Cape Town, for his first outing over the marathon distance. Years later Le Grange said that he had gone over the course the day before and found it "really hilly . . . I just couldn't believe I was going to run so far . . . My longest training run had only been 32 km."

The 22-year-old Le Grange ran an amazing race, and at the end of it the 2:20:00 barrier had fallen. He won by 16 minutes in 2:19:02.2. Scarcely two months later he returned to the same venue for the Republic Festival marathon – and ran even faster! He trounced Olivier by almost 7 minutes in 2:17:51.4.

In between Le Grange's two magnificent runs Johnny Halberstadt who, like many other South African athletes had gone to a US university in order to further his athletic career, finished an excellent third in Boston in 2:22:23. Lamprecht won the SA title in 2:23:38.4 and these three headed the performance list for the year.

Le Grange picked up a leg injury and was out of training for about eight months. In February 1972 he returned to competition: he first ran 30:01.6 over 10000 m and five days later covered 19 447 m in an hour on the soft Bellville grass track. On 4 March he tackled the Durbanville course for the third time. He was not yet at a peak for the marathon and his 69:44 at halfway was too fast. He won in 2:23:36.8 and then started preparing for his first international competition.

Exactly three months later, on 4 June, he lined up in Manchester for the AAA marathon, also the British trial for the Olympic Games in Munich – which, of course, was off limits for the South African star. With him in the field of 279 was an array of stars: the West Germans Lutz Philipp and Paul Angenvoorth, Carlos Peréz ESP, and the Britons Ron

Hill, Bernie Plain, Jim Alder, Bill Adcocks, Don Macgregor, Don Faircloth and Colin Kirkham. The temperature was 13 °C at the early morning start, ensuring fast times. The race developed into a battle between Philipp and Hill which the former won by one second in 2:12:50. In this elite field (24 ran faster than 2:20:00, equalling the most ever in a single race) Le Grange did exceptionally well by finishing eighth, setting his third SA record (2:16:19).

"I didn't feel good," he later commented on his performance. "I knew I could run a lot better. I just hadn't recovered from my flight." (He had only arrived about six days before the race.) He also said that he had never run on such a flat course in his life. "At times I wished there had been a few hills like back home. Then I am sure I would have got nearer the front boys."

Another South African, Dave Hensman, who was studying in England, finished 40th in 2:24:07, placing him fourth on the SA list for the year. A black runner accompanying Le Grange on the tour, Peter Reele, ran 2:41:23.

Then Le Grange crossed the Channel to race in Brussels a week later. This time he not only set an SA record, but also a "world record". No other runner had ever succeeded in running two sub-2:20s within a week. The East German Jurgen Busch twice did 2:17+ within eleven days in 1969 and the same year Derek Clayton clocked 2:17:26 eleven days before his world record 2:08:33.6 in Antwerp. Le Grange showed no ill effects from his race seven days before and won in 2:15:34.6.

When questioned in 1995 about the proximity of the two races, Le Grange said that his schedule had been arranged by the national body. "I ran because I was representing my country."

In May 1981 Bernard Rose would emulate Le Grange with 2:16:14 in Durban and 2:13:01 a week later. In October 1993 the Algerian Mohamed Salmi achieved a fantastic double: he ran a PB 2:13:09 in Lyon and a week later 2:12:47 in Eindhoven.

In March 1973 Le Grange again won the WP marathon (on the Durbanville course) in preparation for an overseas tour. In 14th place, in 2:56:11, was medical student Tim Noakes, who years later would become a sports physiologist of world renown.

Le Grange had one more marathon before he left. It was a historic occasion: white and black marathon runners competed together in the SA Games race, held through the streets of Pretoria on 6 April. It was part of an international

2. In 1971 the first ever "multiracial" athletics meeting in South Africa had taken place in the Green Point Stadium, Cape Town, when for the first time black and white athletes competed against one another in the same events. A large overseas contingent took part. The previous year the IAAF had decided that SA athletes could henceforth only participate internationally in individual competitions. South African athletes still went overseas and competed in the few countries where they were welcome, but in 1976 the country was expelled from the IAAF.

## THE FASTEST SINCE BIKILA

Ferdie le Grange was born in Molteno on 26 August 1948. He went to Stellenbosch University to study medicine and first made his mark as a track runner. In 1970 he ran 14:55.2 to place second in the 5000 m at the Universities Championships. The winner of that race was Johnny Halberstadt, the man who nine years later would break Le Grange's SA marathon record.

Three weeks before his first marathon Le Grange ran 30:27.6 for 10000 m and followed this sixteen days after the marathon with 12 miles, 262 yards for the hour.

At the height of his running career he had to carefully juggle his training and studies. In an interview in *SA Runner* he said in 1979: "You know that road between Bellville and Cape Town? – Voortrekker Road; it's lit up fairly well at night. At nights when I left work at the hospital, I'd go out training – sometimes 10 o'clock, sometimes 12 o'clock. I was really burning the candle at both ends – sometimes only getting a couple of hours sleep a night for five or six consecutive nights."

Despite these difficulties Le Grange turned himself into the fastest marathoner in Africa – and it was the hardship under which he trained that made his achievements all the more extraordinary.

"I never really had much time to train, so the mileage I did was of a good quality. I used to do my long runs of 30-35 km at 2:19 or better pace. No jogging . . ." He did not believe in the methods of Arthur Lydiard and trained "unconventionally for a marathoner".

In 1974, after running the fastest marathon on the continent of Africa, Le Grange retired. He suffered from tendinitis following the race, and this took a long time to heal (he had to abandon a planned overseas tour). He was only 26. "It was a big disappointment," he told the author in an interview, "and difficult to accept. I believe I could have run under 2:10." But he was also busy with his houseman year, and his studies took precedence.

He finished his career with personal bests of 13:46.6 for 5000 m and 28:55.0 for 10000 m – sixth and fourth on the all-time list – and an Africa record for the hour. His 5000 m time, run in Eschweiler in 1973, was only 2.6 seconds slower than the then SA record. Five years later he said: "I love my work, medicine is my life. I'm so busy that I don't get much chance to think about how things could be or how they might have been."

He still ran, but only to keep fit, and only sporadically. There was nothing more to prove.

His sub-2:20 marathons were:

| | | |
|---|---|---|
| 2:12:47 | Port Elizabeth | 23.04.74 |
| 2:13:58 | Manchester | 03.06.73 |
| 2:15:34.2 | Brussels | 11.06.72 |
| 2:15:40 | Durbanville | 02.03.74 |
| 2:16:19 | Manchester | 04.06.72 |
| 2:17:40 | East London | 14.07.73 |
| 2:17:51.4 | Durbanville | 08.05.71 |
| 2:19:02.2 | Durbanville | 06.03.71 |

celebration of athletics in the Pilditch stadium in which athletes from seventeen overseas countries participated over three days.[2] Ten SA records fell. Le Grange's margin was almost 7 minutes as he won in 2:24:12.

On 3 June he was in Manchester for the fifth Maxol marathon. Some of his rivals of 1972 were there again, such as Philipp, Angenvoorth and Faircloth, but there were also East Germany's Eckhard Lesse, Canada's Brian Armstrong and the Japanese Yoshinobu Kitayama and Yoshiaki Morita. Of course, Le Grange was a different runner from 1972.

Sonja Laxton as thousands of spectators have seen her in road races all over the country: always ready with a smile even when competing for a South African title. Laxton set four SA marathon records and won her second SA championship at the age of 44 – twelve years after the first.

Ingrid Kristiansen on her way to winning the London marathon for the fourth time in 1988. Her 2:21:06 world record in this race in 1985 still stood eleven years later. Her eight sub-2:26 marathons are more than any other woman has run. (Touchline Media/Gray Mortimore)

Gelindo Bordin made history in the 1990 Boston marathon when he became the first male Olympic champion to win the race. At the time he was also European champion – a unique achievement. (Touchline Media/Damian Strohmeyer)

The smile says it all: Rosa Mota wins the 1988 Olympic marathon. Her feat of three European titles — the first one in her debut – is unsurpassed in the annals of marathon running. (Touchline Media/Tony Duffy)

He ran with much more confidence, leading at 10 km in 31:56. He was still in front at 15 km (47:27) and 20 km (62:35). Then the runners were drenched by a cloudburst and at 25 km (78:04) Le Grange was spearheading a large group consisting of Lesse, Kitayama, Armstrong, Morita and Philipp. They reached 30 km in 93:16 and it was only then that the South African started to fall back as Lesse pushed the pace. The East German won in 2:12:24, a national record, with Kitayama second in 2:13:29 and Armstrong third, a second behind. Le Grange finished in a superb 2:13:58, the world's tenth fastest for the year.

Before returning to South Africa to claim the national title in 2:17:40 Le Grange showed his splendid form when he ran a PB 28:55.0 for 10000 m in Athens ten days after the Maxol race. This was less than 28 seconds slower than the SA record.

On 24 January 1974 he became the first runner from Africa to exceed 20 km in an hour, breaking the record of none other than Abebe Bikila, when he ran 20 158 m on the Bellville track. Just over five weeks later he won his fourth WP title on the Durbanville course in a course and championship record of 2:15:40. But these were just warm-ups.

He was getting ready for the greatest performance of his career, and he delivered it in the SA Open marathon on 23 April in Port Elizabeth.

After the Durbanville race he had said that he wanted to run 2:12+. He set out to do that in perfect weather, reaching 5 km in 15:23 and 10 km in 31:08. He was already 48 seconds faster than in Manchester – and too fast for Armstrong, who had dropped off the pace. With him was Lesotho's Gabashane Rakabaele, who had finished 12th in the Commonwealth Games marathon in January, but the South African's relentless pressure proved too much and by 20 km (61:59) Le Grange was 41 seconds ahead. His second 10 km had taken only 30:51.

He sped through 25 km in 77:40, still a 2:11:00 pace. Then he started slowing (he would later say that the rough road surface gave him trouble and he developed blisters from an imported pair of shoes that had not been run in adequately) and the next 5 km took him 15:58. In the gathering dusk he held his form beautifully, though, and ran through the finish in the UPE Stadium in 2:12:47. It was a brilliant run which placed him seventh on the world list for the year. Ronnie Brimelow was second in 2:24:49.2 and Derek Preiss third in 2:25:23.6.

This was Le Grange's last serious effort in the marathon – his studies took too much of his time – although he has always kept fairly fit and in 1995 finished 105th in the SA marathon (again in Port Elizabeth!) in 2:46:01. "I had no aspirations – it was nice to be part of it all again." In 1985 he ran the Comrades in 6:44:47 and in 1994 the Two Oceans ultramarathon over 56 km in Cape Town in 3:53:57.

In 1973 Le Grange had been joined under the 2:20:00 barrier by Joe Bellingham, who ran 2:18:05 in Stellenbosch,

and in 1974 two more runners followed: Dave Levick 2:18:41 and Lood Rabie 2:19:22.

A second significant event in 1974, besides Le Grange's run, was the 3:05:02 recorded by fifteen-year-old Suzanne Gaylard (six weeks after she had run 3:10:10). This gave respectability to South Africa's female marathoning and, although it would not be bettered before 1979, it provided the impetus for greater participation by the country's women at a time when internationally Kathrine Switzer and Nina Kuscsik were fighting for women's equality in the marathon. Suzanne's twin sister, Dianne, clocked 3:25:48.

Over the next four years no one came to within 20 minutes of Gaylard's time (except she herself with 3:15:47 in 1976), but runners such as Lettie van Zyl, Alet Kleynhans, Elizabeth Cavanagh and Janet Bailey gradually drew more and more women to races through their performances, modest as they were.

There were no further sub-2:20 times until 10 September 1977, when Brian Chamberlain won the Stellenbosch marathon in 2:18:30. The next day, in faraway Eugene, Oregon, Halberstadt and Bernard Rose finished fifth and ninth in the Nike/OTC marathon, running 2:15:18 and 2:17:46 respectively. Two weeks after his Stellenbosch race Chamberlain easily won the SA Open marathon in 2:19:20 to become the only athlete apart from Le Grange to have more than one sub-2:20.

The day before Chamberlain's victory history was made with the founding of the SA Road Running Association (SARRA) – the body that would oversee and guide the tremendous explosion in road running over the next almost two decades until its unfortunate and traumatic demise in 1994. SARRA achieved immense success in regulating road running in the country, setting standards, developing officials and administrators, and promoting the sport at all levels. Under the able leadership of Mick and Cheryl Winn it gave SA road running a name for excellence in sports administration.

One of South Africa's most talented runners, Matthews Batswadi, became the first black athlete to be honoured with Springbok colours. The next year all black athletes who were members of official South African contingents overseas since 1971 were retrospectively awarded Springbok colours.

In 1978 Chamberlain improved further, to 2:15:25.8 in the Stellenbosch marathon, but on the penultimate day of the year he was passed on the performance list by newcomer Kevin Shaw, who clocked 2:14:02 to win the Sea of Galilee marathon. Halberstadt again ran well in Eugene, finishing seventh in 2:16:21. He did something even Le Grange could not do: he ran three sub-2:20s in one year (the others were 2:19:36 in winning the SA marathon[3] and 2:19:53 – a

---

3. This was the first time a single national title race was held after years in which blacks and whites had had their own events and, from 1974, also an open championship.

week apart). Three more runners dipped under 2:20:00 for the first time in 1978: Willie Farrell 2:18:47, Craig Hepburn 2:18:19 and Geoff Tribe 2:19:37.

In 1979 Clare Taylor broke the 3-hour barrier for the first time – not once, but twice! She first ran 3:01:32 in Johannesburg and then, on 24 March, 2:57:26 in the Interprovincial marathon in East London. Di Alperstein was second in 2:58:53. On 15 September Taylor, a 22-year-old chartered accountant, won the Stellenbosch marathon in 2:56:28. In three races she had slashed the SA record by 8:34.

The men's race in Stellenbosch was also a magnificent affair. Five athletes ran faster than 2:20:00 – the first time this had happened in a South African marathon. Shaw dearly wanted the SA record and sped the first 5 km from the Vlottenburg wine cellar in an almost incredible 14:34 (2:03:00 pace). He reached halfway in 63:36 – the fastest ever by a South African for the distance! The bearded runner faded badly over the last few kilometres, yet still finished in 2:13:21. Behind him Ben Choeu improved from 2:31:54 to 2:18:17, John Donald ran 2:18:54, Rakabaele 2:19:16 and Rabie 2:19:27.

But Shaw's time was not even among the three fastest of the year! Six days before, Halberstadt had won the battle for the SA record between him, Shaw and Rose when he blitzed the Natal marathon in Durban in 2:12:19 after going through halfway in 66:25. The weather was ideal, but Halberstadt was "feeling emotionally drained" after a week in which he had refused the Springbok colours awarded to him for winning the national cross-country title. He gave the administrative problems regarding a passport for Matthews Motshwarateu to further his studies in the USA as the reason for his decision. After the race, in which he had planned to run sub-2:12, Halberstadt (born on 2 October 1949) also complained about the lack of kilometre marks to monitor his progress and about the fact that he was not allowed a personal second (the race was run on a four-lap course through the city's streets). Geoff Bacon was second in 2:22:06.

The same day Rose finished 11th in Eugene in 2:15:04. In March he had made an attempt on Le Grange's record in the Peninsula marathon in Cape Town, but had to be content with 2:14:41. He beat Rakabaele and Chamberlain.

On 20 October Halberstadt, Rakabaele and Rose contested the SA title in Port Elizabeth. It was a tough battle which Rakabaele, certainly the freshest of the trio, won in 2:12:27. Halberstadt was second in 2:13:10 and Rose third, only 5 seconds behind. Nine runners were under 2:20:00.

In March Farrell had dipped under 2:15:00 with his 2:14:52 in the Buffalo marathon in East London.

The upsurge in the standard could be seen in the fact that four runners, Halberstadt, Rose, Hepburn and Donald, each had three times under 2:20:00. The year ended with no fewer than thirteen runners under the barrier, with eight under 2:18:00.

The decade closed with the all-time list looking quite different than in 1960:

| | | | |
|---|---|---|---|
| 2:12:19 | Johnny Halberstadt | Port Elizabeth | 1979 |
| 2:12:27 | Gabashane Rakabaele | Port Elizabeth | 1979 |
| 2:12:47 | Ferdie le Grange | Port Elizabeth | 1974 |
| 2:13:15 | Bernard Rose | Port Elizabeth | 1979 |
| 2:13:21 | Kevin Shaw | Stellenbosch | 1979 |
| 2:14:52 | Willie Farrell | East London | 1979 |
| 2:15:25 | Brian Chamberlain | Stellenbosch | 1978 |
| 2:16:01 | Craig Hepburn | Port Elizabeth | 1979 |
| 2:16:52 | John Donald | East London | 1979 |
| 2:17:06 | Ben Choeu | Port Elizabeth | 1979 |

The year 1980 started fairly slowly, but when spring arrived, things began happening. On 6 September Bacon, just past his 38th birthday, gave the world a foretaste of what Carlos Lopes would prove in 1984 and 1985 – that age is not a hindrance in the marathon – when he ran to a South African record 2:12:10 in the Eastern Province marathon in Port Elizabeth. He clocked 25:08 for 8 km, 50:01 for 16 km and 1:40:05 for 32 km (despite decimalisation many race organisers in South Africa were still thinking in imperial terms!). The race was held on the same course on which Rakabaele won the SA title the previous year (Bacon then ran 2:18:12, his first sub-2:20). Bacon, a bank manager who was born in Port Elizabeth and received Springbok colours for cross-country as long before as 1967, ran in the colours of one of South Africa's oldest clubs, Durban Athletic Club (DAC). Ironically, the record he broke had been set in his club's centenary marathon!

Five days earlier one of the most remarkable performances in South African marathon history came in the Golden Reef marathon between Johannesburg and Brakpan. Running her first marathon at an altitude of more than 1 700 m, track and cross-country star Sonja Laxton blazed to an Africa record 2:46:33. Laxton proved something of which Bacon and Lopes were also prime examples: that a solid cross-country and track background takes one a long way towards marathon success. The record did not last long as twelve days later Stellenbosch computer science student Judy Ryan, who was born in England in 1961, won the Stellenbosch marathon in 2:44:28. It was her second marathon – in 1978 she had completed the WP marathon on a whim in 3:22:21.

The Stellenbosch race became the first in which three women ran under 3 hours: Isavel Roche-Kelly clocked 2:49:01 and Judy Pace 2:56:38. Halberstadt won the men's race with "only" 2:20:15.

Earlier in the year Taylor had run 2:51:55 in the Peninsula marathon.

A month after Stellenbosch, on 11 October, the SA marathon was contested on a two-lap course at Eerste River on the Cape Flats. In May Natal runner Thompson Magawana (21) had been disqualified in a marathon in Durban after he and several other runners had been directed off the course by mistake and in July he had placed third (2:18:54, the same time as Farrell) in the DAC marathon won in 2:14:30 by Shaw.

In the SA race, run in cool, rainy and windy weather, Magawana seemed oblivious of the reputations of his more famous rivals. He stormed away from the start, leaving Halberstadt, Farrell, Bacon and Rakabaele behind. He sped through 5 km in 15:40 and halfway in 65:32, with a lead of 25 seconds on Halberstadt and Farrell. At 30 km (94:15) he was 31 seconds ahead. When Halberstadt realised that the newcomer (Magawana had run his first marathon the previous year) was not coming back to them, it was too late. Magawana won in 2:12:50, with Halberstadt second (2:13:27) and Farrell third (2:13:43). The standard was the deepest ever seen in the country: nine runners were under 2:20:00 and 42 under 2½ hours. Halberstadt and Farrell were the only two in the top fifteen who did not run personal bests; in ninth place Mark Plaatjes set an SA junior record of 2:19:55.

After the race Magawana commented: "I think I am dreaming. I would have preferred more hills – I don't like flat courses too much."

On 26 October Laxton took the record back when she clocked 2:43:49 for 11th in the New York City marathon won by Grete Waitz in a world record 2:25:41.3.

A year after his record run in the Cape Plaatjes went one better when he won the senior title in Potchefstroom. Magawana finished only tenth. The year's fastest time came from Rose, who ran a PB 2:12:57 to win the DAC marathon, and had three other times under 2:17:00 (among them the 2:13:01 mentioned above). Halberstadt, who on Easter Saturday had won the Two Oceans in a scintillating course record 3:05:37, was fourth in the Nike/OTC race in Eugene, clocking 2:13:02 in very hot weather. Bacon set a national veterans' record of 2:19:03 in Durban.

The most outstanding performance of 1981, though, belonged to a petite female student of the University of Cape Town. Her victory in the 1980 Comrades (in 7:18:00) had shown what Roche-Kelly was capable of, but her brilliant effort of 21 November in the Winelands marathon, on one of the most difficult courses in the country, was simply superb. She beat Laxton's record with her 2:42:27 – a race record which has never been bettered. The vivacious Roche-Kelly, who was 1.55 m tall and weighed 43 kg, was born in Limerick on 28 April 1960 and her preferred sport was horse-riding. She started running in 1979 and entered the Peninsula marathon in March 1980. She had never trained more than about 12 km, yet finished in 3:30:38.

In 1981 she also clocked 2:43:16 to win the Stellenbosch marathon and 2:45:22 in the inaugural SA Championship for women in Durban. Laxton won in 2:44:35, with Beverley Malan third in 2:49:54. It was the first time that three women had run under 2:50:00 in the same race. Less than a month later Roche-Kelly returned to the Comrades and shattered

the "up" record with an astonishing 6:44:35, finishing 76th overall! Tragically her life was cut short in 1985 when she fell under a truck while cycling on a slippery Dublin street.

In 1982 Halberstadt ran 2:11:46 – faster than Bacon's national record – for third in Chicago, but at the time he was banned by the SAAAU because of the prize money ($6 000) he had received in the previous year's Eugene race. The SA body wanted him to deposit the money in the local trust fund,[4] but Halberstadt argued that it had been won in the USA and therefore he had put it in the trust fund there. He was only reinstated as an amateur about three years later.

The fastest time in South Africa came from Rakabaele when he beat Rose after a ding-dong battle in the Interprovincial marathon in Port Elizabeth, 2:11:44 against 2:12:22, both personal bests. Siphiwe Gqele was third in 2:13:56. "I know I can still run faster," Rose said afterwards.

Malan not only won the SA title (2:47:44), but went to New York, where she was 23rd in a PB 2:44:40.

Rose did not wait long to provide proof that he could indeed go faster. He delivered the first fireworks of what would be a tremendous 1983 on 5 March in the Peninsula marathon. This time the dreaded southeasterly wind, also known as the "Cape Doctor", which had so often blown away any chances of fast times on this point-to-point course (running from north to south), stayed away. In fact, a *northwesterly* wind was at the runners' backs, accompanied by drizzle. Rose (29) ran the first half in 65:30 and won by more than 3 minutes in 2:12:10, equalling Bacon's record. Two Springbok rugby captains, Dawie de Villiers and Morné du Plessis, finished in 2:56:48 and 3:19:51 respectively. Malan won the women's race in 2:47:16.

Two weeks later Rose clocked the fastest time ever at high altitude when he won the Sun City marathon in 2:14:45. On the last day of April Kevin Flanegan beat Magawana for the SA title in Durban, 2:16:21 against 2:17:00. On 2 July, using part of the course on which Magawana had won the title three years before, Defence (and ex-Stellenbosch) athlete Johan Dreyer (24) claimed the SA record in his debut when he ran 2:11:42 in Kuils River. Shaw was second in 2:14:32.

Just over two months later, and not very far away, Dreyer's friend Ewald Bonzet set off on *his* debut, the Stellenbosch marathon on 10 September. In typical fashion Bonzet, already a Springbok in track and cross-country, kept everyone guessing about his intentions to finally attempt his first marathon. The Bellville star, born on Christmas day 1951, appeared on the starting line two minutes before the gun went and when he returned 2 hours, 12 minutes and 8 seconds later to the famous Coetzenburg track where he had run his best mile of 3:57.3 in 1977, he became only the fifth runner in history to have run a dream mile and a sub-2:13

---

4. At the time – before "open" athletics, this was the only legitimate way in which athletes could win money. Their prizes had to be deposited into a trust fund, from which they could "draw" to cover expenses.

marathon (the others were Halberstadt, Dick Quax NZL, Emiel Puttemans BEL and Paul Cummings USA). Bonzet, one of the most brilliant runners ever produced in South Africa, had in the first half of the previous decade simultaneously held the SA records for the 5000 m, 10000 m and steeplechase. After his Stellenbosch victory (Rakabaele was second in 2:14:41 and Flanegan third in a PB 2:15:06) he received Springbok colours, making him the first triple Springbok since Barnard.

An interesting aspect of Bonzet's career is that he met Lopes, the 1984 Olympic marathon champion, three times – and beat him twice! Their first two races were the Luanda New Year's Eve race in 1972 and a 3000 m track event two days later, both of which Bonzet won. In 1984 Bonzet, running under an alias, met Lopes again in the Chicago marathon won by Steve Jones in a world record. Lopes was second in 2:09:06 and an off-form Bonzet 21st in 2:17:24. (See p. 96.)

Bonzet had prepared for Stellenbosch with twelve weeks of 180-200 km and did "more speedwork than usual. Now I've shown what I can do."[5] Seven weeks later, clad in the green and gold, Bonzet showed some more. In a howling wind in Port Elizabeth he won the Interprovincial marathon in 2:13:59, beating Rakabaele and Flanegan again, as well as Magawana and Frans Ntaole. Bonzet and Dreyer had reached halfway in 66:50, but an injured Dreyer had to withdraw soon thereafter.

The race was the SA Championship for women, and the title went to Adelene Joubert in a PB 2:48:29. The only woman apart from Joubert and Malan who could dip under 2:50:00 in 1983 was Marion Loveday with her 2:49:45 win in Stellenbosch. The next day Lindsey Weight ran 2:50:04 in Durban. Earlier in the year she had won the "up" Comrades which started there, and in 1984 she would repeat the win, this time finishing in Durban.

The year 1984 was a breakthrough one in more than one respect. For the first time a male runner broke through 2:10:00 and a woman through 2:40:00, and for the first time since the days of Le Grange a South African made the top ten on the world list.

The SA marathon was early in the year, on 31 March. The course in Port Elizabeth was a new one, designed for fast times but unfortunately with a drop of 129 m – much more than the international standard at the time of 2 m/km. With the finish in the UPE Stadium, the start/finish separation was 16.5 km, or 39%. (This course was also used in 1985 and 1986.)

With huge prize money and incentives – at least by SA standards – at stake, the race was fast from the start. This time there was no wind and it was a cool, misty morning.

Plaatjes, the national cross-country champion, led the runners through 8 km in 25:01, 16 km in 49:43 and halfway in 65:21. At 28 km he could not maintain the pace, and Ernest Seleke, Gibeon Moshaba and Ntaole went on alone. Eight kilometres further, climbing the only big hill on the course, the 24-year-old Seleke pulled clear of his rivals. With a R2 000 bonus for breaking 2:10:00 in his sights, he ran the 4 km from 36 to 40 km in close to 3 min/km average, including the 38th km in 2:55. He reached the finish in 2:09:41 and netted total prize money of R4 800. The time placed him sixth on the world list for 1984.

Behind Seleke Ntaole held on for second in 2:12:57, followed by Moshaba (2:13:29) and Plaatjes (2:14:03). Four months later Moshaba would win the SA half-marathon title in 62:37. The women's race, held together with the men's for the first time, again went to Joubert (2:48:46). Monica Drögemöller was second in 2:50:28.

On the last day of June Bonzet surprisingly – considering the weather – decided to run the Bellville marathon (on the course where Dreyer had set his record). The elements were even more against him than the previous year in Port Elizabeth: there was a strong wind and it rained. Yet he raced to a tremendously impressive 2:13:54 (halfway in 65:24), winning by a whopping 10:12.

In 11th place came an even more remarkable performance: 35-year-old Sonja Laxton, the SA half-marathon champion, wiped Roche-Kelly's record from the book with her 2:36:44 (halfway in 76:56). She received an incentive of R5 000 for the record – as well as Springbok colours, joining Bonzet and Barnard as triple Springboks.

In October Plaatjes equalled Rose's Sun City time when he won the Johannesburg marathon in 2:14:45. Laxton ran 2:42:44 to give her the two fastest times of the year. Weight won Stellenbosch in 2:49:13, becoming the seventh woman under 2:50:00. On 2 December Derek May clocked 2:12:53 for second place on the SA performance list when he finished fourth in the TAC marathon in Sacramento.

Plaatjes, extremely disappointed with his effort in the SA marathon, returned to the "Windy City" in 1985 with one goal: to win the national title on 4 May. In ideal conditions he ran almost a minute faster than Seleke in 1984, but in a year that saw the outstanding races in Rotterdam, Chicago and Hiroshima, he finished two places lower on the world list than his countryman had done.

Having been denied entry into the Boston marathon by British runner Geoff Smith (who even resorted to legal action to keep the Wits University physiotherapy student out), Plaatjes vented his anger on the Port Elizabeth course. His time at 16 km was only 13 seconds faster than the previous year, and at halfway 21 seconds faster, but on this occasion there was no falling off the pace in the second half. Helped by the attentions of Willie Mtolo, the strongly built Natalian, tiny Moshaba and Petrus Kekana, Plaatjes stormed through 30 km in 91:38. The Springbok then blitzed the next 2 km

---

5. He had planned to run the Nike/OTC marathon, but was asked by the organisers not to enter because they feared that his presence would have repercussions for the Olympic Games in Los Angeles.

in 5:55 and started climbing the hill where Seleke had decided the race in 1984. He also began surging, and at 38 km it proved too much for Mtolo. Plaatjes entered the stadium still full of running . . . and kicked from 300 m. He broke 2:09:00 by 2 seconds and set off on a joyous victory lap.

A weary Mtolo, a student in his final high-school year from Inanda who had started running fourteen months before, won the silver medal in 2:10:32, a PB by 6:40. (He had won the DAC marathon in September in 2:17:12.) In third Magawana at last improved on his PB of 1980, clocking 2:10:39. The first three runners moved into first, third and fourth on the SA all-time list, with the winner placing fourteenth on the world all-time list.

Later in the year Plaatjes would finish sixth in the SA Half marathon in 62:38 and win the SA cross-country title.

The women started 20 minutes before the men, with Laxton and Joubert chasing each other and the record from the beginning. Laxton, in Springbok colours – the first time a woman competed in Springbok colours in a road race – was 30 seconds ahead at 32 km, but at the top of the hill, at 37 km, Joubert had cut the gap to 10 m. Soon she passed Laxton, and by 41 km was more than a minute ahead. She won her third title in a row and broke Laxton's SA record by 59 seconds with her 2:35:45. Laxton was second, exactly 2 minutes behind, and then followed two more runners under 2:50:00 – the first time this had happened: Liz Eglington 2:47:20 and Drögemöller 2:47:33. Laxton was the only runner in the first ten who did not run a PB.

Joubert also made history by ending the year with three more times under 2:50:00 (2:37:46 in the Peninsula marathon, 2:42:10 in the Johannesburg event and 2:48:00 in Pretoria), as well as 2:50:31. Alas, this was too much, and she was never the same again.

In February Helen Lucre had also gone through the 2:50:00 barrier when she took the Villagers marathon in Hillcrest in 2:47:52 for a Natal record. Later in the year she would score the first of her three successive Comrades wins.

In the Bellville marathon Laxton turned the tables on Joubert, winning in 2:33:35 against 2:35:22, but remeasurement of the course found it to be short.

In 1986 South Africa's marathoners shot right up to world class – a statement which is modified somewhat by the nature of the Port Elizabeth course. While the US (TAC) standard at the time was a maximum drop of 2 m/km from start to finish and a start/finish separation of not more than 10% of the race distance, and the Association of International Marathons (AIMS) recommended a drop of 1 m/km, the South African rule stipulated a maximum drop of 3.55 m/km, with no limit on the start/finish separation. This rule was subsequently changed to conform with international standards, and at the time of writing SA records may only be set on courses that do not drop by more than 1 m/km and have the start and finish not more than 10% of the distance apart.

## A LONG, REMARKABLE CAREER

On 30 June 1984, a cold, wintry morning, a momentous race took place in Kuils River, a sleepy village near Cape Town. Few were there to see it, but when Sonja Laxton started the Bellville marathon in the rain and wind, she embarked on a historic run. A little over 2½ hours later she was back. Only ten men had beaten her and she became the first South African woman to run the marathon faster than 2 hours 40 minutes. What is more, her time of 2:36:44 gave her Springbok colours and this made her the first woman and only the third athlete to earn colours in all three branches of athletics: track and field, cross-country and road running.

Laxton was to run faster still and add to her bag of SA titles, but this was perhaps the climactic moment of a career which is one of the most remarkable in the history of South African athletics. A true sportswoman, Sonja played a huge role in popularising women's running in South Africa.

Sonja van Zyl was born in Ermelo on 6 August 1948. She started running in Port Elizabeth in 1962 and by 1970, as a student at the University of the Witwatersrand, she was running 800, 1500 and 3000 m. In 1971 she won her first SA title, in the 1500 m, and also established her first national record with 4:29.8. The date was 10 April, and the performance earned her Springbok colours for the first time. She would receive the coveted award twelve more times.

Later that year she also won her first SA cross-country title.

Over the next twenty-odd years the modest, soft-spoken Sonja went from strength to strength, setting numerous national and Africa records and winning a total of 21 SA titles. In the seventies she towered head and shoulders above the country's other women runners, to such an extent that between 1971 and 1978 she won sixteen of the 22 SA titles open to her, while in 1975 she simultaneously held the SA records for 1000 m (2:48.0), 1500 m (4:13.1), 1 mile (4:45.0) and 3000 m (9:15.6).

Laxton also competed overseas with distinction, but never realised her full potential in international competition before South Africa's exclusion from the world arena. In 1975 she was second in the AAA Championships 1500 m and the next year fourth in the British cross-country title race.

She then concentrated on road running, and in 1980 ran the New York City marathon, setting her second SA record for the distance. The next year she won her first national marathon title. Twelve years later, at the age of 44, she won again. She has said that she does not really like the marathon, but in 1985 her two duels with Adelene Joubert, in Port Elizabeth and Kuils River, put women's marathoning firmly in the spotlight.

Laxton's SA titles: *1500 m*: 1971-76; *3000 m*: 1973-78; *cross-country*: 1971, 1974-76; *16 km*: 1983; *half marathon*: 1984-85; *marathon*: 1981, 1993.

Her progress at the marathon: 1980: 2:43:49; '81: 2:44:35; '84: 2:36:44; '85: 2:37:45; '86: 2:35:44; '87: 2:42:38; '88: 2:36:59; '89: 2:40:59; '90: 2:41:09; '92: 2:40:12; '93: 2:43:01.

The SA marathon was held on 3 May. In the field were Mtolo, Ernest Tjela (2:15:11 in 1985), Moshaba, Rose, Magawana, Kekana and Zithulele Sinqe, the very talented man who had so nearly won the half-marathon title the previous year (he and Matthews Temane both clocked 62:19 for a national record).

Mtolo led a pack of seven though 8 km in 24:48, but soon after 12 km surged away from his rivals. At 15 km (45:30) he was 12 seconds up on Charles Vilakazi and Moshaba, who were leading Tjela and Willie Mankayi by 17 seconds. The two Springboks, Sinqe and Magawana, were 300 m behind Mtolo, who had not been deemed good enough to receive national colours. The flying Zulu reached halfway in 64:19 –

43 seconds ahead of Moshaba and 71 seconds in front of Sinqe, Magawana and Kekana. Then Sinqe started moving. Over the next 4 km he cut the gap by 8 seconds. Mtolo, the hunted, was running at 2:58/km pace, but Sinqe, the hunter, was covering ground even faster. Their times at 25 km were 76:15 and 77:18 respectively. The leader passed 30 km in 91:06 – 32 seconds faster than Plaatjes had done – but, incredibly, Sinqe had sliced the advantage to 35 seconds! His split for the 5 km between 25 and 30 km was 14:23 against Mtolo's 14:51.

Mtolo got the message and accelerated with the wind at his back. At 35 km his time was 1:45:43 for a 5 km split of 14:37 – but behind him the pursuer in green and gold had done 14:18, faster than 2:52 per kilometre! Sinqe's astonishing surge soon brought him level with Mtolo and what followed was one of those superb, spine-tingling battles that the marathon so often produces. In a duel reminiscent of the 1982 Commonwealth Games race between Robert de Castella and Juma Ikangaa the two warriors fought up the infamous hill into the wind, neither giving an inch. The 39th kilometre took 3:08, and then Sinqe surged. He opened a gap of 20 m, but Mtolo came back, and at 40 km (2:01:24) they were neck and neck once more.

Again the Springbok surged and ran the next kilometre in 3:02, digging deep. This time it was enough, and Mtolo faltered. The last kilometre ticked by in another 3:02, and Sinqe was clear. A wide grin split his face as he ran around the track where before him Le Grange, Seleke and Plaatjes had set their records. Now the record was his: 2:08:04, the world's fourth fastest time ever and only 52 seconds slower than the world record. Mtolo was second in 2:08:15 and Tjela third in 2:11:00.

By the end of the year Sinqe would be relegated to sixth and Mtolo to ninth on the all-time list, but their times were fourth and sixth on the 1986 list – South Africa's best showing since Gibson and Coleman were second and third in 1937. The race was not only a triumph for the runners and SARRA, but also for SA Breweries, whose sponsorship since 1981 had played an indispensable role in elevating the country's top runners to the level they attained in this contest. The Breweries sponsored all national road championships, and in the course of the year national records were also set in the half-marathon title race (Xolile Yawa 61:51 and Colleen Lindeque 71:33).

While the exhilarating runs by Sinqe and Mtolo made South Africa the third best marathon country in the world (taking the times of its top three runners into account) after Japan and Great Britain, the truth was that there was little growth in the standard if one looks a bit deeper. The average of the top ten times on the yearly list did drop from 2:15:41.2 in 1982 to 2:13:11.2 in 1986, but the number of runners under 2:20:00 remained stagnant: 25 in 1983, 34 in 1984, 32 in 1985 and 27 in 1986. In line with their sisters in the rest of the world the women showed progress: seven under 2:55:00

in 1983 and 1984, eleven in 1985 and fourteen in 1986.

Much debate ensued afterwards about the assistance the runners received from the drop in course elevation and the wind, which was from behind for most of the race. An interesting comparison would be Tjela's time in Port Elizabeth and the 2:13:40 he ran two months previously in the Peninsula marathon in Cape Town – also on a point-to-point course but with no drop in elevation. This author thought at the time that the Port Elizabeth course was "worth" about a minute (in windless conditions).

Fifth on the SA list for the year was David Phalatse with the excellent 2:14:28 run at high-altitude Carletonville.

Laxton, now 38, took back the SA record – by a single second – when she won Stellenbosch on 13 September. In the Johannesburg marathon she clocked 2:44:00 to beat an exciting newcomer, Annette Redelinghuys (2:44:30). A total of ten women ran under 2:50:00 during the year, one of them Cassandra Mihailovic in claiming the SA title in 2:45:18.

In 1987 the SA marathon was decided on an internationally acceptable course in Stellenbosch (the same one on which Bonzet ran his 2:12:08), and in ideal conditions the battle of 1986 was re-enacted – this time with a few other players added. At 25 km (78:52) Sinqe and Mtolo, who had both been injured in the run-up to the race, were part of a pack of six which also included Rakabaele and Magawana, but they pulled clear shortly after 35 km (1:48:56) and then Sinqe kicked away from his rival with 800 m remaining.

The recreation officer at the West Driefontein Mine won in 2:10:51 against 2:11:01. Sinqe, who was born in Umtata on 9 June 1963, started running in 1982. His only marathon before the 1986 SA race had been the 1985 Johannesburg event, where he finished second to Plaatjes in 2:15:08.

In third place came the amazing Magawana. Two weeks previously he had won his first Two Oceans in 3:05:31, breaking Halberstadt's course record by 6 seconds, and here he ran 2:12:35. This double must surely rank as one of the most outstanding in the annals of distance running in the world.

Redelinghuys, now Falkson, a psychology researcher specialising in the intellectual development of children, won the women's race in 2:36:13 from Drögemöller (2:40:08) and Laxton (2:42:38). Eight weeks before Falkson had won the Peninsula marathon in 2:39:56.

In November Drögemöller was first in the challenging Winelands marathon in a quick 2:44:02, while the Stellenbosch marathon went to Eglington in 2:44:55. In ninth place on the yearly list was Frith van der Merwe with the 2:51:24 that gave her third in the Hyper-to-Hyper marathon in Pretoria. She was to be the next star.

Also in November, Tjela won a windy Columbus marathon in the US in 2:11:39 for third place on the performance list. Eight months before he had taken the Peninsula marathon in 2:11:47. Another South African scored a victory in the US: May in Houston (2:11:51). The same time was turned in by Sinqe in the Ford marathon in Durban.

In July Sinqe had battled Matthews Temane every step of the way in the SA Half marathon and although he ran the same time as Temane – as in 1985 – he once again had to be satisfied with second place. They clocked 60:11, the world's fastest half marathon ever – but the course dropped 46.5 m. During the year Temane also won the national titles in the 10 km, 15 km, 5000 m on the track and cross-country!

In 1988 Mtolo finally won the SA marathon, beating David Tsebe in 2:10:18 against 2:12:14 in Cape Town on 30 April. Magawana tried to repeat his 1987 double performance, but this time – four weeks after his brilliant Two Oceans victory in 3:03:44 with world records for 30 miles and 50 km en route – he failed to finish. Falkson, in Springbok colours, retained her title with an easy win over Laxton and took her SA record away in the process. The 30-year-old ran a comfortable-looking 2:33:39 to break the record by more than 2 minutes. Earlier in the month she had entered Boston, but was asked to withdraw because of fears of a possible African boycott of the race. Like Plaatjes three years before, she then bounced back with a national record.

Falkson had wanted to run under 2:30:00 in the Los Angeles marathon, but a stomach ailment prevented her from taking part. "I found it difficult to maintain my peak condition and to motivate myself again after the disappointment," she said.

Laxton finished second in 2:40:05 with Eglington third in 2:44:16, while the male veterans' record was broken by Paulus Masilela with a fine 2:17:40. Later in the year Laxton would also set a veterans' record with 2:36:59 in Durban.

Laxton won the Johannesburg marathon in a magnificent 2:41:16. Van der Merwe was second in a PB 2:42:49 and also clocked 2:47:32 and 2:47:45. Drögemöller won Stellenbosch in a PB 2:42:01.

Only seven women ended the year with times faster than 2:50:00, while the 33 men under 2:20:00 were the most since 1984. Plaatjes finished third in Los Angeles (2:10:41) and first in Columbus (2:12:17) to make him South Africa's most successful marathoner of the year. Tjela took the Munich marathon in 2:12:55.

The best marathon runner of 1989, male or female, was undoubtedly Van der Merwe. By the time she turned 25 on 26 May she had already won the SA marathon in 2:30:35 to snatch the record away from Falkson, and recorded 2:40:45 in Benoni, the fastest ever at altitude. She followed this up with 2:39:10 in Knysna for the year's three fastest times.

A new course was used for the SA marathon in Port Elizabeth on 25 February. The drop in elevation was now only 18 m, with the start and finish being 3.48 km apart (8.2%). Van der Merwe raced through halfway in 75:55 and then covered the second half in 74:40.

"Now I have to seriously consider staying away from ultra-marathons, and concentrate on shorter distances," said Van der Merwe, who had won the "up" Comrades the previous year in a course record 6:32:56. Despite these words, and despite the two fast marathons she had already run, she nevertheless competed in both the Two Oceans, setting a course record 3:30:36 and world records for 30 miles (3:01:16) and 50 km (3:08:39) along the way, and the Comrades (finishing 15th overall in an astounding 5:54:43, almost an hour under the previous record), as well as the City to City 50 km ultra-marathon, breaking her world 50 km record with 3:04:30 (at altitude!). With this insane racing schedule she began to place the tremendous strains on her body that would a few years later lead to numerous injury problems and a virtual end to her first-class career – one which, in the marathon at least, sadly never reached its peak. She also won the national 15 km title.

Less than 15 minutes ahead of Van der Merwe in the Comrades, after a titanic battle with eventual winner Sam Tshabalala, was Mtolo – a brave effort, but one that also nothing for his marathon career.

Laxton had two sub-2:44s – 2:40:59 in Durban and 2:43:50 behind Van der Merwe in the SA race. Drögemöller retained her Stellenbosch title in 2:44:42. Fifteen women were under 2:55:00 for the year, but only seven were faster than 2:50:00.

Tsebe was the fastest male with his PB 2:10:47 in the Durban Ford marathon; in the SA race he was beaten by Mtolo, 2:13:13 against 2:13:42. Tsebe's brother Rami, older by two years, was third in the Durban race (2:13:29) behind David and Mtolo (2:13:15). In fifth place was the man universally regarded as the most versatile male runner ever produced in South Africa: Temane clocked a disappointing 2:15:41 in his debut and afterwards offered these sage words: "I have a lot to learn about the distance."

Six weeks before his Durban triumph Tsebe had also won the Port Elizabeth Ford marathon in a PB: 2:10:48. Peter Tshikila was second in 2:10:53. Tsebe was the first South African ever to run two sub-2:11s in one year. In the SA Half marathon he was barely outsprinted by Temane, but ran a PB 61:11.

As the decade closed, the SA all-time list for men was completely different from what it had been at the beginning of the period, with eight of the top ten times run in Port Elizabeth. Twelve men had dipped below 2:12:00:

| | | | |
|---|---|---|---|
| 2:08:04 | Zithulele Sinqe | Port Elizabeth | 1986 |
| 2:08:15 | Willie Mtolo | Port Elizabeth | 1986 |
| 2:08:58 | Mark Plaatjes | Port Elizabeth | 1985 |
| 2:09:41 | Ernest Seleke | Port Elizabeth | 1984 |
| 2:10:39 | Thompson Magawana | Port Elizabeth | 1985 |
| 2:10:47 | David Tsebe | Durban | 1989 |
| 2:10:53 | Peter Tshikila | Port Elizabeth | 1989 |
| 2:11:00 | Ernest Tjela | Port Elizabeth | 1986 |
| 2:11:42 | Johan Dreyer | Kuils River | 1983 |
| 2:11:44 | Gabashane Rakabaele | Port Elizabeth | 1982 |
| 2:11:46 | Johnny Halberstadt | Chicago | 1982 |
| 2:11:51 | Derek May | Houston | 1987 |

The top nine women were under 2:45:00:

| | | | |
|---|---|---|---|
| 2:30:35 | Frith van der Merwe | Port Elizabeth | 1989 |
| 2:33:39 | Annette Falkson | Cape Town | 1988 |
| 2:35:44 | Sonja Laxton | Stellenbosch | 1986 |
| 2:35:45 | Adelene Joubert | Port Elizabeth | 1985 |
| 2:40:08 | Monica Drögemöller | Cape Town | 1989 |
| 2:42:27 | Isavel Roche-Kelly | Stellenbosch | 1981 |
| 2:44:16 | Liz Eglington | Cape Town | 1988 |
| 2:44:28 | Judy Ryan | Stellenbosch | 1980 |
| 2:44:40 | Beverley Malan | New York | 1982 |

Tsebe was even better in 1990. With Mtolo concentrating on the Two Oceans, which he won in 3:10:51, Tsebe easily won his first SA title, clocking 2:09:50 in Port Elizabeth on 24 February to give him eighth place on the world list for the year. John Sebata (2:11:24) was second and Thabiso Moqhali (2:12:37), a citizen of Lesotho who would be second in the Two Oceans, third. The first three all ran personal bests. On 21 July Tsebe beat his brother in the SA Half marathon, both running 61:03 (a PB for both). Seven days later he raced to a 2:12:14 in the Port Elizabeth Ford marathon and on 3 November, six days before his 24th birthday, he was second in the SA 15 km in 43:16.

David had hoped to run sub-2:09 in the SA marathon. Rami set the pace for him to halfway, reached in 64:30, but over the faster second half David could not quite maintain the tempo. Van der Merwe did, and her reward was a magnificent SA record of 2:27:36. It was the fourth fastest time in the world for 1990 – the highest placing a South African woman had earned up to that time. Laxton was second in 2:41:09 and Evelina Tshabalala third in 2:42:52.

At the end of the year Van der Merwe's domination of the performance list was even more complete than in 1989 – she had the *four* fastest times: apart from the SA record she had also run 2:33:09 in Pretoria, 2:33:49 in Benoni and 2:35:05 in Johannesburg – i.e. all at altitude! She was superb in the 56 km Korkie ultramarathon, finishing tenth overall in 3:32:42 only three weeks after her SA marathon win. After the race there was much talk about Van der Merwe achieving "the impossible": a place in the first ten in the Comrades. Accomplished ultrarunner Stewart Peacock expressed the feelings of many of the top male runners (quite a number of whom had been beaten by the fleet lady): "She made me feel like I was standing still. I tried to hold her off, but she just cruised past, and hell man – I'm a reasonably good runner!"

Then a stress fracture struck her down and she missed the Comrades – yet in October she bounced back to win the Foot of Africa half marathon at Bredasdorp, clocking 71:42 on the extremely hilly course.

Second on the list was Drögemöller, who at last broke through the 2:40:00 barrier with the 2:37:19 that gave her victory in the Peninsula marathon. She also won the Two Oceans for the second time.

It was a very successful year for the women, as seventeen were quicker than 2:55:00.

In 1991 the top time on the performance list was 39 seconds slower than in 1990, but three men ran under 2:11:00 compared to only Tsebe the previous year. Joseph Skosana, who had been eighth in the 1990 SA marathon in a PB 2:15:27, this time won the title in 2:10:29, beating Tsebe by 3 seconds. Michael Scout (previous PB 2:18:31) improved by leaps and bounds to 2:10:47 for third, with Moqhali fourth (2:12:14). An amazing performance came from 50-year-old Titus Mamabolo (born 7 January 1941), whose 2:19:29 made him the first-ever master to run a sub-2:20 marathon.

Rayner won the women's race in a fine 2:39:32 to move into sixth on the all-time list. Drögemöller was second in 2:45:26 and Helen Lucre, the only triple winner of the Comrades (1985-87), third in 2:46:22.

Earlier in the year Drögemöller had won the Peninsula marathon in 2:43:13, with Lucre second in a PB 2:44:22. Drögemöller also claimed victory in the Two Oceans, once again beating Lucre. Both Rayner and Lucre had other fast times as well: Rayner was third in the Peninsula race (2:48:43) and Lucre second in the Durban Ford event (2:45:55). Van der Merwe also had two quick wins: 2:42:20 in Johannesburg and 2:42:24 in Welkom, but it was clear that she was not in her 1990 form. This was corroborated by her 29th place in the Comrades in 6:08:19 (two positions ahead of Halberstadt).

In the Durban Ford marathon Skosana was beaten by Jan Tau, who scored his first major win in 2:14:27. Mtolo won the Peninsula marathon in 2:15:39, defeating Tsebe. The performance list for the year still showed no improvement compared to 1988: 31 runners were faster than 2:20:00.

The Olympic year of 1992 had extra significance for South Africa: for he first time in 32 years the country was allowed to compete, and its athletes went to Barcelona with high hopes. Their lack of experience at this level of competition resulted in great disappointment, though. The only athlete who excelled was Elana Meyer with her silver medal in the 10000 m. Her lack of a kick was painfully evident and showed that she would fare much better in longer events such as the half and full marathon.

The South African marathon team was chosen in the national championship race in Cape Town on 28 March. After a few quiet years Sinqe was back and ran an excellent race to finish second (2:11:47) behind Abel Mokibe's PB 2:11:07. Tau (2:11:56, another PB) rounded out the team. Tsebe was only seventh, showing no signs of what he would do later in the year.

Tau ran himself into the team with a devastating surge from 31 km, taking the pace down to 2:52/km. This proved too much for Tsebe, who had been battling with a bout of flu. Sinqe also fell back, but then rallied and eventually passed Tau. Of the reason for his absence from the running scene

Sinqe said: "I was simply bored. Everything was the same. The same races, the same runners. You go to race, and you know who's going to win even before the start."

Mokibe, a 26-year-old apprentice electrician from Tembisa, had carefully trained for the race with weekly totals of up to 155 km. When asked what he would do with his winnings of R12 000, he said: "I will buy a lot of sweets."

The women's race was won by 28-year-old Colleen de Reuck (formerly Lindeque) in her debut. She easily qualified for Barcelona with her 2:31:21 after a 73:30 first half. An injured Van der Merwe stopped after 18 km, leaving Laxton (2:40:12) and debuting Blanche Moila (2:41:05) to take second and third. Drögemöller, who would win the Two Oceans for an unprecedented fourth time three weeks later, was fourth in 2:41:35.

In the heat and humidity of Barcelona the South African marathoners were brought down to earth with a shock. Even the slow initial pace (see p. 109) of the race on 9 August did nothing to make it easier, and only Mokibe could finish. He placed 25th in 2:17:24, 4:01 behind the winner and one place ahead of Aussie De Castella.

In the women's race eight days earlier – an even hotter day – De Reuck had been a very creditable ninth in 2:39:03 (see p. 168).

Putting the Cape Town disappointment behind him, Tsebe went to Berlin for the city's marathon on 27 September. (He had run his first overseas marathon in Honolulu in 1988 under an assumed name and finished second in 2:15:12.) Three months before, Mtolo had become South Africa's first international marathon winner since the country's readmission to the international fold when he won the Enschede race in 2:13:39. In Berlin Tsebe settled into a pack with the more fancied runners from Kenya and Ethiopia – men such as Turbo Tumo, Lameck Aguta, Sammy Nyangincha and Godfrey Kiprotich, as well as Olympic bronze medallist Stephan Freigang – but when they reached the halfway point in 63:04 he backed off slightly. "I knew it was too fast for me."

In the last third of the race Tsebe gradually fought his way back as the frontrunners started paying for their earlier rashness, and took the lead for good at about 32 km. He raced down the Kurfürstendam with the clock at the finish mercilessly ticking off the seconds towards Sinqe's SA record, but his 2:08:07 course record missed by 3 seconds. However, taking the nature of the Port Elizabeth course into consideration, it was obviously a far superior performance. Manuel Matias POR was second in 2:08:38 and Simon Karori KEN third in 2:11:50.

"I think, late next year, if I can find a race like Chicago, I know I can run 2:07," Tsebe said after the race which brought him prize money of about R150 000. No other runner would run faster in 1992 and Tsebe thus became the first South African ever to lead the world list.

Van der Merwe finished 14th in 2:39:24.

Just over a month later the world's spotlight moved to another South African runner in the globe's biggest race. Mtolo's New York win in 2:09:29 over Andrés Espinosa MEX, described on p. 110, remains the most significant marathon victory by a South African runner since the return to world competition. The Zulu from the hills of Natal won $50 000 and a Mercedes and was ranked eighth in the world by *Track & Field News*.

Tsebe, who could not back up his Berlin time by other top-class performances (he ran only 2:16:45 in Honolulu, a totally unnecesary outing), was not ranked. He did win the SA half-marathon title in 63:28. De Reuck took the women's title and they were named South Africa's road runners of the year.

On 6 December Lawrence Peu, winner of the SA Half marathon the previous year in a magnificent 60:58 – the fastest by a South African on an internationally acceptable course – debuted in Fukuoka with a splendid 2:10:29 in second, beating, among others, Dionicio Cerón MEX.

Other international victories during the year were scored by Skosana in Taipei (2:14:43), Scout in Hokkaido (2:16:30) and Jerry Modiga in Macau (2:18:31). Moqhali ran 2:10:55 for seventh in London.

The year had brought the long-awaited breakthrough in the men's standard, with 38 runners under 2:20:00 – the most ever. Sixteen women ran faster than 2:55:00, also a record. Mtolo was ninth on the world list.

On 19 April 1993 Yawa, one of South Africa's best road racers ever (and also the holder of the 10000 m track record with 27:39.65) ran his marathon debut in Boston. He was disappointed with his 14th place in 2:15:28 – far behind winner Cosmas Ndeti KEN – but he beat Tsebe, who was plagued by blistered feet and clocked 2:18:15, and Scout (2:20:57). The previous day Ezael Tlhobo had placed 16th in London in a PB 2:16:53, while Mtolo was fourth in a rain-soaked and wind-swept Rotterdam. The organisers had spent most of their available appearance money on Cerón and Mtolo; the Mexican won in 2:11:08 and the South African ran 2:12:33. Cerón charged away from the tired Mtolo 5 km from the end to overtake leader Simon Robert Naali TAN, and Mtolo was passed by Finn Harri Hanninen. Tau was ninth (2:17:13) and Jabulani Mnguni 17th (2:18:22).

After these three less than stellar races *SA Runner* wrote: "The honeymoon is over for South Africa's marathon runners. Last autumn they looked ready to run the world. Now it's back to the drawing board." Referring to Tsebe's poor performance in Boston, the magazine quoted De Castella about the course (a comment which is also true for marathons in general). "It's experience that counts as much as anything in Boston," said the course record holder. "If you overcook it in the first half you end up crawling home on your hands and knees. There's no way back."

There was some brighter news in June, when Tau, Modiga

and Daniel Mbuli won marathons in Enschede, Melbourne and Stockholm repectively in 2:12:19, 2:15:07 and 2:16:30. In the cold and rainy Australian race South Africans also filled second (Skosana 2:16:40) and third (Piet Ramudzuli 2:18:09) places.

Things got even better in the second half of the year, although Mtolo did not finish the World Championships marathon won by ex-South African Plaatjes (see p. 110). In Berlin on 26 September Yawa proved that Boston had not reflected his true worth when he easily won "Tsebe's race" in 2:10:57, three days before his 31st birthday. The defending champion was third in 2:12:07 after leading for much of the race, while Isaac Tshabalala was tenth in 2:15:01. On the same day a below-form Sinqe ran 2:15:29 for fourth in Amsterdam.

In Fukuoka Gert Thys (22), one of South Africa's best runners over the shorter road distances, repeated Peu's second place of the year before behind Cerón (2:08:51), the year's top-ranked marathoner, in 2:09:31 (see p. 112). It was the fastest SA time in 1993 and good enough for fourth on the world list behind Cerón, Vincent Rousseau BEL (2:09:13 in Reims) and Kim Wan-ki KOR (2:09:25 in Kyongju). In March Thys had run 2:11:40 for third in Otsu (the third-fastest time on the SA yearly list), while Tshikila had been fourth in Los Angeles (2:17:22).

Skosana placed seventh in Honolulu (2:18:19) and Mokibe clocked 2:13:54 in Paris. South Africa's first participation in the World Cup in San Sebastián on 31 October met with disastrous results, as the country's first placer, Johannes Maremane, was only 31st in 2:14:44. In the women's race South Africa did not even have a full team; Moila was 42nd in 2:47:02.

Van der Merwe once again had the top three times of the year: 2:32:01 for fourth in Paris, 2:35:56 for a gallant seventh in the World Championships in Stuttgart (see p. 170), and 2:39:10 in Tiberius. However, the next year she would drop out of the Comrades with two stress fractures. No other woman went under 2:43:00, but Laxton missed by 2 seconds in winning the SA title in Cape Town.

A total of 42 men ducked under 2:20:00, again a record, but only eleven women were under 2:55:00.

For the second successive year Boston in 1994 was the debut of a great South African runner. On 18 April Meyer met Uta Pippig GER and Olympic champion Valentina Yegorova RUS in the famous race. Meyer, holder of the world record for 15 km and winner of the Gasparilla Distance Classic earlier in the year, ran a brilliant race and kept up with Pippig until the German threw in a 5:20 19th mile and pulled away to a course record 2:21:45 (see p. 172).

"After she made a little gap I thought I could close it again," Meyer said later, "but I never could. I really felt great for the first 22.5 miles. But it was very difficult the last part." Towards the end Yegorova passed her and Meyer finished third in 2:25:15, obliterating Van der Merwe's SA record. The time placed her third on the world list for the year – the

highest ever by a South African woman – and 14th on the all-time list. De Reuck was ninth in 2:31:53.

Meyer was just over a minute behind Tsebe, whose 2:24:05 was not even good enough to beat Pippig and Yegorova!

Other international forays by women resulted in 2:42:35 for Grace de Oliveira in Lisbon, 2:47:21 for Jowaine Parrott in Dijon and 2:55:22 for Tshabalala in London.

The six fastest times by men were all recorded overseas. On 6 March Maremane was fifth in Hiroshima in 2:12:10 (on a course that dropped 150 m). Two weeks later Yawa and Sinqe also acquitted themselves well in the Far East by placing seventh and ninth respectively in the Dong-A marathon in Kyongju in 2:11:54 and 2:12:01. It was Sinqe's fastest time for two years.

On 17 April Mtolo returned to Rotterdam with the goal of improving on his fourth position of the year before. He succeeded admirably. The race direction was changed around and the runners had to contend with a headwind for the first half. Vincent Rousseau, the man who had been one place behind Mtolo the year before, was too strong this time and after a split of 29:30 between 25 and 35 km the race was his. The South African won his duel with Hu Gangjun CHN for second; his 2:10:17 was his fastest since winning New York and the best SA time of 1994. After the race Hu tested positive for a banned substance and received a three-month suspension.

The same day Tshikila was 23rd in London in 2:15:01. On 23 October, in his best race since winning the SA title in 1992, Mokibe was fourth in Reims in 2:13:20 (Tau ran 2:18:19).

In New York Peu faded to 12th in 2:17:02 – but he was far ahead of Temane (2:24:00) and Mtolo (a pedestrian 2:27:06). Earlier in the year Peu had fared even worse in Tokyo (2:19:30).

In other international races the results were not much better: Skosana 2:18:37 in Los Angeles; Samuel Molokomme 2:17:45 in London; Owen MacHelm 2:18:39 in Enschede and 2:20:39 in the Commonwealth marathon in Victoria, Canada; Yawa 2:17:05 for 21st in Berlin; Tshikila 2:18:16 in the same race; Elgin Mokale 2:17:51 for third in Amsterdam; Mbuli 2:18:59 in Stockholm; and Warren Petterson 2:19:37 in Eindhoven.

Only 28 men dipped under 2:20:00 and a dismal total of five women under 2:55:00. Meyer's Boston performance earned her the sixth spot on the world ranking list.

The year 1995 started off tragically with the death of Magawana on New Year's Day. The fastest times of 1995 were once again established overseas, showing a definite trend as far as the preferences of South Africa's elite marathoners are concerned. The top four times all came on the same day, 2 April. Yawa topped the list for the first time with his 2:10:22 PB in London, moving him to seventh on the SA all-time list. He ran a fine race behind the flying Cerón, whose 2:08:30 made him the first man in history to clock under 2:09:00 four years in a row, Steve Moneghetti AUS and Antonio Pinto POR. Mtolo (seventh) was more than a minute behind his countryman in 2:11:35, with Johannes Mabitle finishing ninth in a PB 2:11:39.

Across the Channel in Paris Peu made a welcome return to form with a fourth place in 2:11:18.

On 24 September Yawa tried to regain his Berlin crown, but unfortunately for him he found himself in the most amazing marathon of the nineties (see p. 118). Sammy Lelei KEN sped to the second fastest time in history (2:07:02),

with Rousseau not far behind (2:07:20). Yawa's 2:11:58 was good enough only for sixth.

The rest of South Africa's men were again in the shadow of the top four. Mokibe came fifth in Toronto in 2:14:43; Skosana tenth in the World Cup in Athens (2:15:47) and Peter Lebopo 21st in 2:19:37; Sinqe 17th in Tokyo (2:17:02); Tlhobo eighth in Belgrade (2:17:49); and Tshikila 11th in Frankfurt (2:19:34). A promising debut that went awry was that of star half-marathoner John September, who ran 2:19:40 in London.

## THE COMPLETE ATHLETE

There can be no doubt that Elana Meyer is the best female runner ever produced in South Africa – maybe the best runner, period. Born at Albertinia on 10 October 1966 as Elana van Zyl, she became, in the nineties, the country's most successful athlete on the world scene and one of its finest sports ambassadors. In her tremendous career this friendly, warm and accessible athlete has accumulated honours and delivered performances that would require a book of its own to do her justice.

She first attracted attention at Robertson High School and was selected for the Western Province senior team at the age of thirteen. In 1980, six days before her fourteenth birthday, she ran (and won, in 87:10) the Foot of Africa half marathon at Bredasdorp for a lark. She was disqualified because she did not belong to a club.

Eleven years later she would set a world record for the distance, and another three years later win the world title.

In her early years she mostly ran second to Stellenbosch University clubmate Tanya Peckham, but she grittily persevered and was rewarded with Springbok track colours for the first time in 1985; the same year she also received cross-country colours. In 1990 she was honoured with road colours, making her the second female triple Springbok after Sonja Laxton.

Meyer won her first senior SA title in the 3000 m in 1987, the same year in which she set her first SA record, 5:42.15 for 2000 m. She also won the SA 10 km in 1987 and the first of five consecutive (and six overall) cross-country titles.

All in all she has won eighteen national titles: 3000 m in 1987-89 and 1992-93, 10000 m in '91, 1500 m in '92, 10 km in '87, both 15 km and half marathon in 1990-91, and cross-country in 1987-91 and '93. She also won the African Championships 1500 m in 1992-93.

Throughout her career Meyer has remained the complete athlete, balancing the demands – and the benefits – of the three disciplines to continuously advance her physical abilities. Her career has been built on the triple pillars of the perfect personality and attitude for top-level sport, hard and dedicated work, and her quiet yet unshakable faith.

From 1989, when she ran 10 km in an SA record 31:47, she has been without equal on the national road-running scene, but she has also been unbeatable when she ventured onto the track.

She topped the SA performance lists for the 10 km, 15 km and 21.1 km in 1990, 1991, and 1993-95. In 1990 she ran the world's fastest 15 km (48:17) and the next year broke the world records for this distance (46:57 in Cape Town) and the half marathon (67:59 in East London), both times winning the SA title. At the time of writing the former record still stands, while the latter was beaten only in 1995, by one second by Uta Pippig, the woman who defeated Meyer in both her first two marathons. Her third SA road record in 1991 was 31:33 for 10 km, the fastest in the world.

The year 1991 also saw her set SA track records of 8:32.00 for 3000 m, 14:49.35 for 5000 m and 31:33.46 for 10000 m. The records for the two longer distances fell again in 1992: 14:44.15 and 31:11.75 in the dramatic

Olympic final when she won the silver medal behind Derartu Tulu. She had the three fastest times in the world for 5000 m, scoring wins in the DNG meeting in Stockholm and the ISTAF meeting in Berlin with the other two. She ranked first in the world in the 5000 m and second in the 10000 m.

Despite her efforts over the longer distances, she remained quick enough to win the SA 1500 m title in 1992.

The next year she won the Tokyo half marathon (which drops 33 m) in a scintillating 67:22, the world's fastest of the year. She ranked second in the 5000 m.

In 1994 Pippig equalled her half-marathon world record, but in the World Half marathon in Oslo on 24 September the South African was supreme. She led from the start to win easily, smiling as usual, in 68:36. She was also second in the Tokyo race in 69:04, giving her the only two sub-70 times for the year.

She led the world list for 15 km with her 48:11 in winning the Gasparilla race in Tampa, while she won the US 10 km title in 31:39 as part of a highly successful US campaign. She also set a world record 15:10 for 5 km. Her debut marathon time of 2:25:15 in Boston was an Africa record and placed her tenth on the all-time list.

In the World Cross-country Championships she finished sixth in 1993 and fourth in 1994. In the first Commonwealth Games since South Africa's readmission into world athletics she was outkicked in the 10000 m by Yvonne Murray and ranked third in the world.

Coached by Pieter Labuschagne, former adviser to Zola Budd, for the major part of her career, Meyer in 1995 turned to Ewald Bonzet to help her.

The only two blemishes on her record both occurred in major championship 10000 m races. In the 1993 World Championships final in Stuttgart she stepped off the track after having been continuously obstructed with impunity by Kenyan teenager Sally Barsosio, and in the 1995 edition of the meeting in Göteborg she finished fifth after a tactical mistake.

Ironically, her best track race came also in the 10000 m. At the 1994 World Cup meeting in London, the city near where she is based during the European track season, she ran a brilliant race to beat European champion Fernanda Ribeiro in a meeting, national, Africa, Commonwealth and UK all-comers record of 30:52.51. Her lack of a kick made her run a tactically perfect race: she forced the pace from the beginning with kilometres of 3:07.63, 3:03.92, 3:04.23, 3:05.80, 3:04.01, 3:05.65, 3:05.67, 3:06.03, 3:06.34 and 3:03.23. It was the second fastest time of the year (behind Chinese phenomenon Wang Junxia's 30:50.34) and gave Meyer fourth on the all-time list.

Elana has run many a fine race and captivated crowds all over the world, but the enduring image of her career is certainly the way in which she threw down the gauntlet in the Barcelona 10000 m and then, after having been outsprinted by Tulu, whose sizzling kick she could not blunt, run an exuberant victory lap with her rival, draped in the new South African flag and smiling delightedly for all the world to see what pleasure she obtains from life and a race well run. This is the essence of Elana Meyer.

In the World Championships marathon in Göteborg the SA results were again utterly depressing. The best time came from the SA champion, Martin Ndwheni (2:23:42), who had won the national title on a new course in Port Elizabeth in 2:12:32 ahead of Tshabalala (2:13:54) and Temane (2:14:21) – all personal bests.

In New York Moqhali had a good run to finish eighth in 2:12:32. Thys, not near his 1993 form, was 11th in 2:13:28.

Meyer went to Boston once again to challenge Pippig on 17 April. The elements were not quite as helpful as in 1994, although there was a following wind (see p. 174). Meyer had a difficult race, having problems with her water bottles and suffering from cramp in a quadriceps muscle, but she moved up one spot to second, albeit in a slower time (2:26:51) than in 1994. She took revenge on Tecla Lorupe KEN, who had beaten her in the Tokyo half marathon, and Yegorova. Her time placed Meyer second on the world list for 1995.

De Reuck, now living in Boulder, had given birth to a daughter in January and in October delivered one of the best road-running performances of the year when she finished fourth (70:34) in the World Half marathon in Montbéliard. Six weeks later she was a disappointing 14th in New York (2:46:18).

The SA title was won by a debuting Nicole Fuller in 2:37:11, but she then failed to finish the Eindhoven marathon.

In the last two months of the year Maremane (2:13:52) and Modiga (2:16:13) finished second in Lisbon and Macau respectively, while Peu could do no better than 33rd in Fukuoka (2:18:55). Josiah Thugwane (2:16:08) and De Reuck (2:37:29) ended the year with fine victories in Honolulu.

The first salvo of the Olympic year of 1996 was fired by Thys, who in February won the Beppu marathon in a magnificent course record and PB of 2:08:30. Since the start of the nineties the world had seen only eleven men run faster.

At the midpoint of the last decade of the century South Africa could look back on about ninety years of marathoning during which the sport grew immensely to become the popular pastime it is today for thousands of runners, joggers and fitness enthusiasts. The boom that had started in the eighties showed little sign of abating.

While the quality of male performances at the top since the heady days of 1985 and 1986, as well as success in major marathons since South Africa's return to international athletics, lagged well behind the consistently high standard (compared to the rest of the world) of the first half of the century, South Africa has continued to narrow the gap. In 1970 the difference between the averages of the top ten male runners on the SA and the world list was 18:33.8. In 1980 this figure was 5:27.2 and, although the rate of progress over the next decade was much less, the figure in 1990 was down to 4:19.3. In 1995 it was 3:51.3.

It is a fact that the annual number of sub-2:20 runners have not shown much progress during the last few years, but one has to realise that the effects of the country's long isolation from the mainstream of competition and technological advances will take a while to overcome. There is certainly nothing to stop South African marathoners of today and tomorrow from following in the footsteps of Hefferon, McArthur, Coleman, Gibson, Luyt, Mekler and Barnard.

# *The women*
# 25 YEARS OF SUCCESS

IN 1977 THE well-known American marathon runner Nina Kuscsik wrote: "I believe that women have been running prior to the time that men saw fit to record it." Kuscsik related the story of the Greek woman Melpomene who, although her entry had been refused, allegedly ran in the first Olympic marathon in 1896 and finished in about 4½ hours. Greek sportswriters criticised the organisers of the Games for being discourteous in refusing the lady's entry. Kuscsik lamented the fact that Melpomene's "assertiveness" did not inspire other women to make more than only sporadic attempts at marathon-distance runs in the next seventy years.

Of course, women had their own athletic competitions in ancient Greece, held every four years at Olympia. Married women were not allowed to attend the men's games – the punishment for this was sometimes the death penalty. There were no such strictures on unmarried women, though! In the games at Olympia the women participated in a run over 500 Olympic feet, or about 160 metres.

The first organised meeting for women in modern times took place at Vassar College, a private women's college in the US state of New York, on 9 November 1895. Strict security was in place, as can be seen from a newspaper report of the time, quoted by Quercetani in his *Athletics: A History of Modern Track and Field Athletics (1860-1990)*: "Every effort was made to have the programme carried through without publicity. The oval field is admirably adapted to secure the girls from undesired spectators . . . Orders were given to exclude reporters and also all masculine visitors."

Distance running for women was regarded as taboo. In 1917 a Frenchwoman, Alice Milliat, formed the *Fédération Féminine Sportive de France* and when the International Olympic Committee (IOC) refused her request two years later to have women's events on the Olympic programme, she organised an international meeting for women in Monaco in 1921.

Five nations were represented and the programme included a race over 800 m.

The first international body for women's athletics, the *Fédération Sportive Féminine Internationale* (FSFI),[1] was formed that same year, and other international games soon followed. Women participated in the Olympic Games for the first time in 1928 in Amsterdam (they had five events). The longest event was the 800 m, but some runners were so exhausted at the finish that the event was scrapped from subsequent Games, to reappear only in 1960.

In South Africa women ran in the Comrades ultra-marathon in the 1920s (Frances Hayward was the first in 1923), but were only allowed to do so officially in 1975 – the same year that women were given the go-ahead to run road races in Great Britain.

The prevailing attitude about female participation in athletic events in the first half of the twentieth Century was summed up nicely by Helen Manley, an official in the public school system in Michigan, in 1936 (quoted by Kuscsik): "I am against highly trained competition for women athletes. Women are not physically fit for the excitement and strain that this competition affords."

Many experts believed that men's attitudes towards women's participation was caused mainly by cultural prejudice. Women had to have the courage to redefine themselves as human beings, according to the clinical psychologist Bruce Ogilvie. They had to get away from the idea that "horses sweat, men perspire, and women glow".

The first marathon mark of note was established by the British runner Violet Piercy. On 3 October 1926 she ran the Polytechnic marathon course (which was the standard

---

1. The FSFI merged with the International Amateur Athletic Federation in 1936.

42.195 km) in 3:40:22. This was most likely a time trial.

Eight years before, Marie-Louise Ledru, a French runner (not surprisingly, in view of Mme Milliat's efforts), had participated in a marathon, but her time is unknown.

In 1931 the eighteen-year-old Gazella Weinreich from Baltimore, an accomplished dancer, tried to run in the AAU (Amateur Athletic Union) marathon from Laurel to Baltimore, but was refused on the grounds, as AAU Secretary Daniel Ferris put it, that the race would be too much for any woman. Thirty years later Julia Chase (19) and two other women, Chris McKenzie and Dianne Lechausse, ran the Turkey Trot road race over 5 miles in Manchester, Connecticut. The previous year Julia had been refused an entry because she had not pre-entered. However, she saw the same officials take entries from men. In 1961 she entered early, but was rejected because AAU rules forbade "mixed competition". Her coach found that this rule was only valid for track races, so she turned up at the start again – where she found the other two women. Race officials took the women to the back of the start, behind all the men. All three finished and received considerable publicity in the media. (Chase was told not to go through the finish line chute or she would lose her amateur status.)

In 1965 Chase almost became the first woman to run the Boston marathon, but hurt her back in a car accident.

In the meantime the world record had been brought down to below 3:20:00. On 9 December 1963 Merry Lepper USA clocked 3:37:03 in the Western Hemisphere marathon in Culver City on an uncertified course. At the start of the race Lepper (20) and Lyn Carman (26), who had been training together, hid on the sidelines and then jumped in among the men. A race official tried to push them off the course, but Lepper – certainly showing assertiveness – punched him! She said that she had every right to run on a public street. She was timed at the finish by a sympathetic AAU official. Carman stopped after 20 miles.

On 23 May 1964 the Scot Dale Greig ran 3:27:45 over a difficult but certified course at Ryde on the Isle of Wight. She had to start four minutes ahead of the 67 men (of whom only 49 finished!).

At the time, although experts were predicting that since long-distance running is a test of heart and circulation rather than muscular strength, women would be able to compete with men as the distance becomes longer, others were warning women that they would not be able to bear children if they continued.

Judy Mitchell would certainly not have bothered about such prophets of doom. She took part officially in the first Equinox marathon in Alaska in 1963 and completed the course, which included more than 900 m of climbing, in 7:15:04 (the male winner clocked 3:54:22). In 1966 Debbie Haines cut the record to 5:24:30.

Greig's time stood for less than two months, for on 21 July 1964 New Zealander Mildred Sampson ran a brilliant 3:19:33 in the Owairaka marathon in Auckland. Sampson won her country's cross-country title four times.

The year 1966 was a significant one for women's marathoning, because one of the "weaker sex" ran the venerable Boston marathon for the first time. She was 23-year-old Roberta Gibb Bingay, whose postal entry had naturally been rejected. (She had actually wanted to run the year before, but the nurse's shoes she had been training in resulted in two sprained ankles!) She ran the first part of the race in a hooded sweatshirt to remain unnoticed and finished in 3:21:40. Afterwards she was adamant that she was not trying to make a feminist statement: "I ran . . . out of love . . . Running expresses my love of Nature, my delight in being alive." A view, certainly, which women everywhere would applaud.

After the race the male finishers "went to have soup together. I felt a pang at being left out. After all, we had just run the Boston Marathon together. But the doors were shut."

Bingay beat almost 300 men, but race director Will Cloney's male chauvinism inspired him to comment: "Mrs Bingay did not compete in the Boston marathon. She merely ran along the official route while the race was in progress."

Cloney could not realise that "Pandora's box had been opened", as Kuscsik put it.

In 1967 Bingay was back. She was not the only female, though. Kathrine Switzer had entered as K. Switzer, was accepted and given a race number. She did not appear for the (then) required prerace physical examination and started the race unnoticed. She was seen by officials about 6 miles into the race and Jock Semple tried to push her off the course (Cloney could not catch her). Switzer's friend, Thomas Miller (a hammer thrower), retaliated and pushed Semple away, sending him sprawling. Switzer continued and finished in an estimated 4:20:02. Bingay ran 3:27:17.[2]

Semple's explanation was that international rules barred men and women from running in the same race. The Boston race was for men only, although he was "not against women athletes". Shortly after the race Switzer was banned by the AAU for the following four reasons: she had run more than the allowable distance for women, she had run with men, she had fraudulently entered an AAU race, and she had run without a chaperone.

In later years, when she was in the forefront of the fight for women's rights in long-distance running, Kathy Switzer became known as a maverick. At high school and university, when her friends regarded their team sports as "just a game", she was different. "I wanted to train hard, and I wanted to *win*. Team sports . . . were not for me."

After her Boston experience Switzer decided to do something to change the prevailing attitude towards women in

---

2. According to Raymond Krise and Bill Squires in *Fast Tracks: The History of Distance Running*, Gibb was prevented from running across the finish by runners who linked arms in front of the line.

sports – the marathon in particular. But first she completed her studies, and in the meantime people like Fred Lebow, Vince Chiapetta, Kuscsik and Pat Tarnowski were busy convincing the AAU that the rules governing women's competition had to be changed.

In 1971 Kuscsik, Switzer and Tarnowski resolved that they would make it their goal to have a women's marathon in the Olympic Games. Switzer herself only started training seriously for the event in 1973, and in 1975 she finshed second in Boston in 2:51:37 – the ninth fastest time ever run and the fifth fastest by an American.

She described it as the perfect race. "I wasn't even running; the road was coming to me. The pain gave me no sense of fear – only a sense of power, because I knew I was a lot better than the pain."

It was, indeed, the perfect race. She never broke 3 hours again – "My heart wasn't in it after that."

But by that time the face of women's marathoning had already changed. On 6 May 1967, only a few weeks after K. Switzer had made history – albeit illegally, in the eyes of the AAU – a thirteen-year-old Canadian girl, Maureen Wilton, improved on Sampson's time when she clocked 3:15:22 in Toronto. Wilton, 1.47 m tall and weighing 36 kg, was sixth in a field of 28 men.

In Europe the West German coach Doctor Ernst van Aaken had become the promoter of long-distance running for women. Working from the small village of Waldniel (near Dusseldorf) Van Aaken started encouraging and assisting female distance runners, propagating the advantages of long slow distance (LSD) training. On 16 September 1967 the next world record was set in Waldniel, when Anni Pede-Erdkamp FRG recorded 3:07:26 on a 10.6 km loop course. This time stood until 28 February 1970 when the sixteen-year-old Portland girl Caroline Walker ran 3:02:53 in the Trail's End marathon in Seaside, Oregon. The tiny Caroline, who was 1.53 m tall and weighed 40 kg, had trained by running 70 miles per week.

That same year, on 27 September, the first championship race for women was organised by the Road Runners Club of America (men also competed) in Atlantic City. It was a closed race for members of the RRCA and therefore it was unnecessary to get AAU approval. Six women started. The winner was Sara Mae Berman USA in 3:07:10. Berman had won Boston (unofficially, of course) the previous year in 3:22:46, with Elaine Pedersen (3:43+) and Kuscsik (3:46+) following her. In 1970 Berman repeated the feat by running 3:05:07. Kuscsik was second in 3:12:16; Switzer ran 3:44+.

The next star to appear on the scene was the nineteen-year-old Elizabeth "Beth" Bonner USA, and she took the world record to 3:01:42 in Philadelphia on 9 May 1971 to start off a year that was to become a landmark for women. Three weeks later Berman answered with 3:00:35 in the sixth annual Plodder's marathon in Brockton, but the course was found to be nearly a quarter of a mile short.

Despite this disappointment, it was clear that women's marathoning was on the point of a breakthrough. However, nobody was prepared for what was to follow.

On 31 August 1971 in Werribee in the Australian state of Victoria Adrienne Beames AUS smashed the record and gave the first glimpse of what women could really do by finishing behind four men and ahead of ten others in 2:46:30. Beames (28) ran on an out-and-back course in weather not conducive to fast times: it was cold, rainy and windy. Her 5-mile splits were remarkably even until 20 miles when headwinds slowed her: 31:19, 31:31, 31:38 and 31:32. Her task towards the end was further complicated by "four miles of steeply cambered, broken, and stony road surface", according to Martin and Gynn (*The Marathon Footrace*).

With Beames having shown the way, other women soon followed. On 19 September five women started the New York City marathon, among them the three best US marathoners at the time. The competition resulted in Bonner and Kuscsik also breaking through the 3-hour barrier with 2:55:22 and 2:56:04 respectively. Bonner was 34th in the field of 164. Berman was third in 3:08:46. (The previous year Kuscsik had been the only female starter in the first New York marathon, but she failed to finish.)

Before the end of the year Bonner's time was beaten when on 5 December Cheryl Bridges USA smashed her course record for the Culver City marathon by more than 24 minutes! Bridges had been running for six years and trained hard for this particular race. She clocked a spectacular 2:49:40 on the out-and-back course and was now the second fastest woman in history.

Also in 1971 the AAU women's committee increased the legal limit which women could run to 10 miles. That same year Susan Hollander, a student at a Connecticut high school, was good enough to be a member of her school's cross-country and track teams, but she was prohibited by law from being part of the boys' team (the school did not have a girls' team). She brought suit against the Connecticut Interscholastic Athletic Conference – and lost. Judge Clark Fitzgerald ruled that "athletic competition builds character in our boys. We do not need that kind of character in our girls."

In 1972 Boston finally opened its doors officially to women.[3] Nine of them started the race on 17 April, each wearing a race number with a big red "F" in front of it – presumably to assist "near-sighted finishing chute workers", as Krise and Squires put it. The starting line was extended across the sidewalk for the women because the women's committee decreed that women had to start in a different place or at a different time to the men.

It was only a month since Kuscsik had run 2:59:43 at the

---

3. That same year the first women-only road race was held, a race over 6 miles which drew 78 entrants. Eight years later more than 5 000 women would turn up for the event.

Earth Day marathon in New York, but she won again – despite a severe case of diarrhoea. Her time was 3:10:26.4 and the first thing she thought about after crossing the finish line was "to find my warm-up outfit and cover up my source of embarrassment".

RESULT:
1  Nina Kuscscik 3:10:26.4
2  Elaine Pedersen 3:29:05
3  Kathrine Switzer 3:39:50

In August Bridges made an attack on the US record in Terre Haute. She could not quite repeat her performance of Culver City, winning in 2:55:44. It would nevertheless remain as the world's fastest of the year.

The New York race, held on 1 October, was an interesting one. The AAU women's committee told Lebow that the women had to start ten minutes before or after the men – their race had to be a separate event. The women would have none of this and when the gun went off for their start ten minutes ahead of the men, they simply sat down on the line and waited for the men to start! Kuscsik won in 3:08:41.

The race also resulted in a lawsuit against the AAU for practising discrimination in a public place. At the same time another lawsuit was brought against the governing body: women were still required to produce a medical certificate for a marathon while men were not. The AAU was not prepared to go to court and decided that the easiest way out was to increase the legal limit which women could run to the marathon distance. Women could also start from the same line and at the same time as the men.

No European woman had yet run faster than 3 hours, but this was rectified on 29 October when Sarolta Monspart HUN ran 2:59:53.2 in Budapest. The previous European best was the 3:00:47 set by Paola Cacchi ITA on 31 December 1971 in Rome.

On 2 December the American track star Teri Anderson (18) ran her debut marathon on an uncertified course in Topeka in 2:55:45. Three months later Anderson would run even faster on a point-to-point (but certified) course in St Louis when she won the Olympiad Memorial race in 2:53:40. The route included sections of the 1904 Olympic course.

The first national championship for women was held on 28 October 1973 in West Germany. Christa Kofferschlager (later Vahlensieck) won in 2:59:25.6.

In the same month the AAU agreed to a national championship marathon for women.

On 2 December, when Frank Shorter was scoring his third victory in Fukuoka, Michiko "Miki" Gorman, a 38-year-old Japanese-American, won the Culver City race in 2:46:36 for a new US record. It was her first completed marathon (she had dropped out of the previous year's event).

The year 1974 was to be another important one in women's marathoning. On 12 January the 31-year-old Judy Ikenberry won the Mission Bay marathon in San Diego in 2:54:28 (second was Irja Pettinen FIN in a new European record of 2:58:34) and then set her sights on the first US championship. This was run on 10 February in San Mateo, on a flat five-lap course, and Ikenberry won again. Her time was 2:55:17. Two more women dipped under 3 hours: Marilyn Paul 2:58:44 and Peggy Lyman 2:58:55. Kuscsik was fourth in 3:04:11.

In this race a ten-year-old, Mary Etta Boitano, clocked 3:01:15.

Gorman set a new course record for the Boston marathon when she won in 2:47:11, beating Kofferschlager, who ran a European record of 2:53:00. Kuscsik excelled with 2:55:12 in third, with Kofferschlager's countrywoman Manuela Preuss fourth in 2:58:46. It was the first time that four women had run faster than 3 hours in the same race.

The best was yet to come, though. On 22 September Dr Van Aaken organised the first international race for women in Waldniel. There were 45 entries from seven nations, among them nine Americans. It was an exciting and high-quality event, fitting the occasion. Liane Winter FRG, who had run 2:57:44 earlier in the year, was the early leader. She had company later on from Vahlensieck and Chantal Langlacé FRA, but proved to be the stronger in the headwind encountered by the runners along parts of the four-lap course and won in a fine 2:50:31.4, a European record. The host country took the team competition.

RESULT:
1  Liane Winter 2:50:31.4
2  Chantal Langlacé 2:51:45.2
3  Christa Vahlensieck 2:54:40
4  Manuela Preuss 2:55:59.6
5  Jacqueline Hansen USA 2:56:25.2
6  Joan Ullyot USA 2:58:09.2
7  Judy Ikenberry 2:58:47

This race inspired women runners the world over. Five weeks later, on 27 October, Vahlensieck established herself as the world's best when she ran 2:46:24 in Neuf Brisach, breaking Beames's record by 6 seconds. It did not last very long: on the first day of December, at Culver City, Hansen broke the record by almost 3½ minutes when she clocked 2:43:54.5. Hansen, who had won Boston the previous year, was coached by the Hungarian Laszlo Tabori.

She had started running four years earlier to keep fit. Two years later she ran her first marathon in 3:15. "I finished . . . somehow," she said later. "I went the first 20 miles thinking I've got this thing licked. What's the big fuss about? I clipped along at seven minute mile pace until 22 miles, undaunted. The rest of the race I can't remember. It was the hardest thing I have ever done in my life. Back to the drawing board."

Twenty days after Hansen's performance two young American girls ran superbly in Arizona. Marjorie Kaput (16) raced the downhill course from Cave Creek to Scottsdale

Frith van der Merwe took South African marathoning to new heights in 1990 when she became the first SA woman to break through the 2½-hour barrier. She finished seventh in the 1993 World Championship race.

Willie Mtolo (left) and Zithulele Sinqe wage their tremendous duel in the 1986 SA marathon in Port Elizabeth. Sinqe won the first of his two titles in a national record 2:08:04. Six years later Mtolo won the New York marathon. (*Eastern Province Herald*)

At the beginning of 1996 Belayneh Dinsamo's world record 2:06:50, run in Rotterdam in 1988, was still the world's only sub-2:07 marathon. (Touchline Media/Gray Mortimore)

Mark Plaatjes was born in Coronationville, near Johannesburg, but won the world title in 1993 in the colours of his adopted country, the USA. In 1985 he had become the first South African to run a sub-2:09 marathon. (Touchline Media/Gray Mortimore)

David Tsebe's win in the 1992 Berlin Marathon in 2:08:07 made him the first South African ever to lead the annual world list. The runner receiving the drink behind him is his brother Rami.

A relaxed Elana Meyer follows Uta Pippig in her marathon debut, the 1994 Boston race. Meyer finished third, but in 1995 moved up one place when Pippig won again. (Touchline Media/Ace Lyons)

in 2:51:38, followed by Diane Barrett (13) in 2:55:12.

The year 1975 was an even better one than 1974. Winter came to Boston for the race on 21 April. The tall runner was in a class of her own and improved on Hansen's record by winning easily in 2:42:24. Switzer, who had won New York in 1974 in 3:07:29, ran a PB of 2:51:37, with a new star, Gayle Barron, third in 2:54:11.

Van Aaken's principles had Winter run up to 60 km on a Saturday or Sunday. Her circulatory system was "in tremendous condition," Van Aaken said after the race.

The battle of the Germans continued, for a mere two weeks later (3 May) Vahlensieck ran 2:40:15.8 in Dulmen. The book-keeper from Wuppertal beat her nearest rival by nearly 35 minutes.

The New York City marathon on 28 September hosted the second AAU national championship. Kim Merritt led from the start and, although she was joined at one stage by Barrett, she won in a brilliant 2:46:13.8 from Gorman (2:53:02). Barron had another good race, finishing third in 2:57:22.

In the meantime Hansen had been preparing thoroughly for the Nike/Oregon Track Club marathon in Eugene on 12 October. She had been running almost 100 miles per week for more than three months, a regimen which included a large dose of intervals on the track. It paid off, as she became the first women to run faster than 2:40:00. Only ten men beat her 2:38:19!

Two more sub-2:50 times were run before the end of the year. Gorman won at Culver City (7 December) in 2:47:45 and a week later Hansen recorded 2:49:24 in the heat of Honolulu.

When the year ended, the world's women had run thirty sub-2:55 times; eighteen of them in 1975. The all-time list looked like this:

| | | |
|---|---|---|
| 2:38:19 | Jacqueline Hansen USA | 1975 |
| 2:40:15.8 | Christa Vahlensieck FRG | 1975 |
| 2:42:24 | Liane Winter FRG | 1975 |
| 2:46:13.8 | Kim Merritt USA | 1975 |
| 2:46:24 | Chantal Langlacé FRA | 1974 |
| 2:46:30 | Adrienne Beames AUS | 1971 |
| 2:46:36 | Michiko Gorman USA | 1973 |
| 2:49:40 | Cheryl Bridges USA | 1971 |
| 2:50:21 | Diane Barrett USA | 1975 |
| 2:51:21 | Claire Spauwen NED | 1975 |

The 1976 Boston marathon was run in extreme heat, which makes Merritt's winning time of 2:47:10 even more commendable. She beat Gorman (2:52:27) and Dorothy Doolittle (2:56:26).

The second international marathon was held in Waldniel on 2 October. Among the 53 starters were four women who had held the world record. Merritt ran with confidence, taking the field through 10 km in 38:30, 20 km in 77:59 and 30 km in 1:56:54. Vahlensieck accelerated and caught

the American at 38 km. At 40 km (2:36:55) she was well ahead and reached the finish in 2:45:24.4. Behind her the quality of performances was the highest yet seen.

RESULT:
1. Christa Vahlensieck 2:45:24.4
2. Kim Merritt 2:47:11.2
3. Gayle Barron 2:47:43.2
4. Claire Spauwen 2:47:50.4
5. Manuela Angenvoorth (Preuss) 2:48:18.6
6. Sarolta Monspart 2:51:23

There was no world record for women in 1976, but the standard continued to improve. Langlacé again ran well in Neuf Brisach, clocking 2:44:40 on 24 October for a new French record, while on the same day Spauwen won in Korso in 2:50:17. A new Hungarian record was set by Monspart when she ran 2:48:22.2 in Budapest a week later.

The New York marathon took place on the same day as the race in Neuf Brisach. A dramatic change was made to the course, with the event now winding its way through the five boroughs of the city. It started at Fort Wadsworth on Staten Island, crossed the Narrows by way of the Verazzano Bridge, and then went through Brooklyn and Queens, crossed the Queensboro Bridge into Manhattan, traversed the Bronx and finished in Central Park in Manhattan. There were 88 female starters and Gorman, second the year before and now 41 years old, set a course record of 2:39:11. She won by almost 14 minutes from five-time world cross-country champion Doris Brown Heritage USA. Gorman, also trained by Tabori, was now the second fastest woman ever. Heritage had run 2:47:34.8 in Vancouver in May – the fastest debut in history.

It was Gorman who explained the dramatic improvement in women's running in this way: "In comparison to childbirth the marathon is trivial." It was also Gorman who said: "I never thought I'd have such a luxurious life. A healthy husband . . . beautiful little girl . . . Jacuzzi and beer and fruitbowl and Beethoven and Mendelssohn and running . . . Running is the best thing."

The Culver City race was again on the same day as Fukuoka, 5 December, and it incorporated the AAU championship. Barrett, not yet sixteen, battled track star Julie Brown for the title. It was Brown's superior speed that won the race for her as she became the third fastest ever in the USA with 2:45:32.2. Barrett finished in 2:46:23, with Leal Ann Reinhart third in 2:50:36 and Ullyot fourth in 2:51:15. Ullyot, a doctor like Van Aaken, had written a book on women's running and was a leader in the battle for athletics equality for women.

In Honolulu Merritt improved to 2:44:44, while Australia's Elizabeth Richards ran 2:50:26. Barron was third in 2:52:16.

While Bill Rodgers failed to finish the hot 1977 Boston marathon, Gorman (who weighed only 40 kg) won for the second year in a row. Her time was 2:48:33. Second was Marilyn Bevans (2:51:12) and third Lisa Lorrain (2:56:04), who in the previous four months had run 2:51:30 and 2:51:13.

The world record was to fall twice in 1977. The first occasion came on May Day in the Spanish town of Oyarzun, where the Spanish championship was decided. Langlacé, now 22, finished 14th in 2:35:15.4 after 10 km splits of 37:05, 37:57, 36:55 and 37:28.

On 10 September, in West Berlin, Vahlensieck competed in cool conditions and recovered the record with 2:34:47.5. It was the national championship, and Angenvoorth was not far behind: 2:38:09.4. Her husband, Paul, was third in the men's race with 2:15:42. The two women had battled until 33 km, when Vahlensieck's excellently judged pace proved too much for her rival. Her splits were 36:30, 36:32, 36:38 and 37:15. It was Vahlensieck's seventh sub-2:50 – the most by any woman.

This performance meant that the record had been brought down from 2:46:30 to under 2:35:00 in six years.

American women were progressing, too. The day after the Berlin race Merritt set a US record of 2:37:57 in winning the Nike/OTC marathon in Eugene. Barron was second in 2:48:34. It was Merritt's fifth sub-2:50.

On 23 October Merritt met the only other American with five sub-2:50s, Gorman, in New York. The men's field had more than doubled, while the women's had almost tripled, to 228. Apart from a headwind for most of the race, it was good weather for running. Gorman retained her title, although she was almost exactly 4 minutes slower. Gorman, born in China to Japanese parents, ran 2:43:10 and Merritt, twenty years her junior, 2:46:03. Barron was third, as she had been in 1975, in 2:52:19. In fourth place Lauri Pedrinan USA was also under 2:55:00 with her 2:52:32.

The women's AAU championship was contested the same day in Minneapolis. The times were fast, with Reinhart winning in a PB.

RESULT:   1   Leal Ann Reinhart 2:46:34
          2   Cynthia Dalrymple USA 2:49:11
          3   Nina Kuscsik 2:50:22

That same day, in Norway, a brilliant new star appeared on the scene. Ingrid Christensen sped to a superb 2:45:15 in Trondheim to become the eighth fastest woman ever. And the previous day, in faraway New Zealand, Beverley Shingles had set a national record of 2:47:16 in Hamilton.

On 10 December Beames, who had held the world record from 1971 to 1974, won the Fiesta Bowl marathon in 2:46:32 – only 2 seconds slower than the time she had run in 1971. In the interval only nine women had run faster. Susan Kinsey USA was second in 2:46:54.

A wonderful total of 505 women lined up for the Honolulu marathon on 11 December. Prior to 1970 no other race in the world, with the exception of Boston, even had as many male competitors! Race temperature peaked at 29 °C and the humidity at the start was 82 per cent. Once more Barron could not win, her 2:51:18.9 beaten by Dalrymple's 2:48:07.6.

The year 1978 was highlighted by the entry of the cosmetics giant Avon into women's marathoning. Behind it was Switzer, who had persuaded the company to become involved. "I remember the first slide presentation I ever gave to [the chairman of the board] and some of the other Avon executives. It was full of braless women in wet T-shirts – and they loved it!" Avon brought seventeen of the world's top women to its first International Women's Marathon. It took place in Atlanta on 19 March 1978, with 150 women on the starting line. Unfortunately the course was difficult, with two big hills which had to be negotiated twice. Martha Cooksey USA beat her more fancied rivals in 2:46:16, more than 7 minutes faster than her previous best.

Monspart was second in 2:51:40, with Angenvoorth third in 2:51:53. Brown, Merritt, Gorman and Hansen all retired; yet ten women broke 3 hours.

A month later Boston did not disappoint, producing the best race in history. And Barron finally accomplished her goal of winning a major marathon. She completed the race in 2:44:52 and behind her twelve others clocked under 2:55:00 – almost doubling the previous record of seven in the 1977 Minneapolis race.

RESULT:   1   Gayle Barron 2:44:52
          2   Penny De Moss USA 2:45:36
          3   Jane Killion USA 2:47:23
          4   Kim Merritt 2:47:52
          5   Lauri Pedrinan USA 2:48:42

National records were established by Kiyoko Obata JPN 2:52:34, Eleonora Mendonca BRA 2:52:49, Gayle Olinek CAN 2:52:20, Deborah Butterfield BER 2:53:51 and Gabrielle Andersen SWI 2:54:21.

On 10 September Brown set a US record of 2:36:23.1 in Eugene (Patti Lyons was second in 2:41:31.2) and thirteen days later Vahlensieck won the West German championship in Steinweisen in 2:38:32.8, easily beating Winter. She would remain world record holder for another month.

The 1978 New York marathon on 22 October started a new era. Not only were under-the-table payments for the top finishing positions made to the runners, but the Norwegian schoolteacher Grete Waitz won her debut marathon in a world record time of 2:32:30.

Waitz, the world record holder for the 3000 m with 8:45.4, had won the bronze medal in this event at the European Championships earlier in the year. She had been active in track running since 1971 (although her parents really wanted her to play the piano), and in 1974 had been third in the 1500 m at the European Championships. When asked on that occasion whether she intended moving up to the 3000 m, she replied: "No. I've raced the distance once and thought it far too long."

After winning in New York by more than 9 minutes she said: "I'll *never* do that again." But she would win eight more times . . . Waitz had almost retired from running in 1976 after her failure to make the Olympic final in the 1500 m met with considerable disapproval from the Norwegian public. Now she had found her niche, although she was a very unwilling marathoner in the beginning.

Waitz not only shattered the world record, she also demolished an extremely talented field which had quadrupled in size compared to the previous year. Cooksey had set her sights on the world record, while Lebow did not think much of Waitz's presence. He felt she would make a good rabbit! (One has to admit that he was not wrong, except that he obviously did not expect the rabbit to stay ahead.)

Cooksey, who had recently run the fastest ever half marathon by a woman (75:02), took command of the race after 9 miles and led at the halfway point in 77:45. Waitz and Vahlensiek were 30 seconds behind. The Norwegian took the lead on First Avenue, near the 18-mile mark, and ran the second half in a storming 74:15. Cooksey collapsed half a mile from the finish, staggered to her feet, and fell again. Completely spent, she crawled the last few metres; still, she improved her PB by almost 5 minutes.

RESULT:  1  Grete Waitz 2:32:30
         2  Martha Cooksey 2:41:49
         3  Sue Petersen USA 2:44:43

Altogether 42 women broke 3 hours.

In December Switzer announced the creation of the Avon International Running Circuit, which soon had running programmes in ten countries. In 1979, when the second Avon marathon was held in Waldniel, 262 women from 25 countries participated. Switzer's goal was an Olympic marathon for women, and since the IOC required that only sports practised by women in 25 countries and two continents could be included in the Olympic programme, she had realised her dream. When the third Avon race took place in London in 1980 (two days after the Olympic marathon – to make a point!), 27 countries were represented by 234 athletes. This marathon was the first race of any kind to be held through the centre of London.

"What Kathrine was able to do, with Avon's backing," said Kuscsik at the time, "was to . . . put [everything] together in a showcase. The Avon races . . . gave the IAAF something to look at that popped up right in front of them."

Even Adriaan Paulen, Dutch president of the IAAF and an opponent of women's distance running, was convinced. As one observer put it in the magazine *The Runner* in 1981: "Three years ago, if God had come down and told Adriaan Paulen to support women's marathoning, he wouldn't have. So Avon, at Kathy's instigation, went into the Neth-

erlands and spent thousands on a running programme."

Switzer's efforts received criticism from certain quarters, especially people in the US long-distance hierarchy who had been working through established channels to promote the idea of an Olympic marathon for women. "What riles up so many people in long-distance running about Kathy Switzer," said Patricia Rico, the US representative on the women's committee of the IAAF, "is that she perceived herself as having performed a feat – and run a gamut – that no one else has."

Kuscsik's comment was: "Kathy is very clever, and she's a really good PR person. But she's got one quirk – and that's promoting herself."

Be that as it may, on 23 February 1981 the executive board of the IOC voted 7-1 in Los Angeles to add a women's marathon to the Games programme. The one member voting against the proposal was Vitaly Smirnov of the Soviet Union.

"I'm ecstatic," said Kuscsik, chairperson of the women's subcommittee of the long-distance running committee of The Athletic Congress (as the AAU had become known). "And the 5000 and 10000 will follow."[4]

Meanwhile, in December 1978, Lyons had run her third sub-2:45 marathon of the year when she won in Honolulu in 2:43:09.5. Six days later, in University Park, Elizabeth Berry became the second fastest American of 1978 when she clocked 2:41:10.

By the end of the year ten women had run fourteen times under 2:45:00 and Lyons' time in Eugene behind Brown gave her the tenth position on the all-time list. *Track & Field News* ranked Waitz first for the year, followed by Cooksey, Barron, Brown and Lyons.

The 1979 Boston was held on 16 April, only the third time that the race had been run this early in the year. It resulted in the fastest time of the year up to that point – and it would take another world record by the incomparable Waitz to push it into second on the world list.

It was a cool and drizzly day and Bill Rodgers wore both his usual gloves and a woollen cap. He ran 2:09:27 for an American record. Joan Benoit from Cape Elizabeth, Maine, wore a Red Sox cap askew on her short hair – not to protect her from the elements but, as she put it, to remind her to run conservatively and not blow the race, as the Red Sox team normally did in pursuit of the baseball championship! She need not have worried – she did not blow it at all. In fact, she set a US record.

The 21-year-old Benoit, running in a Bowdoin College vest, led fifteen women under 2:50:00 – a record. Lyons, who had to receive a pain-killing injection for a foot injury before the race, covered the first half in an unofficial 74:00

---

4. This would happen in 1980. The first World Road Race Championship over 10 km was staged in 1983 in San Diego. This was changed to 15 km in 1985.

# QUEEN OF THE ROAD

There can be little doubt that Grete Waitz is the greatest female distance runner ever. Born Grete Andersen on 1 October 1953 in Oslo, she started athletics as a high jumper at twelve, but first achieved prominence in her home country when she set a Norwegian 800 m record of 2:05.7 and a European junior record of 4:17.0 for 1500 m in 1971. In 1973 she set a Norwegian 3000 m record of 9:34.2 in what she saw as her last attempt at the distance ("I thought it far too long"). Second in that race was the previous record holder, seventeen-year-old Ingrid Christensen.

In 1974 Andersen won the bronze medal in the European 1500 m. In 1975 the high-school teacher of Norwegian literature, grammar, history and geography improved so dramatically that she set a world record of 8:46.6 in her second 3000 m. In 1976 she improved this to 8:45.4. Although she still regarded herself as a 1500 m runner, at the Olympic Games in 1976 she could not advance from the semifinal despite a PB 4:04.8.

In 1978 she won the world cross-country title on her first attempt, but at the European Championships she had to be content with another bronze, this time in the 3000 m. She ran 8:34.33 in what she considered to be one of her best races ever.

"But the press obviously didn't agree, for they wrote about me as if I had more or less come last. That, plus the fact that some of the girls were proven to have been using drugs, made me feel that it was just no fun any more. Another factor was that the 1980 Olympics wouldn't have a 3000. So I made up my mind that now was the time to call it a day."

Fortunately she spoke to countryman Knut Kvalheim, who had also been disappointed with his performance at the same European Championships. Kvalheim mentioned that he had run the New York marathon the year before, and encouraged Grete to do the same.

She and her husband Jack (his surname was Nilsen; when they married in 1975 they decided to take the surname Waitz) did not have enough money to get to New York and Fred Lebow didn't want to pay for Jack. (Initially he didn't want to pay for Grete either.) "Things sorted themselves out in the end", as Grete put it in a 1985 interview in *Athletics Weekly*, and she surprised the world with a global best in her first marathon.

Grete, confused by the mile distance markers, lost track of how far she still had to run towards the end of the race. "Each time I saw trees, I thought it was Central Park."

The victory changed her life (she had planned to retire after the race) and allowed her to become a full-time runner. She was to win New York another eight times, an unprecedented feat in modern road running.

But at times the fame was too difficult to cope with. Although she admitted that she was in the right place at the right time and that the marathon

had made her famous, she also said in an interview in 1979: "Sometimes I wish I could throw the whole thing away . . . and be a common girl."

In 1979 she retained her world cross-country title and set world records of 31:16 for 10 km and 53:05 for 10 miles. She still competed on the track, though, running the year's fastest 3000 m in Oslo. In 1980 she established world records of 31:00 for 10 km and 48:01 for 15 km (she would improve this to 47:53 in 1984) and won the world cross-country title for the third time in a row.

Although she won the cross-country championship again in 1981, she had to drop out of New York with shin splints after three victories and three world records. In 1982 she was beaten for the cross-country title, but set a world record of 69:19 for the half marathon and a European record of 15:08.80 for the 5000 m.

In 1983 she had a tremendous year: first in the World Cross-country Championship, first in the inaugural World Championships marathon and first in both the London and New York marathons. In the former she equalled the world record.

Two days before the Olympic marathon in Los Angeles Grete changed bedrooms with her brother Jan, and the next day her back was hurting. "I was in the shape of my life [but] by lunch-time I was hobbling about like an 80-year-old. Everything collapsed like a house of cards," she related in *Athletics Weekly*. "When I woke the morning of the race, my back was better [after treatment], but I wasn't mentally prepared to run . . . at all. By the time of the race . . . I had no pain. But there was no aggression – my head wasn't tuned in. Then suddenly, halfway, things started functioning, and I felt the brakes were off; there was nothing holding me back. By then Benoit had a two minutes lead. I closed to within a minute of her, and when I caught sight of her back with about 5 km to go I just for a moment thought I might yet win. But I soon realised it was asking a bit much to haul back a minute over 5 km when somebody's travelling at 2:25 pace! So I just ran for the silver, and I was really delighted when I got it."

After 1984 Waitz continued to compete with success on the road around the world. In 1986 she won the London marathon again in a career-low 2:24:54, the fastest time in the world for the year. In 1987 she could not defend her world title because of injury and in 1988 she dropped out of the Olympic marathon, but finished the year with 2:28:06 in her final New York victory. In her last competitive appearance in New York she finished fourth in 1990 after having suffered from stress fractures in 1989-90.

Waitz won thirteen of her nineteen marathons. She never really liked the marathon, but enjoyed competing in road races. "It was more friendly and social than eight people in a 1500." A statue of her stands outside the famous Bislett stadium in Oslo.

---

(faster than the world record for the distance) and was only caught by Benoit at the foot of Heartbreak Hill. Lyons kept up with her for another mile, but then the tiny Benoit pulled away and raced to a superb 2:35:15, 15 minutes faster than her previous best. The ease of her victory brought predictions that she would soon run sub-2:30.

The first four broke Winter's course record of 1975.

RESULT:
1. Joan Benoit 2:35:15
2. Patti Lyons 2:38:22
3. Sue Krenn USA 2:38:50
3. Elizabeth Hassell AUS 2:39:48

On 23 June New Zealander Lorraine Moller ran 2:37:36.5 in Duluth and on 9 September Benoit came very close to her

Boston time when she won the Nike/OTC marathon in 2:35:41, beating Gillian Adams GBR (2:41:03). Benoit thus became the first woman ever to run two sub-2:40 times in the same year (later in 1979 two more women would follow).

After the race Benoit said: "I'd love to do something else for a while."

Thirteen days later 41-year-old Joyce Smith GBR won the second Avon marathon, in Waldniel, in a magnificent 2:36:27, setting British, Commonwealth and world veterans' records. Merritt was second in 2:39:43. More than 10 000 spectators watched the race in unfavourable conditions.

Smith had been taking part in athletics for 22 years and among her successes were a victory in the World Cross-country Championships and national titles and records for 1500 and 3000 m. The Waldniel marathon was her second;

in the first (the AAA race on 17 June) she had set a British record of 2:41:37.

The next day, in Manchester, Vermont, Lyons showed that her fast first half in Boston was no fluke when she set a world half-marathon best of 74:04.

Then it was time for New York. Waitz, who said that she was "still a track runner" and had retained her world cross-country title earlier in the year, lined up with 1 325 other women. Things had changed for Waitz since her victory the previous year – she now had an endorsement contract from Adidas which enabled her to be a full-time runner. There was no stopping her as she completed the first half in 74:51 and then accelerated. She reached the finish at Tavern on the Green in 2:27:32.6 – the first woman under 2:30:00. Her second half was a fraction slower than 72:41.

"Right now, I feel I can't run any faster. I don't want to run faster anyway. The record was really not that important. I came here to win the race again," Waitz said later. Her victory margin was even bigger than the year before.

RESULT:
1. Grete Waitz 2:27:32.6
2. Gillian Adams 2:38:31
3. Jacqueline Gareau CAN 2:39:04
4. Patti Lyons 2:40:17

The Chicago marathon was run the same day. Waitz's time would have placed her second *overall* there.

On 18 November Smith won the Tokyo marathon in 2:37:48 for her second sub-2:40 of the year. Olinek achieved the same feat in Scottsdale on 1 December when she won in 2:36:12. Her first sub-2:40 of the year had been on 18 February in the Mardi Gras marathon in Metairie, where she ran 2:38:12. (In 1980 she would win in a wind-aided 2:35:12.)

Thirteen women finished the year with times faster than 2:40:00 – ten more than in 1978. Waitz was again ranked first, with Smith, who had won the first three marathons of her career in 1979, second and Benoit third.

At the end of the year this author wrote an article for the magazine *S.A. Runner* which appeared under the title "Women will soon overtake men!" and elicited widespread reaction (from men). The purpose of the article was to point out the phenomenal progress in women's times; the world record having improved by 47 minutes and 50 seconds since 1967 against the men's 30.8 seconds (disregarding Derek Clayton's 2:08:33.6).

"Of course the men's record is ripe for revision and could fall any day . . . but we have been saying this for a number of years . . . If the women continue to improve at the same rate [as from 1973-1979], they will break 2:20 in 1982, 2:15 in 1984 and 2:10 in 1986. No doubt about it, somewhere we must find a 2:05 man."

Famous last words, as they say. The men's record did fall in 1981, but even at the time of this writing it is only 1:44 faster than in 1980 while the women have yet to break

2:21:00 – never mind the 2:20:00 which the calculations at the time predicted for 1982!

Benoit went to Auckland early in 1980 for the Choysa marathon, her fourth outing over the distance. The race was on 3 February, it was run in hot and humid weather, and she won in 2:31:23 for her second US record. It was also the second fastest time ever . . . but by the end of the year it would only be the sixth fastest!

Boston was on 21 April, and it was a controversial affair.

First across the line in a course record 2:31:45 was one Rosie Ruiz, who said that she had been born in Cuba 26 years before. No one had ever heard of her, and she beat Gareau and Lyons – two of the fastest marathoners in history.

At the post-race press conference Rodgers, who had just scored his fourth victory, asked her: "Did you win?" When Ruiz said yes, Rodgers asked: "Who are you?" Everyone was asking the same question.

Rodgers's brother Charlie saw Ruiz finish. "The first thing I did was look at her legs, and I said to myself, 'Uh-oh, we have a problem here.' I mean, it was cellulite city."

Ruiz claimed that she had qualified for Boston by running 2:56:29 in New York, but it soon turned out that she had run part of the way, then took a subway train to the finish and entered the finish chutes. In Boston she had waited among the crowds near the finish before jumping into the race.

The official winner was 27-year-old Gareau, a respiratory therapist from Montreal who liked to take four-day winter hikes with a backpack and sled in the Quebec countryside. She was crowned the winner seven days and 23 hours after crossing the finish line in Boston – after the exhaustive investigations by the organisers had proved that Ruiz was an imposter. Gareau's time of 2:34:28 removed Benoit's course record from the books and was the third fastest time ever. Lyons was second (2:35:08) and Adams third (2:39:17). Benoit was still recovering from an appendectomy and did not run.

On 22 June Smith won her national title in Sandbach by clocking 2:33:32. On 6 September Gareau and Lyons, now Lyons-Catalano after her marriage, met again, this time in the Canadian's home town. The American, who had set a US record of 53:40 for 10 miles two weeks before, was in brilliant form and her surge from 23 km gave her the race as well as a US record of 2:30:57.1. It was an awesome display of power running. Gareau set a national record of 2:31:42 in second.

The next day Moller, who had won the Avon race in London on 3 August in 2:35:11, did likewise in the Nike/OTC marathon in the fourth fastest time ever, 2:31:42 – a Commonwealth record. Marja Wokke NED was not far behind in a national record of 2:32:29 and another New Zealander, Allison Roe, third in 2:34:29. The ubiquitous Adams was fourth.

Waitz returned to New York for the race on 26 October, where she was to meet a very determined Lyons-Catalano.

Waitz started much faster than in her two previous attempts and Lyons-Catalano could not keep contact after 5 miles, covered in 27:00. She was running with her husband Joe and they watched Waitz pull away. The world record holder reached 10 miles in 55:25 (at which point she passed quadruple Olympic champion Lasse Viren) and the halfway mark in 72:30. She was clocked in 94:10 at 17 miles. A mile earlier Lyons-Catalano had left her husband behind and started her charge.

Up ahead Alberto Salazar was flying towards the finish of his first marathon. Waitz was flying, too. She finished in an amazing 2:25:41.3 for her third consecutive world record. Lyons-Catalano, brave as she was, had had no chance, yet she set another US record with her 2:29:33.6. Third was Waitz's compatriot Christensen in a PB of 2:34:24.9. Carol Gould GBR ran 2:35:04.6 for third, beating Adams.

On 16 November Smith ran the third fastest time of the year when she won the Tokyo marathon again, this time in 2:30:27. The 43-year-old Briton had a tremendous battle with Gareau, but drew away after 38 km. Gareau finished in 2:30:58 for a Canadian record. Smith's time was a Commonwealth record and the fastest ever on an out-and-back course (in this case the one used for the 1964 Olympic marathon).

A record nine women finished the year with sub-2:35 times (never before had more than one runner – Waitz, of course – achieved the feat). Waitz ranked first for the third consecutive time, followed by Lyons-Catalano, Moller, Smith and Gareau.

The first significant race of 1981 was the London marathon on 29 March, where the amazing Smith improved even further. She won in 2:29:57, beating Gillian Drake NZL by more than 7 minutes and becoming the third woman under 2½ hours. The previous day Waitz had won her fourth successive world cross-country title.

The weather was perfect for the Boston marathon on 20 April. There were almost 7 000 starters. Among the women Catalano was the clear favourite, but Benoit, Roe and Gareau were also in the field. And then there was Julie Shea USA in her second marathon.

Shea took the early lead, but by 10 miles Catalano was in front. Shea was not content with this and regained the lead for about the next 8 miles. The blonde Roe (24) was well behind them at this stage. Gareau had a hamstring problem and did not attempt to go with the leaders. Benoit was also not having a good day. "At Wellesley, I began to wonder what other sport I could take up. Then I remembered that I was a runner," she said later.

Two miles later than she had wanted to (at the top of the Newton hills) Roe caught Catalano. There was nothing the American record holder could do. "When she passed me, she kept hammering, hammering, hammering. I wanted to keep up, but I couldn't get my legs to turn over. I was running hard; pressing, pushing. Allison just outran me, that's all."

Krise and Squires put it beautifully: "Roe bears down at 20 miles . . . She floats extravagantly high over the road, her track muscles taking the pace in stride. Catalano clings low to the tarmac, knowing only the roads, only that this is HER Boston Marathon, seething with dark passion. Her eyes, normally coals, compress into black diamonds of rage and pain . . . For the first time in Boston history, the women in the crowd see a real women's race. They scream hysterically in a rapture of sisterhood, urging on not Allison Roe but Everywoman Runner."

The New Zealander flashed across the finish in 2:26:46, a course record. Catalano was second for the third year in a row, but set another US record, this time 2:27:51. The first six broke the course record and seven were under 2:35:00 – more than double the previous record.

RESULT:
1. Allison Roe 2:26:46
2. Patti Catalano 2:27:51
3. Joan Benoit 2:30:16
4. Julie Shea 2:30:54
5. Jacqueline Gareau 2:31:26
6. Sissel Grottenberg NOR 2:33:02

After the race Catalano said: "I didn't do anything wrong. The only thing I did wrong was get second, and that's not bad." Roe was surprised with her time: "I really didn't think I could run that fast."

Roe began her athletic career as a high jumper, but when she was eighteen (born 30 May 1956) she became New Zealand's youngest-ever senior cross-country champion. In the 1975 World Cross-country Championships, as Allison Deed, she finished 29th, with her team second. The top Kiwi in that race was Moller who, like Roe, would become a top-notch marathoner. Roe ran her first marathon in 1980 and despite walking often, finished second in 2:51:45 – far behind Benoit's 2:31:23. Her second marathon was in Eugene, where she finished third behind Moller and Wokke.

In November 1980, in the Tokyo marathon, she experienced the ravages of the marathon when she hit the wall at 20 miles. "What I felt was pressure around my shoulders and a dizzy, disoriented feeling. Suddenly my stride rhythm and pattern and everything went to pieces. I was a total wreck."

But in March 1981 she returned to Japan and set a world record of 68:22 for 20 km. And then came Boston . . . Roe thought the undulating Boston course was perfect for her, but she was still surprised by her time. "When I . . . looked up at the clock I thought to myself, 'They must have had a power cut!'"

On 20 June the "other New Zealander", Moller, won the Grandma's marathon in Duluth in 2:29:35.5, becoming the fifth woman to break 2:30:00. Moller was also first in the Nike/OTC race in August, running 2:31:15.

The fourth Avon International marathon was run in hot, humid weather in Ottawa on 23 August. There was a field of

631, of which 40 per cent dropped out because of the conditions. Nancy Conz USA won in 2:36:46 after stomach trouble had forced Benoit to pull off the course. She could not catch Conz again and finished second, 38 seconds behind.

For the first time more than 2 000 women (2 029) started the New York City marathon on 25 October. Roe and Shea were both there, and they were up against the two formidable Norwegians, Waitz and Christensen.

Roe and her coach, Gary Elliott, had made their usual list of "the positive things that we'd done in [our] preparation" as part of Roe's mental tune-up. Among these things, all in the last eight weeks before the race, were: her fastest 10 miles and 10 km (31:26), fastest mile repetition session (average 4:40), fastest 2x2 miles session (9:25, 9:26), fastest 3000 m (8:55), fastest 6x800 m session (average 2:10); she had won the Auckland road championships, Peachtree road race and Sydney's City to Surf in record times and had run the most miles ever in a six-month period.

When the race started, Brown took the lead immediately and passed 10 miles in 55:05, with Waitz and Roe less than 200 m behind. The lead had decreased to just a few metres by the end of the 12th mile, but that was as far as Waitz got. The world record holder was suffering from shin splints and had to call it a day. She encouraged Roe to go after Brown.

Roe did, and also went after Waitz's world record. Brown reached halfway in 71:32, but Roe soon drew level. From there on the New Zealander ran unchallenged, while Brown faded badly, eventually finishing ninth. Roe won in 2:25:28.7, breaking Waitz's record by just under 13 seconds. But in December 1984 the course was found to be short, nullifying Roe's performance (see p. 90). It did not change the significance of the victory by the former high jumper and tennis player, though, for as one observer put it, "Winning Boston changes your running career. Winning New York changes your life."

RESULT:   1   Allison Roe 2:25:28.7
         2   Ingrid Christensen 2:30:08.2
         3   Julie Shea 2:30:11.5

"I was just hoping to win," Roe said later. "I was sorry, though, that Grete had to drop out. I was disappointed that I didn't have her to fight it out with."

Catalano ran two more fast races in 1981, clocking 2:33:30 in Newport and 6 seconds faster in Honolulu. Brown kept her best of the year for December, when she won in Dallas in 2:33:39.7.

The year – and it can be called Allison Roe's year – ended with 33 women under 2:40:00 and twelve under 2:35:00. Four – Roe, Catalano, Moller and Smith – were faster than 2:30:00, making an all-time total of five under this barrier. The two Kiwis headed the ranking, with Catalano third and the first Eastern bloc star, the

Soviet champion Zoya Ivanova, fourth. She had won the European Cup race in Agen in 2:38:58.

The year 1982 was highlighted by the first major regional championship for women, the European marathon, which was scheduled for Athens on 12 September. And it was a European runner who first made her mark. On 16 January Charlotte Teske FRG, whose best was the 2:33:13 which had given her the national title and record in 1981, won the Orange Bowl marathon with the greatest of ease in Miami in 2:29:01.6.

Eight days later Rita Marchisio ITA and Carla Beurskens NED battled each other in Osaka, with the Italian winning in 2:32:55 against 2:34:14. Smith was fifth, but both she and Teske were at the beginning of a great year.

Teske, who had run a world record for 25 km in 1981, lined up for the Boston classic on 19 April (Smith had her sights on London twenty days later). While Salazar and Dick Beardsley waged their titanic struggle at the front, the 32-year-old West German simply ran away from the field – not even Gareau could do anything about it. She was "helped" by the leg cramps that hit Waitz at 23 miles and forced her to drop out (after going through 21½ miles at a pace 3 minutes faster than Roe's New York time), but Teske ran an impressive race and became the first woman to clock two sub-2:30s in one year.[5]

RESULT:   1   Charlotte Teske 2:29:33
         2   Jacqueline Gareau 2:36:09
         3   Eileen Claugus USA 2:38:48

Smith's victory in London on 9 May was just as easy, and by almost the same margin. She was going for 2:27:00 and while she could not manage that, she still ran a PB and national record of 2:29:43. This made her the oldest athlete ever to set a British record. She handed Moller (a disappointing 2:36:15) her first defeat in nine marathons.

On the same day as the European Championships marathon the Nike/OTC race took place in Eugene. While the difficult course in Athens made fast times unlikely, there was no such hindrance in the Oregon city.

Benoit had had surgery to both Achilles tendons in December, but came back with the determination which was her trademark. She first recorded the fastest US time ever for 20 km (69:11), then shattered Waitz's course record for the 7.1-mile Falmouth race by 39 seconds, set a US 10-mile record of 53:18, ran 20 km in 67:40 and set a PB of 85:20 for 25 km.

The little Boston University women's coach was ready for something big. She led from the start and in perfect running weather ended with a US record of 2:26:11, the second

5. It should be noted that Roe's time on the short New York course would have been about 2:26:00 on an accurate course – giving her two times under 2:30:00 for 1981.

fastest ever run. She now had no doubts about her ability: "I have questioned if I could run with Grete and Allison. Now I know I can."

She amazed everyone with her strong finish. "I felt so good it was as if I was running a track race. I had too much left. I thought about sprinting but . . . I didn't want to show-boat."

Benoit won $20 000 for her effort. Laurie Binder USA was second in a PB 2:33:50.

On the same day, many thousands of kilometres away, a woman who was to be one of the most successful marathoners of all time was running her debut. Rosa Mota POR, who had finished 12th in the 3000 m three days earlier, did not want to run the European marathon, but her coach convinced her. "He said that in this heat I would be more at home than my rivals."

Mota's coach was certainly right. She ran in a group of three until only 2 km remained and then surged away. Behind her the heat had already played havoc with the main contenders – all more experienced than the Portuguese.

RESULT:

| | | |
|---|---|---|
| 1 | Rosa Mota POR | 2:36:04 |
| 2 | Laura Fogli ITA | 2:36:29 |
| 3 | Ingrid Kristiansen (Christensen) NOR | 2:36:39 |
| 4 | Alba Milana ITA | 2:38:55 |
| 5 | Carla Beurskens NED | 2:39:23 |
| 6 | Karolina Szabó HUN | 2:40:51 |

Mota's time was a national record. Teske, who had inexplicably run a marathon two weeks earlier, was a dismal 12th in 2:45:18.

On 24 October Teske lined up in New York, together with Kristiansen, Fogli and Beurskens . . . and, of course, Waitz.

The Norwegian had recovered from a fatigue fracture earlier in the year and was ready. "I discovered in September that I was in fantastic condition." Roe had had an Achilles injury and was doing television commentating on the race. (In March she had won a race in Seoul in 2:43:12.)

It was a cool, windy day and Waitz took command almost from the beginning. She reached 7 miles in 40:34, leading Brown, Kristiansen (who earlier in the year had won the Stockholm marathon in 2:34:26), Teske, the Soviets Anna Domoratskaya and Nadyezhda Gumerova, Fogli, Szabó, Shea, Binder and Laura DeWald USA. By 10 miles Waitz was 15 seconds ahead of Brown and she continued to increase her advantage to the finish. Brown improved her PB by more than 5 minutes and became the eighth woman under 2:30:00.

RESULT:

| | | |
|---|---|---|
| 1 | Grete Waitz | 2:27:14 |
| 2 | Julie Brown | 2:28:33 |
| 3 | Charlotte Teske | 2:31:53 |
| 4 | Laura Fogli | 2:33:01 |
| 5 | Ingrid Kristiansen | 2:33:36 |

It was the first marathon Waitz had finished after two drop-outs and she was satisfied: "I think I am in good enough shape to run a world record time, but not today because of the wind."

The percentage of finishers (95.1) was the highest in the history of the race.

The twelve runners under 2:40:00 was also a record for a single race. This helped to swell the total of women who broke the barrier in the course of the year to sixty – almost double that of 1981. The nineteen under 2:35:00 for the year and five under 2:30:00 were also records. (The 1981 Boston marathon still held the record for sub-2:35s, though, with seven.)

The first five on the ranking list for 1982 were Waitz, Benoit, Brown, Mota and Teske.

The year 1983 was the best in the history of women's marathoning. For the first time there was a world title at stake, and for the first time a woman broke through 2½ hours three times in the same year. Not surprisingly, the same woman featured in both instances.

The penultimate day of January brought the first sub-2:30:00 time of the year. Carey May IRL won the Osaka marathon in 2:29:23, beating Teske by more than 6 minutes. The 23-year-old Irishwoman, a student in the USA, set an Irish and course record and improved her PB by more than 7½ minutes.

Fourteen days before, Kristiansen had won the Houston marathon in a course record 2:33:27 and collected $15 000 and a cowboy hat for her efforts. Vahlensieck ran 2:39:09 for seventh.

Teske rebounded on 15 May with a national record of 2:28:32 in Frankfurt, but by that time much faster performances had been produced in London and Boston.

London was first, on 17 April. The weather was ideal: there was no wind, and a slight drizzle came down on the 16 500 competitors. But circumstances were not ideal for Waitz, who about a month earlier had had a brilliant race in England when she won her fifth world cross-country title in Gateshead: her old knee injury gave her some trouble, her thigh muscles cramped, and the usual gaggle of men who like to run with the leading women in order to share their glory on live television hindered her rhythm (the latter problem perhaps contributing to her physical difficulties in the course of the race).

Earlier in the year Waitz had lost a road race in the USA for the first time when Wendy Sly GBR defeated her over 15 km in the Gasparilla event in Tampa. Waitz ran 48:30, and now she set out to improve on her world marathon record. She covered the first 5 miles in 27:41, 10 miles in 55:17, and reached halfway in 72:25. At 15 miles she was timed in 82:56 and at 20 miles in 1:51:05. She finished in 2:25:28.7, 12.6 seconds under the record.

No one could stay with her, but her fast pace pulled Mary O'Connor NZL to 2:28:20 – a nice present for the schoolteacher's 28th birthday two days later. O'Connor's previous best was 2:44:53!

The next day, on the other side of the Atlantic, Boston saw the most spectacular women's marathon in history.

Benoit had also been beaten by Sly earlier, although she set a US 10 km record of 31:44 in the process. In Boston she went after the world record – her aim was to run 2:23-something. She clocked 31:50 at 10 km, a time which had been bettered in open competition only twice by an American (herself). It was a 2:14:00 pace! She reached 10 miles in 51:30, and this scared her somewhat. But "I felt good and thought, 'What the heck?'"

She developed blisters, but still went through halfway in 68:23 – 47 seconds faster than the US record for the distance she would set in September! The question now was: what would happen on the Newton hills?

She had a side stitch at 15 miles, but "took some water, collected myself and moved on". Two miles further Roe, who was never in contention, dropped out with leg cramps. Benoit found the last part of the race hard: "I ran those last few miles really hurting in general."

Benoit's furious pace was too much even for Gareau, who ran a PB and national record but finished almost 7 minutes behind the Amercian's world record.

RESULT:  1  Joan Benoit 2:22:43
         2  Jacqueline Gareau 2:29:28
         3  Mary Shea USA 2:33:24

Benoit's performance was called "sublime", but there was also criticism as some observers pointed out that she had been accompanied all the way and given assistance by New Zealand marathoner Kevin Ryan. Benoit replied that Ryan was covering the leading woman in the race for a local television station and that he had only joined her at 10 km after following Roe and then realising his mistake. "By that time I . . . had already established the pace for myself. Kevin did give me some split times. He also gave me water and words of encouragement. However, so did other runners on the course."

Nine days earlier Mota had claimed her second major victory when she set another national record by winning in Rotterdam in 2:32:27.

On 5 June Brown ran the race of her life in Santa Monica. It was the Avon International marathon, the TAC Championship and the US selection race for the World Championships and, as *Track & Field News* put it, there was "*no* tailwind, *no* men . . . for pacing help, *no* big crowd to cheer every mile of the way and . . . a net *gain* in elevation". Brown's 2:26:26 was the fastest ever in a women-only race. In second Vahlensieck showed that she could still perform well by clocking 2:33:22, beating runners like Fogli, Smith and Binder.

The first World Championships marathon was held on 7 August in Helsinki. The race started at 15:05 and Waitz was dominant from the outset. She had recently run 48:44 for 15 km and had fully recovered from her London effort. She passed 10 km in 36:14 in the company of Brown and three Soviets, one of them Raisa Smekhnova, as well as Teske, Gareau and Fogli. Making a surprise appearance in the leading group was US newcomer Marianne Dickerson in her fourth marathon. She had run 2:33:44 in the trials.

The time at 15 km was 54:24, with Gareau leading and Waitz and the main group 8 seconds behind. At 17 km something unexpected happened. Regina Joyce IRL took the initiative and quickly opened a gap of 35 m. Waitz did not react and the others stayed with her. After the race Dickerson was to ask: "Whose pace judgment would you pick, Grete Waitz's or Regina Joyce's?"

Joyce's pace judgment took her to a lead of 125 m at one stage (her splits at 20, 25 and 30 km were 71:39, 89:10 and 1:47:36), but by 30 km it was down to about 10 m. Then the Norwegian star, who was running with Brown, Dickerson and Smekhnova, made the decisive move. She dramatically increased the pace and stormed through the next 5 km in 16:51 . . . and she was all alone. Miraculously, she increased the tempo even further, covering the last full 5 km of the race in 16:22. She reached 40 km in 2:20:52, 2:22 ahead of Smekhnova.

Waitz majestically entered the Olympic Stadium with no rival in sight and finished in 2:28:09, a superb time in the hot and humid conditions. It was a typically imperturbable Waitzian performance. She had once described herself thus in an interview: "Sometimes people look at me and because I am not always smiling and laughing they think I am sad. I'm not sad. I'm not. I'm maybe a little cool. Not impulsive, but controlled. That's the word. Controlled."

Outside the stadium Dickerson and the Soviet were fighting it out for the silver medal. The American was gaining rapidly. She noticed that Smekhnova's "legs were like jelly going up the hill. I was just hoping she wasn't a 1:58 half-miler." Smekhnova was indeed a sub-4:00 1500 m runner, but it did not help her much. She reached the track with a lead of 7 m and the two women sprinted for the line. With 90 m left Dickerson powered past. Behind them Mota improved once again, but it wasn't enough for a medal.

RESULT:  1   Grete Waitz NOR 2:28:09
         2   Marianne Dickerson USA 2:31:09
         3   Raisa Smekhnova URS 2:31:13
         4   Rosa Mota POR 2:31:50
         5   Jacqueline Gareau CAN 2:32:35
         6   Laura Fogli ITA 2:33:31
         7   Regina Joyce IRL 2:33:52
         8   Tuija Toivonen FIN 2:34:14
         9   Joyce Smith GBR 2:34:27
         10  Lutsia Byelyayeva URS 2:34:44

The ninth place by the 45-year-old Smith, the oldest runner in the race, was a formidable feat. Achilles tendon problems had forced Brown, one of the big favourites, to drop out at 37 km. May was 13th, Vahlensieck 19th, O'Connor 34th, while both Teske and Langlacé failed to finish.

The next month nineteen-year-old Akemi Masuda JPN just missed 2½ hours when she won the Nike/OTC marathon in 2:30:30, a national record in her third marathon, while on 16 October Mota got her fourth consecutive PB and national record when she was first in the America's marathon in Chicago in 2:31:12. Gareau was second (2:31:36), Dorthe Rasmussen DEN third (2:31:45) and New Zealander Anne Audain, who had been running very well on the US circuit, fourth in a debut 2:32:14.

A week later it was raining in New York, but it did not seem to bother Waitz as she won for the fifth time. She had no trouble disposing of Moller early on and won by almost 5 minutes in 2:27:00 – an unprecedented third sub-2:30 for the year. Fogli was second (2:31:49, a national record), Priscilla Welch (38) third (2:32:31) and Vahlensieck sixth (2:35:59).

The year ended with 121 women under 2:40:00 – more than double that of 1982 – and 32 under 2:35:00. Seven ran faster than 2:30:00. In each of these cases it was the most ever. No single race had yet seen more than two runners under the 2:30:00 barrier.

The all-time list showed twenty runners faster than 2:32:00 and there were 22 times by eleven runners faster than 2:30:00. Waitz owned six of these and Teske (3) was the only other runner with more than two. The list looked like this (only six times dated from before 1983):

| | | | |
|---|---|---|---|
| 2:22:43 | Joan Benoit USA | 1983 | |
| 2:25:28.7 | Grete Waitz NOR | 1983 | |
| 2:26:26 | Julie Brown USA | 1983 | |
| 2:26:46 | Allison Roe NZL | 1981 | |
| 2:27:51 | Patti Lyons-Catalano USA | 1981 | |
| 2:28:20 | Mary O'Connor NZL | 1983 | |
| 2:28:32 | Charlotte Teske FRG | 1983 | |
| 2:29:23 | Carey May IRL | 1983 | |
| 2:29:28 | Jacqueline Gareau CAN | 1983 | |
| 2:29:35.5 | Lorraine Moller NZL | 1981 | (10) |
| 2:29:43 | Joyce Smith GBR | 1982 | |
| 2:30:08.2 | Ingrid Kristiansen NOR | 1981 | |
| 2:30:11.5 | Julie Shea USA | 1981 | |
| 2:30:30 | Akemi Masuda JPN | 1983 | |
| 2:31:09 | Marianne Dickerson USA | 1983 | |
| 2:31:12 | Rosa Mota POR | 1983 | |
| 2:31:13 | Raisa Smekhnova URS | 1983 | |
| 2:31:37 | Monika Lövenich FRG | 1983 | |
| 2:31:45 | Dorthe Rasmussen DEN | 1983 | |
| 2:31:49 | Laura Fogli ITA | 1983 | (20) |

Waitz once again ranked first (and seventh overall among the world's top women), followed by Benoit, Dickerson, Smekhnova and Mota.

Then it was time for 1984 – the historic first Olympic year

for the women's marathon. With the Games marathon relatively early (5 August), most of the serious contenders were saving themselves for a supreme effort in Los Angeles. On 15 January Kristiansen put the first card on the table with a PB 2:27:51 in Houston – a few months after giving birth to her first child. The course was a double loop "through the concrete canyons of this monument to construction companies", as the *Track & Field News* reporter put it. The Norwegian won first prize of $20 000 plus a life insurance policy of $100 000.

Fourteen days later an interesting race took place in Osaka. The winner in her maiden international outing was the first top marathoner to come out of East Germany, Katrin Dörre (22). She improved her national record from 2:37:31 to 2:31:41 and beat a fine field: Masuda was second in 2:32:05, while Szabó finished third, Rasmussen fourth, Welch sixth and Roe, coming back from her injury, seventh (2:38:36).

On 16 April Moller won Boston in 2:29:28 (Roe dropped out) and on 13 May Kristiansen ran her second sub-2:30 of the year, a scintillating 2:24:26 to win London. While most other runners were careful not to over-race, the strong Norwegian apparently had no such qualms. In March she had been fourth in the World Cross-country Championships (one place behind Waitz) and a week before London she had beaten Waitz and South Arican-turned-Briton Zola Budd over 10 km in 31:25. The previous week she had handed Waitz her first defeat by a Norwegian in twelve years when she won the national cross-country title. Now Kristiansen was ready for a major marathon effort.

She reached halfway in 70:52 and maintained her pace until 35 km (1:58:15), when she started to slow. The wind was also troublesome, but at the finish she still recorded a new national record of 2:24:26, supplanting Waitz. The race had the largest field ever for a marathon: 18 270.

| RESULT: | 1 | Ingrid Kristiansen 2:24:26 |
|---|---|---|
| | 2 | Priscilla Welch 2:30:06 |
| | 3 | Sarah Rowell GBR 2:31:28 |

Three other fast races were held on the same day. In Ottawa Sylvia Ruegger won the Canadian championship in the fastest debut ever (2:30:37), in Baku Ivanova won the Soviet title (2:31:11), and in Frankfurt Teske ran 2:31:16.

The previous day, in the aptly named Olympia, Washington, Benoit won the US trial in 2:31:04 a mere seventeen days after arthroscopic surgery on her right knee. Her knee troubles had started in March and became so severe that she couldn't run. After a variety of measures to try to solve the problem, it was finally decided to operate on 25 April. Five days later Benoit ran 55 minutes without pain. Then she started to do too much, and injured her left hamstring by overcompensating. On 5 May she found it impossible to run. Again everything conceivable was tried

– even sitting in a bathtub with ice cubes! This time electrical stimuli did the trick – up to nine hours a day of it. On 8 May Benoit ran 17 miles – "she needed it for her head," her coach, Bob Sevene, said. Her trials victory – after which the tears of relief flowed – was called one of the greatest examples of courage ever seen in sport.

Six days after the trials, with the hamstring still sore, she said: "I'm still pretty beat from the marathon, but I'm really raring to go. Usually at this time of the year I'm burned out. But, because of the injuries and days off, I'm ready."

The best field ever assembled stood on the start line in the Santa Monica City College stadium at 08:00 for the first Olympic marathon for women. There was Benoit, whose last marathon loss came in November 1981 to Teske. There was Waitz, who had been beaten by Benoit in their only duel over the distance but had set a world record of 47:52 for 15 km in February. There was Kristiansen, but had she not run too hard earlier in the year? And there was Mota, who had improved in each of her four marathons and always ran well in the heat. With them at the start were excellent runners like Audain, Fogli, Gareau, Moller, Ruegger, Teske and Brown. In short: eleven of the fourteen fastest women in history.

The race started slowly – it seemed as if everyone was fearing the effect of the heat and the infamous LA smog which hung over the city. The first mile took all of 6:28.

"I promised myself months ago that I'd run my race and nobody else's," Benoit said in an interview later, "and that's exactly what I did. I did not want to take the lead [but] I didn't have any second thoughts because I was in control. I said, 'You feel too good to blow this, so stay on top of your game.'"

And that's what she did after 14 minutes of running. She led at the 5 km mark in 18:15, with Waitz, Mota, Kristiansen, Moller, Welch, Brown and Audain 6 seconds behind. Then followed Smith, Rowell, Ruegger and Lisa Martin AUS in her third marathon.

At 10 km the time was still exceedingly slow (35:24), but Benoit was stamping her authority on the race. Kristiansen was 4 seconds in arrears, just ahead of Waitz, Moller and Mota in that order.

"I thought, I should go with Benoit," Mota would say later. "But Ingrid and Grete are here. They should know what they are doing. Who am I to take the lead?"

All the top runners seemed to be mesmerised by Waitz, afraid to do anything on their own. Johan Kaggestad, Waitz's coach, put it well, if somewhat indelicately: "Everyone was frightened of Grete. If Grete would have gone to the rest room on the course, Julie Brown would have gone with her."

Then Benoit, who in the last two weeks before the race had stayed in Eugene, picked raspberries and made jam, increased the pace to 5:15 per mile and reached 15 km in 51:46. The last 5 km had taken only 16:22 and she was 51 seconds ahead of Waitz, Moller and Ruegger, who were just ahead of Mota, Kristiansen, Welch and Martin. All the main contenders were apparently waiting for Benoit to succumb to the heat, but the world record holder was running with increasing confidence.

If the others were hesitant, at least she was going for the gold. "This was not going to be another Helsinki," Sevene had said, "It was not gonna be sit around and wait for Grete to win."

"I didn't want to follow because I thought the pace was too fast," Waitz would say later, "and I was worried about the heat over the last 6 or 7 miles." There was also another problem which she admitted to when pressed. The day before the race Waitz had woken up with back spasms. She received treatment and on race day the pain was much better, but not fully gone. "I tried not to think about it, but after 25 km the pain went down to my legs. I just couldn't run faster."

Kristiansen, who like Waitz was trained by Kaggestad, didn't take Benoit's gradual acceleration seriously: "I knew she had been hurt, and I hoped she'd break down and come back to us."

Benoit, running in a white cap, had no intention of coming back. She covered the 5 km sections from 15 km in remarkably even pace considering the conditions, even though she was feeling quite tired towards the end: 16:46 (20 km in 68:32; the second 10 km took only 33:08!), 16:52, 16:59, 17:18 and 17:33. She reached halfway in 71:54. Her lead over Mota at 25 km was 1:50, with Waitz, Ruegger and Fogli a second further back. After another second followed Kristiansen and Toivonen, and then Martin and Moller. Benoit's time at 30 km was 1:42:23, with the gap to Waitz, Kristiansen and Mota still 1:50. Fogli was next and then Ruegger.

It was just after this point that Waitz set out after Benoit. The world champion covered the 5 km between 30 and 40 km in 16:59 – 19 seconds faster than the American. Kristiansen was now 20 seconds behind Waitz. Waitz gained another 4 seconds over the next 5 km, but she was still 1:27 behind. Over the last 2.195 km she could gain only another second.

As a smiling Benoit finished amid the roar of 77 000 spectators, her arms aloft, Waitz was also on the track, a lap behind. The tiny American became the first Olympic champion, capping an amazing recovery over the previous three months. Her time was a world best for a women-only marathon.

Despite the adverse conditions the standard of performances fitted the occasion, with nine runners under 2:30:00. Mota had overtaken Kristiansen at 38 km to take the bronze medal and was rewarded with her fifth consecutive PB. Welch, who had started running only five years before, set a British record.

RESULT:

1. Joan Benoit USA 2:24:52
2. Grete Waitz NOR 2:26:18
3. Rosa Mota POR 2:26:57
4. Ingrid Kristiansen NOR 2:27:34
5. Lorraine Moller NZL 2:28:34
6. Priscilla Welch GBR 2:28:54
7. Lisa Martin AUS 2:29:03
8. Sylvia Ruegger CAN 2:29:09
9. Laura Fogli ITA 2:29:28
10. Tuija Toivonen FIN 2:32:07

Mota's bronze was Portugal's first-ever women's medal. Smith, the oldest athlete at the Games at 46, was eleventh, Teske 16th, O'Connor 27th, May 28th, Brown 36th, while Audain, Gareau and Masuda did not finish.

One place behind Brown came the Swiss Gabriella Andersen-Schiess. In a scene reminiscent of 1908, Andersen-Schiess, suffering from heat exhaustion, staggered around the track of the Coliseum, zigzagging from side to side. Her tortuous effort caused intense debate about whether she should have been stopped, but the officials decided that her health was not in danger and allowed her to continue amid loud encouragement from the crowd. She received emergency treatment and by the next day had recovered.

"Joan took a chance," Waitz said, "and I didn't. I ran a good race but she ran a great one."

And the champion made it sound easy: "I don't know how to say this without sounding cocky, but it was a very easy run for me. Nobody came with me . . . and I can't complain." She had come quite a long way since the days when she was embarrassed that someone would see her run: "I'd walk when cars passed me. I'd pretend I was looking at the flowers."

## A RUNNER AND A PERSON

When Joan Benoit once said that she did not consider herself a marathoner, she was asked what she did consider herself. "Sometimes a runner. But most times, a person." Another time, when she was extending her nineteenth-Century house in Freeport, Maine, just before her marriage, she said: "The building gives me something other than running to concentrate on. I found out long ago that I couldn't be happy thinking about running morning, noon and night."

But despite the fact that her nonrunning activities like knitting, cooking, making jam, collecting stamps and enjoying the outdoors are just as important to her, Benoit – later Samuelson after her marriage to Scott – will always be remembered as the greatest American road runner and the first Olympic marathon champion.

She was born on 16 May 1957 in Cape Elizabeth, Maine, and competed with moderate success on the track until 1978 (16:22.5 for 5000 m). (At school she was, like Ingrid Kristiansen, a skier until she broke a leg and started running.) In October of that year she set her first US road record, 33:15 for 10 km. On 27 January 1979 she won a 10 km race in Bermuda and lined up the next day for the marathon with the idea of running half of it as a training run. On the spur of the moment she completed the race in second place, clocking 2:50:54. The next day she could hardly walk – the start of the Achilles problems that would plague her for the rest of her career.

But those problems were in the future. Less than three months later the Bowdoin College student ran a sensational Boston. She won in a US record 2:35:15 and shot into fourth place on the all-time list behind Grete Waitz, Christa Vahlensieck and Chantal Langlacé.

This amazing run provided the springboard for a career on the road and track and over the country which reached dizzy heights, but she also experienced severe disappointments through countless injuries. Benoit, however, was nothing but tenacious and rebounded every time.

In 1980 she lost her US record to Patti Catalano. In 1981 she improved her best time but was beaten by Allison Roe and Catalano in Boston. She also lost two other marathons, but claimed the US 10000 m track title and set US half-marathon records of 73:26 and 71:16.

In December she underwent surgery on both Achilles tendons, but two days later – with casts on both legs – she started working out on a stationary cycle! By August 1982 she was in fine form again, shattering Waitz's record in the Falmouth race and setting a world record 53:18 for 10 miles. Then she reclaimed the US marathon record with 2:26:11 in Eugene.

In 1983 she was fourth in the World Cross-country Championship and then set a US 10 km record of 31:44. "I feel I'm in my best shape ever right now and I'm looking forward to running a marathon," she said after the record. Less than a month later she improved her marathon time by 3½ minutes to win Boston in a phenomenal world record 2:22:43. It was her tenth marathon.

She wanted to run the 3000 m at the first World Championships, but could not make the US team. Instead, she was selected for the Pan American Games, where she won the event. She ended the year with US records of 31:37 for 10 km and 69:10 for the half marathon.

For the US Olympic trial she was doing some of the hardest training of her career. Called by her coach, Bob Sevene, "the toughest atlete I have ever seen", Benoit was running more than 100 miles a week (including one track session). Then she was struck by a severe knee injury. But her indomitable will carried her through the trial race. Less than three months later she faced Waitz and Kristiansen in Los Angeles – and beat them soundly.

"I think the injury was a blessing in disguise," she said after her victory. "I believe I was in the best shape of my life right before the knee injury, I think I would have had the race of my life at the Olympic Trials and I think I would have had nothing left for this race. So I feel the injury and the timing were perfect."

About six weeks later, on 16 September, she broke the world half-marathon record with 68:34 in Philadelphia. She lost only two races in 1984, indoors over 1 mile and 3000 m.

In 1985 she won five major races on the US circuit, including Falmouth again in a course record. In Chicago she convincingly beat Kristiansen, who earlier in the year had broken her world record with 2:21:06 in London, but fell 15 seconds short of the world mark.

Her next marathon was New York in 1988, where she finished third. Earlier in the year she had to withdraw from the Olympic trial, and injury problems continued to hamper her running. In 1989 she was ninth in Boston, but she was still not healthy. She only returned two years later – and clocked a remarkable 2:26:54, the fastest fourth-place time ever. Later in the year she was sixth in New York.

Her second child, son Anders, was born in 1990.

Benoit is renowned for her sense of humour and occasional outrageousness (she used to sneak up on people and bite them on the rear). She once belonged to the Maine Rowdies, a running club renowned as "one of the hardest-partying organizations in existence". Joan was the only female member – admitted because none of the other members could beat her.

But Benoit is also a very private person whose sense of self goes far beyond her exploits in the world spotlight; one who is proud that her Olympic victory showed people that it is always possible to triumph over adversity.

Fifteen days before the Olympic marathon Dörre, whose chances for Olympic success were killed by her country's boycott, had run what proved to be the fifth fastest time of the year in Grünau – 2:26:52. The first quick time after the Games came from another athlete who was boycotted out of the Olympics when Smekhnova clocked 2:29:10 in Vilnius on 7 October.

On 23 September Moller won the Avon marathon for the third time. The seventh edition of the event was held in Paris, the Kiwi claiming first in 2:32:44. Beurskens was second 9 seconds behind, with Teske third and Vahlensieck fourth.

Mota went to Chicago for the America's marathon on 21 October and produced one of the best races ever. It was cold when the runners got under way at 08:45, and the wind and rain made fast times seem very unlikely. But after 3 miles the wind was at the runners' backs, and both Steve Jones and Mota started chasing the clock. Jones's efforts would net him the world record, while Mota broke Benoit's world best for a loop course. The previous year Mota had won despite suffering cramps; this time she struggled in the unpleasant conditions as Kristiansen set the early pace (15 km in 51:14). But Mota took the lead before 10 miles and achieved a comfortable win over Martin; both clocking national records.

RESULT:
1 Rosa Mota 2:26:01
2 Lisa Martin 2:27:40
3 Ingrid Kristiansen 2:30:21
4 Dorthe Rasmussen 2:30:42

On 28 October, a steaming day in New York with humidity in the 90s, Waitz scored her sixth (and second slowest) win, running 2:29:30. Veronique Marot GBR was second in 2:33:58 (she had also been fourth in London in an almost identical time) and Fogli third.

The year's performance list showed a record 55 runners under 2:35:00 and eleven under 2:30:00. Eight of these had dipped below 2½ hours for the first time – among them Kristiansen, who equalled Waitz's feat of 1983 with three sub-2:30s. The first five in the Olympic marathon were ranked in that order, with the absent Dörre placed sixth. Benoit was also placed fifth on the overall ranking list of the world's top female athletes.

The first major race of 1985 was the inaugural World Cup marathon, held in Hiroshima on 13 April. Dörre scored her sixth win in seven marathons in 2:33:30 from Ivanova and Szabó, with Italy taking the team competition. But much earlier than that, on the sixth day of the year, Ruegger had recorded the first sub-2:30 of 1985 when she finished first in Houston in a national record of 2:28:36. She beat compatriot Gareau, who ran 2:29:32. Three weeks later May ran even faster: 2:28:07 in Osaka.

Two days after the Hiroshima event Lisa Weidenbach USA won Boston in 2:34:06. Three weeks earlier she had set a new US record over 30 km; here she won by more than 8 minutes over a weak field.

All these races, important as they were, were just preliminaries for the big one: London.

One day after Carlos Lopes had sped to a world record of 2:07:12 in Rotterdam, it was Kristiansen's turn. The Norwegian not only wanted to break Benoit's record; she also wanted to break the 2:20:00 barrier. The previous summer she had become the first woman to run under 15 minutes for 5000 m when she clocked 14:58.89 in Oslo. She had trained through the Nordic winter by running on a treadmill in the kitchen of her home in the same city.

In the British capital she set a quick pace from the start (she was allowed to start with the elite men), and was on her own after 5 miles (26:22). Her 10 km splits to 30 km were 32:52, 33:38 and 32:48 (99:18), projecting to a finishing time of 2:19:40. Then the inevitable happened: she slowed and needed 34:00 for the last full 10 km. She covered the 2 195 m to the finish in 7:48. "Over the last 7 km I slowed down and lost more than a minute," she said afterwards. But she still smashed the American's record by 1:37. Rowell finished exactly 7 minutes behind her in a British record, also winning the national championship.

RESULT:
1 Ingrid Kristiansen 2:21:06
2 Sarah Rowell 2:28:06
3 Sally Hales GBR 2:28:38

Kristiansen was only 12:50 behind Steve Jones – the closest a woman has ever finished to the top man in a major marathon. The 15 841 finishers were a world record for a marathon, but this would be broken by 40 in the Big Apple later in the year.

The Frankfurt race on 19 May was again fast. Beurskens, who had been second to May in Osaka in 2:31:11, won in 2:28:37. On 15 September the 23-year-old Dörre scored her second major victory of the year when she won the European Cup race in Rome in 2:30:11.

On 20 October both Steve Jones and Joan Samuelson – as Benoit had become after her marriage – tried to reclaim their world records in Chicago. Earlier in the year Samuelson had won the Falmouth race for the sixth time, setting a course record, and she had been running well. Kristiansen, who during the track season had set a world record of 30:59.42 for 10000 m in Oslo and thus became the first athlete, man or woman, to hold the world records for the 5000 m, 10000 m and marathon simultaneously, was there to challenge her. So were Mota, Beurskens and Dörre. As usual, Samuelson was not intimidated. She set off like lightning, running the first mile in 5:09 and the second in 5:07! Kristiansen went with her, but Mota (who had beaten the Norwegian in all three of their previous encounters) prudently stayed behind.

# IN THE ZÁTOPEK MOULD

When Ingrid Kristiansen set her world record of 2:21:06 in the 1985 London marathon she had already been the world's top long-distance track runner since 1981. Her talents were spotted early, and in 1971, when only fifteen, Ingrid Christensen represented Norway in the 1500 m at the European Championships. "I was a little girl, the other runners were big, and after two and a half laps I fell over," she recalled. She then concentrated on skiing, because "in Norway, skiing is the big sport. Skiers are much better known than runners." In the 1978 World Championships cross-country skiing event she finished 21st. But by 1981 she had turned her attention to running, and the next year came third in the first European Championships marathon. This started her on the trail blazed by compatriot Grete Waitz – a journey that would bring her Zátopek-like success as the most versatile female distance runner the world has ever seen.

In 1981 she set her first world best, 15:28.43 for 5000 m (then not yet an official event). Three years later she was the first woman under 15 minutes when she clocked 14:58.89 and in 1986 she ran a superb 14:37.33. Exactly a month before this performance she had also run a world record for 10000 m: 30:13.74. The previous year she had become the first woman under 31 minutes with 30:59.42.

In 1987 she won the first World Championships 10000 m – just as she had done in the previous year's European Championships. A bone fracture in her right foot caused her to drop out of the 1988 Olympic 10000 m.

Kristiansen, who was born in Trondheim on 21 March 1956, ran her first marathon in her birthplace in 1977, clocking 2:45:15. By 1983 she had improved to 2:33:27 and the next year she finished one place short of a medal in the first Olympic marathon for women.

She was disappointed with the 1984 Olympic marathon, "because in that race I didn't use my head. I do another person's race and I lose the whole thing . . ."

Her magnificent marathon time in 1985 made her the first athlete, man or woman, to hold the world records for the 50000 m, 10000 m and marathon simultaneously. By winning the world cross-country title in 1988 (she was third in 1985 and 1987) she also became the first (and so far only) world champion in track, cross-country and road (she had won the 15 km world

title in 1987 and would retain it in 1988).

In 1983 she won the Houston marathon in a personal best just five weeks after giving birth to her and husband Arve's first child, son Gaute. Three months later she set a European record 2:24:26 in winning the 1984 London marathon. Her daughter Marte was born in 1990.

She set a variety of world records over shorter distances on the road: 30:59 for 10 km in 1989, 47:17 and 50:37 for 15 km and 10 miles in 1987, and 68:32 for the half marathon in 1989. (Her 67:59 in 1986 was on a course 220 m short.)

At the height of her career Kristiansen was going all out to become the first woman under 2:20:00. "Every year I go for 2:20:00," she said in an interview in *Track & Field News*. "You have to train and train some more. You have to keep on going if you want to be on top."

Kristiansen, who has a degree in medical engineering, said that she trained 225 km per week – "for weeks". Most of it was done at a fairly slow pace, between 4:15-4:20 per kilometre. "If I want to run a marathon under 2:20:00, I must run 5:15-5:18 miles. So three or four times a week I do 10-30 km on a treadmill at that pace. I never go on the track to train for the marathon."

Running on the treadmill was not as boring as people might think; actually it was much more pleasant than going outside into the harsh northern winter, with temperatures below freezing. "Outside it may be cold and dark, dangerous with snow and cars. But I run here, with no wind, and my husband sitting nearby reading the paper and my little boy playing alongside."

Her last major marathon win was New York in 1989 – the year she also won Boston and ran the two fastest times in the world. Her five fastest marathons average an almost incredible 2:23:11.6 – a time beaten by only two other women in a single race! These five races were all in the top twenty on the all-time list at the end of 1995:

| | | |
|---|---|---|
| 2:21:06 | London | 1985 |
| 2:22:48 | London | 1987 |
| 2:23:05 | Chicago | 1985 |
| 2:24:26 | London | 1984 |
| 2:24:33 | Boston | 1989 |

The leading duo went through 10 km in 32:51, trading water bottles despite the tremendous battle they were fighting. They reached 15 km in 49:00 – 50 seconds faster than Kristiansen in London and sub-2:18 pace. They slowed somewhat, but still timed 69:33 at halfway (Kristiansen's London split was 70:10). At about 18 miles Samuelson saw signs along the road reading "Go Maine" (her home state) and "Bowdoin College"; shortly thereafter she surged ahead. Kristiansen caught up by 19 miles, but at 20 miles and again at 21 the American accelerated. The last surge (put in despite stomach problems) was too much for the gallant Kristiansen. She let go ("My legs felt heavy, not like in London," she would say later), and Samuelson went after the world record.

After the race she would say: "We are all eyeing 2:20; me and Ingrid and Rosa Mota. When you talk about 2:20, you really are talking about 2:18-2:19. And that's a darn fast time for anybody."

Samuelson averaged 5:24 for the last two full miles in a desperate attempt to get the record, but missed by 15 seconds. It

was a world best for a loop course, though, shattering the previous best (2:26:01) of the woman who came third here. Mota chased the faltering Kristiansen hard towards the end, but failed to catch her by 24 seconds. They were part of the greatest mass finish ever in a race other than the Olympics: the first five ran under 2:29:00, and only Kristiansen's world record would top these five times on the world list.

Samuelson's 5 km splits were 16:05, 16:46, 16:09, 16:44, 17:15, 17:01, 16:48 and 17:01. Her fastest mile was the sixth, which she sped in 5:04, and the slowest the 23rd (5:35).

RESULT:
1 Joan Samuelson 2:21:21
2 Ingrid Kristiansen 2:23:05
3 Rosa Mota 2:23:29
4 Carla Beurskens 2:27:50
5 Veronique Marot 2:28:04

Mota, Beurskens and Marot all set national records, Mota for the seventh time in seven races! Dörre did not finish.

"It's a completely different ballgame, running with someone right on your tail," Samuelson commented later. "I didn't feel as in control in this race as in some others. Around 15 km, I was concerned that maybe I had gone out too fast, even though I felt smooth and fluid up to that point . . . this was a very tough race mentally because Ingrid always was right there. [At 20 miles] I was wondering whether I should make a pitstop, but I was pulling away then and the problem passed. I felt very good the last five miles."

Samuelson and Jones both missed the $50 000 bonus for a world record, but both still earned that amount for their wins.

Seven days later Waitz, who had performed well on the US road circuit during the year, won New York for the seventh time. She had hoped for cool weather, but it was warm and she also had to cope with diarrhoea. She and Martin ran the final two sub-2:30s of the year.

The battle between New York and Chicago for the top stars was evident in Waitz's words: "I would not trade my New York victories for fast times in Chicago. The victory is mine forever; a record is meant to be broken."

RESULT:
1 Grete Waitz 2:28:34
2 Lisa Martin 2:29:48
3 Laura Fogli 2:31:36

In the last two months of the year Dörre and Beurskens each scored one more victory, in Tokyo and Honolulu respectively.

Samuelson's decisive victory over Kristiansen gave her first spot on the ranking list, with Mota third, Dörre fourth and Waitz fifth. For the first time since 1980 the number of sub-2:35 times declined (there were 45), but the twelve under 2:30:00 were a record.

Kristiansen was to have a brilliant 1986, with world records for both 5000 and 10000 m and a win in Boston, as well as the honour of being named Road Runner of the Year, but the fastest time of 1986 would belong to another Norwegian, if barely.

This time Dörre sped the first sub-2:30 of the year when she ran 2:29:33 in Nagoya and then repeated the victory in Karl Marx Stadt in April, albeit in a much slower time.

Marathon Weekend in April set the tone for the major competitions of the year – the top stars were avoiding one another. The London marathon was on 20 April, and Waitz ran what was to prove the world's fastest time in 1986, a PB 2:24:54. O'Connor was second in 2:30:52, while Marot did not finish.

The next day Boston offered $30 000 for a win, plus bonuses for world and course records, as well as time-related incentives. Kristiansen again had sub-2:20 as her goal and although she covered the first 5 miles in a magnificent 26:00, it did not last. At the half marathon she was still on course with 69:44, but then started to look uncomfortable and slowed drastically to 1:48:51 at 20 miles. She finished in 2:24:55, one second behind Waitz's London time. Beurskens was second in a national record 2:27:35; no one else could

break 2:32:00. Vahlensieck was seventh in 2:33:40, beating Moller by one place. Martin failed to finish.

Samuelson was skipping the marathon for the year after heel surgery in November, but was doing well over shorter distances – often in second place. Early in April Mota had broken her world record for 10 miles by running 53:09; Samuelson replied in the same month with a US record of 53:18. In May she set a US record of 84:43 for 25 km. Eight days later Waitz beat her over 12 km (breaking the American's course record by 70 seconds), 38:45 against 39:10, and thirteen days after that she was defeated by Kristiansen over 10 km, 31:45 against 33:03. A comebacking Roe, who had had hamstring surgery in September 1984, ran 35:30.

After this race Kristiansen said in an interview: "I think Grete is afraid to run as fast as she must to break 2:20. She is afraid to try, but if she tried I think she could do it. She wants to *win* races."

In the first Commonwealth Games marathon, held in Edinburgh on 1 August, Martin redeemed herself by winning in a national record of 2:26:07.

RESULT:
1 Lisa Martin AUS 2:26:07
2 Lorraine Moller NZL 2:28:17
3 Odette Lapierre CAN 2:31:48
4 Lizanne Bussières CAN 2:35:18
5 Lorna Irving Sco 2:36:34
6 Angela Pain Eng 2:37:57

Later the same month, on 26 August, Europe's best met in Stuttgart for the continent's championship race. Four years before Mota had stunned the world with her debut victory in the championship; this time she was a known factor as one of the world's top marathoners. Kristiansen was not running; four days later she would win the first major 10000 m championship ever contested. Dörre went into the race with an unprecedented ten successive wins since 1982.

Beurskens stayed with Mota until 20 km (68:19) on the tough course with "surroundings not particularly inspiring", as one reporter put it, and then the defending champion drew away. By 25 km she was 1:48 ahead of the Dutchwoman, and by 30 km (1:43:43) she was exactly 3 minutes ahead of Fogli, who had passed Beurskens. Over the next 5 km Mota stretched her lead to 4:35, reaching 35 km in 2:01:56. The Italian cut the gap to 3:57 at 40 km, which Mota passed in 2:20:44, and again finished second, as she had done in Athens – but this time more than 4 minutes behind.

RESULT:
1 Rosa Mota POR 2:28:38
2 Laura Fogli ITA 2:32:52
3 Yekaterina Khramenkova URS 2:34:18
4 Sinikka Keskitalo FIN 2:34:41
5 Jocelyne Villeton FRA 2:35:17
6 Bente Moe NOR 2:35:34

Beurskens was seventh, while Dörre and Marot once again did not finish.

On 26 October Kristiansen won the $40 000 first prize in the America's marathon in Chicago with 2:27:08 (plus a reputed $40 000 appearance money), with Maria Lelut FRA, winner of the Paris marathon in May, second in a national record of 2:29:51. On the same day Agnes Sipka HUN clocked 2:28:51 in Budapest.

A week later Waitz took New York for the eighth time – fifth in a row – as one of a field of 20 502 (for the first time more than 3 000 women took part). Never before had any woman stuck with her in New York as far as Fogli's 15 miles, but thereafter the 33-year-old Norwegian simply ran away from her to another comfortable victory. Fogli was passed by Martin to finish third for the third consecutive year (after two fourths and a second). In fact, the first three finished in the same order as in 1985.

| RESULT: | 1 | Grete Waitz 2:28:06 |
|---------|---|---------------------|
|         | 2 | Lisa Martin 2:29:12 |
|         | 3 | Laura Fogli 2:29:44 |

Villeton again performed well, finishing fourth in 2:32:51. Vahlensieck excelled with a ninth place.

In an interview in *The Runner* Martin discussed her feelings about the 1985 race: "Last year I ran with her for 11 miles, and I looked across at this woman they made a statue of in Oslo, and I was thinking, 'Wow!' And she took off and I was thinking, 'Wow!' I thought about it afterwards, and you have to knock people off pedestals before you can beat them."

Mota won the Tokyo marathon on 16 November in 2:27:15, her fastest of the year (Dörre was second in 2:31:54), and Beurskens the Honolulu race in 2:31:02.

At the end of the year, which could be called the Year of Money (see p. 100) and which saw 53 runners under 2:35:00 and ten under 2½ hours, the sub-2:25 club had four members: Samuelson, Kristiansen, Mota and Waitz. In the course of the year the latter three had each won two major races, but never met. In the introduction to its rankings, *Track & Field News* wrote that this was because of what fans would call "ducking" and accountants and agents "maximizing earnings". The magazine ranked Waitz first for the sixth time, followed by Kristiansen (who was ranked fourth overall) and Mota. Martin was fourth and Fogli fifth.

The next global championship, for the world title, was held in 1987. The year would see no dramatic improvement in standard, and started relatively slowly with Nagoya on 1 March again the first to produce a sub-2½ hour time – not by Dörre, though. It came from Beurskens, who won in 2:28:27.

In January, in two battles of the "M's", Moe had beaten Marot in Houston by exactly 3 minutes in 2:32:36 and Moller defeated Martin in Osaka by 19 seconds in 2:30:40.

On 5 April Martin broke Mota's world (and course) record in the Cherry Blossom 10 miles in Washington by running 52:23. On the same day Kristiansen showed that she was seriously taking aim at the 2:20:00 barrier when she won the Norwegian half-marathon title in Sandnes in an almost unbelievable 66:40. (It was run on an aided course which has never been certified; the time – which no woman has yet broken – has thus not been ratified as a world record.)

A week later a Soviet newcomer, Yelena Tsukhlo, ran 2:29:50 in Uzhgorod the day after the Soviet record holder, Ivanova, had clocked 2:30:39 in Seoul to win the World Cup race. The race was run on the 1988 Olympic course and Ivanova, who had been second behind Dörre in the first edition of the race, beat Lelut by almost a minute. Dörre ran faster than in 1985, yet finished third. In eighth was an East German who would make her mark in the next decade: Uta Pippig (2:34:48). She had run her first marathon (2:47:42) in 1984; this was her fourth.

In Boston on 20 April, a cool day with drizzle, Mota showed her class once more by scoring a very decisive win in a fast race. She blitzed the first mile in 5:03 and went through 10 km in under 33 minutes. She was followed home by two Belgians, Agnes Pardaens clocking a national record.

| RESULT: | 1 | Rosa Mota 2:25:21 |
|---------|---|-------------------|
|         | 2 | Agnes Pardaens 2:29:50 |
|         | 3 | Ria van Landeghem 2:29:56 |

Samuelson, who was pregnant, had planned to run, but picked up a serious thigh injury. She had her sights on the 1988 Olympic marathon.

On 10 May Kristiansen, who had been third in the World Cross-country Championships, took another shot at the elusive 2:20:00 in the London marathon. She had torn a calf muscle two days before the race but, never one for half measures, blazed through 15 km in 47:32 (faster than the world record for the distance). Near the 18-mile mark her leg started to cramp and her pace fell off. She still won by more than 4 minutes from Welch, who at 42 set an amazing British record of 2:26:51. Kristiansen's 2:22:48 was the fourth fastest ever run. Marot was third in 2:30:15.

On 7 June the Soviets staged a remarkable national championship race in Mogilyov. Khramenkova won in 2:28:20 and a plethora of fast times followed: Tsukhlo 2:28:53, Lyutsia Belyaeva 2:30:25, Irina Bogacheva 2:30:33, Lyubov Svirskaya 2:30:43. The ten runners under 2:35:00 equalled the record set in the 1984 US Olympic trial (and the World Championships the previous year!). Thirteen days later Pippig, who was born on 7 September 1965 in Leipzig, won her country's title in Leipzig in 2:30:50.

The World Championships marathon was held in Rome on 29 August. With Waitz out because of injury and Kristiansen concentrating on the 10000 m (which she won), Mota was the overwhelming favourite. She asserted herself over the 41 other competitors immediately and was already well in the lead by the time they exited the stadium. In 1983 she had finished fourth, but this time there was no stopping her and she won the gold medal by more than 7 minutes, running the second fastest time ever in a women-only race.

While experienced runners such as Martin, Lelut and Marchisio fell by the wayside behind her in the heat and others like Khramenkova (in her third marathon in five months), Ivanova, Tsukhlo, Norway's hope Moe and Villeton chased her in vain, Mota ran on serenely. Her splits for the 5 km sections were superbly even: 17:15, 16:48, 17:02, 17:07, 17:03, 17:28, 17:20 and 17:29.

Villeton, in fourth, accelerated from 25 km and although she gained 2:15 on Ivanova over the next 10 km, she was too far behind and had to be satisfied with the bronze medal.

RESULT:

| | | | |
|---|---|---|---|
| 1 | Rosa Mota | POR | 2:25:17 |
| 2 | Zoya Ivanova | URS | 2:32:38 |
| 3 | Jocelyne Villeton | FRA | 2:32:53 |
| 4 | Bente Moe | NOR | 2:33:21 |
| 5 | Yelena Tsukhlo | URS | 2:33:55 |
| 6 | Yekaterina Khramenkova | URS | 2:34:23 |
| 7 | Nancy Ditz | USA | 2:34:54 |
| 8 | Sinikka Keskitalo | FIN | 2:35:16 |
| 9 | Karolina Szabó | HUN | 2:36:18 |
| 10 | Miyuki Yamashita | JPN | 2:36:55 |

"I want to dedicate this race to Grete," Mota said. "Even though I don't know her too well, the comradeship that exists among marathoners has brought us close together." Waitz had wished Mota well on the morning of the race. "She said she hoped I would win the race."

Pippig was 14th, Pardaens 15th and Marot 22nd.

Between Rome and New York Langlacé, Gareau and Vahlensieck all won races, the Canadian being the fastest with 2:32:52. On 11 October Sylvie Bornet FRA ran away from the field in the Twin Cities marathon in Minneapolis to win in 2:30:11.

Three weeks later, on 1 November, Waitz's absence in New York was conspicuous. Welch was in great form and passed halfway on course record pace – 72:17 – but then slowed to a 2:30:17 victory over the French runners Françoise Bonnet (2:31:22) and Villeton (2:32:03). Roe failed to finish.

"I think old age is a social disease that people think they cannot overcome," said Welch, who started running when she was 34 and smoking a pack of cigarettes a day. "For those who really want to go for it, I hope this will be an inspiration."

Two weeks later in Tokyo Dörre won the sixth of her seven marathons in Japan (her only loss came in the 1986 Tokyo affair), setting a national record of 2:25:24 in the ideal conditions. Beurskens set the pace until halfway (72:32), but then Dörre caught her and the two ran together until 34 km,

when the East German sped ahead. Beurskens also set a national record, 2:26:34; Ivanova was third in 2:27:57.

A month later Beurskens took the Honolulu marathon in 2:35:11.

The year's performance list showed relative stagnation at the top – there were again ten women under 2:30:00 and only Kristiansen could dip below 2:25:00. Mota was ranked ahead of the Norwegian after her two excellent victories, and they were followed by Ivanova, Dörre and Beurskens.

In *Athletics: The International Track and Field Annual 1988/9* David Martin wrote that performance standards of 2:20:00 for men and 2:55:00 for women were comparable. There were then 1 061 sub-2:55 performances by 713 different runners representing 44 nations. The USA was clearly the world's foremost marathon nation, with 303 sub-2:55s – the Soviet Union had 85 and Great Britain 69.

The Olympic year 1988 began in earnest on 31 January with Martin's wonderful 2:23:51 in Osaka, a world best for a loop course and the seventh fastest time ever. It was a tremendous performance in ideal weather and Martin easily beat Misako Miyahara, who set a Japanese record of 2:29:37.

The second major Japanese race of the year, in Nagoya on 6 March, resulted in the first world-class time by a Chinese woman when 22-year-old Zhao Youfeng ran 2:27:56 for an Asian record. Behind her Beurskens (2:28:58) again broke through 2½ hours, with Birgit Stephan GDR (2:29:19) doing it for the first time.

On 17 April Kristiansen won her fourth London title in 2:25:41, her slowest time yet in the British capital – but she had just finished a marvellous month of racing. On 20 March she had retained her world 15 km crown and six days later she had also successfully defended her world cross-country championship. She was alone under 2:30:00 – Ann Ford GBR was second in 2:30:38.

The next day, in Boston, Mota also made a perfect defence of her title, winning easily in 2:24:30, her second-best time. It was clearly meant as a warning to anyone who had designs on the gold medal in Seoul. Four other runners were under 2:31:00, headed by the national record 2:29:26 of Finland's Tuija Jousimaa, whose previous best was 2:32:07. Lapierre was third (2:30:35), Welch fourth (2:30:53) and Bussières fifth (2:30:57).

On the last day of April Dörre gave notice of her intentions for the Olympic marathon with a 2:28:28 win in the European Cup race in Huy, Belgium. But she could not have been too complacent, because Smekhnova finished only 12 seconds behind, with Ivanova third in 2:29:37. And on 26 June another Soviet, Tatyana Polovinskaya, won the national title in 2:28:02. Earlier in the month Waitz had claimed her national title, contested in Stockholm, in 2:28:24.

On 1 May Margaret Groos became the fourth American to run under 2:30:00 when she won the US Olympic trial in Pittsburgh in 2:29:50. Samuelson, who had been injured earlier in the year, did not run.

The world's women were ready for the Olympic marathon on 23 September. Already there were sixteen under 2:30:00 – four more than in any previous year.

Waitz had won the Great North Run in July, clocking 68:49, but then had to have arthroscopic surgery to her knee – like Benoit in 1984. She, too, recovered, but the Olympic marathon proved a disaster for the Norwegian ace. Kristiansen limited herself to the 10000 m (the first time this event was contested at the Olympics), where she dropped out after having been plagued by various problems all year.

Mota was running in her 13th marathon, but if the unlucky number worried her, she did not show it. And with nine victories under her belt, there was no need to worry. The small Portuguese runner stayed in the lead group from the beginning, but never took the initiative before 30 km.

## A UNIQUE TRIPLE

Rosa Mota was born on 29 June 1958 in Foz do Douro. The tiny runner (she weighed 45 kg at her peak) represented Portugal on the track, including nine European Cup matches, and won fourteen national titles: seven in cross-country, three in the 1500 m, two in the 3000 m, and one each in 800 m and 5000 m. Between 1974 and 1987 she set 24 national records at distances from 1500 m to the marathon. Seven of these were in the marathon, and they came in her first seven marathons!

Mota's first marathon was at the 1982 European Championships after she had finished 12th in the 3000 m. She then ran twelve successful marathons (winning nine) before failing to finish at Osaka in 1989. In 1983 she clocked a world record 66:56 for 20 km. Her best half-marathon time is 69:23, run in 1990.

Her last marathon win (the 14th in 21 races over the distance) came in the 1991 World Cup, where she ran 2:26:14. Her record in major competitions is unsurpassed in the history of the event: three European titles, one world title (plus a fourth place), one Olympic title (plus a bronze medal), one World Cup win. Other important victories were: Rotterdam 1983, Chicago 1983 and '84, Tokyo 1986, Boston 1987, '88, and '90, Osaka 1990. Mota's feat of three European marathon titles (1982, 1986 and 1990) has not been equalled by anyone, man or woman.

Of the marathon she said: "For me the marathon always is a fight against my opponents, not the clock. The courses and weather are so different that nothing really is comparable. It's impossible to judge the value of a performance so for me all that matters is winning."

In 1984 she was second to compatriot Aurora Cunha in the World 10 km Championship, while in 1986 they finished in the same positions in the 15 km title race.

In 1995 Mota was elected to Portugal's parliament.

Mota's first seven marathons were:

| 2:36:04 | 1 | European Championships | 120982 |
|---|---|---|---|
| 2:32:27 | 1 | Rotterdam | 090483 |
| 2:31:50 | 4 | World Championships | 070883 |
| 2:31:12 | 1 | Chicago | 161083 |
| 2:26:57 | 3 | Olympic Games | 050884 |
| 2:26:01 | 1 | Chicago | 211084 |
| 2:23:29 | 3 | Chicago | 201085 |

The average of her five fastest marathons is 2:24:48.2 – second only to that of Ingrid Kristiansen (see p. 158).

The pack clicked off the kilometres with monotonous regularity: 17:10, 17:03 and 17:17 for 51:30 at 15 km. Among the thirteen were Mota, Waitz, Martin and Dörre, the big favourites.

They continued at the same tempo, running the next two 5 km sections in 17:16 and 17:09 (85:55 at 25 km). The group was still intact, but over the next 5 km (17:18) five runners separated themselves. Four went ahead and one dropped out. It was Waitz, her race run and with that her last chance for an Olympic gold.

The four who now focused on the task of getting the three medals were Mota, Martin, Dörre and Polovinskaya. The next 5 km was the slowest of the entire race at 17:56, with Dörre and Mota slightly in the lead. Then the Soviet let go, and with 4 km remaining, Mota surged. The gold medal – the first of the Games – had an owner.

She covered the last full 5 km in 17:01 and reached 40 km in 2:18:10. At the finish she was 13 seconds ahead of Martin, who had shaken off the East German. Although Mota's time was slower than Samuelson's in 1984, it was a much closer race than in Los Angeles, with only 2:04 separating the first six. But only six were under 2:30:00 compared to nine in 1984.

"I'm so happy I don't want to think about the bad times," Mota said, referring to the strained relations between her and her fiancé/coach Jose Pedrosa and the Portuguese federation.

RESULT:
1 Rosa Mota POR 2:25:40
2 Lisa Martin AUS 2:25:53
3 Katrin Dörre GDR 2:26:21
4 Tatyana Polovinskaya URS 2:27:05
5 Zhao Youfeng CHN 2:27:06
6 Laura Fogli ITA 2:27:49
7 Danièle Kaber LUX 2:29:23
8 Maria Curatolo ITA 2:30:14
9 Zoya Ivanova URS 2:30:25
10 Angela Pain GBR 2:30:51

Polovinskaya, Zhao, Fogli and Kaber set national records. Villeton finished 19th, Beurskens 33rd, Moller 34th and Jousimaa 41st. Moe dropped out. The last finisher was timed in 3:42:23.

On the day the male marathoners were fighting it out for Olympic gold, Van Landeghem won the Twin Cities marathon in a national record 2:28:11 (10 minutes faster than the top Belgian ran in Seoul), while a week later Renata Kokowska POL clocked 2:29:16 in West Berlin. On 30 October Weidenbach ran one second slower in Chicago.

When it was time for New York on 6 November Waitz was ready once more. She faced a number of Olympians, among them Fogli, Szabó, Moe and Polovinskaya. And Samuelson. The American record holder was meeting Waitz for the first time since Los Angeles and running her first marathon in three years. At 14 miles stomach cramps forced Samuelson to pull over to the side of the road and she was passed by Fogli. Samuelson came back with a vengeance, but at 21 miles, in a dramatic turn of events, a volunteer at a water station accidentally knocked her down. That was that. Although the tough American tried her utmost after the incident, she was still 74 seconds in arrears at the finish. But everything considered, it must rank as one of her best races.

RESULT: 
1 Grete Waitz 2:28:07
2 Laura Fogli 2:31:26
3 Joan Samuelson 2:32:40

It was the 35-year-old Waitz's ninth victory and Fogli's fifth placing in the top three. Her runs in New York, two silver medals in the European Championships and high placings both in Los Angeles and Seoul made the Italian one of the most consistently stellar performers of the eighties. Polovinskaya and Welch dropped out. The race had 22 405 finishers – 484 less than in London.

The increase in standard in the Olympic year could be seen in the 1 150 performances under 2:55:00. The women running these times came from 61 nations, showing the wide spread of top talent. The general growth in popularity of the marathon was pointed out by Martin in *Athletics '89/90*: "The combination of [a] large population center, flat course, cool weather, good organization, and aggressive sponsorship marketing are essential for the long-term success of [big-city] races. The successful co-existence of both aspects of the sport – élite-level and participant-oriented – if carefully nurtured by race directors worldwide, will ensure the popularity of [the marathon] in years to come."

The number of runners under 2:35:00 were the highest ever at 91; so were those under 2:30:00 at 22. The number under 2:25:00 (two) did not show any progress, however. This would not change before the advent – under somewhat suspicious circumstances – of the Chinese in 1993.

Mota was ranked first for the second year in a row, followed by Martin, Dörre, Kristiansen and Polovinskaya.

The post-Olympic year was a quiet one, the major championship race being the World Cup. January and February were marked by a couple of near misses of the 2:30:00 barrier – by Marot (2:30:16 in Houston), Moller (2:30:21 in Osaka) and Frith van der Merwe RSA (2:30:35 in Port Elizabeth). Then, on 5 March, Zhao won Nagoya in 2:28:20, with New Zealand newcomer Marguerite Buist second in 2:29:09, a PB by more than 5½ minutes. On the same day, in Los Angeles, Ivanova beat Mota (suffering from sciatic nerve problems) in 2:34:42. The Olympic champion, who had to retire from the Osaka race, ran 2:35:27 – the slowest since her debut.

Later in March Kristiansen set a world record of 68:31 for the half marathon (covering the first 10 km in 31:36) and she went to Boston as the favourite. She had no trouble winning – only 25 men finished in front of her! The Norwegian's time was 2:24:35, more than a minute faster than anyone else would run all year. Buist improved marginally to 2:29:04 in second. Kim Jones USA was third in 2:29:34 to become the fifth fastest American ever.

The fastest American was ninth in 2:37:52 – Samuelson was still troubled by persistent hip, knee and hamstring injuries which she felt had been brought on by her returning to running too soon after giving birth to daughter Abigail in 1987. "I've been spending as much time in physical therapy as in running," she said. She declared that she would "let Mother Nature do the healing", cut her training and see if the problem cleared up on its own.

Two days earlier the World Cup race in Milan had delivered a surprising result. The virtually unknown American Sue Marchiano improved on her PB by nearly 4 minutes and won in 2:30:48. Behind her came such luminaries as Miyahara (second in 2:35:16), Pippig and Khramenkova. "I went out to run 2:30:00 at my own pace," said the 34-year-old former school teacher. "When I saw the others weren't bothering, I forgot all about them."

That same day Elena Murgoci ROM set a course record of 2:32:03 in Rotterdam.

A week later, on 23 April, Marot beat a strong field in London with a national record of 2:25:56. Mota's countrywoman Aurora Cunha blazed through the first half in 70:52, but then faded badly to allow Marot to take the lead at 21 miles. In second Wanda Panfil set a Polish record, with Rasmussen clocking a Danish record in fourth.

RESULT: 
1 Véronique Marot 2:25:56
2 Wanda Panfil 2:27:05
3 Aurora Cunha 2:28:11
4 Dorthe Rasmussen 2:29:34

Other sub-2:30s before the two major US races were recorded by Kazue Kojima JPN (2:29:23 in Paris), Lyubov Klochko URS (2:28:47 in Belaya Cerkov), Päivi Tikkanen FIN (2:28:45 in West Berlin) and Mun Gyung-ae PRK (2:27:16 in Beijing).

In Chicago on 29 October Weidenbach, who in June had set a US record of 48:28 for 15 km, became the fourth fastest American and won $55 000 with her 2:28:15. The defending champion beat Beurskens (who in December would win in Honolulu) by more than 2 minutes; Panfil was sixth, Villeton eighth, Buist ninth and Khramenkova 11th.

A week later Weidenbach was passed on the US list by Jones, who ran 2:27:54 in New York, yet finished more than 2 minutes behind Kristiansen's course record. The Norwegian broke Waitz's record by 12 seconds with her 2:25:30 – the second fastest time of the year behind her own Boston performance. She went for the world record again, speeding through halfway in 69:59 before being slowed by stomach cramps. Once again Fogli was third (2:28:43).

Jones's time came only four weeks after winning the Twin Cities marathon in 2:31:42. She later said that she was going for the "family record" in New York – her husband Steve's best was 2:27:43.

As could be expected, 1989 was not nearly as good a year as 1988. Only fourteen runners broke 2:30:00 and Kristiansen was the only one under 2:25:00. She ranked first – for the first time, despite being world record holder! – with Marot second (the only blemish in her year was a seventh in Tokyo in November), Jones third, Weidenbach fourth and Panfil fifth. Jones's four marathons of the year – in itself unusual for someone on the ranking list – averaged an amazing 2:30:25.

The phenomenal growth in women's marathoning – even though it was not evident right at the top – could be seen when comparing the 10th, 50th and 100th performer on the world list for each year of the previous decade:

|      | 10th    | 50th    | 100th   |
|------|---------|---------|---------|
| 1980 | 2:35:05 | 2:44:28 | 2:49:08 |
| 1981 | 2:33:13 | 2:42:12 | 2:45:47 |
| 1982 | 2:33:36 | 2:38:44 | 2:43:19 |
| 1983 | 2:31:12 | 2:36:31 | 2:38:52 |
| 1984 | 2:29:10 | 2:34:49 | 2:37:29 |
| 1985 | 2:28:38 | 2:35:27 | 2:38:17 |
| 1986 | 2:29:51 | 2:34:41 | 2:37:58 |
| 1987 | 2:29:56 | 2:33:22 | 2:37:06 |
| 1988 | 2:28:40 | 2:31:56 | 2:35:29 |
| 1989 | 2:28:45 | 2:30:35 | 2:37:04 |

At the close of the decade only four of the times on the all-time list at the end of 1983 still made the list:

| 2:21:06 | Ingrid Kristiansen NOR | 1985 |      |
|---------|------------------------|------|------|
| 2:21:21 | Joan Benoit USA        | 1985 |      |
| 2:23:29 | Rosa Mota POR          | 1985 |      |
| 2:23:51 | Lisa Martin AUS        | 1988 |      |
| 2:24:54 | Grete Waitz NOR        | 1986 |      |
| 2:25:24 | Katrin Dörre GDR       | 1987 |      |
| 2:25:56 | Véronique Marot GBR    | 1989 |      |
| 2:26:26 | Julie Brown USA        | 1983 |      |
| 2:26:34 | Carla Beurskens NED    | 1981 |      |
| 2:26:46 | Allison Roe NZL        | 1981 | (10) |
| 2:26:51 | Priscilla Welch GBR    | 1987 |      |
| 2:27:05 | Tatyana Polovinskaya URS | 1988 |    |
| 2:27:05 | Wanda Panfil POL       | 1989 |      |
| 2:27:06 | Zhao Youfeng CHN       | 1988 |      |
| 2:27:16 | Mun Gyong-ae PRK       | 1989 |      |
| 2:27:49 | Laura Fogli ITA        | 1988 |      |
| 2:27:51 | Patricia Catalano USA  | 1981 |      |
| 2:27:54 | Kim Jones USA          | 1989 |      |
| 2:27:57 | Zoya Ivanova URS       | 1987 |      |
| 2:28:06 | Sarah Rowell GBR       | 1985 | (20) |

The new decade started with a bang in Osaka on 28 January when Mota showed she was healthy again and scored a clear victory over Katsuyo Hyodo, 2:27:47 against 2:29:36. The Japanese girl had challenged Mota at 30 km, but the Portu-

guese was too strong and experienced. Valentina Yegorova URS, in her fourth marathon, also finished under 2½ hours with 2:29:47. Three days later Martin ran even faster in the Commonwealth Games in Auckland when she won by almost 8 minutes, a much bigger margin than she had enjoyed in 1986 when she won the first title. The high humidity and temperature made her performance an excellent one.

RESULT:
1 Lisa Martin AUS 2:25:28
2 Tani Ruckle AUS 2:33:15
3 Angela Pain Eng 2:36:35
4 Sally Ellis Eng 2:37:46
5 Deborah Noy Eng 2:39:01
6 Andri Avraam CYP 2:39:19

On 24 February the first sub-2:30:00 in Africa came in Port Elizabeth when Van der Merwe retained the national title in 2:27:36 (see p. 136). This would be the fourth fastest time of 1990.

On 4 March Panfil, who would be just ahead of Van der Merwe on the yearly list, won in Nagoya in 2:31:04 (Martin did not finish). In the meantime, Mota was getting ready to regain her Boston crown on 16 April. She started the race on world record pace, reaching 10 miles in 54:03 with an unassailable lead.

"At one point, my coach [husband Pedrosa] said, 'No one is behind; enjoy and don't kill yourself.'" Mota ran the rest of the way relaxed and finished in 2:25:24, winning $50 000. Behind her a tough battle was fought among Pippig, surprising American Maria Trujillo (PB of 2:32:09) and Kamila Gradus POL. Trujillo was second until 21 miles, when Pippig passed her and ran on to a West German record. (She had moved to West Germany in January and had trained for Boston in the Colorado mountains.)

RESULT:
1 Rosa Mota 2:25:24
2 Uta Pippig 2:28:03
3 Maria Trujillo 2:28:53
4 Kamila Gradus 2:28:56

Behind them followed three stars: Jones, Marot and Ivanova, with Vahlensieck 13th and Fogli and Tikkanen unable to finish.

Mota's performance would remain the fastest of the year – the first time that she headed the yearly performance list. Only six days later she did the inexplicable: she started the London marathon. Not surprisingly, she dropped out – as did Waitz and Cunha. (Both Kristiansen and Samuelson were expecting their second child.)

It was a tremendous race, with Panfil clocking a national record which put her in ninth place on the all-time list. She won by exactly 1½ minutes, beating one of the strongest fields in years. Two Chinese women finished in the top six.

RESULT:
1. Wanda Panfil 2:26:31
2. Francie Larrieu Smith USA 2:28:01
3. Lisa Weidenbach 2:28:16
4. Zhao Youfeng 2:29:35
5. Yekaterina Khramenkova 2:29:45
6. Xie Lihua CHN 2:30:18

That same day in Rotterdam Beurskens set a course record of 2:29:47, with Pippig's countrywoman Iris Biba 52 seconds behind.

The Pittsburgh marathon on 6 May had an interesting first prize – a thousand dollars for each full mile plus a dollar for each of the remaining yards. The $26 385 went to Conceiçao Ferreira POR (2:30:34).

In July Ivanova made amends for her disappointment in Boston by winning the Goodwill Games marathon in Seattle in 2:34:38. Three other Soviets, however, went to Split for the European Championships to tackle the woman who had won both previous marathon titles: Mota.

The two-time defending champion had one of the toughest races of her career – this time even her usual ally, the heat, seemed to work against her. The race was run on a difficult four-lap course with a testing climb. Mota took the lead before the runners left the stadium and established a considerable lead, but then started to weaken and was caught by Yegorova at 35 km. The two exchanged a few words and then Mota pulled away. It was not easy, though, and over the last 500 m in the stadium she continued to glance over her shoulder to check the distance between her and the Soviet. She won her third gold medal by a tiny margin – 5 seconds.

RESULT:
1. Rosa Mota POR 2:31:27
2. Valentina Yegorova URS 2:31:32
3. Maria Lelut-Rebelo FRA 2:35:51
4. Emma Scaunich ITA 2:37:19
5. Judit Földingné HUN 2:37:55
6. Françoise Bonnet FRA 2:39:04

Both the other two Soviets, Khramenkova and Klochko, failed to finish.

On 30 September Pippig won her first major marathon when she ran 2:28:37 in Berlin. She had to put everything into it, as Kokowska finished only 13 seconds behind. Beurskens ran 2:30:00 in third. On the same day, in Beijing, Zhao won the gold medal at the Asian Games in 2:35:19.

A week later Fogli scored a rare win in Venice, running 2:38:33, and another week later Bornet was the victor in the Twin Cities marathon in 2:29:22, a national record. On 28 October Cunha won Chicago in 2:30:11.

On 4 November Panfil scored her third major victory of the year in a very hot New York. The 31-year-old Pole pulled away from her rivals after 9 miles and seemed set for a comfortable win, but over the last 3 miles she slowed dramati-

cally. Jones, who was a minute behind her at 20 miles, was moving closer with every step. Panfil, in a replay of Mota in the European race, glanced back frequently as the American charged at her. In the end Jones ran out of distance and finished with the same gap as Yegorova had in Split: 2:30:45 against 2:30:50. She beat all but two US men, however!

"I think I ran as fast as I could today," Jones said later. "Five seconds is a long time."

Dörre was third in 2:33:21. Waitz, who had been training for only three months after a pelvic stress fracture, was fourth in her slowest time ever, 2:34:34.

In ninth place Swede Evy Palm, 48 years old, ran 2:38:00. Ivanova was seventh and Marot 11th.

In December Beurskens won her fifth Honolulu marathon. Her times never varied by more than about 4 minutes: 2:35:51 in 1985, 2:31:02 in '86, 2:35:11 in '87, 2:31:50 in '89 and now 2:33:34.

The year ended with no athlete under 2:25:00 – the first time since 1982. There were 74 under 2:40:00 and sixteen under 2:30:00 – both second only to 1988.

Mota, who was third on the overall ranking list, was ranked first in the marathon for the third time, more than any other runner except Waitz (with six). Panfil, Ondieki (as Martin was known after her marriage to Kenyan track star Yobes Ondieki), Pippig and Larrieu Smith followed. Van der Merwe became the first South African to be ranked with her ninth place.

The year 1991 belonged to Poland and was also characterised by the growing participation of eastern European athletes in the West as the global political dispensation changed. The first important race, on 13 January in Marrakech, set the tone for the rest of the year. The time (2:38:05 by Izabela Zatorska POL) was slow, but this was merely a preliminary to what Poland's number one, Panfil, would deliver in Boston on 15 April – only the third time in history that the classic race was held so early in the month.

Panfil, Jones and Pippig were the favourites, but most of the spotlight fell on two new mothers – who were also the two fastest marathoners in history. Kristiansen and Samuelson were both in good shape and they ran accordingly. Kristiansen did what she liked best: taking the lead. She was followed closely by Panfil and Samuelson. The first 10 km went by in 31:43. Near the 15 km mark the American suddenly took the lead and forged ahead. Receiving tremendous support from the spectators, Samuelson ran through halfway in a quick 70:53.

Panfil did not like the noise of the crowd. "The noise was a bit of a distraction, and played a role in my decision to move early. Also, I sensed that Kristiansen wasn't herself; she kept dropping and flexing her arms."

The Pole surged hard after 14 miles. "Once I broke away I just tried to relax, focus, run the course. I was feeling good, so I just went with it."

After the hills she faced a cool headwind, which caused

her leg muscles to tighten. But she kept pressing on, while behind her Jones made her usual late-race charge and passed Samuelson in the last 2 miles to finish in a PB. Both Pippig and Gradus also finished strongly, the German just beating Samuelson. Panfil's time was a national record and elevated her to fifth on the all-time list.

RESULT:
1 Wanda Panfil 2:24:18
2 Kim Jones 2:26:40
3 Uta Pippig 2:26:52
4 Joan Samuelson 2:26:54
5 Kamila Gradus 2:26:55
6 Ingrid Kristiansen 2:29:24

It was the first time in history that five women had run under 2:27:00 in the same race, and also the first time (outside of the Olympics) that six had broken 2½ hours. The third Polish runner, Malgorzata Birbach, was eighth in 2:32:13, giving Poland an amazing three-person average of 2:27:49 – the highest ever by a country in a single race.

Samuelson ran her fastest marathon since her 2:21:21 in 1985. She was the only one of the first five who did not set a PB. Before the race she had said: "I'm not looking beyond this race. For me to continue, it's necessary to run under 2:30:00." After the race, injury-free for the first time in years, she said that she had been thinking of making the US team in the 10000 m rather than the marathon. "I think it would be more of an achievement to go to another Olympics in a different event," she said in an interview in *Track & Field News*. "The top priority now is the family. I'll be honest with you . . . I'll do what's best for them. What's best for all of us."

Before Boston Dörre had won the Osaka marathon on 27 January in 2:27:43, while the Los Angeles race in March went to Cathy O'Brien USA in a PB 2:29:38. Yuko Arimori JPN was second behind Dörre in a national record of 2:28:01 and Chen Qingmei CHN third in 2:29:44.

Six days after Boston Mota again proved her superiority in major championship races when she won the World Cup marathon, incorporated in the London event, in 2:26:14. She ran in the front of the pack until 14 miles and then cleverly broke away at a refreshment point. Unbeknown to her and the rest of the world this was to be her last completed marathon.

The 38-year-old Larrieu Smith, who earlier in the year had set a US record over 10000 m, established a PB in London for the second year in a row, finishing second in 2:27:35 ahead of Yegorova (2:28:18), Dörre (2:28:57) and Lelut (2:29:04). The Soviets won the team competition.

Then attention focused on the World Championships marathon in Tokyo, run on 25 August. The question was: Could Mota do it once more? Her record suggested that she was the favourite, but it was also suggested that she might not have recovered completely from surgery to remove an abdominal cyst after the London race . . . and, of course,

there was the new danger: Panfil. There were also Dörre, who had won seven of eight marathons in Japan (and fifteen of 21 altogether), the Japanese themselves, Kristiansen, and the other two Poles, Kokowska and Gradus.

The race started at 07:00 and it was aleady warm and humid. The 38 competitors did not relish the uncomfortable conditions, but Mota nevertheless immediately took the lead. A lead group of fifteen formed around her and they went through 5 km in a slow 17:53. The leaders passed 15 km in 53:04, with Panfil, Dörre, Grottenberg and Biba prominent. Gradus led at halfway in 74:49.

Meanwhile Mota had started struggling, experiencing abdominal pain caused by breathing difficulties. Not long afterward she stopped and abandoned the race. (Other stars who would drop out were Marot, Fogli, Cunha, Yegorova and Rasmussen.)

The group thinned out gradually to five, and then Manuela Machado POR and Arimori fell behind at 35 km. The medals were to be decided among Panfil (like Mota coached by her husband, the Mexican track runner Mauricio Gonzalez), the little-known Japanese Sachiko Yamashita, who had turned 27 five days before and came into the race with a PB of 2:31:02 run in Nagoya in March, and Dörre.

"The second half . . . was very difficult," Dörre said later. "I tried to sprint with Wanda at 39 km, but I just couldn't keep up with her."

At 40 km (2:22:24) Yamashita, receiving vociferous support from the crowds along the road, surged in an attempt to get away, but it was in vain. Panfil stayed with her and at 41 km made her own break. She quickly opened a gap of 40 m and increased this to the finish. She and Yamashita were the only ones to run under 2:30:00; only 24 finished.

RESULT:
1 Wanda Panfil POL 2:29:53
2 Sachiko Yamashita JPN 2:29:57
3 Katrin Dörre GER 2:30:10
4 Yuko Arimori JPN 2:31:08
5 Maria Lelut-Rebelo FRA 2:32:05
6 Kamila Gradus POL 2:32:09
7 Manuela Machado POR 2:32:33
8 Ramilya Burangulova URS 2:33:00
9 Iris Biba GER 2:33:48
10 Sally Ellis GBR 2:35:09

One national record was set – by the Honduran runner Gina Coello, who ran 3:00:03 in 23rd.

On 29 September Kokowska, who did not finish in Tokyo, showed the country's depth when she won Berlin in 2:27:36. She had to run a course record (breaking Pippig's) and PB to relegate Jones to another second place, in 2:27:50. Toivonen was third in 2:28:49. A month later, on 27 October, Irina Bogacheva, another member of the strong corps of Soviet runners, notched a victory in Carpi, clocking a PB 2:28:57. In second Scaunich won the Italian national title in

2:30:26. That same day Midde Hamrin-Senorski SWE won Chicago in 2:36:21 – 6 seconds slower than her winning time in Stockholm earlier in the year.

A week later the New York extravaganza marked the debut of a formidable track, road and cross-country runner. Elizabeth McColgan GBR had won two Commonwealth 10000 m golds, had set a world record of 30:39 for 10 km in 1989 and in Tokyo had scored an overwhelming victory in the 10000 m. In June she had become the second fastest runner ever over the distance with her 30:57.07; three months before that she had been third in the World Cross-country Championships. Earlier in the year she had given birth to a daughter; now she was ready for a good marathon.

Before the race she said that she could run 2:24:00, but would go only as fast as was necessary to win. "I'm here to win." The 27-year-old Scot started the race in the company of Samuelson and Ondieki (also a new mother), but at 17 miles the American could not maintain the tempo and fell back. At 22 miles there was a surprise when Soviet Olga Markova joined the two leaders and promptly tried to take the lead. The headstrong McColgan wanted none of it and surged away. Two miles further she was 70 m ahead and at the finish her margin was 55 seconds. Her 2:27:32 was the fastest debut ever.

McColgan wasn't shy about her future. "All the signs are there," she said about the possibility of her running sub-2:20.

Markova was second (2:28:18, a PB) and Ondieki third (2:28:53). Samuelson, suffering from asthma-related fluid loss, finished a disappointing sixth in 2:33:48. For the first time more than 5 000 women (5 204) finished the race.

The last sub-2:30 of the year was run by Sally Eastall GBR in Sacramento on 8 December when she won in 2:29:29.

The 22 runners under 2:30:00 for the year equalled the record number of 1988. Panfil was the only one to join the sub-2:25 club, which now had six members. The most prolific member was Kristiansen with six of the fourteen times. The best performances by the three top Polish runners, Panfil, Gradus and Kokowska, averaged 2:26:16 – 47 seconds better than the Americans' 2:27:03.

McColgan, ranked first in the 10000 m, also ranked seventh in marathon. Above her on the list were the undefeated Panfil (who had also set a Polish record of 31:53.83 for 10000 m on the track), Mota, Yamashita, Dörre, Jones and Larrieu Smith.

In 1992 the dominant Poles were surpassed by runners from the former Soviet republics and Japan, the latter showing the same prowess as their male counterparts had done five or six years before. The Marrakech race was again won by Zatorska, 1:36 faster than the previous year, but in Osaka fourteen days later, on 26 January, the first Japanese warning came when Yumi Kokamo won in 2:26:26, eclipsing McColgan's world best for a debut. Kokamo, only twenty years old, had run 20 km in 67:10 in November; here she beat an immensely strong field with an Asian record and earned a place on the Japanese Olympic team for Barcelona. The first three Japanese all broke Arimori's national record set the previous year in the same race; Matsuno did so in her debut. But in Barcelona Arimori would have the last laugh.

RESULT:
1 Yumi Kokamo 2:26:26
2 Akemi Matsuno 2:27:02
3 Katrin Dörre 2:27:34
4 Yoshiko Yamamoto JPN 2:27:58
5 Wang Xiuting CHN 2:28:56
6 Junko Asari JPN 2:28:57

Eight runners finished under 2½ hours – second only to the 1984 Olympic marathon. Kristiansen, who in September had collapsed after winning the Great North Run half marathon, pulled out at 30 km, placing a question mark against her Olympic chances.

That same morning, not far away, McColgan achieved the world's fastest time for the half marathon when she ran 67:11 on the point-to-point and slightly downhill Tokyo course.

On 1 March the former Soviets replied to the Japanese when Madina Biktagirova of Belarus won the Los Angeles marathon in a course record 2:26:23, improving on her previous best by precisely 6 minutes. Ironically, considering the 1984 boycott by the Soviet Union of the Olympic Games held in the same city, the race was the trial for the selection of the Unified Team of ex-USSR republics, who would compete as a single entity for the last time in Barcelona. The other two members of the team would be Ramilya Burangulova (2:28:12) and Yegorova (2:29:41), but while the Olympic race would turn into a triumph for Yegorova, it would end in humiliation for the Los Angeles winner. Germany's Kerstin Pressler finished third in 2:29:40.

On 5 April Cunha easily won the Rotterdam marathon in 2:29:14, breaking Beurskens's course record.

A week later Dörre had a much tougher task in London, beating Kokowska by only 20 seconds in 2:29:39. Olympic champ Mota did not finish.

On 20 April in Boston another ex-Soviet athlete came to the fore – quite literally, as Markova (23) ran the fastest time of the year . . . and more. The former army sergeant was by no means the favourite for the race, because both defending champion Panfil and Pippig were there, as well as Yamamoto. Panfil was aiming for Samuelson's course record of 2:22:43 and set out quickly. She reached 5 miles in 26:02 and the half marathon in 70:32, comfortably in the lead. But as the temperature climbed, her tempo slowed, and at 18 miles Markova drew alongside.

She did not stay long, pulling away decisively to finish in 2:23:43 – a national record and the seventh fastest time ever run. Behind her Panfil, only a shadow of her 1991 self, was also caught by the chasing pack. In second place Yamamoto equalled Kokamo's national record set in Osaka.

RESULT:  1  Olga Markova 2:23:43
2  Yoshiko Yamamoto 2:26:26
3  Uta Pippig 2:27:12
4  Manuela Machado 2:27:42
5  Malgorzata Birbach 2:28:11
6  Wanda Panfil 2:29:29

Markova expressed the hope that her performance would give her a berth to Barcelona, even though she did not run in Los Angeles. "They have changed rules before, now maybe they will change them for me."

They did not. When the third Olympic marathon for women started at 18:30 on 1 August Markova was absent, and so were Mota, who was injured, McColgan and Pippig, who were concentrating on the 10000 m (they would finish fifth and seventh six days after the marathon), Kristiansen, Matsuno and Yamamoto. The favourites were Ondieki, who in June had run the fastest 10000 m of the year, a national record 31:11.72, Dörre and Kokamo. Panfil, the world champion, had seemed off form and was an unknown factor.

At the start the temperature was 29 °C (5 degrees higher than in Tokyo) and the humidity in the 70s. It was clearly a time for caution. They started slowly, with Ondieki marginally ahead in the group of twelve at 5 km (17:58). The next 5 km was even slower (18:29) and then the pace dropped further: 19:01 for a time of 55:28 at 15 km. Ondieki was still in front and reached 20 km in 74:09 (previous 5 km in 18:41).

Then the 28-year-old Yegorova took over and increased the tempo. She passed 25 km in 91:38 after 5 km in 17:29 and that proved too much for the Australian. She stepped off the course soon afterwards and said that she had been drinking too much. This she changed later to the accusation that her water bottles had been tampered with.

Yegorova ran a remarkable 5 km from 25 to 30 km, taking just 16:41 to cover this section – 2:21:00 pace! This broke her clear of the others to such an extent that she had a minute's lead at 30 km.

She was running through the streets of the old part of the city before the torturous climb up Montjuïc hill to the stadium. What she did not know was that behind her the 26-year-old Arimori was running hard – much harder than Yegorova herself. Where Yegorova had chased Mota in the 1990 European race, she was now the hunted, and at 35 km the hunter caught her. The Japanese could not break away and a titanic struggle ensued, with neither prepared to give in as they fought up the long hill.

Only 300 m from the gates of the stadium Yegorova put in a desperate surge ("With the stadium in sight I knew I was going to win") and drew away to claim the gold – only the second victory of her career. Her winning margin of 8 seconds was the smallest in the 96 years of Olympic marathoning. The 37-year-old Moller ran the best race of her life at championship level just four days after the death of her former husband, US marathoner Ron Daws.

Biktagerova finished fourth in 2:35:39, but was disqualified four days later for use of the drug norephedrine.

RESULT:  1  Valentina Yegorova EUN 2:32:41
2  Yuko Arimori JPN 2:32:49
3  Lorraine Moller NZL 2:33:59
4  Sachiko Yamashita JPN 2:36:26
5  Katrin Dörre GER 2:36:48
6  Mun Gyong-ae PRK 2:37:03
7  Manuela Machado POR 2:38:22
8  Ramilya Burangulova EUN 2:38:46
9  Colleen de Reuck RSA 2:39:03
10  Cathy O'Brien USA 2:39:42

The tiny Yegorova (1.56 m, 52 kg), who hailed from Cheboksary, the capital of the Russian republic of Chuvash, said in an interview that she had not found the conditions too hot. When asked what the outcome would have been had Mota been present, she said: "It would have been the same; the conditions were perfect for me."

Marot was 16th, Panfil 22nd (a dismal 2:47:27) and Kokamo 29th (2:58:18), while Cunha did not finish.

On 30 August Olga Appell MEX, who also did not finish the Olympic race, won in Sapporo in 2:30:22 and on 27 September Pippig ran the exact same time when winning the Berlin marathon (35 seconds ahead of Kokowska). On 11 October Xie took the Beijing race in 2:28:53 on a day which featured six major marathons around the world. In the most significant one, in Columbus, Samuelson won her first marathon in seven years with a 2:32:18 effort.

It seemed as if her aches and allergies were something of the past. "I've got a good allergist now, and I'm working on the biomechanics and my asthma to run controlled," the US record holder said in an interview in *Running Stats*.

A week later Khramenkova won her third major race of the year in Lisbon and another week later Rosanna Munerotto ITA was first in Carpi in 2:29:34.

On the first day of November Ondieki was ready to make amends for her failure in Barcelona. Behind her when she toed the line on a cool day in New York was a training spell of six weeks of 150 miles per week at an altitude of more than 2 000 m in Flagstaff. With her were Markova, then living in Gainesville, Yamamoto, Gradus and Jones.

But the Australian was confident. "I've trained too long and too hard to come here and run 2:30:00," she said. She showed her intentions immediately after the first mile went by in 6:10 by speeding up. By 4 miles she was already a minute in front! She went by 10 km in 33:46 and halfway in 71:45, 2 minutes ahead of Markova. The more difficult second half was only slightly slower and she stopped the clock in 2:24:40, a course record and second fastest performance of 1992. It was an emphatic victory, the second fastest time of her career and almost 2 minutes ahead of the world list leader. Markova was runner-up for the second year in a row.

RESULT:
1 Lisa Ondieki 2:24:40
2 Olga Markova 2:26:38
3 Yoshiko Yamamoto 2:29:58

"New York is the jewel in the crown," said the woman who won the silver medal in Seoul. "It's the one I've always wanted to win."

Nine-time winner Waitz accompanied Lebow, who had had surgery for cancer, on his first five-borough race (he had last run it in 1970). They finished in 5:32:34, both overcome with emotion.

McColgan skipped this race and went to Tokyo for her second marathon, where on 15 November she gained just as significant a victory as Ondieki: she not only defeated the Olympic champion by almost 4 minutes, but also two other top Olympians. The Scot's time was 2:27:38, 6 seconds slower than the previous year in New York. Dörre clocked 2:30:05, Burangulova 2:30:34 and Yegorova 2:31:27.

On 13 December Beurskens won Honolulu for the sixth time, running 2:32:13.

The number of runners who broke 2:35:00 (85) was the highest since 1988, while the 23 under 2:30:00 was a new record. For the first time since 1988 two women ran sub-2:25.

Yegorova, who had run four marathons in the course of the year (she was 12th in Paris), was ranked first – "not a clear No. 1", as *Track & Field News* put it – with Ondieki, who had completed only one, second. Then came Markova, McColgan and Dörre.

China's year. That is the best desciption of 1993, a World Championships year. Many people doubted the excellent performances of "Ma's Army", as the group of brilliant women coached by Ma Junren were called, and tales about stimulant abuse, an inhuman training regimen and magic foods (such as caterpillar fungus) were rife. Questions were asked worldwide, among them these three by *Track & Field News*:

"Why are the women suddenly so good while the men remain so average? The skeptical answer is because anabolic steroids work better on women than men.

"Why don't the Chinese compete on the international circuit? The skeptical answer is because they can in that manner avoid drug testing, just as the old Soviet/DDR machine did.

"Can IAAF out-of-competition testing be effective in a nation with strict border controls, or do bureaucratic delays give enough advance warning that counter-measures can be applied to doped athletes? The skeptical answer is that the Soviet Bloc was good at this dodge too."

At the end of the year Dr David Martin of the Department of Cardiopulmonary Care Sciences at Georgia State University, an eminent running historian and scientist, cautioned in *On the Roads*, the official publication of the US Road Running Information Center, that the world was doing itself no favours by condemning the Chinese as frauds and taunting the system that produced them. He wrote: "I, like others, look forward to learning more about 'the Chinese system'. If it is a brutal and ruthless program of over-training that, coupled with clandestine ergogenics, brings short-term success and terrible embarrassment once the entire scheme is uncovered, let's learn from it, and move on. If, on the other hand, it is a fascinatingly succcessful system of doing old things better and doing new things well, then again, let's learn from it, and enjoy."

He also pointed out that Japanese runners were successful because they focused on a long period of high-volume training "to raise their $VO_2$-max, increase blood volume, and quicken lactate threshold". This was exactly what the Chinese were doing.

In February 1994 the IAAF announced that it had conducted random testing of thirteen of Ma's athletes, and all of them had tested negative. A year later Ma's group was breaking up – the coach's iron discipline had proved too much. Said Wang Junxia, his star pupil: "We simply couldn't take it any longer. We had absolutely no freedom. We were all on the brink of going crazy. The pressure was too intense; we couldn't take it."

Once again, before the Chinese appeared on the scene, it was the early Japanese races that produced the fireworks. For the third time in a year a Japanese woman clocked 2:26:26 (equalling the Asian record) when Asari won the Osaka race on 31 January in exactly the same time that gave Kokamo the victory in 1993. Once again the second runner was appearing in her first marathon – and Tomoe Abe JPN missed Kokamo's world best for a debut by one second! The 21-year-old Abe, a waif 1.50 m tall and weighing 38 kg, led at 30 km (after Kokowska had set the pace to a halfway time of 72:45) and then tried to break away. She dropped everyone except Asari, and with 400 m left followed the lead car off course. Abe corrected herself quickly, but that was enough for Asari to sprint ahead and win by one second.

Asari surpassed her PB by 2:31 and said: "In the last half of the race, all I could think of was winning." Yamamoto ran her fourth consecutive sub-2:30 with 2:29:41 in third. Biktagirova was eighth, while Kokowska again could not finish.

The Poles were still a force, however, for on 7 March Gradus won in Nagoya, albeit by only 15 seconds. The first four all ran under 2:29:00: Gradus 2:27:38, Matsuno 2:27:53, Burangulova 2:28:03, Eriko Asai JPN 2:28:22. Beurskens was fifth in 2:30:10.

Earlier, on 24 January, American Kristy Johnson had won the Houston marathon in 2:29:05.

Then the Chinese hit the world scene. On 4 April in Tianjin eight runners crashed through the 2:27:00 barrier – an almost incredible occurrence if one bears in mind that in the 1984 Olympic race the eighth placer had run 2:29:09 and in the 1992 Osaka marathon eighth place was 2:29:53. Never before had more than five runners broken 2:27:00 in a single race – and these eight were all from the same country!

What made the times even more stupendous was the fact that the first seven ran their first marathon and that the winner, Wang Junxia, was only twenty years old. Her time was the ninth fastest ever run.

According to reports Wang covered the last 12 km of the out-and-back uncertified[6] course 19 seconds faster than Kristiansen's world record for the distance (38:35).

RESULT:
1 Wang Junxia 2:24:07
2 Qu Yunxia 2:24:32
3 Zhang Linli 2:24:42
4 Zhang Lirong 2:24:52
5 Zhong Huandi 2:25:36
6 Ma Liyan 2:25:46
7 Wang Yanfang 2:26:36
8 Xie Lihua 2:26:38

Martin commented that he had studied the 5 km split times for the top thirty finishers and could find "no problems".[7] He pointed out that the Chinese stars were not unfamiliar names, as the world press had made them out to be. For instance, Zhong had been fourth in the 1992 Olympic 10000 m and according to Martin one had to "remember that China, unlike many Western nations, publishes, at best, annual 25-deep only lists. Thus many good performances simply don't get documented."

Later in the year, after the Chinese had overwhelmed the rest of the world in the long-distance events at the World Championships in Stuttgart and then stormed to a fabulous fourteen world records at the National Games in Beijing,[8] *Track & Field News* wrote that there were "only a finite number of synonyms for 'unbelievable'". Concerning the drug suspicions, the magazine reminded its readers about the case of the Canadian sprinter Ben Johnson who had passed many tests over the years while taking drugs. "Highly efficient flushing/masking agents obviously exist."

The magazine quoted Martin: "If they never begin to duplicate these performances, will we be left saying they were on drugs? What if they run even faster next year? What then?"

On 18 April the London marathon produced a "normal" result. It was a very strong field, one of the most talented of the year. In what must rank as one of the best runs of her career Dörre beat everyone, including the heavy favourites,

McColgan and Ondieki. The latter two did not have a good word for each other; the race was described as a perfect grudge duel. But they had no answer when the defending champion caught them just before the 18-mile mark. Dörre had been running metronomically consistent miles, all between 5:42 and 5:46.

"When I saw her, she looked good," said Ondieki. "I knew she hadn't spent what I had in the first half." McColgan dropped behind after 20 miles and although Ondieki tried to keep contact, the German was too strong in the closing stages. It was McColgan's first defeat and her slowest time.

RESULT:
1 Katrin Dörre 2:27:09
2 Lisa Ondieki 2:27:27
3 Liz McColgan 2:29:37

After the race Dörre summed up the situation: "When two people are arguing so much then the third person is happy."

The next day in Boston Markova had her chance to take revenge on Yegorova (and show the Russian selectors a thing or two). Jones, Panfil, Samuelson, Weidenbach and Machado were also in attendance, but the defending champion was in a class of her own. Markova took the lead after 2 miles, with the Olympic champion just behind. Panfil again had difficulties from early on with the fast pace (10 miles in 54:31). It was a hot day and soon the pace was telling; by halfway Markova was alone in 71:41. Yegorova was already 100 m behind, and falling further behind as the miles slipped by. She dropped out at 22 miles.

There was no stopping Markova, and she won by 4:33 in 2:25:27 – the fastest non-Chinese time of the year. Samuelson was sixth in 2:35:43. Panfil also failed to finish.

In Stuttgart Dörre was up against the Japanese trio of Asari, Abe and Matsuno, as well as two strong ex-Soviets, Burangulova and Biktagirova. The top Chinese were conspicuous by their absence – Wang and Zhong were running the 10000, Qu and the two Zhangs the 3000.

The marathon took place on the hot and humid morning of 15 August. American Jones set the initial pace (5 km in 18:10), leading a group of eighteen. Jones was running comfortably, yet was irritated by her rivals clipping her heels and generally running too close to her. But at the 30 km water point disaster struck.

"I felt very good even up to 25 km," Jones said. "I was doing fine and feeling good at 30 km, then I got tripped up. That's where I lost it mentally."

That was the point where Machado took the lead, putting a Portuguese vest at the head of a major championship field for the first time since the heyday of Mota. Asari went with her. Soon Machado was 30 m in front, but then Asari started to move up as Machado began to struggle, her strength gone. The Japanese closed the gap, and at 36 km she pulled away – much more easily than Machado had done earlier. She ran the final 7 km almost a minute faster than Machado.

6. I.e., not certified by an IAAF/AIMS measurer.
7. The men's race was won in what Martin called a "perfectly reasonable" 2:11:10.
8. Wang ran 3000 m in 8:06.11 and 10000 m in 29:31.78 (previous records 8:22.62 and 30:13.74). In the latter event she sped the *last* 3000 m in 8.17.47. The second half of the race took her only 14:26, compared to the existing world record of 14:37.33.

The slim 22-year-old Asari won by 51 seconds and could not believe her good fortune. "I can't believe I just won the World Championship," she said, and added that her coach had told her to make her move at 36 km. "It wasn't till I got inside the stadium I was sure I would win."

RESULT:
1 Junko Asari JPN 2:30:03
2 Manuela Machado POR 2:30:54
3 Tomoe Abe JPN 2:31:01
4 Ramilya Burangulova RUS 2:33:03
5 Madina Biktagirova BLR 2:34:36
6 Katrin Dörre GER 2:35:20
7 Frith van der Merwe RSA 2:35:56
8 Kim Jones USA 2:36:33
9 Kamila Gradus POL 2:36:48
10 Firia Sultanova RUS 2:37:59

On 26 September Yamamoto won the Amsterdam marathon in 2:29:12 and on the same day Kokowska scored the best win of her career when she took the Berlin marathon. She had a marvellous record in this race: first in 1988, second in 1989 and 1990, first in 1991 with a course record, and second in 1992. This time she set another course record, 2:26:20, in beating another Portuguese star, world cross-country champion Albertina Dias in her first marathon (2:26:49). Malgorzata Sobanska POL was third (2:29:21).

On the last day of October Wang returned to the marathon, winning the World Cup in San Sebastián in 2:28:16. The race was run on a fast three-lap course. Wang was followed by three team-mates: Zhang Linli 2:29:42, Zhang Lirong 2:29:45 and Ma Liyan 2:30:44. Of course, they easily won the team competition. The Chinese complained of the effects of the National Games the previous month, and of injuries. "We were very tired today," Wang said.

Fourteen days later Pippig finally came into her own. The 28-year-old medical student had set personal bests for 3000, 5000 and 10000 m on the track earlier in the year, but was disappointed with her ninth place in the Stuttgart 10000 m and prepared for New York at altitude in Boulder. She dominated a not-too-strong field in New York, revelling in the warm conditions. She blasted the first half in 71:21 and was on course record pace until 22 miles, but then slowed. She still finished in a PB 2:26:24, blowing kisses to the crowd, with Appell second in a national record 2:28:56. They were the only two under 2½ hours. Pippig won $20 000 first prize, $20 000 time bonus and a Mercedes Benz. Fogli finished 14th, while Jones was the victim of an asthma attack and landed in hospital.

"I'm very happy . . ." the winner said. "And I'm sure I can run faster." Prophetic words indeed.

On 21 November Yegorova bounced back in Tokyo, winning in a PB 2:26:40 – only her third victory in fourteen marathons. Ondieki dropped out at halfway, covered in 72:46, and Yegorova assumed the lead with Dörre and Asai.

Within the next 5 km both the German and the Japanese were gone, and Yegorova ran alone to the finish. Mari Tanigawa JPN was second in 2:28:22 (also a PB) and Dörre third in 2:28:52. In eighth place Alina Ivanova, the 1991 world champion in the 10000 m walk who had the same coach as Yegorova, ended her debut in 2:35:16.

It came as no surprise that the 41-year-old Beurskens won Honolulu for the seventh time, running 2:32:20 – 7 seconds slower than in 1992.

With that a record – and controversial – year came to a close. A total of 99 athletes ran faster than 2:35:00, there were 29 under 2:30:00, and four (the Tianjin quartet) under 2:25:00. The eight under 2½ hours in Tianjin were the same number as in Osaka in 1992.

The sub-2:25 club now had eleven members, who had run twenty times under the barrier:

| 2:21:06 | Ingrid Kristiansen NOR | 1985 |
| 2:21:21 | Joan Benoit USA | 1985 |
| 2:23:29 | Rosa Mota POR | 1985 |
| 2:23:43 | Olga Markova RUS | 1992 |
| 2:23:51 | Lisa Martin AUS | 1988 |
| 2:24:07 | Wang Junxia CHN | 1993 |
| 2:24:18 | Wanda Panfil POL | 1991 |
| 2:24:32 | Qu Yunxia CHN | 1993 |
| 2:24:42 | Zhang Linli CHN | 1993 |
| 2:24:52 | Zhang Lirong CHN | 1993 |
| 2:24:54 | Grete Waitz NOR | 1986 |

Wang was ranked as the best athlete in the world for 1993, but the top marathon spot went to the world champion, Asari (only tenth on the performance list). Wang was second, followed by Markova, Pippig and Abe.

The first really significant race of 1994 was not a marathon, but a half marathon. On 20 March in Kyoto Pippig slashed the official world record to 67:59,[9] showing that she was in superb form and that a fast marathon in the course of the year was likely.

Earlier the Marrakech course had produced a quick time when Adriana Barbu ROM clocked 2:29:21, but on the same day in Osaka Abe was even quicker. In perfect weather she broke the triple deadlock in the Japanese record by beating one of the record holders, Asari, in 2:26:09 . . . but the situation was only partly resolved, for in second place Nobuko Fujimura, Asari's training partner and fourth in the race the previous year (clocking 2:30:02), ran exactly the same time to force a new two-way record tie!

The first 10 km was covered in 34:29, the second in 34:26 and the third in 35:08. Abe took the lead at 40 km, with the clock showing 2:18:31, and took Asari and Fujimura with her. It was only a desperate sprint on the track that brought

9. Pippig equalled the time recorded by South African Elana Meyer in East London in 1991. Meyer's time was never ratified as a world record because, despite later efforts by this author to obtain the timing documentation of the race, the timing sheets could not be traced.

Abe the victory. Her 5 km splits were 17:19, 17:11, 17:17, 17:09, 17:52, 17:16, 17:07, 17:21, with 7:37 for the last 2.195 km.

Abe thus took revenge for her defeats in the 1993 race and the World Championships, where Asari had beaten her. The world champion finished third – only a second behind in 2:26:10. Eight runners ran faster than 2½ hours – the same as in the 1992 race and in Tianjin in 1993. In fourth place Mitsuyo Yoshida equalled the previous record of 2:26:26; Asahina was fifth (2:27:51), Noriko Kawaguchi sixth (2:28:08), Yuka Terunuma seventh (2:28:26) and Sobanska eighth (2:29:06). They all set personal bests – Terunuma by as much as 9 minutes. Markova could only finish tenth; Kokowska dropped out.

Seven days later Appell, who had run 68:34 for the half marathon in Tokyo the previous year (behind Meyer's 67:22) and had become a US citizen nine days before, improved on her national record when she won in Los Angeles. Her earnings for her victory by almost 9 minutes were $15 000 plus a Mercedes.

Asai took the Nagoya marathon in "only" 2:30:30, but then her countrywoman Asahina set matters straight as far as the Japanese record was concerned when she ran to an emphatic win in Rotterdam on 17 April – and gained the course record into the bargain. Asahina, fourth in the World Half-marathon Championship the previous year and due to marry marathoner Koichi Takahashi in July, had predicted before the event that she would run 2:25:00, and that is what she did. The 24-year-old Asahina did not let the wind trouble her (unlike Osaka, there were men to shelter her most of the way).

RESULT:
1  Miyoko Asahina 2:25:52
2  Ritva Lemettinen FIN 2:29:16
3  Carla Beurskens 2:29:43

That same day strong winds held Dörre to a 2:32:34 title defence (and third win in a row) in London. Ondieki was second again. "It was the hardest of the three races mentally," the winner said. "The first two years I was not the favourite; this year I felt the pressure." It was Dörre's 17th marathon victory. The Chinese, widely expected to come and shatter the 2:20:00 barrier, pleaded illness and failed to show.

The next day the scene shifted to Boston and the smiling face of the attractive Ms Pippig. It was to be the best Boston ever. Making her debut was world 15 km record holder Meyer, who later in the year would win the world half-marathon title. Pippig had a slight cold the week before the race and mostly stayed indoors, but on race day she was ready. Next to her on the starting line was not only Meyer, winner of the silver medal in the 10000 m in Barcelona, but also Olympic champion Yegorova, Jones, defending titlist Markova, Dias and Alena Peterková TCH, whose PB of 2:30:36 was run in 1991.

The lead group went through 3 miles in 15:29 and 5 miles in 26:43, and at halfway De Reuck led in a quick 70:48. The first to let go were Markova and Peterková; then Dias, De Reuck and Yegorova. Pippig and Meyer were on their own and staged a magnificent duel on the Newton hills. After 89 minutes Pippig drew away, but a kilometre further the tough little South African pulled her back. In the 19th mile Meyer finally succumbed. Pippig looked behind her a few times and then set out after the course record, running hard between 21 and 24 miles. At one stage it looked as if even the world record was within her grasp, but she could not quite make it. She ran the last mile in 5:23 and raced down the final straight with her by now trademark blowing of kisses to the crowd. Her halves were very even: 70:48 and 70:57.

"I think today I've become less afraid of the Chinese," Pippig remarked later. It was her 17th marathon.

Behind her Yegorova ran strongly over the final 6 miles and caught a gallant Meyer to finish 1:48 behind Pippig. Amazingly the first seven set national records; Meyer's time was also an Africa record.

RESULT:
1  Uta Pippig 2:21:45
2  Valentina Yegorova 2:23:33
3  Elana Meyer 2:25:15
4  Alena Peterková 2:25:19
5  Carmen de Oliveira BRA 2:27:41

Pippig received $95 000 for her win and course record, and her time was the third fastest ever run. The first three recorded the world's fastest times for the year. When assessing these times the very favourable conditions of a following wind and the downhill nature of the course must be remembered. (See also p. 114.)

This reservation of course does not diminish the competitive aspect of the race, which made it, after Osaka, the highlight of the year. Markova did not finish.

Of the marathon Pippig has said that she tried to protect herself from any fear of the distance by not thinking of the 35th kilometre. She also believes that there is a direct connection between mental and physical performance. In an interview in *Runner's World* she said that training "is like a bow that you pull back as far as possible to shoot the arrow at an exact point in time . . . Sometimes you can't hold the bowstring back any longer. Or you can overpull it."

Dörre was the favourite for the European marathon, run on 7 August in Helsinki. The race started at 11:00 after it had rained early in the morning. The temperature was 28 °C, but the humidity only 47% – much lower than during the rest of the week. The runners started relatively slowly, and a large pack was together until 18 km. They had covered the first 10 km in 36:13 and 15 km in 54:14.

At 18 km Machado made a break. Maria Curatolo ITA tried to go with the Portuguese, but soon had to admit defeat. Machado, who had run her first marathon in 1988 and would be 31 two days after the race, reached 20 km in 71:38 and halfway in 75:25. Barbu now accelerated and quickly passed the flagging Italian. She began to cut the gap to Machado, but after 4 km her effort proved too much and she was repassed by Curatolo.

Machado went through 30 km (where Dörre dropped out) in 1:46:04 and 40 km in 2:21:43. She finished in 2:29:54 to claim Portugal's fourth victory in the four European title races held. It was a satisfying win for the durable Portuguese, who had been second in the World Championships but had often been beaten by better runners. She had started the year quietly with seventh in Nagoya, but followed that up with an excellent 75:54 for 20 km.

RESULT:
1 Manuela Machado POR 2:29:54
2 Maria Curatolo ITA 2:30:33
3 Adriana Barbu ROM 2:30:55
4 Ornelia Ferrara ITA 2:31:57
5 Anuta Catuna ROM 2:32:51
6 Ritva Lemettinen FIN 2:33:05

Twenty days later an unimpressive field of only sixteen runners contested the Commonwealth marathon in Victoria, British Columbia. Angelina Kanana KEN led by 15 seconds at halfway in 74:11, but with 10 km to go Bussières took the lead. She held it for about 8 km and was then passed by her team-mate Carole Rouillard, who went on to win in a PB.

RESULT:
1 Carole Rouillard CAN 2:30:41
2 Lizanne Bussières CAN 2:31:07
3 Yvonne Danson Eng 2:32:24
4 Karen Macleod Sco 2:33:16
5 Nyla Carroll NZL 2:34:03
6 Angelina Kanana KEN 2:35:02

On 25 September Dörre-Heinig (she had married her coach, Wolfgang Heinig) made amends for her poor showing in Helsinki when she won Berlin in a course record 2:25:15. It was also a PB – breaking her 2:25:24 run seven years earlier. Rocio Rios set a Spanish record 2:29:00 in second.

On 6 November high humidity reigned in New York and this was reflected in the times. While most attention focused on Biktagirova, Appell, Peterková (who would test positive for Nandrolone in June 1995 and receive a four-year ban) and Jones, it was a Kenyan runner in her first marathon who had the last say. The tiny 21-year-old Tecla Lorupe, weighing only 40 kg, started slowly, running the first mile in 6:15 – 15 seconds behind the leading group. The group was led at various stages by Anne Marie Letko USA, Appell, Dias, Lemettinen and Jones, and they had a lead of a full 48 seconds on the Kenyan at halfway (Catuna in front in 74:12).

Dias, Biktagirova, Catuna and Letko then increased the tempo, but behind them Lorupe was running even faster. Before the clock showed 2 hours she had joined them. At 18 miles the Russian drew away from the others – all but Lorupe, that is. The Kenyan post office auditor stayed with her for a mile and then made a move of her own. Biktagirova was helpless, and a relaxed-looking Lorupe went on to snap the tape held by Waitz. She was the first Kenyan woman to win such a major marathon, and she was immensely happy.

"I was so happy when I came here because everyone was like my mother and my father – they were so friendly. Women in Kenya have talent also. They try to discourage women, but I wanted to show them."

RESULT:
1 Tecla Lorupe 2:27:37
2 Madina Biktagirova 2:30:00
3 Anne Marie Letko 2:30:19

The only other sub-2:28 times of the year were turned in by Franziska Moser SUI, who won the Frankfurt race in 2:27:44, and Tanigawa, who was first in Paris (2:27:55). Johnson took the Chicago marathon, but more significant was the runner in sixth place: Samuelson in 2:37:09. Wang Junxia won Beijing in 2:31:11 and Yegorova Tokyo in 2:30:09. Beurskens won her eighth Honolulu (2:37:06), this time counting Asai and Fogli among her victims.

The 98 runners under 2:35:00 were one fever than in 1993, while the number under 2:30:00 (26) were three down on the previous year. Five of the top ten on the performance list came from Japan. Pippig was ranked first (eighth overall), followed by Yegorova and Abe. There were four more Japanese in the top ten on the ranking list: Fujimura (4), Asari (5), Asahina (7) and Yoshida (10).

The World Championships year of 1995 started with an early sub-2:30 when 39-year-old Tatyana Pozdnyakova UKR won the Houston marathon on 15 January in 2:29:57. On 5 March Nadia Prasad FRA, who had failed to finish the previous Boston and New York events, won $15 000 and a Mercedes with her 2:29:48 in difficult conditions in Los Angeles. With the Osaka marathon called off because of the Kobe earthquake, the first really fast time of the year came on 12 March in Nagoya. The Japanese were surprised by a Pole: Gradus won in a course record 2:27:29 (she also owned the previous record). She was followed by debuting Yukari Komatsu in 2:29:41. "Now I will concentrate in training to get a medal in Atlanta," Gradus said.

For the London marathon on an earlier-than-usual 2 April Dörre requested a halfway split of 73:30. Her main rival in a bid for a fourth title was McColgan, who reportedly was receiving £450 000 for appearing in three London marathons. But McColgan had had knee surgery and would not be a factor. "It was hard to get it right because I'm coming from nothing," she would say after the race in which she finished fifth in 2:31:14. Ondieki pulled out in the week before the race with an Achilles problem.

Jones took the early lead and broke away from the others.

She held it until the 16th mile, when Machado and Kokowska caught her. They were joined by Sobanska and Lemettinen, and Machado decided that it was becoming somewhat crowded. She surged from 30 km, but accomplished nothing. Sobanska and Lemettinen held on and although Machado thought at 40 km that she could still win, she had no answer to Sobanska's kick in the final mile. The Pole won in a PB, while Lemettinen, who had been on the fourteenth floor of a hotel in Osaka when the earthquake hit nearby Kobe, set a national record.

RESULT: 
1 Malgorzata Sobanska 2:27:43
2 Manuela Machado 2:27:53
3 Ritva Lemettinen 2:28:00

A week later three Romanians won the medals in the World Cup marathon in Athens and broke Mota's thirteen-year-old course record: Catuna 2:31:10, Lidia Simon 2:31:46, Cristina Pomacu 2:32:09.

Pippig returned to Boston for the defence of her title in the 99th edition of the famous race on 17 April. The 9 416 runners again had a cool wind blowing from behind when they set off at noon. It was thought that the German's main opposition would come from the two African runners, Meyer and Lorupe. In January Lorupe had beaten Meyer in the Tokyo half marathon (68:39 against 68:58) and in the Lisbon half marathon she had run 18 seconds faster to beat Catuna, McColgan and Lemettinen. Yegorova was also in the field.

But Pippig, who had decided to delay her medical studies for two years, was up to the challenge. She took the lead immediately, with Meyer and Yegorova behind her. Pippig passed 10 miles in 54:21 and halfway in 71:23, still with the same company. Lorupe was 40 m in arrears, but joined them before 25 km (84:48). On the Newton hills the Olympic champion fell off the pace; she would eventually land up in hospital. At 20 miles Meyer and Lorupe collided in their search for their water bottles at a refreshment station and lost about 50 m. They worked their way back to the leader, but expended valuable and unnecessary energy. Soon Lorupe found the pace too much and dropped behind.

"I don't want to say Heartbreak Hill is easy," Pippig later said, "but it is just a little hill compared to how we train." The South African took the lead at one stage, but with just more than 6 km remaining she suffered a cramp in her quadriceps and had to stop briefly to massage it. That was all Pippig needed; she sped away and despite swirling winds and blisters over the final miles she ran to the finish unchallenged in the fastest time of the year (and her eighth marathon win). Lorupe slipped to ninth (2:33:10).

RESULT: 
1 Uta Pippig 2:25:11
2 Elana Meyer 2:26:51
3 Madina Biktagirova 2:29:00

"Not so fast like last year," Pippig remarked. "The race was tactical. The conditions were not so good [and] I had some blisters on my feet. I lost a lot of time in the last 15 km."

Meyer, while admitting that Pippig was the best marathoner in the world, said: "I'm very happy. At least I went from 3rd to 2nd. I'm sure I'll improve on my time. I still believe the marathon will be my best event in the future."

On the last day of the month Kanana won the Shell-Hanse marathon in Hamburg by almost 10 minutes. The previous year she had set a Kenyan record of 2:29:59 here, but this had been surpassed by Lorupe's great run in New York. Kanana reclaimed the record with her 2:27:23.

The top women did not go to Göteborg for the World Championships marathon on 5 August. Pippig wasn't there, Meyer and Lorupe were running the 10000 (Lorupe would win bronze), and the Japanese sent a less-than-exciting squad. One runner who was there was Machado, and she would continue the Portuguese domination of major championship marathons – as well as add another laurel to her own career.

While the race was a triumph for Machado, the Swedish officials were left with a lot of egg on their faces.

The runners had to negotiate four laps of the Ullevi Stadium before going out on the roads – but, inexplicably, they did only three laps! What is more, this error wasn't noticed until long after the race had finished, so it was impossible to correct it at the end when the competitors returned to the stadium. This made the finishing times entirely meaningless.

The 43 runners started at 15:10 in sunny, 24 °C weather. Prasad took the lead, followed by Kanana. They passed 5 km (in reality 4.6 km) in 16:45 – a 2:33:38 pace on a full course. But their stay in the limelight was short-lived, as those who could run well in the heat soon took command. Machado and Catuna drew away from a group of eight just after 15 km and went past halfway in 72:32, well in the lead. Behind them came Sachiyo Seiyama JPN, Monica Pont ESP and Simon.

Over the second half the Portuguese and Romanian fought a seesawing battle, each trying to shake off the other. They were 92 seconds in front, and behind them the field was stringing out, with most of the runners just trying to survive the testing conditions. On the final of three loops, after one hour, 44 minutes of running, Machado surged and opened a gap of 30 m. Catuna came back and tried to get away, but Machado surged for the last time at 40 km and pulled away to a comfortable victory. It came two days to a year after her European Championships victory.

She did not worry too much about the course length debacle. When she heard the following morning that the course had been short, she said: "The goal was to win. Really, I knew I was going to win from the beginning. I've been running 170-180 km per week. This had made me very strong." She had run the true second half in 73:07 and her time on a standard course would have been about 2:27:03, a PB.

RESULT:
1  Manuela Machado POR 2:25:39
2  Anuta Catuna ROM 2:26:25
3  Ornella Ferrara ITA 2:30:11
4  Malgorzata Sobanska POL 2:31:10
5  Ritva Lemettinen FIN 2:31:19
6  Monica Pont ESP 2:31:53
7  Linda Somers USA 2:32:12
8  Sonja Krolik GER 2:32:17
9  Sachiyo Seiyama JPN 2:33:07
10  Lidia Simon ROM 2:33:18

Jones was 16th, while Kanana and Prasad failed to finish. Machado's victory meant that Portugal (read: Mota and Machado) had won seven of the last twelve European and World Championships and Olympic Games marathons; they also finished second, third and fourth once each, and seventh twice. Machado's record was seventh in the '91 Worlds and '92 Olympics, second in the '93 Worlds, and first in both the '94 Europeans and '95 Worlds.[10]

After her Göteborg win she said: "The important thing here is the medal. This is what I wanted. I'm not too concerned about the monetary prizes in other marathons."

Someone who apparently is concerned about these things is Pippig, who on 24 September won $21 000 in Berlin. Her 2:25:37 was close to her Boston time, and her victory was much easier. She allowed Kanana to lead until 30 km (1:42:14), sometimes by as much as 12 seconds. The Kenyan reached 5 km in 16:46, 10 km in 33:26 and 15 km in 50:19 (a 2:21:30 pace). Then the German resident of Boulder put her foot on the pedal and ran away to win by more than 2 minutes. Kanana (2:27:41) just missed her national record, but Rakyia Maraoui MAR (2:28:17) set one in third.

On 15 October Lemettinen scored the best win of her career when she easily beat Jones in Chicago in 2:28:39. On the same day Ana Isabel Alonso, who had run 70:43 in the World Half-marathon Championship, set a Spanish record of 2:26:51. She broke the record of Rios, who was second in 2:28:20. A week later in Reims Russia's Alla Zhilyayeva, who had been fifth in the half marathon, clocked an auspicious debut 2:27:38. Five runners were under 2:30:00; Stefania Statkuviene LIT was second in 2:28:43.

Lorupe made amends for her poor Boston showing in New York on a cold, windy 12 November. Like male winner German Silva she had suffered a tragic personal loss – only hers came in the week before the race when she heard that her sister had died in Kenya. She ended the race crying. It was an easy victory, though: she broke away from Machado with three miles in 5:29, 5:18 and 5:24 on First Avenue.

10. Four days later Machado's countrywoman Fernanda Ribeiro would win the 10000 m and follow that up another three days later with a silver medal in the 5000 m.

RESULT:
1  Tecla Lorupe 2:28:06
2  Manuela Machado POR 2:30:37
3  Lieve Slegers BEL 2:32:08

A week later the Tokyo marathon produced a thrilling and much faster race. Asari (who fell at 38 km) and Yegorova kicked past debutante Mariko Hara JPN in the last 100 m on the track in National Stadium, Asari winning in 2:28:46. The Olympic champion was 2 seconds behind, and 2 seconds ahead of Hara. Naomi Yoshida JPN was fourth (2:28:56).

Earlier in November Chinese Jiang Bo (16) had clocked 2:32:18 in Dailin. At about the same time Kristiansen, whose career had started eight years before Jiang was born, announced that recurring injury problems made it impossible for her to continue competing internationally.

The 110 runners under 2:35:00 and 33 under 2½ hours in 1995 were both records, surpassing the 1993 totals of 99 and 29.

In what is essentially only a quarter century of worldwide participation, women's marathoning has progressed by leaps and bounds. Only 29 years ago the world record was 3:15:22; at the end of 1995 the record was faster than the men's record in 1947. As recently as 1955 the top time on the men's world list was slower than Kristiansen's current world record. At the beginning of 1996 seven countries had national records faster than 2:25:00.

As can be seen in the following table of performers on the annual world lists, the women's standard is showing the same levelling off that is evident in the men's performances over the last few years but, in contrast to the men, the women did not experience an upturn in 1994. In 1995 there was some progress lower down the list, though.

|      | 10th | 50th | 100th |
| --- | --- | --- | --- |
| 1980 | 2:35:05 | 2:44:28 | 2:49:08 |
| 1986 | 2:29:51 | 2:34:41 | 2:37:58 |
| 1987 | 2:29:56 | 2:33:22 | 2:37:06 |
| 1988 | 2:28:40 | 2:31:56 | 2:35:29 |
| 1989 | 2:28:45 | 2:30:35 | 2:37:04 |
| 1990 | 2:28:56 | 2:33:19 | 2:36:48 |
| 1991 | 2:27:43 | 2:32:58 | 2:35:40 |
| 1992 | 2:27:42 | 2:32:20 | 2:36:14 |
| 1993 | 2:26:26 | 2:31:32 | 2:35:04 |
| 1994 | 2:26:26 | 2:31:57 | 2:35:07 |
| 1995 | 2:28:00 | 2:31:48 | 2:34:30 |

At the end of 1995 the all-time list was dominated by runners from Europe and Asia. The 2:20:00 barrier remained as elusive as ever, with the world record still 66 seconds away from the breakthrough. Thirteen runners had run 22 times faster than 2:25:00, with Kristiansen's six being by far the most by any woman (Benoit had half that). An all-time list as at the end of 1995 appears in the Results and Statistics section on p. 190.

# RESULTS AND STATISTICS

## Olympic Games

Distance is 42.195 km unless indicated otherwise. Current ATFS (Association of Track & Field Statisticians) abbreviations for countries are used, such as RSA for Republic of South Africa (although the country became a republic only in 1961). All lists are as at the end of 1995.

### 1896 (ATHENS, 10 APRIL, 40 KM)

1. Spiridon Louis GRE — 2:58:50
2. Charilaos Vasilakos GRE — 3:06:03
3. Gyula Kellner HUN — 3:09:35

### 1900 (PARIS, 19 JULY, 40.26 KM)

1. Michel Theato FRA — 2:59:45
2. Emile Champion FRA — 3:04:17
3. Ernst Fast SWE — 3:37:14

### 1904 (ST. LOUIS, 30 AUGUST, 40 KM)

1. Thomas Hicks USA — 3:28:53
2. Albert Corey USA — 3:34:52
3. Arthur Newton USA — 3:47:33
9. **Lentauw RSA**
12. **Yamasani RSA**

### 1908 (LONDON, 24 JULY)

1. John Hayes USA — 2:55:18.4
2. **Charles Hefferon RSA** — **2:56:06**
3. Joseph Forshaw USA — 2:57:10.4

### 1912 (STOCKHOLM, 14 JULY, 40.2 KM)

1. **Kenneth McArthur RSA** — **2:36:54.8**
2. **Christian Gitsham RSA** — **2:37:52**
3. Gaston Strobino USA — 2:38:42.4

### 1920 (ANTWERP, 22 AUGUST, 42.75 KM)

1. Johannes Kolehmainen FIN — 2:32:35.8
2. Juri Lossmann EST — 2:32:48.6
3. Valerio Arri ITA — 2:36:32.8

### 1924 (PARIS, 13 JULY)

1. Albin Stenroos FIN — 2:41:22.6
2. Romeo Bertini ITA — 2:47:19.6
3. Clarence DeMar USA — 2:48:14
19. **Harry Phillips RSA** — **3:07:13**

### 1928 (AMSTERDAM, 5 AUGUST)

1. Boughera El Ouafi FRA — 2:32:57
2. Manuel Plaza CHI — 2:33:23
3. Martti Marttelin FIN — 2:35:02
40. **Marthinus Steytler RSA** — **2:57:21**

### 1932 (LOS ANGELES, 7 AUGUST)

1. Juan Carlos Zabala ARG — 2:31:36
2. Samuel Ferris GBR — 2:31:55
3. Armas Toivonen FIN — 2:32.12

### 1936 (BERLIN, 9 AUGUST)

1. Kitei Son JPN — 2:29:19.2
2. Ernest Harper GBR — 2:31:23.2
3. Shoryu Nan JPN — 2:31:42
6. **Johannes Coleman RSA** — **2:36:17**
8. **Henry Gibson RSA** — **2:38:04**
27. **Thomas Lalande RSA** — **2:57:20**

### 1948 (LONDON, 7 AUGUST)

1. Delfo Cabrera ARG — 2:34:51.6
2. Thomas Richards GBR — 2:35:07.6
3. Etienne Gailly BEL — 2:35:33.6
4. **Johannes Coleman RSA** — **2:36:06**
6. **Sydney Luyt RSA** — **2:38:11**

### 1952 (HELSINKI, 27 JULY)

1. Emil Zátopek TCH — 2:23:03.2
2. Reinaldo Gorno ARG — 2:25:35
3. Gustaf Jansson SWE — 2:26:07
10. **Wallace Hayward RSA** — **2:31:50.2**
11. **Sydney Luyt RSA** — **2:32:41**
19. **William Keith RSA** — **2:34:38**

### 1956 (MELBOURNE, 1 DECEMBER)

1. Alain Mimoun FRA — 2:25:00
2. Franjo Mihalic YUG — 2:26:32
3. Veikko Karvonen FIN — 2:27:47
14. **Mercer Davies RSA** — **2:39:48**

### 1960 (ROME, 10 SEPTEMBER)

1. Abebe Bikila ETH — 2:15:16.2
2. Rhadi Ben Abdesselem MAR — 2:15:41.6
3. Barrington Magee NZL — 2:17:18.2
13. **Keith James RSA** — **2:22:58.6**

### 1964 (TOKYO, 21 OCTOBER)

1. Abebe Bikila ETH — 2:12:11.2
2. Basil Heatley GBR — 2:16:19.2
3. Kokichi Tsuburaya JPN — 2:16:22.8

### 1968 (MEXICO CITY, 20 OCTOBER)

1. Mamo Wolde ETH — 2:20:26.4
2. Kenji Kimihara JPN — 2:23:31
3. Michael Ryan NZL — 2:23:45

### 1972 (MUNICH, 10 SEPTEMBER)

1. Frank Shorter USA — 2:12:19.8
2. Karel Lismont BEL — 2:14:31.8
3. Mamo Wolde ETH — 2.15.00.4

### 1976 (MONTREAL, 31 JULY)

1. Waldemar Cierpinski GDR — 2:09:55
2. Frank Shorter USA — 2:10:45.8
3. Karel Lismont BEL — 2:11:12.6

### 1980 (MOSCOW, 1 AUGUST)

1. Waldemar Cierpinski GDR — 2:11:03
2. Gerard Nijboer HOL — 2:11:20
3. Satymkul Dzhumanazarov URS — 2:11:35

### 1984 (LOS ANGELES, 12 AUGUST)

1. Carlos Lopes POR — 2:09:21
2. John Treacy IRL — 2:09:56
3. Charlie Spedding GBR — 2:09:58

#### Women (5 August)

1. Joan Benoit USA — 2:24:52
2. Grete Waitz NOR — 2:26:18
3. Rosa Mota POR — 2:26:57

### 1988 (SEOUL, 2 OCTOBER)

1. Gelindo Bordin ITA — 2:10:32
2. Douglas Wakiihuri KEN — 2:10:47
3. Ahmed Salah DJI — 2:10:59

#### Women (23 September)

1. Rosa Mota POR — 2:25:40
2. Lisa Martin AUS — 2:25:53
3. Katrin Dörre GDR — 2:26:21

### 1992 (BARCELONA, 9 AUGUST)

1. Hwang Young-jo KOR — 2:13:23
2. Koichi Morishita JPN — 2:13:45
3. Stephan Freigang GER — 2:14:00
25. **Abel Mokibe RSA** — **2:17:24**

#### Women (1 August)

1. Valentina Yegorova RUS — 2:32:41
2. Yuko Arimori JPN — 2:32:49
3. Lorraine Moller NZL — 2:33:59
9. **Colleen de Reuck RSA** — **2:39:03**

# World Championships

### 1983 (Helsinki, 14 August)

| | | |
|---|---|---|
| 1. | Robert de Castella AUS | 2:10:03 |
| 2. | Kebede Balcha ETH | 2:10:27 |
| 3. | Waldemar Cierpinski GDR | 2:10:37 |

#### Women (7 August)

| | | |
|---|---|---|
| 1. | Grete Waitz NOR | 2:28:09 |
| 2. | Marianne Dickerson USA | 2:31:09 |
| 3. | Raisa Smekhnova URS | 2:31:13 |

### 1987 (Rome, 6 September)

| | | |
|---|---|---|
| 1. | Douglas Wakiihuri KEN | 2:11:48 |
| 2. | Ahmed Salah DJI | 2:12:30 |
| 3. | Gelindo Bordin ITA | 2:12:40 |

#### Women (29 August)

| | | |
|---|---|---|
| 1. | Rosa Mota POR | 2:25:17 |
| 2. | Zoya Ivanova URS | 2:32:38 |
| 3. | Jocelyne Villeton FRA | 2:32:53 |

### 1991 (Tokyo, 1 September)

| | | |
|---|---|---|
| 1. | Hiromi Taniguchi JPN | 2:14:57 |
| 2. | Ahmed Salah DJI | 2:15:26 |
| 3. | Steve Spence USA | 2:15:36 |

#### Women (25 August)

| | | |
|---|---|---|
| 1. | Wanda Panfil POL | 2:29:53 |
| 2. | Sachiko Yamashita JPN | 2:29:57 |
| 3. | Katrin Dörre GER | 2:30:10 |

### 1993 (Stuttgart, 14 August)

| | | |
|---|---|---|
| 1. | Mark Plaatjes USA | 2:13:57 |
| 2. | Lucketz Swartbooi NAM | 2:14:11 |
| 3. | Bert van Vlaanderen HOL | 2:15:12 |

#### Women (15 August)

| | | |
|---|---|---|
| 1. | Junko Asari JPN | 2:30:03 |
| 2. | Manuela Machado POR | 2:30:54 |
| 3. | Tomoe Abe JPN | 2:31:01 |
| **7.** | **Frith van der Merwe RSA** | **2:35:56** |

### 1995 (Göteborg, 12 August)

| | | |
|---|---|---|
| 1. | Martin Fiz ESP | 2:11:41 |
| 2. | Dionicio Cerón MEX | 2:12:13 |
| 3. | Luiz dos Santos BRA | 2:12:49 |
| **32.** | **Martin Ndwheni RSA** | **2:23:42** |
| **36.** | **Isaac Tshabalala RSA** | **2:24:42** |
| **45.** | **Matthews Temane RSA** | **2:31:24** |

#### Women (5 August; 400 m short)

| | | |
|---|---|---|
| 1. | Manuela Machado POR | 2:25:39 |
| 2. | Anuta Catuna ROM | 2:26:25 |
| 3. | Ornella Ferrara ITA | 2:30:11 |

# World Cup

### 1985 (Hiroshima, 14 April)

| | | |
|---|---|---|
| 1. | Ahmed Salah DJI | 2:08:09 |
| 2. | Takeyuki Nakayama JPN | 2:08:15 |
| 3. | Djama Robleh DJI | 2:08:26 |

Teams: 1. Djibouti, 2. Japan, 3. Ethiopia

#### Women (13 April)

| | | |
|---|---|---|
| 1. | Katrin Dörre GDR | 2:33:30 |
| 2. | Zoya Ivanova URS | 2:34:17 |
| 3. | Karolina Szabó HUN | 2:34:57 |

Teams: 1. Italy, 2. USSR, 3. East Germany

### 1987 (Seoul, 12 April)

| | | |
|---|---|---|
| 1. | Ahmed Salah DJI | 2:10:55 |
| 2. | Taisuke Kodama JPN | 2:11:23 |
| 3. | Salvatore Bettiol ITA | 2:11:28 |

Teams: 1. Italy, 2. Japan, 3. France

#### Women (11 April)

| | | |
|---|---|---|
| 1. | Zoya Ivanova URS | 2:30:39 |
| 2. | Maria Lelut FRA | 2:31:27 |
| 3. | Katrin Dörre GDR | 2:31:30 |

Teams: 1. USSR, 2. East Germany, 3. France

### 1989 (Milan, 16 April)

| | | |
|---|---|---|
| 1. | Metaferia Zeleke ETH | 2:10:28 |
| 2. | Dereje Nedi ETH | 2:10:36 |
| 3. | Gianni Poli ITA | 2:10:49 |

Teams: 1. Ethiopia, 2. Italy, 3. France

#### Women (15 April)

| | | |
|---|---|---|
| 1. | Sue Marchiano USA | 2:30:48 |
| 2. | Miyako Miyahara JPN | 2:35:16 |
| 3. | Uta Pippig GDR | 2:35:17 |

Teams: 1. USSR, 2. USA, 3. China

### 1991 (London, 21 April)

| | | |
|---|---|---|
| 1. | Yakov Tolstikov URS | 2:09:17 |
| 2. | Manuel Matias POR | 2:10:21 |
| 3. | Jan Huruk POL | 2:10:21 |

Teams: 1. Great Britain, 2. Portugal, 3. Poland

#### Women

| | | |
|---|---|---|
| 1. | Rosa Mota POR | 2:26:14 |
| 2. | Francie Larrieu Smith USA | 2:27:35 |
| 3. | Valentina Yegorova URS | 2:28:18 |

Teams: 1. USSR, 2. Italy, 3. France
(Staged in conjunction with the London Marathon.)

### 1993 (San Sebastián, 31 October)

| | | |
|---|---|---|
| 1. | Richard Nerurkar GBR | 2:10:03 |
| 2. | Severino Bernardini ITA | 2:10:12 |
| 3. | Kebede Gemechu ETH | 2:10:16 |
| **31.** | **Johannes Maremane RSA** | **2:14:44** |
| **47.** | **Jacob Ledwaba RSA** | **2:18:11** |
| **57.** | **Adam Motlagale RSA** | **2:20:24** |
| **60.** | **Piet Ramudzuli RSA** | **2:22:00** |
| **75.** | **Daniel Mbuli RSA** | **2:36:13** |

Teams: 1. Ethiopia, 2. Italy, 3. Great Britain, **11. South Africa**

#### Women

| | | |
|---|---|---|
| 1. | Wang Junxia CHN | 2:28:16 |
| 2. | Zhang Linli CHN | 2:29:42 |
| 3. | Zhang Lirong CHN | 2:29:45 |
| **42.** | **Blanche Moila RSA** | **2:47:02** |
| **49.** | **Jean Rayner RSA** | **2:55:01** |
| **52.** | **Helen Lucre RSA** | **3:10:01** |

Teams: 1. China, 2. Spain, 3. Russia; **South Africa incomplete team**

### 1995 (Athens, 9 April)

| | | |
|---|---|---|
| 1. | Douglas Wakiihuri KEN | 2:12:01 |
| 2. | Takahiro Sunada JPN | 2:12:16 |
| 3. | Davide Milesi ITA | 2:14:09 |
| **10.** | **Joseph Skosana RSA** | **2:15:47** |
| **21.** | **Peter Lebopo RSA** | **2:19:37** |
| **27.** | **Michael Scout RSA** | **2:20:58** |

Teams: 1. Italy, 2. France, 3. Spain, **6. South Africa**

#### Women

| | | |
|---|---|---|
| 1. | Anuta Catuna ROM | 2:31:10 |
| 2. | Lidia Simon ROM | 2:31:46 |
| 3. | Cristina Pomacu ROM | 2:32:09 |
| **49.** | **Esme Koopman RSA** | **3:00:41** |

Teams: 1. Romania, 2. Russia, 3. Italy; **South Africa incomplete team**

# Commonwealth Games

From 1930 to 1950 the championships were called the British Empire Games; from 1954 to 1962 the British Empire and Commonwealth Games; from 1966 to 1970 the British Commonwealth Games; thereafter the Commonwealth Games.

### 1930 (HAMILTON, 21 AUGUST)

| | | |
|---|---|---|
| 1. | Duncan Wright Sco | 2:43:43 |
| 2. | Samuel Ferris Eng | no time |
| 3. | John Miles CAN | no time |

### 1934 (LONDON, 7 AUGUST)

| | | |
|---|---|---|
| 1. | Harold Webster CAN | 2:40:36 |
| 2. | Donald Robertson Sco | 2:45:08 |
| 3. | Duncan Wright Sco | 2:56:20 |

### 1938 (SYDNEY, 7 FEBRUARY)

| | | |
|---|---|---|
| 1. | **Johannes Coleman RSA** | **2:30:49.8** |
| 2. | Albert Norris Eng | 2:37:57 |
| 3. | **Henry ('Jack') Gibson RSA** | **2:38:20** |

### 1950 (AUCKLAND, 11 FEBRUARY)

| | | |
|---|---|---|
| 1. | Jack Holden Eng | 2:32:57 |
| 2. | **Sydney Luyt RSA** | **2:37:02.2** |
| 3. | Jack Clarke NZL | 2:39:26.4 |

### 1954 (VANCOUVER, 7 AUGUST)

| | | |
|---|---|---|
| 1. | Joseph McGhee Sco | 2:39:36 |
| 2. | **Jack Mekler RSA** | **2:40:57** |
| 3. | **Johannes Barnard RSA** | **2:51:49.8** |

### 1958 (CARDIFF, 24 JULY)

| | | |
|---|---|---|
| 1. | David Power AUS | 2:22:45.6 |
| 2. | **Johannes Barnard RSA** | **2:22:57.4** |
| 3. | Peter Wilkinson Eng | 2:24:42 |
| 13. | **Martinus Wiid RSA** | **2:36:00** |

### 1962 (PERTH, 29 NOVEMBER)

| | | |
|---|---|---|
| 1. | Brian Kilby Eng | 2:21:17 |
| 2. | David Power AUS | 2:22:15.4 |
| 3. | Rodney Bonella AUS | 2:24:07 |

### 1966 (KINGSTON, 11 AUGUST)

| | | |
|---|---|---|
| 1. | James Alder Sco | 2:22:07.8 |
| 2. | William Adcocks Eng | 2:22:13 |
| 3. | Michael Ryan NZL | 2:27:59 |

### 1970 (EDINBURGH, 23 JULY)

| | | |
|---|---|---|
| 1. | Ronald Hill Eng | 2:09:28 |
| 2. | James Alder Sco | 2:12:04 |
| 3. | Donald Faircloth Eng | 2:12:19 |

### 1974 (CHRISTCHURCH, 31 JANUARY)

| | | |
|---|---|---|
| 1. | Ian Thompson Eng | 2:09:12 |
| 2. | John ('Jack') Foster NZL | 2:11:18.6 |
| 3. | Richard Mabuza SWA | 2:12:54.4 |

### 1978 (EDMONTON, 11 AUGUST)

| | | |
|---|---|---|
| 1. | Gidamis Shahanga TAN | 2:15:39.8 |
| 2. | Jerome Drayton CAN | 2:16:13.5 |
| 3. | Paul Bannon CAN | 2:16:52 |

### 1982 (BRISBANE, 8 OCTOBER)

| | | |
|---|---|---|
| 1. | Robert de Castella AUS | 2:09:18 |
| 2. | Juma Ikangaa TAN | 2:09:30 |
| 3. | Mike Gratton Eng | 2:12:06 |

### 1986 (EDINBURGH, 1 AUGUST)

| | | |
|---|---|---|
| 1. | Robert de Castella AUS | 2:10:15 |
| 2. | Dave Edge CAN | 2:11:08 |
| 3. | Steve Moneghetti AUS | 2:11:18 |

#### Women

| | | |
|---|---|---|
| 1. | Lisa Martin AUS | 2:26:07 |
| 2. | Lorraine Moller NZL | 2:28:17 |
| 3. | Odette Lapierre CAN | 2:31:48 |

### 1990 (AUCKLAND, 30 JANUARY)

| | | |
|---|---|---|
| 1. | Douglas Wakiihuri KEN | 2:10:27 |
| 2. | Seve Moneghetti AUS | 2:10:34 |
| 3. | Simon Robert Naali TAN | 2:10:38 |

#### Women (31 January)

| | | |
|---|---|---|
| 1. | Lisa Martin AUS | 2:25:28 |
| 2. | Tani Ruckle AUS | 2:33:15 |
| 3. | Angela Pain Eng | 2:36:35 |

### 1994 (VICTORIA, 28 AUGUST)

| | | |
|---|---|---|
| 1. | Steve Moneghetti AUS | 2:11:49 |
| 2. | Sean Quilty AUS | 2:14:57 |
| 3. | Mark Hudspith Eng | 2:15:11 |
| 15. | **Owen MacHelm RSA** | **2:20:39** |

#### Women (27 August)

| | | |
|---|---|---|
| 1. | Carole Rouillard CAN | 2:30:41 |
| 2. | Lizanne Bussières CAN | 2:31:07 |
| 3. | Yvonne Danson Eng | 2:32:24 |

# African Games

### 1973 (LAGOS, 14 JANUARY)

| | | |
|---|---|---|
| 1. | Mamo Wolde ETH | 2:27:32 |
| 2. | Lengissa Bedane ETH | 2:28:16 |
| 3. | Richard Mabuza SWA | 2:34:17.7 |

### 1978 (ALGIERS, 27 JULY)

| | | |
|---|---|---|
| 1. | Richard Mabuza SWA | 2:21:53 |
| 2. | Dereje Nedi ETH | 2:23:08 |
| 3. | Gebru Gurmu ETH | 2:27:35 |

### 1987 (NAIROBI, 10 AUGUST)

| | | |
|---|---|---|
| 1. | Belayneh Dinsamo ETH | 2:14:47 |
| 2. | Dereje Nedi ETH | 2:15:27 |
| 3. | Kebede Balcha ETH | 2:16:07 |

### 1991 (CAIRO, SEPTEMBER)

| | | |
|---|---|---|
| 1. | Tena Negere ETH | 2:31:17 |
| 2. | Ernest Tjela LES | 2:31:42 |
| 3. | Allaoua Khéllil ALG | 2:32:29 |

### 1995 (HARARE, 17 SEPTEMBER)

| | | |
|---|---|---|
| 1. | Nicholas Nyengere ZIM | 2:20:08 |
| 2. | Honest Mutsairo ZIM | 2:20:15 |
| 3. | Simon Bisiligilwa TAN | 2:20:21 |

#### Women

| | | |
|---|---|---|
| 1. | **Jowaine Parrott RSA** | **2:55:09** |
| 2. | Emebete Abosa ETH | 3:01:53 |
| 3. | Elgenesh Alemu ETH | 3:08:43 |

### 1934 (TURIN, 9 SEPTEMBER)

| | | |
|---|---|---|
| 1. | Armas Toivonen FIN | 2:52:29 |
| 2. | Thore Enochsson SWE | 2:54:35.6 |
| 3. | Aurelio Genghini ITA | 2:55:03.4 |

### 1938 (PARIS, 4 SEPTEMBER)

| | | |
|---|---|---|
| 1. | Väinö Muinonen FIN | 2:37:28.8 |
| 2. | Squire Yarrow GBR | 2:39:03 |
| 3. | Henry Palmé SWE | 2:42:13.6 |

### 1946 (OSLO, 22 AUGUST)

| | | |
|---|---|---|
| 1. | Mikko Hietanen FIN | 2:24:55 |
| 2. | Väinö Muinonen FIN | 2:26:08 |
| 3. | Yakov Punko URS | 2:26:21 |

### 1950 (BRUSSELS, 23 AUGUST)

| | | |
|---|---|---|
| 1. | Jack Holden GBR | 2:32:13.2 |
| 2. | Veikko Karvonen FIN | 2:32:45 |
| 3. | Feodosiy Vanin URS | 2:33:47 |

### 1954 (BERNE, 25 AUGUST)

| | | |
|---|---|---|
| 1. | Veikko Karvonen FIN | 2:24:51.6 |
| 2. | Boris Grishayev URS | 2:24:55.6 |
| 3. | Ivan Filin URS | 2:25:26.6 |

### 1958 (STOCKHOLM, 24 AUGUST)

| | | |
|---|---|---|
| 1. | Sergey Popov URS | 2:15:17 |
| 2. | Ivan Filin URS | 2:20:50.6 |
| 3. | Fredrick Norris GBR | 2:21:15 |

### 1962 (BELGRADE, 16 SEPTEMBER)

| | | |
|---|---|---|
| 1. | Brian Kilby GBR | 2:23:18.8 |
| 2. | Aurele Vandendriessche BEL | 2:24:02 |
| 3. | Viktor Baikov URS | 2:24:19.8 |

### 1966 (BUDAPEST, 4 SEPTEMBER)

| | | |
|---|---|---|
| 1. | James Hogan GBR | 2:20:04.6 |
| 2. | Aurele Vandendriessche BEL | 2:21:43.6 |
| 3. | Gyula Toth HUN | 2:22:02 |

### 1969 (ATHENS, 21 SEPTEMBER)

| | | |
|---|---|---|
| 1. | Ronald Hill GBR | 2:16:47.8 |
| 2. | Gaston Roelants BEL | 2:17:22.2 |
| 3. | James Alder GBR | 2:19:05.8 |

### 1971 (HELSINKI, 15 AUGUST)

| | | |
|---|---|---|
| 1. | Karel Lismont BEL | 2:13:09 |
| 2. | Trevor Wright GBR | 2:13:59.6 |
| 3. | Ronald Hill GBR | 2:14:34.8 |

### 1974 (ROME, 8 SEPTEMBER)

| | | |
|---|---|---|
| 1. | Ian Thompson GBR | 2:13:18.8 |
| 2. | Eckhard Lesse GDR | 2:14:57.4 |
| 3. | Gaston Roelants BEL | 2:16:29.6 |

### 1978 (PRAGUE, 3 SEPTEMBER)

| | | |
|---|---|---|
| 1. | Leonid Moseyev URS | 2:11:57.5 |
| 2. | Nikolay Penzin URS | 2:11:59 |
| 3. | Karel Lismont BEL | 2:12:07.4 |

### 1982 (ATHENS, 12 SEPTEMBER)

| | | |
|---|---|---|
| 1. | Gerard Nijboer HOL | 2:15:16 |
| 2. | Armand Parmentier BEL | 2:15:51 |
| 3. | Karel Lismont BEL | 2:16:04 |

#### Women

| | | |
|---|---|---|
| 1. | Rosa Mota POR | 2:36:04 |
| 2. | Laura Fogli ITA | 2:36:29 |
| 3. | Ingrid Kristiansen NOR | 2:36:39 |

### 1986 (STUTTGART, 30 AUGUST)

| | | |
|---|---|---|
| 1. | Gelindo Bordin ITA | 2:10:54 |
| 2. | Orlando Pizzolato ITA | 2:10:57 |
| 3. | Herbert Steffny FRG | 2:11:30 |

#### Women (26 August)

| | | |
|---|---|---|
| 1. | Rosa Mota POR | 2:28:38 |
| 2. | Laura Fogli ITA | 2:32:52 |
| 3. | Yekaterina Khramenkova URS | 2:34:18 |

### 1990 (SPLIT, 1 SEPTEMBER)

| | | |
|---|---|---|
| 1. | Gelindo Bordin ITA | 2:14:02 |
| 2. | Giovanni Poli ITA | 2:14:55 |
| 3. | Dominique Chauvelier FRA | 2:15:20 |

#### Women (27 August)

| | | |
|---|---|---|
| 1. | Rosa Mota POR | 2:31:27 |
| 2. | Valentina Yegorova URS | 2:31:32 |
| 3. | Maria Lelut FRA | 2:35:51 |

### 1994 (HELSINKI, 14 AUGUST)

| | | |
|---|---|---|
| 1. | Martin Fiz ESP | 2:10:31 |
| 2. | Diego Garcia ESP | 2:10:46 |
| 3. | Alberto Juzdado ESP | 2:11:18 |

#### Women (7 August)

| | | |
|---|---|---|
| 1. | Manuela Machado POR | 2:29:54 |
| 2. | Maria Curatolo ITA | 2:30:33 |
| 3. | Adriana Barbu ROM | 2:30:55 |

# Pan-American Games

### 1951 (BUENOS AIRES, 6 MARCH)

1. Delfo Cabrera ARG — 2:35:00.2
2. Reinaldo Gorno ARG — 2:45:00
3. Luis Velazquez GUA — 2:46:02.8

### 1955 (MEXICO CITY, 19 MARCH)

1. Doroteo Flores GUA — 2:59:09.2
2. Onesimo Rodriguez MEX — 3:02:25.6
3. Luis Velazquez GUA — 3:05:25.2

### 1959 (CHICAGO, 2 SEPTEMBER)

1. John Kelley USA — 2:27:54.2
2. Jim Green USA — 2:32:16.9
3. Gordon Dickson CAN — 2:36:18.6

### 1963 (SAO PAULO, 4 MAY)

1. Fidel Negrete MEX — 2:27:55.6
2. Gordon McKenzie USA — 2:31:17.2
3. Peter McArdle USA — 2:34:14

### 1967 (WINNIPEG, 5 AUGUST)

1. Andrew Boychuk CAN — 2:23:02.4
2. Agustin Calle COL — 2:25:50.2
3. Alfredo Penaloza MEX — 2:27:48.2

### 1971 (CALI, 5 AUGUST)

1. Frank Shorter USA — 2:22:40
2. Jose Gaspar MEX — 2:26:30
3. Hernan Barreneche COL — 2:27:19

### 1975 (MEXICO CITY, 20 OCTOBER)

1. Rigoberto Mendoza CUB — 2:25:02.9
2. Charles Smead USA — 2:25:31.6
3. Thomas Howard CAN — 2:25:45.5

### 1979 (SAN JUAN, 14 JULY)

1. Radames Gonzalez CUB — 2:24:09
2. Luis Barbosa COL — 2:24:44
3. Rick Hughson CAN — 2:25:34

### 1983 (CARACAS, 28 AUGUST)

1. Jorge Gonzalez PUR — 2:12:43
2. Cesar Mercado PUR — 2:20:29
3. Miguel Cruz MEX — 2:21:11

### 1987 (INDIANAPOLIS, 9 AUGUST)

1. Ivo Rodrigues BRA — 2:20:13
2. Ronald Lanzoni CRC — 2:20:39
3. Jorge Gonzalez PUR — 2:21:14

#### Women

1. Maricarmen Cardenas MEX — 2:52:06
2. Debbie Warner USA — 2:54:49
3. Maribel Durruty CUB — 2:56:21

### 1991 (HAVANA, 3 AUGUST)

1. Alberto Cuba CUB — 2:19:27
2. José Santana BRA — 2:19:29
3. Radamés González CUB — 2:23:05

#### Women

1. Olga Avalos (Appell) MEX — 2:43:36
2. Maribel Durruty CUB — 2:46:04
3. Emperatriz Wilson CUB — 2:48:48

### 1995 (MAR DEL PLATA, 25 MARCH)

1. Benjamin Paredes MEX — 2:14:44
2. Mark Coogan USA — 2:15:21
3. Luiz da Silva BRA — 2:15:46

#### Women

1. Maria Trujillo USA — 2:43:56
2. Jennifer Martin USA — 2:44:10
3. Emma Cabrera MEX — 2:46:36

# Asian Games

### 1951 (NEW DELHI, 11 MARCH)

1. Chota Singh IND — 2:42:58.6
2. Katsuo Nishida JPN — 2:49:03
3. Surat Singh IND — 2:53:49.3

### 1954 (MANILA)

No marathon

### 1958 (TOKYO, 29 MAY)

1. Lee Chang Hoon KOR — 2:32:55
2. Myitung Naw BUR — 2:42:46
3. Nobuyoshi Sadanaga JPN — 2:43:44

### 1962 (JAKARTA, 29 AUGUST)*

1. Masayuki Nagata JPN — 2:34:54.2
2. Mohamed Jousef PAK — 2:43:02
3. Myitung Naw BUR — 2:49:37.1

### 1966 (BANGKOK, 15 DECEMBER)

1. Kenji Kimihara JPN — 2:33:22.8
2. Morio Shigematsu JPN — 2:35:04.2
3. Lee Sang Hoon KOR — 2:40:56

*) The 1962 Games were declared unofficial by the International Amateur Athletic Federation (IAAF) as entries from Israel and Taiwan were prohibited. The IAAF did not grant a permit for the 1978 Games as Israel was not invited.

### 1970 (BANGKOK, 15 DECEMBER)

1. Kenji Kimihara JPN — 2:21:03
2. Yoshiro Mifune JPN — 2:24:20.8
3. Kang Myung Kwang KOR — 2:26:47.8

### 1974

No marathon

### 1978 (BANGKOK, 17 DECEMBER)*

1. Mineteru Sakamoto JPN — 2:15:29.7
2. Chang Sop Choe PRK — 2:15:57.4
3. Chun Son Goe PRK — 2:16:10.3

### 1982 (NEW DELHI, 2 DECEMBER)

1. Kim Yang-kon KOR — 2:22:21
2. Fumiaki Abe JPN — 2:24:09
3. Seetharama Kukkappa IND — 2:25:07

### 1986 (SEOUL, 5 OCTOBER)

1. Takeyuki Nakayama JPN — 2:08:21
2. Hiromi Taniguchi JPN — 2:10:08
3. Ryu Jae-Sung KOR — 2:16:55

#### Women

1. Eriko Asai JPN — 2:41:03
2. Misako Miyahara JPN — 2:41:36
3. Weng Yanmin CHN — 2:42:21

### 1990 (BEIJING, 30 SEPTEMBER)

1. Kim Won-tak KOR — 2:12:56
2. Shimizu Satoru JPN — 2:14:46
3. Choi Chol-ho PRK — 2:18:18

#### Women

1. Zhao Youfeng CHN — 2:35:19
2. Kumi Araki JPN — 2:35:34
3. Lee Mi-ok KOR — 2:36:31

### 1994 (HIROSHIMA, 9 OCTOBER)

1. Hwang Young-cho KOR — 2:11:13
2. Toshiyuki Hayata JPN — 2:11:57
3. Kim Jae-ryong — 2:13:12

#### Women

1. Zhong Huandi CHN — 2:29:32
2. Zhang Lirong CHN — 2:36:27
3. Nobuko Fujimura JPN — 2:37:03

Race date is 19 April and country is USA unless indicated otherwise. South Africans in the first ten are shown.

| | | |
|---|---|---|
| 1897 | John J. McDermott | 2:55:10 |
| 1898 | Ronald J. McDonald | 2:42:00 |
| 1899 | Lawrence J. Brignolia | 2:54:38 |
| 1900 | James J. Caffrey CAN | 2:39:44.4 |
| 1901 | James J. Caffrey CAN | 2:29:23.6 |
| 1902 | Samuel A. Mellor | 2:43:12 |
| 1903[1] | John C. Lorden | 2:41:29.8 |
| 1904 | Michael Spring | 2:38:04.4 |
| 1905 | Frederick Lorz | 2:38:25.4 |
| 1906 | Timothy Ford | 2:45:45 |
| 1907 | Thomas Longboat CAN | 2:24:24 |
| 1908[1] | Thomas P. Morrissey | 2:25:43.2 |
| 1909 | Henri Renaud | 2:53:36.8 |
| 1910 | Frederick Cameron CAN | 2:28:52.4 |
| 1911 | Clarence H. DeMar | 2:21:39.6 |
| 1912 | Michael Ryan | 2:21:18.2 |
| 1913 | Fritz Carlson | 2:25:14.8 |
| 1914[1] | James Duffy CAN | 2:25:01.2 |
| 1915 | Edouard Fabre CAN | 2:31:41.2 |
| 1916 | Arthur V. Roth | 2:27:16.4 |
| 1917 | William Kennedy | 2:28:37.2 |
| 1918 | Camp Devens Service Team | 2:24:53 |
| 1919 | Carl W.A. Linder | 2:29:13.4 |
| 1920 | Peter Trivoulidas | 2:29:31 |
| 1921 | Frank Zuna | 2:18:57.6 |
| 1922 | Clarence H. DeMar | 2:18:10 |
| 1923 | Clarence H. DeMar | 2:23:37.4 |
| 1924 | Clarence H. DeMar | 2:29:40.2 |
| 1925 | Charles L. Mellor | 2:33:00.6 |
| 1926 | John C. Miles CAN | 2:25:40.4 |
| 1927 | Clarence H. DeMar | 2:40:22.2 |
| 1928 | Clarence H. DeMar | 2:37:07.8 |
| 1929 | John C. Miles CAN | 2:33:08.6 |
| 1930 | Clarence H. DeMar | 2:34:48.2 |
| 1931[1] | James P. Henigan | 2:46:45.8 |
| 1932 | Paul de Bruyn GER | 2:33:36.4 |
| 1933 | Leslie S. Pawson | 2:31:01.6 |
| 1934 | David Komonen CAN | 2:32:53.8 |
| 1935 | John A. Kelley | 2:32:07.4 |
| 1936 | Ellison M. Brown | 2:33:40.8 |
| 1937 | Walter Young CAN | 2:33:20 |
| 1938 | Leslie S. Pawson | 2:35:34.8 |
| 1939 | Ellison M. Brown | 2:28:51.8 |
| 1940 | Gérard Côté CAN | 2:38:28.6 |
| 1941 | Leslie S. Pawson | 2:30:38 |

| | | |
|---|---|---|
| 1942 | Bernard J. Smith | 2:26:51.2 |
| 1943[2] | Gérard Côté CAN | 2:28:25.8 |
| 1944 | Gérard Côté CAN | 2:31:50.4 |
| 1945 | John A. Kelley | 2:30:40.2 |
| 1946[1] | Stylianos Kyriakidis GRE | 2:29:27 |
| 1947 | Yun Bok Suh KOR | 2:25:39 |
| 1948 | Gérard Côté CAN | 2:31:02 |
| 1949 | Karl Gosta Leandersson SWE | 2:31:50.8 |
| 1950 | Kee Yong Ham KOR | 2:32:39 |
| 1951 | Shigeki Tanaka JPN | 2:27:45 |
| 1952 | Doroteo Flores GUA | 2:31:53 |
| 1953[1] | Keizo Yamada JPN | 2:18:51 |
| 1954 | Veikko Karvonen FIN | 2:20:39 |
| 1955 | Hideo Hamamura JPN | 2:18:22 |
| 1956 | Antti Viskari FIN | 2:14:14 |
| 1957[1] | John J. Kelley | 2:20:05 |
| 1958 | Franjo Mihalic YUG | 2:25:54 |
| 1959[1] | Eino Oksanen FIN | 2:22:42 |
| 1960 | Paavo Kotila FIN | 2:20:54 |
| 1961 | Eino Oksanen FIN | 2:23:39 |
| 1962 | Eino Oksanen FIN | 2:23:48 |
| 1963 | Aurele Vandendriessche BEL | 2:18:58 |
| 1964[1] | Aurele Vandendriessche BEL | 2:19:59 |
| 1965 | Morio Shigematsu JPN | 2:16:33 |
| 1966 | Kenji Kimihara JPN | 2:17:11 |
| 1967 | David McKenzie NZL | 2:15:45 |
| 1968 | Ambrose Burfoot | 2:22:17 |
| 1969[3] | Yoshiaki Unetani JPN | 2:13:49 |
| 1970[1] | Ronald Hill GBR | 2:10:30 |
| 1971 | Alvaro Mejia COL | 2:18:45 |
| 1972[4] | Olavi Suomalainen FIN | 2:15:39 |
| | Nina Kuscsik | 3:08:58 |
| 1973[5] | Jon Anderson | 2:16:03 |
| | Jacqueline Hansen | 3:05:59 |
| 1974[6] | Neil Cusack EIR | 2:13:39 |
| | Michiko Gorman | 2:47:11 |
| 1975[3] | William Rodgers | 2:09:55 |
| | Liane Winter FRG | 2:42:24 |
| 1976 | Jack Fultz | 2:20:19 |
| | Kim Merritt | 2:47:10 |
| 1977[2] | Jerome Drayton CAN | 2:14:46 |
| | Michiko Gorman | 2:48:33 |
| 1978[4] | William Rodgers | 2:10:13 |
| | Gayle Barron | 2:44:52 |
| 1979[5] | William Rodgers | 2:09:27 |
| | Joan Benoit | 2:35:15 |
| 1980[3] | William Rodgers | 2:12:11 |
| | Jacqueline Garreau CAN | 2:34:28 |
| 1981[1] | Toshihiko Seko JPN | 2:09:26 |

| | | |
|---|---|---|
| | Allison Roe NZL | 2:26:46 |
| 1982 | Alberto Salazar | 2:08:51 |
| | Charlotte Teske FRG | 2:29:33 |
| 1983[2] | Greg Meyer | 2:09:01 |
| | Joan Benoit | 2:22:43 |
| 1984[5] | Geoff Smith GBR | 2:10:34 |
| | Lorraine Moller NZL | 2:29:28 |
| 1985[6] | Geoff Smith GBR | 2:14:05 |
| | Lisa Weidenbach | 2:34:06 |
| 1986[3] | Robert de Castella AUS | 2:07:51 |
| | Ingrid Kristiansen NOR | 2:24:55 |
| 1987[1] | Toshihiko Seko JPN | 2:11:50 |
| | Rosa Mota POR | 2:25:21 |
| 1988[2] | Ibrahim Hussein KEN | 2:08:43 |
| | Rosa Mota POR | 2:24:30 |
| 1989[4] | Abebe Mekonnen ETH | 2:09:06 |
| | Ingrid Kristiansen NOR | 2:24:33 |
| 1990[5] | Gelindo Bordin ITA | 2:08:19 |
| | Rosa Mota POR | 2:25:24 |
| 1991[6] | Ibrahim Hussein KEN | 2:11:06 |
| | Wanda Panfil POL | 2:24:18 |
| 1992[1] | Ibrahim Hussein KEN | 2:08:14 |
| | Olga Markova RUS | 2:23:43 |
| 1993 | Cosmas Ndeti KEN | 2:09:33 |
| | Olga Markova RUS | 2:25:27 |
| 1994[2] | Cosmas Ndeti KEN | 2:07:15 |
| | Uta Pippig GER | 2:21:45 |
| | **3. Elana Meyer RSA** | **2:25:15** |
| | **9. Colleen de Reuck RSA** | **2:31:53** |
| 1995[4] | 1. Cosmas Ndeti KEN | 2:09:22 |
| | 2. Moses Tanui KEN | 2:10:22 |
| | 3. Luiz dos Santos BRA | 2:11:02 |
| | *Women:* | |
| | 1. Uta Pippig GER | 2:25:11 |
| | **2. Elana Meyer RSA** | **2:26:51** |
| | 3. Madina Biktagirova BLR | 2:29:00 |

### Course distances

1897-1923: 24 miles, 1232 yards
1924-1926: 26 miles, 209 yards
1927-1952: 26 miles, 385 yards
1953-1956: 25 miles, 938 yards
1957-present: 26 miles, 385 yards

### Race dates

| | |
|---|---|
| 1. 20 April | 4. 17 April |
| 2. 18 April | 5. 16 April |
| 3. 21 April | 6. 15 April |

# New York

| | | |
|---|---|---|
| Country is USA unless indicated otherwise. | | |
| 1970* | Gary Muhrcke | 2:31:38.2 |
| 1971 | Norman Higgins | 2:22:54.2 |
| | Elizabeth Bonner | 2:55:22 |
| 1972 | Sheldon Karlin | 2:27:52.8 |
| | Nina Kuscsik | 3:08:41.6 |
| 1973 | Thomas Fleming | 2:21:54.8 |
| | Nina Kuscsik | 2:57:07.2 |
| 1974 | Norbert Sander | 2:26:30.2 |
| | Kathrine Switzer | 3:07:29 |
| 1975 | Thomas Fleming | 2:19:27 |
| | Kim Merritt | 2:46:14.8 |
| 1976 | William Rodgers | 2:10:09.6 |
| | Michiko Gorman | 2:39:11 |
| 1977 | William Rodgers | 2:11:28.2 |
| | Michiko Gorman | 2:43:10 |
| 1978 | William Rodgers | 2:12:11.6 |
| | Grete Waitz NOR | 2:32:29.8 |

| | | |
|---|---|---|
| 1979 | William Rodgers | 2:11:42 |
| | Grete Waitz NOR | 2:27:32.6 |
| 1980 | Alberto Salazar | 2:09:41 |
| | Grete Waitz NOR | 2:25:41.3 |
| 1981 | Alberto Salazar | 2:08:12.7** |
| | Allison Roe NZL | 2:25:28.7** |
| 1982 | Alberto Salazar | 2:09:29 |
| | Grete Waitz NOR | 2:27:14 |
| 1983 | Rod Dixon NZL | 2:08:59 |
| | Grete Waitz NOR | 2:27:00 |
| 1984 | Orlando Pizzolato ITA | 2:14:53 |
| | Grete Waitz NOR | 2:29:30 |
| 1985 | Orlando Pizzolato ITA | 2:11:34 |
| | Grete Waitz NOR | 2:28:34 |
| 1986 | Gianni Poli ITA | 2:11:06 |
| | Grete Waitz NOR | 2:28:06 |
| 1987 | Ibrahim Hussein KEN | 2:11:01 |
| | Priscilla Welch GBR | 2:30:17 |
| 1988 | Steve Jones GBR | 2:08:20 |

| | | |
|---|---|---|
| | Grete Waitz NOR | 2:28:07 |
| 1989 | Juma Ikangaa TAN | 2:08:01 |
| | Ingrid Kristiansen NOR | 2:25:30 |
| 1990 | Douglas Wakiihuri KEN | 2:12:39 |
| | Wanda Panfil POL | 2:30:45 |
| 1991 | Salvador Garcia MEX | 2:09:28 |
| | Elizabeth McColgan GBR | 2:27:32 |
| 1992 | **Willie Mtolo RSA** | **2:09:29** |
| | Lisa Ondieki AUS | 2:24:40 |
| 1993 | Andrés Espinosa MEX | 2:10:04 |
| | Uta Pippig GER | 2:26:24 |
| 1994 | German Silva MEX | 2:11:21 |
| | Tecla Lorupe KEN | 2:27:37 |
| 1995 | German Silva MEX | 2:11:00 |
| | Tecla Lorupe KEN | 2:28:06 |

*) Nina Kuscsik was the only female starter but she failed to finish.

**) The course was later found to be 148 m short.

# Fukuoka

| | | |
|---|---|---|
| Country is Japan unless indicated otherwise. | | |
| 1947 | Toshikazu Wada | 2:45:45 |
| 1948 | Saburo Yamada | 2:37:25 |
| 1949 | Sinzo Koga | 2:40:26 |
| 1950 | Shunji Koyanagi | 2:30:47 |
| 1951 | Hiroyoshi Haigo | 2:30:13 |
| 1952 | Katsuo Nishida | 2:27:59 |
| 1953 | Hideo Hamamura | 2:27:26 |
| 1954 | Rainaldo Gorno ARG | 2:24:55 |
| 1955 | Vaikko Karvonen FIN | 2:23:16 |
| 1956 | Keizo Yamada | 2:25:15 |
| 1957 | Kurao Hiroshima | 2:21:40 |
| 1958 | Nobuyoshi Sadanaga | 2:24:01 |
| 1959 | Kurao Hiroshima | 2:29:34 |
| 1960 | Barry Magee NZL | 2:19:04 |
| 1961 | Pavel Kantorek TCH | 2:22:05 |
| 1962 | Toru Terasawa | 2:16:18.4 |

| | | |
|---|---|---|
| 1963 | Jeff Julian NZL | 2:18:00.6 |
| 1964 | Toru Terasawa | 2:14:48.2 |
| 1965 | Hidekuni Hiroshima | 2:18:35.8 |
| 1966 | Mike Ryan NZL | 2:14:04.8 |
| 1967 | Derek Clayton AUS | 2:09:36.4 |
| 1968 | Bill Adcocks GBR | 2:10:47.8 |
| 1969 | Jerome Drayton CAN | 2:11:12.8 |
| 1970 | Akio Usami | 2:10:37.8 |
| 1971 | Frank Shorter USA | 2:12:50.4 |
| 1972 | Frank Shorter USA | 2:10:30 |
| 1973 | Frank Shorter USA | 2:11:45 |
| 1974 | Frank Shorter USA | 2:11:31.2 |
| 1975 | Jerome Drayton CAN | 2:10:08.4 |
| 1976 | Jerome Drayton CAN | 2:12:35 |
| 1977 | Bill Rodgers USA | 2:10:55.3 |
| 1978 | Toshihiko Seko | 2:10:21 |
| 1979 | Toshihiko Seko | 2:10:35 |
| 1980 | Toshihiko Seko | 2:09:45 |

| | | |
|---|---|---|
| 1981 | Rob de Castella AUS | 2:08:18 |
| 1982 | Paul Ballinger NZL | 2:10:15 |
| 1983 | Toshihiko Seko | 2:08:52 |
| 1984 | Takeyuki Nakayama | 2:10:00 |
| 1985 | Masanari Shintaku | 2:09:51 |
| 1986 | Juma Ikangaa TAN | 2:10:06 |
| 1987 | Takeyuki Nakayama | 2:08:18 |
| 1988 | Toshihiro Shibutani | 2:11:04 |
| 1989 | Manuel Matias POR | 2:12:54 |
| 1990 | Belayneh Dinsamo ETH | 2:11:35 |
| 1991 | Shuichi Morita | 2:10:58 |
| 1992 | Tena Negere ETH | 2:09:04 |
| | **2. Lawrence Peu RSA** | **2:10:29** |
| 1993 | Dionicio Cerón MEX | 2:08:51 |
| | **2. Gert Thys RSA** | **2:09:31** |
| 1994 | Boay Akonay TAN | 2:09:45 |
| 1995 | Luiz dos Santos BRA | 2:09:30 |

# London

| | | |
|---|---|---|
| Country is Great Britain unless indicated otherwise. | | |
| 1981 | Dick Beardsley USA & | |
| | Inge Simonsen NOR (tie) | 2:11:48 |
| | Joyce Smith | 2:29:57 |
| 1982 | Hugh Jones | 2:09:24 |
| | Joyce Smith | 2:29:43 |
| 1983 | Mike Gratton | 2:09:43 |
| | Grete Waitz NOR | 2:25:28.7 |
| 1984 | Charlie Spedding | 2:09:57 |
| | Ingrid Kristiansen NOR | 2:24:26 |

| | | |
|---|---|---|
| 1985 | Steve Jones | 2:08:16 |
| | Ingrid Kristiansen NOR | 2:21:06 |
| 1986 | Toshihiko Seko JPN | 2:10:02 |
| | Grete Waitz NOR | 2:24:54 |
| 1987 | Hiromi Taniguchi JPN | 2:09:50 |
| | Ingrid Kristiansen NOR | 2:22:48 |
| 1988 | Henrik Jörgensen DEN | 2:10:20 |
| | Ingrid Kristiansen NOR | 2:25:41 |
| 1989 | Douglas Wakiihuri KEN | 2:09:03 |
| | Véronique Marot | 2:25:56 |
| 1990 | Allister Hutton | 2:10:10 |
| | Wanda Panfil POL | 2:26:31 |

| | | |
|---|---|---|
| 1991 | Yakov Tolstikov URS | 2:09:17 |
| | Rosa Mota POR | 2:26:14 |
| 1992 | António Pinto POR | 2:10:02 |
| | Katrin Dörre GER | 2:29:39 |
| 1993 | Eamonn Martin | 2:10:50 |
| | Katrin Dörre GER | 2:27:09 |
| 1994 | Dionicio Cerón MEX | 2:08:53 |
| | Katrin Dörre GER | 2:32:34 |
| 1995 | Dionicio Cerón MEX | 2:08:30 |
| | Malgorzata Sobanska POL | 2:27:43 |

# Rotterdam

| | | |
|---|---|---|
| 1981 | John Graham GBR | 2:09:28 |
| | Marja Wokke HOL | 2:43:23 |
| 1982 | Rodolfo Gomez MEX | 2:11:57 |
| | Mathilde Heuing FRG | 2:54:03 |
| 1983 | Rob de Castella AUS | 2:08:37 |
| | Rosa Mota POR | 2:32:27 |
| 1984 | Gidamis Shahanga TAN | 2:11:12 |
| | Carla Beurskens HOL | 2:34:56 |
| 1985 | Carlos Lopes POR | 2:07:12 |
| | Wilma Rusman HOL | 2:35:32 |
| 1986 | Abebe Mekonnen ETH | 2:09:08 |
| | Ellinor Ljungros SWE | 2:41:06 |

| | | |
|---|---|---|
| 1987 | Belayneh Dinsamo ETH | 2:12:58 |
| | Nelly Aerts BEL | 2:41:24 |
| 1988 | Belayneh Dinsamo ETH | 2:06:50 |
| | Hong-Yan Xiao CHN | 2:37:46 |
| 1989 | Belayneh Dinsamo ETH | 2:08:40 |
| | Elena Murgoci ROM | 2:32:03 |
| 1990 | Hiromi Taniguchi JPN | 2:10:56 |
| | Carla Beurskens HOL | 2:29:47 |
| 1991 | Robert de Castella AUS | 2:09:42 |
| | Joke Kleyweg HOL | 2:34:18 |
| 1992 | Salvador Garcia MEX | 2:09:16 |
| | Aurora Cunha POR | 2:29:14 |

| | | |
|---|---|---|
| 1993 | Dionicio Cerón MEX | 2:11:06 |
| | **4. Willie Mtolo RSA** | **2:12:33** |
| | **9. Jan Tau RSA** | **2:17:13** |
| | Anne van Schuppen HOL | 2:34:15 |
| 1994 | Vincent Rousseau BEL | 2:07:51 |
| | **2. Willie Mtolo RSA** | **2:10:17** |
| | Miyoko Asahina JPN | 2:25:52 |
| 1995 | Martin Fiz ESP | 2:08:57 |
| | Monica Pont ESP | 2:30:34 |

# World record progression

### Men

| | | | |
|---|---|---|---|
| 2:55:18.4 | John Hayes USA | Shepherd's Bush | 240708 |
| 2:52:45.4 | Robert Fowler USA | Yonkers | 010109 |
| 2:46:52.6 | James Clark USA | New York | 120209 |
| 2:46:04.6 | Albert Raines USA | New York | 080509 |
| 2:42:31 | Harry Barrett GBR | Shepherd's Bush | 260509 |
| 2:40:34.2* | Thure Johansson SWE | Stockholm | 310809 |
| 2:38:16.2* | Harry Green GBR | Shepherd's Bush | 120513 |
| 2:36:06.6 | Alexis Ahlgren SWE | Shepherd's Bush | 310513 |
| 2:32:35.8 | Johannes Kolehmainen FIN | Antwerp | 220820 |
| 2:29:01.8 | Albert Michelsen USA | Port Chester | 121025 |
| 2:27:49 | Fusashige Suzuki JPN | Tokyo | 310335 |
| 2:26:44 | Yasuo Ikenaka JPN | Tokyo | 030435 |
| 2:26:42 | Kitei Son JPN | Tokyo | 031135 |
| 2:25:39 | Yun Bok Suh KOR | Boston | 190447 |
| 2:20:42.2 | James Peters GBR | Chiswick | 140652 |
| 2:18:40.2 | James Peters GBR | Chiswick | 130653 |
| 2:18:34.8 | James Peters GBR | Turku | 041053 |
| 2:17:39.4 | James Peters GBR | Chiswick | 260654 |
| 2:15:17 | Sergey Popov URS | Stockholm | 240858 |
| 2:15:16.2 | Abebe Bikila ETH | Rome | 100960 |
| 2:15:15.8 | Toru Terasawa JPN | Beppu | 170263 |
| 2:14:28 | Leonard Edelen USA | Chiswick | 150663 |
| 2:13:55 | Basil Heatley GBR | Chiswick | 130664 |
| 2:12:11.2 | Abebe Bikila ETH | Tokyo | 211064 |
| 2:12:00 | Morio Shigematsu JPN | Chiswick | 120665 |
| 2:09:36.4 | Derek Clayton AUS | Fukuoka | 031267 |
| 2:08:33.6 | Derek Clayton AUS | Antwerp | 300569 |
| 2:08:18 | Robert de Castella AUS | Fukuoka | 061281 |
| 2:08:05 | Steve Jones GBR | Chicago | 211084 |
| 2:07:12 | Carlos Lopes POR | Rotterdam | 200485 |
| 2:06:50 | Belayneh Dinsamo ETH | Rotterdam | 170488 |

*) Run on a track.

### Women

| | | | |
|---|---|---|---|
| 3:40:22* | Violet Piercy GBR | Chiswick | 031026 |
| 3:37:07** | Merry Lepper USA | Culver City | 161263 |
| 3:27:45 | Dale Geig GBR | Ryde | 230564 |
| 3:19:33 | Mildred Sampson NZL | Auckland | 210764 |
| 3:15:22 | Maureen Wilton CAN | Toronto | 060567 |
| 3:07:26 | Anni Pede-Erdkamp FRG | Waldniel | 160967 |
| 3:02:53 | Caroline Walker USA | Seaside | 280270 |
| 3:01:42 | Elizabeth Bonner USA | Philadelphia | 090571 |
| 2:46:30 | Adrienne Beames AUS | Werribee | 310871 |
| 2:46:24 | Chantal Langlacé FRA | Neuf Brisach | 271074 |
| 2:43:54.5 | Jacqueline Hansen USA | Culver City | 011274 |
| 2:42:24 | Liane Winter FRG | Boston | 210475 |
| 2:40:15.8 | Christa Vahlensieck FRG | Dulmen | 030575 |
| 2:38:19 | Jacqueline Hansen USA | Eugene | 121075 |
| 2:35:15.4 | Chantal Langlacé FRA | Oyarzun | 010577 |
| 2:34:47.5 | Christa Vahlensieck FRG | West Berlin | 100977 |
| 2:32:29.8 | Grete Waitz NOR | New York | 221078 |
| 2:27:32.6 | Grete Waitz NOR | New York | 211079 |
| 2:25:41.3 | Grete Waitz NOR | New York | 261080 |
| 2:25:28.7 | Grete Waitz NOR | London | 170483 |
| 2:22:43 | Joan Benoit USA | Boston | 180483 |
| 2:21:06 | Ingrid Kristiansen NOR | London | 210485 |

*) Believed to be a time trial
**) Uncertified course

# South African record progression

| Men | | | |
|---|---|---|---|
| 2:56:06 | Charles Hefferon | Shepherd's Bush | 240708 |
| 2:42:58.2 | Kenneth McArthur | Cape Town | 051110 |
| 2:41:35 | Marthinus Steytler | Durban | 130528 |
| 2:38:32 | Johannes Coleman | Durban | 161135 |
| 2:31:57.4 | Johannes Coleman | Port Elizabeth | 110436 |
| 2:30:45 | Jackie Gibson | Bloemfontein | 270337 |
| 2:25:31.8 | Jan Barnard | Port Elizabeth | 310554 |
| 2:21:37.2 | Jan Barnard | Port Elizabeth | 061056 |
| 2:20:42.5 | De Villiers Lamprecht | Stellenbosch | 240966 |
| 2:20:21 | Willie Olivier | Cape Town | 310568 |
| 2:19:02.2 | Ferdie le Grange | Durbanville | 060371 |
| 2:17:51.4 | Ferdie le Grange | Durbanville | 080571 |
| 2:16:19 | Ferdie le Grange | Manchester | 040672 |
| 2:15:34.2 | Ferdie le Grange | Brussels | 110672 |
| 2:13:58 | Ferdie le Grange | Manchester | 030673 |
| 2:12:47 | Ferdie le Grange | Port Elizabeth | 230474 |
| 2:12:19 | Johnny Halberstadt | Durban | 090979 |
| 2:12:10 | Geoff Bacon | Port Elizabeth | 060980 |
| 2:12:10 | Bernard Rose | Cape Town | 050383 |
| 2:11:42 | Johan Dreyer | Kuils River | 020783 |
| 2:09:41 | Ernest Seleke | Port Elizabeth | 310384 |
| 2:08:58 | Mark Plaatjes | Port Elizabeth | 040585 |
| 2:08:04 | Zithulele Sinqe | Port Elizabeth | 030586 |

| Women | | | |
|---|---|---|---|
| 3:10:10 | Suzanne Gaylard | Stellenbosch | 140974 |
| 3:05:02 | Suzanne Gaylard | King William's Town | 261074 |
| 3:01:32 | Clare Taylor | Johannesburg | 030279 |
| 2:57:26 | Clare Taylor | East London | 240379 |
| 2:56:28 | Clare Taylor | Stellenbosch | 150979 |
| 2:51:55 | Clare Taylor | Cape Town | 080380 |
| 2:46:33 | Sonja Laxton | Johannesburg | 010980 |
| 2:44:28 | Judy Ryan | Stellenbosch | 130980 |
| 2:43:49 | Sonja Laxton | New York | 261080 |
| 2:43:16 | Isavel Roche-Kelly | Faure | 120981 |
| 2:42:27 | Isavel Roche-Kelly | Stellenbosch | 211181 |
| 2:36:44 | Sonja Laxton | Kuils River | 300684 |
| 2:35:45 | Adelene Joubert | Port Elizabeth | 040585 |
| 2:35:44 | Sonja Laxton | Stellenbosch | 130986 |
| 2:33:39 | Annette Falkson | Cape Town | 300488 |
| 2:30:35 | Frith van der Merwe | Port Elizabeth | 250289 |
| 2:27:36 | Frith van der Merwe | Port Elizabeth | 240290 |
| 2:25:15 | Elana Meyer | Boston | 180494 |

# Annual fastest performers

The fastest male and female runner in the world and the top three in South Africa (where available) are given for each year. The position of the top South African on the world list, if the performance was in the first ten, is also given.

| WORLD | | SOUTH AFRICA | |
|---|---|---|---|
| **1924** | | | |
| 2:36:10 | Shizo Kanaguri JPN | | |
| **1925** | | | |
| 2:29:01.8 | Albert Michelsen USA | | |
| **1926** | | | |
| 2:34:25.4 | Iivari Rotko FIN | | |
| 3:40:22 | Violet Piercy GBR | | |
| **1927** | | | |
| 2:31:11 | Albert Michelsen USA | | |
| **1928** | | | |
| 2:32:57 | Boughera El Ouafi FRA | 2:41:35 | Marthinus Steytler |
| **1929** | | | |
| 2:30:57.6 | Harry Paine GBR | | |
| **1930** | | | |
| 2:34:45 | Clarence DeMar USA | | |
| **1931** | | | |
| 2:32:35 | Albert Michelsen USA | | |
| **1932** | | | |
| 2:31:31 | Tanji Yahagi JPN | 2:42:28.4 | Thomas Lalande |
| **1933** | | | |
| 2:31:01.6 | Leslie Pawson USA | | |
| **1934** | | | |
| 2:31:30 | Patrick Dengis USA | | |
| **1935** | | | |
| 2:26:42 | Kitei Son JPN | 2:38:32 | Johannes Coleman |

| WORLD | | SOUTH AFRICA | |
|---|---|---|---|
| **1936** | | | |
| 2:28:32 | Kitei Son JPN | 2:31:57.4 | Johannes Coleman (4) |
| | | 2:32:09 | Jackie Gibson (5) |
| | | 2:36:18 | Thomas Lalande |
| **1937** | | | |
| 2:30:38 | Manuel Dias POR | 2:30:45 | Jackie Gibson (2) |
| | | 2:32:08 | Johannes Coleman (3) |
| | | 2:37:29 | Hardy Ballington |
| **1938** | | | |
| 2:30:27.6 | Patrick Dengis USA | 2:30:49.8 | Johannes Coleman (2) |
| | | 2:38:20 | Jackie Gibson |
| **1939** | | | |
| 2:28:51.8 | Ellison Brown USA | 2:35:07 | Jackie Gibson |
| **1940** | | | |
| 2:27:29.6 | Ellison Brown USA | 2:37:30 | Johannes Coleman |
| **1941** | | | |
| 2:30:38 | Leslie Pawson USA | | |
| **1942** | | | |
| 2:26:51.2 | Joseph Smith USA | | |
| **1943** | | | |
| 2:28:25.8 | Gérard Côté CAN | | |
| **1944** | | | |
| 2:31:50.4 | Gérard Côté CAN | | |
| **1945** | | | |
| 2:30:40.2 | John A. Kelley USA | | |

| WORLD | | SOUTH AFRICA | |
|---|---|---|---|
| **1946** | | | |
| 2:29:27 | Stylianos Kyriakidis GRE | 2:39:02 | Wally Hayward |
| **1947** | | | |
| 2:25:39 | Yun Bok Suh KOR | 2:39:27 | Sydney Luyt |
| **1948** | | | |
| 2:31:02 | Gérard Côté CAN | 2:32:30 | Johannes Coleman (7) |
| | | 2:38:11 | Sydney Luyt |
| **1949** | | | |
| 2:28:39.4 | Salomon Kononen FIN | 2:34:16.5 | Sydney Luyt (9) |
| **1950** | | | |
| 2:29:09.4 | Feodosiy Vanin URS | 2:37:02.2 | Sydney Luyt |
| **1951** | | | |
| 2:28:07.4 | Veikko Karvonen FIN | 2:35:42.2 | Sydney Luyt |
| **1952** | | | |
| 2:20:42.2 | Jim Peters GBR | 2:31:50.2 | Wally Hayward |
| | | 2:32:41 | Sydney Luyt |
| | | 2:34:38 | Bill Keith |
| **1953** | | | |
| 2:18:34.8 | Jim Peters GBR | 2:35:59 | Sydney Luyt |
| | | 2:37:52 | Trevor Allen |
| **1954** | | | |
| 2:17:39.4 | Jim Peters GBR | 2:25:31.8 | Jan Barnard (7) |
| | | 2:28:58 | Jack Mekler |
| | | 2:31:50 | Gerald Walsh |
| **1955** | | | |
| 2:21:21.6 | Veikko Karvonen FIN | 2:36:17 | Gerald Walsh* |
| | | 2:36:39.6 | Jan Barnard |
| | | 2:39:28 | Jack Mekler |
| **1956** | | | |
| 2:18:04.8 | Paavo Kotila FIN | 2:21:37.2 | Jan Barnard (8) |
| | | 2:38:55 | Mercer Davies |
| | | 2:42:58 | David Dodds |
| **1957** | | | |
| 2:19:50 | Sergey Popov URS | 2:33:06.8 | Jack Mekler |
| | | 2:33:29.2 | Mercer Davies |
| | | 2:36:24 | Gerald Walsh |
| **1958** | | | |
| 2:15:17 | Sergey Popov URS | 2:22:57.4 | Jan Barnard |
| | | 2:30:45 | Martinus Wiid |
| | | 2:32:32 | Jack Mekler |
| **1959** | | | |
| 2:17:45.2 | Sergey Popov URS | 2:27:52 | Keith James |
| | | 2:34:17 | Jan Barnard |
| | | 2:36:00 | Floris Visser |
| **1960** | | | |
| 2:15:16.2 | Abebe Bikila ETH | 2:22:58.6 | Keith James |
| | | 2:26:47.4 | Martinus Wiid |
| | | 2:32:03.4 | Jack Mekler |
| **1961** | | | |
| 2:18:54 | Takayuki Nakao JPN | 2:24:37.8 | Martinus Wiid |
| | | 2:31:28 | Oelof Vorster |
| | | 2:38:51 | Jack Mekler |
| **1962** | | | |
| 2:16:09.6 | Yu Mang Hyang PRK | 2:27:57 | Oelof Vorster |
| | | 2:35:19 | Mercer Davies |
| | | 2:37:27 | Henry Dunga |
| **1963** | | | |
| 2:14:28 | Leonard Edelen USA | 2:27:18.2 | Oelof Vorster |
| | | 2:27:19.5 | Jon Lang |
| | | 2:29:29 | Wilf Thring |

*) Walsh was officially timed in 2:22:28 at the marathon mark during a 38-mile race from King William's Town to East London. Mercer Davies was second in 2:24:28.

| WORLD | | SOUTH AFRICA | |
|---|---|---|---|
| **1964** | | | |
| 2:12:11.2 | Abebe Bikila ETH | 2:27:08 | Jon Lang |
| | | 2:27:28 | Dave Wassung |
| | | 2:27:53.4 | Jack Mekler |
| 3:19:33 | Mildred Sampson NZL | | |
| **1965** | | | |
| 2:12:00 | Morio Shigematsu JPN | 2:26:31 | De Villiers Lamprecht |
| | | 2:27:30 | Willie Olivier |
| | | 2:29:20.8 | Tom Malone |
| **1966** | | | |
| 2:13:45 | Alastair Wood GBR | 2:20:42.5 | De Villiers Lamprecht |
| | | 2:25:59 | David Piper |
| | | 2:26:15 | Willie Olivier |
| | | 3:39:27 | Sarie v.d. Westhuizen |
| **1967** | | | |
| 2:09:36.4 | Derek Clayton AUS | 2:22:20 | Willie Olivier |
| | | 2:23:32 | Bennett Makgamathe |
| | | 2:24:13 | Gerhard Dekkers |
| 3:07:26 | Anni Pede-Erdkamp FRG | | |
| **1968** | | | |
| 2:10:47.8 | William Adcocks GBR | 2:20:21 | Willie Olivier |
| | | 2:23:36 | Gerhard Dekkers |
| | | 2:26:02 | Deon Dekkers |
| **1969** | | | |
| 2:08:33.6 | Derek Clayton AUS | 2:25:23 | David Piper |
| | | 2:25:57 | David Kirkby |
| | | 2:26:11 | Willie Olivier |
| **1970** | | | |
| 2:09:28 | Ronald Hill GBR | 2:24:49 | Johnny Halberstadt |
| | | 2:25:42 | David Hensman |
| | | 2:28:16 | David Piper |
| 3:02:53 | Caroline Walker USA | | |
| **1971** | | | |
| 2:11:08.8 | Derek Clayton AUS | 2:17:51.4 | Ferdie le Grange |
| | | 2:22:23 | Johnny Halberstadt |
| | | 2:23:38.4 | De Villiers Lamprecht |
| 2:46:30 | Adrienne Beames AUS | | |
| **1972** | | | |
| 2:10:30 | Frank Shorter USA | 2:15:34.2 | Ferdie le Grange |
| | | 2:23:22 | Willie Farrell |
| | | 2:23:36 | Dave Bagshaw |
| 2:55:44 | Cheryl Bridges USA | 3:27:00 | T. Lombaard |
| **1973** | | | |
| 2:11:12.6 | John Farrington AUS | 2:13:58 | Ferdie le Grange (10) |
| | | 2:18:05 | Joe Bellingham |
| | | 2:22:29 | Chris Hoogsteden |
| 2:46:36 | Michiko Gorman USA | | |
| **1974** | | | |
| 2:09:12 | Ian Thompson GBR | 2:12:47 | Ferdie le Grange (7) |
| | | 2:18:41 | Dave Levick |
| | | 2:19:22 | Lodewyk Rabie |
| 2:43:54.5 | Jacqueline Hansen USA | 3:05:02 | Suzanne Gaylard |
| | | 3:25:48 | Dianne Gaylard |
| **1975** | | | |
| 2:09:55 | William Rodgers USA | 2:20:23 | Willie Farrell |
| | | 2:21:44 | Brian Chamberlain |
| | | 2:21:56 | Derek Preiss |
| 2:38:19 | Jacqueline Hansen USA | 3:33:49 | Lettie van Zyl |
| | | 3:35:07 | Elizabeth Cavanagh |
| | | 3:37:18 | Alet Kleynhans |
| **1976** | | | |
| 2:09:55 | Waldemar Cierpinski GDR | 2:21:17 | Derek Preiss |
| | | 2:23:47 | Andrew Greyling |
| | | 2:24:01 | Gordon Shaw |
| 2:39:11 | Michiko Gorman USA | 3:15:47 | Suzanne Gaylard |
| | | 3:37:22 | Marie-Jean Duyvejonck |
| | | 3:42:23 | Alet Kleynhans |

| WORLD | | SOUTH AFRICA | |
|---|---|---|---|
| **1977** | | | |
| 2:10:55.3 | William Rodgers USA | 2:15:18 | Johnny Halberstadt |
| | | 2:17:46 | Bernard Rose |
| | | 2:18:30 | Brian Chamberlain |
| 2:34:47.5 | Christa Vahlensieck FRG | 3:27:12 | Lettie van Zyl |
| | | 3:35:17 | Janet Bailey |
| | | 3:36:15 | Thea Claassen |
| **1978** | | | |
| 2:09:05.6 | Shigeru Soh JPN | 2:14:02 | Kevin Shaw |
| | | 2:15:25.8 | Brian Chamberlain |
| | | 2:16:21.1 | Johnny Halberstadt |
| 2:32:29.8 | Grete Waitz NOR | 3:08:18 | Clare Taylor |
| | | 3:13:58 | Di Alperstein |
| | | 3:22:21 | Judy Ryan |
| **1979** | | | |
| 2:09:27 | William Rodgers USA | 2:12:19 | Johnny Halberstadt |
| | | 2:13:15 | Bernard Rose |
| | | 2:13:21 | Kevin Shaw |
| 2:27:32.6 | Grete Waitz NOR | 2:56:28 | Clare Taylor |
| | | 2:58:53 | Di Alperstein |
| | | 3:12:50 | Cheryl Jorgenson |
| **1980** | | | |
| 2:09:01 | Gerard Nijboer HOL | 2:12:10 | Geoff Bacon |
| | | 2:12:50 | Thompson Magawana |
| | | 2:13:27 | Johnny Halberstadt |
| 2:25:41.3 | Grete Waitz NOR | 2:43:49 | Sonja Laxton |
| | | 2:44:28 | Judy Ryan |
| | | 2:49:07 | Isavel Roche-Kelly |
| **1981** | | | |
| 2:08:18 | Robert de Castella AUS | 2:12:57 | Bernard Rose |
| | | 2:13:02 | Johnny Halberstadt |
| | | 2:14:12 | Ben Choeu |
| 2:26:46 | Allison Roe NZL | 2:42:27 | Isavel Roche-Kelly |
| | | 2:44:35 | Sonja Laxton |
| | | 2:49:54 | Beverley Malan |
| **1982** | | | |
| 2:08:51 | Alberto Salazar USA | 2:11:46 | Johnny Halberstadt |
| | | 2:12:22 | Bernard Rose |
| | | 2:13:56 | Siphiwe Gqele |
| 2:26:11 | Joan Benoit USA | 2:44:40 | Beverley Malan |
| | | 2:46:52 | Isavel Roche-Kelly |
| | | 2:50:16 | Louise Sinclair |
| **1983** | | | |
| 2:08:37 | Robert de Castella AUS | 2:11:42 | Johan Dreyer |
| | | 2:12:08 | Ewald Bonzet |
| | | 2:12:10 | Bernard Rose |
| 2:22:43 | Joan Benoit USA | 2:47:16 | Beverley Malan |
| | | 2:48:29 | Adelene Joubert |
| | | 2:49:45 | Marion Loveday |
| **1984** | | | |
| 2:08:05 | Steve Jones GBR | 2:09:41 | Ernest Seleke (6) |
| | | 2:12:53 | Derek May |
| | | 2:13:29 | Gibeon Moshaba |
| 2:24:26 | Ingrid Kristiansen NOR | 2:36:44 | Sonja Laxton |
| | | 2:48:46 | Adelene Joubert |
| | | 2:49:13 | Lindsay Weight |
| **1985** | | | |
| 2:07:12 | Carlos Lopes POR | 2:08:58 | Mark Plaatjes (8) |
| | | 2:10:32 | Willie Mtolo |
| | | 2:10:39 | Thompson Magawana |
| 2:21:06 | Ingrid Kristiansen NOR | 2:35:45 | Adelene Joubert |
| | | 2:37:45 | Sonja Laxton |
| | | 2:47:20 | Liz Eglington |
| **1986** | | | |
| 2:07:35 | Taisuke Kodama JPN | 2:08:04 | Zithulele Sinqe (4) |
| | | 2:08:15 | Willie Mtolo (6) |
| | | 2:13:51 | Petrus Kekana |

| WORLD | | SOUTH AFRICA | |
|---|---|---|---|
| **1986** (continued) | | | |
| 2:24:54 | Grete Waitz NOR | 2:35:44 | Sonja Laxton |
| | | 2:44:30 | Annette Redelinghuys |
| | | 2:45:18 | Cassandra Mihailovic |
| **1987** | | | |
| 2:08:18 | Takeyuki Nakayama JPN | 2:10:51 | Zithulele Sinqe |
| | | 2:11:01 | Willie Mtolo |
| | | 2:11:51 | Derek May |
| 2:22:48 | Ingrid Kristiansen NOR | 2:36:13 | Annette Falkson |
| | | 2:40:08 | Monica Drögemöller |
| | | 2:42:38 | Sonja Laxton |
| **1988** | | | |
| 2:06:50 | Belayneh Dinsamo ETH | 2:10:18 | Willie Mtolo |
| | | 2:10:41 | Mark Plaatjes |
| | | 2:12:14 | David Tsebe |
| 2:23:51 | Lisa Martin AUS | 2:33:39 | Annette Falkson |
| | | 2:36:59 | Sonja Laxton |
| | | 2:42:01 | Monica Drögemöller |
| **1989** | | | |
| 2:08:01 | Juma Ikangaa TAN | 2:10:47 | David Tsebe |
| | | 2:10:53 | Peter Tshikila |
| | | 2:13:13 | Willie Mtolo |
| 2:24:33 | Ingrid Kristiansen NOR | 2:30:35 | Frith van der Merwe |
| | | 2:40:59 | Sonja Laxton |
| | | 2:44:42 | Monica Drögemöller |
| **1990** | | | |
| 2:08:16 | Stephen Moneghetti AUS | 2:09:50 | David Tsebe (8) |
| | | 2:11:24 | John Sebata |
| | | 2:13:11 | David Phalatse |
| 2:25:24 | Rosa Mota POR | 2:27:36 | Frith van der Merwe (4) |
| | | 2:37:19 | Monica Drögemöller |
| | | 2:41:09 | Sonja Laxton |
| **1991** | | | |
| 2:08:53 | Koichi Morishita JPN | 2:10:29 | Joseph Skosana |
| | | 2:10:32 | David Tsebe |
| | | 2:10:47 | Michael Scout |
| 2:24:18 | Wanda Panfil POL | 2:39:32 | Jean Rayner |
| | | 2:42:20 | Frith van der Merwe |
| | | 2:43:13 | Monica Drögemöller |
| **1992** | | | |
| 2:08:07 | David Tsebe RSA | 2:08:07 | David Tsebe (1) |
| | | 2:09:29 | Willie Mtolo (9) |
| | | 2:10:29 | Lawrence Peu |
| 2:23:42 | Olga Markova RUS | 2:31:21 | Colleen de Reuck |
| | | 2:39:24 | Frith van der Merwe |
| | | 2:40:12 | Sonja Laxton |
| **1993** | | | |
| 2:08:51 | Dionicio Cerón MEX | 2:09:31 | Gert Thys (4) |
| | | 2:10:57 | Xolile Yawa |
| | | 2:12:07 | David Tsebe |
| 2:24:07 | Wang Junxia CHN | 2:32:01 | Frith van der Merwe |
| | | 2:43:01 | Sonja Laxton |
| | | 2:46:13 | Belinda Roux |
| **1994** | | | |
| 2:07:15 | Cosmas Ndeti KEN | 2:10:17 | Willie Mtolo |
| | | 2:11:54 | Xolile Yawa |
| | | 2:12:01 | Zithulele Sinqe |
| 2:21:45 | Uta Pippig GER | 2:25:15 | Elana Meyer (3) |
| | | 2:31:53 | Colleen de Reuck |
| | | 2:42:35 | Grace de Oliveira |
| **1995** | | | |
| 2:07:02 | Samuel Lelei KEN | 2:10:22 | Xolile Yawa |
| | | 2:11:18 | Lawrence Peu |
| | | 2:11:35 | Willie Mtolo |
| 2:25:11 | Uta Pippig GER | 2:26:51 | Elana Meyer (2) |
| | | 2:37:11 | Nicole Fuller |
| | | 2:37:29 | Colleen de Reuck |

# South African champions

The winners of the segregated championships for white and black runners in the period 1962-1971 are given. In 1974 the first "open" championship (in which white and black athletes ran together) was held, but there was also a closed championship for whites only. For the years 1974-1976 the open champion is given first, followed by the winner of the whites-only race. In 1977 there was also a race for blacks only; its winner is given after the other two. From 1978 there was only one race, open to all (men). In the first three years of the official women's championship (1981-1983) the women ran at a separate venue, thereafter the sexes ran together.

| Year | Name | Time | Venue |
|------|------|------|-------|
| 1908 | Kenneth McArthur | 3:18:27.4 | Cape Town |
| 1909-22 | Not held | | |
| 1923 | Harry Phillips | 3:12:06 | Johannesburg |
| 1924 | Harry Phillips | 3:10:41.8 | Durban |
| 1926 | Marthinus Steytler | 2:48:18 | Johannesburg |
| 1928 | Declared no race | | Cape Town |
| 1929 | W. Victor | 3:21:26.8 | Kimberley |
| 1930 | Marthinus Steytler | 2:57:35.2 | Johannesburg |
| 1931 | W. Victor | 3:00:32.6 | Bloemfontein |
| 1932 | William Cochrane | 3:03:38 | Durban |
| 1933 | C. van der Wath | 3:08:48 | Cape Town |
| 1934 | D. Pivalizza | 3:20:00 | Queenstown |
| 1935 | Jackie Gibson | 2:52:40.4 | Pretoria |
| 1936 | Johannes Coleman | 2:31:57.4 | Port Elizabeth |
| 1937 | Jackie Gibson | 2:30:45 | Bloemfontein |
| 1938 | Arthur Hampton | 2:46:56.2 | Cape Town |
| 1939 | Jackie Gibson | 2:35:07 | Krugersdorp |
| 1940 | Johannes Coleman | 2:37:30 | Durban |
| 1941-45 | Not held | | |
| 1946 | Wally Hayward | 2:39:02 | Kimberley |
| 1947 | Carl Pace | 2:57:41 | Bulawayo |
| 1948 | Johannes Coleman | 2:32:30 | Port Elizabeth |
| 1949 | Sydney Luyt | 2:34:16.5 | Queenstown |
| 1950 | Bill Keith | 2:41:21 | Kimberley |
| 1951 | Sydney Luyt | 2:35:42.2 | Pretoria |
| 1952 | Wally Hayward | 2:37:00.5 | Cape Town |
| 1953 | Nic Slabbert | 2:46:52.8 | Salisbury |
| 1954 | Jack Mekler | 2:35:25.1 | Johannesburg |
| 1955 | Jan Barnard | 2:36:39.6 | Pretoria |
| 1956 | Jan Barnard | 2:37:36 | Bloemfontein |
| 1957 | Jack Mekler | 2:33:06.8 | Queenstown |
| 1958 | Jan Barnard | 2:28:04 | Pretoria |
| 1959 | Keith James | 2:44:45 | Durban |
| 1960 | Keith James | 2:29:14.6 | Bloemfontein |
| 1961 | Martinus Wiid | 2:24:37.8 | Paarl |
| 1962 | Oelof Vorster | 2:48:05.7 | Queenstown |
| | Henry Dunga | 2:37:27 | Umtata |
| 1963 | Jon Lang | 2:27:19.5 | Bloemfontein |
| | Henry Dunga | 2:42:47.8 | Welkom |
| 1964 | Jon Lang | 2:27:08 | Port Elizabeth |
| | Matthew Kanda ZIM | 2:29:26.6 | Silverton |
| 1965 | Sonny van Antwerp | 2:30:43.8 | Potchefstroom |
| | Bennett Makgamathe | 2:31:25.2 | Welkom |
| 1966 | Oelof Vorster | 2:33:07 | Bloemfontein |
| | Clifford Malope | 2:28:53 | Libanon |
| 1967 | William Jardine | 2:33:07.1 | Cape Town |
| | E. Tsukudu | 2:29:20 | Welkom |
| 1968 | Joe Bellingham | 2:27:23.8 | Germiston |
| | Matthew Kanda ZIM | 2:27:24.8 | Libanon |
| 1969 | Jeff Julian NZL | 2:28:23.4 | Bloemfontein |
| | Matthew Kanda ZIM | 2:34:36.6 | Nigel |
| 1970 | Darrell McLean | 2:39:52.6 | Pretoria |
| | Clifford Malope | 2:34:12.9 | Welkom |
| 1971 | De Villiers Lamprecht | 2:23:38.4 | East London |
| | Robson Mrombe ZIM | 2:32:13 | Libanon |
| 1972 | William Brown | 2:28:13 | Stilfontein |
| 1973 | Ferdie le Grange | 2:17:40 | East London |
| 1974 | Ferdie le Grange | 2:12:47 | Port Elizabeth |
| | Dave Morrison | 2:21:51 | Stilfontein |
| 1975 | Mike Tagg GBR | 2:19:47 | Stellenbosch |
| | Doug Schaefer | 2:25:56 | Pretoria |
| 1976 | Gabashane Rakabaele LES | 2:23:49 | Stellenbosch |
| | Brian Chamberlain | 2:26:33.2 | Pretoria |
| 1977 | Brian Chamberlain | 2:19:20 | Durban |
| | Brian Chamberlain | 2:29:10 | Bloemfontein |
| | Frans Ntaole | 2:25:38 | Welkom |
| 1978 | Johnny Halberstadt | 2:19:36 | Springs |
| 1979 | Gabashane Rakabaele | 2:12:27 | Port Elizabeth |
| 1980 | Thompson Magawana | 2:12:50 | Eerste River |
| 1981 | Mark Plaatjes | 2:16:17 | Potchefstroom |
| | Sonja Laxton | 2:44:35 | Durban |
| 1982 | Gabashane Rakabaele | 2:17:36 | Durban |
| | Beverley Malan | 2:47:44 | Port Elizabeth |
| 1983 | Kevin Flanegan | 2:16:21 | Durban |
| | Adelene Joubert | 2:48:29 | Port Elizabeth |
| 1984 | Ernest Seleke | 2:09:41 | Port Elizabeth |
| | Adelene Joubert | 2:48:46 | |
| 1985 | Mark Plaatjes | 2:08:58 | Port Elizabeth |
| | Adelene Joubert | 2:35:45 | |
| 1986 | Zithulele Sinqe | 2:08:04 | Port Elizabeth |
| | Cassandra Mihailovic | 2:45:18 | |
| 1987 | Zithulele Sinqe | 2:10:51 | Stellenbosch |
| | Annette Falkson | 2:36:13 | |
| 1988 | Willie Mtolo | 2:10:18 | Cape Town |
| | Annette Falkson | 2:33:39 | |
| 1989 | Willie Mtolo | 2:13:13 | Port Elizabeth |
| | Frith van der Merwe | 2:30:35 | |
| 1990 | David Tsebe | 2:09:50 | Port Elizabeth |
| | Frith van der Merwe | 2:27:36 | |
| 1991 | Joseph Skosana | 2:10:29 | Durban |
| | Jean Rayner | 2:39:32 | |
| 1992 | Abel Mokibe | 2:11:07 | Cape Town |
| | Colleen de Reuck | 2:31:21 | |
| 1993 | Josiah Thungwane | 2:14:25 | Cape Town |
| | Sonja Laxton | 2:43:01 | |
| 1994 | Daniel Radebe | 2:15:06 | East London |
| | Grace de Oliveira | 2:46:00 | |
| 1995 | Martin Ndwheni | 2:12:32 | Port Elizabeth |
| | Nicole Fuller | 2:37:11 | |

# Chronological list of SA sub-2:13 times

The list includes performances in South Africa by athletes from neighbouring countries such as Lesotho and Swaziland at a time when they were resident in this country and registered with South African clubs. These times are indicated with an asterisk.

| Time | Name | | Place | Date |
|---|---|---|---|---|
| 2:12:47 | Ferdie le Grange | | Port Elizabeth | 230474 |
| 2:12:19 | Johnny Halberstadt | | Durban | 090979 |
| 2:12:27* | Gabashane Rakabaele | | Port Elizabeth | 201079 |
| 2:12:10 | Geoff Bacon | | Port Elizabeth | 060980 |
| 2:12:50 | Thompson Magawana | | Faure | 111080 |
| 2:12:57 | Bernard Rose | | Durban | 020881 |
| 2:11:44* | Gabashane Rakabaele | | Port Elizabeth | 010582 |
| 2:12:22 | Bernard Rose | | Port Elizabeth | 010582 |
| 2:12:10 | Bernard Rose | | Cape Town | 050383 |
| 2:11:42 | Johan Dreyer | (10) | Kuils River | 020783 |
| 2:12:08 | Ewald Bonzet | | Stellenbosch | 100983 |
| 2:09:41 | Ernest Seleke | | Port Elizabeth | 310384 |
| 2:12:57* | Frans Ntaole | | Port Elizabeth | 310384 |
| 2:08:58 | Mark Plaatjes | | Port Elizabeth | 040585 |
| 2:10:32 | Willie Mtolo | | Port Elizabeth | 040585 |
| 2:10:39 | Thompson Magawana | | Port Elizabeth | 040585 |
| 2:08:04 | Zithulele Sinqe | | Port Elizabeth | 030586 |
| 2:08:15 | Willie Mtolo | | Port Elizabeth | 030586 |
| 2:11:00* | Ernest Tjela | | Port Elizabeth | 030586 |
| 2:11:51 | Derek May | (20) | Houston | 180187 |
| 2:10:51 | Zithulele Sinqe | | Stellenbosch | 020587 |
| 2:11:01 | Willie Mtolo | | Stellenbosch | 020587 |
| 2:12:35 | Thompson Magawana | | Stellenbosch | 020587 |
| 2:11:47* | Ernest Tjela | | Cape Town | 070387 |
| 2:12:14* | Ernest Tjela | | Port Elizabeth | 010887 |
| 2:11:51 | Zithulele Sinqe | | Durban | 300887 |
| 2:10:41 | Mark Plaatjes | | Los Angeles | 060388 |
| 2:10:18 | Willie Mtolo | | Cape Town | 300488 |
| 2:12:14 | David Tsebe | | Cape Town | 300488 |
| 2:12:17 | Mark Plaatjes | (30) | Columbus | 131188 |
| 2:10:48 | David Tsebe | | Port Elizabeth | 290789 |
| 2:10:53 | Peter Tshikila | | Port Elizabeth | 290789 |
| 2:10:47 | David Tsebe | | Durban | 100989 |
| 2:09:50 | David Tsebe | | Port Elizabeth | 240290 |
| 2:11:24 | John Sebata | | Port Elizabeth | 240290 |
| 2:12:37* | Thabiso Moqhali | | Port Elizabeth | 240290 |
| 2:12:14 | David Tsebe | | Port Elizabeth | 280790 |
| 2:10:29 | Joseph Skosana | | Durban | 200791 |
| 2:10:32 | David Tsebe | | Durban | 200791 |
| 2:10:47 | Michael Scout | (40) | Durban | 200791 |
| 2:12:14* | Thabiso Moqhali | | Durban | 200791 |
| 2:11:07 | Abel Mokibe | | Cape Town | 280392 |
| 2:11:47 | Zithulele Sinqe | | Cape Town | 280392 |
| 2:11:56 | Jan Tau | | Cape Town | 280392 |
| 2:08:07 | David Tsebe | | Berlin | 270992 |
| 2:09:29 | Willie Mtolo | | New York | 011192 |
| 2:10:29 | Lawrence Peu | | Otsu | 140393 |
| 2:12:33 | Willie Mtolo | | Rotterdam | 180493 |
| 2:12:19 | Jan Tau | | Enschede | 130693 |
| 2:10:57 | Xolile Yawa | (50) | Berlin | 260993 |
| 2:12:07 | David Tsebe | | Berlin | 260993 |
| 2:09:31 | Gert Thys | | Fukuoka | 051293 |
| 2:12:10 | Johannes Maremane | | Hiroshima | 060394 |
| 2:11:54 | Xolile Yawa | | Kyongju | 200394 |
| 2:12:01 | Zithulele Sinqe | | Kyongju | 200394 |
| 2:10:17 | Willie Mtolo | | Rotterdam | 170494 |
| 2:12:32 | Martin Ndwheni | | Port Elizabeth | 110395 |
| 2:10:22 | Xolile Yawa | | London | 020495 |
| 2:11:35 | Willie Mtolo | | London | 020495 |
| 2:11:39 | Johannes Mabitle | (60) | London | 020495 |
| 2:11:18 | Lawrence Peu | | Paris | 020495 |
| 2:11:56 | Xolile Yawa | | Berlin | 240995 |

# Chronological list of SA sub-2:45 times

| Time | Name | | Place | Date |
|---|---|---|---|---|
| 2:44:28 | Judy Ryan | | Stellenbosch | 130980 |
| 2:43:49 | Sonja Laxton | | New York | 261080 |
| 2:44:35 | Sonja Laxton | | Durban | 020581 |
| 2:43:16 | Isavel Roche-Kelly | | Faure | 120981 |
| 2:42:27 | Isavel Roche-Kelly | | Stellenbosch | 211181 |
| 2:44:40 | Beverley Malan | | New York | 241082 |
| 2:36:44 | Sonja Laxton | | Kuils River | 300684 |
| 2:42:44 | Sonja Laxton | | Johannesburg | 101084 |
| 2:37:46 | Adelene Joubert | | Cape Town | 230285 |
| 2:35:45 | Adelene Joubert | (10) | Port Elizabeth | 040585 |
| 2:37:45 | Sonja Laxton | | Port Elizabeth | 040585 |
| 2:42:10 | Adelene Joubert | | Johannesburg | 101085 |
| 2:35:44 | Sonja Laxton | | Stellenbosch | 130986 |
| 2:44:00 | Sonja Laxton | | Johannesburg | 101086 |
| 2:44:30 | Annette Redelinghuys | | Johannesburg | 101086 |
| 2:39:56 | Annette Falkson | | Cape Town | 070387 |
| 2:36:13 | Annette Falkson | | Stellenbosch | 020587 |
| 2:40:08 | Monica Drögemöller | | Stellenbosch | 020587 |
| 2:42:38 | Sonja Laxton | | Stellenbosch | 020587 |
| 2:44:50 | Sonja Laxton | (20) | Johannesburg | 210687 |
| 2:44:55 | Liz Eglington | | Stellenboch | 120987 |
| 2:44:02 | Monica Drögemöller | | Stellenbosch | 211187 |
| 2:33:39 | Annette Falkson | | Cape Town | 300488 |
| 2:40:05 | Sonja Laxton | | Cape Town | 300488 |
| 2:44:16 | Liz Eglington | | Cape Town | 300488 |
| 2:36:59 | Sonja Laxton | | Durban | 280888 |
| 2:42:01 | Monica Drögemöller | | Stellenbosch | 100988 |
| 2:41:16 | Sonja Laxton | | Johannesburg | 101088 |
| 2:42:49 | Frith van der Merwe | | Johannesburg | 101088 |
| 2:40:45 | Frith van der Merwe | (30) | Benoni | 220189 |
| 2:30:35 | Frith van der Merwe | | Port Elizabeth | 250289 |
| 2:43:50 | Sonja Laxton | | Port Elizabeth | 250289 |
| 2:39:10 | Frith van der Merwe | | Knysna | 150789 |
| 2:40:59 | Sonja Laxton | | Durban | 100989 |
| 2:44:42 | Monica Drögemöller | | Stellenbosch | 160989 |
| 2:33:49 | Frith van der Merwe | | Benoni | 280190 |
| 2:27:36 | Frith van der Merwe | | Port Elizabeth | 240290 |
| 2:41:09 | Sonja Laxton | | Port Elizabeth | 240290 |
| 2:42:52 | Evelina Tshabalala | | Port Elizabeth | 240290 |
| 2:37:19 | Monica Drögemöller | (40) | Cape Town | 030390 |
| 2:35:05 | Frith van der Merwe | | Johannesburg | 220490 |
| 2:44:59 | Jean Rayner | | Milnerton | 150990 |
| 2:33:09 | Frith van der Merwe | | Pretoria | 101190 |
| 2:43:13 | Monica Drögemöller | | Cape Town | 160291 |
| 2:44:22 | Helen Lucre | | Cape Town | 160291 |
| 2:42:24 | Frith van der Merwe | | Welkom | 090391 |
| 2:39:32 | Jean Rayner | | Durban | 200791 |
| 2:42:20 | Frith van der Merwe | | Johannesburg | 271091 |
| 2:31:21 | Colleen de Reuck | | Cape Town | 280392 |
| 2:40:12 | Sonja Laxton | (50) | Cape Town | 280392 |
| 2:41:05 | Bance Moila | | Cape Town | 280392 |
| 2:41:35 | Monica Drögemöller | | Cape Town | 280392 |
| 2:43:09 | Grace de Oliveira | | Cape Town | 280392 |
| 2:39:03 | Colleen de Reuck | | Barcelona | 010892 |
| 2:39:24 | Frith van der Merwe | | Berlin | 270992 |
| 2:39:10 | Frith van der Merwe | | Tiberius | 060193 |
| 2:43:01 | Sonja Laxton | | Cape Town | 200393 |
| 2:32:01 | Frith van der Merwe | | Paris | 250493 |
| 2:35:56 | Frith van der Merwe | | Stuttgart | 150893 |
| 2:25:15 | Elana Meyer | (60) | Boston | 180494 |
| 2:31:53 | Colleen de Reuck | | Boston | 180494 |
| 2:42:35 | Grace de Oliveira | | Lisbon | 271194 |
| 2:37:11 | Nicole Fuller | | Port Elizabeth | 110395 |
| 2:26:51 | Elana Meyer | | Boston | 170495 |
| 2:37:29 | Colleen de Reuck | | Honolulu | 101295 |

# Chronological list of world sub-2:09 times

| | | | | |
|---|---|---|---|---|
| 2:08:33.6 | Derek Clayton AUS | | Antwerp | 300569 |
| 2:08:18 | Robert de Castella AUS | | Fukuoka | 061281 |
| 2:08:51 | Alberto Salazar USA | | Boston | 190482 |
| 2:08:53 | Dick Beardsley USA | | Boston | 190482 |
| 2:08:38 | Toshihiko Seko JPN | | Tokyo | 130283 |
| 2:08:55 | Takeshi Soh JPN | | Tokyo | 130283 |
| 2:08:37 | Robert de Castella AUS | | Rotterdam | 090483 |
| 2:08:39 | Carlos Lopes POR | | Rotterdam | 090483 |
| 2:08:59 | Rod Dixon NZL | | New York | 231083 |
| 2:08:52 | Toshihiko Seko JPN | (10) | Fukuoka | 041283 |
| 2:08:55 | Juma Ikangaa TAN | | Fukuoka | 041283 |
| 2:08:05 | Steve Jones GBR | | Chicago | 211084 |
| 2:08:09 | Ahmed Salah DJI | | Hiroshima | 140485 |
| 2:08:15 | Takeyuki Nakayama JPN | | Hiroshima | 140485 |
| 2:08:26 | Djama Robleh DJI | | Hiroshima | 140485 |
| 2:07:12 | Carlos Lopes POR | | Rotterdam | 200485 |
| 2:08:16 | Steve Jones GBR | | London | 210485 |
| 2:08:33 | Charles Spedding GBR | | London | 210485 |
| **2:08:58** | **Mark Plaatjes RSA** | | **Port Elizabeth** | **040585** |
| 2:07:13 | Steve Jones GBR | (20) | Chicago | 201085 |
| 2:08:08 | Djama Robleh DJI | | Chicago | 201085 |
| 2:08:48 | Robert de Castella AUS | | Chicago | 201085 |
| 2:08:10 | Juma Ikangaa TAN | | Tokyo | 090286 |
| 2:08:29 | Belayneh Dinsamo ETH | | Tokyo | 090286 |
| 2:08:39 | Abebe Mekonnen ETH | | Tokyo | 090286 |
| 2:08:43 | Takeyuki Nakayama JPN | | Tokyo | 090286 |
| 2:07:51 | Robert de Castella AUS | | Boston | 210486 |
| **2:08:04** | **Zithulele Sinqe RSA** | | **Port Elizabeth** | **030586** |
| **2:08:15** | **Willie Mtolo RSA** | | **Port Elizabeth** | **030586** |
| 2:08:21 | Takeyuki Nakayama JPN | (30) | Seoul | 051086 |
| 2:07:35 | Taisuke Kodama JPN | | Beijing | 191086 |
| 2:07:57 | Kunimitsu Itoh JPN | | Beijing | 191086 |
| 2:08:39 | Juma Ikangaa JPN | | Beijing | 191086 |
| 2:08:27 | Toshihiko Seko JPN | | Chicago | 261086 |
| 2:08:18 | Takeyuki Nakayama JPN | | Fukuoka | 061287 |
| 2:08:33 | Abebe Mekonnen ETH | | Tokyo | 140288 |
| 2:08:42 | Juma Ikangaa TAN | | Tokyo | 140288 |
| 2:08:47 | Jörg Peter GDR | | Tokyo | 140288 |
| 2:08:49 | Robert de Castella AUS | | Tokyo | 140288 |
| 2:06:50 | Belayneh Dinsamo ETH | (40) | Rotterdam | 170488 |
| 2:07:07 | Ahmed Salah DJI | | Rotterdam | 170488 |
| 2:08:44 | Wodajo Bulti ETH | | Rotterdam | 170488 |
| 2:08:43 | Ibrahim Hussein KEN | | Boston | 180488 |
| 2:08:44 | Juma Ikangaa TAN | | Boston | 180488 |
| 2:07:35 | Abebe Mekonnen ETH | | Beijing | 161088 |
| 2:07:40 | Hiromi Taniguchi JPN | | Beijing | 161088 |
| 2:08:57 | Alejandro Cruz MEX | | Chicago | 301088 |
| 2:08:20 | Stephen Jones GBR | | New York | 061188 |
| 2:08:40 | Belayneh Dinsamo ETH | | Rotterdam | 160489 |
| 2:08:01 | Juma Ikangaa TAN | (50) | New York | 051189 |
| 2:08:19 | Gelindo Bordin ITA | | Boston | 160490 |
| 2:08:16 | Stephen Moneghetti AUS | | Berlin | 300990 |
| 2:08:32 | Gidamis Shahanga TAN | | Berlin | 300990 |
| 2:08:53 | Koichi Morishita JPN | | Oita | 030291 |
| 2:08:36 | Dionicio Cerón MEX | | Oita | 020292 |
| 2:08:47 | Hwang Young-cho KOR | | Oita | 020292 |
| 2:08:14 | Ibrahim Hussein KEN | | Boston | 200492 |
| **2:08:07** | **David Tsebe RSA** | | **Berlin** | **280992** |
| 2:08:38 | Manuel Matias POR | | Berlin | 280992 |
| 2:08:51 | Dionicio Cerón MEX | (60) | Fukuoka | 051293 |
| 2:08:55 | Stephen Moneghetti AUS | | Tokyo | 130294 |
| 2:08:33 | Manuel Matias POR | | Kyongju | 200394 |
| 2:08:34 | Kim Wan-ki KOR | | Kyongju | 200394 |
| 2:07:51 | Vincent Rousseau BEL | | Rotterdam | 170494 |
| 2:08:53 | Dionicio Cerón MEX | | London | 170494 |
| 2:07:15 | Cosmas Ndeti KEN | | Boston | 180494 |
| 2:07:19 | Andrés Espinosa MEX | | Boston | 180494 |
| 2:08:08 | Jackson Kipngok KEN | | Boston | 180494 |
| 2:08:09 | Hwang Young-cho KOR | | Boston | 180494 |
| 2:08:28 | Arturo Barrios USA | (70) | Boston | 180494 |
| 2:08:35 | Boay Akonay TAN | | Boston | 180494 |
| 2:08:47 | Bob Kempainen USA | | Boston | 180494 |
| 2:08:31 | António Pinto POR | | Berlin | 250994 |
| 2:08:50 | Sammy Nyangincha KEN | | Berlin | 250994 |
| 2:08:30 | Dionicio Cerón Mex | | London | 020495 |
| 2:08:33 | Stephen Moneghetti AUS | | London | 020495 |
| 2:08:48 | António Pinto POR | | London | 020495 |
| 2:08:57 | Martin Fiz ESP | | Rotterdam | 230495 |
| 2:07:02 | Samuel Lelei KEN | | Berlin | 240995 |
| 2:07:20 | Vincent Rousseau BEL | (80) | Berlin | 240995 |
| 2:08:57 | António Pinto POR | | Berlin | 240995 |

# Chronological list of world sub-2:26 times

| | | | | |
|---|---|---|---|---|
| 2:25:41.3 | Grete Waitz NOR | | New York | 261080 |
| 2:25:28.6 | Grete Waitz NOR | | London | 170483 |
| 2:22:43 | Joan Benoit USA | | Boston | 180483 |
| 2:24:26 | Ingrid Kristiansen NOR | | London | 130584 |
| 2:24:52 | Joan Benoit USA | | Los Angeles | 050884 |
| 2:21:06 | Ingrid Kristiansen NOR | | London | 210485 |
| 2:21:21 | Joan Samuelson USA | | Chicago | 201085 |
| 2:23:05 | Ingrid Kristiansen NOR | | Chicago | 201085 |
| 2:23:29 | Rosa Mota POR | | Chicago | 201085 |
| 2:24:54 | Grete Waitz NOR | (10) | London | 200486 |
| 2:24:55 | Ingrid Kristiansen NOR | | Boston | 210486 |
| 2:25:21 | Rosa Mota POR | | Boston | 200487 |
| 2:22:48 | Ingrid Kristiansen NOR | | London | 100587 |
| 2:25:17 | Rosa Mota POR | | Rome | 290887 |
| 2:25:24 | Katrin Dörre GDR | | Tokyo | 151187 |
| 2:23:51 | Lisa Martin AUS | | Osaka | 310188 |
| 2:25:41 | Ingrid Kristiansen NOR | | London | 170488 |
| 2:24:30 | Rosa Mota POR | | Boston | 180488 |
| 2:25:40 | Rosa Mota POR | | Seoul | 230988 |
| 2:25:53 | Lisa Martin AUS | (20) | Seoul | 230988 |
| 2:24:33 | Ingrid Kristiansen NOR | | Boston | 170489 |
| 2:25:56 | Véronique Marot GBR | | London | 230489 |
| 2:25:30 | Ingrid Kristiansen NOR | | New York | 051189 |
| 2:25:28 | Lisa Martin AUS | | Auckland | 310190 |
| 2:25:24 | Rosa Mota POR | | Boston | 160490 |
| 2:24:18 | Wanda Panfil POL | | Boston | 150491 |
| 2:23:43 | Olga Markova RUS | | Boston | 200492 |
| 2:24:40 | Lisa Ondieki AUS | | New York | 011192 |
| 2:24:07 | Wang Junxia CHN | | Tianjin | 040493 |
| 2:24:32 | Qu Yunxia CHN | (30) | Tianjin | 040493 |
| 2:24:42 | Zhang Linli CHN | | Tianjin | 040493 |
| 2:24:52 | Zhang Lirong CHN | | Tianjin | 040493 |
| 2:25:36 | Zhong Huandi CHN | | Tianjin | 040493 |
| 2:25:46 | Ma Liyan CHN | | Tianjin | 040493 |
| 2:25:27 | Olga Markova RUS | | Boston | 190493 |
| 2:25:52 | Miyoko Asahina JPN | | Rotterdam | 170494 |
| 2:21:45 | Uta Pippig GER | | Boston | 180494 |
| 2:23:33 | Valentina Yegorova RUS | | Boston | 180494 |
| **2:25:15** | **Elana Meyer RSA** | | **Boston** | **180494** |
| 2:25:19 | Alena Peterková TCH | (40) | Boston | 180494 |
| 2:25:15 | Katrin Dörre GER | | Berlin | 250994 |
| 2:25:11 | Uta Pippig GER | | Boston | 170495 |
| 2:25:37 | Uta Pippig GER | | Berlin | 240995 |

# World all-time lists

## Men

| | | | |
|---|---|---|---|
| 2:06:50 | Belayneh Dinsamo ETH | | 1988 |
| 2:07:02 | Samuel Lelei KEN | | 1995 |
| 2:07:07 | Ahmed Salah DJI | | 1988 |
| 2:07:12 | Carlos Lopes POR | | 1985 |
| 2:07:13 | Steve Jones GBR | | 1985 |
| 2:07:15 | Cosmas Ndeti KEN | | 1994 |
| 2:07:19 | Andrés Espinosa MEX | | 1994 |
| 2:07:20 | Vincent Rousseau BEL | | 1995 |
| 2:07:35 | Taisuke Kodama JPN | (9) | 1986 |
| 2:07:35 | Abebe Mekonnen ETH | | 1988 |
| 2:07:40 | Hiromi Taniguchi JPN | | 1988 |
| 2:07:51 | Robert de Castella AUS | | 1986 |
| 2:07:57 | Kunimitsu Itoh JPN | | 1986 |
| 2:08:01 | Juma Ikangaa TAN | | 1989 |
| **2:08:04** | **Zithulele Sinqe RSA** | | **1986** |
| **2:08:07** | **David Tsebe RSA** | | **1992** |
| 2:08:08 | Djama Robleh DJI | | 1985 |
| 2:08:08 | Jackson Kipngok KEN | | 1994 |
| 2:08:09 | Hwang Young-cho KOR | | 1994 |
| 2:08:14 | Ibrahim Hussein KEN | (20) | 1992 |
| 2:08:15 | Takeyuki Nakayama JPN | | 1985 |
| **2:08:15** | **Willie Mtolo RSA** | | **1986** |
| 2:08:16 | Steve Moneghetti AUS | | 1990 |
| 2:08:19 | Gelindo Bordin ITA | | 1990 |
| 2:08:27 | Toshihiko Seko JPN | | 1986 |
| 2:08:28 | Arturo Barrios MEX | | 1994 |
| 2:08:30 | Dionicio Cerón MEX | | 1995 |
| 2:08:31 | António Pinto POR | | 1994 |
| 2:08:32 | Gidamis Shahanga TAN | | 1990 |
| 2:08:33 | Charles Spedding GBR | (30) | 1985 |

## Women

| | | | |
|---|---|---|---|
| 2:21:06 | Ingrid Kristiansen NOR | | 1985 |
| 2:21:21 | Joan Samuelson USA | | 1985 |
| 2:21:45 | Uta Pippig GER | | 1994 |
| 2:23:29 | Rosa Mota POR | | 1985 |
| 2:23:33 | Valentina Yegorova RUS | | 1994 |
| 2:23:43 | Olga Markova RUS | | 1992 |
| 2:23:51 | Lisa Martin AUS | | 1988 |
| 2:24:07 | Wang Junxia CHN | | 1993 |
| 2:24:18 | Wanda Panfil POL | | 1991 |
| 2:24:32 | Qu Yunxia CHN | (10) | 1993 |
| 2:24:42 | Zhang Linli CHN | | 1993 |
| 2:24:52 | Zhang Lirong CHN | | 1993 |
| 2:24:54 | Grete Waitz NOR | | 1986 |
| **2:25:15** | **Elana Meyer RSA** | | **1994** |
| 2:25:15 | Katrin Dörre GER | | 1994 |
| 2:25:19 | Alena Peterková TCH | | 1994 |
| 2:25:36 | Zhong Huandi CHN | | 1993 |
| 2:25:46 | Ma Liyan CHN | | 1993 |
| 2:25:52 | Miyoko Asahina JPN | | 1994 |
| 2:25:56 | Veronique Marot GBR | (20) | 1989 |
| 2:26:09 | Tomoe Abe JPN | | 1994 |
| 2:26:09 | Nobuko Fujimura JPN | | 1994 |
| 2:26:10 | Junko Asari JPN | | 1994 |
| 2:26:20 | Renata Kokowska POL | | 1993 |
| 2:26:26 | Julie Brown USA | | 1983 |
| 2:26:26 | Yumi Kokamo JPN | | 1992 |
| 2:26:26 | Yoshiko Yamamoto JPN | | 1992 |
| 2:26:26 | Mitsuyo Yoshida JPN | | 1994 |
| 2:26:34 | Carla Beurskens NED | | 1987 |
| 2:26:36 | Wang Yanfang CHN | (30) | 1993 |

# South African all-time lists

## Men

| | | | | |
|---|---|---|---|---|
| 2:08:04 | Zithulele Sinqe | | Port Elizabeth | 030586 |
| 2:08:07 | David Tsebe | | Berlin | 270992 |
| 2:08:15 | Willie Mtolo | | Port Elizabeth | 030586 |
| 2:08:58 | Mark Plaatjes | | Port Elizabeth | 040585 |
| 2:09:31 | Gert Thys | | Fukuoka | 051293 |
| 2:09:41 | Ernest Seleke | | Port Elizabeth | 310384 |
| 2:10:22 | Xolile Yawa | | London | 020495 |
| 2:10:29 | Lawrence Peu | | Fukuoka | 061292 |
| 2:10:29 | Joseph Skosana | | Durban | 200791 |
| 2:10:39 | Thompson Magawana | (10) | Port Elizabeth | 040585 |
| 2:10:47 | Michael Scout | | Durban | 200791 |
| 2:10:53 | Peter Tshikila | | Port Elizabeth | 290789 |
| 2:10:55 | Thabiso Moqhali | | London | 120492 |
| 2:11:00 | Ernest Tjela | | Port Elizabeth | 030586 |
| 2:11:07 | Abel Mokibe | | Cape Town | 280392 |
| 2:11:24 | John Sebata | | Port Elizabeth | 240290 |
| 2:11:39 | Johannes Mabitle | | London | 020495 |
| 2:11:42 | Johan Dreyer | | Kuils River | 020783 |
| 2:11:44 | Gabashane Rakabaele | | Port Elizabeth | 010582 |
| 2:11:46 | Johnny Halberstadt | (20) | Chicago | 260982 |
| 2:11:51 | Derek May | | Houston | 180187 |
| 2:11:56 | Jan Tau | | Cape Town | 280392 |
| 2:12:08 | Ewald Bonzet | | Stellenbosch | 100983 |
| 2:12:10 | Geoff Bacon | | Port Elizabeth | 060980 |
| 2.12.10 | Bernard Rose | | Cape Town | 050383 |

## Women

| | | | | |
|---|---|---|---|---|
| 2:25:15 | Elana Meyer | | Boston | 180494 |
| 2:27:36 | Frith van der Merwe | | Port Elizabeth | 240290 |
| 2:31:21 | Colleen de Reuck | | Cape Town | 280392 |
| 2:33:39 | Annette Falkson | | Cape Town | 300488 |
| 2:35:44 | Sonja Laxton | | Stellenbosch | 130986 |
| 2:35:45 | Adelene Joubert | | Port Elizabeth | 040585 |
| 2:37:11 | Nicole Fuller | | Port Elizabeth | 110395 |
| 2:37:19 | Monica Drögemöller | | Cape Town | 030390 |
| 2:39:32 | Jean Rayner | | Durban | 200791 |
| 2:41:05 | Blanche Moila | (10 | Cape Town | 280392 |
| 2:42:27 | Isavel Roche-Kelly | | Stellenbosch | 211181 |
| 2:42:35 | Grace de Oliveira | | Lisbon | 271194 |
| 2.42.52 | Evelina Tshabalala | | Port Elizabeth | 240290 |
| 2:44:16 | Liz Eglington | | Cape Town | 300488 |
| 2:44:22 | Helen Lucre | | Cape Town | 160291 |
| 2:44:28 | Judy Ryan | | Stellenbosch | 130980 |
| 2:44:40 | Beverley Malan | | New York | 241082 |
| 2:45:18 | Cassandra Mihailovic | | Port Elizabeth | 030586 |
| 2:45:56 | Helene Joubert | | Durban | 150991 |
| 2:46:13 | Belinda Roux | (20) | Lisbon | 281193 |
| 2:46:24 | Winsome Norval | | Port Elizabeth | 030586 |
| 2:47:03 | Anne Blunden | | Port Elizabeth | 030586 |
| 2:47:05 | Laura Hofer | | Port Elizabeth | 030586 |
| 2:47:21 | Jowaine Parrott | | Dijon | 021094 |
| 2:47:43 | Pat Lithgow | | Durban | 100989 |

# SELECTED BIBLIOGRAPHY

## BOOKS

Alexander, Morris: *The Comrades Marathon Story*. Juta & Company Ltd., Cape Town/Wynberg/Johannesburg, 1976 (2nd edition).

Castellini, Ottavio: *Marathon Handbook 1991*. N.p., 1991.

Clayton, Derek: *Running to the Top*. Anderson World, Inc., Mountain View, 1980.

Costill, David L.: *A Scientific Approach to Distance Running*. Track & Field News, Los Altos, 1979.

DeMar, Clarence: *Marathon*. The New England Press, Shelburne, 1981.

Gambaccini, Peter: *The New York City Marathon. Twenty-five Years*. Rizzoli International Publications, Inc., New York, 1994.

Giller, Norman: *Marathon Kings*. Pelham Books Ltd., London, 1983.

Gretton, George: *Out in Front*. Pelham Books, London, 1968.

Gynn, Roger: *Guinness Book of the Marathon*. Guinness Superlatives Ltd., Enfield, 1984.

Hill, Ron: *The Long Hard Road. Part One* and *Part Two*. Ron Hill Sports Ltd, Hyde, 1981.

Kamper, Erich: *Lexikon der 12 000 Olympioniken*. Leykam-Verlag, Graz, 1975.

Kök, Nejat, Magnussen, Rooney, Potts, D.H., and Quercetani, R.L. (comp.): *Track & Field Performances through the Years. Volume 3, 1945-1950*. Association of Track & Field Statisticians, Florence, n.d.

Krise, Raymond, and Squires, Bill: *Fast Tracks. The History of Distance Running since 884 B.C.* The Stephen Greene Press, Brattleboro/Lexington, 1982.

Kuscsik, Nina: "The History of Women's Participation in the Marathon" in Paul Milvy (ed.): *The Marathon: Physiological, Medical, Epidemiological, and Psychological Studies*. The New York Academy of Sciences, New York, 1977.

Le Roux, Gert (ed.): *90 Goue Jare/90 Golden Years*. SA Amateur Athletic Union, Pretoria, n.d.

Lovesey, Peter: *The Kings of Distance. A Study of Five Great Runners*. Eyre & Spottiswoode, London, 1968.

Lovesey, Peter: *The Official Centenary History of the Amateur Athletic Association*. Guinness Superlatives Ltd., Enfield, 1979.

Magnussen, Rooney, Potts, D.H., and Quercetani, R.L. (comp.): *Track & Field Performances through the Years. Volume 2, 1937-1944*. Association of Track & Field Statisticians, Florence, n.d.

Martin, David E., and Gynn, Roger W.H.: *The Marathon Footrace. Performers and Performances*. Charles C. Thomas, Springfield, 1979.

Matthews, Peter: *The Guinness Book of Track & Field Athletics Facts & Feats*. Guinness Superlatives Ltd., Enfield, 1982.

Matthews, Peter: *The Guinness Encyclopedia of International Sports Records and Results*. Guinness Publishing Ltd., Enfield, 1993 (3rd edition).

Moore, Kenny: *Best Efforts: World Class Runners and Races*. Doubleday & Company, Inc., Garden City, 1982.

Nelson, Cordner: *Track and Field. The Great Ones*. Pelham Books, London, 1970.

Noakes, Tim: *Lore of Running*. Oxford University Press, Cape Town, 1985.

Parker, John: *The Frank Shorter Story*. Runner's World Magazine, Mountain View, 1972. Runner's World Booklet of the Month No. 18.

Prokop, Dave (ed.): *The African Running Revolution*. World Publications, Mountain View, 1975. Runner's Booklet Series No. 47.

Quercetani, R.L.: *A World History of Track and Field Athletics 1864-1964*. Oxford University Press, London/New York/Toronto, 1964.

Quercetani, R.L., and Magnussen, Rooney (comp.): *Track & Field Performances through the Years. Volume 1, 1929-1936*. Association of Track & Field Statisticians, Florence, n.d.

Quercetani, Roberto L.: *Athletics. A History of Modern Track and Field Athletics (1860-1990). Men and Women*. Vallardi & Associati, Milan, 1990.

Rodgers, Bill (with Joe Concannon): *Marathoning*. Simon and Schuster, New York, 1980.

Runner's World Magazine: *The Boston Marathon*. World Publications, Mountain View, 1974. Runner's Monthly Booklet No. 10 (revised).

Track & Field News: *Olympic Track & Field*. Tafnews Press, Los Altos, 1979.

Wallechinsky, David: *The Complete Book of the Olympics*. Aurum Press Ltd., London, 1992.

Watman, Mel (comp.): *Encyclopaedia of Track and Field Athletics*. Robert Hale Ltd., London, 1981 (5th edition).

Zur Megede, Ekkehard, and Hymans, Richard: *Progression of World Best Performances and IAAF Approved World Records*. International Athletic Foundation, Monaco, 1991.

## MAGAZINES, NEWSPAPERS AND PERIODICALS

*Athletics* (followed by year). *The International Track and Field Annual**

*Athletics International*

*Athletics Weekly*

*) This publication, as well as *SA Athletics Annual* on the next page, has appeared under various titles over the years.

*Die Burger*
*Hoofstad*
*Huisgenoot*
*IAAF Bulletin*, No. 50, 1985
*Leichtathletik*
*Marathon and Distance Runner*
*Olympic Review*, No. 109-110, November/December 1976
*On the Roads*
*Runner's World* (SA and US editions)
*Running*
*Running Stats*
*Running Times*
*SA Athlete*
*SA Athletics Annual* (followed by year)
*SA Runner*
*SA Runner/Tri-Cycling*
*SA Sports Illustrated*
*The Cape Argus*

*The Runner*
*Topsport*
*Track & Field News*

## OTHER SOURCES

Correspondence with David Martin, Roger Gynn and Peter Matthews.
Information on course measurements of SA championship races provided by Cheryl Winn and Cliff Hopkins.
Official results of various SA marathons.
Research by Doug Coghlan on the history of SA athletics.
Research by Gert le Roux on SA marathoning.
Research by Floris van der Merwe on South Africa's participation in the Olympic and Commonwealth Games.
Telephonic interview with Ferdie le Grange.